Communications
in Computer and Information Science   320

T0188815

Yuyu Yuan   Xu Wu   Yueming Lu (Eds.)

Trustworthy Computing and Services

International Conference, ISCTCS 2012
Beijing, China, May 28 – June 2, 2012
Revised Selected Papers

 Springer

Volume Editors

Yuyu Yuan
Xu Wu
Yueming Lu
Beijing University of Posts and Telecommunications, China
E-mail: yyy1012@gmail.com, {wux,ymlu}@bupt.edu.cn

ISSN 1865-0929   e-ISSN 1865-0937
ISBN 978-3-642-35794-7   e-ISBN 978-3-642-35795-4
DOI 10.1007/978-3-642-35795-4
Springer Heidelberg Dordrecht London New York

Library of Congress Control Number: 2012954492

CR Subject Classification (1998): K.6.5, K.4.4, C.2.0-2, C.2.4, D.2.5, D.4.6, E.3,
H.2.7, F.2.2

Typesetting: Camera-ready by author, data conversion by Scientific Publishing Services, Chennai, India

Printed on acid-free paper

Springer is part of Springer Science+Business Media (www.springer.com)

Preface

Trusted computing and services is one of the most challenging technologies today and is the core technology of cloud computing that is currently the focus of international competition; its standardization work is the premise and guarantee of the technology's successful application and promotion in industry. The International Standard Conference on Trustworthy Computing and Services (ISCTCS) is hosted by the Key Laboratory of Trustworthy Distributed Computing and Service (BUPT), Ministry of Education, and the Beijing Products Quality Supervision and Inspection Institute in order to lay the foundation for the establishment of the Trusted Computing Service Standards Working Group. Scholars, experts, and corporate leaders from all around the world have a chance to share ideas on technologies involved in trustworthy computing and services, their evolution, application, and industrialization.

The main topics of ISCTCS include: architecture for trusted computing systems, trusted computing platforms, building trusted systems, network and protocol security, mobile network security, network survivability and other critical theories and standard systems; credible assessment, credible measurement and metrics, trusted systems, trusted networks, trusted mobile networks, trusted routing, trusted software, trusted operating systems, trusted storage, fault-tolerant computing and other key technologies; trusted e-commerce and e-government, trusted logistics, trusted Internet of things, trusted cloud and other trusted services and applications.

The conference began with an opening ceremony and the conference program featured five welcome speeches, three keynote speeches, and two presentations by local and international experts. During the 2-day program, all paper presentations were given in four parallel sessions. The conference ended with a closing ceremony. The conference received more than 278 papers, each paper was carefully reviewed by the Program Committee members. Finally, 92 papers were selected.

On behalf of the Organizing and Program Committees of ISCTCS 2012, we would like to express our appreciation to all authors and attendees for participating in the conference. We also thank the sponsors, Program Committee members, supporting organizations, and helpers for making the conference a success. Without their efforts, the conference would not have been possible.

Finally, we hope everyone who attended enjoyed the conference program and also their stay in Beijing. We firmly look forward to the impact of ISCTCS 2012 in promoting the standardization work of trusted computing and services.

July 2012

Yuyu Yuan
Xu Wu
Yueming Lu

Conference Organization

The International Standard Conference on Trustworthy Computing and Services (ISCTCS 2012) was organized by the Key Laboratory of Trustworthy Distributed Computing and Service of BUPT, Ministry of Education, and sponsored by the Beijing Products Quality Supervision and Inspection Institute.

General Chair

Yaoxue Zhang

Chinese Academician of Engineering, Director of Academic Committee of Key Laboratory of Trustworthy Distributed Computing and Service (BUPT), Ministry of Education, President of Central South University

Technical Program Committee Chair

Yuyu Yuan

Deputy Director of the Key Laboratory of Trustworthy Distributed Computing and Service (BUPT), Ministry of Education

Workshop Chair

National University of Defense Technology, China

Publication Chair

Xu Wu

Deputy Director of Library, BUPT, Key Laboratory of Trustworthy Distributed Computing and Service (BUPT), Ministry of Education

Finance Chair

Beijing University of Posts and Telecommunications, China

Registration Chair

Beijing University of Posts and Telecommunications, China

Main Organizers

Beijing University of Posts and Telecommunications, China
Zhejiang University, China
Nanjing University, China
Ecole de Technologie Superieure, Canada

ISCTCS Technical Program Committee

Jorgen Boegh	Beijing University of Posts and Telecommunications, China
Witold Suryn	Ecole de Technologie Superieure, Canada
François Coallier	Ecole de Technologie Superieure Coallier, Canada
Regina Colombo	CTI, Brazil
Mary Theofanos	National Institute of Standards and Technology (NIST), USA
Jean Bérubé	Standards Council of Canada, Canada
Enrico Viola	P.I.C.O., Italy
Yukio Tanitsu	IBM Japan, Ltd., Japan
Seok Kyoo Shin	Telecommunications Technology Association, Korea
Alain Renault	CRP Henri Tudor, Luxembourg
Juan Garbajosa	Technical University of Madrid, Spain
Nigel Bevan	Professional Usability Services, UK
Shirley Lacy	ConnectSphere, UK
Xin Chen	Nangjing University, China
Jianwei Yin	Zhejiang University, China
Cong Wang	Ministry of Education; Beijing University of Posts and Telecommunications, China
Xu Wu	Beijing University of Posts and Telecommunications; Ministry of Education, China
Tie Jun Lv	Beijing University of Posts and Telecommunications, China
Yue Ming Lu	Beijing University of Posts and Telecommunications, China
Chun Lu Wang	Beijing University of Posts and Telecommunications, China
Tian Le Zhang	Ministry of Education; Beijing University of Posts and Telecommunications, China

Chuan Yi Liu	Ministry of Education; Beijing University of Posts and Telecommunications, China
Dong Bin Wang	Ministry of Education; Beijing University of Posts and Telecommunications, China
Jin Cui Yang	Ministry of Education; Beijing University of Posts and Telecommunications, China
Yang Yang Zhang	Ministry of Education; Beijing University of Posts and Telecommunications, China

Table of Contents

XII Table of Contents

Software Trustworthiness: Past, Present and Future

Mitra Nami and Witold Suryn

École de technologie supérieure, Montréal, Canada
mitra.nami.1@ens.etsmtl.ca, witold.suryn@etsmtl.ca

Abstract. Software controls an increasing number of complex technical systems, ranging from Internet-based e-health and e-government applications to embedded control systems in factories, cars, and aircrafts. Even though the quality assurance budgets of software makers are increasing, program failures happen quite often. The successful deployment of software systems depends on the extent to which we can justifiably trust them. Academia, government, and industry have conducted several efforts with the aim of providing a view of trustworthiness in software from system construction, evaluation and analysis. This paper investigates the previous and present activities that have been performed to achieve software trustworthiness and suggests some guidelines for future activities. The proposed approach uses the novel behaviouristic model for verifying software trustworthiness based on scenarios of interactions between the software and its users and environment [1].

Keywords: software, trustworthiness, quality, security.

1   Introduction

Introduction of Internet and wireless broadband networks together with service-oriented architectures has great impact on the composition of interactive services using web technologies and web services. The inter-relationships and inter-dependencies between formerly stand-alone systems and networks have created complexities in the infrastructures of our society that have never existed before [29]. These complex systems and networks have been granted access to massive amounts of personal and business data, information and content in ways, which are difficult to understand and control by users [29]. Moreover these complex systems often behave in unexpected ways that are not easily predictable from the behavior of their components. In recent years we have witnessed an increasing number of accidents and attacks on the Internet and on applications and databases, which have been produced by system misbehavior, or cyber attacks. Cyber attackers disrupt the service and steal personal or confidential business data for financial gain or other purposes by using denial of service attacks, viruses, phishing, spyware and other malware. These attacks will impact e-market on an international scale and create mistrust [29].

Apart from external attacks, there are some other possible causes for software to fail. Some of these are:

Y. Yuan, X. Wu, and Y. Lu (Eds.): ISCTCS 2012, CCIS 320, pp. 1–12, 2013.
© Springer-Verlag Berlin Heidelberg 2013

- change of the program source code,
- modification of its context by updating libraries or changing its configuration,
- modification of its test suite.

Any of these changes can cause differences in program behaviour. In general, program paths may appear or disappear between executions of two subsequent versions of a system. Software testing is a way to find faults in software. It is a process of supplying a system under test with some values and making conclusions on the basis of its behavior.

The most significant weakness of testing is that the functioning of the tested system can, in principle, only be verified for those input situations, which were selected as test data. According to Dijkstra [18], testing can only show the existence but not the non-existence of errors. Proof of correctness can only be produced by a complete test, i.e. a test with all possible input values, input value sequences, and input value combinations under all practically possible constraints what is practically impossible.

The solution proposed in this paper is an alternative approach, applying a novel behavioristic model for verifying software trustworthiness by capturing system's functional and quality requirements. The approach is introduced by generation of statecharts from scenarios with the following specific benefits:

- end user can validate the transition of software behavior into path representations.
- real (observed) behavior of the software under investigation is recorded.
- Reference (expected) behavior of software is compared with the real behavior of the software under investigation.
- the observed behavior and its discrepancy from reference behavior for the software under investigation can be analyzed and interpreted.
- the approach can be applied in the process of certifying software trustworthiness

The structure of this paper is as follows:

Section 1 presents a brief introduction. Section 2 contains review of the background on past and present activities for achieving software trustworthiness. In section 3, the approach proposed by the authors is presented. Then the methodology is explained in section 4. The advantages of proposed method in supporting and advancing the achievement of software trustworthiness are presented in section 5 and discussion about the future challenges of software trustworthiness is in section 6. Finally the conclusion is presented in section 7.

2   Software Trustworthiness: Past, Present

The literature related to trust and software trustworthiness attributes and factors from different views can be categorized into following sub-categories:

1- National Science and Technology Council (NSTC) in United States concentrates on high confidence systems and cyber-physical systems that are categorized into physical, biological, and engineered systems whose operations are integrated, monitored, and/or controlled by a computational core. Components are networked at every scale. Computing is "deeply embedded" into every physical component, possibly even into materials. The computational core is an embedded system, usually demanding real-time response, and is most often distributed. The behavior of a cyber-physical system is a fully integrated hybridization of computational (logical) and physical action [20]. In this category, the emphasis is on safety, stability, and performance attributes [20]. Center for National Software Strategy Steering Group (NSG) has also identified software trustworthiness as the most important focus of future research [19]. The report is intended to be a ten-year program to achieve the vision, and goals stated, namely: "Achieving the ability to routinely develop and deploy trustworthy software, products and systems, while ensuring the continued competitiveness of the U.S. software industry" [19].

2- Avizienis et al. have defined the dependability as the reliance that can justifiably be placed on the service that the system delivers [21]. Dependability has become an important aspect of computer systems since everyday life increasingly depends on software. Although there is a large body of research in dependability, architectural level reasoning about dependability is only just emerging as an important theme in software engineering. This is due to the fact that dependability concerns are usually left until too late in the process of development. Additionally, the complexity of emerging applications and the trend of building trustworthy systems from existing untrustworthy components are urging dependability concerns to be considered at the architectural level. Some of these building blocks are commercial off-the-shelf components (COTS), legacy systems, and component systems of systems-of-systems. This category emphasizes the availability, reliability, safety, integrity, and maintainability. Lemos et al. have recognized fault prevention, fault removal, fault tolerance and fault forecasting as important quality attributes for dependable systems [22]. Fault prevention, also known as rigorous design, aims at preventing the occurrence or the introduction of faults. Fault removal, also known as verification and validation, aims at reducing the number or severity of faults. Fault tolerance, aims at delivering correct service in the presence of faults. Fault forecasting, also known as system evaluation, aiming at estimating the present number, the future incidence, and the likely consequences of faults.

3- A group of multinational technology and consulting firms such as Compaq, HP, IBM, Intel and Microsoft formed the Trusted Computing Platform Alliance (TCPA) [25]. Their belief is that the totality (hardware, firmware, software) of the components is responsible for enforcing a security policy so that the system operates as expected [25].

- Those against will say the computer minimizes the control of user on data and software. It is seen as harmful or problematic to small and open source software developers [23].
- Those in support will say the computer operates as the owner/operator expects.

The group eventually grew to over 190 members, to focus on "improving trust and security on computing platforms" and later was being replaced by the Trusted Computing Group (TCG). It concentrates on hardware and software security and use cryptography to maintain security [25].

4- Microsoft developed an integrated process called trustworthy computing for improving the security of commercial software as it is being developed. Microsoft believes that there are three facets for building more secure software: repeatable process, engineer education, and metrics and accountability [24]. In Microsoft's experience, the benefits of providing more secure software (e.g., fewer patches, more satisfied customers) outweigh the costs [24].

5- Trusted Computer National Evaluation Criteria (TCNEC) restricted trustworthiness based on security as the only attribute to consider [10].

6- Other researchers have different views. For example, Parnas *et al*, define software trustworthiness as level of appropriateness of using software engineering techniques to reduce failure rates, including techniques to enhance testing, reviews, and inspections [11]. In the study of Trustworthy Software Methodology (TSM) originally by US National Security Agency, software trustworthiness was defined as "the degree of confidence that exists to meet a set of requirements [17].

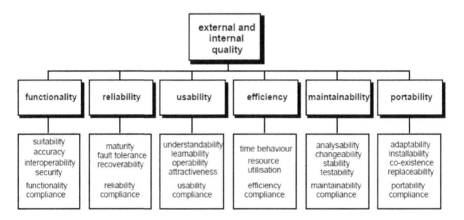

Fig. 1. ISO 9126 characteristic and sub-characteristic, source: [12]

7- On other hand ISO 9126-1 defines a quality model via a set of quality attributes [12]. It recognizes six major characteristics of software quality attributes such as functionality, reliability, usability, efficiency, maintainability and portability and each characteristic has sub-characteristic as shown in Fig. 1. Recently, there is the tendency to add security and interoperability to the set of ISO 9126 qualities, as recognized in the new set of ISO 25000 standards. Security and operability are already present in ISO 9126 standard, but only as "sub –characteristics" of functionality. All the quality attributes are equally important, but most of literature agreed that software trustworthiness encompasses the reliability, security, and safety of software system or service [15] [16], as well as fault-tolerance and stability.

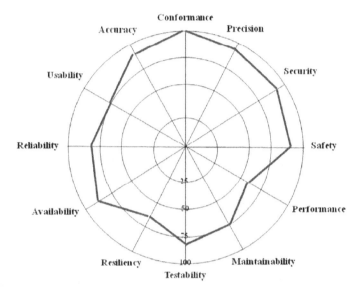

Fig. 2. Trustworthy factor, source: [13]

8- Boland et al. have used an approach to quantify risk and used quality attributes as software trustworthiness factors and represented it by Kiviat Chart as shown in fig. 2 [13]. They have defined the trustworthy factor as: TI = Tactual / Tmaximum, with values of TI between "0"and "1" ("0" being totally untrustworthy and "1" being completely trustworthy, so TI is "normalized"). Tactual is the actual measure of trustworthiness, and Tmaximum, is the potential maximum trustworthiness possible [13].   There are many other classical studies that take quality attributes as the starting point and some of these discussions also include measurement and evaluation of a particular aspect along with tool support.

9- Hurlbut's thesis surveyed and compared nearly sixty different scenarios, use case, policy formalisms and models [26][27].

These efforts are attempting to improve software trustworthiness but:

- they are limited to quality factors of software system or service or
- they are related to specific software system or service or

- they are related to specific domain or
- they are confined in a specific way of handling software trustworthiness.

By comparing the above literature, it can be concluded that the cognition of software trustworthiness is not uniform among researchers and industry. The belief behind the proposed model is that software trustworthiness is a property of a product, which depends on the perception that users have of the qualities of the product (such as reliability, performance, etc.) and functionality of software system or service. On other hand, the user's perception of software trustworthiness of the software systems and services depends, among others, on the following factors:

- Context of usage
- Completeness of required functionalities of product
- Proper quality-cost ratio
- Post-sale maintenance and service
- Pre and post-sale training
- Documentation

In the proposed model, all of these factors are taken into account, and then are prioritized based on the context of use and other important factors from user point of view. The literature on formal methods and model validation techniques are presented in previous study on finding a way to model software trustworthiness by using Finite State Machine (FSM) and scenarios [1].

3   Proposed Approach

The approach is based on Rolland's definition of scenarios along four different views as shown in Fig.1 where each view captures a particular relevant aspect of scenarios. These four views are explained below [2]:

- Content: what is the knowledge in scenario? Scenarios are used to model interactions between the user and the software system and its environment. These interactions are either domain-related or environment-related. Sometimes there are internal actions, which are important for a scenario, but they are not immediately visible during the interaction with the user. Therefore, it is also important to model the impact of user interactions on the software system's data [7].
- Purpose: why scenario is used? The scenarios are used to model system requirements as a basis for comparing recorded behavior of software system with its expected behavior. Moreover, they can be used for validation by analysts, testers and end users.
- Lifecycle: how to manipulate a scenario? As the number of use cases and the number of scenarios per use case increases, the total number of scenarios increases which causes scalability problem. As the number of scenarios and states is augmented, the modeling of the behavior of a large software system becomes more difficult. For example, if a software

system has 100 use cases and each use case has 10 important scenarios on average, it would be necessary to keep a total of 1000 scenarios consistent at all times even when the requirements change. To accommodate all of these scenarios, each use case should be modeled by a statechart diagram and therefore generate all scenarios for that use case [7].

- Form: in which form is a scenario expressed? Both informal and formal notations can be used for describing the semantics of scenarios. Informal notations are used for expressiveness and formal notation is used for proof of correctness. Precise specifications with a suitable degree of formalism can be used to capture requirements in an unambiguous way and to enable the generation of a fully functional model, which can help users to validate requirements [7].

Each specific scenario will be characterised according to these four views.

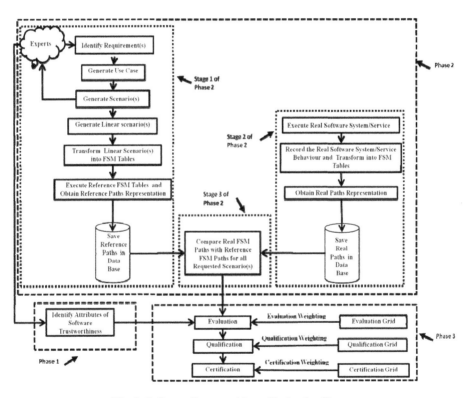

Fig. 3. Software Trustworthiness Evaluation Process

4   Methodology

The behavioristic model consists of three activities or phases, namely: identifying attributes of software trustworthiness, developing a formal behavioristic model, evaluating the trustworthiness (Fig. 3). The development of the formal behavioristic model is further divided into 3 following stages:

Stage 1 – Transforming Reference Requirements to FSM
- identification of reference requirements
- extraction of reference functionalities and quality attributes
- generation of reference use cases
- extraction of reference scenarios
- automatic transformation of any hierarchical (tree format) scenarios to non hierarchical (linear format) scenarios
- generation of reference FSM tables from each non hierarchical (linear format) scenarios
- execution of reference FSM tables to obtain the reference path representation
- saving reference path representation into reference database.

Stage 2 – Recording Real Software System or Services Behavior
- execution of real software system or services
- recording of the real behavior into real FSM tables
- executing of real FSM tables and obtaining the real path representation
- saving real path representation into real database.

Stage 3 – Comparing Real Behavior with Reference Behavior
- reading real path representation from real database
- reading reference path representation from reference database
- comparing reference path representation with real path representation
- analyzing and interpreting of observed behavior and its discrepancy from reference behavior for the software system or services under investigation

5   Advantages of Proposed Approach

In order to gain confidence about behavior of software, its functional and quality requirements have to be captured, which involve creating intentional, structural and behavioral models. UML offers scenario-based and state-based modeling. Using FSM and generating a statechart model from the scenarios can solve redundancy, repetition and scalability problems [3][4][5][6][7] and provides the following benefits [7]:

- flexibility of using scenarios and state machines to generate state chart
- informal and formal specification removes ambiguity
- supports changes in requirements

The specific benefits of proposed behavioristic model are:

- end user can validate the transition of software behavior into path representations.
- real behavior of the software under investigation is recorded.

- reference behavior of software is compared with the real behavior of the software under investigation.
- the observed behavior and its discrepancy from reference behavior for the software under investigation can be analyzed and interpreted.
- the approach can be applied in the process of certifying software trustworthiness

6 Software Trustworthiness: Future

Software trustworthiness encompasses activities with different objectives, such as exposing deviations from user's requirements, assessing the conformance to a standard specification, evaluating robustness to stressful load conditions or to malicious inputs, measuring given attributes such as performance or usability, estimating the operational reliability and so on. Besides, it could be carried on according to a controlled formal procedure or rather informally and ad hoc (exploratory testing).

As a consequence of this variety of aims and scopes, a multiplicity of meanings for the term "software trustworthiness" arises, which has generated many peculiar research challenges.

To organize the latter into a unifying view, the common denominator has to be identified and defined as the attributes and factors that will contribute to the trustworthiness of the software system or service under investigation. It is important to note that not only the quality attributes that are important for software trustworthiness are taken into account, but also the domain of software systems or services as well. The domains (or classification) of software systems or services is introduced by Suryn et al [28] as: Financial Transaction Systems, Transaction Applications Systems, Management Information Systems, Decision Support Systems, Telecommunication Systems, Network Management Systems, Information Management Systems and Industrial Support Systems. The importance of quality attributes based on type of IT systems and services is also used from Suryn et al [28]. The context of use is taken into consideration as the third perspective. It can be found out by answering to the following questions.

- WHO will use the software (Users and Roles)?
- WHAT will be done with the software (Functional Requirements)?
- WHERE the software will be used (Environment)?
- HOW the software will be used (Quality Requirements)?
- WHEN in the product lifecycle the software will be evaluated for software trustworthiness?

We can trust a software system only when it behaves as it is intended to behave and depends on the extent to which we can justifiably prove the correctness of service execution. As software systems grow, they transform into complex systems that often behave in unexpected ways that are not easily predictable from the behavior of their components. Unpredictable software systems are hard to debug and hard to manage. Some of the sources of these misbehaviors that need further research can be categorized into the following topics:

6.1   Security

There are open research areas, which need further research efforts such as [29]:

- continuous and real time assessing and managing the security level of software
- proactively developing new protection schemes
- protecting against intrusions, attacks and cascading effects on interconnected software
- cross-border, cross-organizational, scalable distributed mechanisms for self-organizing, self-healing and self-learning protection mechanisms.

6.2   Privacy

There are open research areas, which need further research efforts such as [29]:

- new privacy models and information control paradigms; privacy enhancing technologies
- new frameworks and architectures integrating for managing personal information and for data sharing and exchange under users' control
- understanding how trust relates to reputation formation, monitoring, evolution and management
- developing novel trustworthy and usable means that take account of the situation and context and help users make informed decisions about which information, services, software and systems they can trust

6.3   Cyber Security

There are open research areas which need further research efforts such as [30]:

- scalable trustworthy software
- enterprise-level metrics for measuring the overall software trustworthiness
- software evaluation life cycle
- detecting, monitoring and countering insider threats
- detecting, monitoring and countering malware
- early detecting, monitoring and countering malicious behaviour
- survivability of time-critical systems
- situational understanding and attack attribution

7   Conclusion

Software trustworthiness is a lively, difficult and richly articulated research discipline. In this paper the goal was to provide a useful overview of current and future challenges and try to cover the ongoing and foreseen research directions for further researches as well as introduce a new behavioristic model for tackling those challenges.

The proposed behavioristic model is a novel methodology for dynamic evaluation and estimation of software trustworthiness. It is intended to allow an analyst to build an integrated requirements model with informal and formal action specifications. The support for changing requirements and interaction between statechart modifications and the scenario model makes the important part of the overall concept. Furthermore, the scenario simulation and a provable evidence for confirming required functionality and quality address the industrial applicability of this research. The other new dimension of this research is its application in the process of certifying software trustworthiness, being actually the subject of standardization project of ISO/IEC JTC1 SC7 – System and software engineering.

References

1. Nami, M., Suryn, W.: From Requirements to Software Trustworthiness using Scenarios and Finite State Machine, Montreal (2012)
2. Rolland, C., et al.: A proposal for a scenario classification framework. Requirements Engineering Journal 3(1), 23–47 (1998)
3. Bordeleau, F., Corriveau, J.-P.: From Scenarios to Hierarchical State Machines: A Pattern based Approach. In: Proceedings of OOPSLA 2000 Workshop: Scenario Based Round-trip Engineering (October 2000)
4. Leue, S., Mehrmann, L., Rezai, M.: Synthesizing ROOM Models From Message Sequence Charts Specifications. In: Proc. 13th IEEE Conf. on Automated Software Engineering (1998)
5. Mäkinen, E., Systä, T.: An Interactive Approach for Synthesizing UML Statechart Diagrams from Sequence Diagrams. In: Proceedings of OOPSLA 2000 Workshop: Scenario Based Round-trip Engineering (October 2000)
6. Whittle, J., Schumann, J.: Generating Statechart Designs From Scenarios. In: Proceedings of OOPSLA 2000 Workshop: Scenario Based Round-trip Engineering, October 2000, Tampere University of Technology, Software Systems Laboratory, Report 20 (2000)
7. Behrens, H.: Requirements Analysis and Prototyping using Scenarios and Statecharts. In: Proceedings of ICSE 2002 Workshop: Scenarios and State Machines: Models, Algorithms, and Tools (2002)
8. DACS, Software Project Management for Software Assurance: A State-of-the-Art-Report (September 30, 2007)
9. DACS, and IATAC, Software Security Assurance: A State-of-the-Art-Report (July 31, 2007)
10. Department of Defence, National Computer Security Center, Trusted Computer System Evaluation Criteria. DOD 5200.28 STD (1985)
11. Parnas, D., et al.: Evaluation of safety-critical Software. UCA 4 33(6), 635–648 (1990)
12. ISO/IEC Standard No. 9126: Software engineering – Product quality; Parts 1–4. International Organization for Standardization (ISO) / International Electrotechnical Commission (IEC), Geneva, Switzerland (2001-2004)
13. Boland, T., et al.: Toward a Preliminary Framework for Assessing the Trustworthiness of Software. National Institute of Standards and Technology (November 2010)
14. Zheng, Z., et al.: Complexity of Software trustworthiness and its dynamical statistical analysis methods. Science in China Series F" - Information Sciences 52(9), 1651–1657 (2009), doi:10.1007/s11432-009-1043-4

15. Hertzum, M.: The importance of trust in software engineers' assessment and choice of information sources. Information and Organization 12, 1–18 (2002)
16. Bernstein, L.: Trustworthy software systems. SIGSOFT Software Engineering Notes 30, 4–5 (2005)
17. Amoroso, E., Taylor, C., Watson, J., Weiss, J.: A process-oriented methodology for accessing and improving Software Trustworthy. In: Proceedings of the 2nd ACM Conference on Computer and Communication Security, Virginia, USA, pp. 39–50 (1994)
18. Dijkstra, E.W., Dahl, O.J., Hoare, C.A.R.: Structured programming. Academic Press (1972)
19. http://www.cnsoftware.org/nsg (visited on April 24, 2011)
20. Gill, H.: High Confidence Software and Systems: Cyber-Physical Systems Progress Report: Semantics Perspective. National Science Foundation, Second Workshop on Event-based Semantics (2008)
21. Avizienis, A., Laprie, J.-C., Randell, B.: Fundamental Concepts of Dependability, Technical Report 739., Department of Computing Science. University of Newcastle upon Tyne (2001)
22. De Lemos, R., Gacek, C., Romanovsky, A.: ICSE 2002 Workshop on Software Architectures for Dependable Systems (Workshop Summary). ACM Software Engineering Notes 28(5) (November 2003)
23. Oppliger, R., Rytz, R.: Does trusted computing remedy computer security problems? IEEE Security & Privacy 3(2), 16–19 (2005)
24. Mundie, C., et al.: Trustworthy Computing. Microsoft White Paper (October 2002)
25. Safford, D.: The Need for TCPA, IBM Research (October 2002), http://www.ibm.com (last visited April 30, 2011)
26. Hurlbut, R.: A Survey of Approaches for Describing and Formalizing Use Cases, Technical Report 97-03, Department of Computer Science. Illinois Institute of Technology, USA (1997), http://www.iit.edu/~rhurlbut/xpt-tr-97-03.html
27. Hurlbut, R. R.: Managing Domain Architecture Evolution Through Adaptive Use Case and Business Rule Models" Ph.D. thesis. Illinois Institute of Technology, Chicago, USA (1998), http://www.iit.edu/~rhurlbut/hurl98.pdf (visited on May 10, 2012)
28. Suryn, W., Trudeau, P.O., Mazzetti, C.: Information Systems and their Relationship to Quality Engineering
29. Security, Privacy and Trust in the Future Internet, Issues for discussion, http://www.future-internet.eu/fileadmin/documents/bled_documents/Issues_TSD_Future_Internet_-_08_03_02.pdf (visited on May 10, 2012)
30. Dept. of Homeland Security, A Roadmap for Cybersecurity Research (November 2009), http://www.cyber.st.dhs.gov/docs/DHS-Cybersecurity-Roadmap.pdf (visited on May 10, 2012)

A New Measurement Method for Software Trustworthiness Based on Rough Sets

Yuyu Yuan[1,2], Qiang Han[1,2,3], and Sun Qi[4]

[1] School of Computer Science, Beijing University of Posts and Telecommunications, Beijing,
China
[2] Key Laboratory of Trustworthy Distributed Computing and Service (BUPT),
Ministry of Education, Beijing, China
[3] School of Computer Science and Engineering, Beifang University of Nationalities, Yinchuan,
China
{yyy1012,nxhanq}@gmail.com
[4] School of Computer Science and Technology, Southwest University for Nationalities,
Chengdu, China

Abstract. Usually, software trustworthiness represents the consistency of software behavior and its claim. Addressing to the measurement method of software trustworthiness, this paper propose a new measurement method for software trustworthiness based on rough sets. In detail, we firstly define the formal representation of software trustworthiness according to its definition. Secondly, we introduce relative measurement method about rough sets and its application approaches in measurement for software trustworthiness. Thirdly, a new measurement method for software trustworthiness is presented which use rough sets to measure the similarities between the software behavior and its claim. Finally, we make the conclusion of this paper and discuss some research area in software trustworthiness in future.

Keywords: Software, Trustworthiness, Measurement Method, Rough Sets.

1 Introduction

Under the rapid evolvement of scalability and complexity of modern distributed software, the traditional measurement method for software quality focusing on stable software documents could not solve the problem on dynamic evolvement of software quality and users' preference on their favorite characteristics on software. Addressing to solve the problem mentioned above, we present a new measurement method concentrated on measure the similarity between software behavior and its claim through Black-box testing. Based on some works completed partially early, in this paper, we continue to put forward research method following with relative approaches by rough sets. The remainder of this paper is consists of the three sections: Section 2 discusses the related research works on measurement approaches; Section 3 illustrate the new measurement method from its formal representation to calculus and algorithm for

Y. Yuan, X. Wu, and Y. Lu (Eds.): ISCTCS 2012, CCIS 320, pp. 13–19, 2013.

software trustworthiness; Section 4 conclude the whole paper and point out research areas in future.

2   Related Research on Measurement Approaches

Resent years, much intelligence computational approaches have been presented to solve varies problem in Software Engineering. Among those approaches, measurement approaches is a branch research area focusing on measurement problem about almost every stage in Software Engineering. In ref.[1], an overview was introduced about major research plan of trustworthy software, which pointed out that research plan has increasingly importance on modern information society, and as a core scientific problem in that plan, measurement of software trustworthiness is proposed to find intent regular rules hidden in relative between software defects and its trustworthiness. In ref.[2], the authors given a survey on research progress of measurement on object-oriented software, from scope and history of quality of object-oriented software to technologies and corresponding tools of quality measurement, the reference summarized several primary research issues on object-oriented software measurement. However, for the aim of research in ref.[2] is software quality, so it mainly discuss static measurement method instead of dynamic measurement method which is the majority of measurement method on software trustworthiness. As the fundamental technology of software trustworthiness measurement, constructing software behavior models is the hot point of research work for a long time. In ref.[3], the authors presented a software behavior model based on system objects. In that reference, inspired by finite state automata, the authors proposed a model of software behavior based on system objects which is resolved from the parameters of system calls. In that model, the behavior of system is represented by its object along with semantic information, so as to solve irrelevant semantics between different traces using the semantic information. Addressing to research evolution strategy for e-Science, ref.[4] put forward an uncertainty enhanced trust evolution strategy. In that strategy, a series definition about trust value space, trust concept space and trust cloud were proposed based on subjective trust concept and cloud model theory [5], and a method to assess trust level is presented by the authors of ref.[4]. Complexity and scalability are the main reason due to trustworthiness of software could not be controlled well as the early stage of static and closed development environment. To reveal the essential characteristics of software trustworthiness evolutionary complexity, the ref.[6] discuss and explain the basic scientific problems in software trustworthiness and the dynamical mechanism under the effect of various internal and external factors. In additionally, the authors of ref.[7] also advanced an invariant-measure based assessment method of software trustworthiness by statistical indices through using the dynamical statistical analysis methods.

In our early research works [8-10], we present some measure calculus about software trustworthiness. According to the definition about software trustworthiness, some formal representation of software trustworthiness is given.

3   A New Measurement Method for Software Trustworthiness

3.1   Formal Representation of Software Trustworthiness [10]

Assume that X is a finite collection of *STD* or *SED* [9-10]. A trustworthiness concept hierarchy is a collection of partitions, $P_1,...,P_r$. Here P_k is called the kth level partition. The fundamental property of the concept hierarchy is that each class (granular or cluster) in a lower level partition is fully contained in one class of the next more coarse as we go up.

We note that for $m > k$ we have $q_m < q_k$. For any class in the kth level, T_{kj}, there exists a class in the mth level, T_{mi} such that $T_{kj} \subseteq T_{mi}$. Then with $m > k$ we have for any T_{mi} that $T_{mi} = \bigcup_{j \in S_{mi/k}} T_{kj}$ where $S_{mi/k} \subseteq \{1,...,qk\}$. In addition, every element T_{mi} in matrix represents **a set of** (R, H) [9-10] occurring with **average probability** r_{mi}, **average weight** w_{mi} and composition mode c_{mi} of its sublevel classes. Every element T_{mi} has two components: Q and H. $T_{mi}.Q = Card(T_{mi})$, $T_{mi}.H$ means its value contributes to $T_{(m+1)j} \left(T_{mi} \subseteq T_{(m+1)j} \right)$.

Formally we have Matrix T as the collection of partitions:

$$
\begin{bmatrix}
P_{Top}(1,1,\wedge / \vee) \\
\cdot \\
P_r : T_{r1}(r_{r1}, w_{r1}, c), T_{r2}(r_{r2}, w_{r2}, c),...,T_{rqr}(r_{rqr}, w_{rqr}, c) \\
\cdot \\
P_2 : T_{21}(r_{21}, w_{21}, c), T_{22}(r_{22}, w_{22}, c),...,T_{2q2}(r_{2q2}, w_{2q2}, c) \\
P_1 : T_{11}(r_{11}, w_{11}, \wedge), T_{12}(r_{12}, w_{12}, \wedge),...,T_{1q1}(r_{1q1}, w_{1q1}, \wedge)
\end{bmatrix} \tag{1}
$$

3.2   Software Trustworthiness Measurement Algorithm with Calculating $R_{SED/STD}$

According to the formulas (1) presented above, we now propose a new measurement algorithm different from Ref.[9]. The aim is to archive a recommendation to the users at services selection time according to trustworthy software running condition in Ref.[10].

Here the algorithm is illustrated as follows:

0: Initialization: $T_{stt}(s)$, P_{STD}, P_{SED}, R_{STD}, R_{SED}; Transform P_{STD} and P_{SED} into Concept Matrix T^1, T^2 of Hierarchy Trustworthiness with every element' component Q and H initialized to Zero for initial and runtime software trustworthiness respectively.

Stage1: Calculate $T_{sit}(s)$.

1:    $i = j = k = 1$

2:    **for each** partition R_{Ti} in P_{STD} :

3:        **for each** level partition P_k in T^1 :

4:            **for each** class T_{kj} in P_k :

5:                **if** $\forall(x, y) \in R_{Ti} \Rightarrow (x, y) \in T_{kj}$

6:                    $T_{kj}.Q = T_{kj}.Q + Card(R_{Ti})$

7:                **endif**

8:            **endfor**

9:        **endfor**

10:    **endfor**

11:    $j = k = 1$

12:    **for each** level partitions P_k in T^1 :

13:        **for each** class T_{kj} in P_k :

14:            **if** $\left(T_{kj}.Q > 0\right) \& \left(T_{(k+1)i}.c = \wedge\right) \& \left(T_{kj} \subseteq T_{(k+1)i}\right)$

15:                $T_{(k+1)i}.H = T_{(k+1)i}.r \times \sum_j \left(T_{kj}.H \times T_{kj}.w\right)$

16:            **else if**

17:                $\left(T_{kj}.Q > 0\right) \& \left(T_{(k+1)i}.c = \vee\right) \& \left(T_{kj} \subseteq T_{(k+1)i}\right)$

18:                $T_{(k+1)i}.H = Max\left(T_{kj}.H\right) \times T_{(k+1)i}.r$

19:            **endif**

20:        **endfor**

21:    **endfor**

22:    $T_{sit}(s) = T_k.H$

Stage2: Calculate $T_{srt}(s)$

23:    $i = j = k = 1$

24:    **for each** partition R_{Ei} in P_{SED} :

25:        **for each** level partitions P_k in T^2 :

26:            **for each** class T_{kj} in P_k :

27:                **if** $\forall(x, y) \in R_{Ei} \Rightarrow (x, y) \in T_{kj}$

28:                    **if** $T_{kj}.Q > 0$

29:                        $0 \rightarrow T_{kj}.Q$ **else**

30:                        $T_{kj}.Q = T_{kj}.Q + Card(R_{Ei})$

31:                    **endif**

32:          **endif**

33:        **endfor**

34:      **endfor**

35:    **endfor**

36:    $j = k = 1$

37:    **for each** level partitions P_k in T^2 :

38:        **for each** class T_{kj} in P_k :

39:            **if** $\left(T_{kj}.Q > 0 \right) \& \left(T_{(k+1)i}.c = \wedge \right) \& \left(T_{kj} \subseteq T_{(k+1)i} \right)$

40:            $T_{(k+1)i}.H = T_{(k+1)i}.r \times \sum_j \left(T_{kj}.H \times T_{kj}.w \right)$

41:            **else if**

42:            $\left(T_{kj}.Q > 0 \right) \& \left(T_{(k+1)i}.c = \vee \right) \& \left(T_{kj} \subseteq T_{(k+1)i} \right)$

43:            $T_{(k+1)i}.H = Max\left(T_{kj}.H \right) \times T_{(k+1)i}.r$

44:            **endif**

45:        **endfor**

46:    **endfor**

47:    $i = j = k = 1$

48:    **for each** partition R_{Ti} in P_{STD} :

49:      **for each** level partition P_k in T^1 :

50:        **for each** class T_{kj} in P_k :

51:            **if** $\exists (x, y) \in R_{Ti} \Rightarrow (x, y) \in T_{kj}$

52:            $R_{STD} = R_{STD} + T_{kj}.r \times T_{kj}.w$

53:            **endif**

54:        **endfor**

55:      **endfor**

56:    **endfor**

57:    $i = j = k = 1$

58:    **for each** partition R_{Ei} in P_{SED} :

59:      **for each** level partition P_k in T^2 :

60:        **for each** class T_{kj} in P_k :

61:            **if** $\exists (x, y) \in R_{Ti} \Rightarrow (x, y) \in T_{kj}$

62:            $R_{SED} = R_{SED} + T_{kj}.r \times T_{kj}.w$

63:            **endif**

64:        **endfor**

65:      **endfor**

66:    **endfor**

67:    $R_{SED/STD} = \left(R_{SED} / R_{STD} \right).$

68:    **for each** row and **each** column in T^1, T^2 :

69:    calculate $\sum \overline{\overline{Cong}}^{w1}$ [10].

70:    calculate $\sum \overline{\overline{Cong}}^{w2}$ [10].

71:    **endfor**

72:    calculate $\overline{\overline{Cong}}^{w3}$ of formula (28) [10].

73:    calculate $T_{srt}(s) = \overline{\overline{Cong}}^{w3} \times T_{sit}(s)$

Stage3: Generate Recommendation

74:    **if** $T_{sit}(s) \geq T_{srt}(s) \geq T_{stt}(s)$

75:        $Recommending = 'True'.$

76:    **else** $Recommending = 'False'.$

77:    **output**: $Recommending$.

Algorithm End.

4   Conclusion and Future Working

Address to congruence measurement problem of software trustworthiness, this paper put forward a new algorithm of software trustworthiness based on our early work and this paper mainly focus on the generation of kernel component of formula of software trustworthiness in runtime (i.e. the ratio of environment of software test to software runtime).

Following works we think should include the illustrating of congruence formula and evaluation of software trustworthiness, and the experiment of theories mentioned above.

Acknowledgement. This paper is supported by National Natural Science Foundation of China (91118002), National High Technology Research and Development Program of China (863 Program, 2011AA01A204).

References

1. Liu, K., Shan, Z., Wang, J., He, J., Zhang, Z., Qin, Y.: Overview on Major Research Plan of Trustworthy Software. Bulletin of National Science Foundation of China 22(3), 145–151 (2008)

2. Zhou, Y., Xu, B.: Research Progress on Metrics of Object-Oriented Software. In: Proceedings of CCF, pp. 49–59 (2010)
3. Fu, J.M., Tao, F., Wang, D., Zhang, H.G.: Software behavior model based on system objects. Journal of Software 22(11), 2716–2728 (2011)
4. Du, W., Cui, G.H., Liu, W.: An uncertainty enhanced trust evolution strategy for e-Science. Journal of Computer Science and Technology 25(6), 1225–1236 (2010)
5. Li, D.Y., Meng, H.J., Shi, X.M.: Membership clouds and membership cloud generators. Journal of Computer Research and Development 32(6), 1315–1320 (1995)
6. Zheng, Z.M., Ma, S.L., Li, W., et al.: Complexity of software trustworthiness and its dynamical statistical analysis methods. Sci. China Ser. F-Inf. Sci. 52(9), 1651–1657 (2009)
7. Zheng, Z.M., Ma, S.L., Li, W., et al.: Dynamical characteristics of software trustworthiness and their evolutionary complexity. Sci. China Ser. F-Inf. Sci. 52(8), 1328–1334 (2009)
8. Yuan, Y., Han, Q.: Data Mining based Measurement Method for Software Trustworthiness. In: IEEE IPTC 2010, pp. 293–296 (2010)
9. Yuan, Y.Y., Han, Q.: A Software Behavior Trustworthiness Measurement Method based on Data Mining. International Journal of Computational Intelligence Systems 4(5), 817–825 (2011)
10. Yuan, Y.Y., Han, Q.: A Data Mining based Measurement Method for Software Trustworthiness. Chinese Journal of Electronics 21(1), 13–16 (2012)

Service Behavior Trustworthiness Management

Yuyu Yuan[1,4,5], Yangyang Zhang[1,2], and Jing Liu[3]

[1] Beijing University of Posts and Telecommunications, Beijing, R.P. China
[2] China Electronics Standardization Institute, Beijing, R.P. China
[3] Olympic Branch, China Everbright Bank CO., LTD
[4] Key Laboratory of Trustworthy Distributed Computing and Service (BUPT),
Ministry of Education, Beijing, China
[5] Yuyu Yuan, No 10, Xitucheng Road, Haidian District, Beijing, China
yyy1012@gmail.com

Abstract. As we move to a world where our information assets reside on the Web, the issue of service trust adds a new set of dimensions to the age-old problem of belief and trust in content. The ability to measure and evaluate service behavior trustworthiness becomes increasingly important. This paper presents a service behavior trustworthiness management system. This system could help third parties to develop and implement a framework for monitoring and managing the trustworthiness of service behavior. An overview, relate concepts and methods of the system are proposed in this paper. We also discuss a case study of this system and potential practical value of the proposed system in e-bank applications.

1   Introduction

For more than one hundred thousand years, if a user wanted to get a service, he should find a service provider. How can he trust this service provider? If he didn't know him directly, he had to know him through the social network. This social network is formed by lots of persons or organizations; we call them entities. If the user trusts this channel, he can trust the service provider, and the service provider provides service to the user.

Now we are in the information technology age. Users also need to find trustworthy service providers. It is the same as for one hundred thousand years ago. But there is the difference that in the information technology based applications every possible entity has an agent. In the trust channel lots of agents attend. A user not only needs to evaluate the entity channel, he also needs to evaluate the agent channel. His job is complicated and huge. But fortunately, he can use information technology to measure, evaluate and certify the service provider's behavior.

2   Related Concept

There are two definitions of **Trust**.
   Trust is the behavior X exhibits if he or she believes that Y will behave in X's best interest and not harm X. [1]

Y. Yuan, X. Wu, and Y. Lu (Eds.): ISCTCS 2012, CCIS 320, pp. 20–25, 2013.
© Springer-Verlag Berlin Heidelberg 2013

In this definition the trust is a behavior, which is the behavior X exhibits. The condition is: X believes that Y will behave in X's best interest and not harm X. But here is a problem. How could X confirm that Y will behave in X's best interest or not harm X. We think X should know Y over time or get information about Y from some way. This means that X should know Y's trustworthiness value.

Trust can be defined as user's thoughts, feelings, emotions, or behaviors that occur when they feel that an agent can be relied upon to act in their best interest when they give up direct control. [1]

This definition tells us that trust behavior happens when a trustor gives up direct control. If a trustor can control, the trustor doesn't need the trustee. But if trustor gives up direct control, he should know the trustworthiness value.

Trust is always the basis of a society. We trust a pilot, and we can take an airplane. IT service becomes an important means to provide service. IT service has evolved from closed and centralized environments to open and distributed environments.

Users enjoy an IT service without ownership of the system, so control of an IT service has moved from users to software service providers. Customers give up direct control of an IT service, so they need know the service providers trustworthiness.

IT service behavior trustworthiness adds new dimensions to the old age problem of trustworthiness in traditional services. The need for IT service behavior trustworthiness management has emerged.

What is IT Service behavior trustworthiness management? Now we give an explanation word by word.

IT Service means a service based on the use of information technology.

Behavior is the way in which an IT service functions or operates. We can also think that behavior is a service providers use software and systems to provide a special act or operates; the purpose is to complement a service.

Trustworthiness of IT service is the demonstrated ability of the service provider to deliver a correct service while adhering to a set of stated (and commonly agreed) principles.

Management includes specification, monitoring, measurement and evaluation of the IT service behavior trustworthiness.

Why do we need behavior? What is the relationship between service and behavior? We can get some elicitation from Fractals. Fractals are typically self-similar patterns. Fractal things can be split into parts, each of which is a reduced-size copy of the whole. Service also can be seen as a recursion of subservices and behavior. Our goal is to find the patterns of service that can be monitored, measured, and evaluated. Trustworthiness can be measured or be evaluated on the pattern of service behavior rather than on the attributes in the quality model. For example, Mail system is system. Mail service is service. Service Behavior is sending mails, receive mails, deleting mails and so on. Service providers are Google Company, yahoo, Hotmail and so on. Mail systems have different service behaviors. Service behavior depends on time. Some Service provider read your mails or deleted your mails. Some service providers do not respond. So customers enjoy service behavior, he cares for service behavior trustworthiness. The mail system has a send function and responds quickly. But the service provider didn't operate; that means service behavior has low trustworthiness. The mail system can delete mails and read mails. But the service provider did this. This means service behavior has low trustworthiness.

3   Related Work

There is some similar concepts; we will show they are different. They are dependability, reliability, safety, security, privacy, and quality.

Dependability to describe the availability performance and its influencing factors: reliability performance, maintainability performance and maintainability support performance. [2]

IEC 61907 defines dependability as availability performance and it influencing factors.

Reliability: a degree to which a system, product or component performs specified functions under specified conditions for a specified period of time. [3]

Security: degree to which a product or system protects information and data so that persons or other products or systems have the degree of data access appropriate to their types and levels of authorization. [3]

Safety: Freedom from unacceptable risk. [4]

From the definitions of dependability, reliability, security and safety, we know these terms are system properties whereas trustworthiness involves properties of the service provider. Trustworthiness is also related to moral values. These terms are only related to technical issues.

Privacy: The right of individuals to control or influence what information related to them may be collected and stored and by whom and to whom that information may be disclosed. [5]

The definition of privacy is from ISO 7498. Privacy is also important for trustworthiness. Privacy does not cover trustworthiness, but it is included in the trustworthiness concept.

Quality: Degree to which a set of inherent characteristics (3.5.1) fulfills requirements (3.1.2). [6]

Finally we can compare trustworthiness with quality. We look at the definition of quality from ISO 9000. The definition of quality is concerned with quality in general. Quality is related to the current version of software and system, so it is static. Trustworthiness is related to accumulate historical records, so it is dynamic.

It is clear that trustworthiness of IT service behavior is a dynamic property. It changes over time. Trustworthiness is about the ability of the IT service provider to deliver a specified service. Each time the service is delivered the trustworthiness may change. But trustworthiness is also about not lying, cheating, stealing, and so on. This is related to moral values. Therefore trustworthiness is completely different from the other terms.

4   Monitor

There are two kinds of monitoring methods to collect the trustworthiness data. If an IT service wants to prove it is trustworthy, it needs to give a standard interface to be monitored. This is like interior monitoring methods. The other way is exterior on time. Testers like customers to collect the trustworthiness data while using the IT service. In this a monitoring method; there are three roles: IT services provider, monitor, and trusted third party.

For the interior monitoring method, we have three ways to implement the monitor. The first one uses trusted computing techniques to construct a trusted execution environment. Any untrusted behavior is detected and reported to a trusted third party. It is up to the trusted third party to evaluate and verify the trustworthiness of the IT service. The second way is to analyze and audit the service log. In this approach, the internal implementation of the IT service is a black box. And through analyzing and auditing the service behavior recorded on the log, the trustworthiness of the IT service can be calculated. The third way is to hook the service behavior in which some specified API of the service should be open to an external monitoring entity. When the above APIs are invoked by the service provider, they are also bypassed and recorded to the trusted third party.

Here further analysis, e.g. finite state machine based behavior logical analysis, are done.

5   Measure

When we get trustworthiness data, the next job is to measure service behavior trustworthiness value. We need to complete three steps to measure service behavior trustworthiness values. Firstly, we should build a standard service behavior database. Secondly, we should formalize service behavior. Thirdly, we should compare standard behavior and real behavior obtained from the monitoring process. A standard service behavior database is the core of measuring service behavior trustworthiness. The database will be very huge, but it should be a simple Pattern. This pattern is decided by the formal language to describe service behavior. For the third step, comparing standard behavior and real behavior, our doctoral student Qiang Han have a public paper, "A Data Mining Based Measurement Method for Software Trustworthiness" [7]. In this paper presents a method that applies a software trustworthiness measure to the dynamic behavior feature datasets generated at software running time compared with the static attribute feature datasets generated at software testing time in order to make recommendations for users at service selection time under the environment of SaaS.

Trustworthy behavior will have some characteristics. If we want to find its nature pattern, we should abstract it from some example real trustworthy behavior. Below are the ten kinds of trustworthy behavior; their relationships are as shown in the Figure 1.

1) **Real/Reality:** Service provider realizes **real-name** system
2) **Claims:** Service provider **claims** the behavior of the service offered
3) **Feedback:** Each request has a **response**, even if it is unreasonable demand
4) **Compensation:** If evidence is enough, the service provider would **pay for its fault**
5) **Complaints:** Users have the opportunity to express their **views**
6) **Privacy:** Sensitive information is well **protected**
7) **Traceable:** Each behavior is recorded and can be **traced**
8) **Evaluate:** Service provider has basic ability to **evaluate** the trustworthiness of **partners**
9) **Consistence:** Service provider is able to prove the **consistence** between the actual service and the claimed service behavior
10) **Monitor:** Service provider does indeed design **monitoring** interfaces

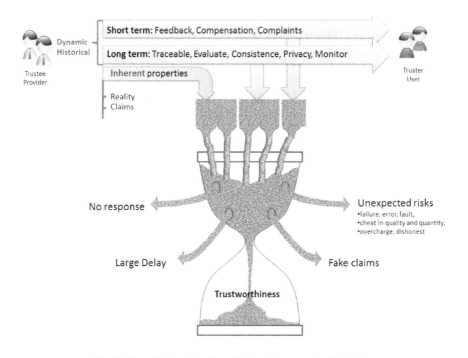

Fig. 1. The relationship of ten kinds of trustworthy behavior

6   Evaluate

IT service behavior trustworthiness evaluation is the practice part of SBTM. Different persons have different risk acceptance level. We can give an evaluation process for different persons. That means the same trustworthiness value will cause different trust degree. We will public another paper about this topic.

7   Scenario: e-Bank

Now we will describe a scenario of a Service Behavior Trustworthiness Management application. Bob want to find an e-bank to management his money. There are lots of e-banks, not only one. Bob should choose one e-bank to manage his money. Which e-bank can he trust? Somebody or some organization should tell him. This organization should have the ability to measure all the e-banks by using information technology. This organization should have a monitor system, which can collect trustworthy interior or exterior data from of service system. The e-bank trustworthiness value will change over time. The custom is depending on the value to choose the e-bank. The customers chose the e-bank with highest trustworthiness value. This trend forces other e-banks to get trustworthiness values. If they want to get this trustworthy value, they need to open the required interface to the monitor organization. This system running fee will be paid by customers and service provider. SBTM make the peoples life easy and simple.

8   Conclusion

Trust is the basis of society. IT service becomes an important means to provide service. This paper presents a system, which is service behavior trustworthiness management. This system could help third parties to develop and implement a framework for monitoring and managing the trustworthiness of service behavior. The overview, related concepts and methods of the system are proposed in this paper. We also discuss a case study of this system and the potential practical value of the proposed system in e-bank applications.

Acknowledgment. This work is supported by National Natural Science Foundation of China under Grants No. 91118002 and National High-tech R&D Program (863 Program) No. 2011AA01A204.

References

1. Patrick, A.S.: Building Trustworthy Software Agents. IEEE Internet Computing, 46–53 (November 2002)
2. IEC 61907:2009 Communication network dependability engineering, IEC (2009)
3. ISO/IEC25010:2011Systems and software engineering — Systems and software Quality Requirements and Evaluation (SQuaRE) — System and software quality models, ISO/IEC (2011)
4. IEC TS 62443-1-1-2009 Industrial communication networks - Network and system security - Part 1-1: Terminology, concepts and models, IEC (2009)
5. ISO 7498-2 Information processing systems - Open Systems Interconnection - Basis reference model - Part 2: Security architecture, ISO (1989)
6. ISO 9000 Quality management systems - Fundamentalsand vocabulary, ISO (2005)
7. Yuan, Y., Han, Q.: A Data Mining Based Measurement Method for Software Trustworthiness. Chinese Journal of Electronics 21(1), 13–16 (2012)

Research on Identifying Method of Covert Channels in Database System

Yao Pang, Xiaoxiao Zhang, Luwei Sun, and Weimin Ding

Nation Center for Quality Supervision and Inspection of Chinese Information Processing
Products, Beijing, China
Beijing Products Quality Supervision and Inspection Institute, Beijing, China
{stmsc,cissiezh,bqi_xd}@126.com,
dingweimin@sohu.com

Abstract. At present, the security level of DBMS in our country fails to satisfy the need of development and it's an urgent task to improve the safety performance of the relational database systems. The analysis and research on covert channels are vital to raising the security level of DBMS in our county. In this paper, we study the identifying method of covert channels in database system and propose a more efficient, more authentic and safely isolated identifying method of covert channels, which contributes to the follow-up process.

Keywords: database system, covert channel, identifying method.

1   Introduction

With the rapid development of information technology and the extensive application of database, data security has aroused high concern of the society. People attach great importance to the security of operating system and network and ignore the security of the database. They think that the secure operating system and network can guarantee the data security. However, for all relational database system, one can bypass the security mechanism of the operating system easily and connect to the database directly with the right query tool. Therefore, we should not only care about computer and network security, but also devote more attention to database security.

In the "Trusted Computer System Evaluation Criteria" (for short "TCSEC") [1] promulgated by America's Department of Defense (DOD) in 1985, data security [2] is classified into seven levels of four groups (D, C1, C2, B1, B2, B3, A)   [3]. According to TCSEC expanded to the database system by TDI, the database systems meeting the standard of the B1 level are called secure database systems or trusted database systems, and those meeting the standard of the B2 or higher level are called high reliability systems [4].

The database management system security level has been far from being able to meet the needs of the business websites of our enterprises and our government in China, so it is necessary to improve the safety performance of our existing relational DBMS to B2 level, or even B3 level to meet the needs of database security.

Y. Yuan, X. Wu, and Y. Lu (Eds.): ISCTCS 2012, CCIS 320, pp. 26–33, 2013.

According to TCSEC, to meet the B2 level, the DBMS must analyze the covert channel on the basis of B1 level. Thus the analysis and research on covert channels are important to enhance the security level of database system. This paper studies the covert channel identification method of the database system.

2   Concept of Covert Channel

In TCSEC the covert channel is defined as follow: A channel which allows processes pass information in the way of violating system security policy [5]. Under normal circumstances, the access of subject to the object through the regular path probably uses the TCB to check in the access path. However, there are various irregular paths in real applications and they constitute illegal access channels, which are covert and hard to check with TCB, named as covert channels [6].

Experts generalize the work principle of the covert channel [7]: in security systems, according to the predetermined way of encoding, the subjects or processes with relatively high security level change the properties of shared resources and make the change visible to the subjects or processes with relatively low security level, to transmit information which violates the system security policy, where the subjects or processes with high security level are called senders, those with low security level are called receivers [8].

3   Research on Method of Identifying Covert Channels in Database

As the basis of subsequent processing of the covert channels, identifying covert channels plays a vital role. This paper focuses on the research on the identification method of database system covert channel and improves the SRM of Kemmerer.

3.1   Determine the Properties of Shared Resources

First of all, identify all statements and the visible or modifiable properties of the shared resources according to Kemmerer method.

In order to find all the operation primitives and shared resource properties, we need to traverse the database system. Firstly, we go through all the resource properties in the system and determine the operation primitives and the shared resource properties according to the different operations to the properties from the sending processes and receiving processes, aiming at traversing all the operation primitives and shared resources properties in the database system.

We'll get a lot of resource properties after traversing the database. It's certain that such large amount of data will increase the difficulty of analyzing the covert channels. The key to solving the problem is reducing the number of properties for constructing shared resource matrix, so we filter the properties with three conditions:

(1) It is a shared variable (directly visible or directly variable)

(2) It can reflect the change of shared resource properties, i.e., the indirect visibility of the shared resource property depends on it.

(3) Or we can change the status or value of the shared resource property through it.

3.2   Constructing the Shared Resource Matrix

We construct the shared resource matrix [9] and apply operating of transitive closure to it.

3.3   Refine the Shared Resource Matrix

Firstly, we need refine the flow of information to exclude the matrix items that can't meet the condition of the covert channel, as shown in Table 1.

(1) The user's input and system's input are merged into one line respectively, which are labeled as u - in and u – out.

(2) Influent property of the information flow.

(3) The conditions producing sub-information flow are shown in Table 3-1: G1 = G（called when the condition is true）, G2 = NOTG（called when the condition does not hold）, G3 = TRUE（called when unconditionally）

Table 1. Table of sharing resources matrix

Resource property variables	Operation（G1）	Operation（G2）	Operation（G3）
S1	R		
S2		R	
T1	M	M	R
G	R	R	
u – in（input）	R	R	R
u – in（output）			M

3.4   Analyze the Security Level of the Operation Primitives and the Shared Resource Properties

The covert channel is in violation of mandatory access control mechanism. Mandatory access marks data with secret level. The tag and data is inseparable no matter how the data is copied. Only the users that comply with the security classification marking requirements can manipulate data, thus a higher level of security is realized. B2 level DBMS has data mandatory access, in which every database master / object has a security level, thus read/write operations from subject to the object can be determined by the security level signs and safe range mark. Since covert channel is an information channel in which primitives communicate with primitives of lower security level through sharing resources [10], we can analyze a pair of operation primitives according to the security levels, and the primitives meeting the following conditions must have potentially covert channels.

(1) For a column that contains a R or M in the matrix, the security level of TCB primitives represented by row which labeled as R should be lower than the security level of TCB primitives represented by row which labeled as M.

(2) If there are covert channels, it must go against with the mandatory access control mechanism (the mandatory access control mechanism is required in security system of B1 level). Then the security level between operation primitives and shared resources is that: only when the hierarchical categories of operational primitives are less than or equal to the hierarchical categories of shared resource properties, the primitives can read the shared resource properties. Only when the hierarchical categories of operational primitives are larger than or equal to those of the shared resource properties, the primitives can write the shared resource properties. Therefore, there are potential covert channels for the shared resource represented by this column only when the security levels of operational primitives and shared resources properties meet this condition.

According to the principle that the covert channels exist and mandatory access control strategy, for two processes between which there are covert channels, the greater the difference of security levels is, the more serious consequences the covert channels bring. So we should not only analyze the security levels of operational primitives and shared resources properties, but also analyze the difference of security level between different operational primitives at the same time.

(1) If the difference between the security levels of operational primitives is relatively large, we should focus on the case that there are potential covert channels.

(2) If the difference between the security levels of operational primitives is relatively small, we can shift our attention targeted.

Since there are many operational primitives and shared resources properties in a system, we will get a lot of triple sequences of the covert channels. In order to analyze and get reliable potential covert channels correctly in such mass data, we should focus on the important information, thus make the covert channel identification work more effectively.

3.5   Combining the Covert Channel Triples Sequence

Merge the triples sequence of the covert channel we get as below:

(1)If the triples sequence of a covert channel occur several times, then merged them into a triples sequence of the covert channel.

(2) If an operation has both read operation and write operation, and the write operation depends on the read operation, then we can merge the operations as the triples of the write operation.

The file system specification requires that a file must be opened before reading, locked before writing. Therefore, in a sequence of operations, if the ReadFile operation succeeds, the OpenFile operation must be done before ReadFile operation. Similarly, if a WriteFile operation succeeds, the LockFile operation must be done before WriteFile operation. The ReadFile operation depends on the OpenFile operation, the WriteFile operation depends on the LockFile operation. So we do not consider the interdependence [11] between the operations.

(3) According to the definition [12] of covert channel, a covert channel is the channel to allow the process of transmitting information in violation of system security policy.

Each process has a private Buffer property and any operation does not allow a process to modify or refer the buffer property of another process. Therefore, the sender and receiver must be the same process in a covert channel based on buffer property.

So for all the triples sequences, if different covert channels triples have same send primitive and receive primitive, then it shows there exists some channels acting upon different shared resource properties between the sender and the recipient. If we merge the different shared resource properties, then we get a property containing all the properties.

(4) Ensure that the covert channel triples sequences are relatively independent, and reduce the interdependence

Merge the triples sequences that have the same shared resource properties, but different recipient or sender because of transitive relation. Therefore, in the subsequent analysis on such triples sequence, we can ignore the sender and the receiver that is obtained by passing temporarily and analyze the covert channel that got by passing only after the covert channel between the initial sender and the initial recipient establishes.

The above merge operations of covert channel is based mainly on the constant repetition and interdependence between triples sequence, where we merge the interdependent triples sequences without excluding the possibility that a potential covert channel triples sequence besides the repeat sequence is a real covert channel. These merge operations can significantly reduce the number of covert channel triples sequences that need to be analyzed in the follow-up operations. After a covert channel is determined through follow-up analysis, we'll judge the sequences merged with the covert channel.

3.6   Remove the Invalid Covert Channel Triples Sequences

Not every potential covert channel can be used to transmit the illegal information. We'll do some analysis according to the classified channel type in Kemmerer method, to remove the invalid covert channel triples sequences.

(1)The channel is useless, i.e., there is another legitimate channel between the sender and the receiver of the covert channel

If the sender of a potential covert channel is asked to have the security level to send some information to another legal resource when it accesses the shared resource properties, and the recipient of the potential covert channel is asked to have the security level to receive some information from the same legal resources when it accesses the shared resource properties, then there exist other legal channels between the sender and the receiver of the covert channel, thus the potential covert channel is useless.

(2)The channel that can't provide any useful information to the recipient

If the operation that the receiver performs on the shared resource properties depend on the operation that the sender performs on the shared resource properties, or the operation that the receiver performs on the shared resource properties does not change over the change of the shared resource properties i.e., the channel can't get useful information and can only transfer the information known by the operation, then the channel can't be took as a potential covert channel.

(3)The channel requiring that the sender and the receiver are same

If a covert channel requires that the sender and the receiver are same, the properties that the sender and the receiver operate can't be considered as a shared resource property. According to why the covert channels exist, if there is no shared resource, there will be no covert channel, i.e., the channel will not provide any useful information for the dissemination of information. Therefore, the channel is not a potential covert channel.

(4)The channel can be used to transfer illegal information

If the channel does not meet any of the three conditions above, and can construct the real-life scene of the covert channel, the channel can be used to transfer illegal information.

If the operation between the sender and receiver depends on another legal channel, the operation between the sender and receiver will depend on the inspection of the TCB, therefore, this channel will not transmit information that violate the system security policy, thus it can't be used as a covert channel; the channel, where the sender can't provide useful information to the recipient, can't pass the illegal information either, thus it can't be took as a covert channel; the shared resources is a prerequisite for the existence of covert channels, so the channel between the sender and receiver that do not have the share resources is invalid covert channel. Based on the above analysis, the operation that removes the invalid covert channels does not remove the real covert channels.

3.7   Construct Covert Channel Real Scenarios

Above identified covert channels are all potential covert channels, because some conditions to constitute the shared resource matrix may never be satisfied in the real system. may also be in the actual scene, some variable/visible system calls to shared system resources are not allowed to invoke not all TCB primitives are allowed to be called by ordinary users in general scenarios either, so we need to construct a real application scenario for each potential covert channel [13].

3.8   Comparing with SRM

(1) We first compare the steps and the result is shown in Table 2.

Table 2. Table of contrast

Step	SRM	Improved method
First	Directly determine the shared resource properties	Analyze the shared resource properties, determine the shared resource properties
Second	Hand-construct shared resource matrix	Construct a shared resource matrix
Third	Analyze all the triples sequence	Refine the shared resource matrix
		Analyze the security level of the primitives and shared resources
		Merge triples sequence
		Remove invalid triples
Fourth	Constructing real scenarios	Constructing real scenarios

As we can see clearly from Table 2, the improved method of shared resource matrix refines the analysis steps and makes the potential covert channel which we get more authentic.

(2) Improved efficiency of analysis

Constructing matrix with our algorithm overcomes the drawback of low efficiency and high error rate in manual constructing.

(3) Increased authenticity

Analyzing shared resource properties with TCB primitives excludes the improper shared resources. The merge or delete operation to the triple sequence improves the probability of being real covert channel.

(4) Enhanced security isolation

We analyze the security level of the shared resource properties and the operation primitives and achieve enhanced security isolation.

4   Conclusion

At present, data security receives serious attention. The covert channel in DBMS will be a security risk with the mandatory access control realized. On the research of the covert channel, identifying the potential covert channel is the starting point for all subsequent work; because only the covert channels are identified correctly can we take effective measures to deal with the security problem. Therefore, identifying the potential covert channels is an urgent task. It is also important and difficult for our study.

References

1. G A/T 389-2002. Database management system technology requirement in computer information system classified security protection
2. Li, D.-F., Xie, X.: The Research and Realization of Database security Technology 1, 1–2 (2008)
3. Liang, T.: Search of Security Evaluation Criteria. Mini-micro Systems 27(4), 2 (2006)
4. Computer system security standards. High Performance Computer Technology 06, 61–62 (2001)
5. Dept.of Defence. Trusted Database Management System Interpretation. National Computer Security Center, 12 (1985)
6. Binge, C.: Using an Information Flow Graph to Identify and Analyze Covert Channels. Journal of Harbin Engineering University 05, 742–744 (2006)
7. Denning, D.E.: A Lattice Model of Secure Information Flow. Communications of the ACM 19(5), 236–243 (1976)
8. Filsinger, J.: Integrity and the audit of trusted database management systems. IFIP Transactions A: Computer Science and Technology A21, 349–365 (1993)
9. Le, Z., Fu, P.: Security Mechanisms and Implementation of Class-B1 Networks. Computer Engineering and Applications 18, 54–56 (2001)
10. http://blog.csdn.net/begtostudy/archive/2006/12/18/1448216.aspx
11. Kemmerer, R.A.: Shared resource matrix methodology: A practical approach to identifying covert channels. ACM Transactions on Computer Systems (1983)
12. Ju, S., Song, X.: On the Formal Characterization of Covert Channel. In: Chi, C.-H., Lam, K.-Y. (eds.) AWCC 2004. LNCS, vol. 3309, pp. 155–160. Springer, Heidelberg (2004)
13. Kemmerer, R.A.: Shared Resource Matrix Methodology: A Practical Approach to Identifying Covert Channels. ACM Transactions on Computer Systems 1(3), 256–277 (1983)

Software Testing is Necessary But Not Sufficient for Software Trustworthiness

Mitra Nami and Witold Suryn

École de technologie supérieure, Montréal, Canada
mitra.nami.1@ens.etsmtl.ca, witold.suryn@etsmtl.ca

Abstract. In the past decades, software verification generally was about 40-50% of the total development costs of any software system [12], yet few users are satisfied with reliability of their software. Even though the quality assurance budgets of software makers are increasing, program failures with possible data loss happens quite often. This paper investigates the reasons why software testing is not enough for assuring software trustworthiness and is a follow up of previous study on finding a way to model software trustworthiness by using Finite State Machine (FSM) and scenarios [1]. The approach uses the novel behavioristic model for verifying software trustworthiness based on scenarios of interactions between the software and its users and environment presented in our previous paper [1]. The approach consists of interactions of examples or counterexamples of desired behavior and supports incremental changes in requirements or scenarios.

Keywords: software, trustworthiness, quality, security.

1 Introduction

When there is sufficient credible evidence to believe that the software system will meet a set of given requirements, it would be considered trustworthy [1]. In order to gain confidence about behavior of software, we need either:

- to test software to validate whether software behaves as intended and identifies potential malfunctions.

or

- to capture its functional and quality requirements, which involve creating behavioral models.

The latter is introduced in this paper by scenario-based and state-based modeling while the former is widely used in industry for quality assurance. Software testing is used to locate software failures. There are several possible causes for a software failure. Some of them are:

- change of the program source code,
- modification of its context by updating libraries or changing its configuration,
- modification of its test suite.

Y. Yuan, X. Wu, and Y. Lu (Eds.): ISCTCS 2012, CCIS 320, pp. 34–44, 2013.
© Springer-Verlag Berlin Heidelberg 2013

Any of these changes can cause differences in program behavior. In general, program paths may appear or disappear between executions of two subsequent versions of a system. Some of these behavioral differences are expected by developers while some are not expected and could be problematic. Furthermore, the degree to which a behavioral change might be problematic is different from system to system. Some of behavioral changes may only become apparent over time as there are interactions between current and future changes. Software testing is used to find faults in software. It is a process of providing some values to the system under test and making conclusions on the basis of its behavior. A test case consists of inputs together with the expected results. Although generating test inputs can be as simple as selecting numbers randomly, deriving the corresponding expected results is often labor intensive. However the most significant weakness of testing is that the behavior of the tested system can only be verified for those input situations which were provided in the test data. According to Dijkstra [13], testing can only show the existence but not the non-existence of errors. Only a comprehensive test plan with all possible input values, input value sequences, and input value combinations under all practically possible constraints can prove the correctness of that program. Because there are numerous possible input situations, execution of a comprehensive test is not possible. In practice only a subset of all possible input value, input value sequences, and input value combinations is chosen in the test plan.

With the growing size of software projects, and the complexity of testing object-oriented code, there are applications with millions of combinations of states and paths. It's impossible for quality assurance to test every possible state, every possible data value, and every possible path through the code.

System testing will always miss something. The more complex the system, the more defects will likely be missed. When the software isn't sufficiently tested, the released version of software will have unknown number of bugs. Fig. 1 presents percentage of defects introduced and found at different stages of software testing and the cost related to repairing defects at each stage. As it is shown, there defects that are still present after release of the software.

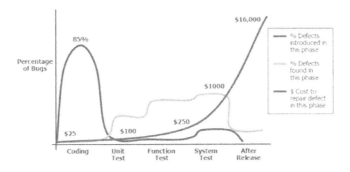

Fig. 1. Percentage of defects found at different stages of software testing, Source: [17]

The choice of best possible subset with most error-sensitive test data is very important. If for any reason error-sensitive data are not part of test data, then the probability of detecting errors within the software diminishes. Fig 2 shows that as the software system becomes more complex, the available testing technology cannot offer suitable tool to find defects and the gaps grows.

The testing activities consist of test case design, test execution, monitoring, test evaluation, test planning, test organization, and test documentation but most important activity is test case design [14].

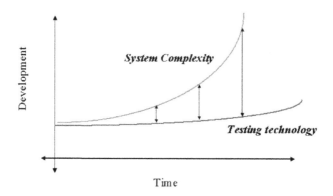

Fig. 2. The gap between system complexity and the available testing technology Source: [18]

Systematic test case design is necessary to good test quality because it defines the type and scope of the test. Automation of test case design is difficult because:

- formal specifications for the generation of test cases for functional testing is not available, symbolic execution has limits,
- testing the temporal behavior of systems is difficult or impossible, and also
- testing safety constraints are difficult or impossible

Therefore, test cases have to be defined manually, which affects the efficiency and effectiveness of the executed test.

This paper is about an alternative approach, which is a novel behavioristic model for verifying software trustworthiness by capturing system's functional and quality requirements. The approach is introduced by generation of statecharts from scenarios with the following specific benefits:

- end user can validate the transition of software behavior into path representations.
- real (observed) behavior of the software under investigation is recorded.
- Reference (expected) behavior of software is compared with the real behavior of the software under investigation.
- the observed behavior and its discrepancy from reference behavior for the software under investigation can be analyzed and interpreted.
- the approach can be applied in the process of certifying software trustworthiness

The structure of this paper is as follows: Section 1 presents a brief introduction. Section 2 contains review of the background. In section 3, the methodology is explained. Transformation of scenarios to state machines is discussed in section 4, while section 5 presents specification language for actions, events and transitions. Section 6 presents discussions on incremental changes in requirements or scenarios. Finally section 7 presents the conclusion.

2   Background

A program failure is caused by a fault, that is, a defect in the code, informally called a bug. Testing is a way to find faults in software. It is a process of supplying a system under test with some values and making conclusions on the basis of its behavior. A test case consists of inputs together with the expected results. Although generating test inputs can be as simple as selecting numbers randomly, deriving the corresponding expected results is often labor intensive.

Testing criteria define what should be tested and when the objective of testing is achieved. For example, statement coverage requires that every statement in the program be executed at least once during testing. Test sets may be chosen according to a number of different testing criteria.

The testing criteria can be compared based on their relative effectiveness and cost. The effectiveness of a criterion is determined by its ability to detect faults. Since the number of faults can be infinite, emphasize is on detecting a limited subset of faults. Alternatively, emphasize may be on the behavior instead of the code and attempt to systematically cover the entire domain of a system.

Testing criteria can be classified into program-based and specification-based categories. Program-based (or white-box) testing is based on the code without consideration of design. Thorough white-box testing is expensive for large software systems. Additionally, it provides no information about whether the code is doing what it is supposed to be doing [16].

In contrast, specification-based (or black-box) testing derives test cases from the specification of a system. A specification provides valuable information about the intended behavior of the implementation, and therefore about the expected test results [15].

Automated test generation from formal specifications improves the ability to test software that has to be highly reliable, as well as lower the cost of testing off-the-shelf software.

On other hand, there are many studies on using statechart for capturing scenarios. Some of these are as follows:

Eshuis has introduced a translation from UML activity diagrams to FSMs [9] and Labeled Transition System (LTS) semantics for UML statecharts [21]. In both approaches, model-checking techniques are used to verify properties such as data integrity, absence of conflicts and consistency.

Uchitel et al. developed a technique for generating one LTS for each Message Sequence Chart (MSC) specification [22]. Their approach requires additional input, which is a high-level message sequence chart (hMSC) that specifies how the MSC scenarios are to be flowcharted. The approach does not take into account the negative scenarios and it is not user friendly because the states are labeled by numbers.

Whittle and Schumann proposed a technique for generating UML statecharts from sequence diagrams that capture scenarios [19]. Their technique requires scenario interactions to be annotated by pre and post conditions on global state variables expressed in the Object Constraint Language (OCL). Kruger et al. proposed a technique for translating MSCs into statecharts [20]. Their technique also requires state information as additional input (in this case, through MSC conditions). In both cases it is unclear whether the end-users are able to provide such additional information.

Mäkinen and Systä developed an interactive approach for synthesizing UML state-charts from sequence diagrams that capture positive scenarios [4]. Their Minimally Adequate Synthesizer (MAS) use grammatical inference and asks the user trace questions in order to avoid undesirable generalization. A trace question is a path in the state machine local to specific agent. MAS focus on single agents; generalization must be done independently for each software agent. Trace questions may be quite hard to understand by the end user, as they do not show global system behaviors.

Van Lamsweede and Willmet developed an inductive learning technique for generating goal specifications in Linear Temporal Logic (LTL) from positive and negative scenarios expressed in MSC-like form [6]. The resulting state machine is very difficult for validation. Also end user has to provide pre and post conditions of scenario interactions.

Christophe Damas et al. [8] take both positive and negative scenarios as input and synthesize an LTS covering all positive scenarios and exclude all negative scenarios. The synthesis procedure extends grammar induction techniques developed in [23] and [6]. Their induction learning procedure is interactive and incremental, which makes it possible to integrate missing scenarios.

Hsia et al [3] and Mäkinen and Systä [4] have studied reverse engineering and forward engineering from scenarios to statechart model and back from the statechart to scenarios by using a statechart driver. Behrens [5] has used scenarios and state-charts for requirements analysis and prototyping.

Finally among existing tools, there are transition systems that form the operational basis for model-checking tools such as FDR [2], LTS Analyzer [10] and the CADP tool set [11], which analyze a transition system for properties of interest (such as deadlock or livelock freedom) or mutually compare two given specifications. STAMP [5] allows the analyst to capture a scenario, traversing state diagram, starting at initial state, adding states and state transitions with associated actions for scenarios.

All of the above-mentioned researches were carried out for purposes other than evaluation of software trustworthiness, namely either for requirements engineering, automatic testing or automatic developing of software system, but their common important point is that they all attempt to address the subject of the software behavior.

3   Methodology

The proposed approach is based on Rolland's definition of scenarios along four different views where each view captures a particular relevant aspect of scenarios.

3.1   Scenario Structure

These four views are explained below [24]:

- Content: what is the knowledge in scenario? Scenarios are used to model interactions between the user and the software system and its environment. These interactions are either domain-related or environmental-related. Sometimes there are internal actions, which are important for a scenario, but they are not immediately visible during same interaction with the user. Therefore, it is also important to model the impact of user interactions on the software system's data [5].
- Purpose: why scenario is used? The scenarios are used to model system requirements as a basis for comparing recorded behavior of software system with its expected behavior. Moreover, they can be used for validation by analysts, testers, and end users.
- Lifecycle: how to manipulate a scenario? As mentioned in section 1, as the number of use cases and the number of scenarios per use case increases, the total number of scenarios increases which causes scalability problem. As the number of scenarios and states is augmented, the modeling of the behavior of a large software system becomes more difficult. For example, if a software system has 100 use cases and each use case has 10 important scenarios on average, it would be necessary to keep a total of 1000 scenarios consistent at all times even when the requirements change. To accommodate all of these scenarios, each use case should be modeled by a statechart diagram and therefore generating all scenarios for that use case [5].
- Form: in which form is a scenario expressed? Both informal and formal notations can be used for describing the semantics of scenarios. Informal notations are used for expressiveness and formal notation is used for proof of correctness. Precise specifications with a suitable degree of formalism can be used to capture requirements in an unambiguous way and to enable the generation of a fully functional model, which can help users to validate requirements [5].

Each specific scenario will be characterized according to these four views.

3.2   Developing a Formal Behavioristic Model

The behavioristic model consists of three activities or phases, namely: identifying attributes of software trustworthiness, developing a formal behavioristic model, evaluating the trustworthiness (Fig. 3). The development of the formal behavioristic model is further divided into 3 following stages:

A. Stage 1 – Transforming Reference Requirements to FSM

- identification of reference requirements
- extraction of reference functionalities and quality attributes

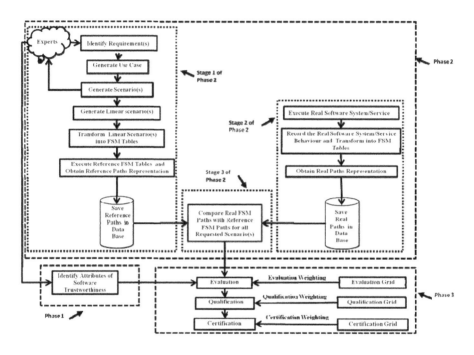

Fig. 3. Software Trustworthiness Evaluation Process

B. Stage 2 – Recording Real Software System or Services Behavior

- execution of real software system or services
- recording of the real behavior into real FSM tables
- executing of real FSM tables and obtaining the real path representation
- saving real path representation into real database.

C.   Stage 3 – Comparing Real Behavior with Reference Behavior

- reading real path representation from real database
- reading reference path representation from reference database
- comparing reference path representation with real path representation
- analyzing and interpreting of observed behavior and its discrepancy from reference behavior for the software system or services under investigation

4   Transformation of Scenarios to State Machine Notation

A scenario can be represented as a path consisting of state nodes and transition edges through the statechart diagram. Statechart diagrams have different types of actions that are performed within the state such as [24]:

- entry actions
- input actions triggered by input conditions that do not cause state changes
- exit actions

Or cause state transitions such as:

- transition actions which is a kind of input Action but is bound to a transition

A new scenario is written by adding states and state transitions to the state machine incrementally, in such a way that the requested scenario becomes executable as a path through the same statechart diagram. It should be noted that all those states and state transitions belong to the same use case. The following additional information is needed to generate scenarios and statecharts [5]:

- any actions or events causing a trigger or state transitions such as clock events, pressing a button or selecting a menu item
- any action or events related to entering or choosing a data input or a change to data such as completing a form or selecting a data item from a dropdown menu or trigger of timer or guard condition
- the object status of the system at the beginning state of scenario execution

It is possible to start from the object status of the system at the beginning state and execute each user actions, events and transitions in the path in order to get to the current status of the system. In this way all scenarios can be reproduced [5].

5   Specification Language

In the UML, the semantics of actions, events and transition can be specified in Action Specification Language (ASL). It is an implementation independent language for specifying processing within UML model. It can be used for specifying action and event semantics and guard conditions formally and creating executable models [25].

6   Incremental Changes in Requirements or Scenarios

Incremental change in requirements cause huge changes in test case design, test execution, monitoring, test evaluation, test planning, test organization, and test documentation which makes software testing inefficient and ineffective. Building behavioristic model for the same system with the same changes, do not cause as much overhead and costs because changed scenarios are incorporated incrementally to the proposed model. Comparison of the reference and real behavior of the system, before and after implied changes, might show discrepancies, which can be resolved by applying incremental changes. These changes are categorized into following subsections:

6.1   Statechart Incremental Changes

An incremental change in the requirements may lead to adding/removing/changing of states to/from statechart which causes changes to the real path which in turn causes discrepancies between the reference path and real path and will have negative impact on software trustworthiness.

6.2   Scenario Incremental Changes

An incremental change in requirements may cause adding/ removing/changing of a scenario or scenario parts. Applying these incremental changes into a model should be accompanied by necessary modification to statechart so that the real path or reference path generated from it has the same required behavior otherwise the discrepancies between the reference path and real path will have negative impact on software trust-worthiness.

6.3   Impacts of Incremental Changes

6.3.1 Impacts of Statechart Incremental Changes
After each modification of the requirements, some incremental changes might have caused by following problems [5]:

- undesired modifications to the statechart might have had undesired effects on some scenarios.
- desired modifications of the statechart that have caused scenarios to follow a different path in the state diagram than reference path, causing the associated scenarios to behave differently.
- In both cases, the discrepancies between the reference path and real path will have negative impact on software trustworthiness.

6.3.2 Impacts of Scenario Incremental Changes
The effects of a scenario modification are in the following forms [5]:

- result change
- path change
- user input change

All above changes will cause real path to change and therefore there will be some discrepancies between the behavior of reference and real paths. These discrepancies will have negative effect on software trustworthiness.

7   Conclusion

Software testing can only show the existence but not the non-existence of errors. A test with all possible input values, input value sequences, and input value combinations under all practically possible constraints is not practical. Therefore software testing can be necessary but not sufficient for software trustworthiness. The proposed behavioristic model is a novel methodology for dynamic evaluation and estimation of software trustworthiness. The model is built of an integrated requirements model with informal and formal action specifications. The support for changing requirements and interaction between statechart modifications and the scenario model makes the important part of the overall concept. Furthermore, the scenario simulation and a provable evidence for confirming required functionality and quality address the industrial applicability of this research. The other new dimension of this research is its application in the process of certifying software trustworthiness, being actually the subject of standardization project of ISO/IEC JTC1 SC7 – System and software engineering.

References

1. Nami, M., Suryn, W.: From Requirements to Software Trustworthiness using Scenarios and Finite State Machine, Montreal (2012)
2. Roscoe, A.W.: The Theory and Practice of Concurrency. Prentice-Hall, Pearson (2005)
3. Hsia, P., et al.: Formal Approach to Scenario Analysis. IEEE Software 11(2), 33–41 (1994)
4. Mäkinen, E., Systä, T.: An Interactive Approach for Synthesizing UML Statechart Diagrams from Sequence Diagrams. In: Proceedings of OOPSLA 2000 Workshop: Scenario Based Round-trip Engineering (October 2000)
5. Behrens, H.: Requirements Analysis and Prototyping using Scenarios and Statecharts. In: Proceedings of ICSE 2002 Workshop: Scenarios and State Machines: Models, Algorithms, and Tools (2002)
6. Oncina, J., Garcia, P.: Regular Languages in Polynomial Update Time. In: Reze de la Blanca, N., Sanfeliu, A., Vidal, E. (eds.) Pattern Recognition and Image Analysis, pp. 49–61. World Scientific (1992)
7. Dupont, P.: Incremental Regular Inference, Grammatical Inference. Learning Syntax Form Sentences, 222–237 (1996)
8. Damas, C., et al.: Generating Annotated Behavior Models from End-User Scenarios. IEEE Transactions on Software Engineering 31(12) (December 2005)
9. Eshuis, R.: Symbolic model checking of UML activity diagrams. ACM Transactions on Software Engineering and Methodology 15(1), 1–38 (2006)
10. Magee, J., Kramer, J.: Concurrency: State Models & Java Programs. John Wiley & Sons (1999)
11. Garavel, H., Mateescu, R., Lang, F., Serwe, W.: CADP 2006: A Toolbox for the Construction and Analysis of Distributed Processes. In: Damm, W., Hermanns, H. (eds.) CAV 2007. LNCS, vol. 4590, pp. 158–163. Springer, Heidelberg (2007)
12. Pressman, R.S.: Software Engineering: A Practitioner's Approach, 3rd edn. McGraw-Hill (1992)
13. Dijkstra, E.W., Dahl, O.J., Hoare, C.A.R.: Structured programming. Academic Press (1972)

14. Wegener, J., Pitschinetz, R.: TESSY – Yet Another Computer-Aided Software Testing Tool? In: Proceedings of the Second International Conference on Software Testing, Analysis and Review, Bruxelles, Belgium (1994)
15. Goodenough, J.B., Gerhart, S.L.: Toward a theory of test data selection. IEEE Transactions on Software Engineering 1(2), 156–173 (1975)
16. Hayhurst, K.J., Veerhusen, D.S., Chilenski, J.J., Rierson, L.K.: A practical tutorial on modified condition/decision coverage. Technical Report NASA/TM-2001-210876, NASA (May 2001)
17. Applied Software Measurement, Capers Jones (1996)
18. Voas, J.: Software Testing Past, Present, and Future, http://www.rstcorp.com
19. Whittle, J., Schumann, J.: Generating Statechart Designs From Scenarios. In: Proceedings of OOPSLA 2000 Workshop: Scenario Based Round-trip Engineering, October 2000, Tampere University of Technology, Software Systems Laboratory, Report 20 (2000)
20. Hertzum, M.: The importance of trust in software engineers' assessment and choice of information sources. Information and Organization 12, 1–18 (2002)
21. Eshuis, R., Wieringa, R.: Requirements Level Semantics for UML Statecharts. In: Proceedings of Formal Methods for Open Object-Based Distributed Systems IV, Stanford, California (2000)
22. Uchitel, S., Kramer, J.: A Workbench for Synthesizing Behavior Models from Scenarios. In: Proc. of the 23rd IEEE International Conference on Software Engineering (ICSE 2001), Toronto, Canada (May 2001)
23. Dupont, P.: Incremental Regular Inference, Grammatical Inference. Learning Syntax Form Sentences, 222–237 (1996)
24. Rolland, C., et al.: A proposal for a scenario classification framework. Requirements Engineering Journal 3(1), 23–47 (1998)
25. Wilkie, I., et al.: UML Action Specification Language (ASL) Reference Guide (2001), http://www.kc.com/download/index.html

A Measurement Model for Trustworthiness of Information System Based on Third-Party Testing Data

Jiaping Zuo, Pei Ren, and Hao Kong

National Application Software Testing Labs,
Zhongguancun Software Park, Beijing, China
zuojp@bsw.net.cn

Abstract. Measurement of trustworthiness is the foundation of trusty management, which is involved in multiple stages of design, development, operation and maintenance. From the view of third-party testing, trustworthiness of the information system is a comprehensive measurement of multiple software quality characteristics. This article describes how to establish the measurement Model based on Testing Data through the number of defects, damage, possible threats and other factors from application-level third-party testing results.

Keywords: software trustworthiness, measurement model, Third-Party testing.

1   Introduction

With the rapid advancement of computer technology, information system has penetrated into all fields of the world. However, a variety of software systems were often been interrupted and brought great losses to economy. Therefore, in the end of the late 1980s, the international community launched the discussion and research on the trustworthiness of the software.

Measurement of trustworthiness is the foundation of trusty software management; the original basis meaning of trustworthiness has extended from the security to other quality attributes of reliability, maintainability, efficiency, availability [1]. As a national the third-party testing center in China, about 1000 systems have been tested annually; the focus of the research is how to provide customers with the trusty measurement information through third-party application testing results. This article provides a measurement model of trustworthiness for software system based on testing data.

2   Measurement Framework

Each type of information system has its different business objectives, we should set up measurement of trustworthiness in line with characteristics of business systems, as Fig. 1 displays.

Y. Yuan, X. Wu, and Y. Lu (Eds.): ISCTCS 2012, CCIS 320, pp. 45–51, 2013.
© Springer-Verlag Berlin Heidelberg 2013

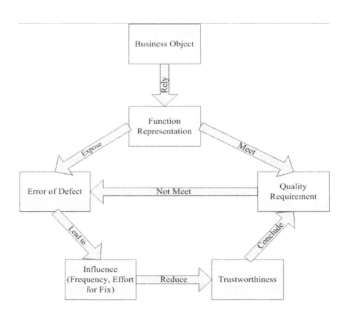

Fig. 1. Measurement model

This measurement model assesses the trustworthiness of the information systems mainly based on defects found in the third-party testing, including the amount, extent of the damage and the possible impact of them.

3   Measurement Methods

3.1   Evaluation of Trustworthiness

Initial researchers located trustworthiness on the only property in security, and then the TSM (Trusted Software Methodology) project organized by several U.S. government agencies and organizations defined the extended definition to 'The confidence of the software to meet the established requirement' in 1994[2]. Researchers have reached a consensus that trustworthiness is a comprehensive nature, in general, including security, reliability, integrity, availability, maintainability, etc... According to ISO 9126 and ISO 15408, our center choice Function, Reliability, Efficiency, Maintainability and Security as the characteristics of quality evaluation model. These quality characteristics have the following meanings:

Table 1. Quality Characteristics

Characteristics	Definition
Function	A set of attributes that bear on the existence of a set of functions and their specified properties. Including: Suitability, Accuracy, Interoperability, Security, Functionality and Compliance [3].
Reliability	A set of attributes that bear on the capability of software to maintain its level of Efficiency under stated conditions for a stated period of time. Including: Maturity, Fault Tolerance, Recoverability, Reliability and Compliance [3].
Efficiency	A set of attributes that bear on the relationship between the level of Efficiency of the software and the amount of resources used, under stated conditions [3].
Maintainability	A set of attributes that bear on the effort needed to make specified modifications. Including: Analyzability, Changeability, Stability, Testability, Maintainability and Compliance [3].
Security	Including protection of information and property from theft, corruption, or natural disaster, while allowing the information and property to remain accessible and productive to its intended users [5].

3.2   Weights of the Quality Characteristics (is)

Different information systems has different requirements of software trusty property,. so different weights should be based on the information system internal characteristics. The establishment of the weights generally first determines the value of the first layer of the quality characteristics, and then determines the value of the sub layer. Since the ultimate results are calculated by weighted add up, so the value range is controlled between 0.0 and 1.0.

The following Table 2 revealed a weights model for Automatic Office system:

Table 2. Quality Characteristics Weights

Quality Characteristics		Sub Characteristics	
Characteristic	Weights (ωi)	Feature	Weights (ωij)
Functionality	0.3	Suitability	0.4
		Accuracy	0.4
		Interoperability	0.2
Reliability	0.3	Maturity	0.5
		Fault tolerance	0.5
Efficiency	0.2	Time properties	0.7
		Resource properties	0.3
Maintainability	0.1	Changeability	1
Security	0.1	Technical requirements	0.6
		Management requirements	0.4

3.3   Defect Level (Si)

With the hierarchical processing in accordance on severity of the defects, different levels represent high or low degree of error according to the potential impact. The greater the rating value, the higher the severity. Table 3 provides a kind of defect severity assignment method for functional testing.

Table 3. Defect Weights

Severity	Definition	Weights
S1	Resulting in system collapses, crashes, memory leaks, loss of data or damage, the main business processes breakpoint.	4
S2	Not accomplishing major modules, business processing error.	3
S3	Not correctly implementing the defined function.	2
S4	General error or imperfect implementation of functions.	1

For efficiency testing, if the value of cost resource exceeds the specified value, and cause a system collapses, set the Weight as 4, or the system still be able to run, set as 2. For security defects, potential completely damage is set at 4, serious damage at 3, general damage at 2, and minor damage at 1.

3.4   Degree of Influence (Ei)

The harm caused by the defect is related to its frequency of occurrence and the user's attention; here use Degree of influence to express. Table 4 lists a number of Influence Factors on functionality, reliability, maintainability, efficiency and security. Each factor assignments were taken from 1 to 5, the greater the value, indicating that the higher the degree of the factor.

Table 4. Degree of influence

Quality Characteristics	Influence Factor	Explanation
Functionality (T1)	Degree of importance of the functions or requirements (T11)	E.g. for banking systems, function of data exchange of external systems are the most important.
	Operating frequency (T12)	Regular business operation is common, system level operation's frequency is relatively low.
	Difficulty of repairing (T13)	Resource cost of defect-repair.
Reliability (T2)	Degree of importance and capacity of the lost data, or the level of system failure (T21)	E.g. Entire-Database-Level data loss has the highest degree. The entire system failure has the highest degree, while the module at the edge set low.

Table 4. (*continued*)

Quality Characteristics	Influence Factor	Explanation
	Operating frequency (T22)	Similar to T12
	Recoverability degree of restore after the failure (T24)	E.g. using more recovery time cost, set higher value.
Maintainability (T3)	Degree of importance of the functions which cannot run after the system upgrade (T31)	Similar to T11
	The frequency of modify or upgrade (T32)	Similar to T12
	Degree of difficulty to recover to its previous state (T33)	Similar to T24
Efficiency (T4)	Degree of the failure to reach the requirement (T41)	E.g., set a value of 3 when only 60 concurrent users supported, versus 100 users required.
	Difficulty of repairing (T 42)	Similar to T13
Security (T5)	Frequency of threaten occurrence (T51)	the frequency of occurrence is high for 5, almost impossible for 1[4].
	The difficulty of the repair defect (T52)	Similar to T13

The measurement may be determined based on historical statistics or industry experience. We can judge the degree of influence (Ei) of each defect, according to the geometric mean values of each factor, and rounded.

$$Ei= \sqrt[n]{T_{ij}} \tag{1}$$

3.5   Calculate the Measurement Value

With the following formula, multiply and weighted add up each Defect level (Si) and the Degree of influence (Ei) of quality sub-features, and then rounded handle. The more the number of defects, the greater the level value, the greater the degree of influence, the higher the measurement value, the lower the trustworthiness is.

$$A=\sum_{i=1}^{k1} \left(\sum_{j=1}^{k2} \left(\sum_{l=1}^{n} S_{ijl} * E_{ijl} \right) * w_{ij} \right) * w_i \tag{2}$$

I - 1~k1, k1 Number of the layer 1 quality characteristics involved in the calculation
J - 1~k2, k2 Number of the layer 2 features involved in the calculation

L - Number of defects of each sub feature
Sijl - The level of defects for each defect
Eijl - The degree of the impact of each defect
Wij - The weight of each feature

4   Related Work

Based on this model, we tested 10 OA systems and calculate metrics, according to this model and ISO/IEC 9126-1 model separately. In ISO/IEC 9126-1 model, the highest score is 1, the software has higher quality with greater score. For comparison, we did preprocessing for the trustworthiness measurement value. With max trustworthiness measurement values of 10 projects as the denominator (Amax), the normalized conversion formula is

$$B=1-Ai/Amax \qquad (3)$$

Higher value of B means higher trustworthiness. Calculation results are shown in Fig. 2 with the consistent overall trend of the software quality expressed by the two models. With the use of ISO/IEC 9126-1 measurement model, its value tends to 0.5 and the differentiations are not obvious from the system 6 to 10. Trustworthiness model takes into account the degree of influence of defects, and still is able to express the difference of system in terms of the trustworthiness. Therefore, using the evaluation model proposed in this article, we can express the trustworthiness of software system in delicate and explicit way.

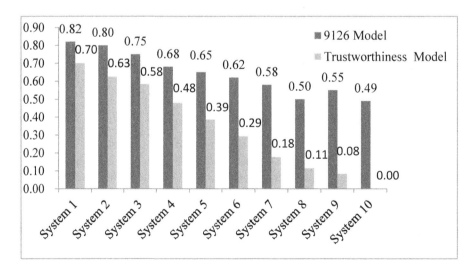

Fig. 2. Values based on 9126 model and trustworthiness model

5   Conclusion

This article describes how to establish a comprehensive measurement model covers the various attributes of the trustworthiness from the perspective of the test as a third-party independent testing center. This model is intuitive to use and easy to try and has been used to some kind of industries to measure the trustworthiness value before the system's launch. With this model we can provide users with relatively comprehensive and intuitive testing results for risk measurement of system through the short-term and rapid evaluation, and also can provide the measurement methods of trustworthiness for system's upgrades and improvement.

According to the characteristics of various information systems in the future practice, we will further improve this model to make sure it could reflect the trustworthiness of the information system more accurately and detailed. The same time we will collect information systems data in the same industry and establish reasonable benchmarks to lay the foundation of understanding of the overall trustworthiness level of the industry and measuring the single information system.

For example, select one or two key industries, at least data of the 100 key projects to establish baseline database to measure the distribution of grading the trustworthiness of the measured value of such information systems in order to provide users with a more intuitive measurement conclusion.

Acknowledgements. This work was supported by projects: Software Quality Evaluation Standard project (Item Number: 201010237) and Software quality testing standards for research based on trusted computing (Item Number: 201210262-01).

References

1. Zhang, Y.: The Trustworthiness software attributes and their metrics (May 2010)
2. Amoroso, E.: A process-oriented methodology for assessing and improving software trustworthiness. In: Proceeding of the 2nd ACM Conference on Computer and Communication Security, Virginia, USA, pp. 39–50 (1994)
3. ISO/IEC 9126-1:2001 Software engineering - Product quality - Part 1: Quality model
4. GB/T 20984:2007 Information security technology—Risk Measurement Specification for information security

Overview of Monitor Selection in Computer Networks

Nafei Zhu, Jiaping Zuo, Yue Zhou, and Wei Wang

National Application Software Testing Labs, Zhongguancun Software Park, Beijing, China
{stmsc,bqizgb,wangwei}@126.com, zuojp@bsw.net.cn

Abstract. With the development of the computer networks, network measurement becomes more and more important and complicated. It may need to deploy many monitors and send many packets, which will introduce impact on the performance of the network. So, it is very meaningful to design network measurement architecture to get as much as the network information using as little as the measurement cost with sophisticated monitors selection, which is referred as the problem of monitor selection. The problem of monitor selection for flow and failures as well as delay is related in this paper. The technologies are dived into three categories which are based on the Graph Theory and the Mathematical Programming as well as the Group Betweenness Centrality theory. This division is coincident with the characteristics of the monitor selection technologies. Then, we go into the main research methods and results referring to each of the three categories. At last, we talk about the further research direction regarding the shortcomings of the present methods.

Keywords: Monitor Selection, Graph Theory, Mathematical Programming, Group Betweenness Centrality Theory.

1 Introduction

The sound development of the computer networks needs powerful network measurement as the foundation stone. But there are a lot of tradeoffs in the network measurement. Network measurement is focused on the traffic and the performance parameters, such as end to end bandwidth and delay as well as packet drop rate. Then, according to this information, the operators can analyze the connection and reliability as well as security of the network. First, the distribution and performance of the network traffic are the fundamental of the network design and optimization. Second, the performance got from network measurement is the basis to provide service. Third, traffic analysis can be used to design and maintain measurement tools. Fourth, network measurement can be used to detect network failure, bottleneck and anomaly as well as QoS (Quality of the Service) test. Fifth, persistent measurement can detect abnormal traffic and illegal entry to attain the overall safety of the network. But the measurement of the network, even just the measurement on the backbone of an ISP (Internet service providers), needs a lot of cost. With the growing of the bandwidth, it is more and more difficult to sample the links, so does the data analysis of the samples. Using as little measurement devices as possible is important to cut down the expense of the deployment as well as the maintenance of the devices while

Y. Yuan, X. Wu, and Y. Lu (Eds.): ISCTCS 2012, CCIS 320, pp. 52–59, 2013.

accomplishing the demand of the measurement. At the same time, sending as little probing packets as possible which traverse as little route paths as possible is crucial to reduce the impact on the network load and performance. So, it is very meaningful to design network measurement architecture with the least overhead to get network information.

In Section 2, we talked about the systems of network measurement. In Section 3, technology for monitor selection is related and its relative researches are included in section 4. Applications of monitor selection are talked about in Section 5. Conclusion and the problems of the monitor selection nowadays are remarked in Section 6.

2   Systems of Network Measurements

In order to explore the global network, many foreign scientific institutions have gradually established their measurement frameworks in different size. For example, two projects carried out by National Laboratory Applied Network Research (NLANR), AMP (Active Measurement Project) and PMA (Passive Measurement and Analysis), have more than 150 monitors and 20 monitors all around the world, respectively. AMP measures the network loop delay, packet loss rate, topology, and throughput performance parameters in an active way. It is designed to measure and analyze the performance of the network nodes interconnected by high speed links. PMA takes a passive way to measure the network. It studies the robustness of the Internet in detail, and collaborates with every monitor to provide high performance network service. NIMI, CAIDA, Surveyor [1] and other measurement projects [2-3] have their own monitor nodes all around, as well. They made a great exploration for the establishment of a scalable measurement framework of Internet. The traffic monitoring devices include SNMP agent [4], RMON [4] and NetFlow [5]. The delay measurement devices include PING, Traceroute, and Pathchar [6] as well as Skitter [7] and so on.

There are many measurement and estimation systems with elaborately deployed monitors. IDMaps is the first implement used to estimate the distance between network hosts [8]. According to a known distance graph, it estimates the delay between any two network hosts from some known nodes by the spanning tree algorithm. KING is another implement with the same aim as that of the IDMaps, but uses the recursive DNS query. According to the distance between DNS and the host, and the distance between the two DNS connected to the two hosts, KING is able to calculate the delay between these two hosts [9]. Zhang B., TS Eugene Ng, made a systematic study on the analysis, modeling and synthesis of the network delay space for the first time. They quantified the network delay space and developed a delay synthesizer called DS2, which can provide a large range of delay space and still maintain certain accuracy [10]. Sharma P., Xu Z.C., develop a network proximity estimating system called Netvigator [11]. It accurately finds the nearest point of a given node by utilizing the enhanced landmark clustering technique, which is to find the nearest node by the distance information of the landmark with the identification information from the routers. Agarwal S. and Lorch J.R. designed Htrae using the far-reaching trace in delay estimating of game matching [12]. In this system, the node location is embedded into network coordinate system, and we chose a reasonable initial network coordinate to determine how the new machines added to the system based on their locations. Using this method, we can make the whole system converge more quickly and make the predicted errors be lower than that of the state based delay estimation systems.

3   Technology for Monitor Selection

Researches on the architecture of the network measurement system are mainly focus on the deployment or selection of the monitors. The main theoretical approaches for the monitor selection include the Graph Theory and the Mathematical Programming as well as the Group Betweenness Centrality [13].

3.1   Graph Theory

Some studies are based on graph theory. As early as the 2000 IEEE INFOCOM, Jamin S. [14] proposed a method to select monitors for delay measurement. In this paper, the author mainly studied the monitor deployment problem in IDMaps. The principle of monitor selection is to minimize the overall distance between the hosts to their nearest monitors, so as to make the measurement or estimation more accurate. This problem can be induced as two issues in Graph theory: One is K-HST [15] (K-Hierarchically well Separated Trees), distributing the two nodes in the largest distance to different collections each time, and making the distance in each collection smaller than the given value while find the minimize number of the collections. The other one is Minimum K-Center [15], for which the number of the collections is given, and then minimizes the largest distance of every collection. These two issues and their solutions require full awareness of topology. So, some researchers came up with a new heuristic algorithm to select the monitors with a partly topology knowledge. Breitbart Y. [16] made a research on the deployment of network traffic monitors and the selection of network delay monitors. For the SNMP is deployed on the router, the deployment problem is reduced to the vertex covering problem in Graph theory. Based on the Flow Conservation (the sum of the traffic flowing into the node is approximately the same as the sum of the traffic flowing out of the node), the vertex cover problem is then changed into the weak vertex cover problem which can be solver using near optimal heuristic algorithm. And then according to the partitioned flow conversation theory, this problem is converted to the Partitioned Weak Vertex Cover to solve with partly topology knowledge. Horton J.D. [17] showed that a network with n nodes requires as many as (n+1)/3 points to detect each link in the shortest distance routing strategy, and may require at least (n-1)/3 points in the worst case, by using graph theory. The author uses arity as basis for the monitor selection.

3.2   Mathematical Programming

There are some studies based on mathematical programming. Zhang H. and Antonio N. studied the issue of optimal deployment of NetFlow for traffic monitoring [18]. They point out there is no need to monitor all the traffic and part of it is enough, which will cut down a lot of cost. So, with a coverage rate requirement, monitor selection problem can be converted to an Integer Liner Programming. The recommended coverage rate is 95%, for they calculated that it will reduce the costs by 55% of which when the coverage rate is 100%. Suh K. studied the issue of tradeoff between price and profit [19]. And he also studied the optimization problem with packet samples and links failures, which are both mapped to some NP hard problems with near optimal solutions. Cantieni G. R. proposed a method that could solve the deployment position and sampling rate for each monitor at one time [20]. They designed an overall monitoring profit function, and then proposed an optimization algorithm to solve this function. The input of the algorithm is the network topology, route matrix and communication pairs. The output is the optimal location of monitors and their sampling rates. Chaudet C. proposed a mix model for traffic monitoring to optimize the coverage rate, and then make the problem to be a mixed integer programming problem [21].

3.3   Group Betweenness Centrality

As to the Group Betweenness Centrality (Betweenness Centrality), it is a new method proposed to be used in monitor selection recently. Betweenness Centrality is a metric for the significance level of a unit in society in sociology area. Researches based on GBC include [13] and [22]. This selection method depends on the significance of the nodes in the network. We select the nodes which make the biggest contribution to the significance of their monitors set. Besides, W.J. Alden got that by using less test points we can even detect every packet with a better chance [23]. At the same time, deploying the monitors on the links among ASes is better than deploying many monitors on the links in the same AS.

3.4   Remarks about the Three Methods

For all the three methods introduced above, we now give an overall comment about them in my opinion. The principle of graph theory method is to model the whole network as a graph, so the problem of node selection is converted to the selection of some points according to the degrees or other special aims. But as related above, this method always needs the whole topology knowledge, which is a limitation to scalability. As to the mathematical programming method, it is to model the selection problem to be an optimization problem and then solve it using the optimization algorithm. But it always can only get a near optimal solution. GBC method mainly selects the monitors based on their significances according to the GBC theory of the sociology which would be not completely suitable for the computer networks. These three methods consider the monitor selection problem from different angles of view, but they have some relations to each other. Some of the monitor selection problems using graph theory method can be converted to be and solved by optimization method. And the GBC method is the essence of the other two methods to some extent.

4   Related Researches about Monitor Selection

There are also some other related researches, such as BGP monitors selection, hierarchical network measurement architecture as well as mobile agent deployment. In interior, many colleges have done researches on these subjects. There are papers about the monitor selection from 2003 to 2008 of National University of Defense Technology. Among these work, Liu X.H. and Cai Z.P. analyzed the bandwidth measurement model and the hierarchical network monitor model with bandwidth and delay constraints using the weak vertex coverage method [24].

Hu C.C. of Tsingua University studied traffic measurement of NIDS system and proposed the distributed NIDS system considering the tradeoff between deployment cost and coverage rate [25]. Zhang J. of The PLA Information Engineering University studied the problem of traffic monitor selection and proposed a universal model for optimal deployment of network flow monitor [26]. Jiang H.Y. of HuNan University proposed a distributed algorithm for monitor selection in network traffic measurement with finding the weak vertex cover of a graph [27]. The algorithm does not require the information of the whole network topology. H. He of Harbin Institute of Technology proposed a monitor deployment scheme based on delay cluster [28]. Ge H.W. of JiangNan University proposed a hybrid optimization algorithm for efficient monitor selection in traffic measurement [29].

5   Application of Monitor Selection

The study of the selection or deployment of monitors mainly has three applications, which are deploying the monitors for network traffic and delay measurement and estimation, and selecting the monitors for failure detection. Generally speaking, traffic monitoring is passive and the monitors are deployed on links, while delay measurement and failure detection is active and the monitors are deployed on the routers.

5.1   Traffic Measurement

Typical studies of monitor selection for flow or traffic measurement include [18], [20], [30], but all the methods focus on constant network traffic, which is not the reality apparently. Hu C.C. studied the optimized deployment of the traffic monitors in a network with a random traffic [31]. He modeled the traffic as a random process, and proposed the hybrid intelligent algorithm.

5.2   Failure Detection

Typical studies based on the selection of failure detection points include the studies of Natu M. and Agrawal S. considering failure detection as an activity process and considered the invalidation of the monitors themselves [32-33]. They proposed an algorithm to solve this problem with full knowledge of router information. Each regular node has at least K separate links to monitors, so the monitor system can detect as many as K disabled links. Shipra A. [34] studied the issue of the failure links and deduced the disable links from the measurement of route path degree. Also, he studied the selection of traffic monitors and failure detection as well as failure diagnosis based on collection covering theory in a passive way. Nguyen H. and Tirana P. studied the issue of detecting the error of links [35]. They sought the minimum set of monitors and spread the detection packages of collection nodes all over the net links. They reinstalled some possible monitors, and worked out the most optimized detection packages collection according to these monitors, and finalized the location of points on the basis of these probe collection.

5.3   Delay Measurement

As for the selecting of delay monitors, Breitbart Y. proposed a monitoring framework. In this framework, a NOC measures the delay with the source routing manner. It required that the probes sent out by NOC cover every link (cover here means two probes respectively measures the two endpoints of the link and get the delay from their difference). The goal of selecting the monitors is to minimize the sum of the links that all the probes pass. The author maps the issue to FLP (Facility location problem) NP-complete and provides a approximate optimal solution algorithm. Bejerano Y. and Rastogi R. provided a solution with two stages to decrease the delay monitor price [36]. First, they figure out the minimum nodes collection is the nodes collection which could detect all the net links even with the links invalidated. Then, they boiled it down to collection covering with greedy algorithm. Furthermore, they proposed greedy approximation algorithms that achieve a logarithmic approximation factor for the station selection problem and a constant factor for the probe assignment problem. These approximation ratios are provably very close to the best possible bounds for any algorithm.

6   Conclusion

In order to explore the global network, many scientific institutions have gradually established their measurement systems in different size. But, the more the measurements are, the more obvious of the bad effects on the network performance are. So, it is very meaningful to design the network measurement architecture with the least overhead to get as much the network information as possible. As a whole, the methods to deploy monitors are divided into three categories which are based on the graph theory and based on the mathematical programming as well as the Group Betweenness Centrality theory. This division is suitable for the characteristics of the monitor selection technologies. The main methods and results referring to these three categories are also talked about. Though many new methods are proposed and good results are gained as to the problem of monitor selection, there are still some points not perfect and need a further study. First, almost all the methods proposed are just evaluated by experiments not the real network, so we need further study on valuation with the real network. Second, none of the works related above can adjust the set of selected monitors to cog with the estimation accuracy requirement such as delay estimation accuracy, which is very important to make the estimation more efficient. So, in the future, we could design a dynamic monitor selection method to solve this problem. Third, the studies above seldom consider the essence of relationship among the network parameters they devoted effort to measure such as flow and delay. In my opinion, the essence relationship among them is valuable to the problem of monitor selection.

Acknowledgements. This work was supported by projects, Software Quality Evaluation Standard (No. 201010237) and Software Quality Testing Standards for Research Based on Trusted Computing (No. 201210262-01) .

References

1. Kalidindi, S., Zekauskas, M.J.: Surveyor: An Infrastructure for Internet Performance Measurements. In: INET 1999, vol. 32, pp. 532–539. IEEE Communication Society (1999)
2. Paxson, V., Mahdavi, J., Adams, A., Mathis, M.: An Architecture for Large-scale Internet Measurement. IEEE Communications 36(8), 48–54 (2001)
3. Claffy, K., Monk, T.E., McRobb, D.: Internet tomography. Nature, Web Matters (1999)
4. William, S.: SNMP, SNMPv2, SNMPv3, and RMON 1 and 2, 3rd edn., pp. 233–237. Addison Wesley (2009)
5. Cisco System: NetFlow services and application. Cisco System White Paper (1999)
6. Jacobsen, V.: Pathchar – A Tool to Infer Characteristics of Internet Paths (1997)
7. Cooperative Association for Internet Data Analysis (CAIDA),
   `http://www.caida.org/`
8. Francis, P., Jamin, S., Jin, C., Jin, Y.: IDMaps: A global internet host distance estimation service. IEEE/ACM Trans. Networking 9(1), 525–540 (2001)
9. Gummadi, K.P., Saroiu, S., Gribble, S.D.: King: Estimating Latency between Arbitrary Internet End Hosts. In: ACM IMW 2002, Marseille, France, vol. 36(2), pp. 346–351 (2002)
10. Zhang, B., Eugene Ng, T.S., Nandi, A., Riedi, R., Druschel, P., Wang, G.H.: Measurement-based Analysis, Modeling, and Synthesis of the Internet Delay Space. In: 6th Internet Measurement Conference (IMC), Rio de Janeiro, Brazil, vol. 29(4), pp. 85–98 (2006)
11. Sharma, P., Xu, Z.C., Banerjee, S., Lee, S.J.: Estimating network proximity and latency. In: Proceedings of the ACM SIGCOMM 2006, Pisa, Italy, vol. 13(7), pp. 41–50 (2006)
12. Agarwal, S., Lorch, J.R.: Match making for online games and other latency-sensitive P2P systems. In: ACM SIGCOMM 2009, Barcelona, Spain, vol. 7, pp. 677–682 (2009)
13. Borgatti, S.P., Everett, M.G.: A graph-theoretic perspective on centrality. Social Networks 28(4), 466–484 (2006)
14. Jamin, S., Jin, C., Jin, Y., Raz, D., Shavitt, Y., Zhang, L.: On the placement of Internet instrumentation. In: IEEE INFOCOM 2000, vol. 35(8), pp. 295–304. IEEE Communication Society (2000)
15. Hochbaum, D.S.: Approximation Algorithm for NP-Hard Problems, pp. 231–233. PWS Publishing Company, Boston (1997)

16. Breitbart, Y., Chan, C.Y., Garofalakis, M., Rastogi, R., Silberschatz, A.: Efficiently monitoring bandwidth and latency in IP networks. In: EEE INFOCOM 2001, vol. 32(5), pp. 933–942. IEEE Communication Society (2001)

17. Horton, J., Lopez-Ortiz, A.: On the number of distributed measurement points for network tomography. In: ACM SIGCOMM IMC, vol. 27(3), pp. 204–209. ACM Press (2003)

18. Zang, H., Nucci, A.: Optimal NetFlow Deployment in IP Networks. In: 19th International Teletraffic Congress (ITC), Beijing, China, vol. 14(2), pp. 621–630 (2005)

19. Suh, K., Guo, Y., Kurose, J., Towsley, D.: Locating network monitors: Complexity, heuristics and coverage. In: IEEE INFOCOM, vol. 34(5), pp. 1564–1577 (March 2005)

20. Cantieni, G.R., Iannaccone, G., Barakat, C., Diot, C., Thiran, P.: Reformulating the Monitor Placement problem: Optimal Network-Wide Sampling. In: CoNeXT, vol. 37(8), pp. 312–318 (2006)

21. Chaudet, C., Fleury, E., Lassous, I., Hervé, Voge, M.E.: Optimal Positioning of Active and Passive Monitoring Devices. In: CoNeXT, vol. 23(4), pp. 93–124 (2005)

22. Dolev, S., Elovici, Y., Puzis, R., Zilberman, P.: Incremental Deployment of Network Monitors based on Group Betweenness Centrality. Information Processing Letters (2009)

23. Dolev, S., Elovici, Y., Puzis, R.: Routing Betweenness Centrality. Technical Report (2009)

24. Liu, X.H., Yin, J.P., Tang, L.L., Zhao, J.M.: A Monitoring Model for Link Bandwidth Usage of Network based on Weak Vertex Cover. Journal of Software 15(4), 545–549 (2004); (in Chinese with English abstract)

25. Hu, C.C., Zhen, L.: On the Deployment Strategy of Distributed Network Security ensors. In: IEEE ICON, vol. 32(3), pp. 25–31. IEEE Press, Singapore (2005)

26. Zhang, J., Zhang, H., Wu, J.X.: Universal Model for Optimal Deployment of Network Flow Monitor. Journal of Chinese Computer Systems 14(6), 397–401 (2008); (in Chinese with English abstract)

27. Jang, H.Y., Li, W., Lin, Y.P., Zhang, Q.H.: A Distributed Algorithm for Monitor2Node s Selection in Net Traffic Measurement. Journal of Natural Science of Hunan Normal University 28(3), 1–21 (2006); (in Chinese with English abstract)

28. He, H., Hu, Z.M., Yun, C.X.: Network Latency Clustering for Detector Placementon Macroscopical Prewarning. Journal on Communications 2(1), 119–124 (2006); (in Chinese with English abstract)

29. Ge, H.W., Peng, Z.Y., Yue, H.B.: Hybrid Optimization Algorithm for Efficient Monitor Nodes Selection in Network Traffic. Application Research of Computers 4(9), 397–401 (2009); (in Chinese with English abstract)

30. Jackson, A.W., Milliken, W., Santivanez, C.A., Condell, M., Strayer, W.T.: A Topological Analysis of Monitor Placement Network Computing and Applications. In: Sixth IEEE International Symposium on Digital Object, vol. 56(5), pp. 323–328 (2007)

31. Hu, C.C., Liu, B., Liu, Z., Gao, S., Wu, D.O.: Optimal Deployment of Distributed Passive Measurement Monitors. In: ICC 2006, pp. 621–626 (2006)

32. Natu, M., Sethi: Probe Station Placement for Fault Diagnosis. In: IEEE GLOBECOM, pp. 125–129 (2007)

33. Agrawal, S., Naidu, K.V.M., Rastogi, R.: Diagnosing Link-level Anomalies Using Passive Probes. In: IEEE INFOCOM, pp. 465–470 (2007)

34. Cohen, R., Raz, D.: The Internet Dark Matter—On the Missing Links in the AS Connectivity Map. In: IEEE INFOCOM 2006, pp. 226–232. IEEE Communication Society (2006)

35. Nguyen, H.X., Thiran, P.: Active Measurement for Multiple Link Failures Diagnosis in IP Networks. In: Barakat, C., Pratt, I. (eds.) PAM 2004. LNCS, vol. 3015, pp. 185–194. Springer, Heidelberg (2004)

Verification of Requirement Analysis Method for System Based on ISO/IEC 9126 Six Quality Characteristics

Kazuhiro Esaki

HOUSEI University Faculty of Science and Engineering
Kees959@hotmail.com

Abstract. In order to take the profit based on the success of new product development. It is very important to define the quantitative quality requirement of new system product during system design phase. For the purpose of define the target quality of product, the method of quantitative quality requirement definitions based on ISO/IEC 9126 quality model that includes six characteristics is widely recognized, which are defined from the view point of customer satisfaction. However, independency of each characteristic is not sure and the suitability of method by using these six quality characteristics for quality requirement is not certified statistically. In this paper, we propose the result of verification about effectiveness of quantitative quality requirement definition from the view point of six characteristics defined in ISO/IEC9126.

Keywords: System, Software, Quality requirement, Quality evaluation, Quality model, Quality in use, Quality characteristic, Quality measure, Requirement process, Evaluation process, Customer, developers, acquirers, Target product.

1 Introduction

In order to take the profit based on the success of new product development. It is very important to define the non-functional requirement and realize the real needs in to the new product during possible early stage of development. On the other hand, the requirements analysis is a very difficult to work because it is non-formulaic and demands much of product designers' technical perceptiveness, sense in balance and experiences. Analysis of non-functional requirements of a product has been conducted through questionnaires and interviews with customers. Traditionally, survey items on questionnaires were selected either from previous questionnaires or based on survey investigator's personal experience with and preference of product requirements.

This lack of structure and incompleteness in the traditional survey introduced missing or biased product requirements and errors in prioritizing requirements to implement in the non-functional requirement analysis of a product, resulting in failing to assure the completeness of the non-functional requirement analysis of a product. The quality model in the standard ISO/IEC 9126 (This standard has revised to ISO/IEC 25010:2011 [2]) presents the six quality characteristics. These six characteristics are

Y. Yuan, X. Wu, and Y. Lu (Eds.): ISCTCS 2012, CCIS 320, pp. 60–68, 2013.

defined based on the model of Boehm [3] or McCall [4], or from the view point of a stakeholder's wide experience, which are considered as necessary and independent from user's point of view. Through analyzing customer requirements based on these six quality characteristics, it becomes possible to perform complete and objective evaluation of customer requirements for a system product. Although a certain level of improvement is expected in the completeness of describing product quality objectives by using the ISO/IEC 9126 quality model, the ambiguity and lack of verification of the ISO/IEC9126 quality model make it impossible to assure that quality objectives of a product are completely described to satisfy the customer quality requirements.

Above assumption, this study verifies the validity of using the six quality characteristics descried in ISO/IEC9126, however, currently ISO/IEC9126 is widely recognized and used in world wide.

In recent years, an increasing number of consumers post their reviews on a web site.

This study focuses on negative reviews of system products posted by consumers, classifies and analyzes such reviews based on the six quality characteristics.

For example, an online negative review may relate to a serious concern that affects the operation of the PC, or it may relate to a relatively minor concern that does not affect the operation of the system, but expresses personally preference.

In other words, different online negative reviews carry different levels of importance (i.e., different degrees of customer quality requirement). Therefore, the degree of customer dissatisfaction may not be accurately obtained by simply classifying online negative reviews into the six quality characteristics.

2 Outline and Concept of SQuaRE Series

2.1 Frame Work of SQuaRE

Figure1. Show the total framework of system and software quality requirements and evaluations [1]. Stakeholders have kind of needs about evaluation for system and software development and acquisition. In order to perform development, at first specify the requirement for product from the view point of stakeholder's needs should be performed by using ISO/IEC 25030[6]. After development, developer should evaluate the product based on the requirement specification of product by using ISO/IEC 25040[8] in order to assure the developed product. Usually, stakeholders needs include both functional requirements and non-functional requirement. Non-functional requirement could include quality requirement and other requirement such as hardware, data, and business requirement so on. Quality requirement can be defined from the view point of six quality characteristics included in the quality model descried in ISO/IEC 9126 (ISO/IEC 25010[2])and ISO/IEC 25020[5].

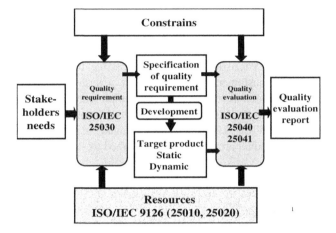

Fig. 1. Framework of Quality Requirement and Evaluation for System and Software Product

2.2   View Point of Software Quality Requirement Definition

In defining the customer quality requirements of a system product, through identifying and clearly differentiating customer quality requirements of a system product based on the quality model and only through setting quality objectives of a system product in the product design phase, it becomes possible to assure the integrity and completeness in describing customer quality requirements of a system product and to avoid incorrectly prioritizing or missing quality objectives of a product resulting in improvement in accuracy of describing customer quality requirements.

Fig. 2 show the structure of the Software Quality Model defined in ISO/IEC 9126.

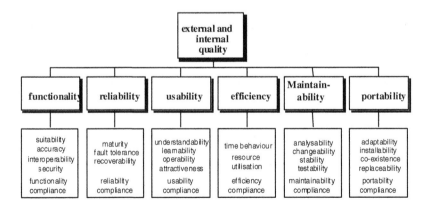

Fig. 2. Software product quality model-ISO/IEC9126

Following is the definition of six characteristics such as Functionality, Reliability, Usability, Efficiency, Portability and Maintainability.

a)Functionality
The capability of the software product to provide functions which meet stated and implied needs when the software is used under specified conditions.

b)Reliability
The capability of the software product to maintain a specified level of performance when used under specified conditions.

c)Usability
The capability of the software product to be understood, learned, used and attractive to the user, when used under specified conditions.

d)Efficiency
The capability of the software product to provide appropriate performance, relative to the amount of resources used, under stated conditions.

e)Maintainability
The capability of the software product to be modified.
Modifications may include corrections, improvements or adaptation of the software to changes in environment, and in requirements and functional specifications.

f)Portability
The capability of the software product to be transferred from one environment to another.

3   Summaries

This study first collects customer complaints, i.e., expression of customer dissatisfaction, posted on a review website where customers who actually purchased personal computer related products post their reviews. The study, then, classifies the posted customer complaints based on the six quality characteristics defined in the ISO/IEC9126 quality model, obtains from questionnaires a weight for each quality characteristic to represent how important the quality characteristic is to the customer, applies the weights to the six quality characteristics, and quantifies the degree of customer dissatisfaction for each quality characteristic.

The study, then, performs correlation analysis of the degree of customer satisfaction over the six quality characteristics for each system product and verifies that the six quality characteristics are mutual independent and that the approach of using the six quality characteristics helps understand the customer satisfaction.

In addition, the study performs multiple-regression analyses in which the degree of customer satisfaction for one of the six quality characteristics is chosen as an objective variable and the degrees of customer satisfaction for the remaining five quality characteristics are chosen as an explanatory variable.

Furthermore, the study develops a model that actually predicts the degree of customer satisfaction of a particular quality characteristic from the remaining five quality characteristics. Finally, the study discusses the validity of ISO/IEC 9126 quality model based on the significance of the developed prediction model.

3.1   Target Data

In recent years, due to the explosion of the Internet, purchasing behaviors of customers have significantly changed. For example, an increasing number of customers order a product directly from an electric commerce site without visiting brick-and-motor shops while remaining at home. The quality of the service that the online distribution system provides may be evaluated by the degree of satisfaction of the customers who have actually purchased products through the online distribution system.

The degree of customer satisfaction [9] is a measure used in marketing that represents how a product or service produced by a company meets or surpasses customer expectation. While questionnaires may help understand the impression of customers who actually purchased and used the product or service (such as understanding which aspects of a product customers are satisfied with), face-to-face interviews with customers may enable understanding potential issues of the product or service in more concrete terms. This study focuses on online reviews posted on the Internet, an effective alternative to face-to-face interviews of customers, and uses the online negative reviews of a system product as data to investigate.

This study also focuses on laptop computers. Reasons for choosing laptop computers are as follows. First, laptop computers have characteristics that correspond to the six quality characteristics of the ISO/IEC9126 quality model.

Second, there is a large amount of data available on the non-functionality requirements of lap top computers on online review websites. Third, available data are relatively easy to collect. The reason for focusing on is that laptop computers are semiconductor products whose product life cycle is very short. Laptop computers released in different years might differ significantly in their quality; quality of a lap top computer released in a given year may improve significantly from that of a lap top release in the previously year. Then, this study only collects online negative reviews regarding the laptop computers that were released in 2011.

3.2   Un-Satisfaction Data of Product

This study collects and uses online reviews of products posted at a website, kakaku.com [9] as customer's expression of his/her dissatisfaction of system products. This study counts the number of online negative reviews for each of the six quality characteristics. For instance, this study considers an online review of "slow operation, frustratingly slow" as customer's expression of his/her dissatisfaction in the efficiency quality characteristic and counts it towards the number of online negative reviews for this quality characteristic. This study also considers an online review of "too heavy to carry, battery capacity" as customer's expression of dissatisfaction in the usability characteristic and counts it towards the number of online negative reviews for this quality characteristic. This study collects and classifies online negative reviews based on the six quality characteristics in this manner. The study excludes online negative reviews for products that received less than 4 online reviews in order to remove potential bias due to the small number of online reviews.

Furthermore, for each product, this study obtains the degree of customer dissatisfaction for each of the six quality characteristics taking into account both the online negative reviews from the website and the importance of (i.e., weight for) each quality characteristic obtained from questionnaire.

For example, the degree of customer satisfaction for the efficiency quality characteristic is quantitatively obtained as follows.

$$\mathbf{t_1} \;=\; 1 - \;\frac{\alpha_1 \;\times\; (\text{Number of negative reviews of efficiency})}{n} \qquad (3\text{-}1)$$

Add your equation here where n is the number of online reviews of a given product, and α_1 is the weight for the efficiency quality characteristic determined from the questionnaires. This study obtains the degree of customer dissatisfaction for the other five quality characteristics in a similar manner.

The study additionally conducts questionnaires with customers to identify attributes of PCs that are important to customers and obtains the quantitative difference (i.e., a weight) among the identified attributes.

By applying the weight for each of the six quality characteristics, this study quantitatively calculates the degree of customer satisfaction.

The questionnaires asked customers the question of "in purchasing a note-type PC, what attributes are important?" and have the customers assign a numeric number between 1 and 6 based on the importance as shown in Table 1. In addition, this study determines the weight for each of the six quality characteristics; the weight is 1 for the most important quality characteristic, and the weights for the other quality characteristics are normalized in the range of from 0 to 1.

Table 1. Importance of quality requirement by each characteristic

	Question of Attribute	Requirement Ratio
Functionality	**Display method**	0.2133
Usability	**Wait, Battery capacity**	1.0000
Reliability	**Production Country, Maker**	0.4814
Efficiency	**Transaction speed, Response**	0.1037
Portability	**Number of USB port**	0.1340
Maintainability	**Customer service, Expand Memory slot**	0.4814

3.3   Data Analysis Process

This study conducts the analysis as follows.

[Step 1] Among the online reviews posted on kakaku.com [9], this study identifies 35 online reviews for the products that were released in 2011 and received 4 or more online reviews. This study counts the number of online reviews in each of the six quality characteristics among the 35 identified online reviews.

[Step 2] This study conducts questionnaires with 100 students and asks "in purchasing a laptop, what attributes are important?" Using the result of the survey, this study quantitatively obtains the level of importance (i.e., the degree of customer quality requirement) for each of the six quantity characteristics.

[Step 3] The level of importance (i.e., the degree of customer quality requirement) obtained in Step 2 is normalized with the highest value to be 1 and with the other values between 0 and 1. The resulting normalized values of the level of importance are called "weights."

[Step 4] The number of online negative reviews in each of the six quality characteristics obtained in step 1 is multiplied by the weight for the quality characteristic obtained in step 3. The degree of customer dissatisfaction is quantitatively obtained by equation (3-1). The degree of customer satisfaction is obtained by subtracting the degree of customer dissatisfaction from 1.

[Step 5] In obtaining the degree of customer satisfaction for each of the six quality characteristics in Step 4, this study considers two cases; one where the weight of each quality characteristic is considered, and the other where it is not. This study, then, performs correlation analysis between these two cases for each of the six quantity characteristics.

[Step 6] From the result in step 5, this study examines correlation and independence between the six quality characteristics, as well as the additivity of the degree of customer satisfaction for each of the six quality characteristics.

[Step 7] The study performs multiple-regression analysis in which the degree of customer satisfaction for one of the six quality characteristics obtained in step 4 is chosen as an objective variable and the degrees of customer satisfaction for the other five quality characteristics are used as explanatory variables.

[Step 8] Using the results from step 7, this study analyzes variance for each of the six quality characteristics, multiple-regression coefficients and determination coefficients, to verify a causal relationship between the objective variable and explanatory variables.

[Step 9] Using the results from step 8, the study develops a model that predicts the results in step 8, the results of variance analysis of the six quality characteristics, and the degree of customer satisfaction for one of the six quality characteristics from the remaining five quality characteristics. The study also confirms the significance of the prediction model using F-Test in the multiple-regression analysis.

4   Verification of Effectiveness of Quality Requirement Definition Based on the Six Characteristics

4.1   Verification of Independency among Six Characteristics

Table2 show that the result of correlation analysis based oh the Step5 in clause 3.3. From Table2, there is not a correlation among each customer satisfaction from the view point of six characteristics and independency of each are recognized.

Since the correlation coefficient is small (at most 0.3), there is no apparent correlation among the six quality characteristics. In other words, the degree of customer satisfaction for each of the six quality characteristics is independent of each other.

Table 2. Correlation Matrix between six characteristics

	Functionality	Usability	Reliability	Efficiency	Portability	Maintainability
Functionality	1.0000	0.1924	-0.2180	0.0313	0.2811	-0.1110
Usability	0.1924	1.0000	0.0297	0.1014	0.1406	-0.0940
Reliability	-0.2180	0.0297	1.0000	-0.1763	0.0467	0.2076
Efficiency	0.0313	0.1014	-0.1763	1.0000	-0.2528	-0.0570
Portability	0.2811	0.1406	0.0467	-0.2528	1.0000	0.1046
Maintainability	-0.1110	-0.0940	0.2076	-0.0570	0.1046	1.0000

4.2   Multiple Regression Analysis

Table3 show the result of multiple-regression analysis based oh the Step6 in subclause 3.3. From Table 3, Multiple-regression analysis for the other five quality characteristics shows that the maximum value of the multiple-regression coefficients and the determination coefficients are 0.422 and 0.178, respectively. Since these values are small, this study confirms that no causal relationship exists among the six quality characteristics. Table 3 shows the F values that indicate the significance of the multiple-regression analyses for each of the six quality characteristics. These values are obtained in step 8 described in the previous sub clause 3.3. In addition, multiple-regression analysis of the customer satisfaction between a given quality characteristic and the other five quality characteristics show that the maximum value of F-test is 1.26. Since it is less than 5% significance level $F_0=2.545$, this study confirms that there is no significance in predicting the degree of customer satisfaction for one quality characteristic and that for any of the other five quality characteristics.

Table 3. Result of Multiple regression Analysis

	Functionality	Usability	Reliability	Efficiency	Portabilty	Maintainabilty
Multiple regression ratio	0.4078	0.2788	0.3445	0.3374	0.4228	0.2694
R2	0.1663	0.0777	0.1187	0.1139	0.1787	0.0726
F Value	1.1567	0.4889	0.7810	0.7452	1.2622	0.4537

5   Concluding Remarks

This study verifies the validity of the introduced method of quantitatively obtaining customer quality requirements using the customer satisfaction and using weights for the degree of customer requirements for each of the six quality characteristics included in the quality model descried in ISO/IEC 9126. In the introduced method, the classified customer satisfaction is confirmed to be independent from each other and have no additivity. Then, total quality evaluation indicator of system could be produced by accumulation of quantitative customer satisfaction, which is introduced from the view point of each six characteristics. In the future work, the author plans to develop a model to quantitatively predict the degree of customer satisfaction from the attributes that the product should achieve.

Acknowledgments. The authors express appreciations to Mr. Kentaro Tai and Mr. Takamitsu Matumoto at Graduate School of Factory of Science and Engineering HOUSEI University. The authors are also grateful to members of production system research office who their contributions and support to make the discussion.

References

1. ISO/IEC 25000: Software engineering–Software product Quality Requirements and Evaluation (SQuaRE) – Guide to SQuaRE, Int'l Organization for Standardization (2005)
2. ISO/IEC 25010: Software engineering–System and software Quality Requirements and Evaluation (SQuaRE) – System and software Quality Model (2011)
3. Boehm, B.W., et al.: Quantative Ev. of Software Quality. In: 2nd ICSE, pp. 596–605 (1976)
4. McCall, J.A., et al.: Factors in Software Quality. RADC TR-77369 (1977)
5. ISO/IEC 25020: Software engineering–Software product Quality Requirements and Evaluation (SQuaRE)–Measurement reference model and guide, Int'l Organization for Standardization (2007)
6. ISO/IEC 25030: Software engineering–Software product Quality Requirements and Evaluation (SQuaRE)–Quality requirement, Int'l Organization for Standardization (2007)
7. Boegh, J.: A New Standard for Quality Requirements. IEEE Computer Society (2008)
8. ISO/IEC 25040: Software engineering–System and software Quality Requirements and Evaluation (SQuaRE)– Evaluation process (2011)
9. Kakaku.com, http://www.kakaku.com

A Trustworthy Storage Framework on the Cloud

Xiang Yao[1,2] and Wenbin Yao[1,2]

[1] School of Computer Science, Beijing University of Posts and Telecommunications, Beijing, China
[2] Key Laboratory of Trustworthy Distributed Computing and Service (BUPT), Ministry of Education, Beijing, China
{xyao,yaowenbin}@bupt.edu.cn

Abstract. The security of important data is a great issue in distributed storage system, especially when the data is stored on the cloud where risk increases and traditional encryption with key may not be secure enough. To deal with the problem, an expanded efficiency secret splitting algorithm (EESSA) is proposed to strengthen the security of data which is not only for long-term storage but also for sharing. Three key technologies are used in EESSA to guarantee security: file manipulation is used to split file to guarantee the data not be obtained by the unauthenticated users; asymmetric cryptosystem is designed to make a secure communication channel to transfer the feature information; security controller makes the whole secure process under the control. The security of the algorithm is proved theoretically, while its feasibility and efficiency is confirmed by experiments.

Keywords: trustworthy storage, secure sharing, information dispersal, asymmetric cryptosystem.

1 Introduction

With the development of information technology, security and reliability of file storage is becoming an important issue. Distributed storage system is a common application for file storage which needs to guarantee security and reliability. The fault-tolerance mechanism in distributed storage system provides a safeguard making it possible that the system will survive when the system malfunctions including error correcting code, group communication server, and fault detection.

Secret sharing is a mechanism to guarantee reliability in distributed storage system. It divides a secret into n shares hold by n users, and the collaboration of some shares may recover the secret so the secret can be recovered if limited numbers of shares lost. Shamir proposed a secret sharing algorithm based on (n, k) threshold problem [1], making contribution to solving data leak problem because of single point`s vulnerability. In addition, secret sharing scheme have been widely applied in electronic auction, electronic voting, multi-signature [2-4], etc.

Secret sharing mechanism also provides an approach to protecting file confidentiality on the server, but if the attacker gets enough parts, the file can be reconstructed. Furthermore, with cloud storage getting more popular, users may not trust the provider

Y. Yuan, X. Wu, and Y. Lu (Eds.): ISCTCS 2012, CCIS 320, pp. 69–77, 2013.
© Springer-Verlag Berlin Heidelberg 2013

of the cloud. Traditionally, the privacy relies on encryption with key which can be cracked by brute-force so that it's not good for long-term storage, especially when on the cloud where computing ability is much higher because of distributed computing. To solve this issue, POTSHARDS [5] was proposed using secret sharing to split a file into fragments in the first step, then redundancy encoding to make shares instead of encryption algorithm. But this project has a storage overhead problem. To solve these problems, Chen [6] proposes ESSA based on the knight`s tour problem. The algorithm provides a better security and greater efficiency than encryption. In fact, the owner doesn`t need to open detail of the algorithm. It is similar to an encryption algorithm while the security doesn`t only depend on the key, but also depends on the secret details. So, it can only be used for security storage, but cannot be used for sharing files in distributed system which is a common requirement.

In order to solve this problem that traditional encryption with key may not be secure enough with storage on the cloud where risk increases, we proposed a trustworthy storage framework, EESSA, an expanded efficient secret splitting algorithm. It realizes the function of sharing files with particular part in distributed storage system. It also gives a solution to avoid file leak and some errors. Nonrepudiation is also guaranteed. Meanwhile, users only need to save their own private key.

The rest of this paper is organized as follows: Section 2 will introduce the architectural of EESSA. Section 3 will give details about EESSA. Section 4 will make some analyzes and discussion about security and efficiency with some proof and experiment. Section 5 will conduct a conclusion.

2   Architectural of EESSA

2.1   Structure of EESSA

EESSA is composed of three modules, which are file manipulation, cryptosystem, and server controller, respectively. The structure is shown in fig.1.

Fig. 1. Structure of EESSA

File manipulation is a mechanism to manipulate files which will be shared. It is made up of three modules, which are digital right management, splitting, and feature information of file.

Digital Rights Management (DRM): Digital rights management is used to reduce the possibility of document leak. If document leak takes place, the owner can observe it according to the watermarking. Digital watermarking algorithms are commonly used for different types of file, such as image, audio, video, text, software. Users choose algorithm according to the file type.

Splitting: Splitting is an approach to ensure the security of file. The method is based on ESSA. Some improvements were made to strengthen security, such as decreasing grain size and adding parity bit. The implement will be shown in 3.1.

FIF (Feature Information of File): FIF is used to transfer information from file owner to receiver. It records splitting method, file information and signature. The receiver uses FIF to verify signature, reconstruct file and verify integrity.

Cryptosystem is designed to share files securely with two modules: encryption/decryption and key management. In detail, asymmetric cryptosystem is selected to make it possible to share files with particular party.

Encryption/Decryption: Encryption and decryption are the mechanism to make it secure for process of sharing.

Key Management: Key management is used to guarantee that all users in the system can share files with any other one in the system.

Security Controller controls the sharing process with management and judgment. It consists of server management and server judgment.

Server Management: When the owner uploads the file and FIF, the server will know this uploading. Then the server notices the *receiver* to download.

Server Judgment: When the receiver considers the verification of signature or file integrity is invalid, it uploads the signature or the hash value and requests the server to judge. The server can verify the signature directly and verify the hash value by asking the owner. If the verification is invalid, then the server requests the owner to repeat uploading. Otherwise, the server requests the receiver to repeat operations.

2.2   Work Flow Chart of EESSA

Suppose there is a distributed system with n users, u_1 u_2 $\ldots$ u_n. The file owner (set as u_1) needs to share file securely with the receiver (set as u_2). EESSA is designed to make it possible to share files with particular party securely. There are three parties in the system, which are owner, receiver and server, respectively.

Owner: The owner owns the file and hopes to share file with a particular party with secure.

Receiver: The receiver gets file which is shared by the owner.

Server: The server manages the system and stores the file and other information such as FIF and receipts. The server also provides a communication channel for every legal user to use. In addition, the server judges the disagreement about file sharing between owner and receiver.

The flow chart of EESSA is shown in Fig.2. The following paragraphs will explain the process of EESSA.

Before sharing, key generation and key storage must be done (Details in 3.2). u_1 must ensure P_{u_2} is available. u_1 signs on some test information with S_{u_1}, and encrypts it with P_{u_2}. If u_2 can get the test information, than he can ensure u_1 is legal, than he send a receipt to u_1. Then u_1 can ensure u_2 is legal.

When pre-sharing is done, sharing process can start. The owner applies DRM on the file, splits the file; generates FIF, encrypts it and uploads it with the file; notice the server who is the receiver. The server notices the receiver to download file and FIF. The receiver decrypts FIF and verifies the signature. If the verification is valid, then the receiver reconstructs the file verifies its integrity; otherwise, the receiver requests the server to judge. The server judges by the information given by the receiver to decide whether FIF is wrong. If it's wrong, then requests the owner to repeat uploading, otherwise to request the receiver to repeat downloading.

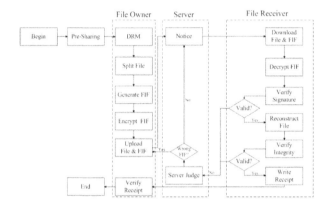

Fig. 2. Flow Chart of EESSA

3   Key Technologies of EESSA

In this section, three key technologies of EESSA will be explained, which are optimization of splitting method, asymmetric cryptosystem in EESSA and the feature information of file (FIF) used to transfer information respectively.

3.1   Optimization of Splitting Method

The splitting method in EESSA is based on ESSA with optimization.

Firstly, to offer better security, EESSA dispersal the segment in bit level.

Besides, fault-tolerant capability of file is also strengthened. In EESSA, the last bit of scramble matrix will be set as parity check bit which can not only used to check error, but also used to make semantic cryptanalysis more useless because some bytes are separate in different matrix.

In addition, some type of file has a static file header. According to the header and the split file, the splitting method can be got. In EESSA, scramble matrix is filled with bits. As it`s difficult to distinguish this '1' from that '1', analysis will be no effective.

In file type of txt format, although file header doesn`t exist, the statistical regularity also works. For example, the word "the" appears frequently, so an analysis of the position of character 't', 'h', 'e' will have a considerable possibility to find true order. When the scramble matrix is filled with bits, it's difficult to analyze from frequency.

3.2   Feature Information of File (FIF)

Feature Information of File (FIF) contains the Knight's tour, file information and signature. Suppose selecting 8×8 chessboard with the starting point $(3, 4)$, the length of FIF for will be set as 4096 bits, 384 bits for Knight's tour ($64*6=384$ bit), 3200 bits for file information, and 512 bits for signature (using RSA).

Table 1. Components of FIF (8*8 chessboard)

Splitting Method	File Information	Signature
384bits	3200bits	512bits

Coding

The method of splitting must be transferred in sharing. Since the security of splitting method is based on difficulty to get Knight's tour, how to share the Knight's tour becomes important. So there will be a coding with fault-tolerant mechanism.

Coding of Directions

The path is coded according to the directions. There're eight directions for knight to move at most. Encode the eight directions called C for 000, 001, 010, 011, 100, 101, 110, and 111 clockwise.

Fault-Tolerant Mechanism

According to the formula $2^p \geq p+d+1$ [7] (p stands for the number of check bits, d stands for the number of data bits), in EESSA, three check bits are needed. Generator matrix G is used to describe the method of coding.

$$G = \begin{pmatrix} 1 & 0 & 0 & 1 & 1 & 0 \\ 0 & 1 & 0 & 1 & 0 & 1 \\ 0 & 0 & 1 & 0 & 1 & 1 \end{pmatrix}$$

The code word C' after second coding will be implemented by the equation

$$C' = C \cdot G$$

Parity-check matrix H is:

$$H = \begin{pmatrix} 1 & 1 & 0 & 1 & 0 & 0 \\ 1 & 0 & 1 & 0 & 1 & 0 \\ 0 & 1 & 1 & 0 & 0 & 1 \end{pmatrix}$$

A valid code word C' must meet the equation:

$$C' \cdot H^T = 0$$

If an error occurs on the a data bit of C', then $C' \cdot H^T \neq 0$ If there is only one-bit error, check the column of generate matrix G, and the error bit will be found.

Security Mechanism

File information and signature are attached to FIF to provide security mechanism.

File information is used to describe file so the receiver can check whether the file is true or not. It contains file name, the owner's name, modification time and something related to the file, the SHA-1 value of original file is included too.

Signature is used to convince users that FIF comes from an authorized party. The owner signs on Knight's tour and file information with private key. And the receiver uses the corresponding public key to verify the signature.

Convenient Management of File
The owner may need to reconstruct file while they may have deleted before. As a user can own a large scale of files with different splitting method, how to manage the splitting method for different files is an issue. In EESSA, the owner don`t need to save all the splitting methods, but the private key instead. FIF with information of path can be encrypted by using the owner`s public key and be saved in the server.

3.3   Asymmetric Cryptosystem

Asymmetric Cryptosystem is used to make it possible to share files with particular party since it can give an approach to make communication without key exchange.

Key Management
Key management consists of key generation of key storage.

Key Generation
Each user have two keys – public key (recorded as P_{u_i}) and private key (recorded as S_{u_i}) for u_i. Users generate key pairs and send the public key with the cryptosystem information C_{u_i} to the server. Public key is free to get while private key is hold by the user itself. It's difficult to deduce private key from the public key.

Key Storage
The server receives public keys from users, and repeats detection.

If (C_{u_i}, P_{u_i}) is the same as (C_{u_j}, P_{u_j}), then request u_i and u_j to change their key pairs. When all users are ready, servers generate a key table for users to look up.

4   Analysis

The security and efficiency of EESSA is analyzed with mathematical proof and experiments.

4.1   Security

The security of the framework comes from two aspects: one is the security of splitting method; the other one is security of asymmetric encryption system.

Security of Splitting Method
To ensure security, a splitting method cannot be reused so that known plaintext attack and chosen plaintext attack is no effective. And by the reason mentioned in 3.1, semantic cryptanalysis is less useful and the adversary can only do brute-force.

There is no efficient algorithm to crack the knight`s path because it`s a NP problem. The number of permutation in 8×8 chessboard is 64! =1.269e+89, while the key space of AES-256 is only 2^{256} =1.158e+77. Suppose time cost per trial in AES-256 is similar to one in EESSA in brute-force, the EESSA (8×8) is providing better security when the adversary don`t have dictionary for knight`s path.

However, the number of knight`s tour in 8×8 chessboard is given by [8], which is almost 3.4e+11. Brute force will be effective if the adversary get all paths. The size of chessboard is increased to make secure even though the dictionary of path is leak.

$$F_{n,n} = \Omega(1.3535^{n^2})$$ (1)

($F_{n,n}$ represents the number of knight`s path in $n\times n$ chessboard [9])

Table 2. Relationship between the number of path and n

n	Lower Bound Magnitude of $F_{n,n}$
8	2.6e+8
24	5.2e+75
48	7.6e+302

When n equals to 24, $F_{n,n} \geq c \cdot 10^{75}$, which is as the same magnitude as the key space of AES-256. However, constructing the dictionary also costs an amount of time, enhancing the difficulty of brute-force. If n equals to 48, the security level is higher.

Security of Asymmetric Encryption System
The security of asymmetric encryption system depends on the encryption algorithm. The common algorithm is RSA and NTRU. NTRU is chosen as an example to analysis. According to the S. Bu [10], distributed attack to NTRU is useless. So the security of asymmetric encryption system is guaranteed.

4.2   Efficiency

A series of experiments were designed to show that EESSA has a high efficiency. The asymmetric encryption algorithm is RSA. In the experiments, the time cost by path generation is ignored because the path is stored in local place. The data capacity is 10 Mbytes and I/O time is not calculated. The size of chessboard is $n\times n$.

Time Cost in EESSA
If n equals to 8, 24, and 48, the time cost in splitting are separately 1.53s, 1.58s, 1.59s; the time cost by encryption of FIF using RSA are separately 0.36s, 0.79s, 2.20s. Total time cost are separately 1.89s, 2.37s, 3.79s.

Compare with AES
The time cost in AES encryption is 10.58s while the time cost in RSA encryption of AES's key and signature is 0.39s. Total time cost is 11.97s. It is shown in Fig.3.

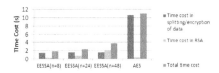

It's clear that the time cost in EESSA is less than that in AES, because in AES, the encryption steps will be executed for several rounds which spend much time.

Fig. 3. Time cost between EESSA and AES

In conclusion, compared to AES, a very common encryption algorithm, EESSA provides higher security and higher efficiency when n is set as 48. And the security level can be advanced by the increase of parameter n with little efficiency decrease.

5   Conclusions

We propose a trustworthy storage framework on the cloud with EESSA, an expanded efficient splitting algorithm. The framework can solve the problem that traditional encryption with key is not secure enough with storage on the cloud where risk increases. And EESSA can also give a way to share files with secure. The key technologies used in EESSA are file manipulation, asymmetric cryptosystem and security controller. The security of the framework is proved to be better than AES encryption and as series of experiment are conducted to show the efficiency is better.

Acknowledgement. This study is supported by the National High Technology Research and Development Program ("863"Program) of China (2012AA012600) the Fundamental Research Funds for the Central Universities (BUPT2011RCZJ16) and China Information Security Special Fund (NDRC).

References

1. Shamir, A.: How to share a secret. Communications of the ACM 22(11), 612–613 (1979)
2. Schoenmakers, B.: A Simple Publicly Verifiable Secret Sharing Scheme and Its Application to Electronic Voting. In: Wiener, M. (ed.) CRYPTO 1999. LNCS, vol. 1666, pp. 148–784. Springer, Heidelberg (1999)
3. Kikuchi, H. (M+1)st-Price Auction Protocol. In: Syverson, P.F. (ed.) FC 2001. LNCS, vol. 2339, pp. 341–363. Springer, Heidelberg (2002)
4. Lal, S., Kumar, M.: A Directed-Threshold Multi-Signature Scheme. Cryptography and Security ACM-class (2004)
5. Storer, M.W., Greenan, K.M., et al.: POTSHARDS: secure long-term storage without encryption. In: Proceedings of the USENIX Annual Technical Conference, pp. 1–14. USENIX Association, Santa Clara (2007)
6. Chen, Z., Yao, W.-B., Xiao, D., Wu, C.-H., Liu, J.-Y., Wang, C.: ESSA: An Efficient and Secure Splitting Algorithm for Distributed Storage Systems. China Communications 7(4), 89–95 (2010)
7. Singleton, R.: Maximum distance q-nary codes. IEEE Transactions on Information Theory 10(2), 116–118 (1964)

8. Löbbing, M., Wegener, I.: The Number of Knight's Tours Equals 33,439,123,484,294 - Counting with Binary Decision Diagrams. The Electronic Journal of Combinatorics 3(1), 5 (1996)
9. Kyek, O., Parberry, I., et al.: Bounds on the number of knight's tours. Discrete Applied Mathematics 74(2), 171–181 (1997)
10. Bu, S., Xu, X., et al.: Analysis on Security of NTRU Public Key Cryptosystem. Computer Engineering and Applications 38(24), 3 (2002)

Progress in Study of Encrypted Traffic Classification

Zigang Cao[1,4], Shoufeng Cao[2], Gang Xiong[3], and Li Guo[3]

[1] Beijing University of Posts and Telecommunications, Beijing, China
caozg@bupt.edu.cn
[2] National Computer Network Emergency Response Technical Team / Coordination Center of China
csf@cert.org.cn
[3] Institute of Information Engineering, Chinese Academy of Science
{xionggang,guoli}@iie.ac.cn
[4] Key Laboratory of Trustworthy Distributed Computing and Service (BUPT), Ministry of Education, Beijing, China

Abstract. The rapid increase in encrypted network traffic recently has become a great challenge for network management, and study of encrypted traffic classification provides basic technical support for effective network management and network security. The basis and problems of encrypted traffic classification are introduced first. Next, the main research progresses of encrypted traffic classification are summarized. Finally, the future trend is put forward.

Keywords: traffic classification, encrypted traffic, flow statistical properties, machine learning, host behavior.

1   Introduction

Network traffic classification is the essentialrequirement for network management. In general, the focus is on accurate classification and detailed classification. With the rapid development of Internet network, the scale of traffic itself has become much larger, the speedmuch higher, and components much more complex. Accordingly, traffic classification technology has developed from traditional port-based classification to signature-based Deep Packet Inspection(DPI) classification, and recently hastransferred to flow-based statistical classificationand host-based behavior classification, which experienced a realistic demand-driven development process.

Since 2006, Peer to Peer(P2P) applications has been trying to breaking limit of Internet Service Providers(ISPs) gradually bythe use of encryption and protocol obfuscation techniques, and the public have paid much more attention to privacy protection, which both resulted in a substantial increase of encrypted applications and traffic. As the traditional DPItechniquewas powerless for encrypted traffic classification, new methods were tried, making the classification a central issueof traffic classification. In the next period of time, with the rapid increasing bandwidth and computing capabilities, encryption applications will be more and more. Meanwhile, the deployment of IPv6 makes IPSEC implementationat the network layer much easier, which will further promote the raise of encryption applications and traffic.

Y. Yuan, X. Wu, and Y. Lu (Eds.): ISCTCS 2012, CCIS 320, pp. 78–86, 2013.

Therefore, encrypted traffic classification will still be the focusin the next few years.From the perspective ofpublished results, a lot ofspecific work of encrypted traffic classification has been carried out recent years. Meanwhile, important issues and challenges faced by encrypted traffic classification are still to be resolved, or donebetter.

The rest of this paper is organized as follows.Section2 introduces the category of encrypted traffic, classification requirements, the basic classification methods and the main challenges. In section 3, the main progressesin study of encrypted traffic classification in recent years were reviewed. Section 4 concludesthe paper with the summary of challenges in the field and suggestions of possiblefuture work.

2   Basics of Encrypted Traffic Classification

2.1   Category and Classification Requirements

Encrypted traffic being publicly studied can be roughly divided into the following categories: Secure Shell (SSH), Virtual Private Network (VPN), Secure Sockets Layer (SSL), encrypted P2P and encryptedVoice over Internet Protocol(VoIP) traffic, not including private protocols. It should be noted that there may be a cross between two types of them. For example, SSL VPN can be grouped into both SSL and VPN, and Skype belongs to both encrypted P2P and encrypted VOIP.

Classification requirementsare accuracy, real-time, and robustness.

Accuracy: Reflect the ability to the classification to the correct classification of encrypted traffic, which means both accurate classification of encrypted and unencrypted traffic and accurate fine-grainedclassification of encrypted traffic internally.

Real-time: Reflect the ability of classification methodto quickly identify online encrypted traffic.

Robustness: Reflect the abilityto overcome asymmetric routing, packet loss and packet retransmissionof the network or protocol anomaly factors, as well as in face of traffic morph or obfuscationand classify encrypted traffic effectively.

Besides, there are some most commonly used quantitative metrics, namely:

True Positive (TP): members of class A correctlyclassifiedasbelonging to class A. And Percentage of TP, TPR = TP / (TP + FN).

True Negative (TN): members of otherclasses correctly classified as not belonging to class A. And Percentage of TN, TNR = TN/ (FP + TN).

False Negative (FN): members of class A incorrectly classified as not belonging to class A.And Percentage of FN, FNR = FN / (TP + FN)=1-TPR.

False Positive (FP): members of otherclasses incorrectly classified as belongingto class A.And Percentage of FP, FPR = FP / (FP + TN)=1-TNR.

Detection Rate (DR) = Recall = TP / (TP + FN), equivalent to the TPR.

Precision = TP / (TP + FP), and Accuracy = (TP + TN)/(TP + TN + FP + FN).

F-measure = 2 * Recall * Precision / (Recall + the Precision).

2.2   Basic Classification Methods

Peter Dorfinger [1] divided encrypted traffic classification research into two directions, which are packet-based classification and classification based on host/social information.The difference is that the former uses a single flowto implement classification, while the other uses host behavior to do it. The former can be called flow-based classification, and the latter is classification based on host behavior.

Flow-based classification mainly refers to the methods based on flow statistical properties, which are usually called statisticalmethods.There are also some techniques that use a combination of IP header properties and flow statistical properties. The most commonly used attributes arepacket length, packet direction, and packet inter-arrival time, etc.

Machine learning (ML), which isthe most common method to connect feature setswith classification, can be subdivided into unsupervised learning, supervised learningand semi-supervised learning.T. Nguyen et.al [2] had a very good summary of machine learning in traffic classification, so no more details will be discussed here. Common used machine learning methods include Support Vector Machine (SVM), the NaïveBayes, K-Means,AutoClass, C4.5 decision tree and neural networks etc. Some mathematical methods such as Gaussian Mixture Model (GMM), Hidden Markov Model (HMM) and maximum likelihood classification were used too. In addition, information theory and processing methods are employedinthe feature set-sprocessingfor encrypted traffic classification, such as time domain and frequency domain correlation [3], entropy estimation based on the first packet of a flow [1] and flow similarity of the same type traffic internally.

Classification based on host behavior is to analyze the behavioral characteristics ofdifferent types of applications from the host perspective, which mainly depends on the connection patterns of the different types of applications.Traffic is generally divided into coarse-grained classes, such as P2P and web. This approach becomes useless when the flows of transport layer are encrypted or connection information is incomplete, and the use of Network Address Translation (NAT)in the network will make it not so powerful. Since its coarse-grained result cannot meet the fine-grained need of many traffic managers, there is not much research on it.

As forthe two types of classification methods above,the general steps are feature extraction, modeling, followed by sample training, and classifyingthe traffic to be tested. Given that certain encrypted traffic can carry a variety of applications and refinement of classification requirements of different applications within the encrypted tunnel,classification is usually carried out in two steps.The first step is to identify specific type of encrypted traffic and other traffic(generally unencrypted traffic), and the second is to do fine-grained classification according to the characteristics of different applications in the encrypted traffic.

2.3   Problems in Classification

How to Achieve Effective Classification. Thebasic requirement of traffic classification is precise and detailed classification.However, there has been no statement that there is some method that can be used in the real complex and fast-changed traffic environment for a long time and do accurateand efficient work on encrypted traffic classification. Table 1 below is an overview of the current mainstream classification methods used for encrypted traffic.

Table 1. Comprasion of methods for encrypted traffic classification

Classification methods	Port-based	Payload-based	Statistical classification	Host behavior based
Accuracy	Low	Low	Higher	Higher
Real-time	High	Middle	Higher	Higher
Robustness	Low	Low	Higher	Higher
Advantages	Simple,small computational overhead	No	Robustness, accuracy, fine-grained	Simple,small computational overhead
Disadvantages	Low accuracy, cannot be used alone	Almost useless, privacy risk	Large computational over-head,a lot of training,not stable when traffic changes	Coarseclassification,useless when transport layer encrypted, degradation in case of NAT
Status	Not in use	Not in use	Under test	Under test

From the table above we can see that there is still a long way to go in the study of effectiveclassification of encrypted traffic.

Theory and Practical Issues of Statistical Classification. Issues mainly includethe impacts of asymmetric routing, missing packets, retransmission in a flow, or lack of the initial few packetson statistical classification, the impact of the differences between offline environmentand online or evenhigh-speed environment on classification performances, as well as classification in countermeasure scenes. The answers to these questionswill promotebest practices in the real encrypted traffic classification.

How to Obtain Ground Truth of Data Sets. Ground truth (GT)in traffic classification refers to the true information ofeach flow or packet belonging to the right application or categories. When researchers want to validate their algorithms, the data setsused must have GT. Besides the single pure flowsgenerated in certain controlled environments and manual annotation, the automatic methodsto get GT aremostly based on port and DPI technology to label flows, so the accuracy is not trustworthy. The resultsof open source or commercial products cannot be taken as real GT, neither. Therefore, how to label the data to obtain GT as accurately as possibleis a challenge.

3   Main Progresses in Classification

Most widely used methodsin encrypted traffic classification are similar around the world. SSH, Skype and encrypted P2P are paid more attention by researchers of all encrypted traffic types. Study of SSH and SSLtraffichas been refined to distinguish the applicationscarried in the encryptedtunnels, and classification of encrypted Skype VoIP flowsfocuses on identifying its traffic and obtaining sensitive information.Fine-grained classification of P2P applications accords withQuality of Service(QoS) of network management.The main progresses are summarized as follows.

3.1   Achieving Effective Classification

Alshammari et.al[4] usedfive ML algorithms to classify SSH and Skype traffic, and results showed that C4.5 decision tree classifier was the best. Bacquet C.et.al [5] compared performances of five unsupervised clustering algorithmsin identifying SSH traffic and found that Multi-Objective Genetic Algorithm (MOGA)presented a good overall performance in DR, FPR, the establishment and operation of the model.

The difficulty in SSH and SSL traffic classification is to distinguish the applications within encrypted tunnel. The current studies are based on a hypothesis: the encryptedtunnelonly carries a single type of application at the same time. Tan et.al [6] proposed a method usingmaximum likelihood classifier to classify SSH tunnel traffic, in which the SSH Tunnel flow boundarywasidentifiedfirstly, and then only the statistical information of the continuous L-packets after the border was used to classify the applications in the SSH tunnel.

As for encrypted P2P traffic classification, most methods are using machine learning algorithms based on flow statistical properties. Besides, there are some methods using a combination of payload and flow characteristics. But the payload is forcontent statistical properties, rather than fingerprint matching. Hjelmvik et.al [7] showed the validity of Statistical Protocol Identification(SPID)algorithm for the classification of P2P obfuscationtraffic in a comprehensive and detailed way, and the most useful statistical properties for several typical protocols were summarized.

Encrypted VOIP classification not only helps to provide better network service quality, but alsoaid to find flaws in the protocols to enhance safety further. Yildirimet.al[8]used a machine learning method to classify VoIP and non-VoIP traffic in the IPSEC tunnel, and proved by experimentsthe importance ofidentifying the VoIP application and give high priority to it to improve QoS. Andrew M. White[9] revealeda new privacy threat that parts of the VOIP conversation could be unmaskedby segmenting an observed packet stream intosubsequences representing individual phonemes and classifyingthose subsequences by the phonemes they encode.

As for exploration of new methods, Charles V-Wright, etc. in[10] used visual motifs to show the differences of the transient and steady-state behaviors of different application protocols, which was used to identify encrypted trafficand new applications. Recently, the team of Dalhousie University in Canada applied genetic programming to encrypted traffic classification and achieved good results. As the latest progress of the team, an extended MOGA in [11] was used in feature selection and cluster count optimization for K-Means, and results showed that DR got an increase of 2% to 5%, while the FPR did not increased significantly. Their results fully demonstratedthe advantages of genetic programming.

3.2   Solving Problems in Statistical Classification

On the effects of asymmetric routing on statistical classification, M. Crotti et.al [12]compared the capability of unidirectional classifierswith the ones of bidirectional classifiers in extracting informationfrom the features of half-flows. The results showed that bidirectional classifiersworked better substantially in FP decreaseinstead of TP increase. The significance was that the statistical classifiers may face a constraint with half-flow of a single direction, and the relationship between the two half-flows can be studied for better classification.

As for loss of part of the packets in a flow or lackof the initial packets of it, there is no good solution. In [13],multiple short sub-flows extracted from a full flow were used to train Naive Bayes ML algorithm in order to optimize the use of it. The results showed thatcompared with training on the entire flow, training in this way could get better performance, which also provided a possible solution for the problem.

As for the impact of differences between offline and online environment on classification performance, the problem needs to be further resolved. M. Crotti et.al [14] explored the problem of determining the optimum working parametersfor statistical classifiers, and proposed a procedure to do it.Results indicated that the automatic parameter optimization was essential, and revealed that some of the properties used in classification algorithms need to be further studiedbeforethey were put into practice.

On the countermeasuretechniques for statistical classification, Charles Wrightet.al [15]proposed a method to defeat statistical traffic analysisalgorithms by optimally-morphingone class of traffic tolook like another one. This method used convex optimization techniques to modify the packetsreal-timewhile incurring much less overheadthan padding. Recently in [16], a model was proposed to obfuscate the traffic from Tor [17] clientsto Tor bridges in Skype video protocol. It can be predicted that anti-classification techniques will be more and more in future.

3.3   Obtaining Ground Truthof Data Sets

M. Canini et.al[18]presented a methodology and detailed the design of a technical-frameworkGround Truth Verification System (GTVS) thatsignificantlyimproved-theefficiencyincompiling theapplication trafficgroundtruth. The specific approach was to monitor the host kernel, associatethe packetswithapplications and combine it with DPI mechanisms. M. Dusiet.al [19] compared the ground truth collected by tools based on the port and DPI techniques and that through the application layer error-free GTcollection tool, and results show that the error rates of GTobtained by the port and DPI were 91% and 26% respectively. Work still need to be done further.

3.4   Encrypted Traffic Classification Based on Host Behavior

In 2005, based on previous research result of identifying the types of P2P applications using connection patterns, T. Karagianniset.al [20]proposed a traffic classification method based on host transport layer behavior patterns, which is called BLINC. The method analyzed host behaviors at three levels: social, functional and application.

A heuristic classification method based on the activities of network hosts was proposed in [21], which focused on classifying those "long" flows that transferred most of the bytes across a network.The heuristic analysis of the flow was in four aspects: the source host, the destination host, further connections between the hosts, and the flow activity. The experimental results show thatsimilar accuracies could be achieved in real-time as were developed in the offline process.

Although the method is not fine-grained enough, but the small computational overhead make it useful in real-time coarse-grained classification of the backbone network traffic or combined with some fine-grained methods to get better performance.

4   Summary and Future Works

Encrypted traffic classification is one of the most challenging problems in traffic classification field. With the rapid growing of Internet traffic, the use of encryption technology will become a general problem of traffic classification. Besides the basic problem that there are no standards for traffic class definitions and comparison metrics, classification in case of packet loss, unidirectional flow, and trafficmorphing attack etc.is the focus of challenges. Meanwhile, with a large number of applications using encryption techniques, another obstacle is how to fine-grained classifythe traffic of a wide variety of differentapplications. Regarding of the differences between traffic in the lab environment and online real environment, especially in the high-speed network, and fast change of traffic characteristics, how to make those useful methods performing well in the experimental environment maintaintheir good abilities whenapplied to real online scenes is a problem worthy of study.

The current research basically concentrates on the specific methods of statistical analysis andextraction of a variety of behavioral characteristics. In our opinion, a combination of coarse-grained classification methods based on host behavior and other fine-grained ones based on flow statistical properties, or classification methods based on host behaviorsupported by other technical means of the active validation, etc., may get betterresults. It is worthtrying to use the randomness property of encrypted traffic in information theory for classification, too. Introducing intelligent machine learning methods to the classification of encrypted traffic may also be one of the better solutions.

Acknowledgements. The work in this paper is supported by the "Strategic Priority Research Program" of the Chinese Academy of Sciences(Grant No. XDA06030200) and the National High-Tech Research and Development Plan "863" of China (Grant No. 2011AA010703) and the National Natural Science Foundation (Grant No. 61070026).

References

1. Dornger, P.: Real-Time Detection of Encrypted Traffic based on Entropy Estimation, Master Thesis (2010)
2. Nguyen, T., Armitage, G.: A Survey of Techniques for Internet TrafficClassification using Machine Learning. IEEE Communications Surveysand Tutorials 10(4), 56–76 (2008)
3. Lu, Y., Zhu, Y.: Correlation-Based Traffic Analysis on Encrypted VoIP Traffic. IEEE Journal on Parallel and Distributed Systems, 45–48 (2010)
4. Alshammari, R., Zincir-Heywood, A.N.: Machine Learning Based Encrypted Traffic Classification: Identifying SSH and Skype. In: Proceedings of the 2009 IEEE Symposium on Computation Intelligence in Security and Defense Applications, Ottawa (2009)
5. Bacquet, C., Gumus, K., Tizer, D., Zincir-Heywood, A.N., Heywood, M.I.: A Comparison of Unsupervised Learning Techniques for Encrypted Traffic Identification. Journal of Information Assurance and Security 5, 464–472 (2010)
6. Tan, X., Su, X., Qian, Q.: The Classification of SSH Tunneled Traffic Using Maximum Likelihood Classifier. In: 2011 International Conference on Electronics, Communications and Control, ICECC (2011)
7. Hjelmvik, E., John, W.: Breaking and Improving Protocol Obfuscation.Technical report, Chalmers University of Technology (2010)
8. Yildirim, T., Radcliffe, P.: VoIP Traffic Classification in IPSec Tunnels. In: 2010 International Conference on Electronics and Information Engineering, ICEIE (2010)
9. White, A., Matthews, A., Snow, K., Monrose, F.: Phonotactic Reconstruction of Encrypted VoIP Conversations: Hookt on fon-iks. In: IEEE Symposium on Security and Privacy (SP), pp. 3–18 (2011)
10. Wright, C.V., Monrose, F., Masson, G.M.: Using Visual Motifs to Classify Encrypted Traffic. In: Proceedings of the 3rd International Workshop on Visualization for Computer Security, VizSEC 2006 (2006)
11. Bacquet, C., Zincir-Heywood, A.N., Heywood, M.I.: Genetic Optimization and Hierarchical Clustering applied to Encrypted Traffic Identification. In: IEEE Symposium on Computational Intelligence on Cyber Security, pp. 194–201 (2011)
12. Crotti, M., Gringoli, F., Salgarelli, L.: Impact of Asymmetric Routing on Statistical Traffic Classification. In: Proceedings of the 7th IEEE Global Communications Conference (GLOBECOMM 2009), Honolulu, USA (2009)
13. Nguyen, T., Armitage, G.: Training on multiple sub-flows to optimizethe use of Machine Learning classifiers in real-world IP networks. In: Proc. IEEE 31st Conference on Local Computer Networks,Tampa,Florida, USA (2006)
14. Crotti, M., Gringoli, F., Salgarelli, L.: Optimizing Statistical Classifiers of Network Traffic. In: Proceedings of the 6th Wireless Communications & Mobile Computing Conference (IWCMC 2010), Caen, France (2010)
15. Wright, C., Coulls, S., Monrose, F.: Traffic Morphing: An efficient defense against statistical traffic analysis. In: Proceedings of the 14th Annual Network and Distributed Systems Symposium, NDSS (2009)
16. Moghaddam, H.M., Li, B., Derakhshani, M., Goldberg, I.: SkypeMorph: ProtocolObfuscation for Tor Bridges. Technical report, University of Waterloo (2012)
17. Tor Project, https://www.torproject.org/
18. Canini, M., Li, W., Moore, A.W., Bolla, R.: GTVS: Boosting the Collection of Application Traffic Ground Truth. In: Papadopouli, M., Owezarski, P., Pras, A. (eds.) TMA 2009. LNCS, vol. 5537, pp. 54–63. Springer, Heidelberg (2009)

19. Dusi, M., Gringoli, F., Salgarelli, L.: Quantifying the accuracy of the ground truth associated with Internet traffic traces. Elsevier Computer Networks (COMNET) 55(5), 1158–1167 (2011)
20. Karagiannis, T., Papagiannaki, K., Faloutsos, M.: BLINC: Multilevel Traffic Classification in the Dark. In: Proc. of the Special Interest Group on Data Communication Conference (SIGCOMM 2005), Philadelphia, PA, USA (2005)
21. Hurley, J., Garcia-Palacios, E., Sezer, S.: Host-based P2P flow identification and use in real-time. ACM Trans. Web 5(2), Article 7, 27 pages (2011)

Trustworthiness: From a Social Phenomenon to Internet Technology

Jørgen Bøegh[1,2]

[1] School of Software Engineering, Beijing University of Posts and Telecommunications,
Beijing, China
[2] Key Laboratory of Trustworthy Distributed Computing and Services (BUPT),
Ministry of Education,
Beijing, China
jorgen@bupt.edu.cn

Abstract. Trustworthiness is an important concept in human life. This paper discusses trustworthiness from a human social point of view. Today trustworthiness has become equally important for IT services. A definition of trustworthiness is proposed. It is shows that this definition is both consistent with our intuitive understanding and suitable for IT services. The definition leads naturally to a formula useful for describing and measuring trustworthiness.

Keywords: Trustworthiness, IT services, neurobiology, social science, measurement.

1   Introduction

Trust and trustworthiness are important concepts in our daily life. Every day we have to evaluate the trustworthiness of other people. This has always been the case during the history of human life. It is not so easy to explain why we trust some people and why we consider someone to be trustworthy. However, we are not in doubt when we have to decide whether or not a person is trustworthy. We have a fairly good intuition for trustworthiness evaluation.

Usually we trust people that we already know, for example our wife or husband and our close friends. This is not surprising because we have years of experience with their abilities and moral values. We know exactly when we can trust them.

Sometimes we also trust people we do not know. For example, we trust strangers on the street to give us directions when we don't know the area very well. We trust taxi drivers in a city not familiar to us, for example to bring us safely from the airport to our hotel.

Today we also face the trustworthiness problem in a completely different environment: the IT world. It is difficult to make a judgment of trustworthiness when we use computers and access websites on the Internet. Here our intuition does not work well. It is very difficult to decide whether a service offered on a web site is trustworthy. We urgently need to find solutions to help us to evaluate the trustworthiness in the world of IT services.

Y. Yuan, X. Wu, and Y. Lu (Eds.): ISCTCS 2012, CCIS 320, pp. 87–93, 2013.
© Springer-Verlag Berlin Heidelberg 2013

In this paper we will discuss how to move from the normal human understanding of trustworthiness to a concept that is also useful for IT services.

2   The Human Brain

The history of human life goes more than 2 million years back in time and probably started in Africa. During these many years evolution has created a human brain, which is unique among living organisms [1]. One particular aspect of importance in that respect is that humans live together in groups. There are several advantages of this social arrangement. One is that groups can provide better security from enemies, better choice of wife, and more reliable access to food. The other side of the coin is that mates and food are also available to competitors from within the group.

Living together in groups requires many social skills. Our brain has developed mechanisms for managing these social skills. Some skills are related to cooperation and other skills are related to competition. The evolution of our brain happened in a complex and dynamic interplay between these two opposing factors. This is the reason why humans have developed mechanisms for behaving in two different ways.

One mechanism is related to working together and helping others. This is the nice side of the human behavior. The other mechanism is related to lying, cheating, manipulating and forcing others to behave in a specific way by use of threats or some other form of pressure or force. This is the bad side of the human nature. Therefore we need to know who we is trustworthy and this is exactly the reason why we have developed a strong intuition for trustworthiness evaluation.

There are two sides of trust and trustworthiness in human societies.

One side is our ability to make individual judgments of trustworthiness. Deciding whether a stranger is trustworthy is one of the most important decisions routinely faced in social environments. Perceived trustworthiness determines whether to approach or avoid the person. In most part of human history this decision could mean the difference between life and death. This is why trustworthiness evaluation is a built-in function in the human brain. When we meet a person we mainly use features of that persons face to make a trustworthiness evaluation.

The other side is concerned with the social mechanisms. Social structures provide mechanisms that may ensure and enhance trustworthy behavior of people. This is necessary because we have the above mentioned abilities for lying, cheating, and manipulating others.

The posture of the body is important, but the human face is the most important part when evaluating another person. The face provides a large variety of important social signals. It can tell if the person is old or young, male or female, sad or happy, angry or scared, and so on. These signals are important for social interaction and we are very good at reading them.

We process information about features of a face in a specialized area of the brain, called the amygdala. The amygdala is an almond-shape set of neurons located deep in the brain. The processing in the amygdala is very fast, less than 100 milliseconds [2]. This is enough time to form an impression of a stranger; also to evaluate the trustworthiness of the person. The face has some specific features we use when making the trustworthiness decision. These features include the form of the inner eyebrows, cheekbones, and chin [3].

It is remarkable that we largely base the trustworthiness evaluation of a person on characteristics of the person's face. People generally agree when evaluating trustworthiness of others. Therefore it is correct to say that it is a built-in algorithm. The ability to decide who is trustworthy is essential. However, it is not clear whether these features of a person's face actually relate to the character of that person.

3   Social Mechanisms

In addition to the individual ability to evaluate trustworthiness we have also developed social mechanisms that strongly influence trustworthiness. This section discusses some of these mechanisms.

3.1   Social Control Mechanisms

The human social structures have resulted in the evolution of a set of social control mechanisms which ensure that people behave trustworthy. These mechanisms are mainly based on fear.

One of these mechanism is punishment. If there is a high probability for detection when cheating, and detection will cause severe punishment, then most people will be trustworthy. The fear of punishment is one of the main reasons for a person to be trustworthy.

Another mechanism is related to reputation. The fear of getting a bad reputation is a strong motivation for being trustworthy. The reputation mechanism works well in groups where people know each other. It also works in an environment where reliable feedback is available. Fear of losing a reputation may actually be the best enforcer of trustworthiness.

3.2   Trustworthiness Enhancing Mechanisms

The human social structures have also developed mechanisms for enhancing trustworthiness. This probably happened because high levels of trust correlate with prosperity in a society. These social mechanisms enhance trustworthiness by reducing the risk of entering into a transaction.

The use of contracts is one approach to enhance trustworthiness. Contracts enable people to make explicit what they count on another person to do, and in return for what. Should they not do just that, then the contract tells what damages can be extracted from them. Contracts are useful because they are sanctioned by a powerful entity like a state. In most societies today only the state has the necessary, legitimate power for doing this. The state will enforce fulfillment of contracts by means of legal systems.

Insurance is another way of enhancing trustworthiness. Insurances are usually provided by private companies. If our trust is misused then we will be partly compensated by the insurance company. Therefore the risk decreases and the trustworthiness increases.

3.3   Risk and Betrayal

When speaking about trust there are two further concepts to consider: risk and betrayal.

Risk is essential when talking about trusts. If there is no risk, there is no reason to trust. Risk is actually a complex concept with many facets. Risk is usually defined as a combination of the probability that something will go wrong and the magnitude of harm if it actually goes wrong. However, there is no consensus in the literature about the precise definition. We will not discuss risk in further details here.

Trust is also related to betrayal. Betrayal means the intention to act against the best interest of the person who trusts. When dealing with other people there is always a possibility that we will be cheated, misused, or even killed. In that case we are betrayed. On the other hand, when using a machine we rely on its safety and reliability; but if it causes an accident due to a technical failure we will not claim that we have been betrayed. It is only when there is a specific intention to act against the best interest of the user that we talk about betrayal. Hence a machine cannot betray a user. There must be a possibility of betrayal; otherwise there is no need to trust.

4   Definition of Trustworthiness

We propose a definition of trustworthiness in this section. It is based on the definition originally proposed by [4]. The main difference is that the explicit mentioning of betrayal, i.e. acting against the best interest of the person who trusts, is not included. The reason follows from the above discussion: there must be a possibility of betrayal. In addition, the "best interest" is subjective; it depends in the individual who trust. The definition proposed here avoids this subjectivity. It also takes into account principles from the human social world discussed in the previous sections. The new definition is suitable for IT services and still reflects our human intuitive understanding [5].

Definition: Trustworthiness is the demonstrated ability of the service provider to perform a specified action while adhering to a set of stated and commonly agreed principles.

The definition includes some concepts which need further explanation. The first concept is the "demonstrated ability". It is about competence of the service provider. Competence is demonstrated by showing objective evidence of the service provider's ability to perform the claimed service. Without objective evidence the service provider is not trustworthy. If the service provider cannot demonstrate the necessary competence to conduct the claimed service, then we should not use the service.

Secondly, when providing the service, some stated and agreed principles must be followed. These principles are concerned with being honest, being predictable, and behaving according to agreed moral values. If a service is not honest and predictable, and if it does not comply with agreed moral values, then it is not trustworthy.

The third concept of the definition to highlight is "a specified action". This is the service claim. The service claim describes the functionality of the IT service provided as well as the quality characteristics of this service. The claim also states the principles that will be followed when providing the service. The claim is similar to a contract.

4.1   Trustworthiness Evaluation

The definition of trustworthiness asks for evidence in terms of the "demonstrated ability". This offers some guidance on how to evaluate trustworthiness. Trustworthiness evaluation can be split into two distinct components, which can be evaluated independently:

1.   Objective evidence of capability
2.   Historical evidence of performance

Objective evidence of capability represents an initial evaluation. This evaluation is done before the IT service is commissioned. To conduct this evaluation, both the service and the set of principles must be specified. This specification is what we above called the service claim. Based on this specification we can check whether the service provider can demonstrate the necessary capabilities to perform the service.

The second component, the history, requires a continuous evaluation. This evaluation is done every time the service is used. To conduct this evaluation continuous monitoring of service provision is needed. It is an obvious requirement that the service provider must provide the necessary interfaces to enable continuous monitoring and measurement of the service in question.

The definition of trustworthiness can be expressed as a symbolic formula:

$$\text{Trustworthiness} = \text{Capability} + \Sigma \, \Delta \, \text{Performance} \qquad (1)$$

The capability represents the initial evaluation. The IT service provider must present the evidence necessary for conducting this evaluation.

Performance represents the behavior of the service. The evaluation is based on measuring the difference between claimed service and the actual service. Whenever a user is using the IT service, this difference is measured.

Combining these two evaluation components gives a dynamic expression of the trustworthiness of an IT service. We can conclude that trustworthiness is a behavioral concept. It changes over time based on how services are actually performed.

The definition of trustworthiness applies the "contract" concept in form of service claims. A service claim describes in detail the service offered, the "specified action", and the "set of stated principles" that will be adhered to. The purpose of a contract is to make service claims explicit and to make breaches easy to establish.

The definition of trustworthiness also includes the "reputation" concept. Reputation is established as the users' collective measure of deviations. It is derived by measuring the difference between claimed service and actual service for each usage of the service.

4.2   Design for Trustworthiness

In addition to the contract and reputation concepts directly related to the proposed definition, the IT services should be developed following certain design principles. These principles guide the developer to design the IT service so that it appears trustworthy in the view of users. This reflects the human evaluation of a person's face to decide the level of trustworthiness of that person. The human evaluation is based on specific features of the face. Similarly, we quickly make a judgment of a web site based on its features. In [6] four basic principles that communicate trustworthiness of e-commerce Web sites are identified:

1. Quality of Web design including professional appearance and clear navigation (competence)
2. Comprehensive, correct and up-to-date content and product selection (competence)
3. Connectivity to the rest of the Web; linking to a third party add credibility (competence)
4. Up-front disclosure of all aspects of the customer relationship like shipping charges (principles)

The first three principles are indicators of the competence of the service provided. The fourth principle is an indicator of the adherence to a set of commonly agreed principles.

5   Conclusion

Trustworthiness is an important concept in the social life of human beings. Now trustworthiness has become equally important for IT services in the Internet world. We have analyzed the concept in order to get a better understanding of the human intuition. Based on this analysis we have proposed a definition of trustworthiness in accordance with the human intuition and suitable for IT services as well. The definition can be expressed as a formula that shows how trustworthiness can be measured.

The next step in our research will be, starting with the formula, to develop the specific measures needed for establishing an IT service behavior trustworthiness management system. An important step will be to derive a specification language for IT service behavior claims. The specification language must be able to express both functional and non-functional aspects of service behavior as well as principles for service provision. Furthermore, the static and the dynamic components of the evaluation process must be described in detail.

References

1. Tooby, J., Cosmides, L.: The Psychological Foundations of Culture. In: Barkow, J., Cosmides, L., Tooby, J. (eds.) The Adapted Mind: Evolutionary Psychology and the Generation of Culture. Oxford University Press, New York (1992)
2. Engell, A.D., Haxby, J.V., Todorov, A.: Implicit Trustworthiness Decisions: Automatic Coding of Face Properties in the Human Amygdala. Journal of Cognitive Neuroscience 19(9), 1508–1519 (2007)
3. Todorov, A., Said, C.P., Engell, A.D., Oosterhof, N.N.: Understanding evaluation of faces on social dimensions. Trends in Cognitive Sciences 12(12), 455–460 (2008)
4. Mayer, R.C., Davis, J.H., Schoorman, F.D.: An integrative model of organizational trust. Academy of Management Review (20), 709–734 (1995)
5. Bøegh, J., Yuan, Y.: Towards a Standard for Service Behavior Trustworthiness Management. In: Proc. Second International Conference on Digital Information and Communication Technology and its Applications (2012)
6. Nielsen, J.: Trust or Bust: Communicating Trustworthiness in Web Design, Jacob Nielsen's Alertbox (1999), http://www.useit.com/alertbox/990307.html

Introduction of Quality Requirement and Evaluation Based on ISO/IEC SQuaRE Series of Standard

Kazuhiro Esaki[1,*], Motoei Azuma[2], and Toshihiro Komiyama[3]

[1] HOUSEI University Faculty of Science and Engineering
Kees959@hotmail.com
[2] Convener, ISO/IECJTC1/SC7/WG6 and SQuaRE Series Prime Project Editor
Emeritus Professor, Waseda University, Tokyo Japan
azumam@waseda.jp
[3] SW Process Innovation and Standardization Div., NEC Corp. Tokyo, Japan
t-komiyama@bk.jp.nec.com

Abstract. ISO/IEC 25030[1] was published in 2007 and ISO/IEC25040[2] was published in 2011. JTC1/SC7/WG6 is currently developing ISO/IEC 25041 based on ISO/IEC 25030[1], 25040[2] and previous ISO/IEC 14598-3, -4, and -5. ISO/IEC 250nn SQuaRE series set of standards can be used for quality requirement and evaluation project. This paper introduces the ISO/IEC 25030[1], 25040[2] and 25041 for specifying quality requirements and evaluation of systems and software products for development and acquisition of them.

Keywords: Systems and software quality, Quality requirement, Quality evaluation, Quality model, Quality in use, Quality characteristic, Quality measure, Internal measure, External measure, Evaluation process, developers, acquirers, independent evaluators, development, acquisition, Static product, Dynamic product.

1 Introduction

As the use of information technology grows, the information technology brought remarkable innovation to human society. Especially critical information systems, such as security critical, human life critical, economically critical and safety critical, are now indispensable and vital foundation to our society and companies. If we wish to realise the sustainable and felicitous society in such a life environment, we have to realize the high-quality information systems. In order to set out adequacy of the developing information system projects and to secure the quality of the project, quality requirements and evaluation of system and software is extremely important. The ISO/IEC published ISO/IEC 25030[1], [8] which is useful for specifying systems and software product quality requirements and 25040[2] is useful for evaluating systems and software product quality. ISO/IEC SC7/WG6 is currently developing ISO/IEC 25041: Evaluation Guide for Developers, Acquires and Independent Evaluators.

---

* Corresponding author.

Y. Yuan, X. Wu, and Y. Lu (Eds.): ISCTCS 2012, CCIS 320, pp. 94–101, 2013.

In this paper, the concept, framework of these standards and its application are introduced.

2   Outline and Concept of SQuaRE Series

2.1   Organization of SQuaRE

▶International standards developed by ISO/IEC JTC1 SC7 include ISO/IEC 250nn SQuaRE (Software Product Quality Requirements and Evaluation) series of standards. The purpose of the SQuaRE series of standards is to assist developing and acquiring software products with the specification of quality requirements and evaluation.

▶Figure 1 shows the organization of the SQuaRE series of standards defined in ISO/IEC 25000[6]. It includes five core divisions: quality management, quality **model**, quality measurement, quality requirements, and quality evaluation, as well as SQuaRE Extension division.

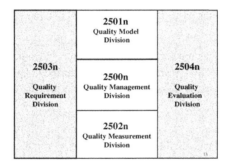

Fig. 1. Organisation of the SQuaRE series of international standards -ISO/IEC 25000[6]

The SQuaRE set of standards supports two main processes i.e. software quality requirements specification and software quality evaluation. It also provides two main tools such as software quality models and measures in order to support software quality requirements and evaluation processes.

2.2   Conceptual Model of Quality Requirement and Evaluation

Figure2 shows the conceptual model of system and software quality requirements and evaluations.

▶Stakeholders have needs for evaluation for systems and software development and acquisition. In order to perform development, designer should specify the quality requirement based on functional requirements for product from the view point of stakeholder's. After development, developer should evaluate the product based on the quality requirement specification of product in order to assure the developed product.

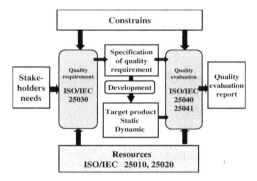

Fig. 2. Conceptual model of quality requirement and evaluation

▸Quality requirements can be specified during the process defined in ISO/IEC 25030[1] for each quality characteristics and sub-characteristics descried in ISO/IEC 2501n[3],[4] using quality measures ISO/IEC 25020[5].

▸Quality evaluation can be performed by using ISO/IEC 25040[2] and 25041 for each quality characteristics descried in ISO/IEC 2501n[3],[4] and ISO/IEC 25020[5] based on the quality requirements.

▸ISO/IEC 25030[1] provide the requirements and recommendations for defining quality requirements specification from selected and defined stakeholder's needs. The specified quality requirements should be used as the criteria of system and software product evaluation.

▸ISO/IEC 25040[2] provides the standardized common evaluation process for systems and software products quality evaluation based on the quality requirements, which are defined by using ISO/IEC 25030[1].

▸ISO/IEC 25041 provides the quality evaluation guides for developers, acquirers and independent evaluators from the view point of each stakeholder's role and responsibility by using common evaluation process described in ISO/IEC 25040[2].

2.3   Quality Models

▸Figure 3 shows the target entities of the quality models and the related entities. The SQuaRE series provides Quality in Use model and Systems and Software Products Quality Model (ISO/IEC 25010[3]), as well as Data Quality Model (ISO/IEC 25012[4]).

▸Any system, in general, composes hierarchical structure. ISO/IEC 25010[3] define human-computer system as the highest level. It includes the information systems, which can include users and other technical and physical environments, such as machines and buildings. The information system includes the target computer system and can also include one or more other computer systems and communication systems. The product quality model focuses on the target computer system that includes the target software product. The data quality model focuses on the target computer system that includes the target data.

▶ISO/IEC 25010[3] defines quality in use model, which focuses on the total human-computer system that includes the target computer system and target software product from the users' viewpoints. The target computer system also includes computer hardware, non-target software products, non-target data, and target data.

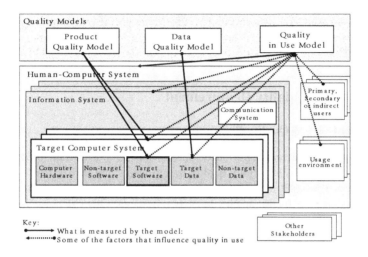

Fig. 3. Target of quality models -ISO/IEC 25010:2011[3]

▶ISO/IEC 25010[3] also provides the product quality models. ISO/IEC 25012[4] defines the data quality model descried in figure3. Its can be used by developers, acquirers, and independent evaluators, as well as users of the information system.

▶The system and software product quality model defines eight quality characteristics: functional suitability, performance efficiency, compatibility, usability, reliability, security, maintainability and portability. Each characteristic is composed of a set of related subcharacteristics.   ISO/IEC 25010[3] replaced ISO/IEC 9126-1 quality model, which defined six quality characteristics
ISO/IEC25010 defines additional quality characteristics, compatibility and security as the system level: The quality in use model defines five characteristics such as effectiveness, efficiency, satisfaction, freedom from risk, and context coverage.
▶The software quality in use view is related to a specific application of the software in its operational environment, for carrying out specific tasks by specific users. System and software quality provides a view of the dynamic properties related to the execution of the software on computer hardware and applying an operating system or static properties that typically are available during the development.

2.4   Quality Measurement

Currently, ISO/IEC JTC1/SC7/WG6 is developing international standards on quality measures as ISO/IEC 2502n SQuaRE – Quality measurement division. ISO/IEC 25021 provides the quality measure element, which replaces TR25021 and is used for constructing software quality measures. ISO/IEC 25022, 25023 and 25024 provides the quality measures, which intended to provide quality measures for product quality, quality in use and data quality.

▸The quality measures defined in ISO/IEC 2502n are useful for quantifying the quality requirements based on the result of quality requirement specifications by using ISO/IEC 25030[1] for each quality characteristics defined in ISO/IEC 25010[3].

3   Outline of Quality Requirement

3.1   ISO/IEC 25030 Quality Requirement

In order to perform development successfully, it is very important to define non-functional requirements, especially quality requirements and realize the real needs in to the developed product during possible early stage of the development. However, there is a tendency to focus on functional requirements rather than quality requirement. If software quality requirements are not stated clearly, it may cause the software product inconsistent with user expectations and poor quality. On the other hand, it is very difficult to analyse the requirements successfully because there is no widely accepted analysis method, and depends on sense and experiences of the analyst. Analysis of non-functional requirements of a product has been conducted, in many cases, through questionnaires and interviews with customers.

Traditionally, survey items on questionnaires were selected either from previous questionnaires or based on survey investigator's personal experience and preference about the product. This incomplete approach in the traditional survey resulted in missing or biased and erroneous product requirements. It caused failing to assure the completeness of the non-functional requirement analysis of a product.

Based on this observation, It was decided that ISO/IEC 25030[1] provides the method for quality requirements analysis and definition by using the quality model defined in ISO/IEC 25010[3] and 25020[5].

▸Usually, stakeholders' needs for systems and software should be selected and transformed into both functional requirements and non-functional requirements. Non-functional requirements could include quality requirements and other requirements such as hardware, data, and business requirements so on.

▸ISO/IEC 25030[1] mainly focuses on software quality and applies to organizations in their role as both acquirers and developers. However, it does not cover specification of other requirements. Figure 4 shows an example of categorization of system requirements based on the consideration of figure3.

System requirements	Software requirements	Software product requirements	Inherent property requirements	Functional requirements	
				Software quality requirements	Quality in use requirements
					External quality requirements
					Internal quality requirements
			Assigned property requirements	Managerial requirements including for Example Requirements for price, delivery date, Product future, and product supplier	
		Software development requirements	Development process requirements		
			Development organisation requirements		
	Other system requirements	Include for example requirements for computer hardware, data, mechanical parts, and human business processes			

Fig. 4. System requirements categorisation -ISO/IEC 25030[1]

▸Software requirements include software product requirement and software development process requirements. Software product requirements include inherent property requirement of software and assigned property requirements of software. Inherent property requirement of software include functional requirements and software quality requirements. Functional requirements include the application domain specific requirements as well as functional requirements that support quality requirements. Software quality requirements include requirements for quality in use, external and internal quality. Assigned property requirements of software may include price and delivery date of software. Software development requirements may include requirements for artifacts, development processes, project, development organization, and developers.

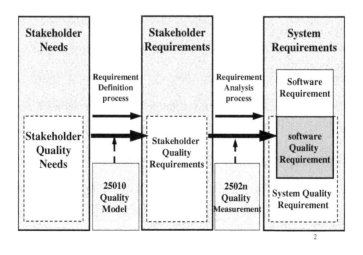

Fig. 5. Software quality requirement definition analysis -ISO/IEC 25030[1]

▸Figure5. shows the software quality requirement definition process and analysis process descried in ISO/IEC 25030[1]. Figure 5 shows how software quality requirements are derived as part of the requirements processes defined in ISO/IEC 15288[9]. The definition process focuses on stakeholder requirements to the system. The analysis process assumes some architectural decisions, which makes it possible to identify requirements relevant for the software included in the system.

4   Outline of Quality Evaluation

4.1   ISO/IEC 25040 Quality Evaluation

This International Standard contains general requirements and recommendations for product quality evaluation based on the specified quality requirements. ISO/IEC 25040 provides a standardized common process description, inputs, constraints, resources for, and outcomes of each evaluation process for evaluating system and software product quality and states the requirements for the application of this process. ISO/IEC 25040[2] defines the process based on the evaluation process in ISO/IEC 14598-1 and replaced it.

▸This standardized process can be used for, such as evaluation of the quality of commercial-off-the shelf software product and custom made software product. It can be used during or after the development and acquisition process. This International Standard establishes the relationship of the evaluation process to the SQuaRE documents as well as shows how each SQuaRE document should be used throughout the activities of the evaluation process.

▸Following are the standardized system and software product quality evaluation process descried in ISO/IEC 25040[2];

(1) Establish the evaluation requirements
(2) Specify the evaluation
(3) Design the evaluation
(4) Execute the evaluation
(5) Conclude the evaluation

This process can be applicable to each stakeholder such as developers, acquirers and independent evaluators, but not limited to them.

4.2   ISO/IEC 25041 Evaluation Guide for Each Role

Currently, this International standard is at the final stage of development and provides the quality evaluation guides, which intended to focus on specific issues related to the developers, acquirers and independent evaluators.

▸This International Standard provides requirements, recommendations and guidelines for system and software product quality evaluation for the application of ISO/IEC

25040[2] common quality evaluation process. It is a short version of ISO/IEC 14598-3, -4, and -5 and replaces them. This proposed standard is not limited to any specific application area, and can be used for quality evaluation of any type of systems and software products.

▸This International Standard defines the roles and responsibilities of each stakeholders such as the developers, acquirers and independent evaluators. Also, this Standard defines the relation ships among the target entity and evaluation activities.

Acknowledgments. The authors express appreciations to editors and co-editors of ISO/IEC 250nn-SQuaRE series of international standard and SC7/WG6 members who contributed to develop the series. The authors are also grateful to Japan's national SC7WG6 members who their contributions and support to make the work of WG6 successful.

References

1. ISO/IEC 25030: Software engineering–Software product Quality Requirements and Evaluation (SQuaRE)–Quality requirement, Int'l Organization for Standardization (2007)
2. ISO/IEC 25040: Software engineering–System and software Quality Requirements and Evaluation (SQuaRE) – Evaluation process (2011)
3. ISO/IEC 25010: Software engineering–System and software Quality Requirements and Evaluation (SQuaRE)– System and software Quality Model (2011)
4. ISO/IEC 25012: Software engineering – Software product Quality Requirements and Evaluation (SQuaRE) – Data Quality model, Int'l Organization for Standardization (2006)
5. ISO/IEC 25020: Software engineering–Software product Quality Requirements and Evaluation (SQuaRE)–Measurement reference model and guide, Int'l Organization for Standardization (2007)
6. ISO/IEC 25000: Software engineering–Software product Quality Requirements and Evaluation (SQuaRE) – Guide to SQuaRE, Int'l Organization for Standardization (2005)
7. ISO/IEC 25001: Software engineering–Software product Quality Requirements and Evaluation (SQuaRE)–Planning and Management, Int'l Organization for Standardization (2007)
8. Boegh, J.: A New Standard for Quality Requirements. IEEE Computer Society (2008)
9. ISO/IEC 15288: Information Technology– Life Cycle Management– System Life Cycle Processes, Int'l Organization for Standardization (2002)

A Survey on the Security of Multihop Ad Hoc Network

Yuan De-yu[1,2], Liu Tong[1,2], Wei Geng-yu[1,2], and Wang Zhi-zhao[1,2]

[1] School of Computer Science, Beijing University of Posts and Telecommunications,
Beijing, China
[2] Key Laboratory of Trustworthy Distributed Computing and Service (BUPT),
Ministry of Education, Beijing, China
yuandeyu@gmail.com, liutong1988@126.com, weigengyu@bupt.edu.cn

Abstract. With the development of wireless network, mobile Ad Hoc networks have been applied in many fields. But the security problem of Ad Hoc network has not been solved very well, and the security system of Ad Hoc network is more difficult to design than other networks because of its particularity. Ad Hoc network's security is a key problem of the Ad Hoc network applications. This article studied Ad Hoc network's security issues from the aspects of key management, routing security, intrusion detection, and trusted computing.

Keywords: Ad Hoc network, network security, trusted computing

1 Introduction

Mobile Ad Hoc network consists of a set of wireless mobile nodes, and is a kind of network system which can rapidly spread to use without relying on the existing fixed communication network facilities. Mobile Ad Hoc network doesn't have any central entity, and each of the nodes cooperate with each other, it communicates, exchanges and shares information and service via a wireless link; network nodes can dynamically, optionally, frequently enter and leave the network, usually without prior warning or notification, and will not affect the other nodes in the network communication. The vision of Ad Hoc network is wireless Internet, that is the user can maintain the network connection at any time, in any way to move.

With the MANET applications become more widely, the security problem has become the important problem demanding prompt solution. The current domestic and international research hot spots of MANET also gradually shifted to the security problem. Since the Ad Hoc network's particularity, this makes Ad Hoc network security problem much more complex than the traditional wired networks. Ad Hoc network's security threats come from the radio channel and network. Wireless channel is vulnerable to eavesdropping and interference. In addition, the network organization form of no center and self-organizing not only makes it easy to suffer from attacks of counterfeiting and fraud, but also puts forward new requirements on the network security architecture.

This article will focus on the Ad-Hoc network's security issues, and research on Ad Hoc network's security solutions that have been proposed.

Y. Yuan, X. Wu, and Y. Lu (Eds.): ISCTCS 2012, CCIS 320, pp. 102–108, 2013.

2   The Security Solutions of Ad Hoc Network

The security of Mobile Ad Hoc network is subjected to the limitations of special conditions, so its security system is more difficult to design compared with other networks. Research institutions and researchers have proposed some solutions for special problems. Currently, researches on Ad Hoc network security issues are mainly concentrated in the aspects of key management and authentication, routing security, and intrusion detection.

2.1   Secure Key Management and Certification

Stajano and Anderson studied Mobile Ad Hoc Networks in depth, and proposed the resurrection duck security model according to the revelation on the biology, which solved the problem of security instantaneous session [1]. This method emphasized the uniqueness of the owner, and when the owner printed a mark to a node, then the node only accepted the control of its owner. When it's necessary, the master can remove this mark, so that the node can accept a new owner. Zhou and Hass proposed a distributed asynchronous key management service model for mobile Ad hoc networks [2]. The model requires the system to have a public / private key pair, which is used for the node's public key certificate signature and verification. It assumes that all nodes of the system know the public key, and trust the system's private key signature for any node's public key certificate. Asokan used a key exchange method based on the shared password[3]. It requires the users prepare to communicate share a weak password beforehand, and then a strong public session key is generated using the password authentication method. In addition, Camp and some others analyzed public key management in mobile ad hoc network model [4]; Sufatrio etc. proposed a scalable authentication framework [5]; Herzberg etc. describes the Proactive public key and signature system [6]; Fasbender etc. introduced the idea of onion routing to secure mobile ad hoc network node location information [7].

2.2   Routing Security

Based on the analysis of conventional security mechanisms in the traditional network routing protocols, Hauser, etc. recognized that the authentication and confidentiality method based on public key encryption mechanism, even for a dedicated router in the wired network also appears too costly, and therefore proposed a method using the hash chain binding public key authentication to reduce the security overhead in the kind of traditional LSR (Link State routing) routing protocols [8]. Zapata proposed SAODV routing protocol, and the using of public key authentication and hash chain mechanism is suggested to enhance the AODV protocol routing security of the discovery process [9]. This makes the feasible attacking node cannot claim a route that does not exist. At the same time, SAODV also add the Hash chain corresponding to the routing hops to the RREQ and RREP, which is used to verify whether the claimed route hop count is correct. Hu etc. proposed the SEAD protocol which also use the Hash chain to protect routing notice information of the mobile ad hoc networks DV (Distance Vector) routing protocol in [10]. Papadimitratos etc. proposed a secure extension for a widely used secure routing protocol of mobile ad hoc networks [11]. Assuming that the two end nodes of each communication share a SA (Security Association) relations, for example, a symmetric key K, after each RREQ packet reaches the destination node, a corresponding MAC (message authentication code) is generated by computing the routing information (using the shared key K) which Hash and encryption algorithm is used. RREQ packet routing information, together with the MAC backtracked to the source node, thus ensured the path information in the routing return process cannot be changed.in order to ensure the security of data transmission, Yi etc. proposed the SAR (Security-Aware Routing) scheme [12], the basic idea is to divide all nodes in the network into a trust level, the nodes with a trust level only the nodes with the same level to forward in the transmission of data. Buchegger etc. inspired by the behavior patterns of bird populations, designed a scheme to improve the overall security of ad hoc network routing scheme through collaboration with each other [13]. This scheme can be used to isolate the bad nodes in the network (the attacker) to ensure the full network security.

2.3   Intrusion Detection

Zhang etc. pointed out that there was not an open computer system which was intrusion immune, and mobile ad hoc network was no exception [14]. The existed intrusion detection methods that developed for the fixed wired network cannot be applied in this new environment. Therefore, a new intrusion detection and response structure that can be applied in mobile ad hoc network is proposed. But what information a routing protocol should include to make intrusion detection more effective was not given, and what is the best anomaly detection model was also not indicated. Kachirski etc. introduced a distributed intrusion detection system based on mobile agent technology [15]. This system can extract useful audit data from multiple network sensors, and then analyze whether the entire network is invaded, and tried to stop the invasion activities. Compared with many intrusion detection systems designed for the wired network, the scheme executed an effective framework to solve the problem of intrusion detection on multiple network layer, and took the distribution characteristics of mobile ad hoc network management and decision-making mechanism into account. Bhargava etc. proposed an intrusion detection model (IDM) to enhance the security of the mobile ad hoc on-demand routing protocols [16]. In this model, each node utilizes an IDM, and used the information of neighbor nodes to detect the error behavior of the neighbors. When the error number of neighbor nodes of a node exceeds a preset threshold, the alarm information is sent to other nodes, and then the process of a global response is started. After the other nodes receiving the alarm information, they will check the local number of errors, and add the results into the response to the node which issued the warning information.

3   Authentication Scheme Based on Trusted Computing

In recent years, the technology of trusted computing has been developed rapidly.TPM modules have been put into production, and more and more networks and devices have embedded them, at the same time, mobile trusted computing technology is becoming one of the trends in the future. And some authentication schemes based on trusted computing in the Ad Hoc network have been proposed.

3.1   Development of Trusted Computing Technology

Formed in 1999, led by Compaq, HP, IBM, Intel and Microsoft, TCPA(Trusted Computing Platform Alliance)focused on computing platform system structure to enhance security. In March 2003, it was reorganized as TCG (Trusted Computing Group), and the idea of trusted computing was put forward. The new model in TCG was based on TPM (Trusted Platform)hardware module.

In October 2004, TCG introduced the concept of trusted computing into mobile field, put forward TMP's (Trusted Mobile Platform) hardware and software system and protocol draft standard. In June 2007, TCG published MTM specification and TCG Mobile Reference Architecture, laying foundation for the development of trusted computing in mobile terminals.

3.2   Network Security Management Model Based on Trusted Computing

TCSM model is based on thoughts of the domain .Nodes in the Ad Hoc network are divided into some small regions according to their location, each region is called a domain, here referred to as a security domain. In every security domain, a node is elected as a DA (Domain Authority).DA usually has higher performance in the domain,and DA is responsible for both node authentication and key management in security domain .A security domain includes DA and other common node, and the key alignment between any two common nodes is completed by DA before the communication. The system architecture of security domain is shown as Fig. 1.

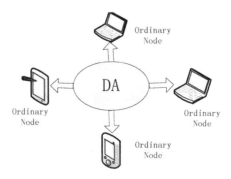

Fig. 1. The system architecture of security domain

Considering that the processing capacity of DA is limited and it may leave the network at any time, DA may be replaced by other nodes in security domain whenever necessary. DA mainly comes from the trusted algorithm which includes the following two definitions.

- **Definition 1:** Define the Basic Score(BS) to measure the performance of each network node.

$$BS = lg\,(F/Fs + M/Ms + N/Ns)$$

Where Fs is the standard value of CPU frequency(GHz); Ms is the standard memory size of the network nodes(MB); Ns is the standard network bandwidth of the network nodes(Mb); F is the actual CPU frequency of the network node(GHz); M is the actual memory size of the network nodes(MB); N is the actual network bandwidth of the network nodes(Mb).

- **Definition 2:** Define the Reputation Credit(RC) to indicate the assessment of one network node by another.

$$RCij = \alpha Rij + \beta BSj \; (i \neq j, i \leq d, j \leq d)$$

R_{ij} is the percentage of the successfully communicated times between node i and node j. BS_j is the BS value of node j. d is the number of network nodes of certain security domain in the Ad Hoc network. $\alpha + \beta = 1$,respectively indicates each proportionin the calculation of R_{ij} and BS_j.

Literature [17] also presents that in order to establish initial trust of the network, a trusted third party DAA Issuer is introduced to prove node's legitimate identity during the initialization stage of the MANET. During the initialization of the network, each node communicates to DAA Issuer through the DAA-Join protocol to prove its identity, and DAA Issuer will issue certificates to each trusted node, after that those nodes no longer need to interact with DAA Issuer.

Literature [18] provides a verifiable platform integrity authentication scheme based on trusted computing technology, the basic idea is that nodes using TPM to measure software and hardware configuration of the platform and extend Hash value of the measurement results to the corresponding PCR and save the storage measurement log (SML); remote nodes use DAA protocol to authenticate node's identity , and recalculate its PCR value according to the storage measurement log and compare it with the PCR value it receives, then judge whether node's platform status and configuration has been tampered , thus realizing the check of node's platform integrity.

4   Conclusion

The ad Hoc network, in a certain level is still a new technology, and many contents are still in research stage. Since Ad Hoc networks with the characteristics of dynamic multi-hop, no center, and self-organizing, a variety of protocols and algorithms based on this kind of environment is also more complex than the traditional network. Until now, many questions still have no satisfactory answers.

Currently there have been more researches about Ad Hoc network's routing problems, but in the future there search of security problems for Ad Hoc network will be more deeply. Mobile Ad Hoc network security should be a comprehensive solution. It should be a fusion of key management, routing security, intrusion detection and other aspects, forming an overall security solution. And security problems should be closely integrated with the routing problem to study together. In the encryption algorithm, ECC encryption system will be more widely applied in the future.

References

1. Stajano, F., Anderson, R.: The Resurrecting Deckling: Security Issues for Ad Hoc Networks. In: Malcolm, J.A., Christianson, B., Crispo, B., Roe, M. (eds.) Security Protocols 1999. LNCS, vol. 1796, pp. 172–182. Springer, Heidelberg (2000)
2. Zhou, L., Hass, Z.J.: Securing ad hoc networks. IEEE Network Magazine 13(6), 24–30 (1999)
3. Asokan, N., Ginzboorg, P.: Key agreement in ad hoc networks. Computer Communications 23, 1627–1637 (2000)
4. Camp, T., Boleng, J., Davies, V.: Mobility models for ad hoc network research. Wireless Communications and Mobile Computing (WCMC), Special issue on Mobile Ad Hoc Networking: Research, Trends and Applications (2002)
5. Sufatrio, Lam, K.Y.: Scalable authentication framework for mobile-IP(SAFe-MIP). Internet draft, IETF (November 1999)
6. Herzberg, A., Jakobsson, M., et al.: Proactive public key and signature systems. In: ACM Security 1997 (1997)
7. Fasbender, A., et al.: Variable and scalable security: protection of location information in mobile IP. In: IEEE 46th Vehicular Technology Conference on Mobile Technology for the Human Race (1996)
8. Hauser, R., et al.: Lowering security overhead in link state routing. Computer Networks (1999)
9. Zapata, M.G.: Secure ad hoc on-demand distance vector(AODV), Routing. Mobile Ad Hoe Networking Group, Internet Draft (August 2001)
10. Hu, Y.-C., Johnson, D.B., Perrig, A.: SEAD: Secure efficient distancevector routing for mobile wireless ad hoc networks. In: Proceeding of the 4th IEEE Workshop on Mobile Computing Systems and Applications, Calicoon, NX (June 2002)
11. Papadimitratos, P., Hass, Z.J.: Secure routing for mobile ad hoc networks. In: SCS Communication Networks and Distributed Systems Modeling and Simulation Conference (CNDS 2002), San AntonioTX (January 2002)
12. Yi, S., Naldurg, P., Kravets, R.: A security aware routing protocol for wireless ad hoc networks. In: he 6th World Multi-Conference on Systems, Cybernetics Andinfornatics, SCl 2002 (2002)
13. Buchegger, S., Le Boudec, J.-Y.: Nodes bearing grudges:towards routing security,fairness, and robustness in mobile ad hoc networks. In: Proceedings of 10th Euromicro Workshop on Parallel, Distributes and Network-based Processing (2002)

14. Zhang, Y., Lee, W.: Intrusion detection in wireless ad hoc networks. In: IEEE Workshop International Conference on Mobile Computing and Networking (MobiCom 2000), Boston, MA, pp. 275–283 (2000)
15. Kachirski, O., Guha, R.: Intrusion detection using mobile agents in wireless ad hoc networks. In: IEEE Workshop on Knowledge Media Networking (KMN 2002), Kyoto, Japan (2002)
16. Bhargava, S., Agraval, D.P.: Security enhancement in AODV protocol for wirelessad hoc networks. In: Vehicular Technology Conference, Atlantic City, NY (October 2001)
17. Kang, Y., Tao, Z., et al.: An Authentication Scheme for Mobile Ad Hoc Networks Based on Trusted Computing. TN929.5 (2010)
18. Hu, R.-L., Li, R., et al.: Trusted Computing-based Authentication Scheme forAd hoc Networks. Computer Engineering 36(12) (June 2010)

Outsourcing Cloud Data Privacy-Preserving Based on Over-Encryption

Bing Rao, Zhigang Zhou, Hongli Zhang, Shuofei Tang, and Renfu Yao

School of Computer Science and Technology, Harbin Institute of Technology, Harbin, China
Raobing2011@pact518.hit.edu.cn, zzgisgod@sina.com,
{zhanghongli,tangshuofei,yaorenfu}@hit.edu.cn

Abstract. Cloud computation allows the users with limited computing power outsource their data to the cloud of large-scale computing power through payment method. However, the security issue has been always the obstacles to the widely use of the computing outsourcing, especially when the end-user's privacy data need to be processed on the cloud. Secure outsourcing mechanisms are in great need to not only protect privacy information, but also protect customers from malicious behaviors by validating the computation result. A mechanism of general secure computation outsourcing was recently shown to be feasible in theory, but to design mechanisms that are practically efficient is a very challenging problem. General research is based on a basic model. The model we used in this paper including Data Owner (DO), Cloud Service Provider (CSP) and End-User (EU). Focus on considering the DO, CSP and EU. Over-encryption is a good method to protect the security of the users' data. Our proposal is based on the application of selective encryption as a means to enforce authorizations. Two layers of encryption are imposed on the data blocks. This paper talks about the over-encryption mechanism and proposes a novel over-encryption mechanism which can protect the security of the data on the Cloud. Last, we do some experiments to verify the performance of our mechanism.

Keywords: cloud, outsourcing, privacy-preserving, over-encryption.

1 Introduction

Since the daily operations of modern corporations heavily depend on their information processing capabilities, the costs and overhead to manage their computation resources start to pose serious challenges to these companies. To free the companies and their personnel from the burden of IT services, the concept of cloud computing has been proposed [1].Cloud Computing provides convenient on-demand network access to a shared pool of configurable computing resources that can be rapidly deployed with great efficiency and minimal management overhead [2].Generalized cloud computing refers to the service delivery and usage patterns. It means the user get the service through network according to demand in an easy extend way. The services refer to information technology (IT), software, network and other service. It means

Y. Yuan, X. Wu, and Y. Lu (Eds.): ISCTCS 2012, CCIS 320, pp. 109–116, 2013.

that the computing power could be a commodity circulating through Internet. A large number of services on infrastructure, platform, and software have been developed and provided by various parties [3]. The service includes follow items.

- SaaS, it means Software-as-a-Service, it is a mode of delivering software over the Internet, users need not to purchase software, but rent the Web-based software to manage the activity of enterprise.
- IaaS, it means Infrastructure-as-a-Service, consumers get computer infrastructure service through Internet.
- PaaS, it means Platform-as-a-Service, the PaaS actually refers to the platform of software development as a service that present to users as a SaaS mode, therefore, PaaS is an application of SaaS mode.
- DaaS, it means Data-as-a-Service, CSP provide the users the service of data storage, inquiry, management and computing, the data include all kinds of text, image, statistics etc.

The development of DaaS promote the development of cloud computing. Data outsourcing is a main expression form of DaaS. A basic advantage of the outsourcing model is that it allows the user no longer limited by the device with limited computing power. Workload outsourcing to the cloud, user can get unlimited computing power through pay when use method. It can reduce the overhead of purchasing hardware and software devices and operation. The continuous growth of the amount of digital information to be stored together with the service providers will be more and more requested to be responsible for the storage and the efficient and reliable distribution of content produced by others, realizing "data outsourcing" architecture on a wide scale. This important trend is particularly clear when we look at the success of services like YouTube, Blogger, MySpace, and many others in the "social networking" environment [4].

Despite the tremendous benefits, outsourcing computation to the commercial public cloud is also depriving customers' direct control over the systems that consume and produce their data during the computation, which inevitably brings in new security concerns and challenges towards this promising computing model [4].On the one hand, the outsourced computation workloads often contain sensitive information, such as the business financial records, proprietary research data, or personally identifiable health information etc [7].To combat against unauthorized information leakage, sensitive data have to be encrypted before outsourcing [8] so as to provide end-to-end data confidentiality assurance in the cloud and beyond. Cloud security play an important role in the development of the cloud computing.

2   Base Model

Cloud computing has get attention of many people. The benefit of the cloud computing is obvious. It can provide content storage service and other service at any time. Enterprise could reduce the cost by using cloud platform. User could rent the platform, software, hardware device provide by the CSP.A popular form of data outsourcing mode include data owner, cloud computing service provider and end-user. Owner is the actual owner of the data who has full right of the data.CSP provide the services of storage, science computing and inquire etc.EU is the actual user of the data. The EU must get the access of corresponding data before using the data. The structure relationship of the DaaS model shows in Figure 1.

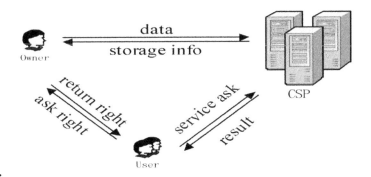

Fig. 1. Structure relationship of the DaaS model

Owner encrypts the data and storage into CSP, then CSP return the storage information of the Owner. In order to query the data, EU must apply for permission of the data to the Owner first. Owner grant the EU based on EU's legitimacy. After getting the permission of the Owner, EU will ask CSP service through sending service request. CSP return results of the request to EU after verifying EU's right.

Our study is based on the above model. The model above exist some shortcomings and security problem. This paper elaborates the problem and security hazard caused by the above model and propose a novel and feasible solution. In order to solve the security hazard exist in the model, the paper use the over-encryption. This paper conducts a detailed description of the over-encryption and proposes a solution to avoid the cloud not encrypt the data. The main idea is modify the protocol of over-encryption and lazy revocation method and modify the storage address of the updated data. The main contribution of this paper is threefold. First (Section 3), we elaborate the problem of the base model and propose a solution. Second (Section 4), we elaborate the importance and essential of the over-encryption and find the problem of the over-encryption. Third (Section 4), we propose a new protocol of over-encryption.

3   Threat Model

This section talks about the security hazard and the problem of the base model.

3.1   Problem Assuming

We introduce a DaaS model in section 2, the scenario of the data owner to write and user to read is a very common example in data outsourcing. Figure 1 provides an abstract illustration of this scenario. The data Owner store a lot of information in the CSP. But he CSP is not entirely credible. To enable secure and efficient access to outsourced data, investigators have tried to integrate key derivation mechanisms [9-12] with encryption-based data access control. Here the Owner encrypts the data before sending to the CSP.

Here we assume the minimum information storage unit is the so-called "block"."Block" is an abstract concept and has different meanings in different system. In order to provide a fine granularity access control, the encryption is based on the "block" level and for the same "block" the key is certain. Only the owner can make updates to the outsourced data. Here the operations include updates to data blocks, and deletion, insertion, and appending of blocks. We also assume that there exist pre-distributed secrets between data owner and service provider, and between data owner and end-users [1]. The key distribution and update problem is beyond the scope of this paper and we refer interested readers to existing approaches such as [5].

The outsourced data can be accessed by different EUs who are distributed all over the network. Since the EUs may use devices with weak processing capabilities such as PDAs, we need avoid computationally expensive operations such as asymmetric encryption of data blocks.

And we want to reduce the amount of information that is stored on the EUs. The access rights of the end users are different and they may change (grant and revocation) as time proceeds. Therefore, right keys must be provided to the end users to control their access [1].

We assume that the service provider is a curious but not malicious model. That means the CSP will not intentionally send wrong data blocks to an EU but it may try to get access to the plaintext of the stored information. To preserve confidentiality of the outsourced data, the owner may ask the service provider to conduct a second level encryption (over-encryption) [6] before the data is sent to the EUs. For providers that refuse to over this service, we adopt the lazy revocation method [7] to reduce information leakage through eavesdropping.

3.2   Threat Model

Different users have different permissions to different data blocks. Some users have permission to the data before it update, but have no permission to the updated data. Every data block has a unique key. The key must be changed after owner updates the data block. The owner must notify all the uses those have the right to the block and send the new key to them. It takes a lot of resource to owner. The owner will be the bottleneck of the system when the number of user become large and this approach is not feasible. To protect the privacy of the data owner demand CSP conduct over-encryption. CSP may omit the second encryption because of the CSP is driven by economic benefits and the privacy of the data is broken.

4   Solution

Before solve the problem we should give the definition of the SLA.

SLA: Service Level Agreement is a contact between the service provider and customers including type and quality of service, customer payment etc. Cloud computing is based on the addition, usage and cost mode of related service on the network. Usually refer to dynamic and scalable virtual resource. That makes the CSP is driven by economic benefit and CSP will maximize the benefit leading to the breaking of the SLA.

This section we propose a solution for the problem above. To provide the privacy of the data block CSP should conduct the second encryption. We propose a novel over-encryption mechanism and DO should process the data blocks to prevent CSP from not conducting the second encryption.

4.1   Over-Encryption

To provide the privacy of data blocks CSP provide a second encryption. When data block is updated and the block key change and inform all the EUs refer to the block which need to consume a lot of resource and overhead. It's not feasible for the DO whose computing power is limited. To solve the problem it demands the CSP encrypt the block in the cloud. There is a unique relationship between each registered users and CSP. Each user corresponds to a unique encryption key and CSP don't know the decryption key. EUs and DO have the decryption key which is created when a new user is registered according to a given algorithm. The EU has the access right apply for the resource can decrypt the data block after the CSP encrypt the block only and it can prevent the EUs from bypass attacks. The CSP will not return the data blocks to the EUs who have been revoked by DO after the block is updated. The block is encrypted by CSP using a unique encryption key can be decrypted by the corresponding EU and other EUs can't decrypt the block after intercepting it. The encryption key will not be changed after the data block is updated. EUs' encryption key and decryption is changed after EUs' right is changed. CSP get the information from DO and preserve the relationship between EU and encryption key. A new relationship will be sent to CSP after the right of the EU is changed. DO also preserve the relationship between EU and decryption key. The decryption is sent to EU when EU submits requires.

4.2   Improved Method

CSP is driven by economic benefit. CSP may not conduct the second encryption because of the saving of computing resource from the perspective of CSP and the privacy of the data block is not protected. We propose a improve method to protect the privacy of the data block. An EU can't get the updated data block after the revoke of the permission. The EU lose privileges will encrypt the updated data block because the encryption key is not changed when CSP omit the second encryption. To this end we carry out the following improvements. The updated data block will be stored separate from the original block. If an EU lose privileges to the updated data block, but he can still access the original block. DO send the new address to EU who has the permission of the updated data when EU submit requires and EU can get the updated data block and decrypt the block using the decryption key sent by DO. DO need not inform each EU when a data block is updated. In order to manage the data block a version control information and block address will be sent to the EU when DO return license to EU.

5   Experiments

In this section we have done some experiments to verify the performance of the over-encryption. In the experiment we adopt the AES-256 and DES-256 encryption algorithm encrypt different data in different sizes. The time consumed by AES and DES in the case of one encryption and over-encryption is shown in figure2 and figure3.

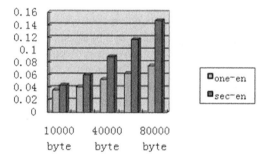

Fig. 2. Time consumed by AES-256 encryption in different sizes in the case of one-encryption and over-encryption

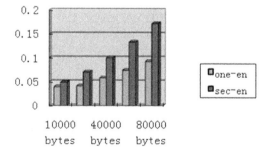

Fig. 3. Time consumed by DES-256 encryption in different sizes in the case of one-encryption and over-encryption

From the figure we could find that the time consumed by over-encryption is not more than twice the time consumed by one-encryption. And we find that the time consumed by encryption is not large. It verifies that the over-encryption is feasible to protect the privacy of data block with little overhead.

6   Conclusions

There is a trend towards scenarios where resource is outsourced to a CSP providing storage capabilities and high-bandwidth distribution service. Thus, secure outsourcing mechanisms are in great need to protect privacy of the data. Such a mechanism was recently shown to be feasible in theory, but to design mechanisms that are practically efficient remains a very challenging problem. This paper adopts the over-encryption mechanism which can protect the privacy of the data. The CSP conduct the second encryption according to the encryption key sent by DO. EU decrypts the data block according to the key sent by DO. And we propose an improved method to prevent the CSP from omitting second encryption.

Acknowledgment. This work is partially supported by the National Grand Fundamental Research 973 Program of China (Grant No. 2011CB302605); the National Natural Science Foundation of China (Grant No. 61173145); High-Tech Research and Development Plan of China (Grant No. 2010AA012504, 2011AA010705). The authors also gratefully acknowledge the helpful comments and suggestions of the reviewers, which have improved the presentation.

References

1. Wang, W.C., Li, Z.W.: Secure and Efficient Access to Outsourced Data. In: ACM Workshop on Cloud Computing Security, New York, pp. 55–66 (2009)
2. Mell, T.P., Grance.: Draft Nist Working Definition of Cloud Computing (2010), \
   http://csrc.nist.gov/groups/SNS/cloud-computing/index.html
3. Open Crowd Cloud Taxomy (2009),
   http://www.opencrowd.com/views/cloud.php
4. Security Guidance for Critical Areas of Focus in Cloud Computing (2009),
   http://www.cloudsecurityalliance.org
5. Blaze, M.: Key Management in an Encrypting File System. In: Proceedings of the USENIX Summer Technical Conference, pp. 27–35 (1994)
6. di Vimercati, S.D.C., Foresti, S., Jajodia, S., Paraboschi, S., Samarati, P.: Over-encryption: Management of Access Control Evolution on Outsourced Data. In: Proceedings of the International Conference on Very Large Data Bases, pp. 123–134 (2007)
7. Kallahalla, M., Riedel, E., Swaminathan, R., Wang, Q., Fu, K.: Plutus: Scalable Secure File Sharing on Untrusted Storage. In: Proceedings of the USENIX Conference on File and Storage Technologies, pp. 29–42 (2003)
8. Cong, W., Kui, R., Jia, W.: Secure and Practical Outsourcing of Linear Programming in Cloud Computing. In: IEEE International Conference on Computer Communications, pp. 820–828 (2011)

 9. Chen, T., Chung, Y., Tian, C.: A novel key Management Scheme for Dynamic Access Control in a User Hierarchy. In: IEEE Annual International Computer Software and Applications Conference, pp. 396–401 (2004)
10. Chien, H., Jan, J.: New Hierarchical Assignment without Public Key Cryptography. Computers & Security 22(6), 523–526 (2003)
11. Lin, C.: Hierarchical Key Assignment without Public-key Cryptography. Computers & Security 20(7), 612–619 (2001)
12. Zhong, S.: A Practical Key Management Scheme for Access Control in a User Hierarchy. Computers & Security 21(8), 750–759 (2002)

The Measurement and Analysis of KAD Network

Dong Wang, Hui He, and Jiantao Shi

School of Computer Science and Technology, Harbin Institute of Technology, Harbin, China
wangdong_first@163.com, hehui@hit.edu.cn,
shijiantao@pact518.hit.edu.cn

Abstract. KAD protocol is the most widely used P2P protocol, and the study of KAD is significance to improve the performance of DHT network. We introduce the KAD measurement system based on active detection, and measuring search path and node k-bucket of KAD network. Then we analyze the common prefix of node ID that stores keyword, hops of searching keyword and k-bucket. Finally, we draw some conclusions as follows. The node that stores less-popular keyword has a longer common prefix. The number of search hop usually is few and the search efficiency is very high. The coverage of k-bucket is large and the node well knows other node that is near to itself. All these indicate that searching and storing resources in KAD network is effective.

Keywords: KAD, measurement system, search path, common prefix, hop, k-bucket.

1 Introduction

Distributed hash table (DHT) is a good design of peer-to-peer (P2P) network, it can make the search process more effective. Although there have been some DHTs, such as Chord [1], Can [2] and Pasty [3], all of them have not been large-scale applicated. So at early stage, the researches of DHT are simulation, analysis and deploy on a small-scale. In recent years, with large-scale application of the Kademlia [4] network, it provides the experimental platform to research various properties of DHT network. Kademlia protocol is a DHT protocol based on XOR and in IPTPS of year 2002, it's proposed by Petar Maymounkov and David Mazieres of New York University, it uses distributed application layer network to store and retrieve information. In many of P2P protocols, Kademlia protocol is most widely used, and its principles and achieve are very simple. The current popular P2P applications, such as eMule [5], Bitcomet, Bitspirit and Azure, have adopted Kademlia as its assisted-search protocol. Therefore, the study of Kademlia is significant to improve the search strategy of DHT network.

Kademlia network is changing randomly, and new nodes can join the network anytime and old nodes can leave the network at the same time. To quickly get the network online-node, we need to design a kind of efficient crawler, and thus we can accurately analyze various characteristics of Kademlia. At present, many researchers have designed a variety of crawlers to measure and analyze Kademlia. Locher compared the node activity of eDonkey network and Kademlia network, he found the

Y. Yuan, X. Wu, and Y. Lu (Eds.): ISCTCS 2012, CCIS 320, pp. 117–123, 2013.
© Springer-Verlag Berlin Heidelberg 2013

number of search requests in eDonkey network was far greater than in Kademlia network, and he concluded that eDonkey network was more popular than Kademlia network. Yu measured the routing table of Kademlia, he found the duplication of the Kademlia node ID, and if ID repeated more, the keyword search was less efficient. Pietrzyk measured shared files of the Kademlia users, he found that Kademlia had been popular now and users got large amount of data from the Kademlia network daily. Zhou et al. measured the Kademlia node, they found that the routing table size remained stable, there were DNS server attacks in the Kademlia network and so on.

In this paper, we measure and analyze some characteristics of the KAD network, which publish and search resources in eDonkey network. In section 2, the KAD background is introduced. In section 3, the measurement of KAD network based on active detective is given, which includes search path and k-bucket of the KAD node. In section 4, we analyze the KAD network from the common prefix, the search hop and K bucket of the node. Our conclusions of this paper are summarized in section 5.

2   KAD Background

In this paper, the KAD protocol of eMule is measured and analyzed, which is a DHT routing protocol based on Kademlia protocol. eMule is an open-source P2P software, which connects to a file-sharing network called eDonkey. eDonkey has a huge number of online users, and KAD is responsible for publishing and searching resources [6] in the eDonkey network.

2.1   KAD Node State

Every node in KAD network has a 128-bits ID as an identifier, and eMule uses the MD4 hash algorithm to randomly generate a no-duplicate ID. In KAD network, each node is regarded as a leave of the binary tree, and the position of each node is uniquely identified by the shortest prefix. KAD protocol ensures that each node knows at least one other node. In this premise, each node can find any other node by its ID, and this routing process is achieved by XOR distance.

2.2   Distance between KAD Nodes

In KAD network, every node can store the (key, value) pair [7], and the key is a 128-bits identifier. Each node that has joined the KAD network will be allocated a node ID value in the 128-bits namespace, the value is stored in the node whose ID value is same as or closest to ID value of the key. Calculating the distance between node x and node y is based on the mathematical XOR binary operation, and the distance between x and y is x XOR y. Given any node x and the distance d, there will always be a node y, and the distance between x and y is just d. In addition, One-Way ensure that all queries of the same key value will gradually converge to the same path, no matter where the position of start node is.

2.3 *K*-Bucket of KAD Node

KAD node routing table is built up by the list that called *k*-bucket. This is similar to Tapestry technology, and its routing table is also constructed by using a similar method. For $0 \leqq i < 128$, each node stores the information of node which have the distance range $[2^i, 2^{i+1})$, these information consist of some (IP address, UDP port, Node ID) pairs (KAD network mostly uses UDP to exchange information). Such a list is called a *k*-bucket, and the node information in *k*-bucket are ordered by last-seen time, less-recently seen nodes are put on the head, most-recently seen nodes are put on the tail. Each *k*-bucket has no more than *k* data items.

3   KAD Measurement System Based on Active Detection

The experimental system is mainly achieved by modifying the eMule client code. The system measures two aspects of KAD network [8]: KAD network search path and KAD node *k*-bucket. KAD network search path is found by using the mechanism of KAD network routing query, this part records the entire path in the process of searching for the target node. It mainly measures the availability of the KAD search and finds some characteristics of the KAD network. *K*-bucket of KAD network node is detected [9] by using some special nodes and querying the corresponding nodes from other clients, this part can obtain a certain number of layers of the other client's *k*-bucket. It mainly measures the characteristics of the *k*-bucket [10].

3.1   Finding Search Path

KAD network search path is found by using the mechanism of KAD network routing query, and this mechanism can record the nodes that more and more closer to the target node. Finally, we can find the node that is closest to the target node. This part completely records all the KAD nodes that appear in the process of querying, and it is shown in figure 1.

3.2   Detecting *K*-Bucket of KAD Node

Detecting *k*-bucket of KAD Node also uses the mechanism of KAD network routing query. This part detects the deepest layer of *k*-bucket, the information can be used to analyze the query of KAD network node and resource search. As mentioned above, the KAD network is a DHT network based on XOR. If we want to construct an ID value whose prefix is the same as the other one, we can make this 128-bits node XOR the special 128-bits node. These special 128-bits nodes have the following characteristics, the bits of prefix are all 0 and the rest are all 1. In this case, bit that XOR 0 is unchanged, bit that XOR 1 is negation. Finally, the prefix of the constructed node is the same as the node to be detected. According to this thought, *k*-bucket of KAD node detection algorithm is given below.

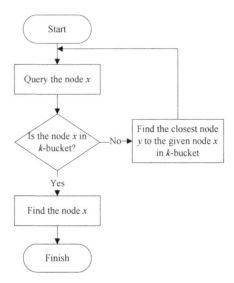

Fig. 1. Mechanism of KAD network routing query. After one node receives the query of the node x, it will find whether the node x is in its k-bucket. If yes, it directly returns the node x, if no, it returns the closest node y to the given node x in k-bucket, then continues to query.

```
Input:  Detected Node IP, Detected Node Port, Detected
Node ID
Output: Request Data Packet of KAD Node k-bucket
Data peer: struct{IP address, port number, kadID}
Data: shared list Peer = list of peer elements
Data int position = 0
Data list ids = list of n properly chosen kid elements
1 Peer.add(seed);
2 while position < size(Peers) do
3   for i = 1 to n do
4   destkadID = Peer[position].kadID ⊕ ids[i]
5   send route requests(destkadID) to Peer[position];
6   ++position;
7 end;
```

4   Analysis of Measurement Results

4.1   Common Prefix of Node ID

In KAD network, the distance calculation is based on XOR metric. So if a node and the target node have a longer common prefix, then it indicates that the node is closer to the target node and more likely to be searched. Through analyzing different target keyword search paths, we get the distribution of bits in common between the target node and the closest node, which is shown in figure 2. The maximum number of bits in common is 30, and there is a higher proportional distribution in 8 and 20. Further analyzing the target keyword, we know that the keyword that has 8 bits in common is more-popular now, while the keyword that has 20 bits in common is less-popular now. It indicates that the node that stores less-popular keyword has a longer common prefix than the node that stores more-popular keyword. In KAD network, when user queries the keyword, he tends to request the node that has a longer common prefix at first. So this storage mechanism makes the node that stores the less-popular keyword has a longer common prefix, then these keywords can be searched more easily. In a word, it enhances the effectiveness of KAD network resources storage.

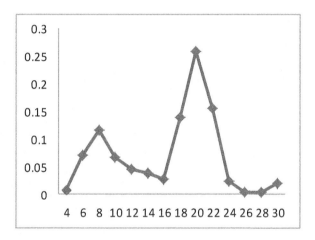

Fig. 2. Distribution of bits in common. In the figure, the abscissa represents the number of bits in common, the ordinate represents the proportional distribution. The maximum number of bits in common is *30*, and there are two peaks in *8* and *20*.

4.2   Hop of Searching Target Node

When searching the target node by the KAD routing mechanism, each time user needs to request the closer node to the target node, and finally finds the target node. So each intermediate node is a hop. By analyzing the hops of different target keyword search paths, we get the distribution of search hops, which is shown in figure 3. The maximum number of hop is 11, so it indicates that the search process of KAD network converges quickly, and the efficiency of search is higher. The proportional distribution is higher in 1 hop, 5 hops and 9 hops, so it proves the correctness of first conclusion above. Because more-popular keyword has a shorter common prefix, it can be searched by using less hops, while less-popular keyword has a longer common prefix, it can be searched by using more hops. This conclusion also ensures that the less-popular keyword can be searched more easily.

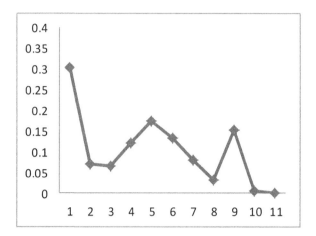

Fig. 3. Distribution of search hops. In the figure, the abscissa represents the number of hop, the ordinate represents the proportional distribution. The maximum number of hop is *11*, and there are three peaks in *1* hop, *5* hops and *9* hops.

4.3   *K*-Bucket

By using the crawler, we crawl many different nodes in k-bucket. Through analyzing these nodes in k-bucket, we discover that there are 15 bits in common between the closest node in k-bucket and the target node. So the coverage of k-bucket is large and the node well knows other node that is near to itself. In this case, k-bucket ensures that routing query converges quickly. Besides, in order to do not store the dead node in k-bucket, the k-bucket will be refreshed every once in a while, the dead node will be taken out and the alive node will join. So the speed and performance of searching in KAD network are high-efficiency.

5   Conclusions

In this paper, we use active detection technology to measure the KAD network, including search path and node k-bucket. We draw some conclusions as follows. In KAD network, the node that stores less-popular keyword has a longer common prefix. The number of search hop usually is few and the search efficiency is very high. The coverage of k-bucket is large and the node well knows other node that is near to itself, so routing query converges quickly. These conclusions prove that KAD network search is effective, and provide some references for further studying and improving the performance of the DHT network.

Acknowledgment. This work is partially supported by the National Grand Fundamental Research 973 Program of China (Grant No. 2011CB302605); the National Natural Science Foundation of China (Grant No. 61173145); High-Tech Research and Development Plan of China (Grant No. 2010AA012504, 2011AA010705). The authors also gratefully acknowledge the helpful comments and suggestions of the reviewers, which have improved the presentation.

References

1. Stoica, I., Morris, R., Karger, D., Kaashoek, M., Balakrishnan, H.: Chord: A scalable Peer-to-peer lookup service for Internet applications. In: Proc. ACM SIGCOMM, pp. 149–160 (2001)
2. Ratnasamy, S., Handley, M., Karp, R., Shenker, S.: A scalable content-addressable network. In: Proc. ACM SIGCOMM (2001)
3. Rowstron, A., Druschel, P.: Pastry: Scalable, distributed object location and routing for large-scale peer-to-peer systems. Accepted for Middleware (2001)
4. Maymounkov, P., Mazières, D.: Kademlia: A Peer-to-Peer Information System Based on the XOR Metric. In: Druschel, P., Kaashoek, M.F., Rowstron, A. (eds.) IPTPS 2002. LNCS, vol. 2429, pp. 53–65. Springer, Heidelberg (2002)
5. E-Mule, http://www.emule-project.net
6. Pietrzyk, M., Urvoy-Keller, G., Costeux, J.L.: Digging into KAD users' shared folders. Poster of ACM SIGCOMM (2008)
7. Steiner, M., Biersack, E.W., En-Najjary, T.: Actively monitoring peers in KAD. In: Proc. 6th Int. Workshop on Peer-to-Peer Systems, IPTPS (2007)
8. Steiner, M., En-Najjary, T., Biersack, E.W.: A global view of KAD. In: Proc. Internet Measurement Conf., IMC (2007)
9. Mickens, J., Noble, B.: Exploiting availability prediction in distributed systems. In: Proc. NSDI, San Jose, CA (2006)
10. Saroiu, S., Gummadi, P.K., Gribble, S.D.: A measurement study of peer-to-peer file sharing systems. In: Proc. Multimedia Computing and Networking (MMCN) (January 2002)

Encrypted Traffic Classification
Based on an Improved Clustering Algorithm

Meng Zhang, Hongli Zhang, Bo Zhang, and Gang Lu

School of Computer and Technology, Harbin Institute of Technology, Harbin, China
{zhangmeng2011,zhangbo,lugang}@pact518.hit.edu.cn,
zhanghongli@hit.edu.cn

Abstract. Classification analysis of network traffic based on port number or payload is becoming increasingly difficult from security to quality of service measurements, because of using dynamic port numbers, masquerading and various cryptographic techniques to avoid detection. Research tends to analyze flow statistical features with machine learning techniques. Clustering approaches do not require complex training procedure and large memory cost. However, the performance of clustering algorithm like k-Means still have own disadvantages. We propose a novel approach of considering harmonic mean as distance matric, and evaluate it in terms of three metrics on real-world encrypted traffic. The result shows the classification has better performance compared with the previously.

Keywords: traffic classification, machine learning, k-means clustering.

1   Introduction

With the rapid expansion of application types on the Internet, network traffic classification has drawn significant attention with increasing bandwidth demands from individual users as well as business organizations over the past few years. When concerning quality of service, intrusion detection, security and privacy, effective management of network traffic is essential and necessary. Traditional traffic classification methods include the port-based and payload-based prediction [1]. However, in current network environment, many applications have emerged that utilize obfuscation techniques such as random ports, encrypted data transmission, or proprietary communication protocols, so traditional methods are no longer effective. Machine learning has been considered to intelligently conduct traffic classification.

Traffic statistics of different application types reflect users' behavior while using the network. So research approaches focused on statistical observations and distributions of flow features in the packet traces. The flow statistical information without packet payloads can be achieved by using supervised classification method and unsupervised classification method. Supervised classification, such as C4.5 decision tree, Bayesian network, SVM and neural network [2], require an intensive training procedure and large storage capacity for model building. Yet clustering algorithms can

Y. Yuan, X. Wu, and Y. Lu (Eds.): ISCTCS 2012, CCIS 320, pp. 124–131, 2013.

work with unlabeled training samples and assign new applications by examining the flows that are grouped to form a new cluster.

In this paper, we consider K-Means clustering, a partition-based algorithm. It has advantages of briefness, efficiency and celerity. However, this algorithm also has its drawbacks. It is incapable of revealing clusters of arbitrary shapes, but non-convex and interwoven clusters can be seen in many applications. Moreover, it depends quite much on initial dots, and different way in choosing initial samples always leads to different outcomes. Therefore, we improve K-Means algorithm by using harmonic mean to reduce the impact on initial determination. Additionally, a new distance matric with high robustness is quoted.

The remainder of the paper is structured as follows. Section 2 reviews related work in traffic classification. An improved clustering approach for traffic classification is proposed in detail in Section 3. Section 4 presents our experiments and results for performance. Finally, the paper is concluded in Section 5.

2 Related Work

Historically, traffic classification is based on well-known port numbers, due to traditional applications using fixed port numbers assigned by IANA. As application design and user behavior rendered, Karaginnis in [3] present that this approach is unreliable for current generation of P2P applications which use dynamic port number or masquerade as well-known applications. Then payload-based research emerged, that inspects packet content on application layer to identify some specific characteristic signatures. Payload inspection technology, sometimes called deep packet inspection (DPI), also face technological and related economic challenges, like encryption, protocol obfuscation or encapsulation [4]. These challenges have motivated researchers to seek machine learning techniques which do not require payload examination.

In supervised traffic classification, training data is needed to produce an inferred model to predict the output class for testing flow. Moore et al. [5] proposed to use Naïve Bayes algorithm to group flows. Williams et al. [6] evaluated the supervised algorithms including naïve Bayes with discretization, naïve Bayes with kernel density estimation, C4.5 decision tree, Bayesian network and naïve Bayes tree. Este et al. [7] applied one-class SVMs to classify traffic. These works require an intensive training procedure for the classifier parameters and cannot discover new network applications. Reversely, the unsupervised methods try to find cluster structure in unlabeled traffic data and assign testing flow to the application-based class of its nearest cluster. McGregor et al. [8] confirmed the ability of using the expectation maximization (EM) algorithm to group flows using transport layer attributes. Zander et al. [9] extended this work by using AutoClass algorithm and analyze the best set of attributes to use. Erman et al. [10] proposed to evaluate K-Means and density-based spatial clustering of applications with noise (DBSCAN) compared with AutoClass algorithm. The experimental results show that both K-Means and DBSCAN work much more quickly than AutoClass. Nevertheless, unsupervised clustering algorithms have difficulty in mapping unlabeled clusters to real network applications. Later, Erman et al. put forward a semi-supervised method in [11], which uses K-Means algorithm to partition flows set that owns scarce labeled flows. However, K-Means clustering algorithm is sensitive with the initial random assignments. Our work focuses on the initial cluster point based on density instead of randomly selection.

3　An Improved K-Means Clustering Algorithm

K-Means clustering algorithm has been proved fast and accurate in network identification. Through repeated iteration, K-Means clustering algorithm partitions the data set into K sections, while K is the desired number of classes which is required pre-specified.

3.1　Determination of the Initial Center

The concept of algorithm is quite simple, only consisting of three steps. Firstly, it selects the K centers of the initial clusters randomly. Each data object is assigned to its most similar class center by calculating the distance between each object and centers. The mean vector (center) for all objects in each cluster is computed instead of the original center. Then this cycle is repeated until the members within clusters no longer change [10]. Time complexity of K-means algorithm is extraordinary low, so it is easy to implement.

But because of the clustering process may terminates in a local optimum, the initial state of clusters will cause significant influence. The stochastic selection of points leads to the fact that the outcome of cluster result is also quite stochastic. While in practical applications, we want initial centers to be decentralized and more typical.

We only use transport layer statistics to identify the traffic. Let $F = \{x_1, x_2, \ldots, x_n\}$ be a set of flows, where each flow x_i has a set of attributes of $\{d_{i1}, d_{i2}, \ldots d_{im}\}$. Meanwhile, the total traffic clusters is known as k. We assign a new distance matric of two flow vector instead of Euclidean distance:

$$D(x, y) = 1 - exp(-\|x - y\|^2) \tag{1}$$

The measurement approach has been proved effective in [12], which has high robustness, that the weight of noise points and outliers is lower. According to the concept, the Harmonic Means of $A = \{a_1, a_2, \ldots a_m\}$ with m numbers is defined as follows:

$$HM = \frac{m}{\sum_{i=1}^{m} 1/a_i} \tag{2}$$

Consequently we have the sum of harmonic mean of the square distance between each object to all centers as the evaluation function:

$$E(x) = \sum_{i=1}^{n} \left(K / \sum_{j=1}^{K} \left(1/D(x_i, c_j) \right) \right)^2 \tag{3}$$

In order to obtain the optimal algorithm, we make the value of the formula derivation equal to 0, so we can get the center of iteration as follows.

$$c_j = \sum_{i=1}^{n} \frac{exp\left(-\|x_i - c_j\|^2\right)}{D\left(x_i, c_j\right)^2 E(x)^2} x_i \Big/ \sum_{i=1}^{n} \frac{exp\left(-\|x_i - c_j\|^2\right)}{D\left(x_i, c_j\right)^2 E(x)^2} \tag{4}$$

In this algorithm, for each object, the evaluation function considers the distances to all centers. The harmonic mean is sensitive when the object is very close to two or more centers at the same time. The algorithm will automatically move the excess center to the area without recent center point, what would create a smaller evaluation function value.

On the other hand, in the iteration of K-Means algorithm, the evaluation function assign to all points of the same weight value. Whereas each point weight value is assigned dynamically on the basis of the harmonic mean value. When a point is far away to any center, the harmonic mean will assign a larger weight to the point. Conversely, when a point is in the nearby of more than one center, it will be assigned a smaller weight value. This approach is insensitive to the initial centers, for each cluster center is linked with all points in iteration.

3.2   Algorithm Description

Steps of initialization in our improved K-Means clustering algorithm are elaborated as follows:

1. A subset of flows data is sampled randomly to form an initial dataset.
2. Using the above method executes center iteration until the center points converge.
3. For all the rest flows, continue K-Means algorithm steps of calculating the distance of each data point to the k *clusters centers, and resolve which cluster it is belong to.*

4   Methodology and Results

In this section, we evaluate the proposed clustering algorithm on two real-world encrypted traffic datasets. One was captured by Computer Network and Information Security Technology Research Center at Harbin Institute of Technology on the campus network gateway in 2011. This dataset has been labeled by Layer 7 filter based on the process of applications. The other is a public dataset for research, which has more than 3 million flows signed of SSH protocol and NOTSSH protocol. Our dataset consists of 25M flows randomly sampled from 5 classes: SKYPE, QQ, SSH, SSL, MSN. In our experiments, 10 percent samples of each class dataset were selected to construct a training set. We also concerned the discrimination between TCP and UDP, so clustering procedures are executed separately.

We use recommended performance metrics to evaluate performance [4]. Precision is the ratio of objects properly attributed to a class over the total number of objects attributed to that class. Recall is the percentage of objects from a given class that are F-measure is used to compare the per-class performance and calculated by:

$$F - measure = \frac{2 \times precision \times recall}{precision + recall} \tag{5}$$

In this work, more than 20 flow statistical features are extracted and listed in Table1. Flows are bidirectional with the first packet determining the forward direction. Meanwhile, flows are of limited duration, and UDP flows are terminated by a time-out, which is assigned as 60 seconds here.

Table 1. Flow attributes

Description	Category	
packet length	forward	
	backward	min, mean, max
inter arrival time	forward	stand deviation
	backward	
duration of the flow		
total packets	forward	
	backward	
total volume	forward	
	backward	
protocol	TCP and UDP	

In the experiment, we assign the simple K-Means randomly generate 20 seeds each time. Fig 1 shows the precision, recall and F-measure for the K-Means algorithm and our improved algorithm on the dataset mixed by 5 kinds of flows. For MSN, SSH and SSL protocol, two algorithms have precision and recall values above 80%, especially the accuracy on MSN is close to 1. But the accuracy of K-Means method on QQ and SKYPE protocol is less than 50%. Obviously, our method increases the F-measure accuracy of QQ protocol at least 10%. Other protocols like SSL and Skype also have an improved identification.

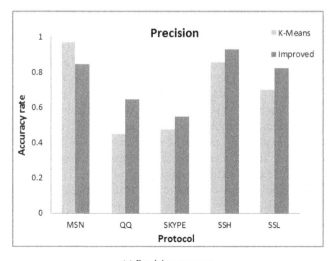

(a) Precision accuracy

Fig. 1. Results on the remix dataset

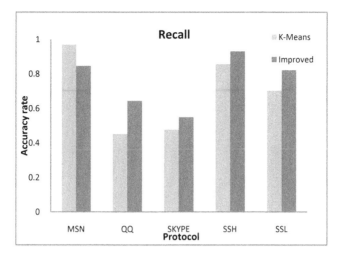

(b) Recall accuracy

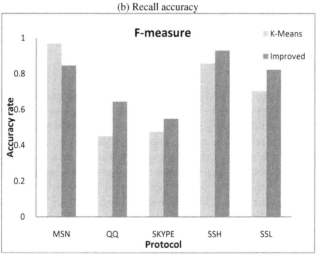

(c) F-measure accuracy

Fig. 1. (*continued*)

In Fig 2, we compare the methods in SSH flows and NOTSSH flows. As the proportion of SSH data is far less than NOTSSH in the real network environment, the precision accuracy is quite low, even cannot reach by 30%. The reason is that many variety protocols have similar statistic information like SSH. Although the accuracy of our improved algorithm decreases a little on the NOTSSH dataset, It is obviously that the improvement of F-Measure accuracy of SSH is from 10 percent to 20 percent. While in regard to K-Means method, it is much lower than 50%.

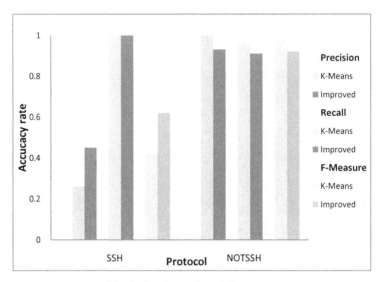

Fig. 2. Results on the public dataset

5   Conclusion

In this paper, we proposed a new approach to improve the drawbacks of K-Means algorithm in traffic classification, through the use of harmonic mean to reduce the impact of random initial clustering centers. On account of each cluster center does not only iterate the points within the same class, but linked with all points in iteration. Moreover, we substitute a new distance measure to Euclidean distance, so that it can reveal clusters of non-convex shapes. Experiments have been carried out on two real-world traffic datasets, and show that the accuracy of encrypted traffic classification can be improved significantly. This approach has no need to execute an intensive training procedure to obtain the optimal parameters, so it can be used to automatic recognize traffic in real time.

Acknowledgment. This work is partially supported by the National Grand Fundamental. Research 973 Program of China (Grant No. 2011CB302605); High-Tech Research and Development Plan of China (Grant No. 2010AA012504, 2011AA010705); the National Natural Science Foundation of China (Grant No. 61173145).The authors also gratefully ac-knowledge the helpful comments and suggestions of the reviewers, which have im-proved the presentation.

References

1. Thomas, K., Konstantina, P., Michalis, F.: BLINC: Multilevel Traffic Classification in the Dark. Computer Communication Review 35(4), 229–240 (2005)
2. Roughan, M., Sen, S., Spatscheck, O., Duffield, N.: Class-of service mapping for QoS: a statistical signature-based approach to IP traffic classification. In: Proceedings of the 4th ACM SIGCOMM Conference on Internet Measurement, New York, USA, pp. 135–148 (2004)

3. Karagiannis, T., Broido, A., Faloutsos, M., Claffy, K.C.: Transport Layer Identification of P2P Traffic. In: Proc. of IMC 2004, Taormina, Italy, pp. 121–134 (2004)
4. Dainotti, A., Pescapé, A., Claffy, K.C.: Issues and Future Directions in Traffic Classification. IEEE Network 26(4), 35–40 (2012)
5. Moore, A.W., Zuev, D.: Internet Traffic Classification Using Bayesian Analysis Techniques. In: SIGMETRIC 2005, Banff, Canada, June 6-10, pp. 50–60 (2005)
6. Williams, N., Zander, S., Armitage, G.: A preliminary performance comparison of five machine learning algorithms for practical ip traffic flow classification. Computer Communication Review 36(5), 5–16 (2006)
7. Este, A., Gringoli, F., Salgarelli, L.: Support vector machines for tcp traffic classification. Computer Networks 53(14), 2476–2490 (2009)
8. McGregor, A., Hall, M., Lorier, P., Brunskill, J.: Flow Clustering Using Machine Learning Techniques. In: Barakat, C., Pratt, I. (eds.) PAM 2004. LNCS, vol. 3015, pp. 205–214. Springer, Heidelberg (2004)
9. Zander, S., Nguyen, T., Armitage, G.: Automated traffic classification and application identification using machine learning. In: Annual IEEE Conference on Local Computer Networks, Los Alamitos, CA, USA, pp. 250–257 (2005)
10. Jeffrey, E., Martin, A., Anirban, M.: Traffic classification using clustering algorithms. In: Proceedings of SIGCOMM 2006, New York, USA, pp. 281–286 (September 2006)
11. Jeffrey, E., Anirban, M., Martin, A., Carey, W.: Identifying and discriminating between web and peer-to-peer traffic in the network core. In: Proceedings of the 16th International Conference, WWW 2007, New York, USA, pp. 883–892 (May 2007)
12. Wu, K.L., Yang, M.S.: Alternative c-means clustering algorithms. Pattern Recognition 35(10), 2267–2278 (2002)

Real-Time Detection of Encrypted Thunder Traffic Based on Trustworthy Behavior Association

Gang Xiong[1,2,3], Wenting Huang[4], Yong Zhao[2], Ming Song[5,6], Zhenzhen Li [2], and Li Guo[2]

[1] Institute of Computing Technology, Chinese Academy of Science
[2] Institute of Information Engineering, Chinese Academy of Science
[3] Graduate University of Chinese Academy of Science
[4] National Computer Network Emergency Response Technical Team, China
[5] Beijing University of Posts and Telecommunications, Beijing, China
[6] Key Laboratory of Trustworthy Distributed Computing and Service (BUPT),
Ministry of Education, Beijing, China
xionggang@ict.ac.cn

Abstract. Thunder, as the most popular P2P download software in China, has token up a large amount of bandwidth. And it is almost impossible to identify the encrypted thunder traffic. This paper proposes a method to detect encrypted Thunder traffic, featuring high precision and small computational cost. At the same time, this method doesn't depend on content inspection, nor does it violate users' privacy, which can be used flexibly in high-speed network environment, and deal with changes of statistical traffic properties. We implement a prototype system based on this algorithm, which can detect multiple versions of encrypted Thunder traffics in real time, achieving a precision rate above 95% and a recall rate above 95%.

Keywords: traffic classification, trustworthy behavior, encrypted traffic, P2P traffic, behavior association, thunder.

1 Introduction

According to related research, Thunder is not only the most popular P2P system in China [1], but also stands out in other regions of the world, such as Europe, Africa and etc. [2]. Besides, Thunder has used protocol confusion and other traffic hidden methods, and currently there is no effective ways to identify its traffic.

2 Related Work

There are four classical types of network traffic detection: port-based, load-based, host-behavior-based and machine-learning-based. Obviously, current detection methods based on port and load are useless for the detection of encrypted traffic. Efforts to detect encrypted P2P traffic mainly concentrate on machine learning based

Y. Yuan, X. Wu, and Y. Lu (Eds.): ISCTCS 2012, CCIS 320, pp. 132–139, 2013.
© Springer-Verlag Berlin Heidelberg 2013

on statistical traffic properties. Related research is still in experimental stage, immature to put into real application [3].

In the field of the host behavior-based traffic classification, the BLINC method proposed by Karagiannis et al is the most typical one [4]. The disadvantage of this method is it's difficult to achieve high classification efficiency in the backbone network. In addition, it needs to apply comprehensive analysis to data collected within a long period of time (up to 10 days), making real-time classification impossible. Xu kai et al introduced the concept of RU value in their traffic classification method [5]. This method can also be seen as traffic classification based on host behavior. Moreover, ILIOFOTOU et al provided a graph-based P2P traffic identification method which is an expansion for BLINC [6]. Its computational cost is still large and it is difficult to achieve real-time classification.

In conclusion, though the host behavior-based method can be used in the inspection for encrypted traffic, all the existing methods need significant amounts of computation and it is hard to make real-time classification.

We focus on relationship of association of traffics between hosts, and introduce a real-time method based behavior association of trustworthy traffic flows.This paper provides an association algorithm that uses the relationship between the hosts. This method avoid a lot of computation and detects the encrypted traffic in real-time.

3   Real-Time Detection Method Based on Trustworthy Behavior Association

The behavioral feature of traffic or host is more commonly used, and is not confused or hidden. In this chapter, we first present trustworthy traffic behavior; then NAT traversal in P2P systems is introduced. Subsequently, we define the various elements necessary in the whole P2P system and abstract basic composition of the P2P systems. Next, the interaction between various elements is described. Finally, based on the relationship between the various elements in the P2P system, we propose a real-time detection method based on trustworthy behavior association.

3.1   Trustworthy Traffic Behavior

In order to hide itself, a lot of encrypted P2P traffic use "Protocol Obfuscation" to evade detection. The terminology "Protocol Obfuscation (fuzzy)" originally came from "eMule" software, which considered protocol confusion a technology that can protect its traffic, reaching the purpose of confusion or "hiding" its own protocol.

Common confusion methods are: port confusion, protocol camouflage, encryption and random filling. In order to ensure the effectiveness of the following association based on traffic behavior, we first make a definition for trustworthy and untrustworthy traffic behavior.

It is possible to determine the Thunder trustworthy behavior as follows.

1. The behavior of DNS accessing the Thunder server;
2. The behavior of accessing the Thunder server to obtain resources;
3. The behavior of communicating with other PEER node.

The untrustworthy Thunder behaviors include:

1. The behavior of having short-flow, ultra-short flow (such as there is only one packet, or only one-way data flow, or light load with only a few bytes)in the communication with other PEER node;
2. The behavior of scanning traffic;
3. The behavior of attacking traffic (such as SYN flood, UDP flood).

In this association algorithm, we add the trustworthy behavior to the association analysis, while untrustworthy behavior is excluded. This greatly reduces unnecessary data in the process of generating association and adds certain attack-proof feature at the same time.

3.2   NAT and P2P System

NAT technology has been widely used in the Internet. NAT traversal technology has become an integral part of mainstream P2P systems [7], and has a significant impact on our host association algorithm.

3.3   Host Behavior Patterns in the P2P System

Basing on the widespread of NAT, we define the various parts that make up the P2P system, making it possible to discuss the relationship between hosts.

We regard all endpoints in the P2P network, including node and server that participate in P2P connections, as hosts. Then host can be represented by the following properties {IP, Htype} [8], where IP is the ip address and Htype refers to the corresponding type of the host, including Server, Peer and Client, that is : Htype $\in$ {Server, Peer, Client}.

Besides the property of the IP addresses, different types of hosts, according to their characteristics in the P2P network, can make their own properties extended as follows:

Server (S): defined as a triple {IP, Proto, Stype}, which sequentially refer to IP address, transport protocol (TCP/UDP), and the server. Server types include NAT server and Ordinary server, that is, Stype $\in$ {NAT, Ordi}.

Node (P): defined as a triple {IP, Port, Proto}, which sequentially refer to IP address, listening port and transport layer protocols (TCP / UDP).

Client (C): defined as a tuple {IP}, attribute to an IP address.

Based on the IP packet information from the network, we can find a new P2P host. For subsequent discussions, we will divide hosts into three categories.

• Server Set (SS): the collection of known servers. SS is a set of specific P2P application server (where the collection is a variable set), and it consists of single server, that is triple {IP, Proto, Stype}.

- Peer Set (PS): the collection of P2P network' nodes. PS is a variable set and it consists of single Peer, which is the triples {IP, and Port Proto}.
- Client Set (CS): CS consists of single client, which is a tuple {IP}.
- Association Set (AS): the collection of associated IP. AS consists of tuple {IP}, including the IP of all the three sets above. That is AS = {IP | IP ∈ the SS ∨ the IP ∈ the PS ∨ the IP ∈ the CS}.

There is a lot of communication in front of packets between the three types of hosts in the P2P networks. These packets reflect the relationship between each host. As the basis of our association algorithm, we assume:

Hypothesis 1: The host that communicates with listening port of a known P2P host is also identified as a host of this P2P system.
Hypothesis 2: The node uses a random port to communicate with ordinary servers.
Hypothesis 3: The node uses a fixed port to communicate with NAT servers in UDP.
Hypothesis 4: The node communicates with other nodes using fixed port via UDP.
Hypothesis 5: The node uses a random port to establish a connection with the other node that has a listening TCP port.

3.4   Traffic Detection Based on the Association of Trustworthy Traffic Behavior

With the five basic hypotheses mentioned above, we propose a traffic detection algorithm based on the host-association. The algorithm starts with a list of servers, and discovers new P2P hosts by observing the network border traffic. And the traffic between P2P hosts will be labeled.

Firstly, we need to filter the traffic that crosses the border router, and the suspicious traffic will be sent to the subsequent association algorithm for analysis. Filtering algorithm is as follows:

At the beginning of the algorithm, AS should not be null, that is, AS ≠Φ, equivalently, SS, PS, CS should not to be null in all. Ensuring continuous operation of the association algorithm, when the program starts, one or several elements of the three collections are initialized based on prior knowledge, and some identified elements are added to the corresponding collection.

Table 1. Filtering Algorithm

```
if( ippkt.SIP ∈ AS ),then
    ippkt.HitS = 1;
Endif
if(ippkt.DIP ∈ AS ),then
    ippkt.HitD = 1;
Endif
if(ippkt.HitS==1 or ippkt.HitD == 1),then
    return True;
Endif
return False;
```

For the first packets in both directions of every connection, filtering algorithm in Table 1 below determines whether the SIP and DIP of the ippkt is in the collection of AS according to the association rules. If so, further association analysis and process will be done after they are classified in to the sub-set of SS, PS and CS (that means the different of the host type). Specifically, the algorithm can be divided into 4 sub-modules: IP hitting Query and Test, server association analysis, client association analysis and node association analysis. And they are shown in the Table 2 to Table 5 respectively.

Table 2. Module 1. IP hitting Query and Test.

```
RetVal=Rule(ippkt, AS);
if (False==RetVal),then
    return;
Endif
if(ippkt.HitS==1 and ippkt.HitD==1) , then
    if(DIP∈CS),then
            Hitip = ippkt.SIP;
    Endif
Else if(ippkt.HitS==1), then
    Hitip = SIP;
Else if(ippkt.HitD==1), then
    Hitip = DIP;
Endif
```

Table 3. Module 2. Server Association Analysis.

```
Hitnum = ippkt.HitD + ippkt.HitS;
if(Hitip∈SS),then:
    if(Hitip.Stype==NAT and
        Hitip.proto==udp),then
        PS=PS∪{notHitip};
Else if(Hitip.SType==Ordi and
        Hitnum==1),then
        CS=CS∪{notHitip};
    Endif
Endif
```

Table 4. Module 3. Client Association Analysis.

```
Hitnum = ippkt.HitD + ippkt.HitS;
if(Hitip∈PS),then
    if(Hitnum==1),then
        if(Hitip.Proto==UDP),then
            if(notHitip.Port==8000),then
                SS=SS∪{notHitip};
                notHitip.Stype    =
NAT;
            Else
                PS=PS∪{notHitip};
            Endif
        Else
            CS=CS∪{notHitip};
        Endif
    Else
        if(Hitip.Proto==UDP),then
            PS=PS∪{notHitip};
        Endif
    Endif
Endif
```

Table 5. Module 4. Node Association Analysis.

```
Hitnum = ippkt.HitD + ippkt.HitS;
if(Hitip∈CS),then
    if (ippkt.Proto==UDP), then
        if(Hitnum==2),then
            if(notHitip.Port==8000),then
                SS=SS∪{notHitip};
                notHitip.Stype = NAT;
            Else
                PS=PS∪{notHitip};
            Endif
        Endif
    Else
        if (Hitnum==2), then
            PS=PS∪{notHitip};
        Endif
    Endif
Endif
```

Note that notHitip.Port in both Table 4 and Table 5 refers to the corresponding port in the ippkt, specifically, SIP corresponds to the Sport, and DIP to Dport.

It should also be noted that elements in these sets have a certain life cycle, once time-out, in other words, it has no refresh by associated packet hit, the element will be age to be deleted.

4   System Implementation and Experimental Results

4.1   Experimental Environment and Traffic Identification System

We get a mirror image of all the traffic from a campus network border router. The network boundary export bandwidth is 400Mbps, with 200Mbps to 300Mbps is used in ordinary time.

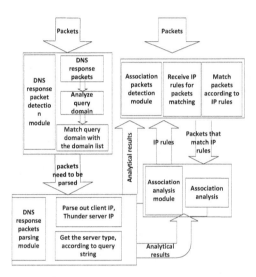

Fig. 1. Traffic detection system based on the host association

As shown in Fig.1, the traffic identification system is mainly divided into four parts: packet inspection module, the DNS response packet detection module, the DNS response parsing module and the host association module.

The host association algorithm is an iterative algorithm, so the start of the algorithm needs an initial input. In Thunder system, parts of the servers have a specific domain name.

DNS response parsing module parses the DNS response packet sent to it, and searches the corresponding server type according to the domain of Thunder server in the message.

With the initial list of servers, the server's IP address is sent to the packet inspection module. This module receives IP address matching rules of the parsing module and associating module, it filters network packets according to the IP address.

The host association module receives the traffic data from packet inspection module, discovers new Thunder hosts in accordance with the previously described association algorithm. The newly found host will be added to the corresponding set by association algorithm. Meanwhile, packet detection module will be required to send back the follow-up traffic of the newly found hosts.

4.2   Result of Verification Experiment

Our main objective in this experiment is to accurately detect Thunder traffic across the boundary in real-time.

We did some reverse analysis on the Thunder client, and studied the detailed structure of the protocol and encryption algorithms [9], [10]. According to the result of the analysis, we found the encryption algorithms that Thunder system used on the UDP packets is reversible from version 5.5.2.252 (released in November 2006) to version 7.2.7.3496 (released in April 2012).

Therefore, we can decrypt all traffic through the network boundary, and take the decrypted traffic as a benchmark. Comparing the results of the association algorithm with the benchmark, we can get results of packets(bytes) precision rate, packets(bytes) recall rate and etc.

Taking Thunder decrypted traffic as a comparing benchmark, we tested and verified the various performance indicators of the host association on a campus network outlet. During the experiment, we decrypted the traffic and performed the association detection algorithm online at the same time. Every five minutes, we compared the results of the association algorithm and decryption. As shown below, in Fig.2, Fig.3 gives the exact statistical results of accuracy rate and recall rate for 24 hours from 14:26 on May 10, 2011 to 14:26 on May 11th.

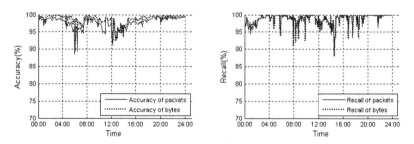

Fig. 2. The accuracy rate and recall rate of host association algorithm

According to our experimental results, accurate rate of the association algorithm basically maintained above 95% at most time, which indicates that other protocol is rarely mistaken as Thunder's traffic by association algorithm.

The recall rate of the association algorithm was validated too. It reflects how much complete the algorithm can identify the total traffic. In the beginning of our experiment, the recall rate was in the process of a rising for some time. This is mainly because some hosts have already been running Thunder software before our experiment. Besides, our association algorithm requires some time to identify host. In addition, the recall rate of the association algorithm can be basically maintained above 95%.

5   Conclusion

We use the association behaviors between the hosts, proposed a new P2P encrypted traffic detection method. The method only observes the trustworthy association between hosts traffic, without inspecting of contents of traffic load achieving a high detection rate. With our prototype system, we tested all Thunder client software, according to the result, the trustworthy association algorithm can detect encrypted traffic of multiple versions in real-time. Meanwhile the average precision rate and the average recall rate reached more than 95%.

Acknowledgements. The work in this paper is supported by the "Strategic Priority Research Program" of the Chinese Academy of Sciences (Grant No. XDA06030200) and the National High-Tech Research and Development Plan "863" of China (Grant No. 2011AA010703) and the National Natural Science Foundation (Grant No. 61070026).

References

1. Download Software Ranking (April 2010),
   http://www.iresearch.com.cn/View/116214.html
2. Schulze, H., Mochalski, K.: Internet Study (2008/2009), http://www.ipoque.com/resources/internet-studies/internet-study-2008_2009
3. Xiong, G., Meng, J., Cao, Z.-G., Wang, Y., Guo, L., Fang, B.-X.: Research Progress and Prospects of Network Traffic Classification. Journal of Integration Technology 1(1), 31–41 (2012)
4. Karagiannis, T., Papagiannaki, K., Faloutsos, M.: BLINC: multilevel traffic classification in the dark. SIGCOMM Comput. Commun. Rev. 35(4), 229–240 (2005)
5. Xu, K., Zhang, Z.-L., Bhattacharyya, S.: Profiling internet backbone traffic: behavior models and applications. In: Proceedings of the 2005 Conference on Applications, Technologies, Architectures, and Protocols for Computer Communications, pp. 169–180. ACM, Philadelphia (2005)
6. Iliofotou, M., Hyun-Chul, K., Faloutsos, M., et al.: Graph-Based P2P Traffic Classification at the Internet Backbone. In: Proceedings of the INFOCOM Workshops 2009, April 19-25. IEEE (2009)
7. Yangyang, L., Jianping, P.: The impact of NAT on BitTorrent-like P2P systems. In: Proceedings of the IEEE Ninth International Conference on Peer-to-Peer Computing, P2P 2009, September 9-11 (2009)
8. Bernaille, L., Teixeira, R., Salamatian, K.: Early application identification. In: Proceedings of the 2006 ACM CoNEXT Conference. ACM, Lisboa (2006)
9. Zhao, Y., Zhang, Z., Wang, Y., et al.: Performance evaluation of Xunlei peer-to-peer network: A measurement study. In: Proceedings of the Consumer Communications and Networking Conference (CCNC 2011). IEEE (January 2011)
10. Yong, Z., Zhibin, Z., Li, G., et al.: XunleiProbe: A Sensitive and Accurate Probing on a Large-Scale P2SP System. In: Proceedings of the 2011 12th International Conference on Parallel and Distributed Computing, Applications and Technologies (PDCAT 2011), October 20-22 (2011)

Security and Trust Model
for Data Disaster-Recovery Service on the Cloud

Zhao Chen[1,2], Wenbin Yao[1,2], and Cong Wang[2]

[1] School of Computer Science, Beijing University of Posts and Telecommunications,
Beijing, China
`chenzhao201@gmail.com, yaowenbin@bupt.edu.cn`
[2] Key Laboratory of Trustworthy Distributed Computing and Service (BUPT),
Ministry of Education, Beijing, China
`wangc@bupt.edu.cn`

Abstract. To cope with the security challenges posed by providing disaster-recovery services on the cloud, a data disaster-recovery model is proposed based on a three-dimension data split scheme. This model presents higher security, data privacy and time efficiency than conventional security methods for cloud storage service. Besides, it will not bring too much extra costs on cloud storage resources. And taking storage price of Amazon S3 as an example, this model only costs less than 20 cents a month for extra storage price as the back-up files are TB level.

Keywords: disaster-recovery, cloud, security, trust, data segment.

1 Introduction

Cloud computing is an innovative information system architecture, which promotes IT capacities over the Internet as a new kind of service. Nowadays, small and medium business (SMB) companies increasingly realize that simply by tapping into the cloud they can gain fast access to the best business applications at a negligible cost, especially when they want to build data disaster-recovery service on the cloud.

As cloud computing becomes more and more popularity, concerns are being voiced about the security issues introduced by building data disaster-recovery service on the cloud[1,2,3]. On the one hand, this service mode may lead to a very low level of trust because service users(SUs) have only limited control on either the cloud system or the upload data. On the other hand, service provider(SP) may be threatened by malicious users like blackmailers.

Some researchers believe that it is not much different from existing practices which can be well managed by traditional techniques[4,5]. And some researchers prefer building trusted third party or protocols for cloud[6,7], which may bring new security problem. However, the specific security requirements are still cloudy to the community. Many consultants and secure agencies have issued warnings on new threats in these services[8]. And the uniqueness of security on the cloud is not recognized.

Y. Yuan, X. Wu, and Y. Lu (Eds.): ISCTCS 2012, CCIS 320, pp. 140–147, 2013.

As a matter of fact, SP who provides a well deployed disaster-recovery on the cloud must satisfy following issues:

1. SP must keep the confidentiality. Although processing full access, the provider, who is considered as an untrustworthy character, cannot reveal users' data.
2. SP must solve the problems of data access and authentication for multiple users.
3. SP and SUs need to solve the data integrity problem. Judgment is needed to solve the suspicion of provider or users when backup data is destroyed.

In this paper, we propose a trust and security model for data disaster-recovery services on cloud. We solve third party disaster-recovery problems by using data split scheme and the trusted protocol. The client of data backup splits the backup files into small pieces and hides unbreakable self-check information in each piece. The self-check information is used to fix the issues of confidentiality, integrity, authentication and access. It is proved that the model has higher security than the model of general encryption and not inferior to erasure codes and secret sharing. A series of experiments and analysis were taken and the conclusion shows that the model does not cost too much on the extra resources of encoding time and storage space.

The organization of this paper is as follows: Chapter 2 presents the model of data processing. Chapter 3 proposes the protocol of security and trust. Chapter 4 analyzes the security, cloud resource costs of this model. Chapter 5 concludes the paper with the limitations and contributions of this work.

2 Disaster-Recovery Model on the Cloud

Cloud storage can promotes disaster-recovery services over the internet. But SP and SU will face a series of security problem like data access, identity authentication, confidentiality, integrity and blackmailer. The layered stack for a typical SaaS disaster-recovery vendor and critical aspects is illustrated in Fig. 1.

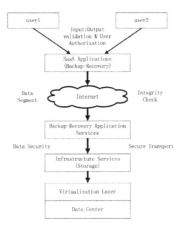

Fig. 1. Security model for data disaster-recovery service based on the cloud

The general idea of handling the security issue in this model is to present a secure data segmenting scheme and trust scheme before data is sent to the cloud. Data is split and self-checked at the SaaS application(SA) before it is sent to SP for integrity check. Then the checked segments are stored on the cloud. Only the legal SU, who has the correct segment information, have access to the backup files.

ESSA[9], which is a security and efficiency data split algorithm. The scheme presented is generalized by ESSA to form a new kind of data segment algorithm, which use ESSA to scramble grouped split matrices and makes unbreakable hash check information of each piece. There are several definitions about ESSA.

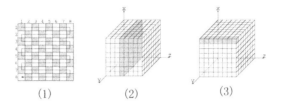

(1)   (2)   (3)

Fig. 2. Data split and scramble. (1)8×8 split matrix contains 512bytes, data is filled as the order of the arrows; (2)$8\times8\times8$ split cub formed by 8 split matrices parallel to coordinate plane xoy ; (3) Data fragment F_{88} contains the bytes belongs to $(8,8)$ of each matrix.

Definition 1: Split matrix. Data is split into pieces which have $m\times n$ bytes, and bytes are filled into a $m\times n$ matrix as order. Fig.2 (1) shows a 8×8 split matrix.

Definition 2: Split cube. Data is split into pieces and fill into different split matrices, all of which can form a cube by the order. Fig.2 (2) shows a $8\times8\times8$ split cube. Each matrix parallel to coordinate plane xoy and $z_i (i\in[1,8])$ is the ith plane.

Definition 3: Data fragment. Get all the bytes from coordinate $(x_i,y_j),i,j\in[1,8]$ of each matrix to form a bytes buffer named as data fragment which is record as $F_{x_iy_j}$. Fig.2 (3) shows a data fragment split from a $8\times8\times8$ cube.

In our new scheme, SA gets backup file to form a $m\times n\times k$ split cube and divides it into p groups. Then SA uses ESSA to scramble each group by different knight's tour path $KTP_e (e\in[1,p])$ which is generated randomly and stored by user. After that, SA uses scrambled groups to build new split cube and splits it into data fragments. Each fragment $F_{x_iy_j}$ has its own coordinate information, which can used to generate unbreakable hash check information. SA calculates 32 byte MD5, which is record as $S_{x_iy_j}$, and scrambles it to form fragment head by (1) which can be shown in Fig.3.

$$f_{x_iy_j}(\alpha)=\sqrt[3]{x_i}\alpha+\sqrt{y_j}\alpha+x_iy_j \tag{1}$$

SA calculates $u_\alpha = \left\lceil f_{x_i y_j}(\alpha) \right\rceil \bmod 32$ as $\alpha = 0$, and put u_α^{th} byte of $S_{x_i y_j}$ into the first byte of fragment head. Then SA calculates u_α while α increases and scramble next byte. If the u_α^{th} byte has already been scrambled, SA will increase α and calculate u_α again until all the bytes are scrambled. Finally, SA inserts $x_i \times m + y_j$ at the position u_{id} calculate by the users identify number where $u_{id} = id \bmod 32$.

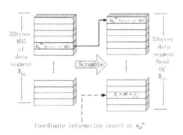

Fig. 3. Generation of data fragment head

SA inserts the self-check head in front of each data fragment and form a new kind of data, which is recorded as data segment. Because it does not contain continues bytes, SP cannot get the useful information of original data. As a result, the security problem of storage and transfer can be solved.

3   Security Protocal Based on Data Segment

Backup service which stores data segments can handle the security problem mentioned above. This section will present how to solve them between SP and SUs.

3.1   Confidentiality

When an attacker or SP gets some data segment of original data, he cannot get useful information because each segment does not contain continue bytes. Even if he has gotten all the data segments, he must deal with the cube recovery problem before he knows the meaning of the SU's data.

Suppose the backup data is split into N fragments, attacker needs to find right size of split matrix in many options which must satisfy $(m,n) \in \{m \times n = N, m \geq 5, n \geq 5\}$ and record as ps. Besides, there will have $s = N!$ kinds of recovery methods if attacker gathered all segments. Although s is large, it may be tried out by attackers when keeping secret for a long period. But SA partitions split matrices into p groups and uses different tour path. Attacker or SP needs to reconstruct original data of each group with the right tour path. So the 'decryption spaces' ds will become a huge space which can be calculated by $ds = ps \times (N!)^p$. For example ds will be 6.719×10^{712} if SA chooses parameter as $m = n = 8$, and make totally 8 groups.

3.2   Integrity

Data segments will face the risk of being changed or destroyed during store in the SP cloud. If it cannot be detected, data will never be recovered. SA uses unbreakable hash check number to check data integrity before reconstructing original data. Because it is scrambled by coordinate information, it cannot be forged unless the attacker gets the right way to generate it. And different segment uses different functions for scrambling. Only legal users who have the right tour path can get the coordinate information from segment head and generate right scramble function.

While reading data from clouds, SA calculates MD5 of each data segment's body part and generates function (1) to scramble it. And SA inserts $x_i \times m + y_j$ at u_{id}. If the number newly generated dose not equal segment head, this segment must be fault.

3.3   Trust without Third Party

SUs still wonder whether the cloud is secure and there are at least two concerns. One is that the users who do not have confidence worry about that their backup data may be disclosed to SP. The other is whether the data that SUs receives from the cloud is integrity[4]. In addition, the repudiation issue may open a door to blackmailers when user turned to be malicious.

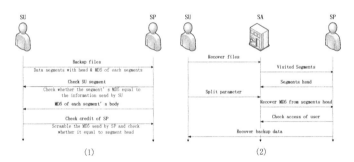

Fig. 4. Interact protocol. (1)Data Integrity check without TTP; (2) Data access check.

Many schemes use trusted third party (TTP) [3] as an intercessor. These schemes bring a lot of risks while transform data and information between the two parts. In our model, confidentiality and integrity can be achieved under the condition that uploading and downloading phase must be handled separately.

We proposed a new protocol without TTP as Fig.4 (1), and the step as follows:

1. SU splits backup files into data segments and sends them with theirs' MD5 to SP.
2. SP gets data segments and theirs' MD5. He will check whether the MD5 of each segment equal to the MD5 sent by SU.
3. SP sends MD5 of each segment body to SU.
4. SU scrambles the MD5 received and check whether it equals to segment head.

Because SP cannot forge segment head, SU can check whether the data received and stored in SP is correct. By checking the data segment's MD5 sent by SU, SP can make sure whether the SU is a blackmailer when data were broken.

3.4   Data access

When SP provides disaster-recovery service for multiple users, data access will become a serious problem. This security policy must be adhered by the SP to avoid intrusion by unauthorized or illegal users. Our scheme uses data segment head to identify whether the visitor is legal. The step is shown in Fig.4(2), and SU must follow these steps to check whether he can visit these data.

1. SU sends request of data recovery to SA and SA send this request to SP.
2. SP reads the data segments head which SA requested and sends it to SA.
3. SU sends recovery function to SA for recovering MD5 from each segment head.
4. SA sends these MD5 of segment body to SP for check and open access to SU.
5. SA recovers the original data to SU.

With this scheme, only legal users can visit and recover the backup files requested.

4   Evaluation and Other Issue

We design a series of experiments to analyze the efficiency of ESSA use a Personal Computer, which has Intel® Core™2 Duo CPU E7500, 2GB RAM and Microsoft Windows XP SP3. Other algorithms used are provided by crypto++ algorithm library 5.6.1.

4.1   Time Request

We compared data processing of our scheme using 8×8 matrix split original data, IDA, Secret Sharing and crypto scheme RC4 while processing 10MB files. As our scheme use 8×8 split matrix to split data into 64 pieces, this experiment compares IDA and Secret Sharing when they also split data into 64 pieces.

Table 1. Time request of data processing scheme

Scheme	Parameter	Time Cost (seconds)
Our Scheme	with 8×8 split matrix	8.92926
IDA	1-64-64	51.0112
Secret Sharing	8-8-64	401.231
RC4	-	5.03427

Table 1 show that our scheme takes great time efficiency while processing data. It is suitable for data disaster-recovery service, especially when processing mass data for service users.

4.2   Storage Requirement

Our scheme only makes $33 \times n$ bytes check information to provide security services, which is more efficiency than any other scheme shown in Table 2. Replication, IDA and Secret Sharing cost different storage space when splitting (data size is L bytes) by $1 - m - n$ threshold. But our scheme can be seen as a $1 - n - n$ scheme enjoys greater storage cost efficiency than them.

Table 2. Time request of data processing scheme

Scheme	Parameter	Storage Cost (bytes)
Our Scheme	$1 - n - n$	$L + 33 \times n$
Replication	$1 - 1 - n$	nL
IDA	$1 - m - n$	nL / m
Secret Sharing	$1 - m - n$	nL

4.3   Cloud Resource Cost

With cloud storage especially for data disaster-recovery services, all customers will pay for storage resource they used. Take Amazon S3 storage system for example (Table 3), storage pricing is changing with the increasing of storage.

Table 3. Storage Pricing of Amazon S3

Data size	Standard Storage	Reduced Redundancy Storage
First 1 TB / month	$0.140 per GB	$0.093 per GB
Next 49 TB / month	$0.125 per GB	$0.083 per GB

According to Table 2, our scheme only cost a little extra storage for segments head. It only associates with the size of split matrix, which also influences on the confidentiality. So it is necessary to concern the extra cost. Then the cost based on Amazon S3 price is shown in Table 4, and $N = 0$ means backup file without our processing.

Table 4. Price of Backup Files

File Size (TB)	Standard Storage ($)			Reduced Redundancy Storage ($)		
	N=0	N=64	N=100	N=0	N=64	N=100
1	143.36	143.62	143.76	95.23	95.40	95.50
50	6415.36	6415.59	6415.71	4259.84	4259.99	4260.08

Table 4 shows that the extra cost storage is less than 20 cents, which can be ignored as the size of backup files become bigger. Thus the our security scheme dose not bring much more costs for users and they can store their backup file in cloud and choose the highest split matrix as they need.

5   Conclusion

This paper presents a data split model for data backup and a set of security protocols for ensuring the confidentiality, integrity and privacy of customers' data when building data disaster-recovery services on cloud. The time cost and storage cost of this scheme is proved to be efficiency and will not bring too much extra costs for service users. Future extensions will be: (1) consider reliability of data disaster recovery services for long-lived sensitive backups; (2) service users always distrust the provider, we insist on provide a disaster-recovery model based on different public clouds and private cloud, so that service provider does not hold all segments; (3) provide detailed analysis and evaluation of the system implementation.

Acknowledgment. This study is supported by the National High Technology Research and Development Program("863"Program) of China(2012AA012600) and the Fundamental Research Funds for the Central Universities (2011RCZJ16) and China High Technology Development Project (NDRC) and China Information Security Special Fund (NDRC).

References

1. Subashini, S., Kavitha, V.: A survey on Security issues in service delivery models of cloud computing. Review Article, Journal of Network and Computer Applications 34, 1–11 (2011)
2. Svantesson, D., Clarke, R.: Privacy and consumer risks in cloud computing. Computer Law & Security Review 26, 391–397 (2010)
3. Pearson, S., Benameur, A.: Privacy, Security and Trust issues Arising from Cloud Computing. In: The 2nd IEEE International Conference on Cloud Computing Technology and Science, pp. 693–702. IEEE Press
4. Feng, J., Chen, Y., Ku, W., Liu, P.: Analysis of Integrity Vulnerabilities and a Non-repudiation Protocol for Cloud Data Storage Platforms. In: The 2010 39th International Conference on Parallel Processing Workshops, pp. 251–258. IEEE Press (2010)
5. Khan, K.M.: Security Dynamics of Cloud Computing. Cutter IT Journal, 38–43 (June/July 2009)
6. Sato, H., Kanai, A., Tanimoto, S.: A Cloud Trust Model in a Security Aware Cloud. In: The 2010 10th IEEE/IPSJ International Symposium on Applications and the Internet, pp. 121–124. IEEE Press (2010)
7. Ahamed, S.I., Sharmin, M.: A trust-based secure service discovery (TSSD) model for pervasive computing. Computer Communications 31, 4281–4293 (2008)
8. Heiser, J., Nicolett, M.: Assessing the Security Risks of Cloud Computing. Gartner Inc. (June 2008)
9. Chen, Z., Yao, W.B., Xiao, D., Wu, C.H., Liu, J.Y., Wang, C.: ESSA: An Efficient and Secure Splitting Algorithm for Distributed Storage Systems. China Communications 04, 89–95 (2010)

Towards Analyzing Traceability of Data Leakage by Malicious Insiders[*]

Xiao Wang[1,2,3,4], Jinqiao Shi[2,4], and Li Guo[2,4]

[1] Institute of Computing Technology, CAS, China
[2] Institute of Information Engineering, CAS, China
[3] Graduate University, CAS, China
[4] Chinese National Engineering Laboratory for Information Security Technologies
{wangxiao,shijinqiao,guoli}@software.ict.ac.cn

Abstract. Data leakage committed by malicious insiders proposes a serious challenge for business secrets and intellectual property. Great efforts have been made to detect and mitigate insider threat. Due to the diversity in the motivations, previous work in this field mostly focuses on designing data holder's data distribution and insider tracing algorithms, with little consideration of malicious insiders' leakage strategies. In this paper, the traitors tracing problem is modeled as an incremental refining multi-step process. For each step, a metric is proposed to measure the efficiency of current tracing status. Theoretical and simulating analysis shows that malicious insiders can adopt sophisticated leakage strategies, which makes it difficult to distinguish them from others and leads to more innocent users involved as suspects. Thus it is important for the data holder to figure out the insiders' leakage strategies and adopt proper tracing scheme to improve the refining process.

Keywords: data leakage, data distribution, insider tracing.

1 Introduction

In the information age, a compelling need is emerging for the secure dissemination of data. Data dissemination plays an important role in our daily life. For example, medical records published by hospitals can help researchers devise new treatments; business information shared between multiple partners can help them respond to business opportunities rapidly. However, data dissemination may also leads to a serious problem of data leakage. The reveal of patients' names or business information can cause serious consequences thus posing a security challenge in the dissemination of data.

From the perspective of leakage protection, ways of data dissemination are classified into two types in this paper. The first type is called data publishing, where the

---

[*] This work is supported by National Natural Science Foundation of China (Grant No.6100174), National Key Technology R&D Program (Grant No.2012BAH37B04) and Strategic Priority Research Program of the Chinese Academy of Sciences (Grant No. XDA06030200).

Y. Yuan, X. Wu, and Y. Lu (Eds.): ISCTCS 2012, CCIS 320, pp. 148–155, 2013.

data holder publishes the data and makes them publicly available. Various methods [13][10] are adopted to anonymize the data and release them with guarantees that the objects in the published data cannot be re-identified while the data remain practically useful. Researches in secure data publishing try to provide a better tradeoff between privacy preservation and data usability.

The second type of data dissemination is called data distribution, where the data holder shares data only with third parties that he trusts. Since the data holder trusts these third parties, he can share the unrevised version of data with them and track malicious insiders (i.e. traitors) when a leakage comes up. For example, in the field of proxies distribution [3][1], proxy addresses are distributed to trusted users directly. In Tor [4] bridge's distribution, the distributor trusts all its users and shares three bridge addresses with each of them [3]. However, compromised users controlled by censors may hide among them, posing a serious threat to the accessibility of these bridges. Once some bridges become inaccessible, the distributor can identify users with whom he shared these bridges as suspected compromised users. One of the most important tasks in data distribution is to design algorithms that help identify malicious insiders efficiently.

This paper focuses on traitors tracing problem in data distribution where supposed honest third parties may leak data objects that the data holder shares with them. The secure data distribution discussed here are studied in many areas such as key predistribution in WSNs [14], proxy distribution in overlay networks [3][9] and traitors tracing in rebroadcasts of movies [5][12][8][7]. Due to the diversity in the motivations, researches in these areas mostly study this problem from the data holder's standpoint, focusing on some specific aspects of data distribution rather than its whole process. In this paper, the traitors tracing problem is modeled as an incremental refining multi-step process, and each step is further considered to have three essential phases. An efficiency metric is proposed to measure the current tracing status in each step. An analysis of tracing efficiency over different scenarios shows how the tracing result is influenced by strategies adopted by both the data holder and malicious insiders. The main contributions of this paper are as follows:

- An incremental refining multi-step model of the traitors tracing problem is presented (Section 2). Each step is further divided into three essential phases (Section 2): data allocation, data leakage and insider tracing.
- A tracing efficiency metric (Section 3) for each step, as well as an analysis over different scenarios (Section 4) is presented. The result shows that, malicious insiders can adopt sophisticated leakage strategies to protect themselves from being identified efficiently. And it's important for the data holder to adopt proper tracing schemes based on insiders' leakage strategies.

2   Traitors Tracing Problem and Model

Fig. 1 reveals a data distribution process with two types of players: a *distributor* who owns the data and shares them with others; *members* who request and get data objects from the distributor. Each member plays the role of either an *honest member* or an *insider*. Compare with the honest members, insiders tend to leak data objects they got.

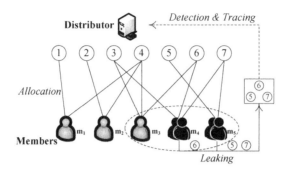

Fig. 1. An simple example of the traitors tracing problem

Traitors tracing problem is considered as an incremental refining multi-step process. Each step contains the following three phases:

1. **Data Allocation:** The distributor shares data objects with each member to satisfy their request. The scheme used by the distributor to allocate different data objects to different members is called *data allocation scheme*.
2. **Data leakage:** Insiders leak data objects they got. The leakage method used by insiders is called *data leakage strategy*. Four different kinds of data leakage strategies are present in Section 4.
3. **Insider tracing:** Based on the leaked data objects, the distributor can identify members with whom he shared these data objects with as suspected insiders (i.e., *suspects set*). The scheme used here is called *insider tracing scheme*. There are also four insider tracing schemes presented in Section 4 corresponding to the four data leakage strategies.

The traitors tracing problem is an incremental refining process consisting of multiple steps presented above. In each step, the data holder can identify some members as suspects. In the next step, the data holder can further exclude few of them from the suspects set, i.e., reduce the size of suspects set. This paper focuses on the single three-phase step, for it is the basis of the whole multi-step traitors tracing process.

Let $D = \{d_1, d_2, \cdots\}$ to be the data objects held by the distributor and $M = \{m_1, m_2, \cdots\}$ to be the members with whom the distributor shares data. D_i is used to denote data objects that the distributor shares with m_i. Insiders are denoted by I, $I \subseteq M$. Data objects leaked by these insiders are denoted by D^*, $D^* \subseteq \bigcup_{m_i \in I} D_i \subseteq D$. Based on the relation between D^* and D_i, the distributor can find some suspected insiders denoted by S. For example, in Fig. 1, $D = \{d_1, d_2, \cdots, d_7\}$, $M = \{m_1, m_2, \cdots, m_5\}$ and $I = \{m_4, m_5\}$. Data objects allocated to each members in M are $D_1 = \{d_1, d_4\}$, $D_2 = \{d_2, d_4\}$, $D_3 = \{d_3, d_4, d_6\}$, $D_4 = \{d_3, d_6, d_7\}$ and $D_5 = \{d_5, d_7\}$. Data objects leaked by I are $D^* = \{d_5, d_6, d_7\}$. As shown in the figure, the distributor traces a suspected insider set $S = \{m_3, m_4, m_5\}$, for each of these suspects knows at least one of the leaked data objects.

Formally, a data allocation scheme is a function $\mathcal{A}: (D, M) \mapsto D_i$ where $i = 1, \cdots, |M|$. The data leakage strategy is also a function $\mathcal{L}: D_i \mapsto D_i^*$ where $m_i \in I$

and $D^* = \bigcup_{m_i \in I} D_i^*$. $\mathcal{T} : (D, D^*) \mapsto S$ denotes the insider tracing scheme. $\mathcal{T}$ is actually a scheme based on the relation between D_i and D^*, i.e., whether $D_i \propto D^*$: if $D_i \propto D^*$, the member m_i is taken as a suspected insider; otherwise, $m_i \notin S$. The relation denoted by $D_i \propto D^*$ is different in different tracing schemes.

3   Traceability and Tracing Efficiency

Traceability is defined as the data holder's ability to trace insiders in the traitors tracing problem. And *tracing efficiency* is defined as a metric to measure the current tracing status of each step. We focus on tracing efficiency in this paper for it's the basis of traceability analysis. In each step, the relation among members, suspects and insiders can be denoted as $M \supseteq S \supseteq I$. The expression "$S \supseteq I$" implies that, there are no false negatives when tracing insiders. This can be achieved by adopt a proper insider tracing scheme, even a "loose" relation between D^* and D_i when making a decision. However, there may be some honest members included in the suspects set, i.e., there exists some false positives. Tracing efficiency can be viewed as the distributor's ability to identify insiders who hide themselves among suspects set. Both the number of insiders and the size of the suspects set should be taken into consideration. In this paper, tracing efficiency in data distribution is defined as the number of insiders divided by the expected size of the insiders' suspects set as show in (1). The maximum value of $TEff$ is 1 which means all the suspects identified by the distributor are insiders. The minimum value of $TEff$ is $|I|/|M|$ which means the distributor identifies every member to be a suspected insider.

$$TEff = \frac{|I|}{\mathrm{E}\{|S|\}} \tag{1}$$

For each honest member, whether $m_i \in S$ (i.e., $D_i \propto D^*$) or not is independent with each other. Let $P_{\mathcal{T}}$ to be the probability of an honest member being judged as a suspected insider (i.e., false positive) under $\mathcal{T}$ tracing scheme. The expected size of insiders' suspects set can be denoted by (2).

$$\mathrm{E}\{|S_{\mathcal{T}}|\} = |I| + (|M| - |I|)P_{\mathcal{T}} \tag{2}$$

4   Tracing Efficiency Analysis

In this section, we present a few scenarios and analyze the tracing efficiency of in a single step under these scenarios. The scenarios presented here include a data allocation scheme, some different data leakage strategies, insider tracing schemes and the combinations of them. We give a theoretical analysis of tracing efficiency under each scenario. Besides, a simulation program written in Python [2] is implemented to simulate the whole three-phase process and produce the simulated tracing efficiency result.

Uniform Random Data Distribution Scheme. Uniform random data allocation scheme is a simple scheme that allocate data objects to each members in M. The distributor is supposed to share a uniformly random subset of size k from D with each member, i.e., $D_i = k$.

Data Leakage Methods and Insider Tracing Schemes. Typically, a leakage can take place in the following four ways:

1. **TS:** A single insider leaks all data objects he got from the distributor. $I = \{m_i\}$ and $D^* = D_i^* = D_i$.
2. **PS:** A single insider leaks part of data objects set he got from the distributor. $I = \{m_i\}$ and $D^* = D_i^* \subseteq D_i$.
3. **TC:** Colluding insiders leak all data objects they got from the distributor. $I = \{m_i, m_j, \cdots\}$ and $D^* = \bigcup_{m_i \in I} D_i^* = \bigcup_{m_i \in I} D_i$.
4. **PC:** Colluding insiders leak part of data objects they got from the distributor. $I = \{m_i, m_j, \cdots\}$ and $D^* = \bigcup_{m_i \in I} D_i^* \subseteq \bigcup_{m_i \in I} D_i$.

Table 1. Tracing insiders under different tracing schemes

	Single Insider(S)	Colluding Insiders(C)
Total Leakage(T)	$D_i = D^*$	$D_i \subseteq D^*$
Partial Leakage(P)	$D_i \supseteq D^*$	$D_i \cap D^* \neq \emptyset$

The four insider tracing schemes corresponding to these different leakage strategies are shown in Table 1. The table also gives conditions to judge a member as suspect using these different tracing schemes, i.e., a specific relation between D_i and D^* formerly denoted by "$D_i \propto D^*$" in Section 2. Suspect sets under different tracing schemes are different. Table 1 shows that, condition in "TS" scheme is strictest and leads to a smaller set of suspects. Conditions in "TC" and "PS" schemes are a little looser. "PC" scheme adopts the loosest condition when judging a member, thus leading to a much larger suspects set when tracing insiders.

Table 2. $P_{\mathcal{T}}$ under tracing schemes $\mathcal{T}$

	Single Insider(S)	Colluding Insiders(C)
Total Leakage(T)	$\dfrac{1}{\binom{|D|}{k}}$	$\dfrac{\binom{|D^*|}{k}}{\binom{|D|}{k}}$
Partial Leakage(P)	$\dfrac{\binom{|D|-|D^*|}{k-|D^*|}}{\binom{|D|}{k}}$	$1 - \dfrac{\binom{|D|-|D^*|}{k}}{\binom{|D|}{k}}$

Theoretic Tracing Efficiency. As shown in Table 2, in each tracing scheme, the probability of an honest member being judged as a suspected insider can be denoted by a function of D, D^* and k. Together with (1) and (2), the theoretic tracing efficiency can be calculated accordingly.

Experiments and Results. The uniform random data allocation scheme, data leakage and insider tracing schemes are implemented to simulate the whole data distribution process. Both the theoretic results and average results over many independent simulation runs are presented in the following experiments.

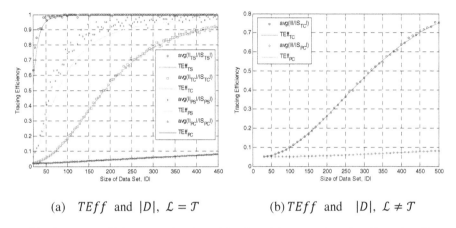

(a) $TEff$ and $|D|$, $\mathcal{L} = \mathcal{T}$ (b) $TEff$ and $|D|$, $\mathcal{L} \neq \mathcal{T}$

Fig. 2. Tracing efficiency as a function of the size of data set, when $\mathcal{L} = \mathcal{T}$ or $\mathcal{L} \neq \mathcal{T}$

The first experiment is used to study the relation between the amount of data objects and tracing efficiency under each scenario. In this experiment, the distributor has a set of $|D|$ data objects from which he shares a random subset of $k=3$ objects with each of the $|M|=1000$ members. All four data leakage strategies are studied in this experiment. The distributor is supposed to know the data leakage strategies used by the insiders and utilize the corresponding insider tracing schemes to trace them, i.e., $\mathcal{L} = \mathcal{T}$. Particularly, when studying the colluding leakage strategies ("TC" and "PC"), we suppose there are $|I|=20$ insiders among $|M|$ members; when studying the partial leakage strategies ("PS" and "PC"), we suppose the insiders randomly leak 2 data objects out of 3. Fig. 2(a) shows how $|D|$ affects the tracing efficiency in data distribution. There are 2 curves for each data leakage strategy (insider tracing scheme) in the plot. The solid curve shows theoretic $TEff$[1]. The other one shows the average of $|I|/|S|$ over 50 independent simulation runs. It reveals that:

1. $|D|$ is positively correlated with the tracing efficiency. The underlying reason is that, as the amount of data objects increase, $P_{\mathcal{T}}$ presented in Table 2 tends to decrease and approach its lower limit of 0. As a result, the increment in $|D|$ can drive $TEff$ to approach its upper limit of 1 (See (1) and (2)).

---

[1] $|D^*|$ in Table 2 is replaced with $E\{|D^*|\}$ when calculating the theoretic tracing efficiency. $E\{|D^*|\}$ can be calculated by a conclusion of the "Occupancy Problem" [6]: $E\{|D^*|\} = |D| - |D|(1 - k^*/|D|)^{|I|}$, in which $k^*=3$ for total leakage and $k^*=2$ for partial leakage in our scenarios.

2. "TS" leads to the best tracing efficiency while "PC" results in the worst one. This can be explained as a result of the different conditions to judge a member as suspect under different scenarios.

The first experiment can help both the distributor and insiders in the following ways: the distributor can try to enlarge its data set to improve the tracing efficiency; while the insiders can adopt "PC" leakage strategy to weaken it.

The second experiment reveals that the tracing scheme of data holder has a significant impact on the tracing efficiency in data distribution. In this experiment, let $k=3$, $|M|=1000$, $|I|=50$ and $\mathcal{L}$="TC". Both "TC" and "PC" tracing schemes are studied here. The theoretic tracing efficiency as well as the average of $|I|/|S|$ over 50 simulation runs are show in Fig. 2(b). It shows that the tracing efficiency under both "TC" and "PC" tracing scheme is positively correlated with the size of data set. However, in this experiment, when "PC" tracing scheme is adopted to trace leakage committed by insiders with "TC" leakage strategy, the tracing efficiency is much lower than it should be.

This experiments shows that, when a loose tracing scheme is adopted to trace leakage committed by insiders with other leakage strategies, it may lead to a much lower tracing efficiency. However, when the insiders' leakage strategy is unknown, the distributor should not adopt a strict tracing scheme because it may bring false negative into the tracing result. Thus, it is important for the data holder to figure out the insiders' leakage strategies and adopt proper tracing schemes.

5   Related Work

In the key predistribution and proxy distribution ares, data distribution phase of the traitors tracing problem is well studied. In [14], the authors introduced a model for key predistribution which is used to assign cryptographic seeds to sensor nodes in WSNs. They also analyzed these schemes in terms of resilience to node capture which causes a key leakage. Tor [4][3] introduced some bridge distribution strategies to prevent adversaries from knowing too many of them. Both [14] and [3] focus on the data allocation phase with the purpose of mitigating data leakage. From the perspective of efficient insider tracing, the authors of [11] considered the design of data allocation schemes as an optimization problem and proposed a series of data distribution strategies that improve the probability of identifying leakage.

In the area of movies rebroadcasting, the traitors tracing problem is modeled as a two-part problem: watermark distribution algorithm and tracing/incrimination [5]. Research in this area tries to provide the center (source of the content) with effective algorithms that help distinguish insiders from all other subscribers.

In this paper, these related researches are furthered by a three-phase model of traitors tracing problem as well as a general tracing efficiency metric of the whole data distribution process.

6   Conclusion and Future Work

This paper gives an incremental refining multi-step model of the traitors tracing problem. Each step is modeled and formalized as a three-phase process. As a metric measure the current tracing status in each step, tracing efficiency is introduced. We also give a few data leakage scenarios that combine a data allocation scheme, different data leakage strategies and insider tracing schemes. Analysis shows that, malicious insiders can adopt sophisticated leakage strategies to protect themselves from being identified efficiently. And it is important for the data holder to figure out the insiders' leakage strategies and adopt proper tracing scheme to improve the refining process.

We hope this paper will encourage additional research in these aspects: (1) analyzing tracing efficiency of data leakage under more practical data allocation scheme; (2) designing and improving algorithms in traitors tracing problem, for the purpose of optimizing the multi-step tracing process.

References

1. Psiphon design overview 1.0,
   `http://psiphon.ca/documents/Psiphon_Design_Overview_1_0.pdf`
2. Python programming language, `http://www.python.org/`
3. Dingledine, R., Mathewson, N.: Design of a blocking-resistant anonymity system. Tech. rep., The Tor Project (2006)
4. Dingledine, R., Mathewson, N., Syverson, P.: Tor: the second-generation onion router. In: Proceedings of the 13th Conference on USENIX Security Symposium, vol. 13. USENIX Association (2004)
5. Fiat, A., Tassa, T.: Dynamic traitor tracing. Journal of Cryptology 14, 211–223 (2001)
6. Gittelsohn, A.: An occupancy problem. American Statistician, 11–12 (1969)
7. Jin, H., Lotspiech, J., Megiddo, N.: Effcient Coalition Detection in Traitor Tracing. In: Jajodia, S., Samarati, P., Cimato, S. (eds.) Proceedings of The Ifip Tc 11 23rd International Information Security Conference. IFIP, vol. 278, pp. 365–380. Springer, Boston (2008)
8. Jin, H., Lotspiech, J., Nusser, S.: Traitor tracing for prerecorded and recordable media. In: Proceedings of the 4th ACM Workshop on Digital Rights Management, pp. 83–90. ACM (2004)
9. McCoy, D., Morales, J.A., Levchenko, K.: Proximax: Measurement-Driven Proxy Dissemination (Short Paper). In: Danezis, G. (ed.) FC 2011. LNCS, vol. 7035, pp. 260–267. Springer, Heidelberg (2012)
10. Nergiz, M.E., Atzori, M., Clifton, C.: Hiding the presence of individuals from shared databases. In: Proceedings of the 2007 ACM SIGMOD International Conference on Management of Data, pp. 665–676. ACM (2007)
11. Papadimitriou, P., Garcia-Molina, H.: Data leakage detection. IEEE Transactions on Knowledge and Data Engineering 23(1), 51–63 (2011)
12. Safavi-Naini, R., Wang, Y.: Sequential traitor tracing. IEEE Transactions on Information Theory 49(5), 1319–1326 (2003)
13. Sweeney, L.: k-anonymity: A model for protecting privacy. International Journal of Uncertainty Fuzziness and Knowledge-Based Systems 10(5), 557–570 (2002)
14. Tague, P., Poovendran, R.: A canonical seed assignment model for key predistribution in wireless sensor networks. ACM Trans. Sen. Netw. 3 (2007)

Dynamic Task Scheduling in Cloud Computing Based on Greedy Strategy

Liang Ma[1,2], Yueming Lu[1,2], Fangwei Zhang[3], and Songlin Sun[1,2]

[1] School of Information and Communication Engineering,
Beijing University of Posts and Telecommunications, Beijing, China
[2] Key Laboratory of Trustworthy Distributed Computing and Service (BUPT),
Ministry of Education, Beijing, China
mal327@sina.com, {ymlu,slsun}@bupt.edu.cn
[3] School of Humanities, Beijing University of Posts and Telecommunications, Beijing, China
zhangfangwei@bupt.edu.cn

Abstract. Task scheduling is essentially an NP-completeness problem in cloud computing and the existing task scheduling strategies can't fully meet its demands. In this paper, a feasible and flexible dynamic task scheduling scheme *DGS* is proposed, which dynamically allocates virtual resources to execute computing tasks and promptly completes the scheduling and execution process by using improved greedy strategy. The simulation platform CloudSim is expanded to realize the proposed scheme and the simulation results show that *DGS* can speed up the tasks' completion time and improve the utilization of cloud resources to achieve load balance.

Keywords: cloud computing, dynamic task scheduling, greedy strategy, load balance, completion time.

1 Introduction

In cloud computing [1], virtualization technology hides the heterogeneity of the resources. They are no longer physical entities but instead a huge resource pool that consists of abundant virtual machines (VMs).The basic mechanism of cloud computing is to distribute computing tasks to the virtual resource pool, which enables a variety of applications to gain computing power, storage and a variety of software services according to their needs [2]. Thus an appropriate task scheduling strategy is needed as a support.

The traditional scheduling schemes usually assume all computing nodes available for processing which is not reliable in some scenarios[3],such as round-robin algorithm, max-min algorithm, min-min algorithm and least-connection scheduling algorithm [4].So they don't meet the characteristics of cloud computing. Fortunately, many efficient scheduling strategies have been proposed by the major cloud computing vendors such as IBM's Tivoli, Amazon's EC2, Microsoft's Dryad and Google's MapReduce[5]. But a uniform standard to evaluate the methods is yet to be achieved. Task scheduling in cloud computing is essentially an NP-completeness problem while heuristic intelligent scheduling algorithms have been quite mature in seeking the optimal

Y. Yuan, X. Wu, and Y. Lu (Eds.): ISCTCS 2012, CCIS 320, pp. 156–162, 2013.
© Springer-Verlag Berlin Heidelberg 2013

solution, such as genetic algorithm, simulated annealing algorithm, ant colony algorithm and so on [6].But with the growing number of tasks and resources, the complexity of these algorithms will become very high.

The current research of dynamic resource allocation and task scheduling mainly focused on dividing onerous tasks into multiple subtasks for optimal solution and migrating VMs for load balance. But in fact the divided subtasks usually can't conduct parallel computing due to strong backward and forward linkages. Furthermore, cloud platform may be suspended because of the mandatory shutdown of the associated VMs during migration process [7].

To address the problems, *DGS* is proposed which is described in detail in section 2.It monitors and calculates the actual amount of resources required by applications, dynamically adjusts virtual resources to increase resource utilization and achieve load balance. Meanwhile, improved greedy strategy is used to dynamically distribute tasks to appropriate computing nodes in order to respond to users quickly. We also conduct performance studies in CloudSim [8] environment and compare the performance of *DGS* with round-robin algorithm and min-min algorithm in section 3.

2   A Feasible and Flexible Dynamic Task Scheduling Scheme *DGS*

According to the above explanation, *DGS* mainly focused on dynamically allocating VMs and distributing tasks by greedy strategy. In order to realize *DGS*, a task scheduling node is divided into four modules to carry on scheduling process, including Service Request Module (SRM), VMs Monitoring and Managing Module (VMM), Routing Analysis Module (RAM) and Task Scheduling Module (TSM).

2.1   Quantification of Tasks and VMs

When the cloud receive the requests of users, TSM will firstly quantify them to computable tasks by the following data structure.

$$Task\{TaskId, TaskIP, Task\ Load, Computing\ Capacity,$$
$$Communication\ Traffic,\ Storage\ Content\}; \tag{1}$$

In (1), *Computing Capacity, Communication Traffic* and *Storage Content* indicate the requirements of each task to the *Computing Power*, *Network Throughput* and *Storage Capacity* of a VM. Corresponding to it, VMs will also be quantified like this.

$$VM\{VM\ Id,\ VM\ IP,\ CPU,\ Memory,\ Computing\ Power,$$
$$Network\ Throughput,\ Storage\ Capacity,\ Running\ Task\}; \tag{2}$$

In this paper, we define the completion time of a task executing on a VM like formula (3).

$$Completion\ time = Computing\ Capacity\ /\ Computing\ Power$$
$$+ Communication\ Traffic\ /\ Network\ Throughput; \tag{3}$$

Assuming the load of a task is L_{task} and the maximum workload of a VM is L_{max}, then the total load of users' requests is L_{total} and the maximum workload of these existed VMs is $L_{bare.}$ Assuming the current workload of a VM is L_{normal}, we define two load factors $Rate_{total}$ and $Rate_{normal}$ to describe the load condition of the whole system and each VM respectively. At the same time, a variable $Rate_{threshold}$ is defined to indicate the threshold rate which is the main criterion to identify whether the system or a VM is overloaded. It's an empirical value here.

$$L_{total} = \sum L_{task};$$ (4)

$$L_{bare} = \sum L_{max};$$ (5)

$$Rate_{total} = L_{total} / L_{bare};$$ (6)

$$Rate_{normal} = L_{normal} / L_{max};$$ (7)

When the problem of load balance is discussed, the load of a server L is often calculated by formula (8), where L_{cpu}, L_{memory}, $L_{network}$ and $L_{storage}$ mean the load of *CPU*, *Memory*, *Network Throughput* and *Storage Capacity*; α, β, γ, $\delta \in [0,1]$and $| \alpha + \beta + \gamma + \delta | = 1$, they represent different weights according to the types of applications.

$$L = \alpha * L_{cpu} + \beta * L_{memory} + \gamma * L_{network} + \delta * L_{storage};$$ (8)

2.2   Dynamic Resource Allocating Method

The main idea of dynamical allocation is to use virtual machine as the minimum resource allocation unit [9]. VMM uses pre-prepared image files with different functions and certain network bandwidth to create new different VMs. As mentioned above, we will dynamically allocate virtual resources in three situations.

First of all, if VMM detects that there is no VM in cloud or the computing power of these VMs is limited, new VMs will be created. It firstly calculates the value of L_{total}, L_{bare} and $Rate_{total}$ through formula (4) (5) (6). Meanwhile the variable $Rate_{threshold}$ here is defined as 0.7to avoid the overload of the whole system when new tasks arrive. If $Rate_{total}$ is smaller than $Rate_{threshold}$, then the existed virtual resources could swimmingly execute the tasks and new VMs don't need to be allocated, or else the number of VMs that we have to create is N so as to ensure the whole network will not overload. N is depicted as follows.

$$N = (L_{total} - L_{bare}) / L_{max};$$ (9)

Secondly, after the fist-timescheduling by greedy strategy, if VMM notices some VMs running in the critical state, it will create new VMs and conduct second-time scheduling. In formula (7), we compute each VM's $Rate_{normal}$ and compare it to $Rate_{threshold}$ which is defined as 1.0 here to avoid the downtime of a VM. If $Rate_{normal}$ is more than $Rate_{threshold}$, the VM is overloaded and VMM will create a new and exactly the same one to it except *VM Id*. Then TSM will assign these tasks in the task queue on the overloaded VM to the two VMs in turn, as shown in Fig.1. If it is still overloaded, the above procedure will be repeated.

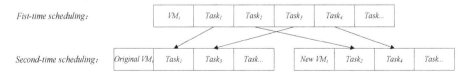

Fig. 1. An example of second-time scheduling

Finally, before executing these assigned tasks, idle VMs will be released to reduce the network load and avoid the waste of resources.

Through the three steps, both the whole network'sworkload and single resource's workload are taken into consideration. In thissituation,resources in cloud will be sufficiently used and network congestion will be avoided.

2.3   Task Scheduling Based on Greedy Strategy

Greedy strategy usually makesthe optimal choice with an optimization measure based on the current situation butregardless of any possible overall situation.It doesn't need to backtrack and the complexity is relatively simple.

Before allocating, TSM will firstly create a Tasks–VMs taboo table, as shown in Fig.4. The left column of the table are tasks which are sorted by computing capacity in decreasing order by SRM and the right column is VMs list.In each row, TSM calls formula (1)(2)(3) to compute the *Completion time*for each task on all VMs and sort the VMs in ascending order.

Table 1. An example of Tasks-VMs taboo table

Tasks	*VMs*				
Task$_2$	*VM$_2$*	*VM$_3$*	*VM$_5$*	*VM$_1$*	*VM...*
Task$_1$	*VM$_4$*	*VM$_2$*	*VM$_3$*	*VM$_5$*	*VM...*
Task$_3$	*VM$_3$*	*VM$_5$*	*VM$_2$*	*VM$_1$*	*VM...*
Task$_4$	*VM$_2$*	*VM$_3$*	*VM$_5$*	*VM$_1$*	*VM...*
...	...				

Then we attempt to assign the task to the VM in the first column of virtual machines list from the first line to ensure thattasks with larger computation quantity will be executed on the VMs with more powerfulexecuting ability. Normally, the chosen VM with strong computing power has already gotsome tasks working on it. Sothe completion time of this being currently assigned task should includetheexecution time of these tasks assigned before if it is assigned to the VM.

Then the current program will be compared to others in whichthis task is assigned to other slightly worse VMs.If the current program is optimal compared to other results, the program is feasible, otherwise we have to choose other optimal programs. In this case, the more sophisticated tasks will be preferentially executed to solve time bottleneck caused by themselves.By recording the parameter *Running Task* of a VM, when there are multiple solutions that can achieve optimal, the task will be assigned to the VM which has the lower resource utilization rate.

In this way, itcannot only quickly complete users' requests but also take fully advantage of the current resources existed in cloud so as to implement asimple load balance.

3   Evaluation

In our work, the simulation platform CloudSim is expanded and applied to realize *DGS*.To have a better view of the advantages of *DGS*, a comparison betweenround-robin algorithm

(RR) and min-min algorithm (MM) is conducted.In initial situation, there are four types of tasks and 15VMsin the system.

Fig.3 shows the comparison of three schemes' completion time inhandling different number of tasks.If the downtime of each VM is not considered, thenthe completion time will grow gradually with the increasing of the number of tasks, just like MM and RR in this figure. But in actual experiments, when the number of tasks increases to 120, many VMs have been overloaded and stopped working. Then *DGS* began to create some new VMs to ensure each VM can work normally and its number is 8 here. Due to creating new VMs to execute the tasks on overloaded VMs, the completion time will be shorter. So the completion time of *DGS*will not grow obviously with the increasing of the number of tasks and it is relatively smoother in Fig.2.

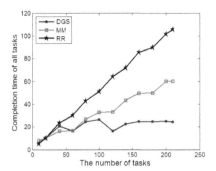
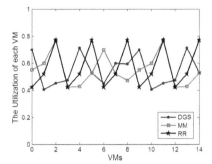

Fig. 2. The comparison of three schemes'   **Fig. 3.** The comparison of three scheme's com-
completion time   pletion time resource utilization with 60 tasks

Fig.3 shows the comparison of three schemes' resource utilization when there are 60 tasks. In this situation, both the whole system and each VM are not overloaded. The resource utilization of three schemes is similar in the figure. So *DGS* doesn't have significant advantageswhen the number of tasks is small.

As shown in Fig.4, when the number of tasks reaches 120, many VMs will be overloaded with the use of MM or RR. And here we set theirutilization to 1, just like the second VM in this figure. Thenthe load of the whole system will become extremely unbalanced. At this time,*DGS* creates8 VMs to make sure no VM is overloaded and the utilization of each VM is relatively more balanced.

When the number of tasks increase to 210, the whole system will be overloaded. Then users' requests will not be respond timely either MM or RR is used. But with *DGS* it can work normally no matter what the number of requests is. In this situation, *DGS* will firstly allocate some new VMs to ensure the whole system is able to work and the number here is 5. Then another 5 new VMs are created during the scheduling process to avoid the overload of each VM. As a result, there are 25 VMs here after the accomplishment of scheduling. As shown in Fig.5, the resource utilization of each VM is high and under the critical point.

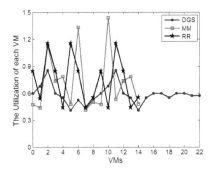
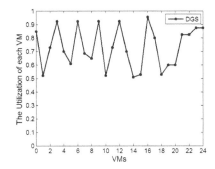

Fig. 4. The comparison of three schemes'

Fig. 5. The resource utilization of DGS resource utilization with 120 tasks with 210 tasks

From the simulation, we can see *DGS* plays a significant role if the number of tasks is large. It can promptly deal with the requests of users and relatively achieve load balance at the same time. With the growing number of tasks, *DGS* will have better-performance and adapt to the characteristics of cloud computing better. But the premise is to consume more hardware resources because more VMs are allocated during the process.

4   Conclusions

In this paper, an efficient dynamic task scheduling scheme based on greedy strategy named *DGS* is proposed to deal with the requests of users as soon as possible on the premise of load balance. Through the expansionofCloudSim, *DGS*has been simulated and the experiment results show that the new scheme can dynamically allocate VMs to reach load balance rate and rapidly finish executing tasks by greedy strategy.Moreover, it's easy to implement in the realistic situation and will achieve great effect. During the research we haven't taken the cost of virtual resources and the prediction of users' requests into consideration.That will be studied in the future research.

Acknowledgments. This research was supported in part by National 863 Program (No. 2011AA01A204), National 973 Program (No. 2011CB302702), P. R. China. Thanks for the great help.

References

1. Armbrust, M., Fox, A., Griffith, R., et al.: Above the Clouds: A Berkeley View of Cloud Computing. Technical Report, No. UCB/EECS-2009-28 (2009)
2. Baomin, X., Chunyan, Z., Enzhao, H., Bin, H.: Job scheduling algorithm based on Berger model in cloud environment. J. Advances in Engineering Software (2011)
3. Xiangzhen, K., Chuang, L., Yixin, J., Wei, Y., Xiaowen, C.: Efficient dynamic task scheduling in virtualized data centers with fuzzy prediction. Journal of Network and Computer Applications 34(4), 1068–1077 (2011)

4. Chauhan, S.S., Joshi, R.C.: A Weighted Mean Time Min-Min Max-Min Selective Scheduling Strategy for Independent Tasks on Grid. In: 2010 IEEE 2nd International Advance Computing Conference on (IACC), pp. 4–9. IEEE Press, Patiala (2010)
5. Dean, J., Ghemawat, S.: MapReduce: Simplified Data Processing on Large Clusters. Communications of the ACM - 50th Anniversary Issue: 1958–2008 51(1), 107–113 (2008)
6. Abdulal, W., Ramachandram, S.: Reliability-Aware Genetic Scheduling Algorithm in Grid Environment. In: 2011 International Conference on Communication Systems and Network Technologies (CSNT), pp. 673–677. IEEE Press, Katra (2011)
7. Warneke, D., Kao, O.: Exploiting Dynamic Resource Allocation for Efficient Parallel Data Processing in the Cloud. IEEE Transactions on Parallel and Distributed Systems 22(6), 985–997 (2011)
8. Calheiros, R.N., Ranjan, R., Rose, C.A.F.D., Buyya, R.: CloudSim: A Novel Framework for modeling and Simulation of Cloud Computing Infrastructures and Services. Technical report (2009)
9. Weiwei, L., James, Z.W., Chen, L., Deyu, Q.: A Threshold-based Dynamic Resource Allocation Scheme for Cloud Computing. J. Procedia Engineering 23, 695–703 (2011)

A Multi-modal Clustering Method for Web Videos

Haiqi Huang[1], Yueming Lu[1], Fangwei Zhang[2], and Songlin Sun[1]

[1] School of Information and Communication Engineering,
Beijing University of Posts and Telecommunications, Beijing, China
hqhuang@bupt.edu.cn
[2] School of Humanities, Beijing University of Posts and Telecommunications, Beijing, China
zhangfangwei@bupt.edu.cn
[3] Key Laboratory of Trustworthy Distributed Computing and Service (BUPT),
Ministry of Education, Beijing, China
{ymlu,slsun}@bupt.edu.cn

Abstract. The prevalence of video sharing websites brings the explosion of web videos and poses a tough challenge to the web video clustering for their indexing. This paper proposes a flexible multi-modal clustering method for web videos. This method achieves web video representation and similarity measurement by integrating the extracted visual features, semantic features and text features of videos to describe a web video more accurately. With the multi-modal combined similarity as input, the affinity propagation algorithm is employed for the clustering procedure. The clustering method is evaluated by experiments conducted on web video dataset and has a better performance than existing methods.

Keywords: multi-modal, modified Hausdorff distance, similarity fusion, affinity propagation Algorithm, average precision.

1 Introduction

With the impetus from advanced coding technique and prevalent social network services, there is an explosion of web videos which mean video clips or user generated videos from video sharing websites. It is crucial to explore a solution to organize this large-scale dataset orderly for video retrieval and accessing applications. Many video sharing websites such as YouTube [1] addressing this problem with categories, which are labeled by uploading users or website editors, costing so much time and labor and encountering a subjective problem due to diverse comprehension of different people. Besides, automatic video categorization based on supervised or semi-supervised machine learning [2] is also proposed to settle the classification issue. However, the effects of majority of machine learning methodologies heavily rely on sufficient and high-quality training sample sets. As an unsupervised method without dependence on human participation and training sets, data clustering has been used for underlying structure, natural classification and compression [4]. Inspired by the utilization of clustering in text area, many researchers introduce clustering methodologies to multimedia retrieval. Clustering of video search results tends to be a tightly concerned research interest due to ambiguous and duplicate results of search engines [3, 5].

The strategy of multi-modal has been gradually adopted to resolve the issue of video representation and applications based on it, making videos described more accurately.

Y. Yuan, X. Wu, and Y. Lu (Eds.): ISCTCS 2012, CCIS 320, pp. 163–169, 2013.

Advances have been reported in the field of multi-modal retrieval system [6], video search reranking [7], web video categorization [8] and so forth. The fusion of multi-modal has been applied to clustering video search results in [9].

In this paper, we research the web video representation and similarity measurement, and present a novel unsupervised web video clustering approach based on integrating low-level visual, semantic and textual features. The proposed framework for multi-modal integration enables us to exploit state-of-the-art clustering algorithms to accomplish the preliminary classification for web videos. The effectiveness of our clustering scheme is validated by comprehensive experiments.

2   A Multi-modal Clustering Method for Web Videos

2.1   Overview

The framework of our multi-modal clustering scheme is illustrated in Fig. 1. Web videos from dataset are represented by their extracted visual, semantic and textual features respectively using vector space model. Similarity between videos is calculated separately for each feature. A fusion of three similarities then will be computed according to our strategies, and works as the input of the Affinity Propagation clustering algorithm. Finally, the clustering results would form the classification for the dataset.

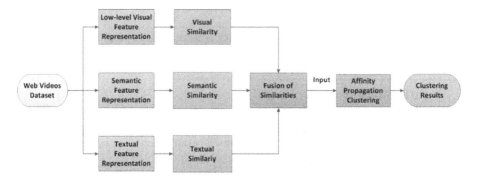

Fig. 1. Framework of proposed multi-modal clustering scheme

2.2   Video Representation

Visual Feature. Color histogram is widely used which represents the number of pixels that have colors in a fixed list of ranges. It is relatively invariant with translation and rotation and varies slowly with the angle of view, making it well suited for recognizing an object in unknown position. However, without shape information, similar objects with different colors may be indistinguishable based solely on color histogram comparisons. Hence we also introduce edge histogram to alleviate this drawback.

Semantic Feature. The video semantic feature means the concept representation for the entire video which can reflect video content. In our scheme, we employ the bag of words model based on extracted SIFT features. Analogous to the Bag of Words in natural language processing, an image can be treated as a document, and features extracted from the local patches in image are considered as the "words". The Scale-invariant feature transform (SIFT) features [10] extracted from the appearance at particular interest points are robust to image scale and rotation, and illumination and minor changes, which make SIFT competent for the descriptor of our BoW model.

Textual Feature. Surrounding textual information is a particular characteristic of web videos which is regarded as a significant supplement to video content, including video titles, tags, descriptions and comments appearing on the related webpage. All of them could give users intuitionistic perception on videos. In consideration of accuracy and relevance, we only introduce titles and tags to the textual feature representation.

2.3   Multi-modality Fusion Strategy

Similarity Measurement for Visual and Semantic Features. Euclidean distance is popularly used to measure the dissimilarity of two vectors composed by features extracted from key frames of video. However, videos usually consist of several key frames and extracting the visual features from which one becomes a complicated issue.

Inspired by this, we treat a video as a set of key frames, and the dissimilarity of two videos is converted into the distance between these two key frame sets. The Modified Hausdorff Distance is introduced to address the issue. Given two finite non-empty key-frame sets M and N, the modified Hausdorff Distance is defined as follow:

$$MHD(M,N) = \max(mhd(M,N), mhd(N,M)), \tag{1}$$

$$mhd(M,N) = \underset{m \in M}{mean}\ \underset{n \in N}{\min}\|m-n\|, \quad mhd(N,M) = \underset{n \in N}{mean}\ \underset{m \in M}{\min}\|n-m\| \tag{2}$$

where $\|x\|$ denotes the normal form of x.

Similarity Measurement for Textual Features. As titles and tags are noisy short texts, method for similarity computation we adopt is somewhat like bag of words: construct a dictionary using all terms existing in texts after preprocessing first; generate a term-document matrix in accordance with the dictionary, and the vector space model using term frequency is employed for textual features representation; finally, the text similarities are computed with normalization used to form the similarity matrix.

Fusion of Similarities. Our multi-modal strategy is embodied with a concise weighted sum of normalized similarities calculated upon different features as:

$$Sim(X,Y) = \alpha * Sim_{visu}(X,Y) + \beta * Sim_{sema}(X,Y) + (1 - \alpha - \beta) * Sim_{text}(X,Y) \tag{3}$$

where $0<\alpha<1$ and $0<\beta<1$ are weights of features.

2.4   Clustering with Affinity Propagation

The popular k-means clustering algorithm is quite sensitive to the cluster amount and the initial selection of cluster centers, so it is usually rerun many times with different k

and initializations to find an optimal solution. For videos which are usually represented by high dimensional features, these optimization-based clustering algorithms are computationally expensive and time-consuming. Affinity propagation (AP) proposed by Frey and Dueck [11] is an iterative clustering algorithm based on passing availability and responsibility messages between data points. Without requirement for precise number of clusters, AP algorithm does not rely on the initialization of cluster centers selection since running AP repeatedly will obtain the same clustering result. In our work, we integrate three features to compute pair-wise similarity matrix following the aforementioned similarity measurement and fusion strategy as the input of AP algorithm. The preference in AP, which can influence the probability of a node to be selected as a cluster identifier and the amount of clusters, is set to be the median of similarities to generate a moderate amount of clusters as customary.

3   Experiment

3.1   Dataset

WEBV [12] consists of more than 80,000 most viewed videos for every month of 15 categories on YouTube [1]. Although labels annotated by users and editors of YouTube are provided in the WEBV dataset, a portion of categories in WEBV are not absolutely exclusive. Inspired by the observation in [8], we improve the categories of YouTube. The self-defined categories as ground truth include: Auto&Vehicle, Animations, Comic, Entertainment, Event, Film, Game, Music, News&Politics, People&Blogs, Pet&Animal, Science&Technology, Sport and Travel.

3.2   Performance Evaluation

The output clusters of our system are compared with manual labeled categories of videos to evaluate the performance. Average precision [13] is adopted as the evaluation criterion for the clustering result. Given n videos divided into c manually labeled categories, the precision of a category k is defined as:

$$P(k) = \frac{\sum_{j=1}^{m_k} |C_{j,k}|}{\sum_{j=1}^{m_k} |C_j|} \tag{4}$$

where |x| denotes the size of set x, m_k identifies the number of clusters containing video clips from category k, C_j represents a generated cluster, and $C_{j,k}$ consists of videos that belong to category k in cluster C_j. The average precision results of all categories are averaged as mean average precision (MAP).

3.3   Methods

Since the WEBV divides data month by month, we pick out one month with 1446 web videos for our clustering experiment. As the features have been provided by the dataset, we compute the visual and semantic similarities by applying our strategy. For textual features, titles and tags are stemmed and numbers and stop words are wiped off. Remaining words constitute the dictionary for vector space model, and afterwards the textual similarity is worked out. As to similarity weightings of the three modalities, we empirically choose weighting combinations for emphases on different features or no emphasis, such as $\alpha=0.15$, $\beta=0.15$, $1-\alpha-\beta=0.7$ with greater textual weighting for emphasis on textual feature. We run affinity propagation algorithm with the weighted sum of similarities as input.

3.4   Results Analysis

Fig. 2 demonstrates a comparison of the performances of different feature weight combinations. Intuitively, none of these weighting combinations could outperform other ones for every categorization. An interesting we noticed was that the clusters produced by our system generally possessed a smaller size than the corresponding manual labeled categories. It seems like that the system tends to generate more than one cluster for videos belong to the same manual labeled category. We deem this as a reflection of the subjectivity of manual categorization. The experiment results indicate that there is no optimum feature weighting combination which can be applied across all sorts of videos in terms of content. Empirical analysis might be a way to determine the optimal weighting scheme.

When two of the three weighting coefficients are assigned with zero value, the scheme can be regarded as single-modal clustering. We compare the performance of our multi-modal method with that using video signature representation and Euclidean Distance similarity measurement in [3]. It can be observed from Fig. 3 that the fusion of multi-modal outperforms not only all of the single-modals, but also the method in [3].

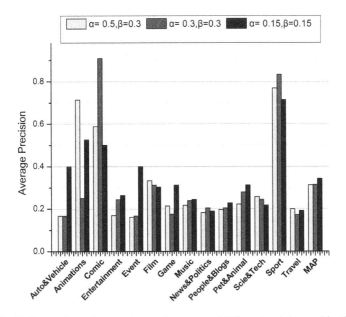

Fig. 2. Comparison of clustering performance of different weight combinations

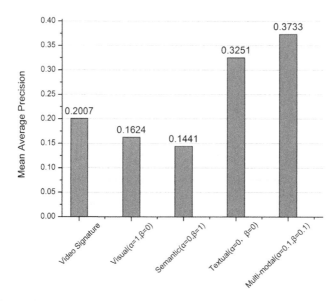

Fig. 3. Comparison of clustering performance of method in [3] and our multi-modal clustering

4   Conclusion and Future Work

Web videos can be regarded as a mixture of videos with huge amount, various qualities, abundant subjects and social information. Our video representation and similarity calculation scheme based on multi-modal strategy have an encouraging performance. Moreover, the affinity propagation algorithm is appropriate for clustering videos with multiple feature information, which is a non-metric similarity mining procedure.

Besides features we adopt in this paper, we deem that audio information is also feasible to describe the web videos as another modal, such as zero cross rate and bandwidth. Furthermore, other clustering algorithms can be explored to substitute for affinity propagation algorithm in our scheme.

Acknowledgement. This research was supported by National 863 Program (No. 2011AA01A205), National 973 Program (No. 2011CB302702), P. R. China.

References

1. YouTube, http://www.youtube.com
2. Brezeale, D., Cook, D.J.: Automatic Video Classification: A Survey of the Literature. IEEE Transactions on Systems, Man and Cybernetics Part C: Applications and Reviews 38(3) (2008)
3. Liu, S., Zhu, M., Zheng, Q.: Mining Similarities for Clustering Web Video Clips. In: International Conference on Computer Science and Software Engineering, pp. 759–762 (2008)

4. Jain, A.K.: Data Clustering: 50 Years Beyond K-means. Pattern Recognition Letters 31(8), 651–666 (2010)
5. Juasiripukdee, P., Wiyartanti, L., Kim, L.: Clustering Search Results of Non-text User Generated Content. In: ICDIM 2010 (2010)
6. Rasiwasia, N.J., Pereira, C., Coviello, E., Doyle, G., Lanckriet, G.R., Levy, R., Vasconcelos, N.: A New Approach to Cross-modal Multimedia Retrieval. In: ACM Multimedia, pp. 251–260 (2010)
7. Wei, S., Zhao, Y., Zhu, Z., Liu, N.: Multimodal Fusion for Video Search Reranking. IEEE Transactions on Knowledge and Data Engineering 99(1), 1191–1199 (2009)
8. Yang, L., Liu, J., Yang, X., Hua, X.S.: Multi-modality Web Video Categorization. In: Multimedia Information Retrieval (MIR), pp. 265–274 (2007)
9. Hindle, A., Shao, J., Lin, D., Lu, J., Zhang, R.: Clustering Web Video Search Results Based on Integration of Multiple Features. World Wide Web 14(1), 1–21 (2010)
10. Lowe, D.G.: Distinctive Image Features from Scale-invariant Keypoints. International Journal of Computer Vision 60, 91–110 (2004)
11. Frey, B.J., Dueck, D.: Clustering by Passing Messages Between Data Points. Science 315(5814), 972–976 (2007)
12. Cao, J., Zhang, Y.D., Song, Y.C., Chen, Z.N., Zhang, X., Li, J.T.: MCG-WEBV: A Benchmark Dataset for Web Video Analysis. Technical Report, MCG-ICT-CAS-09-001, Institute of Computing Technology (2009)
13. Kishida, K.: Property of Average Precision and Its Generalization: An Examination of Evaluation Indicator for Information Retrieval Experiments. Nii technical report (2005)

Incorporate Spatial Information into pLSA
for Scene Classification

Fei Huang, Xiaojun Jing, Songlin Sun, and Yueming Lu

School of Information and Communication Engineering,
Beijing University of Posts and Telecommunications, Beijing, China
Key Laboratory of Trustworthy Distributed Computing and Service(BUPT),
Ministry of Education
mailforhf@gmail.com,
{jxiaojun,slsun,ymlu}@bupt.edu.cn

Abstract. pLSA has been successfully used in scene classification as an intermediate representation of images, but it didn't utilize the spatial information of
an image which is important for scene classification tasks. To improve the accuracy of classification, we proposed a new method which incorporates spatial information coming from neighbor words and topics' position into pLSA. Finally,
an image can be represented by the position distribution of each latent topic,
and subsequently, we train a classifier on the topics' position distribution vector
for each image. Besides, the traditional fold-in heuristic way of pLSA is not necessary and more sophisticated supervised pLSA can be adopted when our no-
fold-in way is used, whichalso givesan accuracy improvement.

Keywords: scene classification, pLSA, spatial information.

1 Introduction

Scene classification aims to analyze images and classify them into semantic meaningful categories. It is not an easy task owing to variability and the semantic gap between
low-level image features and high level semantics.

Earliest studies used low-level features including color, shape and texture for scene
modeling [1][2]. These features were extracted in a global way.Later Bag-of-
Words(BoW)[3] became a dominant representation for images in scene classificationand object categorization tasks,by which images are represented asan orderless collection of local features.The BoW model, however, discards the spatial information of
local descriptors which is important for scene classification. Among the solutions to
this problem, the most successful one is Spatial Pyramid Matching(SPM) [8].

Another strategy for image classification uses an intermediate representation such as
Latent DirichletAllocation(LDA) [4] and probabilistic Latent Semantic Analy-
sis(pLSA) [5]. In [9]Fei-Fei et al. proposed a Bayesian hierarchical model which use
LDA to classify natural scene images. In [7]Sivic et al. used pLSA on sparse features
for recognizing object categories. In [10][12], the combination of pLSA and supervised

Y. Yuan, X. Wu, and Y. Lu (Eds.): ISCTCS 2012, CCIS 320, pp. 170–177, 2013.

classification on sparse or dense features was proposed.pLSA has the ability to solve the problem of "polyseme" and "synonym".However, standard pLSA also cannot make use of spatial information.To address this shortcoming, different methods were proposed in [11][12][13].Our work also aims to add spatial information into pLSA, and we proposes a new scene classification method which improves the accuracy of classification.

The rest of the paper is organized as follows.In Section 2, a new method is proposed to incorporate spatial information coming from neighbor words and topics' position into pLSA.Besides, the fold-in heuristic described in [5] is not necessary for this method when test images are classified and more sophisticated supervised pLSA can be adopted when the no-fold-in way is used.Then, experimental results are presented in Section 3.

2   Proposed Strategy

In this section we describe methods for incorporating spatial information into pLSA. Then we introduce a supervised pLSA incorporating background model.

2.1   pLSA with Paired Words

What is to be discovered is the relation between a specific word and its surrounding eight words in BoW representation. If we take all possible combinations into account, the size will be too large. Inspired by LBP [16], we see a patch as a pixel and compare it with its surrounding words. Each word is compared with its eight neighbors in a 3×3 neighborhood.If a surrounding word is the same with the given word we get a bit 1.And we will get an 8 bit binary string after putting all the eight bits together. Then we convert the 8 bit binary string into a decimal number and get a new variable $V = \{1, 2, ..., 256\}$. Thus, $P(w|z)$ in pLSA becomes $P(w, v|z)$, we have:

$$P(w,v \mid d) = \sum_{z=1}^{K} P(w,v \mid z)P(z \mid d) \qquad (1)$$

And we call it paired words pLSA(pw-pLSA). The graphical model representations of pLSA and pw-pLSA are shown in Fig.1(d)(e). In order to improve the computation efficiency, we need to reduce the dimension of V. As shown in Fig.1(a)(b)(c), we can change V to lower dimensions by using less surrounding words or combining two surrounding words as a compare unit. These methods will reduce V's dimensions to 8 or 16. A similar E-step and M-step of standard pLSA can be used to find $P(w,v \mid z)$.

A similar work in [15] shows a performance improvement by using SPM. But when with pLSA, the improvement of paired words is limited and this will be shown in the next section.

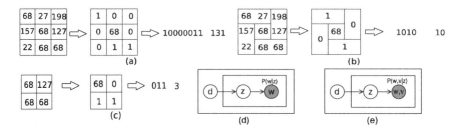

Fig. 1. (a-c): Paired Words Model. (d)(e): Graphical Models of pLSA.

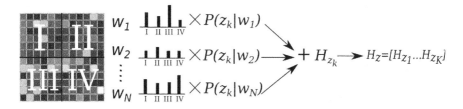

Fig. 2. Topic Position: This figure illustrates how to calculate H_{z_k} and H_z.

2.2   Discover Topics and Their Positions

In order to utilize spatial information, we evenly sample the image into $S \times S$ subregions and label them from 1 to $S \times S$. For any word w_i in this image, its position distribution H_{w_i} over these subregions can be calculated. H_{w_i} is a $S \times S$-dimension vector that represents the number of word w_i occurring in subregions.

After Applying Bayes' theorem on $P(w \mid z)$ and $P(z)$ calculated from pLSA, we get $P(z \mid w)$ which means word w_i makes contribution to topic z_k with weight $P(z_k \mid w_i)$. From $H_{w_i} P(z_k \mid w_i)$, we can get z_k's position distribution coming from word w_i. So we can get topic's position distribution of every image from eq.2.

$$H_{z_k} = \sum_i^M H_{w_i} P(z_k \mid w_i) \tag{2}$$

H_{z_k} is also a $S \times S$-dimension vector. Then we use $H_z = [H_{z_1}, ..., H_{z_K}]$, a $S \times S \times K$-dimension vector, to represent an image. The procedure is shown in Fig.2. For pLSA using paired words, we have $P(z \mid w, v)$ from $P(w, v \mid z)$ and $P(z)$. Then H_{z_k} becomes:

$$H_{z_k} = \sum_i^M \sum_j^V H_{w_i v_j} P(z_k \mid w_i, v_j) \tag{3}$$

$H_{w_i v_j}$ is also a $S \times S$-dimension vector but represents the number of word w_i with v_j in subregions.

Note that in [12][13], $P(z \mid d)$ is calculated on every subregion. This method will have probabilities of topics on every subregions, and our method will get the information about where the topics may appear.In [12], after determining both $P(w \mid z)$ and $P(z \mid d_{train})$, each training image is represented by a K-vector $P(z \mid d_{train})$.When test images are classified, $P(z \mid d_{test})$ are computed by fold-in heuristic described in [5].Different from before, the fold-in step is not necessary for our strategy. In more detail, we have two ways to normalize vector $H_{z_{train}}$ and $H_{z_{test}}$:

- For no-fold-in way, we already have calculated $P(z \mid w)$ or $P(z \mid w, v)$. Both $H_{z_{train}}$ and $H_{z_{test}}$ can be calculated by $P(z \mid w)$ with the method described above.Then they are normalized to unit vectors directly.
- For fold-in way, we need to compute $P(z \mid d_{test})$ in the same way in [12]. That is running same EM with $P(w \mid z)$ or $P(w, v \mid z)$ fixed. After calculating and normalizing H_{z_k} (not H_z), we then multiply normalized H_{z_k} by $P(z \mid d_{train})$ for training images and $P(z \mid d_{test})$ for testing images. It can be seen that $H_z = [H_{z_1}, ..., H_{z_K}]$ is also a normalized vector which can be used to represent a specific image.

After getting $H_{z_{train}}$ and $H_{z_{train}}$ from the two different ways, we train a multiclass discriminative classifier with $H_{z_{train}}$. Then $H_{z_{test}}$ are used to classify images by the classifier trained before.

2.3   Supervised pLSA with Background Language Model

When no-fold-in way is adopted, we can use supervised and more sophisticated pLSA, because we have no need to calculate $P(z \mid d_{test})$ of testing set. In [6], a simple mixture model for text clustering was proposed which is closely related to pLSA.

Inspired by this, we assume there are K common topics in all collections and different background models for every category. Then a supervised pLSA incorporating background model is given:

$$P(w_i \mid d_j) = \lambda P(w_i \mid C_{d_j}) + (1 - \lambda) \sum_{k=1}^{K} P(w_i \mid z_k) P(z_k \mid d_j) \qquad (4)$$

where $P(w_i | C_{d_j})$ denotes the category-specific background model. C_{d_i} means the category d_i belongs to. As we know every document in training set comes from which category , $P(w|C_d)$ for every category can be calculated directly by eq.5.

$$P(w|C_d) = \frac{\sum_{d \in C} n(d,w)}{\sum_w \sum_{d \in C} n(d,w)} \tag{5}$$

Like pLSA, this model can also be estimated by EM algorithm. In E steps we need to calculate $P(C_d | d, w)$ which means the word w in document d is generated by the category background d belongs to, and $P(z|d,w)$ which means the word is generated by topic z. Using Bayes Rule, we obtain the following E steps:

$$P(C_d | d, w) = \frac{\lambda P(w|C_d)P(d)}{\lambda P(w|C_d)P(d) + (1-\lambda)\sum_z P(w|z)P(d|z)P(z)} \tag{6}$$

$$P(z|d,w) = \frac{P(w|z)P(d|z)P(z)}{\sum_z P(w|z)P(d|z)P(z)} \tag{7}$$

By maximize the Q-function we get the M steps:

$$P(w|z) = \frac{\sum_d n(d,w)(1-P(C_d|d,w))P(z|w,d)}{\sum_w \sum_d n(d,w)(1-P(C_d|d,w))P(z|w,d)} \tag{8}$$

$$P(d|z) = \frac{\sum_w n(d,w)(1-P(C_d|d,w))P(z|w,d)}{\sum_w \sum_d n(d,w)(1-P(C_d|d,w))P(z|w,d)} \tag{9}$$

$$P(z) = \frac{\sum_d \sum_w n(d,w)(1-P(C_d|d,w))P(z|w,d)}{\sum_w \sum_d \sum_z n(d,w)(1-P(C_d|d,w))P(z|w,d)} \tag{10}$$

3   Experiment

The 15-scene dataset [17] contains fifteen categories. Most of the scenes in the dataset display large intra-class variability and some indoor scenes have low inter-class variability. Each category of scenes is split randomly into two separate sets of images.Dense SIFT descriptors are computed on 16×16-size patches and the grid spacing is 10 pixels.Then we construct the M-size codebook with K-means. In the classification stage, Support Vector Machine(SVM) is trained using the one-versus-all rule with Radial Basis Function(RBF) kernel.

We first follow the experimental setup in [12] and compare standard pLSA with pw-pLSA. Here we set codebook size M and topics number K in different values and use strategy described in Fig.1(b)(c).Table.1 shows the classification rates:

Table 1. Classification Rates for pLSA and pw-pLSA

	pLSA	pw-pLSA
M=400 K=20 V=8	64.3	65.7
M=400 K=30 V=8	65.2	66.3
M=600 K=20 V=8	65.5	66.7
M=600 K=30 V=8	66.2	66.9
M=400 K=20 V=16	64.3	65.9
M=600 K=20 V=16	65.5	67.1

We know that with the help of neighborhood word, the word becomes more discriminative, but for pLSA it may cause severe overfit, and the classification performance improvement is little and sometimes even worse.

In the experiments for comparing topics' position method and standard pLSA, we don't use pw-pLSA which is time and memory consuming and brings little improvement, and we choose larger M and K. Standard pLSA on training set and testing sets are run to get the values for classification. Then we calculate $H_{z_{train}}$ and $H_{z_{test}}$ using fold-in and no-fold-in ways proposed in Section 2 and train model with them.As in no-fold-in way we have no need to run pLSA on testing set, supervised pLSA can be adopted. Here we use the pLSA incorporating category-specific background model proposed above and calculate the background model 'use eq.5.Table.2 gives the classification results.

We can see that fold-in way and no fold-in way are not much different in performance when S>1, but both have a higher classification rate than standard pLSA. On average, fold-in way gives better results.

As noted in [8], the spatial information indeed improves the performance. And when background model is used, we gain performance improvement on the benefit of the more informative pLSA and more discriminative words. Fig.3 shows the confusion matrix for 15-scene data set when using supervised pLSA and topic position with L=4. It can be seen that the major confusion appears between bedroom, living room and kitchen. This is because the indoor scenes have low inter-class variability.

4   Conclusion

In this paper, we focus on incorporating spatial information into pLSA for scene classification.We propose two strategies to associate location information into the vector which represents a specific image. And unlike other pLSA methods, one of our strategies doesn't need fold-in heuristic. Besides we propose a category specific background model for pLSA and show that supervised pLSA can be adopted to improve performance.

Table 2. Performance(Classification Rates) Comparison Among pLSA, Topic Position Model with fold-in way, no-fold-in way And Supervised no-fold-in way

		pLSA	fold-in	no-fold-in	supervised no-fold-in
S=1	M=800 K=30	66.6	65.6	64.0	65.5
	M=800 K=45	66.5	66.5	65.6	68.0
	M=800 K=60	67.3	67.3	66.3	67.8
	M=1000 K=30	67.4	65.2	66.4	65.2
	M=1000 K=45	68.5	66.5	67.3	68.8
	M=1000 K=60	68.6	67.5	66.1	68.1
	M=1200 K=30	68.2	66.2	66.4	67.1
	M=1200 K=45	68.7	66.9	67.1	67.8
	M=1200 K=60	67.6	67.1	67.7	68.3
S=2	M=800 K=30	-	71.4	71.5	72.7
	M=800 K=45	-	72.1	70.7	73.2
	M=800 K=60	-	71.0	70.1	72.1
	M=1000 K=30	-	73.9	71.2	73.5
	M=1000 K=45	-	74.7	73.3	74.9
	M=1000 K=60	-	73.6	73.7	74.4
	M=1200 K=30	-	72.8	71.1	73.6
	M=1200 K=45	-	74.9	73.2	74.3
	M=1200 K=60	-	73.5	72.0	73.8
S=4	M=800 K=30	-	76.9	76.1	77.2
	M=800 K=45	-	77.6	77.9	78.4
	M=800 K=60	-	78.0	78.3	77.6
	M=1000 K=30	-	77.1	76.3	77.2
	M=1000 K=45	-	78.1	77.9	79.4
	M=1000 K=60	-	78.8	78.0	78.9
	M=1200 K=30	-	77.3	76.7	78.2
	M=1200 K=45	-	78.2	77.6	79.1
	M=1200 K=60	-	77.7	77.3	78.9

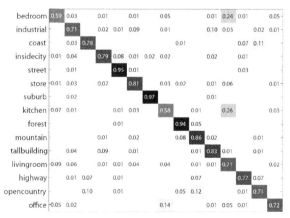

Fig. 3. Confusion Matrix

Acknowledgement. This research was supported in part by NSFC (No. 61143008), National High Technology Research and Development Program of China (No. 2011AA01A204) and Beijing University of Posts and Telecommunications Research and Innovation Fund for Youths

References

1. Szummer, M., Picard, R.W.: Indoor-outdoor image classification. In: CAIVD Workshop, ICCV (January 1998)
2. Vailaya, A., Figueiredo, M., Jain, A., Zhang, H.J.: Image classification for content-based indexing. IEEE Trans. on Image Processing 10(1), 117–130 (2001)
3. Csurka, G., Dance, C.R., Fan, L., Willamowski, J., Bray, C.: Visual categorization with bags of keypoints. In: ECCV, pp. 1–22 (2004)
4. Blei, D., Andrew, Y., Jordan, M.: Latent Dirichlet allocation. Journal of Machine Learning Research 3, 993–1020 (2003)
5. Hofmann, T.: Unsupervised learning by probabilistic latent semantic analysis. Mach. Learning 42, 177–196 (2001)
6. Zhai, C.X., Velivelli, A., Yu, B.: A cross-collection mixture model for comparative text mining. In: Proceedings of the Tenth ACM SIGKDD International Conference on KDD, Seattle, WA, USA, August 22-25 (2004)
7. Sivic, J., Russell, B.C., Efros, A.A., Zisserman, A., Freeman, W.T.: Discovering Objects and Their Locations in Images. In: Proc. ICCV, pp. 370–377 (October 2005)
8. Lazebnik, S., Schmid, C., Ponce, J.: Beyond Bags of Features: Spatial Pyramid Matching for Recognizing Natural Scene Categories. In: Proc. IEEE CS Conf. Computer Vision and Pattern Recognition, vol. 2, pp. 2169–2178 (June 2006)
9. Fei-Fei, L., Perona, P.: A Bayesian Hierarchical Model for Learning Natural Scene Categories. In: Proc. IEEE CS Conf. CVPR, pp. 524–531 (2005)
10. Quelhas, P., Monay, F., Odobez, J.M., Gatica-Perez, D., Tuytelaars, T., Van Gool, L.: Modeling Scenes with Local Descriptors and Latent Aspects. In: Proc. Int'l Conf. Computer Vision, pp. 883–890 (October 2005)
11. Fergus, R., Fei-Fei, L., Perona, P., Zisserman, A.: Learning Object Categories from Google's Image Search. In: Proc. Int'l Conf. Computer Vision, pp. 1816–1823 (October 2005)
12. Bosch, A., Zisserman, A., Munoz, X.: Scene classification using a hybrid generative/dicriminative approach. IEEE Trans. on PAMI (2008)
13. Ergul, E., Arica, N.: Scene Classification Using Spatial Pyramid of Latent Topics. In: ICPR (2010) 1991, 1992
14. Lowe, D.: Distinctive Image Features from Scale Invariant Keypoints. Int'l J. Computer Vision 60(2), 91–110 (2004)
15. Zhang, E., Mayo, M.: Improving Bag-of-Words Model with Spatial Information. In: Proc. IEEE IVCNZ, pp. 1–6 (2010)
16. Huang, D., Shan, C., Ardabilian, M., Wang, Y., Chen, L.: Local Binary Patterns and Its Application to Facial Image Analysis: A Survey. IEEE Transactions on Systems, Man, and Cybernetics 41(6), 765–781 (2011)
17. http://www-cvr.ai.uiuc.edu/ponce_grp/data/

A Trust-Based Data Backup Method on the Cloud

Mingtao Lei[1,2], Wenbin Yao[1,2], and Cong Wang[2]

[1] School of Computer Science, Beijing University of Posts and Telecommunications,
Beijing, China
leimingtao1@163.com, yaowenbin@bupt.edu.cn
[2] Key Laboratory of Trustworthy Distributed Computing and Service (BUPT),
Ministry of Education, Beijing, China
wangc@bupt.edu.cn

Abstract. Data backup method may trigger the problem of the security reduction owing to the same data versions stored in different IDCs. To deal with the problem, the paper proposes a trust-based data backup method on the cloud in which trust value is exploited as the foundation to decide that the replica should be stored to the most trusted nodes. Production node calculates the trust value combining with local trust value and mutual trust value before it carries out the operation of backup. The trusted third party(TTP) is introduced to calculate the local trust value. The production node evaluates the mutual trust value based on the interactive evaluation with the available backup nodes. The trust-based data backup method can guarantee that every replica will be stored on the most trusted node during the time nodes trust each other. The proof shows this method is feasible.

Keywords: data backup, trust model, mutual trust, the third trusted party.

1 Introduction

To protect user's data from disaster, data backup has extensively been developed and it has contributed much on data protection. But at the same time, the method may trigger a problem of security reduction owing to the same data versions stored in different IDCs. Especially, it is more important on the cloud because the data may be stored to distributed storage nodes.

In recent researches, most methods of data backup centered on behavioral characteristics. Li Xiong[1] proposed a trust evaluation model based on the feedback of transaction satisfaction. However, feedback may be delayed and thus produced the trust problem. Tang Wen[2] proposed a trust model based on fuzzy logic to implement the subjective evaluation. However, this subjective evaluation can't avoid deceptive actions and thus malicious node could launch an attack. Cao Hui[3] proposed a trust model based on focus point space which evaluates the credibility of peers through dynamic adjustments of weights, highlights peer reliability and improves the dynamic regulation ability in various fields. However, focus point space didn't propose interactive evaluation. Trust should be built on the basis of subjective trust and objective trust [4-5].

Y. Yuan, X. Wu, and Y. Lu (Eds.): ISCTCS 2012, CCIS 320, pp. 178–185, 2013.

This paper proposed a trust-based data backup method on the cloud, which concentrates on trust value obtained from the calculation of combined local trust evaluation and mutual trust evaluation. The trusted third party (TTP) is introduced to calculate the local trust value. The production node evaluates the mutual trust value based on the mutual evaluation with the available backup nodes.

This paper is organized as follows. Section 2 introduces the architecture of data backup. Section 3 describes theoretical basis of trust in detail. Section 4 defines some rules and regulations about this method. Section 5 cites an example to prove that this method is feasible. Finally, this paper is concluded in Section 6.

2   Architecture of Data Backup

2.1   Network Topology

On the cloud, the network is made up of several production nodes, several backup nodes and a TTP. The network topology of backup process is shown as Fig.1.

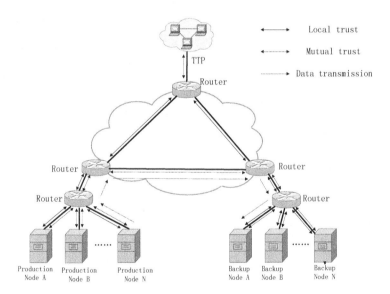

Fig. 1. The network topology of backup process

Production node: Production nodes produce replicas and provide evidence for backup nodes so that they could be tested whether backup nodes will trust them.

Backup node: Backup nodes receive replicas and provide evidence of trust for production node.

TTP: TTP is an abbreviation of the trusted third party. It monitors nodes' status and provides local trust evaluation for every node.

2.2   Process of Data Backup

The process of a trust-based data backup method is shown as Fig.2.

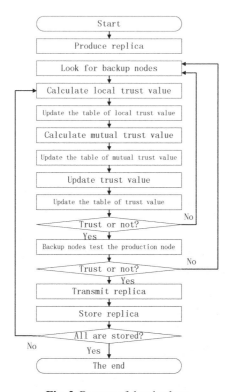

Fig. 2. Process of data backup

3   Theoretical Basis of Trust

3.1   Definition

Definition 1. Local trust value: Under none interaction, local trust value, which is used for the local trust evaluation, is generated by judging operating mode of every node by TTP.

Within a period of time t_1, the TTP broadcasts m messages to every node. These nodes will reply one after another. If message i is replied on time, mark u_i as"1", else mark u_i as "0".At the same time, TTP evaluates the replied results and grades them. w_i stands for the score, $0 \le w_i \le 1, 1 \le i \le m$ .At the end of test, local trust value is calculated as the formula (1).

$$U_j = \frac{1}{m}\sum_{i=1}^{m} u_i \times w_i \qquad (1)$$

Definition 2. Mutual trust value: During the time of interaction, mutual trust value, which is used for mutual trust evaluation, is generated by which one node interacts with the others.

Within a period of time t_1, one node sends m messages to another. If message i is replied on time, mark v_i as "1", else mark v_i as "0".At the same time, the node evaluates the replied results and grades them. x_i stands for the score, $0 \le x_i \le 1$, $1 \le i \le m$ .At the end of test, mutual trust value is calculated as the formula (2).

$$V_j = \frac{1}{m}\sum_{i=1}^{m} v_i \times x_i \qquad (2)$$

Definition 3. Trust value: Trust value, which combines local trust value with mutual trust value, shows how much one node will trust another.

At the end of time t_1, local trust value of node j is U_j, mutual trust value of node j is V_j and the frequency of interaction is c_j. At the end of time t_2, local trust value of node j is U_j', mutual trust value of node j is V' and the frequency of interaction is c_j'. The function $f(\Delta c)$, which is named as CF(correcting function), stands for the tendency that interactive frequency is declining. It is calculated as the formula (3).

$$f(\Delta c) = \begin{cases} 1 & if \quad \Delta c \ge 0 \\ \frac{c_j'}{c_j} & if \quad \Delta c < 0 \end{cases}, \Delta c = c_j' - c_j \qquad (3)$$

Another function $g(x)$ named as AF(attenuation function) stands for the affection which is produced by trust owing to time. $g(x)$ is calculated as the formula (4).

$$g(x) = \begin{cases} kx & if \quad x \le 1 \\ \frac{k}{x} & if \quad x > 1 \end{cases}, k > 0, a > 1 \qquad (4)$$

Trust value is calculated as the formula (5).

$$Z_j = \frac{(U_j \times \prod g(\Delta U) + V_j \times f(\Delta c) \times \prod g(\Delta V))}{2}, \Delta U = \frac{U_j}{U_j'}, \Delta V = \frac{V_j}{V_j'} \qquad (5)$$

3.2   Theorems

Theorem 1. The tendency of increasing range is less than that of before, and the tendency of decreasing range is more than that of before.

Proof:

Trust value is $Z_j = \dfrac{(U_j \times \prod g(\Delta U) + V_j \times f(\Delta c) \times \prod g(\Delta V))}{2}$.

Suppose $\Delta U'' = \dfrac{U_{jt_4}}{U_{jt_3}}$, $\Delta U' = \dfrac{U_{jt_3}}{U_{jt_2}}$, $\Delta U = \dfrac{U_{jt_2}}{U_{jt_1}}$, $t_4 > t_3 > t_2 > t_1$, so do $\Delta V''$, $\Delta V'$ and ΔV .

If $\Delta U'' - \Delta U' \geq \Delta U' - \Delta U$ and $\Delta V'' - \Delta V' \geq \Delta V' - \Delta V$, $g(x)$ is a monotonic increasing function. At that moment, $Z_j'' - Z_j' \geq Z_j' - Z_j$. It shows that the tendency of increasing range is less than that of before.

If $\Delta U'' - \Delta U' \leq \Delta U' - \Delta U$, $\Delta V'' - \Delta V' \leq \Delta V' - \Delta V$, $g(x)$ is a monotonic decreasing function. So $Z_j'' - Z_j' \leq Z_j' - Z_j$. It shows that the tendency of decreasing range is more than that of before.

In conclusion, Theorem 1 is proved.

Theorem 2. If the frequency of interaction between node A and B is decreasing, the trust value of A and B will decrease.

Proof:

The function $f(\Delta c)$, which is defined, stands for the tendency that trust is declining. $f(\Delta c) = \begin{cases} 1 & if \quad \Delta c \geq 0 \\ \frac{c_j'}{c_j} & if \quad \Delta c < 0 \end{cases}$, $\Delta c = c_j' - c_j$. The trust value is as formula (5) shows.

Only considering Δc , if the frequency of interaction between node A and B is decreasing, $c_j'' - c_j' < c_j' - c_j$. At the moment, $f(\Delta c') < f(\Delta c)$. Then, $Z_j' < Z_j$.

In conclusion, Theorem 2 is proved.

4   Rules and Regulations

The process of building trust needs several regulations, including some rules for exception handling.

Rule 1. Trust must be evaluated completely, including trust with each other, trust properly and forecasting trust.

Trust with each other is a concept that production nodes must trust the backup nodes and as well the backup nodes should also trust the production nodes. If trust travels one way, there may be a situation that backup nodes didn't know whether it could be trusted or not. With building an entirely trust completely, nodes could protect themselves from the untrusted nodes.

Trust properly shows the max range that one node trust another. If one node owns a higher trust, it may result in overload operation and rising failure rate. Aiming at solving this problem, the higher trust node should be left behind. With the flow of time, its trust value may decrease and it can be joined once again.

Forecasting trust is to forecast whether one node could trust after a period of time. If the frequency of changing trust value is higher than the frequency of interaction, a case that backup nodes have been untrusted before a replica sent may occur. Production nodes should forecast trust value of backup nodes at the time t_2 before the time t_1, so they could know when they will interrupt the transmission and look for another backup node. This measure could improve efficiency of data backup.

Rule 2. After trust is built, the nodes should evaluate mutual trust randomly so that the trust value should be a variation with the change of trust relationship.

During the interaction between nodes, production nodes will send m messages to tested backup nodes and production nodes will judge these messages. But fraud may appear after testing. So the test should be random. At the moment of time t_1, there is an exception appearing between two trust nodes after they are tested. Continuous m tests will start. If it's true for this exception, the operation of backup will be interrupted and production nodes will look for another trust backup node.

Rule 3. With evaluating dynamically, production nodes should select the best backup node for backup.

Mutual trust value is calculated dynamically. The process of evaluating dynamically shows as follows.

(1)The production node cut this replica into l pieces;
(2)Suppose $x = 1$, y is the time of trust test;
(3)At time $t \times x$, the production node tests backup node of number k;
(4)The production node provides ideal conditions is as $(l_1, l_2, \cdots, l_p)$;
(5)This backup node provides several conditions is as $(l_{k1}, l_{k2}, \cdots, l_{kp})$;
(6)The production node selects the back node which owns the lowest

$$S_k = \frac{1}{p-1}\sum_{i=1}^{p}(l_{ki} - l_i)^2 ;$$

(7)At the end of time $t \times x$, test if the replica has been stored completely;
(8)If this replica has been stored completely, run step 11, else, run step 9;
(9)If $x > y$, run step 11;else, run step 10;
(10) $x + 1$, run step 3;
(11)The end.

5   Experiments

5.1   Analysis Contribution of CF

CF changes with frequency of interface each. Suppose that only frequency changes and every score holds on as "1". Trust changing with interactive frequency shows in Table 1(Only select discrete points).

Table 1. Trust changes with frequency

Time	t_1	t_2	t_3	t_4	t_5	t_6	t_7	t_8	t_9
Frequency	2	3	4	5	6	5	4	3	2
Trust value	1	1	1	1	1	0.917	0.9	0.875	0.833

When the frequency keeps increasing or constant, the trust degree will stay the same. After the frequency begins decreasing, the range of the first decreasing is larger than the other. The case happens because mutual trust evaluation influences greater on trust evaluation. After that, the range of trust evaluation is larger than the last. It shows as Fig.3.

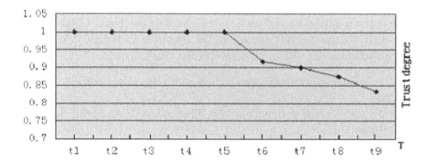

Fig. 3. Trust changes with frequency

5.2   Analysis Contribution of Local Trust Value and Mutual Trust Value

Suppose that $g(x) = \begin{cases} x & if \quad x \leq 1 \\ \dfrac{1}{1.5^x} & if \quad x > 1 \end{cases}$ and mutual trust degree keeps constant. Table

2 shows the influence of local trust value.(Only select discrete points)

Table 2. The influence of local trust value

Time	t_1	t_2	t_3	t_4	t_5	t_6	t_7	t_8	t_9
Local trust	0.5	0.6	0.7	0.8	0.9	0.8	0.7	0.6	0.5
Mutual trust	0.8	0.8	0.8	0.8	0.8	0.8	0.8	0.8	0.8
Trust value	0.65	0.70	0.75	0.80	0.85	0.68	0.57	0.51	0.46

With local trust value increasing, the trust value increases. When local trust evaluation begins to decrease, the trust evaluation begins to decrease too. But the range of decreasing is different at every moment. This case occurs because the influence of local trust values less than the last. It shows as Fig.4.

The computing methods of mutual trust value and local trust value are the same.

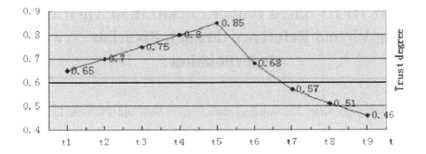

Fig. 4. The influence of local trust value

6   Conclusion

This paper proposes a trust-based data backup method on the cloud which solves the problem of the security reduction owing to the same data versions stored in different IDCs. Also, the paper proposes the method in which trust value is exploited as the foundation to decide that the replica should be stored to the most trusted nodes. The trust-based data backup method can guarantee that every replica will be stored on the most trusted node during the time nodes trust each other.

Acknowledgement. This study is supported by the National High Technology Research and Development Program("863"Program) of China(2012AA012600) and the Fundamental Research Funds for the Central Universities(BUPT2011RCZJ16) and China Information Security Special Fund (NDRC).

References

1. Xiong, L., Liu, L.: PeerTrust: Support reputation-based trust for peer-peer-peer electronic communities. IEEE Trans. on Knowledge and Data Engineer 16(7), 843–857 (2004)
2. Wen, T., Jianbin, H., Zhong, C.: Research on a fuzzy logic-based subjective trust management model. Computer Research and Development 42(10), 1654–1659 (2005) (in Chinese)
3. Hui, C., Zheng, Q.: Trust model based on focus point space. Journal of Tsinghua University (Science and Technology) 51(11) (2011)
4. Borowski, J.F., et al.: Reputation-Based Trust for a Cooperative Agent-Based Backup Protection Scheme. IEEE Transctions on Smart Grid (2011)
5. Tian, L.-Q., Lin, C., Yang, Y.: Behavior trust computation in distributed network. Computer Engineering and Applications (2008)

Active RFID-Based Indoor Localization Algorithm Using Virtual Reference through Bivariate Newton Interpolation

Chenggang Shao, Xiaojun Jing, and Songlin Sun, and Yueming Lu

School of Information and Communication Engineering, Beijing University of Posts and Telecommunications, Beijing, China
Key Laboratory of Trustworthy Distributed Computing and Service (BUPT),
Ministry of Education, Beijing, China
scg_bupt@163.com, {jxiaojun,slsun,ymlu}@bupt.edu.cn

Abstract. At present, the LANDMARC algorithm and the VIRE (Virtual Reference Elimination) algorithm both use RFID technology in indoor localization. VIRE algorithm is a location method by estimating the virtual reference tags based on active RFID. However, the RSSI (Received Signal Strength Indicator) values of virtual reference tags, achieved from the linear interpolation formula in VIRE, are not enough precise according to the RSSI-Distance curve. The proposed algorithm estimates the RSSI values of virtual reference tags by using a nonlinear interpolation, Bivariate Newton interpolation. Simulation results show that the proposed algorithm makes the location accuracy for 69.5% increasing than LANDMARC and 23.3% increasing than VIRE in average.

Keywords: RFID, indoor localization, Bivariate Newton interpolation, location accuracy.

1 Introduction

The existing RFID localization methods are based on the signal strength, which use the received signal strength indication (RSSI, Received Signal Strength Indicator) to determine the location of the object [1]. LANDMARC [2] method is a classic indoor localization algorithm based on active RFID, which uses the reference tags as the position reference points to assist locating. Because the RFID reader reads their RSSI similarly, whose position are close to each other, LANDMARC method finds out those reference tags which are the nearest to the object tag by comparing the RSSI values of the reference tags and the object tag's. It combines the positions of the reference tags with their weight to calculate the objects' position. LANDMARC method has a high positioning accuracy and expandability, and can handle some complex situation. In spite of that, there are still some problems [3], such as in a closed environment, because of the radio signal multi-path effects, which makes the accuracy of its positioning lower. The actual situation requires more reference RFID tags in order to make positioning more accurate. Hence, using LANDMARC method not only increases the cost, but also produces RF interference phenomenon [4].

Y. Yuan, X. Wu, and Y. Lu (Eds.): ISCTCS 2012, CCIS 320, pp. 186–193, 2013.

Based on the inadequacy of LANDMARC algorithm, Y. Zhao and his team put forward a new algorithm, VIRE [5] (Virtual Reference Elimination) algorithm, which is a location method by estimating the virtual tags based on active RFID. The core of VIRE method is determining the RSSI values of each virtual reference tag by a linear interpolation algorithm which is fast and convenient but lack of precision according to the Distance-Loss curve [6]. Consequently, the author proposes a nonlinear interpolation algorithm [7] to calculate the RSSI values of each virtual reference tag which is more close to the RSSI-Distance curve. The simulation results show that the proposed algorithm achieves a higher accuracy compared with LANDMARC and VIRE.

The remainder of the paper is organized as follows. The proposed algorithm will be described in Section 2. Section 3 illustrates the simulation results and the experimental analysis. In Section 4, some conclusion and a short outlook for future work are presented.

2   Proposed Algorithm

2.1   The Model of System

In our model, the RFID readers are put on the four corners, all reference tags are placed into a planar grid, and the object tags are placed in this grid. Fig.1 shows the layout of the model. Suppose that there are M readers, N reference tags and L target tags, and we define RSSI value vector for each reference tag as

$$\vec{S} = (S_1, S_2, \cdots, S_M) \tag{1}$$

where $S_i, i \in [1, M]$ stands for the RSSI value of reference tag received by i-th reader. Similarly define RSSI value vector for each target tag as

$$\vec{T} = (T_1, T_2, \cdots, T_M) \tag{2}$$

where $T_i, i \in [1, M]$ stands for the RSSI value of target tag received by reader i-th reader.

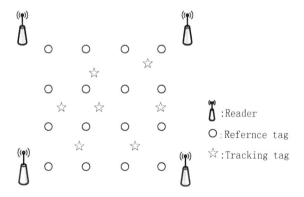

Fig. 1. The layout of the system

The grid can be divided into many small grids. Each grid which is covered by 1four reference tags is separated into the size n × n of virtual grid cells, and each virtual grid cell can be thought of being covered by 4 virtual reference tags which distribute in the corner of the cell. Because the coordinates of the reference tags are known, the coordinates of the virtual reference tags can also be very easy to obtain. After that we use the Bivariate Newton interpolation to get the RSSI values of virtual reference tags directly. Finally, through a series of consideration, we can also get virtual reference tags which can be based on to calculate the location of the object tags by the principle of nearest neighbor.

2.2   Bivariate Newton Interpolation

In the real environment, there is a complex curve between RSSI value and distance, and using direct linear interpolation produces a big error in VIRE, so we use Bivariate Newton interpolation to get the RSSI value of virtual reference tag which is more close to the Distance-Loss curve. We introduce the Bivariate Newton Interpolation algorithm as following.

As we know, the unitary Newton Interpolation is

$$
\begin{aligned}
f(x) = f(x_0) + f[x_0, x_1](x - x_0) + \cdots \\
+ f[x_0, x_1, \cdots, x_m](x - x_0)(x - x_1) \cdots (x - x_{m-1}) \\
+ f[x, x_0, x_1, \cdots, x_m](x - x_0)(x - x_1) \cdots (x - x_m)
\end{aligned} \tag{3}
$$

where $x_i (i = 0,1,2,\ldots,m)$ is the discrete variable, and m-th order difference quotient is

$$
f[x_0, x_1, \cdots, x_m] = \frac{f[x_1, \cdots, x_m] - f[x_0, x_1, \cdots, x_{m-1}]}{x_m - x_0} \tag{4}
$$

In order to extended to bivariate interpolation, we assume that

$$
f(x, y) \in C(R^2), \psi = \{(x_i, y_j) \mid 0 \le j \le n, 0 \le x \le n\} \tag{5}
$$

where $f(x, y)$ is the bivariate function, (x_i, y_i) is the discrete bivariate variable, and we define the following notation

$$
\begin{cases}
f_{v\mu} \triangleq f[x_0, x_1, \cdots, x_v; y_0, y_1, \cdots, y_\mu] \\
X_v \triangleq (x - x_0)(x - x_1) \cdots (x - x_{v-1}) \\
Y_\mu \triangleq (y - y_0)(y - y_1) \cdots (y - y_{\mu-1}) \\
X_0 = Y_0 \triangleq 1
\end{cases} \tag{6}
$$

From the eq.4, the bivariate difference quotient is been got

$$f[x_0, x_1, \cdots, x_v; y] = \sum_{\mu=0}^{n} Y_\mu f_{v\mu} + Y_{n+1} f[x_0, x_1, \cdots, x_v; y, y_0, \cdots, y_n] \qquad (7)$$

Hence, we can get the Bivariate Newton Interpolation according to the eq.6 and the eq.7.

$$f(x, y) = \sum_{v=0}^{m} X_v f[x_0, x_1, \cdots, x_v; y] + X_{m+1} f[x_0, x_1, \cdots, x_m; y] \qquad (8)$$

Finally, the Bivariate Newton interpolation formula can be simplified through the eq.6 and the eq.8.

$$p(x, y) = \sum_{v=0}^{m} \sum_{\mu=0}^{n} X_v Y_\mu f_{v\mu} \qquad (9)$$

In the model of system, the coordinates of the reference tags, (x, y), is easy to know, and the RSSI values of the reference tags, $f(x, y)$, have been got in the eq.1. Hence, we can use the Bivariate Newton interpolation formula, $p(x, y)$, as shows in eq.9 in the condition of having discrete bivariate variable and the bivariate function to calculate the each RSSI value of the virtual reference tag by different readers.

$$\begin{cases} p_1(x, y) = \sum_{v=0}^{N} \sum_{\mu=0}^{N} X_v Y_\mu f_{1v\mu} \\ p_2(x, y) = \sum_{v=0}^{N} \sum_{\mu=0}^{N} X_v Y_\mu f_{2v\mu} \\ \quad \vdots \\ p_M(x, y) = \sum_{v=0}^{N} \sum_{\mu=0}^{N} X_v Y_\mu f_{Mv\mu} \end{cases} \qquad (10)$$

where $p_i(x.y), i = 1, 2, \ldots, M$ is the Bivariate Newton interpolation formula which is used to calculate the RSSI values of the virtual tags by the i-th reader, M is the number of readers, and N is the number of the reference tags.

After we obtain interpolation formula, next to do is the calculation of the RSSI value of each virtual reference tag to each reader. The n-1 virtual reference tags are equally placed between two adjacent real tags. The total number of virtual reference tags will be increased to $(n+1)^2 - 4$, as Shown in Fig.2.

When the virtual reference grid is established, the RSSI value of each virtual reference tag by the k-th reader can be calculated by the eq.10, we define the RSSI value vector for each virtual reference tag as

$$\vec{V} = (V_1, V_2, \cdots, V_Q) \tag{11}$$

where $V_k(x.y) = p_k(x.y), i \in [1,Q]$ stands for the RSSI values of virtual reference tag by i-th reader, and $Q = [(\sqrt{N}-1)n+1]^2$ stands for the number of the total virtual reference tags.

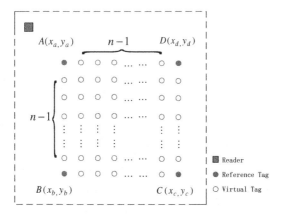

Fig. 2. The establishment of the virtual tags

2.3   Location Implement

So far, we have got vector V, the RSSI values of the virtual tags, and vector T, the RSSI values of the object tags. Hence, for each target tag $p, p \in [1,L]$, we have

$$E_j = \sqrt{\sum_{k=1}^{M}(V_i - T_i)^2}, j \in [1,Q] \tag{12}$$

E_j represents the correlation between the target tag and virtual reference tag j. The smaller the correlation, the closer between the object tag and the virtual reference tag, and vice versa[8]. Therefore, as to the Q virtual reference tags, we get

$$\vec{E} = (E_1, E_2, \cdots, E_Q) \tag{13}$$

identify the k minimum values from E_1 to E_Q which stand for the k nearest virtual reference tags to the object tags. Finally, we can get the estimated coordinates of the target tag as

$$(x, y) = \sum_{i=1}^{k} w_i(x_i, y_i) \tag{14}$$

where (x_i, y_i) are the coordinates of one of the k nearest virtual reference tags with a relevant weight w_i defined as

$$w_j = \frac{\dfrac{1}{E_i^{\ 2}}}{\displaystyle\sum_{i=1}^{k} \dfrac{1}{E_i^{\ 2}}} \tag{15}$$

where $E_i \neq 0$. If $E_i = 0$, we set $E_i = 0.1$.

3   Experiment Analysis

3.1   Simulation Model

In our simulation, 4 reader tags, 25 reference tags and 10 tracking tags are placed in a $16(m) \times 16(m)$ indoor environment (path loss exponent a is 2.2[9]), as illustrated in Fig.3. The distance between two adjacent reference tags is set to $4(m)$ uniformly. Moreover, the number of nearest neighbor reference tags is chosen as $k = 4$ and the whole simulation is conducted with white Gaussian noise [10]. We define as

$$error = \sqrt{(x - x_o)^2 + (y - y_o)^2} \tag{16}$$

Where error represents the location estimation error from the computed coordinate (x, y) to the real coordinators (x_0, y_0) of the target tag, and the results are acquired by repeat the simulation for 500 times in our experiments.

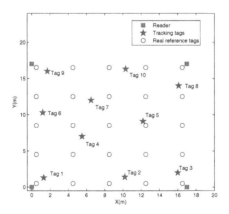

Fig. 3. Layout of simulation environment

3.2   Simulation Results and Analysis

Fig.4 shows that when the number of virtual reference tags which are equally placed between two adjacent real tags $n = 7$, the comparison between the LANDMARC, the VIRE and the improved algorithm on the 10 different locations of the object tags shown in Fig.3. As seen from the figure, the location accuracy of the improved algorithm increases 69.5% over LANDMARC and 23.3% over VIRE in average, and the worst estimation error of the improved algorithm is 0.60m while the average estimation error is 0.35m. Clearly, our algorithm approach provides a higher degree of accuracy than that of LANDMARC and VIRE at all locations.

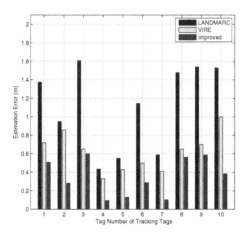

Fig. 4. Comparison between LANDMARC, VIRE and Improved

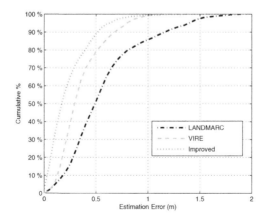

Fig. 5. Cumulative percentiles of error distance with different algorithms

Subsequently, we make a comparison with the performance of different algorithm about the CDF (Cumulative Distribution Function). Fig.5 shows that the improved algorithm provide a more precise location than LANDMRC and VIRE, and it can be seen that more than 80 percentile of error distance is less than 0.41m in the improved algorithm.

4   Conclusion

This paper presented a new active RFID-based indoor localization algorithm based on the concept of the virtual tags. We achieve the virtual tags' RSSI values through the Bivariate Newton interpolation, and the experimental result indicates that location accuracy has promoted 69.5% than LANDMARC and 23.3% than VIRE in average. Our future work is to expand the algorithm to a more wide environmental condition and 3D location algorithm.

Acknowledgement. This work is supported by NSFC(No. 61143008), National High Technology Research and Development Program of China (No. 2011AA01A204), Beijing University of Posts and Telecommunications Research and Innovation Fund for Youths.

References

1. Nikitin, P.V., Martinez, R., Ramamurthy, S., Leland, H., Spiess, G., Rao, K.V.S.: Phase Based Spatial Identification of UHF RFID Tags. In: 2010 IEEE International Conference on RFID, Orlando, USA, pp. 102–109 (April 2010)
2. Ni, L.M., Liu, Y., Lau, Y.C., Patil, A.P.: LANDMARC: indoor location sensing using active RFID. In: Proceedings of the First IEEE International Conference on Pervasive Computing and Communications, pp. 407–415 (March 2003)
3. Ayoub Khan, M., Antiwal, V.K.: Location Estimation Technique using Extended 3-D LANDMARC Algorithm for Passive RFID Tag. In: 2009 IEEE International Advance Computing Conference (IACC 2009), Patiala, India (March 2009)
4. Hekimian-Williams, C., Grant, B., Liu, X., Zhang, Z., Kumar, P.: Accurate localization of RFID tags using phase difference. In: Proc. of IEEE Int' l Conf. on RFID, Orlando, FL (April 2010)
5. Zhao, Y., Liu, Y., Ni, L.M.: VIRE: Active RFID- based Localization using Virtual Reference Elimination. In: 2007 International Conference on Parallel Processing, pp. 56–66 (2007)
6. Almaaitah, A., Ali, K., Hassanein, H.S., Ibnkahla, M.: 3D passive tag localization schemes for indoor RFID applications. In: Proc. of IEEE ICC, Cape Town, South Africa (May 2010)
7. Jain, S., Sabharwal, A., Chandra, S.: An improvised localization scheme using active RFID for accurate tracking in smart homes. In: Proc. of Int' Conf. on Computer Modelling and Simulation, Cambridge, UK (March 2010)
8. Yiming, J., Saad, B., Santosh, P., Prathima, A.: ARIADNE: A dynamic indoor signal map construction and localization system. In: MobiSys 2006- Fourth International Conference on Mobile Systems, pp. 151–164 (2006)
9. Wada, T., Uchitomi, N., Ota, Y., Hori, T., Mutsuura, K., Okada, H.: A novel localization scheme for passive RFID tags; communication range recognition (CRR). In: Proc. of IEEE ICC, Dresden, Germany (June 2009)
10. Reza, A.W., Geok, T.K.: Investigation of indoor location sensing via RFID reader network utilizing grid covering algorithm. Wireless Personal Communications 49, 67–88 (2008)

An Implementation of Trusted Remote Attestation Oriented the IaaSCloud

Chunwen Li[1,2], Xu Wu[1,2,3], Chuanyi Liu[1], and Xiaqing Xie[1,2]

[1] Key Laboratory of Trustworthy Distributed Computing and Service (BUPT)
Ministry of Education, Beijing, China
cy-liu04@mails.tsinghua.edu.cn
[2] School of Computer Science, Beijing University of Posts and Telecommunications,
Beijing, China
[3] Beijing University of Posts and Telecommunications Library, Beijing, China
{chunwenli,wux}@bupt.edu.cn,
happy_christina@qq.com

Abstract. The hosting service model of cloud computing brings trustworthines-sissue of cloud providers, which is a serious obstacle for wider adoption of cloud-based services. Based on open source components of TCG (Trusted Computing Group)and IBM's IMA (Integrity Measurement Architecture), this paper designed and implementeda remote attestation architecture and protocol to verify the trustworthiness of users' virtual machineinIaaS cloud. Meanwhile, as theverification agent, Trusted Third Partyminimized cloud configuration information disclosure, ensured the privacy of cloud.The experiments demonstratedthat this architecture brought little extra cost while provided trustworthiness guarantee.

Keywords: trustworthiness, remote attestation, cloud computing, IaaS, virtual machine.

1 Introduction

There are three types of cloud-based service mode: IaaS (Infrastructure as a Service), PaaS (Platform as a Service) and SaaS (Software as a Service).IaaS virtualizes IT infrastructure (computing, network, storage) to elastic resource pool, which will be used and paid on-demand by cloud service users. Moreover, IaaS modelhas other advantages in the aspects of good scalability, high reliability, and resource dynamical-location.Benefitingfrom these, IT enterprisesgreatly saved costs while enjoyed high quality services, this is the main reason that IaaS model is widely favored by SMEs (Small Medium Enterprises).

However, users lose direct control of their own resources in IaaS model,leading to the concerns of security, privacy, controllability, and trustworthinessissues [1].A survey of Fujitsu in 2010 indicated that89% of the consumers were concerned about who had access to their data, and a similar number said they were becoming more security conscious [2]. Trustworthiness issue hinders the wider application of IaaS for the

Y. Yuan, X. Wu, and Y. Lu (Eds.): ISCTCS 2012, CCIS 320, pp. 194–202, 2013.

large-scale enterprise and data-intensive organizations (e.g. banks, hospitals, government agencies), which will reduce the potential commercial value of cloud computing and obstruct its long-term development. It is significant to solve thetrustworthiness issue ofcloud.

Trusted attestation based on trust computing technology is one of solutions tosolvethe trustworthiness issue,using TPM (Trusted Platform Module) hardware as the trusted root. On the whole, there are mainly three categories of attestation mechanisms.The binary attestation is first proposed by IBM's Sailer [4], who implemented IMA (Integrity Measurement Architecture) to collectintegrity informationto verify the trustworthiness of platform. Based on this idea, PRIMA[5], BIND[6], LKIM[7], Re-DAS[8], and DynIMA[9] modelswereproposed todevelop the binary attestationmechanism.IBM's Jonathan Poritz [10]argued thatSailer'sbinary attestation suffers from limitations ofscalability, privacy and openness, proposed a new branch of verification method named property attestation.Verifier attestedthe high level security properties of platform without receiving detailed configuration data. Then Ahmad-RezaSadeghi[11], Liqun Chen[12], Ulrich Kühn[13], Qin Yu[14], AarthiNagarajan[15], made contribution to develop this model.LI Xiao-Yong[16]pointed out that the two previous methods can't reflect the behavior of platform, which is meaningless to trustworthiness, so they proposed the behavior-based attestation,direct verified the behavioral model of the system or software. Liang Gu [17] proposed a more realistic model-driven behavior-based attestation model. RABBIF [18] combined of behavior validation and integrity of information flow to make an attestation.

In this paper, we designed and realized trustworthiness verification framework for VM (Virtual Machine)inIaaSlayer, based on TCG open source components, IBM's IMA module and openPTS (Platform Trust Services). The attestation mechanismof openPTS is the blend of the three attestation methodspreviously mentioned, which is more practical and with littledefects. On this basis, we expanded verification of a single VM to the IaaS layer, and gave a related attestation protocol participated with a TTP(Trusted Third Party). TTP acted as an agent of trustworthiness attestation to ensure the correctness and reliable of verificationresults,while minimized the cloud configuration information disclosure. The experiments quantitatively gave the extra cost of the trustworthiness attestation frameworkfor the VMs of the IaaS platform, indicated that this frameworkbrought little extra cost on the performance of VM.

The remainder of this paper is organized as follows. The design and analysis of the trustworthiness verification frameworkof VMis describedin section 2. Section 3 presents the attestation architecture and protocol in IaaS platform. The experimental evaluations are discussed in section4. Finally, section 5 makes a conclusion of this paper.

2   The Trustworthiness Verification Framework of VM

2.1   Verification Framework

According to the standard of TCG (Trusted Computing Group), we design and implement this frameworkto verify the trustworthiness of VM on IaaS platform based on open source components of trust computing, as shown in the Fig.1.

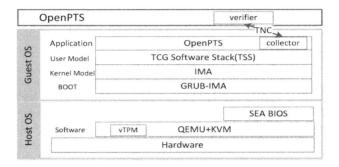

Fig. 1. Trustworthiness verification framework of VM

The host is physicalnode of cloud, and the guest is the VM that user requests to rentresources from cloud provider. In host OS, QEMUacts as the VMM (Virtual Machine Monitor), running VM with the KVMaccelerate module. The vTPM (virtual TPM) module of QEMU is the role of TPM hardware form the point view of VM.SeaBIOS is an open source implementation of X86 BIOS and fulfill the function of the initialization of TPM, SRTM (Static Root of Trust Measurement) and the extend of TCG BIOS, which plays the role of BIOS of VM.

GRUB-IMA is the enhancement of Linux boot loader adding the TCG measurement capability. It measures the grub during the process of loading Grub.

IMA works by hooking into the mmapoperation. Whenever a file is mapped in an executable mode, the IMA hook will first perform and save an SHA1 in the file of IML (Integrity Measurement List).

The TSS (TCG Software Stack) provides an API to operating systems and applications so that they can use the functionality provided by a TPM.

The implementation of remote attestation in this paper is based on openPTS, which is an open source implementation of the TCG PTS standard. OpenPTS combined the ideas of three trustworthiness attestationmechanismsmentioned above to verify the trustworthiness of system.

2.2   Verification Procedure

The validation process includes two steps. Firstly, build trust chain with the TPM as trust root,theintegrityinformation of VM such as BIOS boots sequence, kernel, and system program collected in the startup process.   Secondly, verify the configuration information through openPTS to determine the trustworthiness of the VM.

In the first step, as the startup of the system, thecomponent in the previous procedure measured the next component,extended measurements to TPM's PCRs (Platform Configuration Registers) and updated the PCR value as follows:

$$PCR_{new} = SHA1 \ (PCR_{old} \ || \ Measurement) \tag{1}$$

After this measurement and the current procedure finished,this component transferred control to the next component. This process repeated till the system fully starts up, andfinally generated the IML of the system. After that, whenever a new application loaded to run, IMA measured the program's binary code, then added a new measurementrecord to the end of IML file and extended the measurement to PCR. When verified IML, the measurement valuewas calculated from the first record to the last one, as the way of extending PCR:

$$Measurement_{cal}= SHA1 \ (Measurement_{cal} \ || \ Measurement_{one}) \qquad (2)$$

$Measurement_{one}$ is one of the measurement in IML, $Measurement_{cal}$ is the final measurement needed to compare with PCR value. The compare of final measurement value of IML and PCR value verified the coherence of IML and PCR to find out whether the IML has been tampered. If the final measurement value isequal to PCR value, then the IML is trustworthiness.

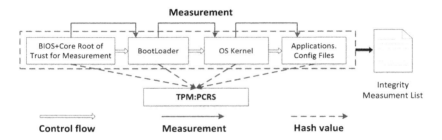

Fig. 2. Build trust chain

The second stepis validation.OpenPTS predefined some platform-independent system behavior model using finite state machine (FSM). The behavior model includes some prerequisites and security properties that systems need to meet. IML consists of the integrity information generated in the process of building trust chain and the related event type. IML eventsdrove system behavior model and generated the machine behavior of the local host, which is stored in the RM (Reference the Manifest) file. At the same time, The TPM PCR value and contents of IML wererecorded in the file of IR (Integrity Report). When the attesting system platform received the validation request from Verifier,it sent the RM and IR files to the Verifier.Verifierused RM to drive the behavior measurement record in the IR file, generated a calculate PCR value PCR', and compared the $PCR'$with the PCR value of TPM. If equal, the IR file is trusted, and thenVerifiercompared the SHA1 digest record in IR to the database recorded the SHA1 digest of trusted processes to find if there was any process not exists in the database. If the entire digests in IR matched with database, the VM was trustworthiness, if not, it is untrusted.

3   The Trusted Attestation of VM on IaaS Platform

3.1   The Attestation Architecture of IaaS Platform

Fig. 3depicts the attestation architecture of IaaS platform, indicating the inter-relationship among Users, CM (Cloud Manager) and TTP (Trusted Third Party). CMmanages cloud node (cloud physical machine) and acts as theintermediary of node and external entity, each node is designed as the framework of Fig. 1. TTP is the attestation agent of users, services to verify the trustworthiness of VM on the node that users request to connect, and reports the verification result to users.Users decide whether or not to connect to the VMthat IaaS provides to this user based on the verification result.

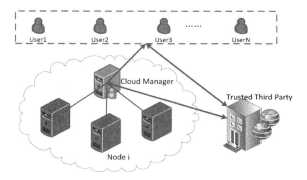

Fig. 3. Attestationarchitecture of IaaS platform

3.2   Attestation Protocolof Request a TrustedVM

Assumption:Users, TTP and CM, save public key of one another, CM and cloud nodes save public key of each other.

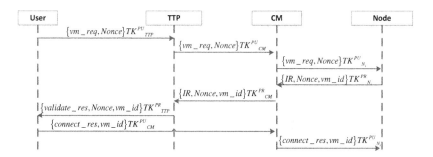

Fig. 4. The protocol of request a trusted VM

The protocol of Fig. 4 is the detail interaction among User, TTP, CM, and VM when users request a VM to the cloud. Users access the VM only after the validation of trustworthinessof the VM form TTP. We used recipient's public key to encrypt the interactivemessages, ensuringthe messageswould not be accessedin transmission process. The recipient used the corresponding private key to decrypt the received messages. The protocol process is as follows:

1. User sendsvm_req with a random number of *Nonce*to TTP for the request of application a VM. *Nonce* is used to ensure communication within a protocol round. TTP transfers the request message to node N_i through CM.
2. Node $N_i$readsvm_reqcontent, running a VM according to user's request configuration, then generates the *IR* file after the startup of system. $N_i$sends the message including*IR*, *Nonce*, and *vm_id*to TTP through CM.
3. TTP validates *IR* using the method mentioned in section 2.2 to achievethe validation results *validate_res*, then sends*validate_res*to user.
4. Userchecks *validate_res*to decide whether or not to use the VM.If the validation does not pass, user will give up the connection to the node N_i hosts this VM, ifthe *validate_res*is "the VM is trustworthiness", user will send the *connection_req* and *vm_id* to N_i through CM.
5. Node Ni receives connection messagefrom CM, allowing user to connect to the trusted VM of label*vm_id*. To this point, the request of a trusted VM is success.

4   Experiments and Discussions

Typically, cloud users rent VM to enjoy IaaS cloud services. The trustworthiness attestation systemmonitors the integrity and behaviors of TVM (Trusted VM), which will surely bring extra cost in performance for TVM. In this section, we used some benchmarks to evaluate the extra performance, and compared performance gap quantitativelybetween TVM and normal VMform the point of micro-benchmark and macro-benchmark (Fig. 5).

The experiments of micro-benchmark are shown as the two charts on top of Fig. 5, reflecting the ratio of performance cost between TVM and normal VM in command execution and computing ability. Thetwo charts on bottom of Fig. 5 belong to macro-benchmark, showing the influence of attestation systemon the file processing ability and database transaction abilityof TVM compared with normal VM.

We selected10 most commonly used Linux commands to test the ratio of execution time in TVM and normal VM. It can be seen from the chartthat, the average time of command execution of TVM is longer than the normal VMby 20%. However, the time is in milliseconds level, so the effects can almost be neglected.

BYTEmark tested the cost of computing ability of TVM, the ratio of comprehensive indexINTEGER INDEX andFLOATING-POINTINDEX is 0.990 and 0.987, so we can see TVM lose little performance in the aspect of computing, because the integrity of measurement only take place at the time when the program starts to run, after this, the execution will not be interfered by the attestation system.

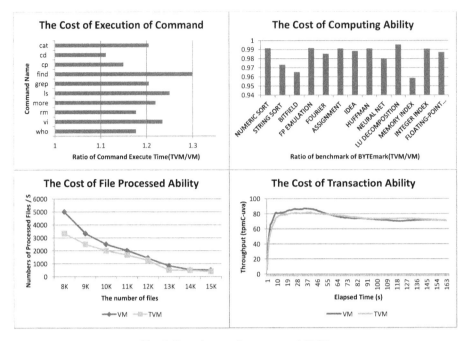

Fig. 5. Experiment of extra cost of TVM

We used two macro-benchmarks, Postmark andTPCC-UVa, to test the loss of file processingcapability and database transaction capability of TVM. The results demonstrate that the transaction capability of TVM is averagely lower than normal VM, but their gap is little.

The experiments proved thattrustworthiness attestationsystemdoes bring TVM some extra performance cost, however, the cost is little for the "measure once on the startupof program"characteristic of the attestation system, and the extra performance cost can be accepted compared to the benefit of assureof the trustworthiness.

5   Conclusion

We designed and implemented a trustworthinessverification framework of a VM based on open source components of TCG and IBM's IMA module, realized the goal to make sure the VM to be trusted, and extended the framework to the IaaS layer with a verification protocol, forming the trustworthiness attestation architecture of IaaS platform. Userverified the trustworthiness of their VM on IaaS with the participation of TTP, which acted as the nonaligned agent to ensure the credibility of the verification result and protected the privacy of cloud. The experiment results indicated thatthough attestation system in the VM brings some extra cost, it can be neglected compared to the benefit of trustworthinessassurance.

Acknowledgments. This study is supported by National Natural Science Foundation of China under Grants No. 91118002 , National High-tech R&D Program (863 Program) No. 2011AA01A204 and National High-tech R&D Program (863 Program): the typical demonstration and application based on eID .

References

1. Robinson, N., Valeri, L., Cave, J., Starkey, T., Graux, H., Creese, S., Hopkins, P.: The Cloud: Understanding the Security, Privacy and Trust Challenges. RAND Corporation, California (2011)
2. Personal Data in the Cloud: the importance of trust, `http://www.fujitsu.com/global/news/publications/dataprivacy.html`
3. Sailer, R., Zhang, X.L., Jaeger, T., Doorn, L.V.: Design and Implementation of a TCG-based Integrity Measurement Architecture. In: 13th USENIX Security Symposium, pp. 223–238. USENIX Association, Berkeley (2004)
4. Jaeger, T., Sailer, R., Shankar, U.: PRIMA:Policy-Reduced Integrity Measurement Architecture. In: Proceedings of the 11th ACM Symposium on Access Control Models and Technologies, pp. 19–28. ACM, New York (2006)
5. Shi, E., Perrig, A., Doorn, L.V.: BIND: A Fine-grained Attestation Service for Secure Distributed Systems. In: 2005 IEEE Symposium on Security and Privacy, pp. 154–168. IEEE Press, New York (2005)
6. Loscocco, P.A., Wilson, P.W., Pendergrass, J.A., McDonell, C.D.: Linux Kernel Integrity Measurement Using Contextual Inspection. In: 2007 ACM Workshop on Scalable Trusted Computing, pp. 21–29. ACM, New York (2006)
7. Kil, C., Sezer, E.C., Azab, A.M., Ning, P., Zhang, X.L.: Remote Attestation to Dynamic System Properties: Towards Providing Complete System Integrity Evidence. In: 39th Annual IEEE/IFIP International Conference on Dependable Systems and Networks, pp. 115–124. IEEEPress, New York (2009)
8. Davi, L., Sadeghi, A.R., Winandy, M.: Dynamic Integrity Measurement and Attestation: Towards Defense AgainstReturn-Oriented Programming Attacks. In: 2009 ACM workshop on Scalable Trusted Computing, pp. 49–54. ACM, New York (2009)
9. Poritz, J., Schunter, M., Herreweghen, E.V., Waidner, M.: Property Attestation—Scalable and Privacy-friendly Security Assessment of Peer Computers. Technical Report 3548, IBM Research Zurich (2004)
10. Sadeghi, A.R., Stüble, C.: Property-based Attestation for Computing Platforms: Caring about Properties, not mechanisms. In: 2004 New Security Paradigms Workshop, pp. 67–77. ACM, New York (2004)
11. Chen, L., Landfermann, R., Löhr, H., Rohe, M., Sadeghi, A.R., Stüble, C.: A Protocol for Property-Based Attestation. In: 1st ACM Workshop on Scalable Trusted Computing, pp. 7–16. ACM, New York (2006)
12. Kühn, U., Selhorst, M., Stüble, C.: Realizing Property-Based Attestation and Sealing with Commonly Available Hard- and Software. In: 2007 ACM Workshop on Scalable Trusted Computing, pp. 50–57. ACM, New York (2007)
13. Qin, Y., Feng, D.G.: Component Property Based Remote Attestation. J. Software 20(6), 1625–1641 (2009)

14. Nagarajan, A., Varadharajan, V.: Modelling Dynamic Trust with Property Based Attestation in Trusted Platforms. In: Foresti, S., Jajodia, S. (eds.) Data and Applications Security and Privacy XXIV. LNCS, vol. 6166, pp. 257–272. Springer, Heidelberg (2010)
15. Li, X.Y., Shen, C.X., Zuo, X.D.: An Efficient Attestation for Trustworthiness of Computing Platform. In: 2006 International Conference on Intelligent Information Hiding and Multimedia, pp. 625–630. IEEE Computer Society, Washington (2006)
16. Gu, L., Ding, X.H., Deng, R.H., Zou, Y.Z., Xie, B., Shao, W.Z., Mei, H.: Model-Driven Remote Attestation: Attesting Remote System from Behavioral Aspect. In: 9th International Conference for Young Computer Scientists, pp. 2347–2353. IEEE Press, New York (2008)
17. Wang, J., Wang, H.H., Tan, C.X.: RABBIF: Remote Attestation Based on Behavior and Information Flow. In: 2nd International Conference on Computer Engineering and Applications, pp. 18–22. IEEE Press, New York (2010)

C-SURF: Colored Speeded Up Robust Features

Jing Fu, Xiaojun Jing, Songlin Sun, Yueming Lu, and Ying Wang

School of Information and Communication Engineering, Beijing University of Posts
and Telecommunications, Beijing, China
Key Laboratory of Trustworthy Distributed Computing and Service (BUPT),
Ministry of Education
fujing19890115@163.com, {jxiaojun,slsun,ymlu}@bupt.edu.cn,
wangyingduke@gmail.com

Abstract. SURF has been proven to be one of the state-of-the art feature detector and descriptor, and mainly treats colorful images as gray images. However, color provides valuable information in the object description and recognition tasks. This paper addresses this problem and adds the color information into the scale-and rotation-invariant interest point detector and descriptor, coined C-SURF (Colored Speeded Up Robust Features). The built C-SURF is more robust than the conventional SURF with respect to rotation variations. Moreover, we use 112 dimensions to describe not only the distribution of Harr-wavelet responses but also the color information within the interest point neighborhood. The evaluation results support the potential of the proposed approach.

Keywords: object recognition, local invariant features, SURF, color images.

1   Introduction

Object recognition using local invariant features involves three main stages: interest points detection, descriptor building, and descriptor matching. Considering all the points in the image for object description is not feasible. Therefore, highly informative points are selected as interest points. More stable interest points mean better performance. For each of these interest points, a local feature descriptor is built to distinctively describe the local region around the interest point, and the final stage is matching the descriptors to decide if this point belongs to the object of interest or not. The matched points are used for further processing such as performing global object recognition or pose estimation.

Current successful local invariant features, such as scale invariant feature transform (SIFT) [1] and gradient location and orientation histogram (GLOH) [2]，the Speeded Up Robust Feature (SURF) operator developed by Bay, Tuytelaars and van Gool [3] is an extension and modification to the previously discussed SIFT operator. SURF aims at better runtime performance of the image feature detector, and preserves the high reliability and accuracy of SIFT, and is proved to be invariant to the scale, viewpoint and illumination changes. DAISY [4], which is inspired from earlier ones such as SIFT and GLOH but can be computed much faster by convolving gradient map to compute

Y. Yuan, X. Wu, and Y. Lu (Eds.): ISCTCS 2012, CCIS 320, pp. 203–210, 2013.
© Springer-Verlag Berlin Heidelberg 2013

the bin values. Although the algorithm attempts to estimate dense depth maps from wide-baseline image pairs, and gives better wide baseline stereo matching results than SIFT and SURF, the 200 dimensionality of the descriptor is a drawback of DAISY. BRIEF [5] is a method proposed by Michael Calonder and Vincent Lepetit which can directly compute a binary descriptor. It compares feature points fast while requiring comparatively small amounts of memory. SULD [6] (Speeded-Up Local Descriptor) is a low dimensions descriptor, which is achieved by summing up the Haar wavelet responses rather than the gradient. SULD approximates or even outperforms previously proposed schemes such as SURF [3] and DAISY [4]. Mikolajczyk and Schmid gave an excellent survey about local region descriptors [7].

Color is an important component for objects recognition. If the color information in an object is ignored, the important source of distinction maybe lost. The objects in Figure (1) will illustrate the point that color information is so important in object recognition. This example explains that how pure gray-based geometric description can cause confusion between two different features.

In this paper, we propose a novel descriptor scheme based on SURF. The built Colored SURF (C-SURF) is more robust and distinctive than SURF. Tests are based on colorful Tableware images. We evaluate the matching performance of SURF and C-SURF. Experiment results show that there are enhancements on the accuracy of image matching. The rest of the paper is organized as follows. In section 2, we describe the SURF algorithm. In section 3, we add color information to SURF. Experimental results are presented in section 4 and concluding remarks are given in section 5.

Fig. 1. An example that illustrates the neglecting of color information may confuse the two magnified corners. The magnified corners in the top pictures show the difference between them. Note the big similarity between the two magnified corners in the bottom pictures, which occurs when discard the color information.

2   SURF Algorithm

SURF, generally, includes four major stages: scale space feature extraction by a fast Hessian detector, extracting the localization of keypoints, orientation assignment, and key point descriptor. It takes use of Lowe's suggestion called Best-Bin-First [1] algorithm, with a distance ratio $0.6-0.8$ between the nearest one and the second nearest feature as a standard to accept a match.

1. SURF feature points detection method is based on scale space theory, it uses the determinant of Hessian matrix as a discriminant to look for local maximum value. For the point $X = \{x, y\}$ in an image I, it can be defined as

$$H(X,\sigma) = \begin{bmatrix} L_{xx}(X,\sigma)L_{xy}(X,\sigma) \\ L_{xy}(X,\sigma)L_{yy}(X,\sigma) \end{bmatrix} \tag{1}$$

Where $L_{xx}(X,\sigma)$ is the convolution of the Gaussian second order derivative with the image I in point X, and that is

$$L_{xx}(X,\sigma) = I * \frac{\partial^2}{\partial x^2} g(\sigma) \tag{2}$$

$L_{yy}(X,\sigma)$ and $L_{xy}(X,\sigma)$ is similar to $L_{xx}(X,\sigma)$. Bay, who proposed using the box filter approximate instead of second-order Gaussian filter [8]. With the integral image described in [10] to speed up the convolution to improve the computing speed. Further solving and getting the Hessian matrix Δ expression:

$$\det(H_{approx}) = D_{xx}D_{yy} - (\omega D_{xy})^2 \tag{3}$$

Then get each spot's response values. ω is recommended as 0.9, as in [12].

2. Setting a threshold to Hessian matrix of the detected extreme points. When the value is bigger than the threshold, non-maxima suppression is used to get the extreme point in the $3 \times 3 \times 3$ neighborhood of three-dimensional. Only the point bigger than the neighboring values of 26 points was chosen as a feature point.
3. SURF descriptor mainly bases on the gray neighborhood statistics information within the interest points, it is obtained by calculating the main direction and the feature vector. Firstly, set feature point as the center, calculate the Harr wavelet responses in x and y direction within a circular neighborhood of radius $6s$ around the interest point, s is the scale at which the interest points are detected. And assign Gaussian weighting coefficient to these responses. Then count the weighted Harr wavelet response with histogram. Accumulate the responses within $60°$ and form a new vector. Select the longest vector in the direction as the main direction of the feature points. U-SURF is the case of SURF that can be used when there is no or little rotation (up to $15°$). U-SURF is faster to compute as it doesn't take the orientation information into account [6].
4. For the extraction of the descriptor, the first step consists of constructing a square region centered around a point $P(x,y)$ and at scale S, the interest point and oriented along the orientation selected in the previous section. The first task is to

construct a square region of size $20s$. Each region is divided into 4×4 square sub-areas. Each sub area could be considered as an area with 4 components. For each sub area, Haar wavelet responses (size of $2s$) are computed at 5×5 regularly spaced samples. By denoting Haar wavelet responses for x and y components d_x and d_y [10], for 25 sample points sum of responses are calculated as:

$$V_{sub} = (\sum d_x, \sum d_y, \sum |d_x|, \sum |d_y|) \tag{4}$$

3   C-SURF

C-SURF algorithm not only keeps the advantages of the pure gray-based geometric description but also adds color information to improve the distinctiveness of the feature set. C-SURF includes four major stages: scale space feature extraction by a fast Hessian detector, extracting localization of key points, orientation assignment, and key point descriptor.

The descriptor describes not only the distribution of Harr-wavelet responses but also the color information within the interest point neighborhood, which outperforms SURF with respect to rotation variations. We rely on the integral image to reduce the computation time [3]. Moreover, we use the second-nearest-neighbor ratio matching strategy [7] to get the matching of descriptors. The region descriptors are robustly matched for each image pair to find the overlapping images to describe the features. The detailed procedures of this method are as follows:

1. Extracting the scale space feature of interest points by using the Fast-Hessian Detector proposed by Herbert Bay [3].
2. Finding the location as well as scale of the interest points.
3. Assigning Orientation.
4. Adding color information to SURF descriptor, so that the descriptor describes not only the distribution of Harr-wavelet responses but also the color information.

The first three stages are the same with SURF. The last stage is described as follows: For the extraction of the descriptor, firstly, constructing a square region centered around the interest point, the size of this window is $20s$. This region is split up regularly into smaller 4×4 square sub-regions. Secondly, it is oriented along the orientation selected in the previous section. Thirdly, for each sub-region, the factors calculated in the SURF descriptor are also calculated here. What's more, we calculate three factors namely $\sum r(x, y), \sum g(x, y), \sum b(x, y)$ for each sub-region. For each interest point $P(x, y)$, $r(x, y), g(x, y) b(x, y)$ represent color value of every pixel. Then, in every sub-region, $r(x, y), g(x, y).b(x, y)$ of every pixel are summed up to form a first set of entries to the feature vector. $\sum r(x, y), \sum g(x, y), \sum b(x, y)$ are weighted with three different factors, α, β, γ. They have different values when the matching images are of different rotation angles, and are set according to a large number of tests. The wavelet responses are invariant to a bias in illumination. Finally, the descriptor vector for each sub-region can be described as:

$$V_{sub} = (\sum d_x, \sum d_y, \sum |d_x|, \sum |d_y|, \sum r/\alpha, \sum g/\beta, \sum b/\gamma) \tag{5}$$

The descriptor is of the length of 112. Figure (2) shows the matching result.

Fig. 2. This shows the matching result, the result is the total matches

4   Experimental Evaluation

4.1   Evaluation Measurement

We use percentage of correct matches, P_c, over all the matches to compare the matching performance of the different methods. P_c is defined as ratio of correct matches T_{CM} to total matches T_M :

$$P_c = 100 \times T_{CM} / T_M \tag{5}$$

If matches are within a neighborhood of each other for 5 pixels, they are considered as correct matches.

   In this paper, the two methods that were used are all based on Matlab. We use the same dataset. The database contains 181 colorful images, which of different rotations. The rotation angle of these images is from 0° to 360°. Test images are all of the same size of 1181×1772 .

   We use the same image dataset to test SURF with color information(C-SURF) and SURF. The dataset includes deformation of rotation. The first experiment is based on the images without rotation, and the second experiment is based on ten pairs of colorful images with different rotation angles (from 0° to 20°). In each of the experiment, table shows the average correct match ratio and the value of α, β, γ .

4.2   Tests without Rotation

In this section, test images have the same rotation. Results of SURF, C-SURF tests are given in Table (1). Figure (3) shows the tests results as a chart.

Table 1. Tests results without rotation. Using images of the same rotation angle, data represents the average correct match ratio and the value of α, β, γ.

	SURF	C-SURF
P_c (%)	97.86%	98.46%
α		18.6
β		18.7
γ		18.7

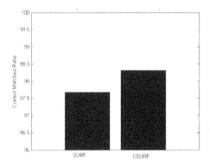

Fig. 3. Tests results without rotation. Using images of the same rotation angle, data represents the average correct match ratio.

As we can see in Table (1), C-SURF increases the average correct match ratio from 97.68% to 98.31% compares with SURF. C-SURF is more robust and distinctive than SURF when two images have the same rotation angle.

4.3   Rotation Tests

The second experiment shows the influence of rotation on the two methods. Ten pairs of colorful images with different rotation angles (from $0°$ to $20°$) are used for testing. Every pair of images will be tested by SURF and C-SURF. In every rotation test, C-SURF has been observed to increase average correct match ratio by $1\%-5\%$ compares with SURF. The accurate rotation tests results and the values of α, β, γ are given in Table (2). Figure (4) shows the tests results as a chart for easier visualization.

Table 2. Rotation comparison. Using ten pairs of images with different rotation angles. Data represents the average correct match ratio of rotation and the value of α, β, γ.

C-SURF	2°	4°	6°	8°	10°	12°	14°	16°	18°	20°
P_c (%)	98.31	99.13	97.22	98.15	97.83	96.23	100.00	97.83	100.00	94.44
α	18.6	18.5	18.3	18.3	18.3	18.2	18.2	18.0	18.0	18.0
β	18.7	18.5	18.6	18.6	18.6	18.6	18.6	18.6	18.6	18.6
γ	18.7	18.5	18.6	18.6	18.6	18.6	18.6	18.6	18.6	18.6

SURF	2°	4°	6°	8°	10°	12°	14°	16°	18°	20°
P_c (%)	97.68	96.40	97.12	95.19	94.59	93.82	93.29	92.62	92.94	94.16

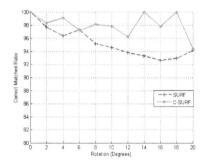

Fig. 4. Rotation comparison. Using ten pairs of images with different rotation angles. Data represents the average correct match ratio of rotation.

C-SURF is represented by the green line that has higher average correct match ratio, and is stable to rotation. SURF is represented by the red line, it has lower average correct match ratio. Therefore the results shows that SURF is not stable as C-SURF to rotation. C-SURF is the preferred method if the rotation angle is from 0° to 20°.

5   Conclusion

In both the rotation tests and the tests without rotation, C-SURF has been shown to increase the average correct matching rate and robust against rotation. According to the experimental results, C-SURF is the preferred method if the rotation angle is from 0° to 20°. Tests based on U-SURF and CU-SURF as well as tests against scale changes will be done in the future work.

Acknowledgement. This work is supported by NSFC (No. 61143008), National High Technology Research and Development Program of China (No. 2011AA01A204), Beijing University of Posts and Telecommunications Research and Innovation Fund for Youths.

References

1. Lowe, D.G.: Distinctive Image Features from Scale-Invariant Keypoints. International Journal of Computer Vision 60(2), 91–110 (2004)
2. Mikolajczyk, K., Schmid, C.: A performance evaluation of local descriptors. IEEE Trans. on Pattern Analysis and Machine Intelligence 10(27), 1615–1630 (2005)
3. Bay, H., Ess, A., Tuytelaars, T., Van Gool, L.: SURF: Speeded Up Robust Features. Computer Vision and Image Understanding (CVIU) 110(3), 346–359 (2008)
4. Tola, E., Lepetit, V., Fua, P.: DAISY: An Efficient Dense Descriptor Applied to Wide-Baseline Stereo. IEEE Transactions on Pattern Analysis and Machine Intelligence 32(5), 815–830 (2010)
5. Calonder, M., Lepetit, V., Özuysal, M., Trzcinski, T., Strecha, C., Fua, P.: BRIEF: Computing a local binary descriptor very fast. IEEE Trans. on Pattern Analysis and Machine Intelligence, 1 (2011)
6. Zhao, G., Chen, L., Chen, G.: A Speeded-up Local Descriptor For Dense Stereo Matching. In: 16th IEEE International Conference on Image Processing, pp. 2101–2104. IEEE Press (2009)
7. Mikolajczyk, K., Schmid, C.: A Performance Evaluation of Local Descriptors. IEEE Trans. on Pattern Analysis and Machine Intelligence 27(10), 1615–1630 (2004)
8. Bay, H., Sunderhauf, N., Protzel, P.: Comparing Several Implementations of Two Recently Published Feature Detectors. In: Proc. of the International Conference on Intelligent and Autonomous Systems, IAV, Toulouse, France (2007)
9. Witkin, A.P.: Scale-space Filtering. In: International Joint Conference on Artificial Intelligence, pp. 1019–1022 (1983)
10. Viola, P., Jones, M.: Rapid object detection using a boosted cascade of simple features. In: 2001 IEEE Computer Society Conference on Computer Vision and Pattern Recognition, pp. 511–518. IEEE Press (2001)
11. Lowe, D.G.: Object recognition from local scale-invariant features. In: International Conference on Computer Vision, Corfu, Greece, pp. 1150–1157 (1999)
12. Burt, P., Adelson, E.: The laplacian pyramid as a compact image code. IEEE Trans. on Communications, 532–540 (1983)

Mining Explainable User Interests from Scalable User Behavior Data

Li Jun[1,2,3], Zuo Xin-qiang[1], Zhou Meng-qi[1], Fan Gong-yuan[1], and Li Lian-cun[1]

[1] State Grid Energy Research Institute, Beijing, 100052, China
[2] School of Computer Science, Beijing University of Post and Telecommunication, Beijing, 100080, China
[3] Key Laboratory of Trustworthy Distributed Computing and Service (BUPT), Ministry of Education, Beijing, China
lijun@software.ict.ac.cn

Abstract. Capturing user interests from big user behavior data is critical for online advertising. Based on the user interests, advertisers can significantly reduce their advertising cost by delivering the most relevant ads for the user.

The state-of-the-art user Behavior Targeting (BT) models treat user behaviors as documents, and thus use topic models to extract their interests. A limitation of these methods is that user behaviors are usually described as unexplainable hidden topics, which cannot be directly used to guide online advertising. To this end, we propose in this paper a systematic User Interest Distribution Mining (UIDM for short) Framework to extract explainable user interests from big user behavior data. In the solution, we first use the Probabilistic Latent Semantic Analysis (PLSA) to discover the relationship between users and their behaviors, which can be described as hidden topics. Then, we construct a mapping matrix between the hidden topics and user interests by manually labeling a feature entity matrix. Experiments on real-world data sets demonstrate the performance of the proposed method.

Keywords: Behavior Targeting, Probabilistic Latent Semantic Analysis, User Category.

1   Introduction

Today, online advertisers are able to collect Internet user behavior data from their page visits, the links they click on, the searches they make and the things that they interact with. These big behavior data motivate them to develop data mining models to identify potential buyers from huge Internet users. As a result, they can deliver their ads to those who are potential buyers, instead of to all Internet users, which greatly reduces their advertising expense.

Behavioral Targeting (BT) has become a popular research area for online advertising. It aims to discover user interests from big user behavior data. Existing BT approaches for capturing user interests can be categorized into two types: classification or clustering of big user behavior data. The former often labels user behavior data to train a user interest classification model, while the latter simply group users into

Y. Yuan, X. Wu, and Y. Lu (Eds.): ISCTCS 2012, CCIS 320, pp. 211–218, 2013.

different interest groups. These methods have their own shortcomings. Classification models need to manually label a large portion of training examples, while the clustering models cannot accurately assign a user having multiple interests.

Recently, topic models have been popularly used to solve BT tasks. These models treat user behaviors as documents, and group user interests into hidden topics. The merit of topic models is to eliminate the ambiguity of interests by semantically clustering similar interests into the same group. The limitation is that the hidden topics are often unexplainable, and thus cannot be directly used to guide the online advertising. This limitation motivates us to develop an explainable user interest model based on the topic models.

Example 1. In an online advertising system, we collect the most recent behavior data of three users u_1, u_2, u_3 as shown in Table 1. Each user's behavior consists of her search keywords in search engines (denoted as ``2" in Table 1) and the web links she clicked (denoted as ``1"). We can observe that user u_1 recently searched three keywords ``cannon, samsung and camera", and clicked a link ``www.cannon.com". The second user u_2 searched a ``jordan" and a ``all-star", and clicked a link ``sports.sina.com/nba". Then, we treat each user as a document, with each behavior decomposed as a couple of words in the document. This way, topic models can be used to learn the hidden topics ``T" behind these behavior data.

Table 1. The behavior data of the three users in Example 1

userid	Recent behavior data	Interest distribution(target)
U1	Cannon:2 www.cannon.com:1 samsung:2 camera:2	Digital:0.8 Sports:0.05 Movie:0.15
U2	Jordan:2 sports.sina.com/nba:1 all-star:2	Digital:0.05 Sports:0.7 Movie:0.25
U3	Comedy:2 movie:2 www.youtube.com:1 jordan:2	Digital:0.05 Sports:0.1 Movie:0.85

However, the hidden topics ``T" are usually unexplainable. Thus, we want to map these topics into explainable user interest categories. For simplicity, we assume that there are only three user interest categories in this problem $Y=\{Digital, Sports, Movie\}$. Therefore, the aim is to obtain user interest categories (i.e., the target interest distribution matrix), as shown in the last column in Table 1, through which we can easily explain the three users' interests. For example, user u_1 is more likely to buy a digital equipment such as a camera, and thus we can recommend cameras ads to her.

In this paper, we present a practical user interest distribution mining (UIDM for short) framework to extract *explainable user interests* from big user behavior data. Technically, the model have the following two steps: (1) it first treats the user-behavior matrix as a document-word matrix, and uses the Probabilistic Latent Semantic Analysis (PLSA) to mine the relationship between users and their behaviors, described as hidden topics. (2) it builds a mapping matrix M between hidden topics and user interests based on a small portion of manually labeled feature entities. Experiments on real behavior data sets demonstrate the performance of the method.

The rest of the paper is structured as follows. Section 2 systematically gives the solution. Section 3 reports experimental results. We conclude the paper in Section 4.

2   Solution

We first introduce the notations used in this paper. Consider a Internet user u, her behavior data x is a set of vectors $X=\{x_1, x_2, ..., x_n\}$, where each vector x_i $(1 < i < n)$ is a bunch of text words representing a query extracted from the search engine or a URL clicked by her. Let $Y=(y_{1(u)}, y_{2(u)}, ..., y_{K(u)})$ be the distribution matrix of her interests, where each $y_{i(u)}$ is her preference on the i_{th} word. The learning task can be described as "learning the mapping function between the behavior data X and the interest distribution matrix Y".

2.1   The Procedure of UIDM

Figure 1 shows the procedure of the UIDM method. In the first step, we use the Bag-of-Words method to extract features from the behavior data, such as the search keywords and the clicked links. Thus, each user can be represented by a collection of documents, and we can apply the semantic analysis method PLSA to model the user interests. However, as the hidden topic extracted by PLSA is a mixture of unexplainable feature entities that cannot be directly used to supervise online advertising, we build a mapping matrix between topics and interest categories. As a result, the learning task is further extended to a new one that *how to map user-topic to user-interest.* In the second step, we build a mapping matrix from the user-topic matrix to the user-interest topic. This requires to label each hidden topics by attaching it explainable user interests. For example, in Figure 1, we build the classification distribution matrix C of all the feature items.

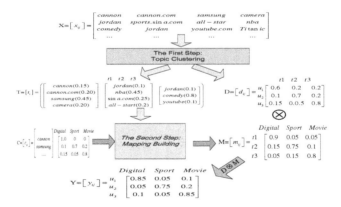

Fig. 1. An illustration of the UIDM method. Two steps are incorporated. The first step maps high-dimension behavior data into low-dimension hidden topics in the latent semantic space. As the hidden topics are unexplainable, the second step converts the user-topic matrix to the user-interest matrix.

2.2   Feature Selection

Generally, user behavior data is heterogeneous and sparse. A data-driven approach is to use granular events as features, such as page views and search queries. The dimensionality of search queries can be unbounded. Common approaches for feature selection evaluate terms according to their ability to distinguish the given user from the whole users, which have been popularly used in text categorization and clustering.

Here we use a frequency-based feature selection method. It first counts the entity frequency in terms of online users. Then, it selects the most frequent entities into the feature space. As the feature entity is often the unique identifier of the current event (e.g., URL or query), it is one level higher than features as the latter is identified by the pair (feature type, entity). In this work, we consider two types of entities: URL, and search. Thus the output of feature selection is two dictionaries.

2.3   Latent Semantic Analysis

In this section, we introduce the semantic analysis algorithm for the user historical actions (queries and clicks). The aim is to find the latent relationship between user and their behavior. Since we treat each query as an term entity, each user can be represented by a bag-of-words.

Formally, given a collection of users $u_i \in U = \{u_1, u_2, ..., u_n\}$, when using PLSA method for clustering, at first a latent topic model, which associates to an unobserved latent variable $z_k \in Z = \{z_1, z_2, ..., z_l\}$ with each occurrence of the behavior t in user u, should be defined. Suppose that $t_j \in T = t_1, t_2, ..., t_m$ is a feature entity, where T represents the vocabulary of all features used by all users. We use T_{u_i} as the set of all feature entities in u_i. This way, we have Eq.~(1),

$$T = \bigcup_{u_i \in U} T_{u_i} \tag{1}$$

Then, we define the co-occurrence matrix $N = cnt(u_i, t_j)$, where $cnt(u_i, t_j)$ describes the number of t_j behaved by u_i. To semantically analysis the user's purchasing preference, latent topic $z_k \in Z = \{z_1, z_2, ..., z_l\}$ is used to build the relationship between user and their behavior. From the user's perspective, topics are strongly related to interest.

From generative model construction point of view, it can be done in three steps:

1. select a user u with probability $P(u)$;
2. choose a latent topic z with probability $P(z|u)$;
3. generate a behavior t with probability $P(t|z)$.

Consider observations (t,u) of behavior features and users is generated independently and the behavior t and user u are conditional independent given the latent topic z. the joint probability $P(t,u)$ of behavior t co-occurrence with user u can be calculated as:

$$P(u,t) = P(u)\sum_{z \in Z} P(z \mid u)P(t \mid z) \tag{2}$$

Based on the Bayes' rule, the above equation can be further rewritten as:

$$P(u,t) = \sum_{z \in Z} P(z)P(u \mid z)P(t \mid z) \tag{3}$$

Eq.4 is the symmetric formulation, where u and t are both generated from the latent class Z in similar ways(using the conditional probabilities $P(u|z)$ and $P(t|z)$. Eq.5 is an asymmetric formulation, where, for each user u, a latent class is chosen conditionally to the user according to $P(z|u)$, and a feature entity is then generated from that class according to probability $P(t|z)$. The graphical model representation is shown in Figure 2.

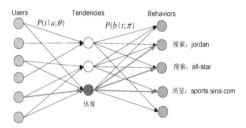

Fig. 2. An illustration of modeling the user behavior in a graphical model

If we treat a user and a feature entity as a document and a term respectively, the PLSA evaluation step of the relationship between user and behavior will be the same problem as text mining. Then best parameters $P(t|z)$, $P(u|z)$ and $P(z)$ can be determined by maximizing the user-behavior log-likehood function.

$$Max = \sum_{i=1}^{n} \sum_{j=1}^{m} cnt(u_i, t_j) \log P(u_i, t_j) \tag{4}$$

Combining Eq.(2) and Eq.(3), we have,

$$Max = \sum_{i=1}^{n} \sum_{j=1}^{m} cnt(u_i, t_j) \log \sum_{k=1}^{l} P(Z_k)P(u_i \mid z_k)P(t_j \mid z_k) \tag{5}$$

In order to solve the above problem, we use the Expectation Maximization(EM) approach which iteratively calculates the two steps.

1. Expectation step(E-step). Based on the current estimates of parameters, compute the posterior probabilities $P(z_k|u_i, t_j)$ for the latent variable.
2. Maximization Step(M-step). Maximize the likelihood function $E[L_c]$, update $P(z_k)$, $P(u_i|z_k)$ and $P(t_j|z_k)$.

At last, our UIDM method evaluates all the $P(z_k|u_i)$ between a user u_i and a topic z_k using Eq.(4).

The topic is unexplainable, and it is unable to explicitly describe denote the interest. The second step builds the bridge between topics and interests. Since the user-topic matrix (T in Figure 1) and the user-topic distribution matrix (D in Fig.1) can be evaluated by the PLSA algorithm with the user-behavior data sets, the original problem can be converted to a new one that *how to get the final user-interest matrix?*

To solve this problem, as the number of labeled feature entities is limited compared to the total feature space. Thus, we propose to use SVM classifiers to predict the interests of all feature entities, and then integrate the predict result with the label feature, and get the feature-interest matrix C, which is shown in Fig.1.

Based on the matrixes C and T, we multiple them by using Eq. (5) to get the topic-interest matrix M, which represents the final user-interest distribution matrix Y.

3   Experiments

In this section, we use real-world Internet user search sessions recorded by a popular commercial search engine to empirically validate the effectiveness of the proposed UIDM method. All experiments were conducted on two Linux servers with Intel Xeon E5620(2.40GHz)*16 CPU and 24GB memory. All the source code and test data can be downloaded from http://streammining.org.

3.1   Data Set

A One-day behavior log data set was collected from a commercial search engine. Specially, the log data contain users' URL clicks, page visits and search queries. A data preprocessing step was applied to remove users that have more than 100 clicks per hour.

Table 2. The interest-category system

Interest category	Number of labeled features
finance	8976
sports	1644
healthy	1738

Table 2 shows the interest-category system. Meanwhile, we label 16,860 URLs for classifier training. In addition, we also label queries by the referred information from the search engine.

3.2   Benchmark Methods and Measures

We implemented two benchmark methods for comparison.

(1) A UIDM method with all feature entities (UIDM): In our experiments, we use base SVM classifiers to predict all the feature entities, and integrate the predicted

results with all labeled feature entities to build the topic-interest matrix M as shown in Figure 1.

(2) Label-based Categories Statistics (LCS for short): In this framework, the interest evaluation is based on the labeled hosts and queries, for every behavior of user u, if this behavior is labeled, we directly update the interest distribution matrix by adding the labeled vector.

The accuracy of our UIDM method is measured by R_{pv} and R_{uv} which are defined as follows:

$$R_{pv}(c,w) = \frac{cnt_{pv}(w,c)}{sum_{pv}(w)} \tag{6}$$

$$R_{uv}(c,w) = \frac{cnt_{uv}(w,c)}{sum_{uv}(w)} \tag{7}$$

where c is the corresponding category, w is the test web site, $sum_{uv}(w)$ is the number of users who visited w. For each web site, the larger the $N_{c(w)}$ is, the more accurate should be observed.

On the other hand, we use P_{avg} to evaluate the total performance of different mining framework, which is defined as follows:

$$P_{avg} = \frac{1}{n}\sum_{i=1}^{n} p(k,i) \tag{8}$$

where n is the scale of label sets, k is the number of categories.

3.3   Experimental Results

We compare the two methods under different parameter settings of topics.

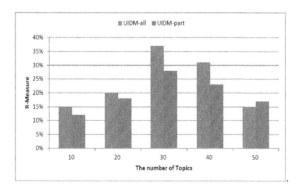

Fig. 3. The result of topic vs. R-Measure

The number of Topic N: To study the impact of N to the final predict accuracy, we use the R-measure, which integrates both interest and behavior, to evaluate UIDM method. Figure 3 shows the averaged R_{pv} and R_{uv} under different topics in our data set. We can observe that in most cases, 13 topics yield the best result. In addition, to reduce memory space, only the results of the top three web sites are provided. The x-axis of the figure stands for the number of topics, and the y-axis stands for precision. To sum up, in terms of R-measure, UDIM always performs better than benchmark methods on our advertising data.

4   Conclusion

Behavior Targeting (BT) plays an important role in online advertising. The state-of-the-art BT approaches uses topic models for user interest mining. These models, albeit effective, are often unexplainable, and thus cannot be directly applied. In this paper, we propose a systematic User Interest Distribution Mining(UIDM) Framework to accurately predict the long-term interests from big user behavior data. UIDM further extends the Probabilistic Latent Semantic Analysis (PLSA) model for better understanding and explanation of user interests. An interesting research direction in the future is to parallelize the PLSA model based on the Map-Reduce procedure to handle big user behavior data.

References

1. Beitzel, S., Jensen, E., Frieder, O., Lewis, D., Chowdhury, A., Kolcz, A.: Improving automatic query classification via semi-supervised learning. In: Fifth IEEE International Conference on Data Mining, p. 8. IEEE (2005)
2. Cao, H., Hu, D., Shen, D., Jiang, D., Sun, J., Chen, E., Yang, Q.: Context-aware query classification. In: Proceedings of the 32nd International ACM SIGIR Conference on Research and Development in Information Retrieval, pp. 3–10. ACM (2009)
3. Cao, H., Jiang, D., Pei, J., Chen, E., Li, H.: Towards context-aware search by learning a very large variable length hidden markov model from search logs. In: Proceedings of the 18th International Conference on World Wide Web, pp. 191–200. ACM (2009)
4. Hu, J., Wang, G., Lochovsky, F., Sun, J., Chen, Z.: Understanding user's query intent with wikipedia. In: Proceedings of the 18th International Conference on World Wide Web, pp. 471–480. ACM (2009)
5. Shen, D., Sun, J., Yang, Q., Chen, Z.: Building bridges for web query classification. In: Proceedings of the 29th Annual International ACM SIGIR Conference on Research and Development in Information Retrieval, pp. 131–138. ACM (2006)

An Improved Design of the Trustworthiness Authentication Mechanism of IaaS

Xu Wu[1,2,3], Xiaqing Xie[1,2], Chuanyi Liu[1], and Chunwen Li[1,2]

[1] Key Laboratory of Trustworthy Distributed Computing and Service (BUPT),
Ministry of Education, Beijing, China
`cy-liu04@mails.tsinghua.edu.cn`
[2] School of Computer Science, Beijing University of Posts and Telecommunications,
Beijing, China
[3] Beijing University of Posts and Telecommunications Library, Beijing, China
`wux@bupt.edu.cn`, `happy_christina@qq.com`, `lichunwen1987@sina.com`

Abstract. By improving resource utilization, cloud computing can greatly save costs and get users considerable profit. However, security issues have emerged as one of the most significant barrier to faster and more widespread adoption of cloud computing. Therefore, this paper focused on the trustworthiness of infrastructure as a service (IaaS) and designed a role-based authentication trustworthiness mechanism to ensure that the different roles in IaaS architecture are trusted. What's more, this paper also considered the interactions between different roles in cloud environment and designed relevant validation protocols. At last, we also designed some benchmarks to evaluate the performance overhead of this mechanism and the results showed the costs can be very little to be neglected.

Keywords: trusted computing, IaaS, trustworthiness authentication mechanism.

1 Introduction

Despite of the advantages cloud computing brings, new problems arise; especially the crisis of trust comes to be a big threat. The clients place computation and data on machines they cannot control, and the provider agrees to run a service whose details clients do not know. It is natural for clients to have concerns about the data confidentiality, security and integrity [1]. On the other hand, the cloud providers also don't know the detailed behaviors or intentions of the services deployed by users while malicious users may theft other users' sensitive data or even destroy the platform.

Since the crisis of trust between cloud providers and clients has emerged as arguably the most significant barrier to faster and more widespread adoption of cloud computing, it's urgent to solve the trustworthiness issue of cloud. Researchers and scholars home and abroad have achieved great progress in the research of trustworthiness of cloud. CERTICLOUD [2] proposed a TPM-based approach to ensure trustworthiness and integrity of infrastructure as a service (IaaS), including one main

Y. Yuan, X. Wu, and Y. Lu (Eds.): ISCTCS 2012, CCIS 320, pp. 219–226, 2013.

protocol: TPM-based certification of a remote resource (TCRR), which offered a way to verify the integrity of remote physical system and to exchange symmetric keys. RepCloud [3] designed a reputation system for managing decentralized attestation metrics in the cloud and further managing trust in the cloud. A flaw of this design is that it didn't offer clear result whether a node is trusted. And myTrustedCloud [4] integrated eucalyptus with the Trusted Computing technology to meet the security requirements of the energy industry. And [5] proposed TCCP (Trusted Cloud Computing Platform) which enables IaaS (Infrastructure as a Service) providers to serve a closed box execution environment that guarantees confidential execution of guest VMs (Virtual Machines). This system allows a customer to verify if its computation will run securely, before requesting the service to launch a VM. The common drawback of current research is that they regard the nodes in cloud as the same, while the nodes play different roles and perform different tasks, and their interaction can be dynamic, transient.

On the basis of above analysis, this paper overcame the shortcomings and designed the trustworthiness authentication mechanism of IaaS to make a difference between nodes in cloud so as to adapt to the requirements of complex cloud environment.

2   The Design of Trustworthiness Authentication Mechanism

2.1   Physical Server Architecture

In order to implement the trustworthiness authentication mechanism, physical servers should be equipped with TPM [9], Integrity Measurement Architecture (IMA) [11] and OpenPTS [12]. According to the Trusted Computing Group (TCG) [10], TPM [9] is a hardware component on the motherboard of a platform and takes on the role of the root of trust. It provides protected data (crypto-graphic secrets and arbitrary data) by never releasing a root key outside the TPM. In addition, TPM provides some primitive cryptographic functions, and mechanism of integrity measurement, storage, and reporting of a platform, from which strong protection capabilities and attestations can be achieved. IMA [11] works by hooking into the mmap operation and it maintains a list of file hash values as well as an aggregate integrity value over this list inside the TPM hardware. Whenever a file is mapped in an executable mode, the IMA hook will first perform and save an SHA1 in the file of Integrity Measurement List (IML). IMA's maintenance of a TPM hardware anchored file measurement list is fundamental to TCG's Platform Trusted Services (PTS). While OpenPTS[12] is a reference implementation of the PTS, and works with other trusted computing open source components, such as BIOS and GRUB-IMA and so on.

2.2   Different Roles in IaaS

This paper focuses on IaaS, in which the cloud provider supplies a set of virtualized infrastructural components such as VMs and storage for customers to build and run applications [7]. Existing open source IaaS cloud includes OpenStack[13], OpenNebula[14] and Nimbus[15] and so on. We primarily chose eucalyptus [8] to research into the trustworthiness authentication protocols mechanism of IaaS, as it supports an industry standard interface (Amazon EC2), and it is one of the world's most widely used IaaS cloud. And this paper also regards the eucalyptus architecture as IaaS typical architecture.

The eucalyptus cloud computing platform has five kinds of roles: Cloud Controller (CLC), Cluster Controller (CC), Walrus, Storage Controller (SC) and Node Controller (NC). The CLC is responsible for exposing and managing the underlying virtualized resources via user-facing APIs; walrus implements scalable "put-get bucket storage" , providing a mechanism for persistent storage, access control of virtual machine images and user data; the CC controls the execution of VMs running on the nodes and manages the virtual networking; the SC provides block-level network storage that can be dynamically attached by VMs; the NC (through the functionality of a hypervisor) controls VM activities, including the execution, inspection, and termination of VM instances.

According to different roles in eucalyptus, this paper also regards the nodes in eucalyptus differently and designs the trustworthiness authentication mechanism accordingly. In detail, this mechanism will not only ensure the single node's trustworthiness, but also the trustworthiness of the inner interactions. Moreover, we also introduce Third Trusted Entity (TTE) as verifier to verify the nodes in the cloud.

2.3 Single Node's Verification

The validation of single node mainly refers to the process of node registration. We describe the protocols that manage the set of nodes of the platform, and design related protocols to secure the cloud environment. Symbols used in the protocols are described as Table 1.

Table 1. Symbol Description Table

Symbol	Description
Node_info	Related information including node_ID, certificates of TPM and the node configuration information.
Node_type	The role of the node, including CLC, CC, and NC.
Cert(A)	The certificate of A.
Hash(A)	The hash value of A.
K_A^{PR}	The private key of A.
K_A^{PU}	The public key of A.
{A}K	Encrypt data A with key K.
$challenge_A$	Unique sequences generated by A.
K_S	Session keys.
ML_A	Measurement List of A's configure information.
Rgt_info	Registration information of specific role, including the host's IP information and so on.
TTE	Third Trusted Entity.

This part takes CLC as an example to describe the validation process. Fig.1 describes the protocols of CLC registration to TTE to be a cloud node.

Step 1, CLC sends a request as *message 1* to the TTE. CLC has to provide the CSP's certificate to prove that the provider is trusted. As the private key of TTE is safe, this message can only be deciphered by TTE. With this message, TTE can get the public key of CLC as well as validate CLC's role in the cloud. If message passes validated, then go to step2.

Step 2, TTE return *message 2* which was signed by TTE to CLC. Those who know the public key of TTE can all decipher this message as:

$$\{ challenge_{CLC}, K_S \} K_{CLC}^{PU}, \{ challenge_{TE} \} K_S$$

Message 1. CLC→TTE: $\{Hash(Cert(CSP)), K_{CLC}^{PU}, \{ challenge_{CLC}, Node\_type \} K_{CLC}^{PR} \} K_{TTE}^{PU}$

Message 2. TTE→CLC: $\{\{challenge_{CLC}, K_S\} K_{CLC}^{PU}, \{ challenge_{TTE} \} K_S \} K_{TTE}^{PR}$

Message 3. CLC→TTE: $\{\{challenge_{TTE}, Node\_info, CL_{CLC}\} K_S \} K_{TTE}^{PU}$

Message 4. TTE→CLC: $\{\{Cert(CLC), ACK\} K_S \} K_{TTE}^{PR}$

Fig. 1. Protocol description of CLC registration

However, only CLC can get the plain text. $Challenge_{CLC}$ is to ensure this message is to reply from TTE to its request, Ks is to get the $challenge_{TTE}$ to establish the communication. By this message, CLC can not only ensure that the message is sent from TTE, but also ensure that the message can only be got by itself.

Step 3, CLC sends its detail information to TTE for the initial validation to help finish this registration. This message is encrypted with Ks to ensure the uniqueness of this session, and then it's encrypted by TTE's public key to ensure its confidentiality.

Step 4, TTE issues the certificate to CLC on condition that the CLC is trusted.

To be sure, the validation of other roles like CC and NC obey to the same protocols, while the role-related information or certificate changes.

2.4   Interactions' Verification between Nodes

The interactions between nodes include the process of secondary node registering to the superior node (e.g., CC registers to CLC, NC registers to CC), and the interaction between the physical host and the VMs.

Registration Protocol. During the construction of cloud, secondary will register to the superior node to be a cloud node. This part takes registration from CC to CLC as an example shown as Fig.2.

Step 1, CC sends its request *message 1* to the CLC; this information is encrypted by the TTE's public key. Only TTE can decipher the message because CC doesn't trust CLC. The message includes CC's certificate to be validated by TTE, and session key as well as $challenge_{CC}$ are signed by CC that CLC cannot forge message because it doesn't know CC's private key.

Step 2, CLC binds message 1 with CLC's certificates and sends all this as message 2 to TTE. TTE has to validate the trustworthiness of both the CLC and CC.

Step 3, after TTE confirms the trustworthiness of CLC and CC, it transfers *message 1* to the form that CLC can decipher or read as *message 3* and sends to CLC.

Validation process:

Message 1. CC→ CLC: $\{Hash\ (Cert\ (CC)),\ \{Ks,\quad challenge_{CC}\ \}\ K_{CC}^{PR}\}\ K_{TTE}^{PU}$

Message 2. CLC→TTE: $\{Hash\ (Cert\ (CC)),\ \{Ks,\quad challenge_{CC}\ \}\ K_{CC}^{PR}\}$
$K_{TTE}^{PU},\ Hash(Cert(CLC))$

Message 3.   TTE → CLC: $\{\{K_{CC}^{PU},\ Ks,\quad challenge_{CC}\ \}K_{CLC}^{PU}\}\ K_{TTE}^{PR}$

Message 4.   CLC→CC: $\{\{Hash\ (challenge_{CC},\ Rgt\_info),\ \{Rgt\_info\}\ Ks\}K_{CLC}^{PR},$
$K_{CLC}^{PU}\}K_{CC}^{PU}$

Fig. 2. Protocol description of registration from CC to CLC

Step 4, CLC gets CC's public key and returns the registration information to CC. In order to ensure confidentiality and integrity of *Rgt_info,* CLC binds it with $challenge_{CC}$ and calculates *hash value.* When CC receive message 4, it can decipher it and get K_{CLC}^{PU}, then get $Hash(challenge_{CC},Rgt\_info),\{Rgt\_info\}Ks$. As *Ks* was generated by itself, it can get *Rgt_info.* At last, CC calculates a new hash value of *{challenge_{CC}, Rgt_info}* to be compared with the received one. It they are consistent, the *Rgt_info* is trusted and the registration is finished.

As for the registration from NC to CC, the process is the same to the registration from CC to CLC, we need to replace CC-related information with NC-related information, and replace CLC-related with CC-related information.

VM Launch Protocol. As the user's application is running in the VMs, so it necessary to validate the trustworthiness of VM from the moment it launches. The user requests to launch a VM, then the CC allocates a physical node (NC), and the NC launch the VM under the monitoring of TTE.

In detail, the process in Fig.3 is as followed:

Step 1, user sends a request as message 1 to the CLC to launch a VM.

Step 2, CLC binds message 1 to CLC's certificates, sends to TTE.

Step 3, TTE confirms that the CLC and user are both trusted, sends the validation result as *message 3* to CLC.

Step 4, CLC sends the *message 4*, which is encrypted by CC's public key, to CC.

Step 5, CC deciphers *message 4*, transfers it to *message 5* and sends to NC.

Step 6, NC deciphers *message 5*, and launches a VM, then sends the VM information to CC. At this moment, NC is sure that CC is trusted, so the data will only be encrypted by CLC's public key to ensure its privacy.

Step 7, CC transfers the data to CLC. CLC is only communicated with CC, but not NC.

Step 8, CLC returns the data to user, and the user can access the VM with the relevant information.

The process of launch is monitored by TPM, and TPM will record this information, generate the ICV and sends it to TTE; only after TTE validates it and the result is trusted, NC returns VM information to the user.

Message 1. User$\rightarrow$ CLC: $\{Hash\ (Cert\ (User)),\ \{Request, challenge_U,\ Ks\ \}K_{User}^{PR}\}$ K_{TTE}^{PU}

Message 2. CLC$\rightarrow$TTE: $\{Hash\ (Cert\ (User)),\ \{Request, challenge_U,\ Ks\ \}K_{User}^{PR}\}$ $K_{TTE}^{PU},\ hash(Cert(CLC))$

Message 3. TTE$\rightarrow$CLC: $\{\{K_{User}^{PU},\ Request, challenge_U, Ks\ \}K_{CLC}^{PU}\}K_{TTE}^{PR}$

Message 4. CLC$\rightarrow$CC: $\{\{VM\_Stat,\ Hash\ (VM\_Stat)\}\ Ks\}K_{CLC}^{PR}.\{$ $Ks,\ challenge_{CLC}\}K_{CC}^{PU}$

Message 5. CC $\rightarrow$NC: $\{\{\{VM\_Stat,\ Hash(VM\_Stat)\}\ Ks\ \}K_{CC}^{PR},$ $challenge_{CC}\}K_{NC}^{PU}$

Message 6. NC $\rightarrow$CC: $\{\{VM\_info\}\ Ks,\ challenge_{CC}\}K_{CLC}^{PU}$

Message 7. CC $\rightarrow$CLC: $\{\{VM\_info\}\ Ks,\ challenge_{CLC}\}K_{CLC}^{PU}$

Message 8. CLC$\rightarrow$User: $\{\{VM\_info\}\ Ks, challenge_U\}K_{User}^{PU}$

Fig. 3. Protocol description of VM launch

3   Results and Discussion

The mechanism proposed by this paper ignored the hardware attack, and TTE is trusted naturally. On this condition, the security of the protocols relies on the safety of private keys. Since the private keys are preserved by TPM, the root of trust, which can well ensure the confidentiality, integrity and undeniability, so the private keys are secure. What's more, this paper also combines symmetrical encryption with asymmetric encryption, thus improving the encryption/decryption efficiency at the same time. In addition, these protocols can avoid replay attack with the help of nonce [16] and session keys, as nonce and session key are both effective only in one session, thus avoiding replay attack. It's should be noted that these protocols can also be against Man-in-the-middle attack.

Practically, the trustworthiness authentication mechanism will bring some extra performance cost. In order to evaluate the cost, we design several benchmarks to do experiments. The control group is the system without our mechanism, and the experimental group is the system with our trustworthiness authentication mechanism. Finally, we focus on the overhead in computing and I/O throughputs.

As for the cost in computing ability, we use the BYTEmark [17], which consists of a number of well-known algorithms, including MEMORY INDEX, BITFIELD and so on. We tested ten frequently used commands and run the benchmark 10 times to get the average value to calculate the ratio of cost between two groups.   Fig.4 shows that the lowest cost is less than 1% by *NUMERIC SORT* while the highest is about 4% by MEMORY INDEX, and the average cost of computing is 1.6%. We can conclude that the cost of computing ability brought by the trustworthiness system can be ignored.

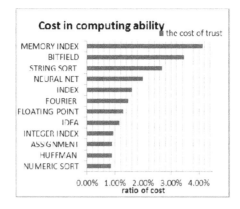

Fig. 4. Experimental on computing overhead

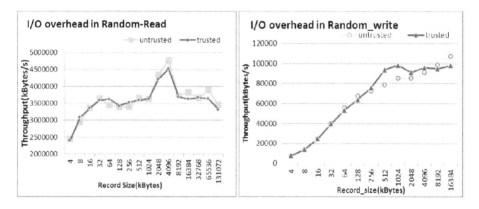

Fig. 5. Experiments on I/O overhead by random read and random write

In order to evaluate the I/O overhead, we used IOzone, a filesystem benchmark tool to test file I/O performance by generating and measuring a variety of file operations like *write, read* and *re-read* and so on. The two charts in Fig.5 are I/O overhead by *Random Read* and *Random Write* respectively and the each chart compares the throughput of two groups. In the experiments, file size is 512M and the record increases. Observing the trend of throughput, the two lines in each chart almost superpose, which indicate that the cost of I/O is very little.

In summary, the cost brought by our mechanism can almost be neglected.

4   Conclusion

This paper proposed a role-based trustworthiness authentication mechanism to ensure that the different roles in IaaS are trustworthy. The main innovative point is to make a difference among different roles in the cloud and design different protocols accordingly. Finally, we analyzed the security of the protocols and designed several benchmarks to evaluate the performance of our mechanism. The experiments indicate that the cost brought by the mechanism can be very little. In the future, our mechanism will cover the other roles in eucalyptus like Walrus and SC, and take consideration of other relevant interactions like the VM migration and so on.

Acknowledgment. This study is supported by National Natural Science Foundation of China under Grants No. 91118002 and National High-tech R&D Program (863 Program) No. 2011AA01A204 and National High-tech R&D Program (863 Program) No. 2012AA01A404.

References

1. Goyal, A., Dadizadeh, S.: A Survey on Cloud Computing. University of British Columbia Technical Report for CS 508 (2009)
2. Bertholon, B., Varrette, S., Bouvry, P.: Certicloud: a novel tpm-based approach to ensure cloud iaas security. In: Proceedings of the 4th International Conference on Cloud Computing (CLOUD 2011), July 4-9, IEEE Computer Society, Washington DC (2011)
3. Ruan, A., Martin, A.: RepCloud: Achieving Fine-grained Cloud TCB Attestation with Reputation Systems. In: Proceedings of the 6th ACM Workshop on Scalable Trusted Computing, New York, NY, USA, pp. 3–14 (2011)
4. Wallom, D., Turilli, M., Taylor, G., Hargreaves, N., Martin, A., Raun, A., McMoran, A.: myTrustedCloud: Trusted Cloud Infrastructure for Security-critical Computation and Data Management. In: Proceedings of the 3th IEEE International Conference on Cloud Computing Technology and Science (CloudCom 2011), Athens, Greece, November 29-December 1, pp. 247–254 (2011)
5. Santos, N., Gummadi, K.P., Rodrigue, R.: Towards Trusted Cloud Computing. In: Proc.of the 1st USENIX Workshop on Hot Topics in Cloud Computing, Berkeley, CA, USA (2009)
6. Takabi, H., Joshi, J.B.D., Ahn, G.J.: Security and Privacy Challenges in Cloud Computing Environments. Technical Report (2010)
7. Takabi, H., Joshi, J.B.D., Ahn, G.J.: Security and Privacy Challenges in Cloud Computing Environments. Technical Report (2010)
8. 2012 Eucalyptus Systems, Inc., http://open.eucalyptus.com
9. Wikimedia Foundation, Inc., http://en.wikipedia.org/wiki/Trusted_Platform_Module
10. Trusted Computing Group, http://www.trustedcomputinggroup.org/
11. David, S., Mimi, Z., Reiner, S.: Using IMA for Integrity Measurement and Attestation. In: Linux Plumbers Conference (2009)
12. OpenPTS (IBM), http://openpts.sourceforge.jp/
13. 2012 Rackspace, US Inc.The OpenStack Project, http://www.openstack.org/
14. OpenNebula Project Leads (OpenNebula.org), http://opennebula.org/
15. Nimbus Home Page, http://www.nimbusproject.org/
16. Wikimedia Foundation, Inc., http://en.wikipedia.org/wiki/Nonce
17. Bytemark Hosting, http://www.bytemark.co.uk/

Research on Simulation and Real-Time Evaluation Method of IoT-Oriented Complex System

Jin-Cui Yang[1,2], Bin-Xing Fang[1,2], Yu-Yu Yuan[1,2], and Meng-Xiao Zhai[1,2]

[1] School of Computer Science and Technology, Beijing University of Posts and Telecommunications, Beijing, China
[2] Key Laboratory of Trustworthy Distributed Computing and Service (BUPT), Ministry of Education, Beijing, China
jincuiyang@sina.com, {fangbx,yuanyuyu}@bupt.edu.cn,
zmxbupt@gmail.com

Abstract. Mathematics and the traditional method faced some limits on the complex system, this paper setup a methodology of simulation and real-time evaluation on the IoT-oriented complex system, introduced in detail about gaining the information of simulation object, establishing the standard mode library, evaluating real-time status and determining the evaluation results.

Keywords: simulation, real-time evaluation, Internet of Things(IOT), complex system.

1 Introduction

With the continuous development of Internet of Things (IOT), the complexity of modern industrial control systems is becoming more and more serious, and the relevant control systems were also updated gradually from the traditional centralized-control system to the distributed-control system. Compared to the traditional centralized-control system, the distributed-control system of IoT is more flexible, more convenient, more reliable and more efficient. However, on the other hand, such update also brought new problems and challenges such as: the problems caused by saturated or overload communication network, data security issues caused by data sharing, and system performance issues. In addition, the distributed control system of IoT demonstrates high requirements in reliability, real-time, extension and coordination. Finally, the diversity of terminal equipment and the complexity of the control equipment can also cause the system error accumulation.

Mathematics and the traditional method faced some limits on the complex system, especially when the complex system features itself as having multiple dimensions, multiple objectives, and involves many factors and non linear relationship. In such scenario, computer simulation was widely used and became the most effective way for the complex systems. This paper is trying to setup a methodology of real-time evaluation on the complex system from the perspective of simulation platform.

Y. Yuan, X. Wu, and Y. Lu (Eds.): ISCTCS 2012, CCIS 320, pp. 227–235, 2013.
© Springer-Verlag Berlin Heidelberg 2013

2   Related Works

The research about complex system real-time evaluation is less, the related works introduced from two aspects: 1) simulation; 2) measure method of vector similarity.

2.1   Simulation

The concept of distributed interactive simulation was first proposed by the American Defense's SIMNET project in the 1980s. Distributed interactive simulation integrates many new contemporary technologies based on computer network technology. It creates the possibility of complex system simulation.

The method of simulation technology for complex system was usually based on AGENT. Mr. R.Boero[1] set up Agent-Based Modeling and Simulation (ABMS), including ABMS basic theory, ABMS formation & method verification, ABMS model testing, and etc. Based on ABMS, Mr. R.Leombruni[2][3] further developed it to the application on economy and social issue. Kennedy and Eberhar set up the particle swarm optimizing algorithmic[4]. G.Wagner, S.C.Bankes, L.Henrickson[5][6][7][8] and others also advanced the simulation theory and method based on agent.

Nowadays，Simulation technology has applied in many fields and acquired wealthy harvest. For example: American economy simulation model –ASPEN series[9] -- developed by American Sandia national laboratory, artificial stock market model –ASM[10]-- developed by SFI research institute, transport analysis simulate system –TRANSIMS-- developed by America Los Alamos national laboratory, land battle simulate system –ISAAC[11]-- developed by America navy campaign command, earth model[12] developed by Delaware university' S.R.Thomas, ameba world model –Ameoba[13]-- developed by bel laboratory.

In china, the research about complex system simulation focus on modeling method and applications, and most of them were for specific projects. Although certain modeling theory and method were set up, the majority of such research was merely the summary and explanation to the foreign papers. The real innovation is less.

2.2   Measure Method of Vector Similarity

Measure method of vector similarity was generally divided into two categories: distance measure method and similarity function method. Distance measure methods include Euclidean Distance, Manhattan Distance, Minkowski Distance, Mahalanobbis Distance[14], and etc. Vector distance should meet the followings[15] [16]:

$X= (x_1, x_2, x_3 \cdots x_n)$, $Y= (y_1, y_2, y_3 \cdots y_n)$, Set distance of vectors X and Y is D (X, Y):

$D(X, Y) \geq 0$，When and only if $X = Y$, the equality holds

$D(X, Y) = D(Y, X)$；

$D(X, Y) \leq D(X, Z) + D(Z, Y)$.

Calculation method of Minkowski Distance is the general calculated Distance form, expressed as: $D(X, Y) = (\sum_{i=1}^{N} |x_i - y_i|^m)^{1/m}$.

Euclidean Distance is the special form of Minkowski Distance (when m=2), which is used widely as a form of distance calculation. However, this method also has its own shortcomings. Due to the uneven distribution of the vector dimensional elements, it will amplify the effect of large error element in the distance metric. Therefore, in the practical application of the Euclidean Distance, people usually make some improvement based on the original, such as the Euclidean Distance measurement methods after standardization. The idea is "to standardize" the vector dimensional elements first before calculating the vector distance, the formula can be described as: $x_i^* = \frac{x_i - m}{s}$, Where x_i^* is the standardized component, m is the mean of component , s is the standard deviation of the component. In a sense, the standardized Euclidean Distance measure method can be regarded as a weighted Euclidean Distance metric (the inverse of the variance as weights).

The similarity function method expresses the extent of similarity between two vectors by function. General methods include: Angle cosine method, Correlation coefficient method and generalized Dice coefficient, generalized Jaccard coefficient and so on. Angle cosine method and Correlation coefficient method are the most widely used one, others are evolution on the basis of angle cosine method, so their nature is similar. Cosine of the angle expresses the size of the angle between two vectors. Before use it, we need treat each element value to be positive so that its range can be within [0,1]. The smaller the angle, the closer the cosine value will be to 1, meaning the two set of vectors is closer. Compared with the distance metric method, the cosine angle method has an advantage of standardizing the vector length[17], therefore, some component parts will not be enlarged during the computing similarity process.

2.3   Evaluation Method

Simulation and real-time evaluation method of complex systems needs to include 1） to gain the information of simulation object； 2) to establish the standard mode library； 3） to evaluate real-time status； 4） to determine the evaluation results. The evaluation process can be shown in fig.1

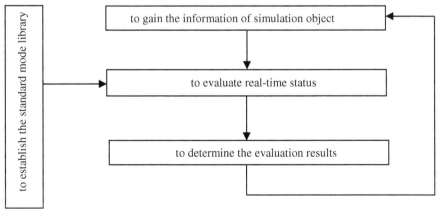

Fig. 1. Simulation and real-time evaluation process

2.4   Gain the Information of Simulation Object

Equipments will produce a variety of signals during operation. The original signal gathered by sensors need to be treated by appropriate mathematical method in order to reflect the working status of equipment. Therefore, it's very importance for simulation and evaluation work that process and analyze characteristic signals by using appropriate method. Currently, signal processing methods have filtering, wavelet transformation, time domain analysis, frequency domain analysis, timing sequence analysis and so on [18]. The signal characteristics and system accuracy requirements need to be considered when choosing signal processing methods.

Thanks to the characteristics of the distributed-control system and the requirements about real-time data, we select the timing sequence analysis method for the correlation research, and establish a timing sequence model.

Within the scientific research scope of timing sequence analysis, timing sequence refers to the generalized and ordered random data. In order to specify timing sequence characteristics of distributed real-time system, the key is to identify the timing order relationship among the system task activities. After establishing the timing sequence model for system task activities, by taking it as characteristic parameter, and combining it with other system parameters and constraints, we finally get the timing sequence characteristic model reflecting the system state under various task activities.

We refer to the definition of the business process model, definite the Timing Sequence Characteristic Model（TSCM）as following:

Definition 1:   TSCM=<P，D，S，Control，Input，Output>, among:

$P=\{p_1, p_2, \ldots, p_n\}$:   the set of task activities;

$D=\{d_1, d_2, \ldots, d_j\}$:   the set of relevant data;

$S=\{s_1, s_2, \ldots, s_k\}$:   the set of resources need to use when system running;

Control: control relationship of timing sequence process model;

Input: input relationship between activity and data. Input $\subseteq P \times D$;

Output: output relationship between activity and data. Output $\subseteq P \times D$;

Every system task activity has an execution time. We can descript task activity from the point of view of execution time:

Definition 2: $\forall p \in P$, $P=\{p_1, p_2, \ldots, p_n\}$, $T_p = [t_p^s, t_p^e]$, among:

T_p: execution time of system task activity p;

t_p^s: Start time of system task activity p;

t_p^e: End time of system task activity p;

$\forall t_p \in T_p$, $0 \leq t_p^s \leq t_p \leq t_p^e$;

If $t_p^s = t_p^e$, then task activity p can be called event (instantaneous event);

If $t_p^s \neq t_p^e$, then task activity p can be called process (continuous event);

For two system task activities at will, we can descript the sequence between two task activities as:

Definition 3:$\forall p_i, \ p_j \in P, \ P=\{p_1, \ p_2, \ \ldots, \ p_n\}$,

$Q(p_i, p_j)$ is the sequence between p_i and p_j,

if there is not sequence between pi and p_j, then $Q(p_i, p_j) = 0$;

$R(p_i, p_j)$ is the interaction between p_i and p_j,

if there is not interaction between pi and pj, then $R(p_i, p_j) = 0$.

2.5   Establish the Standard Mode Library

The evaluation process is actually compared the simulation results with the reference mode that already exists through a set of objective and specific methods or steps, and measure the system current status whether it is normal or not. As the reference for evaluating, standard mode in database is the basis to conduct evaluation.

The establishment of the standard mode library is related with the system's characteristics and requirements. The traditional standard mode library stored fault status standard mode. But with the system complexity increasing, the set of status of system failure is also increased sharply. Any important parameter changes can lead to system failure status. From the set point of view, when the complexity of the system was increased to a certain extent, the system failure status set will become extremely large, and even tends to the status that can't be exhaustive. Furthermore, in the late evaluation process, it will bring a great deal of the workload and burden to the database, and cause inefficiency. Therefore, this paper proposes to establish system standards status set based on the task activity. In other words, the standard mode library is no longer the status set by the system failure mode, on the contrary, it should be a set of predefined set of normal system status mode.

In previous section, we have researched the signal acquisition and mathematical processing of the simulation object, and eventually formed the characteristics mode based on the timing sequence to reflect the status of the system. The premise of an evaluation is to establish the mapping between the characteristics model and the system running status. We will start from the fuzzy mathematical point of view, to establish the process as followings:

(1) Establish the fuzzy relationship matrix R between the characteristics and status, expressed as:

$$R=\{u_r(x_i, y_i); \ x_i \in X, \ y_i \in Y\} \qquad \text{(formula 1)}$$

In formula 1 $Y=\{y_1, \ y_2, \ \ldots, \ y_n\}=\{y_i|i=1, \ 2, \ \ldots, \ n\}$ express the normal status mode set of system, n is the total of status, and n is the total of task activities needed to perform too, because the establishment of the system status is based on a set of pre-divided and defined system task activities, each task activity only corresponds to one system normal status.

$X=\{x_1, \ x_2, \ \ldots, \ x_n\}=\{x_i|i=1, \ 2, \ \ldots, \ n\}$ express the characteristic elements set of various entities of the system (or system equipment components) corresponding to these system status (or system task activity).

The matrix elements $u_r(x_i, y_i)$ express the degree of membership that eigenvector x_i to the status y_i. The classic method to determine membership functions have: fuzzy statistics method, weighted statistic method, the example method, experts method, binary comparison sort method, and etc. The mathematical principles and the specific steps for above methods was already introduced in the literature [19], we will not repeat them here.

(2) Extract system characteristic element, set up the characteristic parameters vector matrix X.

(3) Solve the relationship matrix equation $Y = X \cdot R$, gain the status vector.

2.6   Evaluate Real-Time Status

The purpose of the evaluation is to monitor the system current running status in real-time. In previous section, we discuss the real-time data collection and the standard mode library establishment. These preparations are the premise of the evaluation. Real-time evaluation is to compare the results obtained by the simulation with the standard mode in the database, and to measure and assess the system status mode by analyzing the similarity between them. Details are as followings:

(1) Consistent treatment of the evaluation object

The evaluation standard is the status vector set of the system normal operation, yet the object to be assessed is the characteristics vector set of sample data. They are not consistent in their forms. Therefore, before assessing the difference between them, we need to make the data consistent, so as to ensure semantic consistency of assessment of both sides. In other words, we need transform the real-time characteristics vector to the system status vector by using mathematical mapping method, which we used similarly in the establishment of the standard library steps. We will not repeat it here.

(2) Standard mode library index

The standard mode library is a strict definition status vector set of the system during normal operation. In real-time evaluation process, as time goes on, the task activities that the system needs to execute will change continuously, the system normal operation status will subsequently transform. When evaluating system running status of a moment or a stage, we need to scan the database for status query, to select the appropriate standard status vector for the evaluation review. In the previous section we discussed the timing sequence mode based on the task activity. That means we already determined the time sequence relationship among the activities of system tasks. Meanwhile, standard status in the database is one-to-one correspondence with the task activity, so it provides factors for the status vector query, to determine the status vector by finding task activity. Thanks to the task activity sequence is in order, we can apply binary search algorithm.

(3) Measure vector similarity

Through the comparing and analysis of the advantages and disadvantages of each vector similarity measure method in section 2.2, we will set up a new measure method based on the actual application requirements, which will elaborate the relative variation rather than absolute variation, and finally work out a measure method by comparing the simulation vector to the standard vector.

Let : $X = \{x_1, x_2, ..., x_n\}$: the vector to be evaluated

$Y = \{y_1, y_2, ..., y_n\}$: the standard vector

Similarity measure processes and principles described as follows:

1) define the relative error vector:

$$\lambda=\{\lambda_1, \lambda_2, ... , \lambda_n\}=\{\lambda_i | i=1, 2, ... , n\}, \text{ Among:}$$

$$\lambda_i = \left|\frac{x_i-y_i}{y_i}\right|, \quad i= (1, 2, ... , n)$$

Thanks to the absolute error does not accurately reflect the similarity between the two sets of objects, we need to define the relative error. It is because the element error's impact is not only related to the absolute change but also its own size. For example, assuming that an absolute change is 3, the standard element is 1000, then the error between the compared element and the standard element is negligible; if the standard element is 1, the variation is 3 times of element value, the error become very large.

2) Select the first K largest ones in the vector λ, get the vector:

$$\xi = \{\xi_1, \xi_2, ..., \xi_k\}$$

3) Do weighted average to the vector ξ, get the greatest dissimilarity coefficient

$$\rho_y = \frac{\sum_{j=1}^{k}(k - j + 1)\xi_j}{\sum_{j=1}^{k} j}$$

The largest dissimilarity coefficient is in fact a weighted average process, and different dimensional component of vector applies different weighting coefficient. The greater the relative error, the greater the weighting factor will be. It will highlight the impact of the element with high relative error to determine similarity. The value range of the largest dissimilarity coefficient ρ_y is $[0, +\infty]$, the smaller value of ρ_y, the more similar of two sets of vectors will be. When and only when $\rho_y = 0$, two vectors are identical.

In general case, when measuring vector similarity, two sets of vectors should be treated equally. No emphasis was made on either this set or that set. However, in this paper, the case is a little bit different. The system simulation status vector and the standard status vector in standard mode library can't match the same comparable conditions. The influence of element error should be evaluated on the basis of dimensional parameters of the standard status vector. Therefore its condition does not meet the nature of the conventional similarity measure method. The method in this paper is for a particular application scenario. By using the calculation of the relative error and the weighted method of maximum dissimilarity coefficient, it tends to greatly improve the accuracy and the applicability of the similarity evaluation.

2.7   Determine Evaluation Results

Finally, from the security perspective, we can also determine the level of system security based on evaluation result, which straight feedback the safety status of the system to the user.

We can get the biggest dissimilarity coefficient ρ_y by a proper mathematic method to measure the vector similarity. With such ρ_y value, we can evaluate the similarity degree: the smaller value of ρ_y, the more similar of two sets of vectors will be. As described in the article, the smaller ρ_y means the higher system security level, showing the high similarity of the real-time simulation status with the normal system status in the standard library. By defining the value interval of ρ_y, we can mark each interval as a unique security level. Briefing as the followings:

When $\rho_y \in [0, a]$, system is in security status;

When $\rho_y \in (a, b]$, system is in ordinary security status;

When $\rho_y \in (b, c]$, system is in insecurity status, need alarm, and take appropriate measures;

......

When $\rho_y \in (d, +\infty]$, system is in a serious status of insecurity, need to start an emergency program;

Here $0 \leq a < b < c < d$。

The upper limit value and the lower limit value of the interval a, b, c, d need setting after specific analysis, because different systems have different benchmarks, and the system error tolerance is different too. In this article, we only have a simple description on the evaluation idea. In practice, many details need to be developed and expanded.

3   Summary

This paper setup a methodology of simulation and real-time evaluation on the IoT-oriented complex system, introduced in detail about gaining the information of simulation object, establishing the standard mode library, evaluating real-time status and determining the evaluation results. we definite the Timing Sequence Characteristic Model（TSCM）for gaining the information of simulation object, establish the standard mode library by a set of pre-defined set of normal system status mode, evaluate real-time status by analyzing the similarity between the results obtained by the simulation with the standard mode in the database, determine evaluation results by the biggest dissimilarity coefficient.

Acknowledgements. This paper is supported by The National Natural Science Foundation of China (Grant No. 91118002), and 863 Program (Grant No. 2011AA01A204).

References

1. Boero, R.: Some methodological issues of agent based models in social sciences (2003),
   `http://www.unisi.it/santachiara/aree/conf_phd_econ2003/`
   `conference_siena/papers/boero.pdf`
2. Leombruni, R.: The methodological status of agent-based simulations. LABORatorio R.
   Revelli, Working Paper No. 19 (2002), `http://ssrn.com/abstract=886671`
3. Leombruni, R., Richiardi, M., Saam, N.J., et al.: A common protocol for agent-based social simulation. Journal of Artificial Societies and Social Simulation 9(1) (2006),
   `http://jasss.soc.surrey.ac.uk/9/1/15.html`
4. Kennedy, J., Eberhart, R.: Particle Swarm Optimization. In: Proceedings of IEEE International Conference on Neural Networks, vol. IV, pp. 1942–1948 (2005)
5. Wagner, G., Tulba, F.: Agent-Oriented Modeling and Agent-Based Simulation. In: Jeus-
   feld, M.A., Pastor, Ó. (eds.) ER 2003 Workshops. LNCS, vol. 2814, pp. 205–216. Springer, Heidelberg (2003)
6. Brian, J.L.B., Kiel, D., Elliott, E.: Adaptive agents, intelligence, and emergent human organization: Capturing complexity through agent-based modeling. PNAS 99, 7187–7188
   (2002)
7. Bankes, S.C.: Agent-based modeling: A revolution? PNAS 99(suppl. 3), 7199–7200
   (2002)
8. Henrickson, L., McKelvey, B.: Foundations of "new" social science: Institutional legitimacy from philosophy, complexity science, postmodemism, and agent-based modeling.
   PNAS 99(suppl.3), 7288–7295 (2002)
9. Pryor, R.J., Basu, N., Quint, T.: Development of Aspen: A microanalytic simulation model
   of the U.S. economy. SAND96-0434 Distribution Unlimited Release Category UC-905.
   Sandia National Laboratories (1996)
10. Arthur, W.B., Holland, J.H., LeBaron, B., et al.: Asset pricing under endogenous expecta-
    tions in all artificial stock market. In: The Economy as all Evolving Complex System II,
    pp. 15–44. Addison-Wesley, Reading (1997)
11. Ilachinski, A.: Irreducible semi-autonomous adaptive combat(ISAAC): An artificial-1ife
    approach to land combat. Military Operations Research 5(3), 29–46 (2000)
12. Thomas, R.: An approach to the synthesis of life. In: Langton, C., Taylor, C., Farmer, J.D.,
    Rasmussen, S. (eds.) Artificial Life II, pp. 371–408. Addison-Wesley (1991)
13. Pargellis, A.N.: Digital life behavior in the Amoeba world. Artificial Life 7, 63–65 (2001)
14. Zhang, Y., Liu, Y.-D., Ji, Z.: Vector similarity measurement method. Technical Acous-
    tics 28(4) (August 2009) (in Chinese)
15. Sun, J.-X.: Modern pattern recognition. University of Defense Technology, Changsha
    (2002) (in Chinese)
16. An introduction to data mining [DB/OL] (in Chinese),
    `http://book.csdn.net/bookfiles/327`
17. Tlan, R., Xie, P.: Study on the standardization of similarity evaluation method of chroma-
    tographic fingerprints(Part I). Traditional Chinese Drug Research & Clinical Pharmacolo-
    gy 17(I), 40–42 (2006)
18. He, Z.-J.: Modern signal processing and engineering application. Jiaotong University
    Press, Xi'an (October 2007) (in Chinese)
19. Zhang, T.-Y.: The determine method of Fuzzy membership function. Mechanical Industry
    Press (June 2010) (in Chinese)

A New Manipulation Based Mobility Model for Vehicular Delay Tolerant Networks

Tianle Zhang, Yuyu Yuan, Jørgen Bøegh, and Xu Wu

Key Laboratory of Trustworthy Distributed Computing and Service (BUPT),
Ministry of Education, Beijing, China
{tlezhang,yuanyuyu,Jorgen,wuxu}@bupt.edu.cn

Abstract. In realistic vehicular communication systems, network connections suffer from dynamic mobility and random operations of independent nodes. End to end fully connected path may never exist. VDTNs (Vehicular Delay/Disruption Tolerant Networks) achieve tolerably timely packet delivery by utilization of asynchronous relays among mobile nodes. Mobility pattern has a strong impact on the performance. Unrealistic or unreasonable mobility model may mislead the design and research. In this paper, a driving manipulations based mobility model is proposed to simulate the trajectory of mobile nodes of multi-hop VDTN networks. The proposed model can generate smooth and reasonable trajectory which resembles the real world driving behaviors. It can also output most results of existing models and can be a general option for a wide range of applications. Simulation is conducted to validate the design.

Keywords: vehicular network, mobility, delay tolerant, trajectory.

1 Introduction

The appearance of plenty of intelligent devices equipped for short-range wireless communications enable the ubiquitous vehicular communication. Vehicular ad hoc networks (VANET) have been envisioned to be useful in transport efficiency and safety [1].

However, in realistic vehicular communication systems, connectivity quality of networks may be poor and restricted due to the dynamic mobility, frequent sleep scheduling, failure and disturbance in environment as well as accidents. End to end fully connected paths may never appear due to extremely low duty cycle of links. Most of the existing VANET routing protocols are designed for fully connected networks and would fail when end to end path connection is broken. VDTN (Vehicular Delay/Disruption Tolerant Network) routing provides balance between certain delays and the probability of successful packet delivery in disconnected networks. By shuffling the packet among the vehicles according to carefully designed routing metric and policy, the packet has a high probability of successful forwarding to the target.

VDTN can achieve tolerable packet delivery by utilization of asynchronous relay of mobile nodes. The mobility will have a strong impact on the performance of

Y. Yuan, X. Wu, and Y. Lu (Eds.): ISCTCS 2012, CCIS 320, pp. 236–241, 2013.

VDTN. It will also affect the simulation when we study on VDTN. Unrealistic or unreasonable mobility may mislead the design and research. To get convincible simulation result, a new is needed to achieve smooth and reasonable trajectory of vehicles which is more similar to the realistic world. Simulation is conducted to validate the routing design. Optimal parameters configuration is achieved under certain constraints such as expected packet delivery ratio, expected communication delay, or expected energy consumption. The computation and simulation results validate the proposed methods. The research paves a foundation for VDTN to be deployed over a wider range of application.

In the remainder of this paper, we firstly describe related approaches in section 2, and then we offer driving based mobility model for VDTN in section 3. Section 4 analyzes simulation and computing results. We conclude the paper in Section 5 with future research tasks.

2   Related Works

Since the truth is that persistent full connectivity is not the rule everywhere, further researches are needed in order to overcome the limited connectivity in applications with frequent disruptive scenarios. Delay Tolerant Networks (DTNs) [2] are networks that enable communication suffered from sparse and intermittent connectivity, long and variable delay, high latency, high error rates, highly asymmetric data rate, and even no end-to-end connectivity exist. The DTN Research Group (DTNRG) [3] was chartered as part of the Internet Research Task Force (IRTF), it proposed DTN architecture and protocol.

VANETs assume that end-to-end connectivity and differ from DTNs. As mobility and disruption is very common in VANETs, a kind of Vehicular Delay-Tolerant Networks (VDTNs) [4] is attracting more and more attentions where vehicles communicate with each other and with fixed nodes placed along the roads in order to disseminate messages. VDTNs support also extreme networks through its store-carry forward paradigm, and extend VANETs with DTN capabilities to support long disruptions in network connectivity.

Most of the problems in VDTN arise from the direction and velocity of vehicular mobility that are responsible for a dynamic network topology and short contact durations. There always exists trade-off between high reliability and the fast responsiveness. One way is to maintain the connectivity to achieve highest performance and lowest delay [5, 6]. The other is to maximize the probability of successful transmission at given delay.

Most of the previous works address the former issue. Many evaluation of the connectivity availability were proposed with assumption of the full connectivity without consideration of frequent disruptions and large scale delays [7]. The assumption may not be true in realistic networks.

The connectivity availability has a strong impact on the performance. However the connectivity is intensively coupled with the mobility and activity of vehicular devices in VDTN. The mobility pattern of VANET is quite different from the random waypoint model RWP that is intensively used for ad hoc network simulations [8]. Classical mobility model can be catalogued into two kinds. One is synthetic model which is based on probabilistic parameters of mobility pattern. The other one is statistical model which is based on statics data gathered from realistic ingestion and investigation in real world.

Most papers fall into synthetic model category. Some papers discuss routing protocols using macroscopic model where the mobility pattern is defined by average vehicle speed, traffic density, traffic flow, and net time gap. Some paper focus on the motion details of vehicles, such as individual vehicle speed, moving direction, accelerating, turning, braking etc. For statistical model, the cellular automaton approach [9], combined with road patterns created based on certain maps and traffic volumes data.

3   Model Designs

In this section we firstly propose a driver operation mobility model for VDTN modeling and simulation. We then present a model to evaluate the availability under unreliable and intermittent connectivity due to mobility and activity of vehicles. The formula is given to analyze the availability of VDTN with timeliness and performance requirements. The connectivity availability is defined as the probability of successful multi-hop forwarding through an N-hops path within certain tolerant delay.

The more hops the packets are relayed, the packet will be more possible to reach the target in challengeable dynamic VDTN compared with just holding the packets in buffer. In this paper, we assume that, if dissemination of packets among vehicles along multi hops path will increase the probability of successful packet delivery to the destination. The route and forward process are based on store-wait-forward manner developed in our other works on partially connected routing [10]. When packets are destined to a downstream neighbor who is just leaving the available communication range, packets can be buffered for latterly resumed transmission when neighbor enter the range again. This asynchronous process can be reoccurred repeatedly until the packets arrive at the destination. The process is shown as right part of Fig.1

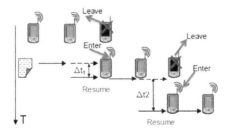

Fig. 1. Packet delivery process in VDTN

Mobility modeling is the basis of routing protocol simulation and the performance evaluation modeling. Because the statistical model involves large scale data ingestion and processing, the modeling may be very costly. However, if synthetic model is based on artificial construction and randomized parameters, the simulated mobile activity may differ from the real scenario. If the mobility model is too arbitrary, the simulation result will be doubted. Most mobility models are synthetic and controlled by customized motion parameters such as speed, direction etc. The parameters are randomized according to certain probabilistic process. These methods will output arbitrary and zigzag trajectory which involves emergent turning and bounced loops which can never be produced by real vehicles. This unreasonable mobility model may mislead the routing design and evaluation molding.

In this paper, we introduce Driver Manipulation based Mobility model (DMM) which uses the key manipulation operations of vehicle to control the moving process. This method can simulate the real physical moving action of vehicle and can output smooth trajectory such as all kinds of reasonable curves which is very similar to the real navigation trace of realistic vehicle. There are only three main parameters of this model. One is the speed V which is bounded to the current status of vehicle. The other is acceleration A which simulates the gas pedal and brake pedal of vehicle. The last parameter is the Wheel steering angle W which simulates the steering left or right process. The different combinations and time series of these key operations can describe almost all possible status and mobility of vehicle. Fig.2 shows the mobility model.

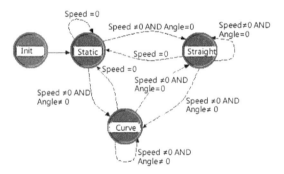

Fig. 2. State machine of vehicle mobility process

4   Simulation Results

The simulation is conducted in network within an area of 1000m×1000m with 200 mobile nodes scattered homogeneously. In the simulation study, all nodes may move according to DMM model with the homogenous parameters. The mobility parameters can be adjusted to different mode with certain combinations of configuration.

Fig.3 shows the simulated trajectory controlled by mobility model. In (a), the model use random speed and random steering angle (-180°~180°) and can output smooth but zigzag trajectory. If the steering angel is confined to (-40°~40°) the trajectory will be more smooth and consistent. In (b), the steadily varying speed and steering angel are used to produce cylindrical spiral. If constant speed and angle are used it will get circle. In (c), constant speed and steadily varying steering angel are used to get asymmetrically cylindrical spiral. In (d), steadily varying speed and steadily varying steering angel are used to get snail curve (vortex curve).

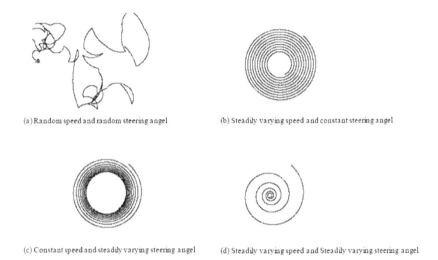

(a) Random speed and random steering angel   (b) Steadily varying speed and constant steering angel

(c) Constant speed and steadily varying steering angel   (d) Steadily varying speed and Steadily varying steering angel

Fig. 3. Simulated trajectory controlled by DMM

5   Conclusions

In this paper, we offer a systematic approach to establish a new mobility model to generate trajectories of mobile nodes in VDTN. By modeling and simulation, different kinds of synthetic trajectory can be constructed to simulate certain scenarios of VDTN. Further work can be done on the performance evaluation based on different mobility pattern in terms of speed, direction, intensiveness, etc. This work helps to achieve routing design for VDTN with mobility, reliability, and timeliness constraints.

Acknowledgements. This work was supported in part by NSFC under Grant Nos. 90818006.

References

1. Ettema, D., Timmermans, H.: Costs of Travel Time Uncertainty and Benefits of Travel Time Information: Conceptual Model and Numerical Examples (2006)
2. Cerf, V., et al.: Delay Tolerant Network Architecture, IETF, RFC 4838 (April 2007)
3. Scott, K., Burleigh, S.: Bundle Protocol Specification. IETF, RFC 5050 (November 2007)

4. Rogerio, P.P., Augusto, C., Rodrigues Joel, J.P.C.: From Delay-Tolerant Networks toVehicular Delay-Tolerant Networks. IEEE Communications Surveys and Tutorials, 1 (September 2011)
5. Zhang, X., Lu, S., et al.: Topology Control for Wireless Sensor Networks. Journal of Software 18(4), 943–954 (2007)
6. Schurgers, C., Tsiatsis, V., Ganeriwal, S., Srivastava, M.: Topology Management for Sensor Networks: Exploiting Latency and Density. In: Proc. ACM MobiHoc Conf. (June 2002)
7. Zhang, T., Li, Z., Liu, M.: Partial Connection Availability Modeling for Wireless Networks. Chinese Journal of Computers 30(4), 505–513 (2007)
8. Bettstetter, C., Resta, G., Santi, P.: The node distribution of the random waypoint mobility model for wireless ad hoc networks. IEEE Transactions on Mobile Computing 2(3), 257–269 (2003)
9. Chopard, B., Luthi, P.O., Queloz, P.-A.: Cellular automata model of car traffic in a two-dimensional street network. Journal of Physics A: Mathematical and General 29(10), 2325–2336 (1996)
10. Zhang, T., Li, Z., Liu, M.: Routing in Partially Connected Wireless Network. Journal of System Simulation 18(10), 2972–2975 (2006)
11. Zhang, T., Yuan, Y., Wu, X., Luo, Z., Wang, C.: A New Routing and Connectivity Availability Metric of Low Duty Cycle Random Sleep Scheduled Multi-hop Wireless Sensor Networks. The Journal of China Universities of Posts and Telecommunications (2011)

A Pervasive Technology Approach
to Social Trustworthiness

Wang Hongqi[1], Zongwei Luo[1], Tianle Zhang[2], Yuyu Yuan[2], and Xu Wu[2]

[1] E-Business Technology Institute,The University of Hong Kong, Hong Kong, China
{wanghongqi,zwluo}@eti.hku.hk
[2] Key Laboratory of Trustworthy Distributed Computing and Service (BUPT),
Ministry of Education, Beijing University of Posts and Telecommunications, Beijing, China
{tlezhang,yuanyuyu,wuxu}@bupt.edu.cn

Abstract. Growing awareness of environmental concerns has been reflected on more and more public's attention on low carbon lifestyles. The awareness and public participation could be further enhanced and encouraged via computer assisted persuasive technologies to present carbon footprint information for products and services. Such technologies could shape public's trust by establishing trustworthiness in carbon footprint information delivered, as carbon footprint itself is highly dynamic which could reflect potential differences between instances of the same product, for example. Trustworthy carbon footprint information would lead and help public to select and choose the product or services to buy. In this paper, we have adopted a persuasive technology approach to deliver and visualize **dynamic** carbon footprint information to encourage public to lead low carbon lifestyle. Mobile phones, Internet of Things networks, and other persuasive technologies are integrated in the prototype system developed to deliver and establish trustworthiness in the public.

Keywords: dynamic carbon footprint, persuasive technology, trust and trustworthiness.

1   Introduction

As the growing concern on environmental considerations, numerous corporations are facing new challenge on carbon management in various business activities. Environmental responsibility will no doubt help enhance enterprises social image. On the other hand, Greener products, services and production will increase market potentials for products and services. The branding value of low carbon development as well as the sustainable development methods would strengthen comparative advantages of environmentally-ware industries, supporting economic transformation by developing a technology rich, high value add, and service oriented low carbon economy.

A few of global companies which provide management services are developing various tools of carbon management. Since carbon management would exert considerable impacts with changes on business activities, effective tools become critical to illustrate and measure the carbon inter-dependencies and inter-impact

Y. Yuan, X. Wu, and Y. Lu (Eds.): ISCTCS 2012, CCIS 320, pp. 242–249, 2013.

among activities. As the carbon management itself is highly dynamic in nature, it presents an excellence case for illustrating the importance of trustworthiness of carbon accounting could enhance enterprises' credibility in meeting the environmental and social responsibilities.

In this paper, we study trustworthiness of dynamic carbon accounting from a perspective of social persuasiveness to establishing trustworthiness for social perception on environmental concerns. Rest of the paper is as follows. In Section 2 dynamic carbon footprint is introduced. In Section 3, persuasive and captology is introduced for trustworthiness. Section 4 is system design and implement to calculate, deliver and visualize dynamic carbon footprint information. Section 5 summarizes the paper with comparative analysis.

2   Dynamic Carbon Footprint

2.1   Life Cycle Assessment for Carbon Footprint

A carbon footprint is defined as the total greenhouse gas emissions caused directly and indirectly by a person, organization, event or product [1]. Exemplary causes of these emissions include electricity production in power plants, transport operations and other industrial and agricultural processes.

There are many national and international standards and tools existing to measure carbon footprint, on which companies can rely to take further eco-friendly activities. Many of these carbon footprinting standards comply with life cycle assessment (LCA), a technique to assess environmental impacts associated with all the stages of a product's life from-cradle-to-grave (i.e., from raw material extraction through materials processing, manufacture, distribution, use, repair and maintenance, and disposal or recycling) [2]. LCA is a well-established field and exists as an international standard in the ISO 14040-14044 series. LCA includes all environmental impacts, i.e. not only GHG emissions qualified by carbon footprint, but also other impacts such as acid rain, summer smog, cancer effects and land use.

2.2   Carbon Footprinting Methods

Generally speaking, carbon footprinting can be achieved on different levels, .e.g. enterprise level, product level and supply chain level. Product level carbon footprint is with higher granularity. Enterprise level carbon footprinting is to evaluate emissions from all activities across a company or a organization, while product level footprinting is the amount of emissions caused by a specific product or service. There are plenty of international standards to estimate enterprise-wide emissions. The Intergovernmental Panel on Climate Change (IPCC) Guidelines for National Greenhouse Gas Inventories make use of Global Warming Potential (GWP) values as indicators to reflect the relative effect of GHG. The Greenhouse Gas Protocol provides guiding principles, practical approaches, scopes, steps and guidelines for Verification for enterprises monitors and manages enterprise-level carbon footprints. On the other hand, lots of standards are applicable for product-level carbon footprinting. A significant one is Publicly Available Specification 2050 (PAS2050), which was published in October 2008 by the British Standards Institute (BSI) and the Carbon Trust. It's based on the process lifecycle approach and currently is one of the comprehensive way to calculate carbon footprints.

With growing concern on environmental considerations in supply chain industries, numerous corporations are facing new challenge on carbon management in supply chains. A few of global companies which provide management services are developing various tools of carbon management. Since carbon management would exert considerable impacts with changes on supply chain activities, effective tools become critical to illustrate and measure the carbon inter-dependencies and inter-impact among activities.

For example, in the supply chain carbon management, it is inevitable to make changes on supply chain activities. Due to these activities have different connections or relationships with each other, some of them change would lead to changes to the rest accordingly. In order to measure these changes, it would require tools to model and represent the inter-connection of activities, as well to calculate the impact to the rest if any activities would change. It is necessary to develop models to represent the inter-connections of supply chain activities and calculate the change impact of carbon intensity caused by carbon management..

2.3   Towards Dynamic Carbon Footprint

Nevertheless, carbon footprinting is highly dynamic, e.g. carbon emissions of some products, which could exert potential difference between instances of the same product. PAS2050 points out where carbon emissions may vary considerably among instances of the same product [5]. The example areas named are [3]:

- Seasonal fruits whose associated emissions vary depending on the season
- Highly variable supply chains, where suppliers are frequently replaced
- The degree of using reused or recycled components in products
- The downstream distribution of products to different locations
- The mode of usage of the product

For instance, fruits bought in different seasons of the year will require different period of chilled storage, which results in carbon footprints that vary over the year.

So, a physical label on the product will not be flexible enough to reflect the dynamic nature of carbon footprints. But it could serve as a link to provide dynamic carbon footprint which could be visualized on mobile handhelds. Some research is being conducted using mobile phones to retrieve and display dynamic carbon footprints, which help end consumers to know the difference among items at the point of sale. The possible scenario could be: a consumer uses his or her mobile phone to touch the tagged product and the carbon footprint information is displayed on the phone, so that multiple instances of the same product with different carbon footprints are correctly presented. The experimental result of the pilot project by SAP has demonstrated this kind of approach.

3   Persuasive Technologies for Trustworthiness

Realizing the crucial importance of guiding people towards low carbon lifestyles and also the incredible pervasion of information and communication technologies, persuasive technologies are adopted in the modern design of solutions changing human attitudes and behaviors to establish trustworthiness, in our case, towards environmental concerns via delivering and visualizing carbon footprint.

Persuasive technology is broadly defined as technology that is designed to change attitudes or behaviors of the users through persuasion and social influence, but not through coercion [6]. Traditionally, such technologies usually involving psychology and rhetoric are widely used in sales, advertising, public health, management and etc. Persuasive technologies can function as 1) tools which can increase people's ability to perform a target behavior by making it easier for restructuring it [7], 2) media which can use both interactivity and narrative to create persuasive experiences that support rehearsing a behavior, empathizing, or exploring causal relationships [7], or 3) social actors which can cue social responses through e.g. their use of language, assumption of established social roles, or physical presence – or as more than one at once [6].

Captology is a special form of persuasive technology and it evolves as the development of information and communication technologies. Captology is short for "computers as persuasive technologies". This area of inquiry explores the overlapping space between persuasion in general (influence, motivation, behavior change, etc.) and computing technology [8]. There is an increasing demand on captology and the field of captology is expanding quickly. Every day more computing products, including websites and mobile apps, are designed to change what people think and do.

There are a number of computing technologies existing that are suitable for the usage of persuasive technologies, particularly captology [9]. Just to name a few, mobile devices, pervasive sensors, social media, artificial intelligence are all potential. Mobile phones are no doubt the significant technology as they are used everywhere, every time, by almost everybody.

4   System Design and Implementation

The system functionality implementation is shown in the following diagram – Figure 1. End consumers could use their mobile phones to capture and display the dynamic carbon footprint information of a product. With social networks, they could publish their purchase information to any social network service (SNS) to let their friends know their "green" purchase decisions. What's more, tips could be provided for them to know about the correct ways to use products and how to dispose products so that the emissions during usage and disposal are minimized. For retailers, from which end consumers are buying products, they should respond efficiently and correctly to consumers' carbon footprint query. Based on a product code inked or tagged, a information repository could be established to capture and later retrieve all associated carbon footprint information during product's manufacturing, transportation, and storage, and so on. For suppliers, manufacturers and distributors, they could record emissions of the products. Logistics service providers are responsible for determining what vehicle types they use to transport products, and the traveling distance which is crucial to estimate emissions caused by transportation. And this is the system we are going to design and implement to illustrate the concept of trustworthy dynamic carbon footprint.

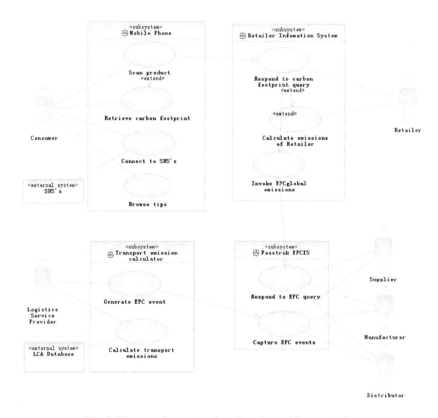

Fig. 1. Use case for system functionality and impmentation

4.1   Network Support for Dynamic Carbon Footprint

A global network like EPCglobal network is necessary to provide the ability to track and trace products, as product information could be captured along its supply chain connected with such networks. By use of this tracking infrastructure, together with product information database and life cycle assessment database, dynamic carbon footprint can be determined.

To integrate the EPCglobal network into our system, we need a software platform Fosstrak. Fosstrak is an open source RFID software platform that implements the EPC Network specifications. It is intended to support application developers and integrators by providing core software components for track and trace applications [10]. Fosstrak provides core components for EPCglobal network based applications and can be used by application developers, system integrators and research groups in academy and industry. There are four fundamental modules in Fosstrak, which are EPCIS Repository, TDT Engine, ALE Middleware and LLRP Commander. In the paper, we'll adopt EPCIS Repository in our system as Fosstrak EPCIS is a complete implementation of the EPCIS standard specification and it is an EPCglobal-certified EPCIS Repository. The scenario for dynamic carbon footprint calculation is shown in Figure 2.

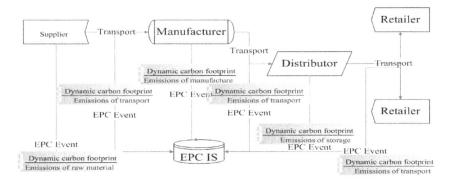

Fig. 2. Illustration for dynamic carbon footprint calculation

4.2   Carbon Footprint Calculation

As the calculation of carbon footprint is a LCA based process, it involves all supply chain participants from the supplier to any retailer. The EPCglobal network can only be applied to products which are previously RFID tagged, thus calculating accurate product carbon footprint cannot only depend on the data captured by the EPCglobal network. For instance, wheat is a raw material to make bread and the carbon footprint emitted by wheat during its growth cannot be derived by the EPCglobal network. Also, the GHG emissions caused by usage of electricity during manufacture processes of products are beyond the control of the EPCglobal network. In these two situations here, GHG emissions should be available from the wheat supplier's and manufacturer's environmental management information systems (EMIS).

However, by incorporating with corresponding EMIS's, emissions can be captured as parameters of EPC events when EPCs of products interact with the EPCglobal network. In this way, relative emissions are associated with EPCs. And combining the result from corresponding EMIS's, we can have our accurate result of product carbon footprint, and then the information can be delivered to consumers.

To track necessary data for GHG emissions, EPC events have to capture additional information. For transport emissions, besides the information of EPC code and time, the additional information needed includes two end locations (start and end locations), vehicle types, travelling distance and the number of transported items. To integrate with Fosstrak EPCIS, EPC events should be compatible with Fosstrak EPCIS so that they can get recognized. We design a EPC event class, called

TransportEPCISDocumentType, that extends Fosstrak EPCIS's EPCISDocumentType class, which is the event object to be captured by Fosstrak EPCIS.

4.3   Sourcemap Integration for Visualization

Now we'll present our system in the delivery of dynamic carbon footprints on mobile phones to reflect the frequent supply chain changes. Nevertheless, we are not just satisfied about the dynamic delivery; at the same time we want our system as a persuasive technology to help consumers lead low carbon lifestyles.

Sourcemap is a web-based tool for visualizing global supply chains and the history behind products in order to allow producers, designers and investigators to plot the probable supply chain of a product in terms of materials, provenance and environmental impact [11]. Also, Sourcemap is a free, community-driven and open source project, and it lets users create, edit and browse maps detailing the supply chain and carbon footprint of a variety of products.

Sourcemap can provide users with a surprisingly profound and educational experience as it visualizes the paths of products from their component sources to manufactures to warehouses and finally to retailers during every stage of their life cycles. This feature makes Sourcemap a very powerful persuasive technology as it gives users a greater understanding of the products' literal origin. Based on this reason, we leverage Sourcemap as a core persuasive technology towards low carbon lifestyles. In addition to display the real carbon footprint value and the carbon intensity, at the same time an attractive map displaying products' origins is also available in our system.

5   Summary and Comparison

In this paper, we first talk about what is carbon footprint and the life cycle assessment approach is the standard way to derive carbon footprint of any product or service. Driven by the requirements of both the increasing number of regulations and end consumers' environmental awareness, we have proposed and adopted persuasive technologies as product instance level to deliver carbon footprint information to their consumers as a way to make their products more competitive. It works well with the dynamic nature of product's carbon emissions, which shows that different carbon footprints can be among the same product.

What's more, to better deliver dynamic carbon footprint, and to better utilizing mobile phones as a better persuasive technology, we make use of Sourcemap to visualize the information of carbon footprint. Sourcemap not only displays the total carbon footprint of a product in terms of the dynamic nature of the product, but also displays where the components of the product originate from and the partial carbon footprint of the product during every stage of its life cycle. This persuasive technology approach provides a convincing way for end consumers to make decisions in an environmental friendly way, and thus help lead low carbon lifestyles.

There are a number of related work in the perspective of dynamic carbon footprint, carbon label and Sourcemap. Compared with these related work, our work differentiates from them in the following ways:

- Like in [3, 4], which are launched by the Auto-ID Labs, we both adopt the same Fosstrak as the EPC IS and the delivery of dynamic carbon footprint both in their work and our work is visualized. However, by leveraging Sourcemap as the user interface, the display of dynamic carbon footprint is a more convincing persuasive technology in light of the traceability and the carbon emissions of every lifecycle stage of a product.
- Compared to [12], which is carried out by SAP Research, our work of the display of dynamic carbon footprint as electronic label is escalated to a powerful map display, which is intuitive and easy understanding.
- In comparison with Sourcemap itself, we simplify the creation of a map and provide a way for the automation of map creation which could make the map more accurate and consistent.

References

1. UK Carbon Trust. Tesco and Carbon Trust join forces to drive forward carbon labeling (2008)
2. Wikipedia (2011), `http://en.wikipedia.org/wiki/Life_cycle_assessment`
3. Dada, A., Staake, T., Fleisch, E.: The potential of the EPC network to monitor and manage the carbon footprint of products, part 1: Carbon Accounting (2010)
4. Dada, A., Rau, A., Konkel, M., Staake, T., Fleisch, E.: The potential of the EPC network to monitor and manage the carbon footprint of products, part 2: Dynamic carbon footprint demonstrators (2010)
5. Carbon Trust, and Defra. Pas 2050:2008 - specification for the assessment of the life cycle greenhouse gas emissions of goods and services. Public Available Specification (2008)
6. Wikipedia (2011), `http://en.wikipedia.org/wiki/Persuasive_technology`
7. Fogg, B.J., Nass, C.: Silicon sycophants: the effects of computers that flatter. International Journal of Human-Computer Studies (1997)
8. Wikipedia (2011), `http://en.wikipedia.org/wiki/Captology`
9. Fogg, B.J.: Persuasive Technologies. Using computers to change what we think and do. Stanford University, Morgan Kaufmann Publishers (2003)
10. Auto-ID Labs, `http://www.fosstrak.org/`
11. MIT Media Lab, `http://tangible.media.mit.edu/project.php?recid=111`
12. Dada, A., Vogel, A.: Dynamic Carbon Labels: A demo using RFID tagged consumer goods and NFC enabled mobile (2008)

Policy-Based De-duplication in Secure Cloud Storage

Chuanyi Liu[1,3,*], Xiaojian Liu[2,3], and Lei Wan[2,3]

[1] Software School, Beijing University of Posts and Telecommunications,
Beijing 100876, China
cy-liu04@mails.tsinghua.edu.cn
[2] School of Computer Science and Technology,
Beijing University of Posts and Telecommunications, Beijing, China
chn19891xj@163.com, wanlei.bupt@gmail.com
[3] Key Laboratory of Trustworthy Distributed Computing and Service (BUPT),
Ministry of Education, China

Abstract. Reducing the amount of data need to be transferred, stored, and managed becomes a crucial for cloud storage. On the other hand, as user data are stored and processed by outsourced cloud provider, encryption becomes a necessary before updating data into the cloud. However, the above two goals are greatly opposed to each other. In order to solve the above conflict, a policy-based de-duplication proxy scheme is proposed in this paper. It suggests a policy-based de-duplication proxy scheme to enable different trust relations among cloud storage components, de-duplication related components and different security requirements. Further proposes a key management mechanism to access and decrypt the shared de-duplicated data chunks based on Proxy Re-encryption algorithms. This paper finally analyses the security of the scheme.

Keywords: Cloud Storage, Encryption, Data De-duplication, Proxy Re-encryption, Convergent Encryption.

1 Introduction

Cloud computing is getting more and more popular as it can provide low-cost and on-demand use of vast storage and processing resources. With the explosive growth of online digital contents [10], cloud storage focuses on effectively coalescing storage resources for better power utilization and cost effectiveness. As the volume of data grows, also increasing is the Total Cost of Ownership (TCO), which includes storage infrastructure cost, management cost and human administration cost. Therefore in cloud storage systems, reducing the amount of data that need to be transferred, stored, and managed becomes a crucial, and it also benefits for application performance, storage costs and administrative overheads [11].

As a result, Data De-duplication [16]˙[17] is an important and popular cost-saving feature for cloud storage. It refers to approaches that use lossless data compression

---

* Corresponding author.

Y. Yuan, X. Wu, and Y. Lu (Eds.): ISCTCS 2012, CCIS 320, pp. 250–262, 2013.

schemes to minimize the duplicated data at inter-file level. It divides each file into a number of non-overlapping chunks and storing only unique chunks on storage devices.

On the other hand, the largest vulnerability in cloud storage model is that the data stored and processed on typical machines that are owned by an entity different from the information owner. Since the data is stored and processed on the cloud infrastructure or platform, which the information owner does not have full control of. In case of the user data being peeked, leaked or modified by the cloud provider or other adversaries, encryption become a necessary before updating data into the cloud.

However, de-duplication and encryption, to a great extent, conflicts with each other. De-duplication takes advantage of data similarity in order to achieve storage reduction. While cryptography makes ciphertext indistinguishable from theoretically random data, i.e., encrypted data are always distributed randomly, so identical plaintext encrypted by randomly generated cryptographic keys will very likely have different ciphertexts which cannot be de-duplicated.

To solve the above conflict, most of current work use convergent encryption [7], [3] to get identical ciphertext from identical plaintext, but the information leakage in such encryption scheme can be unacceptable [7]. What's worse, the convergent encryption gives one deterministic transform from a particular plaintext to the ciphertext, which exposes more vulnerability.

By defining and limiting the ability and the knowledge needed for de-duplication, a policy-based de-duplication proxy scheme is proposed in this scheme. Compared with related work, each data chunk can be encrypted with arbitrary keys, while at the same time achieving comparable performance of de-duplication on unencrypted data.

Contributions of this paper include:

- Data de-duplication supported secure cloud storage model is proposed, based on which the main threats, security requirements and security policy can be made;
- It is proved that a de-duplication scheme without limitation will impair confidentiality and privacy. To gain a certain degree of security assurance, we suggest a policy-based de-duplication proxy scheme to enable different trust relations among cloud storage components, de-duplication related components and different security requirements.
- A novel key management mechanism is proposed for different users or groups in order to access and decrypt the shared de-duplicated data chunks.

2   Related Work

The conflict between de-duplication and encryption was first discovered by Douceur etc. in the Farsite distributed file system [7]. To overcome the conflict, they used the convergent encryption, in which the hash of the data was used as the encryption key, to make identical plaintexts be encrypted to the same ciphertext regardless of which user they belonged to. However, Farsite only worked in the granularity of file-level, so that it could only save space with identical files.

Storer etc. [3] coalesced data at chunk-level, thus achieved de-dup with files that were merely similar as opposed to identical. Furthermore, they presented an on-line de-duplication scheme which saved not only storage space, but also network bandwidth. Storer etc. also used convergent encryption to guarantee the data confidentiality.

However, convergent encryption does leak information that a particular ciphertext, and thus plaintext, already exists. So an adversary can get more potential knowledge by constructing a particular data chunk and checking whether it has already existed on the storage. What's worse, the encryption key is determined if a typical plaintext is given, i.e. the mapping from plaintext to ciphertext is determinate but not random, which is less secure according to semantic security principal.

Most of the following work [2] [6] that considered both security and storage efficiency used the same encryption proposed in [3]. Marques etc. [2] created a hierarchy before backing up the mobile devices into the cloud for performance optimization. Anderson etc. [6] proposed a scheme to identify shared sub-trees of a directory hierarchy, and with a single access to the backup store, it can detect whether an entire subtree is already present.

FadeVersion [5] presented a secure cloud backup system to serve as a security layer on top of today's cloud storage services. Instead of convergent encryption, it used an independent symmetric key to encrypt each file, and each key was encrypted with the version key owned by the versions which contained the very file. But the additional cryptographic key management in data backups cost a lot of performance overhead.

In summary, although the conflict between de-duplication and encryption has been researched for years, there are still challenge problems to solve, such as trading off de-duplication and encryption under different security requirements, protecting from information leakage, lowering performance overhead for additional operations, key management for shared data chunks among large groups of users, etc.

3   De-duplication Supported Cloud Storage Model

There are three distinct players in a typical cloud storage model with de-duplication, as: Client, De-dup Provider and Cloud Storage Provider. Client resides in the user side, and from the users' perspective, de-duplication supported cloud storage system provides the abstract interface of the file-level granularity. It hides the details of actual organization and locations of data from users. De-dup Provider takes charge of de-duplication related metadata management, access control, and key management. Cloud Storage Provider provides storage resources for real data contents.

Architecture and main components for the cloud storage model with data de-duplication is depicted in figure 1, in which Storage Server and Metadata Server are separated. Most decisions on separation or combination of different components are based on security or performance reasons.

In this paper, we deliberately separate de-duplication from storage and define it as a standalone component: De-duplicator. The reasons to do so are also security and performance. First, the security assumption of de-duplicator is different from Storage Server; second, de-duplication is a resource consuming operation as the system needs to maintain a large hash table in memory cache for all data chunks, and the swap of this cache requires a lot of disk I/O operations; Thirdly, not so obvious but reasonable, in the cloud storage scenario, it is not the cloud storage provider but the users have the incentive to reduce the consumed network bandwidth and storage. So a de-duplicator is more on the behalf of users instead of the cloud.

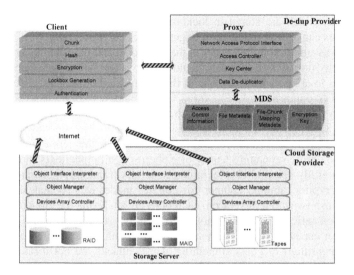

Fig. 1. Architecture for the cloud storage model with de-duplication provision

Files are generated, chunked and encrypted on client side then uploaded to storage server, meanwhile the client submit *Lockbox*es and other metadata information which helps de-duplication to the MetaData Server (MDS), for example, hashes of chunks, or file-chunk mapping table, which are organized into corresponding *Mapbox*. To access those files, clients need to hold corresponding decrypting keys for *Lockbox*es of all chunks. After the chunks have been uploaded to storage servers, the de-duplication proxy checks those metadata of chunks.

4   Threat Model

In cloud storage scenario, the Cloud Storage Provider is considered as "not trustworthy". It is not because the storage service providers could refuse to store data or delete data, after all, if they would not provide service why users would have chosen them?

The threat in this scenario is the security may be impaired in some unnoticed and deniable ways. We take this as our first assumption that the storage service is provided by a "passive adversary" in the sense that the cloud storage provider would not make obviously malicious attack.

So our security concern here is to focus on two attacks. First, the data may be read by unauthorized users, such as curious administrators, hackers, they may access data on storage with unauthorized permissions, or they may be able to illegally get copies out of the storage. Second attack is, the data may be illegally modified and legal users can not technically detect this modification.

As we have seen in Figure 1, the metadata of a file can be divided into the following four types: (1) Security related data, which include access control information such as path name, permission bits and ACL entries; (2) file metadata, which include the metadata or tags to describe the very file; (3) file-chunk mapping metadata, which include the mapping information that connecting file to chunks; and (4) encryption keys of chunks, which are stored in lockboxes and encrypted in the way that only authorized users can access and decrypt to get chunk encryption keys.

The second assumption in this paper is that metadata and data chunks are stored in different security domains so that they could not be comprised at the same time. Our security goal is to assure when only one of them is passive comprised, the security of data would not be comprised.

The security of encrypted data chunks should only rely on the security of the encryption keys which means the adversaries/storage cannot gain any knowledge of the plaintext from ciphertexts without decrypting keys. This is the definition of semantic security [9]. To ensure semantic security of ciphertexts, all ciphertexts should be generated with carefully selected cryptographic materials (randomly generated keys for symmetric encryption, unique counter for counter mode, etc) so that an adversary cannot distinguish two ciphertexts from each other by analysing the ciphertexts.

However, semantic security does not mean absolute security, because the storage service provider can still observe the usage of data chunk (when, who, how often the data is read or written) to guess something. These attacks are not discussed in this paper.

The access control and the security requirements on the stand alone de-duplication proxy is different, the proxy shall be able to access metadata to find out identical data chunks, sending delete commands to storage servers when it find identical chunks, assuring remained chunks could be accessed by all legal users by creating or transforming *Lockbox*es for users. However, the proxy shall not be able to decrypt *Lockbox*es and get decrypting keys, nor the proxy need read access to encrypted chunks on storage server.

5   Proxy Based De-Duplication for the Cloud

In this section, we will describe how client side, storage server, MDS and de-duplication proxy interact to each other in our scheme, and also give detailed descriptions for several cryptographic components that are used in this scheme.

A. Policy and Setup

Suppose the scheme is being used in an enterprise, each user is assigned a *user_id* to identify himself. The enterprise also registers those users to the de-duplication proxy P. A key centre will assign a user A several cryptographic credentials, a key pair, with public key pk_A, private key sk_A, and a root hash key hk which are shared by all users within this key centre. The key center needs to give the de-duplication proxy capabilities (proxy re-encryption keys) to transfer *Lockbox* of user A to other users and capabilities to transfer *Lockbox*es of other users to A (if the capabilities are not commutative).

Files are chunked on client side. For each chunk, user A encrypts it with a symmetric key k, and then encrypts k with pk_A. The user then computes a tag for the plaintext of this chunk $tag = Hash_{hk}(M)$ with key hashed function $Hash$ and key hk. A submits $Enc_{pkA}(k)$ as the lockbox and the tag $Hash_{hk}(M)$ to MDS, uploads $Enc_{pkA}(k)$ to a storage server.

The de-duplication proxy can only de-duplicate data of its registered users based on the capabilities it has received from the key center. The user can decide if he wants de-duplication proxy to de-duplicate some of his data by submitting the tag or not. The users thus can classify data into three categories: not encrypted, encrypted, encrypted without de-duplication. As we can see, not encrypted data impose no cost for encryption but expose the data readable to cloud storage. Encrypted data require users encrypting them on client side and the de-duplication proxy comparing tags, deleting replicated chunks, and transferring *Lockbox*es on server side. Encrypted without de-duplication data would not share content among users but it could raise high cost on storage. How to classify data should be the policy of the enterprise when it decides to use the encrypted storage with de-duplication. By enforcing policies, the enterprises, clients of the storage can gain a balance of cost and security.

B. Proxy Re-encryption

There are already several kinds of proxy re-encryption schemes [12], [13], [14], roughly can be divided into two categories: identity-based proxy re-encryption and type-based proxy re-encryption. Most proxy re-encryption schemes are identity-based, in which the proxy transforms ciphertext from one identity to another identity, or ciphertext that can be decrypted with private key of A to ciphertext that can be decrypted with private key of B. Type-based proxy re-encryption [18] is different in that the proxy key $rk_{A,B,t}$ assigned to each proxy to transform ciphertext are limited by data types t, Only data encrypted under type t $Enc(Msg, t, rk_A)$ can be transformed by the proxy holding correspondent proxy key $rk_{A,B,t}$

Among these identity based or key based schemes, reference [12] is unidirectional, non-transitive and non-transferable. Its security is based on DBDH assumption. The *Lockbox* encryption and regeneration in this paper is based on this scheme. Here we give a short description of the construction.

The global parameters of this scheme include two groups G_1 G_2 and bilinear mapping $e: G_1 \times G_1 \to G_2$. g is one generator of G_1 and $Z = e(g, g)$.

- **Key Generation** (*KG*). User A has a key pair in the form of $pk_A = \left(Z_1^{a_1}, g^{a_2}\right)$ and private key $sk_A = \left(a_1, a_2\right)$.
- **Re-encryption Key Generation (RG).** The key center generate re-encryption key A to another user B $rk_{A \to B} = g^{a_1 b_2}$.
- **First Level Encryption** (E_1). Encrypt a message under pk_A so that only A can decrypt it with sk_A. The ciphertext is $C_{a,1} = \left(Z^{a_1 k}, mZ^k\right)$. To get proxy invisibility, compute $C_{a,2} = \left(Z^{a_2 k}, mZ^k\right)$.
- **Second Level Encryption** (E_2). Encrypt a message under pk_A and the ciphertext can be decrypted not only by A but also can be transformed to ciphertext that can be decrypted by other users, say B. The ciphertext is $C_{a,r} = \left(g^k, mZ^{a_2 k}\right)$.

- **Re-encryption(R).** Anyone can re-encrypt second-level ciphertext for A $c_{a,r}$ into first-level ciphertext for B with $rk_{A \to B}$. From $C_{a,r} = (g^k, m Z^{ak})$, compute $e(g^k, g^{ab_2}) = Z^{b_2ak}$, and publish new ciphertext $c_{b,2} = (Z^{b_2ak}, m Z^{ak}) = (Z^{b_2k'}, m Z')$.

- **Decryption (D_1, D2).** To decrypt a first-level ciphertext $C_{a,i} = (\alpha, \beta)(i=1, 2)$, compute $m = \beta / \alpha^{1/a_i}$. To decrypt a second-level ciphertext $C_{a,r} = (\alpha, \beta)$, compute $m = \beta / e(\alpha, g)^{a_i}$.

C. Encrypted Bloom filters

Zhu, etc. [15] used bloom filters as Summary Vectors to reduce the space of indexes thus reduce the time to swap indexes between memory and disk. As the observation in [15] shows, data chunks access, especially those of backup applications tend to reappear in the same or very similar sequences. If the fingerprints of these chunks are stored in one bloom filter, most likely next fingerprints will locate in the same bloom filter. Basically, a bloom filter is a byte array to store fingerprint information of n data chunks. It uses the location of each bit to represent a part of information of fingerprints. Suppose the length of the bloom filter is m bits, one bit of a bloom filter can represent a number in the range of $(1; 2^m)$. If we have k hash functions to generate k fingerprints for one chunk, and these fingerprints are distributed in $(1; 2^m)$ randomly, we will mark all bits that represent these k fingerprints to 1. The bloom filter thus can be used as a compacted index for this chunk. If we compute k fingerprints of a new chunk, and find correspondent k bits in a bloom filter are marked as 1, then we know the chunk already existed in the storage, the probability that this prediction is wrong (false positive) is

$$\left(1 - e^{-kn/m}\right)^k$$

However, publicly available hash functions that were used to generate bloom filters can also be used by any observer (storage administrator, for instance) to guess original plaintexts. To avoid this security vulnerability, we should use hash functions that were known only to users, in our scheme these functions are keyed hash functions with keys known only to users. We define $H_i(M) = HMACSHA(k_i, M)$, where $k_i = SHA(i \parallel hk)$. hk is the root hash key given to registered users.

D. User revocation

When there is a user is revoked, the bloom filters should be refreshed with new keys, and old fingerprints should be removed from bloom filters. However a bit that was marked by several fingerprints should not be simply set to 0. Fan et al [19] proposed "counting bloom filter", in which an entry is not a bit but a counter of several bits that can count inserted item at this entry.

6   Data Archival and Retrieval Algorithms

In this section the two key procedures is described in our model: data archival and data retrieval.

A.   Archival procedure

As identified in the scheme policy, there are three types of files: not encrypted, encrypted, and encrypted without de-duplication.

For the files encrypted without de-duplication, client will encrypt them by using his public key, and sent to cloud storage provider directly without de-duplication. For the files not encrypted, they will skip all the encryption steps.

For the rest files which are encrypted and need to be de-duplicated, for example $file_1$, the data archival procedure is shown on Figure 2.

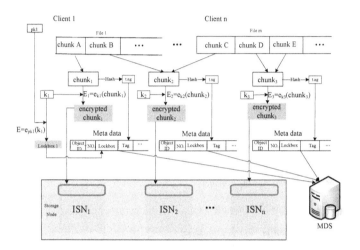

Fig. 2. Data Archival procedure

On client, if file1 needs to be upload to the cloud storage provider, there are following steps before sending its metadata to de-duplication provider:

- File is chunked by its owner, for example, user A.
- A tag is computed for the plaintext of each chunk. $Tag_i = Hash\ (M_i)$ with hash function *Hash*.
- Encrypt each chunk with a random symmetric key k_i. $C_i = Enc_{ki}(M_i)$. (where C_i is the ciphertext of the $chunk_i$)
- Generate the *Lockbox*. $Lockbox = Enc_{pkA}\ (K_i)$. (pkA is the public key of user A)
- Generate the *Mapbox* for the file.
- Send the *Mapbox* to de-dup provider

After the *Mapbox* is sent to de-duplication provider After the *Mapbox* is sent, there are following steps on de-duplication provider:
- Receive the *Mapbox* from the client.
- For each chunk, using the Tag to find out whether it is a duplicate one.
- If no (it is not a duplicate chunk): Mark this chunk as not duplicate.
- If yes (it is a duplicate chunk): Re-encrypt the original Lockbox:

$$Lockbox_{new} = Re\text{-}Enc_{rkB\text{-}>A}(Lockbox_{Bi})$$

(Where, rkB->A is the re-encryption key from user B to user A, $Lockbox_{new}$ is the new Lockbox of this chunk$_i$ for user A, $Lockbox_{Bi}$ is the original one of chunk$_i$ for user B.)

Then add the *object_ids* for this chunk to the *Mapbox*, overwriting the *Lockbox*, and mark this chunk as duplicate.

- Send the changed *Mapbox* back to client.

Finally the client will process following steps to store the data and its metadata:

- Send the chunks which are marked as not duplicate to storage service, and get the *object_ids* from the cloud storage service.
- Add these *object_ids* to the *Mapbox*.
- Send the final *Mapbox* to the metadata server.

```
Retrieve_file algorithm ()
//for Client
on recieve(file_name) from applicatons
{ /* client get the file to be retrieved*/
    send message(ASK_FOR_FileID) to de-dup provider
}
on receive(map_entry) from de-dup provider
{
    Get the Mapbox from the Map Entry
    Get object_id from map
    send(object_id) to cloud storage provider
}
on receive(echunk) from cloud storage provider
{
    chunk_key = decryption(private_key, lockbox)
    chunk = decryption(chunk_key, echunk)
    Put the chunk in the file according to its offset
}
//for de-dup provider
on receive(file_name) from Client

{ /* Client get the Map Entry of the file*/
        Get file_id through looking up the corresponding record in File_Attibutes_Table
        Get map_entry through looking up the corresponding record in File_Chunk_Table
        send(map_entry) to Client
}
//for cloud storage provider
on receive (object_id) from client
{
        Get echunk through looking up the corresponding record in object_id_Table.
        send(echunk) to Client.
}
End Algorithm
```

Fig. 3. Description of the data retrieval algorithm

B. *Retrieval procedure*

As shown in figure 3, when a user needs to download files, the retrieval procedure has the following steps:

- Client sends a retrieval request to de-dup provider to get the *Mapbox* of the file from metadata server.
- Use the *object_id*s in *Mapbox* to get each encrypted chunk from the cloud storage provider.
- Decrypt each chunk by using the private key.
- Rebuild the original file

7   Security Analysis

The evaluation of the secure cloud storage model with data de-duplication is intended to demonstrate that the system is secure in the face of a variety of foreseeable scenarios. First, we examine the attacks that communication channel could take upon the system. Second, we examine the possible security leaks when faced with misbehaviour of malicious cloud storage provider, e.g. cloud storage system administrators with root-level access. Third, we examine the security implications from adversary attacks in the client side.

C. *Communication Channel Attacks*

One adversary may intercept the communication channel between the players. In our scheme, as the chunking and encryption are performed on the client side, and plaintext data is never transmitted in the clear, the interceptor cannot get useful information. Compared with convergent encryption, the chunks transmitted are encrypted by randomly generated symmetric keys, ciphertext based security analysis attack is much harder in our scheme. On the other hand, the lockbox uploaded to the proxy by client is also encrypted by client's public key. Even when an adversary intercepts the channel and get all the metadata of a file, e.g. *Mapbox*, he could only get the encrypted chunk contents and lockboxes of the chunks, which can only been decrypted using the data owner's private key.

If considering an adversary changing the intercepted messages. While it is not explicitly explained in our scheme, the above attack can be largely mitigated through the use of transport layer security (TLS) approaches such as Secure Sockets Layer [20].

D. *Cloud Storage Provider Attacks*

A secure storage system should also provide protection from the attacks in the cloud storage provider. But as discussed in "Threat Model" section, the most important goal of Cloud Storage Provider is to engage more users, so Denial of Service attacks, e.g. powering off the storage servers, refusing to store or deleting the data, don't make any sense.

The main attacks from the cloud storage provider are illegal data leakage or at most data modification. For example, a malicious cloud storage provider can change any data he chooses, resulting in users' incorrect access to their data.

Generally speaking, there are two facets to protect such changes. First, an insider's ability to target specific files can be limited. Second, we would like to make overwriting a value with garbage is generally more detectable. In our scheme, we have limited the adversary's ability to make undetectable changes, as undetected changes require the adversary to obtain the *Mapbox*, which can only be accessed after the very user grant access to the de-duplication provider.

The cloud storage server can leaks some information about users: a malicious cloud storage provider can determine the chunk to which a specific user has access, and the users that have access to a specific chunk, but this is not a serious issue in our system, because the chunk is encrypted and *Mapbox* is kept in metadata server separated from the chunk contents.

In another case, if the cloud storage provider attempt to access the plaintext of the data which stored on storage servers, though he can access any data he choose, he would not know the *Mapbox* and the private key for decrypting the Lockbox, so he still could not leak the user's information.

E. *Client Attacks*

A malicious user may somehow know the *object_id* of other user's data. Then he can access to cloud storage provider to download these data, however, he still lack of the key for decrypting the chunks and the *Mapbox* for rebuilding the file.

If an adversary somehow gets authenticated by the system, for example as user A, then he can access the de-dup provider to get all file *Mapboxes* of user A, however, he doesn't know the private key of user A to decrypt the chunks, the file content of user A is still safe. Only when both the private key of user A is leaked and the authentication mechanism of the system is compromised by the adversary, the data of user A will leak out.

If another key in our model, the chunk key, is compromised, it results in a less drastic information leak. This is due to the fact that an adversary with the chunk key would still need to know the object_id, and be able get authenticated to the MDS in order to rebuild the plaintext of the file.

8   Conclusions

In cloud storage, reducing the amount of data need to be transferred, stored, and managed becomes a crucial, especially for lowering the user cost and bandwidth. So data de-duplication becomes an important and popular cost-saving feature for cloud storage. On the other hand, as user data are stored and processed by outsourced cloud provider, encryption becomes a necessary before updating data into the cloud.

However, the above two goals are greatly opposed to each other. In order to solve the above conflict, this paper proposes a policy-based de-duplication proxy scheme, which allows a policy-based de-duplication proxy scheme to enable different trust relations among cloud storage components, de-duplication related components and different security requirements. The de-duplication proxy can only de-duplicate data of its registered users based on the capabilities it has received from the key center. The user can decide which data will to de-dup by submitting the tags of the data chunks or not.

Based on the above scheme, the data archival and retrieval algorithms are given, further with a key management mechanism to access and decrypt the shared de-duplicated data chunks based on proxy re-encryption.

This paper also gives the security analysis of the scheme. Prototype implementation and experimental evaluation are planed future work.

Acknowledgment. We thank Chunhui Shi for his original and helpful advice on this topic. We also thank Ke Wang and Xiaojian Liu for their feedback and discussion with us. This work is supported by the China NSFC Program under Grant No. 60273006.

References

1. Zheng, Q., Xu, S.: Secure and efficient proof of storage with deduplication. In: Proc. CODASPY 2012, pp. 1–12 (2012)
2. Marques, L., Costa, C.J.: Secure deduplication on mobile devices. In: Proc. OSDOC 2011, pp. 16–29 (2011)
3. Storer, M.W., Greenan, K., Long, D.D., Miller, E.L.: Secure data deduplication. In: Proc. StorageSS 2008, pp. 1–10 (2008)
4. Xu, J., Chang, E., Zhou, J.: Secure Cloud Storage with Encrypted Data using File-Based Authentication. In: IACR (2011), http://eprint.iacr.org/2011/538.pdf
5. Rahumed, A., Chen, H.C.H., Tang, Y., Lee, P.P.C., Lui, J.C.S.: A secure cloud backup system with assured deletion and version control. In: Proc. ICPPW 2011, pp. 160–167 (2011)
6. Anderson, P., Zhang, L.: Fast and Secure Laptop Backups with Encrypted De-duplication. In: Proc. LISA 2010, pp. 29–40 (2010)
7. Douceur, J.R., Adya, A., Bolosky, W.J., Simon, D., Theimer, M.: Reclaiming space from duplicate files in a serverless distributed file system. In: Proc. ICDCS 2002, pp. 617–624 (2002)
8. Harnik, D., Pinkas, B., Shulman-Peleg, A.: Side channels in cloud services: deduplication in cloud storage. IEEE Security & Privacy 8(6), 40–47 (2010)
9. Goldwasser, S., Micali, S.: Probabilistic encryption & how to play mental poker keeping secret all partial information. In: Annual ACM Symposium on Theory of Computing (1982)
10. Gantz, J.F., et al.: The Expanding Digital Universe: A Forecast of Worldwide Information Growth through 2010. In: IDC (March 2007)
11. Nath, P., Urgaonkar, B., Sivasubramaniam, A.: Evaluating the usefulness of content addressable storage for high-performance data intensive applications. In: Proceedings of the 17th International Symposium on High Performance Distributed Computing, Boston, MA, USA (2008)
12. Green, M., Hohenberger, S., Ateniese, G., Fu, K.: Improved proxy re-encryption schemes with applications to secure distributed storage. In: Proceedings of the 12th Annual Network and Distributed System Security Symposium, NDSS (February 2005)
13. Green, M., Ateniese, G.: Identity-Based Proxy Re-encryption. In: Katz, J., Yung, M. (eds.) ACNS 2007. LNCS, vol. 4521, pp. 288–306. Springer, Heidelberg (2007)
14. Blaze, M., Bleumer, G., Strauss, M.J.: Divertible Protocols and Atomic Proxy Cryptography. In: Nyberg, K. (ed.) EUROCRYPT 1998. LNCS, vol. 1403, pp. 127–144. Springer, Heidelberg (1998)
15. Zhu, B., Li, K., Patterson, H.: Avoiding the Disk Bottleneck in the Data Domain Deduplication File System. In: Proceedings of the 6th USENIX Conference on File and Storage Technologies (FAST 2008), pp. 269–282 (February 2008)

16. Liu, C., Lu, Y., Du, D., Wang, D.: ADMAD: Application-Driven Metadata Aware De-duplication Archival Storage System. In: International Workshop on Storage Network Architecture and Parallel I/Os (SNAPI 2008) Held In Conjunction with the 25th IEEE Conference on Mass Storage Systems and Technologies, MSST 2008 (2008)
17. Liu, C., et al.: R-ADMAD: High reliability provision for large-scale de-duplication archival storage systems. In: Proceedings of the 23rd International Conference on Supercomputing, pp. 370–379 (June 2009)
18. Ibraimi, L., Tang, Q., Hartel, P., Jonker, W.: Type-Based Proxy Re-encryption and Its Construction. In: Chowdhury, D.R., Rijmen, V., Das, A. (eds.) INDOCRYPT 2008. LNCS, vol. 5365, pp. 130–144. Springer, Heidelberg (2008)
19. Fan, L., Cao, P., Almeida, J., Broder, A.Z.: Summary Cache: A Scalable Wide-Area Web Cache Sharing Protocol. IEEE/ACM Transactions on Networking 8(3), 281–293 (2000)
20. Weaver, A.C.: Secure sockets layer. Computer 39(4), 88–90 (2006)

A New Method Based on Fuzzy C-Means Algorithm for Search Results Clustering

Fei Wang[1,2], Yueming Lu[1,2,*], Fangwei Zhang[3], and Songlin Sun[1,2]

[1] School of Information and Communication Engineering, Beijing University of Posts and Telecommunications, Beijing, China
[2] Key Laboratory of Trustworthy Distributed Computing and Service (BUPT), Ministry of Education, Beijing, China
wflovest@foxmail.com, {ymlu,slsun}@bupt.edu.cn
[3] School of Humanities, Beijing University of Posts and Telecommunications, Beijing, China
zhangfangwei@bupt.edu.cn

Abstract. The existing Fuzzy C-means (FCM) clustering algorithm can only cluster the web documents samples with a pre-known cluster number c which is impossible in practical situations. A new method based on fuzzy c-means algorithm for search results clustering is proposed in this paper. The new clustering method combines FCM algorithm with Affinity Propagation (AP) algotithm to find the optimal c for search results. It is proved that the new method has a better performance in accuracy than traditional method in search results clustering.

Keywords: clustering algorithm, search engine, results clustering, FCM, similarity measure.

1 Introduction

With the rapid growth of the Internet, search engine has become a crucial tool for retrieving information on the Internet. Due to the facts that many different queries may present a same search intention and a single query may indicate various meanings, search engines often return inconsistent results. Users have to iterate through a long list to locate their desired information, which is often tedious and inefficient [1], [2]. Thus it is important to cluster search results before submitting them to users like famous clustering search engines carrot2 [3] and vivisimo [4].

Considering the huge amount of information on the Internet, linear time clustering algorithms are the best candidates complying with the speed requirement of online clustering [5]. These include the k-means algorithm and FCM algorithm. FCM algorithm is a method of clustering that allows one web document to belong to two or more clusters, so it can reflect the real occasion of search results well. However, FCM algorithm could not be applied without the cluster number c. So, FCM algorithm is

---

* Corresponding author.

Y. Yuan, X. Wu, and Y. Lu (Eds.): ISCTCS 2012, CCIS 320, pp. 263–270, 2013.
© Springer-Verlag Berlin Heidelberg 2013

not well suited for search results clustering, as it is difficult for us to get the value of c before clustering.

A new clustering method combining FCM algorithm with AP algorithm which could predict the value of c is proposed in the paper. Besides, the similarity measure, vector inner product, is applied in the new method to further improve the performance. The experimental simulation proves that the new method has better performance in accuracy than traditional FCM algorithm and is more practical in search results clustering.

2   Proposed Method

2.1   Clustering Algorithm

FCM Algorithm

FCM is a algorithm [6] for cluster analysis in which the allocation of data points to clusters is not "hard" (all-or-nothing) but "fuzzy" in the same sense as fuzzy logic. In other words, the fuzzyness represents the uncertainty that data point i belongs to cluster j. FCM algorithm is based on minimization of the objective function (1):

$$J_m = \sum_{i=1}^{N} \sum_{j=1}^{c} u_{ij}^m \left\| x_i - v_j \right\|^2, 1 \leq m \leq \infty \tag{1}$$

where m is the weighting exponent, the greater m is, the more fuzzy the partition. The u_{ij} is the degree of membership that x_i belongs to cluster j, v_j (i=1,2,$\cdots$,c) is the j-th center of the clusters, and $\|*\|$ is distance expressing the similarity between web page i and the center j. Fuzzy partitioning is carried out through an iterative optimization of the objective function (1), with the update of membership u_{ij} and the cluster centers v_j by:

$$u_{ij} = 1 \bigg/ \sum_{k=1}^{c} \left(\left\| x_i - v_j \right\| \big/ \left\| x_i - v_k \right\| \right)^{2/(m-1)} \qquad v_j = \sum_{i=1}^{N} u_{ij}^m * x_i \bigg/ \sum_{i=1}^{N} u_{ij}^m \tag{2}$$

This iteration will stop when inequality (3) holds. ε is a termination criterion between 0 and 1, whereas k is the iteration steps.

$$\max_{ij} \left\{ \left| u_{ij}^{(k+1)} - u_{ij}^{(k)} \right| \right\} < \varepsilon \tag{3}$$

Affinity Propagation Algorithm

Affinity Propagation (AP) is proposed for image clustering [7]. It works based on similarities between pairs of data points x_i and x_k, and it treats all the data points (x_1, x_2,...,x_N) as potential cluster centers (called exemplars). To find appropriate exemplars, AP accumulates evidence "responsibility" $R(i,k)$ from data point i for how well-suited point k is to serve as the exemplar for point i, and accumulates evidence "availability" $A(i,k)$ from candidate exemplar point k for how appropriate it would be for point i to choose point k as its exemplar. From the view of evidence, the greater $R(:,k)+A(:,k)$ is, the larger probability the point k as a final cluster center [8].

Affinity propagation algorithm has low time complexity. However, when clustering large amount of web documents, AP algorithm would return too much redundant clusters which is not convenient for users to locate their desired information.

2.2   The New Clustering Method

The new clustering method combining FCM with AP algorithm is used to detect the value of c. The main steps are: FCM algorithm is assigned with a relatively large value c and will output c centers of clusters v_j, $j \in [1,c]$). Then the c cluster centers will be clustered by AP algorithm, and an optimal c' centers of clusters $(v_j'$, $j \in [1,c'])$ will be returned as the initial partition of another FCM algorithm procedure.

The new method is composed of the following steps as Fig.1 shows:

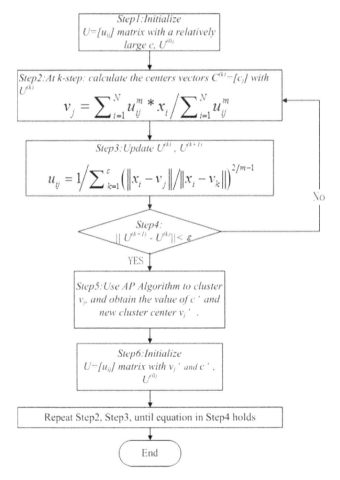

Fig. 1. The procedure of the new clustering method

3   Preprocess Work

3.1   Representation of Web Page

As is shown in Fig.2, web page snippets from search results usually have three parts: title, URL and abstract [9]. The key terms contained in URLs and abstracts are more representative. To construct vector space model to be introduced in 3.2, these key terms such as "ipad" in title and "store" in URL will be assigned triple weight.

Fig. 2. The display form of web page snippets from search results

3.2   Vector Space Model for Search Results

Vector Space Model (VSM) is an algebraic model for representing text documents. In the paper, VSM is constructed to represent top-N web page snippets of search results. The process of constructing VSM is as follows:

$$R = \{ R_1, R_2, \cdots, R_N \} \tag{4}$$

(4) represents the top-N snippets of web pages from search results.

$$\begin{cases} X = \{ x_1, x_2, \cdots, x_N \} \\ X_i = (X_{i1}, X_{i2}, \cdots, X_{in}), (i = 1, 2, \cdots, N) \\ X_{ij} \in [0,1], (i = 1, 2, \cdots, N; j = 1, 2, \cdots, n) \\ \sum_{j=1}^{n} X_{ij} = 1, (i = 1, 2, \cdots, N) \end{cases} \tag{5}$$

(5) is the final vector model of search results. X_i is the constructed vector of web page snippet R_i and each web page snippet has n feature items. X_{ij} is the weight of j-th feature in the i-th web page snippet. In other words, X_{ij} is term frequency of term t_j in web page snippets R_i.

4   Experimental and Evaluation

4.1   Datasets

A typical way to collect datasets is introduced in [10]. For example, when a keyword "apple" is submitted to search engine, a list of pages is returned. Then the search results ranked top-53 are chosen to prepare search results datasets. Besides, the web documents datasets derived from the Open Directory Project (DMOZ) and famous datasets such as IRIS are also simulated in the paper.

The content of datasets mentioned above is described in Table 1.

Table 1. Content of Datasets

Datasets	Categories (number)	Description
IRIS	setosa (50); versicolor (50); virginica (50)	1. Come from the UCI Repository of Machine Learning Databases. 2. Three groups.
Docs_DMOZ	shirt (35); swimwear (33); music (34); photography (25); tobacco (30); auto loans (18)	1. Derived from the Open Directory Project (DMOZ). 2. Six categories.
Results_SE	iphone (22); apple news (19); apple retails (12)	1. Top-53 ranked search results from Carrot2 search engine, Query ="apple". 2. Three manually classified categories.

4.2   Evaluation

As the categories of the datasets are pre-known, the external quality measure [11] such as *Precision* and *Recall* is applied to evaluate clusters. For example, the category "shirt" in Docs_DMOZ, its precision rate P and recall rate R are defined as follows:

$$P(shirt) = S_{correct} \cap S_{compute} / S_{compute} \tag{6}$$

$$R(shirt) = S_{correct} \cap S_{compute} / S_{correct} \tag{7}$$

$S_{correct}$ represents the correct number of web documents in category "shirt", here the $S_{correct}$ of "shirt" equals 35 as shown in Table 1. While $S_{compute}$ represents the number of web documents in cluster "shirt" computed by clustering algorithms. *Precision* and *Recall* is applied in this paper to calculate the accuracy of cluster. The value of *Precision* and *Recall* ranges from 0 to 1, and higher *Precision* and *Recall* suggests higher quality of the clustering results.

4.3   Result Analysis

IRIS Datasets
Considering the fact that IRIS dataset is not sparse matrix, Euclidean distance is applied to compute similarity of vectors, and the clustering results of the new method

and traditional FCM algorithm on IRIS dataset is shown in Table.2 and Table.3. Each of the three categories (I,II,III) in IRIS dataset has 50 data points, and the 50 data points of each category distribute in three clusters (1,2,3). When compared with traditional FCM algorithm, the proposed method has a purity of 0.9667 shown in Table.2, while the traditional FCM algorithm has a purity of 0.8933 shown in Table.3.

Table 2. Result of the new method on IRIS dataset

Cluster / Category	1	2	3
I.setosa	50	0	0
II.versicolor	0	4	46
III.virginica	0	49	1
Purity	(50+49+46)/150=0.9667		

Table 3. Result of traditional FCM algorithm on IRIS dataset

Cluster / Category	1	2	3
I.setosa	50	0	0
II.versicolor	0	3	47
III.virginica	0	37	13
Purity	(50+37+47)/150=0.8933		

DMOZ Document Datasets

The documents datasets derived from the Open Directory Project (DMOZ) is more persuasive to validate the advantage of the new clustering method. The curves in Fig.3 show that almost every cluster generated by the new clustering method has a higher *precision* and *recall* which indicates a better quality cluster.

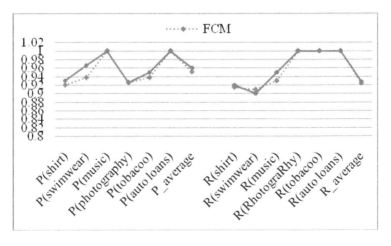

Fig. 3. The comparison of different algorithms on DMOZ document datasets

Search Results Datasets

The new clustering method is also validated on search results. Experiment shows it can not only detect the value of c, but also can improve the performance of clustering to some extent. Fig.4 shows the comparison of the new method with traditional FCM on search results. The curves in Fig.4 shows that the new clustering method has a higher average *Precision* and *Recall* which means a better quality clusters.

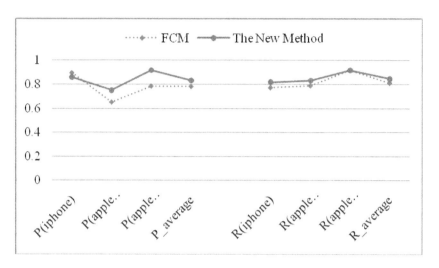

Fig. 4. The comparison of different algorithms on search results

5   Conclusions

In this paper, a new clustering method combining FCM algorithm with AP algorithm for search engines is proposed. According to the simulation, it is effective in predicting the parameter c in FCM clustering algorithm and it is able to promote the accuracy of clusters to some extent.

As to how to initialize the c cluster centers in FCM method in order to get a better quality of web search and accurate rate of classification, a further research will be conducted.

Acknowledgments. This research was supported in part by National 863 Program (No. 2011AA01A205), National 973 Program (No. 2011CB302702), P. R. China. Thanks for the great help.

References

1. Wang, Y., Kitsuregawa, M.: On Combining Link and Contents Information for Web Page Clustering. In: Hameurlain, A., Cicchetti, R., Traunmüller, R. (eds.) DEXA 2002. LNCS, vol. 2453, pp. 902–913. Springer, Heidelberg (2002)

2. Li, J.C., Yao, T.F.: An Efficient Token-based Approach for Web-Snippet Clustering. In: Proceedings of the Second International Conference on Semantics, knowledge, and Grid (SKG 2006) (November 2006)
3. Corrot2 clustering engine, http://search.carrot2.org/
4. Vivisimo clustering engine, http://vivisimo.com/
5. Oren, Z., Oren, E.: Web Document Clustering: A Feasibility Demonstration. In: Proceedings of the 21st annual international ACM SIGIR Conference on Research and Development in Information Retrieval, SIGIR 1998 (August 1998)
6. A Tutorial on Clustering Algorithms : Fuzzy C-means, http://home.dei.polimi.it/matteucc/Clustering/tutorial_html/cmeans.html
7. Frey, B.J., Dueck, D.: Clustering by Passing Messages Between Data Points. Science 315, 972–976 (2007)
8. Wang, K.J., Zhang, J.Y.: Adaptive Affinity Propagation Clustering. Acta Automatica Sinica, Computer and Information Science 33, 1242–1246 (2008)
9. Yang, N., Liu, Y., Yang, G.: Clustering of Web Search Results Based on Combination of Links and In-snippets. In: 2011 Eighth Web Information Systems and Applications Conference, pp. 108–113 (October 2011)
10. Wang, Y., Kitsuregawa, M.: Link Based Clustering of Web Search Results. In: Wang, X.S., Yu, G., Lu, H. (eds.) WAIM 2001. LNCS, vol. 2118, pp. 225–236. Springer, Heidelberg (2001)
11. Oren, Z., Oren, E.: Web Document Clustering: A Feasibility Demonstration. In: Proceedings of the 21st ACM SIGIR, pp. 46–54 (1998)

A Distance Adaptive Embedding Method in Dimension Reduction

Yanting Niu[1,2], Yueming Lu[1,2,*], Fangwei Zhang[3], and Songlin Sun[1,2]

[1] School of Information and Communication Engineering, Beijing University of Posts
and Telecommunications, Beijing, China
[2] Key Laboratory of Trustworthy Distributed Computing and Service (BUPT),
Ministry of Education, Beijing, China
qingorange@126.com, {ymlu,slsun}@bupt.edu.cn
[3] School of Humanities, Beijing University of Posts and Telecommunications, Beijing, China
zhangfangwei@bupt.edu.cn

Abstract. The distribution preservation is a challenge inthe dimension reduction methods. This paper proposes a distance adaptive embedding method (DAE). The DAE method includes the cosine similarity technology and a new distance transformation function. It has the characteristics of easy handling and strong similarity distinction. The DAE method can make small loss value and good cluster discrimination by using the new distance transformation function in the embedding.The experiment results show that the DAE method has a good performance in distribution preservation, better than the performance of the multidimensional scaling method.

Keywords: dimension reduction, clustering, distance adaptive embedding.

1 Introduction

With the rapid development of information technology and its extensive application, the high dimensionality of the data appeared in large numbers. Due to the curse of dimensionality, data analysis in high dimensions becomes a difficult problem [1] [2]. Hence data dimension reduction methods are introduced [3]. For clustered data, cluster preservation becomes critical during the process of dimension reduction. Traditional dimension reduction methods are generally ignored the cluster preservation while reducing the dimensionality of the data[2].

So far, many dimension reduction methods are based on the high-dimensional pair-wise distances computed in the original space. The effect of embedding such distance distributions is the generation of spherical embedding with low or no cluster discrimination power. Given the particular behavior of distances in high dimensions, distance adaptation, i.e. transformation, is required in order to improve the detection of clusters [2].

Our purpose with the distance adaptive embedding method (DAE) is to avoid the spherical embedding and to increase the cluster discrimination capability. We rely on

---

* Corresponding author.

Y. Yuan, X. Wu, and Y. Lu (Eds.): ISCTCS 2012, CCIS 320, pp. 271–278, 2013.

distance analysis and therefore seek a distance distribution based on the cosine similarity [4] [5]technology that reflects a clustered dataset. To enforce it we propose a transformation of distances that is based on a loose identification of the structures. By identifying the relevant relationships between data items and modifying the distances accordingly, we help the traditional dimension reduction methods to preserve clusters.

2   Distance Adaptive Embedding Method

In this part, a detailed description ofthe DAE method is proposed. Given that the DAE method is an improvement of traditional dimension reduction methods in cluster preservation, wefirst give a brief introduction of multidimensional scaling methodwhich is used in the DAE method. For the DAE method, we choose a new distance function based on the cosine similarity technology instead of the common Euclidean distance [6]. By using the new distance function, we define a similar subset which is the prerequisite for the DAE method. Subsection 2.2 focuses on the cosine similarity. On the basis of new distance function, we propose a distance transformation technology and apply it to the multidimensional scaling method.

2.1   Multidimensional Scaling Method

The data dimension reduction can be described as follows:

(i) $X = \{x_i\}_{i=1}^N$, a sample set in the D-dimensional space; $Y = \{y_i\}_{i=1}^N$, a sample set in the d-dimensional space $(d<<D)$ [7].

(ii) Dimension reduction mapping: $M: X \to Y, x \to y = M(x)$, then y is the low-dimensional representation of x[7].

Based on the description of dimension reduction, the problem is to find an accurate mapping of the data which can preservethe original clusters as best as possible.

MDS is a commonmethod to pair-wise distance preservation, which optimizes a loss function of all distances. The loss function has the following general form:

$$L = \sum_{i<j} f\big(g(\delta_{ij}) - d_{ij}\big) \times h\big(g(\delta_{ij}), d_{ij}\big) \tag{1}$$

Where the δ_{ij}represents the distance in the original space and d_{ij}represents distance in the embedded low-dimensional space. The quadratic function is the most commonly employed form for$f$:

$$f\big(g(\delta_{ij}) - d_{ij}\big) = \big(g(\delta_{ij}) - d_{ij}\big)^2 \tag{2}$$

The function$g$ represents the transformation applied on the distances matrix of data in the original high-dimensional space.

The most commonly used loss function is the minimization form:

$$L = \sum_{i<j}\big(\delta_{ij} - d_{ij}\big)^2 \tag{3}$$

The significant drawback is: larger distances have more weight and will be given more importance in the embedding. Thus, the global structure of the data is more or less affected.

MDS models generally use the minimization form of g: $g(\delta_{ij}) = \delta_{ij}$, while always focusing on the design of weighting function h. It is mainly this distance transformation function of the high-dimensional data that is of interest in this paper.

2.2   Cosine Similarity Technology

Given two points x_i and x_j expressed in the vector form. The cosine similarity between them can be measured as follows:

$$similarity(x_i, x_j) = \frac{x_i \circ x_j}{\|x_1\|_2 \cdot \|x_j\|_2} \qquad (4)$$

Where '$\circ$' in formula 4 stands for the inner product of two vectors and $\|*\|_2$ stands for the Euclidean norm of the vector. Clearly the cosine similarity takes values range from -1 meaning exactly opposite to 1 meaning exactly the same, with 0 usually indicating independence, and in between values indicating intermediate similarity or dissimilarity.

In this paper, we define the similarity from 0 to 1, and ignore the dissimilarity which from -1 to 0.

Figure 1 gives an example. There, $\cos\theta$ is the similarity of the two vectors x_i and x_j. Visually, the cosine similarity maps all the point vectors to the unit hyper-sphere (vectors $x_{i,0}$ and $x_{j,0}$ in the Fig. 1).

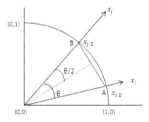

Fig. 1. Cosine similarity

In order to apply this in the DAE method, a distance function that decreases with increasing the cosine similarity is needed. From Fig. 1, to use the length of the line segment AB would be a solution: $(AB) = \|x_{i,0} - x_{j,0}\|_2$. After trigonometric manipulations, the result is

$$\delta(x_i, x_j) = 2 \times \sin{^\theta}/_2$$

$$= \sqrt{2 \times (1 - \cos\theta)}$$

$$= \sqrt{2 \times \left(1 - similarity(x_i, x_j)\right)} \qquad (5)$$

The $\delta(x_i, x_j)$ takes value between 0 and $\sqrt{2}$, based on the limit $0 \leq similarity(x_i, x_j) \leq 1$. Formula 5 defines a distance function that meets the requirement of regressive.

Also noticing that we can use it to respond to range queries: suppose that all the points satisfying the following formula are wanted:

$$similarity(x_i, x_j) \geq \varepsilon \tag{6}$$

Referring to formula 5, the requirement becomes

$$\delta(x_i, x_j) \leq \sqrt{2 \times (1 - \varepsilon)} \tag{7}$$

Define $\sqrt{2 \times (1 - \varepsilon)} = \rho$. Then we get the new requirement:

$$\delta(x_i, x_j) \leq \rho \tag{8}$$

2.3   Distance Transformation Technology

The key of the DAE method is to define a distance transformation function g using the cosine similarity technology. Below we propose a detailed definition.

$U = X \times X$ is the set of all pairs of points (x_i, x_j) for $x_i \neq x_j \in X$. Given a concept of similarity (the cosine similarity defined above), we define U_1 as the subset of the pairs of the similar points and U_2 the subset of the rest of the pairs:

$$U_1 = \{(x_i, x_j) | \delta(x_i, x_j) \leq \rho, 0 \leq \rho \leq \sqrt{2}\} \tag{9}$$

Here we use only the similarity matrix.

Let the transformed distance matrix be represented with $D^* = (\delta_{ij}^*) \in R^{N \times N}$. The new distance δ_{ij}^* is transformed through g, which taking into account the similarity relationships:

$$\delta_{ij}^* = g(\delta_{ij}, U) = \begin{cases} \delta_{ij}^2 & \text{if } (x_i, x_j) \in U_1 \\ \delta_{ij} & \text{if } (x_i, x_j) \in U_2 \end{cases} \tag{10}$$

By applying the transformation function g on the distances, the DAE method tries to preserve all transformed distances δ_{ij}^* as faithfully as possible in the low-dimensional embedding space.

Replacing the original distances δ_{ij} with the new distances δ_{ij}^*, we obtain the new loss function:

$$L = \frac{1}{\sum_{i<j} \delta_{ij}^*} \sum_{i<j} \frac{(d_{ij} - \delta_{ij}^*)^2}{\delta_{ij}^*} \tag{11}$$

The presence of the weighting by $\frac{1}{\delta_{ij}^*}$ naturally reinforces the effect of the transformation function g by increasing the importance of smaller distance values in the embedding. We obtain the new form of loss function by substituting the scaled distances:

$$L = C \sum_{U_1} \frac{(d_{ij} - \delta_{ij}^2)^2}{\delta_{ij}^2} + C \sum_{U_2} \frac{(d_{ij} - \delta_{ij})^2}{\delta_{ij}} = L_1 + L_2 \tag{12}$$

Where C is the constant: $C = \frac{1}{\sum_{i<j} \delta_{ij}^*}$.

The first term L_1 addresses relationship between similar points, $(x_i, x_j) \in U_1$, and L_2 the remainder, $(x_i, x_j) \in U_2$.

Based onformula 10, different values forρ generate different embeddings. When $\rho = 0$, the function g is the same as in MDS, the embedding is equivalent to the original space. When $0 < \rho \le 1$, distances can be perceived as forces in the loss function; a small distance is a force of attraction while a large distance is a force of repulsion. So the cluster preservation is promised in the DAE method.

3   Experiments and Evaluation

As the DAE method aims at making good cluster preservation in dimension reduction, we evaluate it by the visualization method in 2D spaces. Besides, we take the loss value as an evaluation factor. The experiments on real dataset show the evaluation results.

3.1   Dataset

DOCS: It consists of 35 text documents. It has the following 7 groups. Each group has 5 documents.

ABS: Abstracts of computer science technical reports.
BBR: Reports about basketball games.
CAL: 'Call for papers' for technical conferences.
MAT: Five portions of the Bible in King James' Version.
REC: Cooking recipes.
WOR: 'World News', documents about the Middle East.
SAL: Sale advertisement for computers and software.

The distance is based on the cosine similarity. For the documents in same group, their similarity value is very large, while for two documents in different groups, the similarity value is very small. Table 1 shows the similarity of a part of the dataset.

Table 1. Document to document similarity matrix for part of the DOCS dataset

	Abs1	Abs2	Abs3	Bbr1	Bbr2	Bbr3
Abs1	1	0.730	0.617	0	0.013	0
Abs2	0.730	1	0.610	0	0	0
Abs3	0.617	0.61	1	0	0	0
Bbr1	0	0	0	1	0.761	0.890
Bbr2	0.013	0	0	0.761	1	0.807
Bbr3	0	0	0	0.890	0.807	1

3.2   Experiments

In our experiments, first, we use formula 5 to get the distance matrix. Then we make distance transformation to get the δ_{ij}^* matrix based on formula 9 and 10.

For the next step, we run multidimensional scaling on the dataset we import to get a 2-dimensional visualization. The 2-dimensional representation is returned in output dataset.Here we use distance matrix transformed from table1 as the input dataset. Table 2 shows the output dataset.

Based on table 2, the fig.2 gives the distribution result for the output dataset.

Table 2. Output value for the dataset from table1

	Abs1	Abs2	Abs3	Bbr1	Bbr2	Bbr3
x	-1.17928	-0.1805	-1.10086	1.174068	1.078024	1.208549
y	0.35498	-0.38502	-0.36586	-0.00745	-0.00752	-0.01089

Fig. 2. Embedding result for two groups, $\rho = 0.9$

Now we give the visualization results for the whole DOCS dataset.

The original dataset has 7 groups, so the ideal result is that we see 7 clearly discriminated clusters. Here we give different values of ρ.For every value of ρ, we get a visualization result in 2D space as shown in Fig. 3.

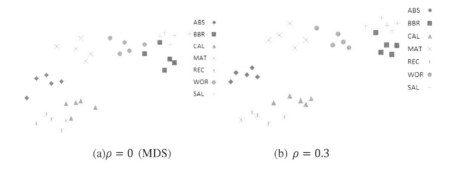

(a)$\rho = 0$ (MDS)   (b) $\rho = 0.3$

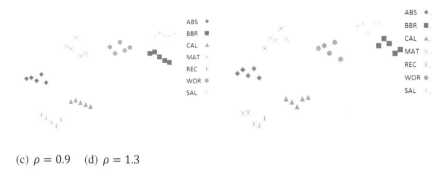

(c) $\rho = 0.9$ (d) $\rho = 1.3$

Fig. 3. Embedding results for DOCS with different values of ρ

The traditional MDS can hardly make clearly discriminated clusters, especial for BBR, REC, WOR, SAL (Fig.3(a)). A document in BBR group in the original space may be assigned to SAL group in the low-dimensionality. When giving a very small value for ρ (Fig.3(b)), the result is better than MDS, but the cluster preservation is still not good, for almost no similar points are based on the definition in subsection 3.2. Just as shown in Fig.3(c), giving a bigger value of ρ, the seven clusters can be well discriminated, and the documents can all be assigned to the right clusters as in the original distribution. This is because the similarity relationships have been well taken into account as described in formula 9 and formula 10, a small distance is a force of attraction while a large distance is a force of repulsion.With the continuing increase of ρ, the result in Fig.3(d) is worse than that in Fig.3(c) .It's because too large value can change the relative distance in the original space. For $\rho = 1.3$, the δ_{ij} which is bigger than 1 but smaller than 1.3 is squared, while the δ_{ij} which is bigger than 1.3 in the original matrix is still the same value. This leads to the relative distance be destroyed. Based on this, we can figure out that bigger value of ρ does not always bring better result. Only when giving an appropriate value, the cluster preservation can be obtained.

Another evaluation factor is the loss value of different values of ρ. Fig. 4 gives the results of the experiment. We use the distance matrix in the low-dimensionality. The loss value is figured out by formula 12.

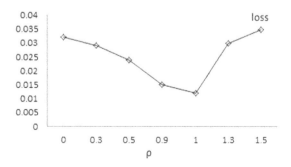

Fig. 4. The loss with varying ρ, for the DOCS dataset

As can be seen in Fig. 4, when $0 \leq \rho \leq 1$, the increasing in ρ significantly decreases the loss value. For $\rho = 0$, this method is just the traditional MDS method, so the first point in the Fig. 4 is the loss of MDS. Within this range of value, because of the DAE method increases the importance given to smaller distance values, with the increasing of ρ, the loss value is decreasing. While for $\rho > 1$, the loss value begins to increase. The reason can be found in the characteristics of square function, which makes the dissimilarity parts have more weight and brings negative effect.

Considering the loss value and the clusters distribution, an appropriate value for ρ can make significant contribution to the distance adaption in dimension reduction.

4   Conclusion

High-dimensional data brings the curse of dimensionality. Dimension reduction methods are proposed to avoid the curse of dimensionality. However, due to specific behaviors of distance measurements in high dimensions, structures in the data are difficult to be preserved.

In this paper, we propose a distance adaptive embedding method which increases the discrimination power of the embedding. A distance function based on the cosine similarity is adopted, and then it is applied to the traditional dimension reduction methods. Based on the new distance function, we define a similar subset. This is the key step of the DAE method as it determines the distance transformation. Experimental results have shown that an appropriate similar definition can generate both a small loss value and a good cluster preservation performance. Certain method for distance adaption is promising in the dimension reduction.

Acknowledgments. This research was supported in part by National 863 Program (No. 2011AA01A205), National 973 Program (No. 2011CB302702), P. R. China. Thanks for the great help.

References

1. Alotaibi, K., Rayward-Smith, V.J., de la Iglesia, B.: Non-metric Multidimensional Scaling for Privacy-Preserving Data Clustering. In: Yin, H., Wang, W., Rayward-Smith, V. (eds.) IDEAL 2011. LNCS, vol. 6936, pp. 287–298. Springer, Heidelberg (2011)
2. Szekely, E., Bruno, E., Maillet, S.M.: High-Dimensional Multimodal Distribution Embedding. In: IEEE International Conference on Data Mining Workshops, pp. 434–441 (2010)
3. Fodor, I.K.: A survey of dimension reduction techniques (2002)
4. Faloutsos, C., Lin, K.J.: FastMap: A fast algorithm for indexing, data-mining and visualization of traditional and multimedia datasets
5. Salton, G., McGill, M.J.: Introduction to Modern Information Retrieval. McGraw-Hill (1983)
6. Osinski, S.: Dimensionality reduction techniques for research results clustering (2004)
7. Wu, X.T., Yan, D.Q.: Analysis and research on method of data dimensionality reduction. Application Research of Computers 26(8) (2009)

Joint Cognitive Access and Power Control in Two-Tie Femtocell Networks

Xiaolong Zhao[1,2], Tiejun Lv[1,2], Yanhui Ma[1,2], and Yueming Lu[1,2]

[1] School of Information and Communication Engineering, Beijing University of Posts and Telecommunications, Beijing, China
[2] Key Laboratory of Trustworthy Distributed Computing and Service (BUPT), Ministry of Education, Beijing, China
{biyuxilan,lvtiejun,mayanhui2010,ymlu}@bupt.edu.cn

Abstract. In this paper, a joint cognitive access and power control algorithm is considered in the macrocell and femtocell networks. The cross-tier interference severely affects the performance of both the macrocell users and the femtocell users. To alleviate the interference, usually the femtocell base station which causes terrible interference to cellular users will be restricted in closed access mode or the cellular users will be regarded as authorized users in open access mode. In contrast, we take the macrocell cellular users nearby the boundary of the femtocell base station as cognitive users to get access to the nearest femtocell base station. Since the femtocell base station causes maximal interference to the cellular users and deters them from communicating with the macrocell base station (MBS). Other contributions of this paper include proposing a simple but effective method to improve the average throughput of the networks for the adaptive system, as well as establishing a distributed power control game model for the all users.

Keywords: femtocell, macrocell, power control, interference.

1 Introduction

With the increase of the data traffic demand in cellular networks today, the surest way to increase the system capacity of a wireless link is by getting the transmitter and receiver closer to each other, which introduces the femtocell base station [1]. Femtocells share spectrum with macrocell networks, which makes cross-tier interference management between femtocell and macrocells essential. Study shows that more than 50% of all voice calls and more than 70% of all data traffic originate indoors [2], while the ultimate link utilization of the home base station (HBS) which is also called femtocell isn't very satisfied in reality [3]. In the downlink, the interests of femtocell users and cellular users are in conflict, with femtocell users preferring closed access mode and cellular users preferring open access mode. The conflict is most pronounced for femtocells near the cell edge, where there are many cellular users and fewer femtocells [4].

Y. Yuan, X. Wu, and Y. Lu (Eds.): ISCTCS 2012, CCIS 320, pp. 279–286, 2013.
© Springer-Verlag Berlin Heidelberg 2013

Many works have been done, such as[1][5][6], however, most of the current works focus on determining the dynamic range of the uplink transmission power of femto-cells, rather than an analytical framework and detailed power control schemes. In [7], a distributed utility-based signal-to-interference-plus-noise (SINR) adaptation algo-rithm for femtocells is proposed. However this algorithm reduces transmission powers of the strongest femtocell interferers only, and after the power allocation, there are still some femtocells can't get their QoS guaranteed. What's more, the power control of the cellular users in the "dead zone" is not proposed in detail.

This work introduces the derivation of the throughput by Eigen function transfor-mation that has been done in a complex way in paper [4]. What's more, we comple-ment the uplink analysis in [7]. The present paper focuses on those cellular users nearby the HBS. A similar utility function is used in this paper with less a multiplica-tion during each iteration algorithm. We take these users as cognitive users to the femtocell users. The HBS broadcasts the system resources occupancy to these cogni-tive users and they adopt the solution of game theory to choose the best RB in order to optimize the throughput of the system.

The rest of this paper is organized as follows: Section 2 describes the system model. Section 3 and 4 presents it. Finally, conclusions are provided in Section 5.

2   System Model

Denote $C \subset \Re^2$ as the circular interior of a macrocell with radius R_c centered at a MBS defined as B_0, and the femtocells located in the interior of the centered macrocell are defined as $B_i (i = 1,2,3...S)$, where S is the number of the femtocells in the area. Cellular users are assumed to be uniformly distributed inside C, while the femtocell users are uniformly distributed around the HBSs.

For the cellular users, we consider multi-level M-ary modulation single carrier transmission that is adapted to the received $SINR$ (denoted as γ), thus each user is assumed to estimate its $SINR$ and provide perfect $SINR$ feedback to the B_0. Dis-cretize the SINR of all cellular users into N regions as $R_n = (\Gamma_n, \Gamma_{n+1}), n = 1, \cdots, N$, where Γ_1 is the minimum $SINR$ providing the lowest discrete rate and $\Gamma_{n+1} = \infty$. Then, the instantaneous transmission rate is $r_n = log(1 + \Gamma_n)$ (in bps/Hz) for $\gamma \in R_n (n \in [1, N])$, with the probability $P\{\Gamma_n \leq \gamma \leq \Gamma_{n+1}\}$. Consequently we obtain the average throughput [4]

$$T = \sum_{n=1}^{N} r_n P\{\Gamma_n \leq \gamma \leq \Gamma_{n+1}\}, \tag{1}$$

if the probability density function (PDF) of the $P(\gamma)$ is continuous, we have

$$T = \int \gamma \cdot p(\gamma) d\gamma. \tag{2}$$

An example of the model is given in Fig. 1.

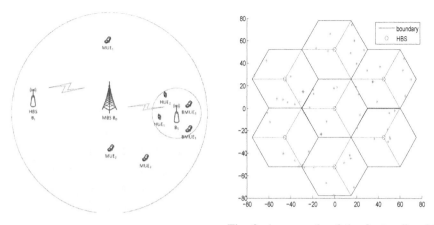

Fig. 1. An example of the model

Fig. 2. An example of the femtocells with BMUE (green *) and HUE (red *)

For the MUEs, whose SINRs don't meet the target's minimum SINR, we combine them with femtocell users into consideration. We assume there are N cellular users in the boundary area and the "dead zone" (BMUEs) whose SINR are inferior to their respective Interference Temperature. We allocate K sub-channels (resource blocks) for each femtocell and suppose that $K \leq N$, so these cognitive users (the second users) chose their RBs by estimating the availability of all RBs allocated by the HBSs. Let the $P(i, j, k)$ be the power between the ith cognitive user and the jth HBS on its kth RB, and the $h(i, j, k)$ be the link gain between the kth RB of the jth HBS and the ith cognitive user. We denote the **A** as the RBs occupation matrix, which implies whether the kth RB of the jth HBS is occupied or not

$$A(j,k) = \begin{cases} 1 & (occupied) \\ 0 & (unoccupied) \end{cases}, \tag{3}$$

An example of the femtocells is given in Fig. 2.

3   Optimization

3.1   The General Macrocell Users (MUE)

We take the uplink into account, let δ^2 be the variance of Additive White Gaussian Noise (AWGN) at B_0, then the SINR γ_i of the ith cellular user (here, the cellular users in the "dead zone" or around the bound of femtocells' interior are not included, which we will discuss in latter sections) can be written as

$$\gamma_i = \frac{p_i h_i}{\sum_{j \neq i} p_j h_j + \sigma^2}, \tag{4}$$

where the p_i is the power of the ith cellular user, and the term h_i is the channel gain between the ith cellular user and the MBS B_0. Do some works to the formula (4), we obtain

$$\gamma_i = \frac{p_i h_i}{\sum_{j \neq i} p_j h_j + \sigma^2} = \frac{p_i h_i / \sigma^2}{\frac{1}{\delta^2} \sum_{j \neq i} p_j h_j + 1} = \frac{SNR_i}{\sum_{j \neq i} SNR_j + 1} = \frac{\alpha_i}{\beta}. \tag{5}$$

We assume no fast shadow fading, numerator and denominator are defined as α_i and β respectively for simplicity, they are both stochastic variables. Since we know the statistical property of the $SNR_i = \alpha_i$ obeys logarithm Gaussian distribution with the mean of μ_α in decibels, and the standard deviation σ_α. So the probability density function (PDF) is

$$f(\alpha_i) = \frac{\xi}{\sqrt{2\pi\sigma_\alpha^2}} exp[-\frac{(10lg\alpha - \mu_\alpha)^2}{2\sigma_\alpha^2}], \tag{6}$$

where the $\xi = 10 / ln10$, so the Eigen function of the α_i defined as $\varphi_{\alpha_i}(\omega)$ is

$$\varphi_{\alpha_i}(\omega) = \int_{-\infty}^{\infty} f(\alpha_i) exp(j\omega\alpha_i) d\alpha_i = e^{j\omega\mu_\alpha - \frac{\xi^2}{2\sigma_\alpha^2}}. \tag{7}$$

We assume the cellular users are independent with each other, and then the Eigen function of the denom is

$$\varphi_\beta(\omega) = \prod_{j \neq i} \varphi_{\alpha_j}(\omega) 2\pi\delta(\omega) = \prod_{j \neq i} \varphi_{\alpha_j}(0) = \zeta. \tag{8}$$

$$\gamma_i \cdot \beta = \alpha_i \leftrightarrow \varphi_{\gamma_i}(\omega) \otimes \varphi_\beta(\omega) = \varphi_{\alpha_i}(\omega), \tag{9}$$

so the problem of solving for the Eigen function of the γ_i can be seen as a channel estimation problem, we defined the $g(\zeta)$ as the probability density coefficient of the SINR of the cellular users that we have obtained by channel estimation.

Therefore, we get the Eigen function of the γ_i defined as $\varphi_{\gamma_i}(\omega)$ by formula (5) ~ (9)

$$\varphi_{\gamma_i}(\omega) = g(\zeta)\varphi_{\alpha_i}(\omega) = g(\zeta)e^{j\omega\mu_\alpha - \frac{\xi^2}{2\sigma_\alpha^2}}. \tag{10}$$

In terms of the relation of the PDF and the Eigen function, we get the PDF of the SINR of the ith cellular user as follow

$$f(\gamma_i) = g(\zeta)f(\alpha_i), \tag{11}$$

then we have the probability for the interval of Γ by formula (2) and (11)

$$P\{\Gamma_n \le \gamma \le \Gamma_{n+1}\} = \int_{\Gamma_n}^{\Gamma_{n+1}} \gamma.f(r)d\gamma. \tag{12}$$

To sum up, we find that without the fast shadow fading, in the uplink the PDF of the cellular users subject to logarithm Gaussian distribution, which is consistent with our intuition. Once we get the probability of users' SINR, we get the throughput.

3.2   The Boundary Macrocell Users (BMUE) and the Femtocell Users (HUE)

We set the parameter τ_i as the minimum SINR level that the BMUE needed in order to connect its primitive station B_0. Therefore, if the BMUE's SINR is below its threshold τ_i, we take it as the cognitive user. Assume the ith cognitive user linked to the jth HBS on its kth RB. Modify the formula in [8] and [9], and then the SINR of this cognitive user is

$$SINR(i,j,k) = \frac{P(i,j,k)h(i,j,k)}{\sum_{j \ne i} \sum_{j \in S} p(j,j,k)h(j,j,k)A(j,k) + \delta^2}, \tag{13}$$

where δ^2 is the background noise. Since we know how to calculate the probability in the formula (1), we simplify it under the assumption that all the probability of the γ_i is the same, then the throughput of the ith cognitive user linked the jth HBS on the kth RB can be written as

$$t(i,j,k) = log[1 + SINR(i,j,k)], \tag{14}$$

and the interference of the primary user linked to the jth HBS on the kth RB from the second users is

$$I_{jk} = \sum_{i \in N} A(j,k)P(i,j,k)h(i,j,k). \tag{15}$$

We model the solution of RBs allocation as a game output. All the cognitive users are the participants, whose strategies are affected by not only their own decisions, but also the others. The key question is how to make a decision that the ultimately strategies of the participants are the optimal strategies, namely achieve the Nash equilibrium. In accordance with the throughput, denote the utility function U_0 standing for the strategy evaluation.

$$U_0(i,j,k) = \sum_{i \in N} \sum_{j \in S} \sum_{k \in K} t(i,j,k). \tag{16}$$

Taking the interference of the primary users into consideration let the jth HBS' total interference of the authorized users be I_{jtot}

$$I_{jtot} = \sum_{k \in K} I_{jk} = \sum_{i \in N} \sum_{k \in K} A(j,k)P(i,j,k)h(i,j,k), \tag{17}$$

then the formula (16) can be written as

$$U(i,j,k) = U_0(i,j,k) - \sum_{j \in S} \alpha_j I_{jtot} = \sum_{i \in N} \sum_{j \in S} \sum_{k \in K} log[1 + \frac{P(i,j,k)h(i,j,k)}{\sum_{j \neq i} \sum_{j \in S} p(j,j,k)h(j,j,k)A(j,j,k) + \delta^2}]$$
$$- \sum_{j \in S} \sum_{i \in N} \sum_{k \in K} \alpha_j A(j,k)P(i,j,k)h(i,j,k), \tag{18}$$

where α_j is the interference coefficient. It's worth noting that since we take the user and the interference into consideration in utility function, the maximization of utility function can be regarded as an exact potential game [8]. If we want to optimal utility efficiency, we should optimize the power of the cognitive users. Do derivation of $U(i,j,k)$ to the power $P(i,j,k)$ by (12) ~ (17)

$$\frac{\partial U(i,j,k)}{\partial P(i,j,k)} = \frac{1}{1+SINR(i,j,k)} \cdot \frac{h(i,j,k)}{\sum_{j \neq i} \sum_{j \in S} P(j,j,k)A(j,k)h(j,j,k) + \delta^2} - \alpha_j h(i,j,k). \tag{19}$$

$$\frac{\partial^2 U(i,j,k)}{\partial P^2(i,j,k)} = \frac{-1}{[1+SINR(i,j,k]^2} \cdot [\frac{h(i,j,k)}{\sum_{j \neq i} \sum_{j \in S} P(j,j,k)A(j,k)h(j,j,k) + \delta^2}]^2 < 0. \tag{20}$$

From the formula (20), we know the utility function is a convex function, so we let formula (19) be ZERO to get the solution of power

$$P(i,j,k) = \frac{1}{\alpha_j h(i,j,k)} - \frac{\sum_{j \neq i} \sum_{j \in S} P(j,j,k)h(j,j,k)A(j,k) + \delta^2}{h(i,j,k)}. \tag{21}$$

If $P(i,j,k) < 0$ then let $P(i,j,k) = 0$. If we consider the fairness to make sure that the SINR constraint of each user will not be too low to continue the transmission, we set a P_{min} power level. The existence of Nash Equilibrium can be seen in paper [10].

4   Simulations

It is assumed that N=20 BMUEs (cognitive users) randomly distributed around the HBS (R=30m) with distance in the range of 3m to 30m. There is one HUE at most on each RB. The initial power of the BMUEs is 100mw and the background noise is $-100dBm$. The link-gain is $h = w/d^4$, where w=0.97 and the scale factor is $\alpha = 200$. The interference to the HUE is shown in Fig.3. From the figure we can see that the interference to the HUE is convergent after the adjustment of the algorithm and the interference gets less at last. The average utility efficiency of one HBS can be seen in Fig.4.

From the Fig.4, we can see before the adjustment is done, the utility function U is less than the initial value, even below the zero, namely the system is unaccepted. That's because the interference is very strong. After the adjustment is finished, the U tends to stable and above the initial value, namely the system is accepted and the performance is improved. Overall, the U_0 is above the U. At the beginning, the utility function U is fluctuant, but after the adjustment of the whole users it's convergent.

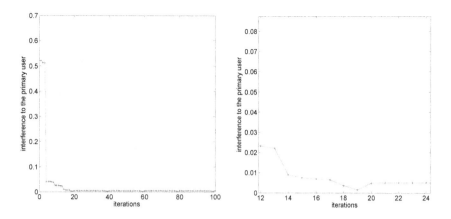

Fig. 3. The convergence of the interference to the HUE

At last, we draw a comparison in Fig.5 of the U_0 with the solution in [7]. Here, we denote the PU0 as the U_0 with the previous solution.

From the Fig.5, we know when the interference is less after the adjustment, our algorithm has the same performance with the solution mentioned in [7], however when the interference is great, we get a better performance. Although we get the same performance after the adjustment as a complement to the users that hadn't been done in detail in that paper, we simplify the algorithm with one multiplication less during each iteration algorithm.

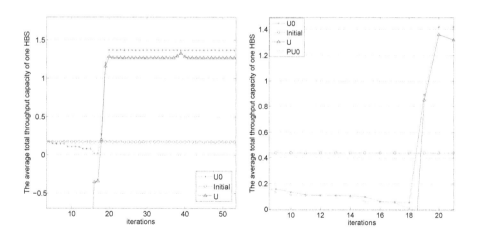

Fig. 4. The average utility efficiency of one HBS   **Fig. 5.** The comparison of U_0

5   Conclusions

From the above analysis, we present the proof of our algorithm. We formulate the throughput of the system without fast shadow fading and the utility function based on the interference and capacity. we take the BMUE as cognitive user to the primary user (HUE), formulate the potential game model and analyze the optimal adaptive power allocation of the cognitive user based on channel selection. The theory analysis and simulation results show the low ultimate interference to the primary user (HUE) guarantees the interests of the HUE and the acceptance of this algorithm. Meanwhile we prove the convergence of this algorithm, interference and utility function included. In future work, we will address more practical scenarios and the fairness of the network.

Acknowledgments. This work is financially supported by the National Natural Science Foundation of China (No. 60972075) and National 863 Project (No.2011AA01A205).

References

1. Damnjanovic, A., Montojo, J., Wei, Y., Ji, T., Luo, T., Vajapeyam, M., Yoo, T., Song, O., Malladi, D.: A survey on 3gpp heterogeneousnetworks. IEEE Wireless Communications 18(3), 10–21 (2011)
2. Chandrasekhar, V., Andrews, J., Gatherer, A.: Femtocell networks:a survey. IEEE Communications Magazine 46(9), 59–67 (2008)
3. Balachandran, K., Kang, J., Karakayali, K., Rege, K.: Cell selection with downlink resource partitioning in heterogeneous networks. In: 2011 IEEE International Conference on Communications Workshops (ICC), pp. 1–6. IEEE (2011)
4. Jo, H., Xia, P., Andrews, J.: Downlink femtocell networks: Open or closed? In: 2011 IEEE International Conference on Communications (ICC), pp. 1–5. IEEE (2011)
5. Claussen, H.: Performance of macro-and co-channel femtocells in a hierarchical cell structure. In: IEEE 18th International Symposium on Personal, Indoor and Mobile Radio Communications, PIMRC 2007, pp. 1–5. IEEE (2007)
6. Chandrasekhar, V., Andrews, J.: Uplink capacity and interference avoidance for two-tier femtocell networks. IEEE Transactions on Wireless Communications 8(7), 3498–3509 (2009)
7. Chandrasekhar, V., Andrews, J., Muharemovic, T., Shen, Z., Gatherer, A.: Power control in two-tier femtocell networks. IEEE Transactions on Wireless Communications 8(8), 4316–4328 (2009)
8. He, H., Chen, J., Deng, S., Li, S.: Game theoretic analysis of joint channel selection and power allocation in cognitive radio networks. In: 3rd International Conference on Cognitive Radio Oriented Wireless Networks and Communications, CrownCom 2008, pp. 1–5. IEEE (2008)
9. Nie, N., Comaniciu, C.: Adaptive channel allocation spectrum etiquette for cognitive radio networks. Mobile Networks and Applications 11(6), 779–797 (2006)
10. Monderer, D., Shapley, L.: Potential games. Games and Economicbehavior 14, 124–143 (1996)

Based on Support Vector and Word Features New Word Discovery Research

Li Chengcheng and Xu Yuanfang

School of Computer and Information Engineering, Inner Mongolia Normal
University, Hohhot, China
nmlcc@sohu.com, xuyuanfang86@126.com

Abstract. Chinese word segmentation is difficult to deal with ambiguity and
unknown words recognition, this paper proposes the new word mode features as
well as various word internal patterns from the training corpus of positive and
negative samples to quantify extraction, and then through the training of support vector machine to get new support vector classification. On the test corpus
with absolute discounting method new candidate extraction and selection, and
with the training corpus to extract word patterns to quantify the new support
vector classification for support vector machine test, through a portion of the
rule filter to get the final word recognition results.

Keywords: natural language processing, support vector machine, word recognition, word feature.

1 Introduction

With the rapid development of the economy, Chinese has also been enriched and
developed continuously, plenty of Chinese new words appear in people's life. New
words appear to bring greater challenges for Chinese word segmentation. New words
in the presence of Chinese word segmentation results in too many "loose string", has a
great effect on word segmentation accuracy [1]. Therefore, new word detection has
become the Chinese automatic word segmentation is one of the difficulties and
bottlenecks. How to identify for Chinese *n*neologism has become an important research topic.

In the new word detection methods, mainly based on rules, based on statistics, two
methods of hybrid method [2] .The rule-based method main idea is based on the word
formation features or design features, establishing rules for professional thesaurus or
pattern library, then by matching rules to discover new words. Based on the statistical
method, the general is the use of statistical methods to extract candidate string, and
then use the language knowledge exclusion is not new word garbage string. Or is the
calculation of correlation, find related degree the biggest character and the character
combination. The rule of the method mainly is confined to one area, and requires the
establishment of rule base. Statistical methods are generally limited to, find a short
new words.

Y. Yuan, X. Wu, and Y. Lu (Eds.): ISCTCS 2012, CCIS 320, pp. 287–294, 2013.
© Springer-Verlag Berlin Heidelberg 2013

This method uses support vector machine (SVM) model as a framework, the training samples for training support vector, using support vector on the test sample to be tested to get initial results, and add rules to get the final result. Support vector machine has high efficiency and good prediction of unknown data, and can effectively integrate a variety of features as well as some Chinese characters morpheme constraint information and other characteristics; the new Chinese words and expressions found the problem also has good applicability.

2   Basic work

2.1   Basic Principles of SVM

Support vector machine is a kind of classification method based on boundary. Its basic principle is that (to 2D data as an example): if the training data according to their classification is assembled in different regions of the planar points. The classification algorithm based on SVM goal is: through training to find these classifications between boundaries, boundary curve is called a non-linear classification, is called linear dividing line. For those data (such as N dimension), they can be viewed as points in an N - dimensional space, while the classification boundary is in an N-dimensional space surface, called the super surface (super than N dimensional space dimension less). Nonlinear classifier using hyper surface type of boundary, while the linear classifier using hyper planes types of boundary [3] .

SVM is based on the linearly separable cases the optimal classification hyper plane proposed [4]. The optimal classification hyper plane is the demands of classification hyper plane can not only two kinds of error separated and to make the two categories in the classification of the largest distance.

2.2   Word Feature Selection

New word identification can be viewed as a linearly no separable classification problems [5], the new words and new words through the hyper plane that separates, so choose how word internal and external features become the key to improve the correct rate.

In this method the identification of new words, word feature selection is a very important link, this article selects the word feature.

- Context information (Context) [6]: in Chinese sentences, words from the words or phrases have a certain relationship between structure, new word is a new word, but it should play a role, so that the sentence structure is more compact, more logical.
- Word probability (IWP) [7]: refers to a Chinese characters morpheme in the corpus with other morphemes to form words by using the probability.
  Characteristic that a Chinese character into words is the Chinese characters morpheme can own characteristics. Defined as:

$$IWP\ (z) = \frac{number(in(z))}{number(all(z))}$$

Where number (in (z)) representing the Z in the article with the word probability, number (all (z)) represents the total number of articles appeared in Z.

- Morphological productivity (MP) [8]: where n (z) for the specific structure of different morphological quantity, N (z) for a given structure. The total time. MP more easily derived words. Defined as:

$$MP\ (z) = \frac{n(z)}{N(z)}$$

- Frequency characteristics (F_F)[9]: on large-scale corpus for word recognition, a new words often appear repeatedly, so words with repeatability, defining a new word occurrence number is n, the N is defined as the total number of words:

$$F_F = \frac{n}{N}.$$

- Mutual information （MI）[10]: assume that A is the length of N text strings, s=$c_1 \ldots c_n$, M and N is the length of n-1 substring, Is M,N mutual information, $f(A)$ represents a text string in the corpus the number of occurrences, M and N substring of the total number of times, we can see that MI (A) is larger, the larger the probability of words:

$$MI\ (A) = \frac{f(A)}{f(M+N) - f(A)}$$

2.3   Corpus Processing and Related Work

The training corpus processing, Context, IWP, MP, MI ,F_F statistics, defined as the word internal models feature table, through the process of corpus segmentation, the segmentation results are negative training example, text extraction, text of the dictionary can be correctly recognized words, namely a neologism, marked as 1. Negative text segmentation is a scattered word, labeled as negative 1, according to the word combination pattern; this paper chooses 1+2, 2+1 and 1+3 mode markers. Identification of positive and negative words in text and internal models feature tables are combined to form a training corpus vector attribute matrix, through the SVM test procedure test to get new words recognition support vector.

Table 1. New words common combination mode

WORD COUNT	THERE MAY BE NEW PATTERN
TWO WORDS	1+1
THREE WORDS	1+1+1 1+2 2+1
FOUR WORDS	1+1+1+1 1+3 3+1 1+2+1 2+1+1

On the test corpus processing, the corpus segmentation, through the above patterns to extract candidate words, through the discount method for screening candidate words, the new word identification support vector and the candidate word vector to construct a matrix through SVM testing to get the final result.

Table 2. Extraction of positive and negative samples

CATEGORY	STRING
POSITIVE CASES	里程碑 转机建制 一国两制　交响曲 星之路　红运当头
NEGATIVE CASES	隐车族 心体谐一 捂地惜建　午动族 养卡人 城铁商圈

We found in the experiments, a lot of new part may be identified into words, and words are not complete, For example: The three words "同名门", "同名", "名门", Through calculation we can see that they are IWP, MP , and F_F difference is not big, the system is likely to name and a cut out, but not with a word recognition, we count them several word appears in the article number, respectively is 28, 27, 31, differ not quite, so when the words in articles appearing in the difference in the number does not exceed a certain value we can think they are the whole existence is a word, the system will cut off the longest string, is "同名门". We define the difference threshold of 5.

Table 3. Ome new characteristics

WORD	IWP	MP	$1/F_f$
同名门	0.893619	0.010866	28
同名	0.902986	0.019826	27
名门	0.927982	0.021067	31

Due to our training sample may not cover all cases; this has not been estimated for some event handling our smoothing, using absolute discounting method, estimation formula:

$$P_r = \begin{cases} m - a/N, & 0 < m \le M \\ a \cdot \dfrac{K - n_0}{N \cdot n_0}, & m = 0 \end{cases}, \quad K = \sum_{m=0}^{M} n_m , \text{ take b=2.}$$

Through our observation, we find that a sentence can be extracted from a plurality of candidate words, for example:

"很多企业举万科模式标识的大旗。"

This sentence contains a new word "万科" in the dictionary, we have to have it removed, so here it as a new word.

After processed dictionary word segmentation has been "举万","万科" and "举万科" three candidate words, after SVM classification results, the three word candidate is likely to have been considered new words. But in fact, there is only one word, "万科" is right. We call these words as mutually exclusive words. The first constraint is to solve the problem of mutually exclusive words. In the above case, we assume that, in the SVM classification, mutually exclusive words with the highest confidence for the final result, namely deviation threshold of 0largest candidate word for the final results.

3   The Experiment Results and Analysis

3.1   Method and Standards

The method adopts the correct rate (P), recall rate (R) [11] and F-measure, the recall rate (R) is a measure of the system to find out new words ability, that all should be identified new word, be system correctly recognized words proportion. Correct rate (P) is a measure of system is not new, i.e. all identified new words new words in correct proportion. F-measure is based on R and P to give a comprehensive evaluation.

$$\text{F-measure} = \left(\beta^2 + 1\right) \times P \times R \Big/ \left(\beta \times P\right) + R \quad (\beta = 1)$$

3.2   The Experimental Results and Analysis

First we with the word patterns MP, IWP and the RBF kernel function as the basic word features for new word detection system is obtained by training the results in order to control foundation After joining Context, MI respectively train again that the training results, in order to draw on new word identification of word internal attributes Classification of image details as well as the system flow chart   refer to Fig.1 and Fig. 2.

Table 4. The experimental results of statistical table

WORD ELEMENT	P (%)	R (%)	F (%)	Change
T(B)	40.78	57.86	47.85	—
T(B+ CONTEXT)	45.72	60.36	52.03	4.18
T(B+MI)	47.78	60.86	53.53	5.68
T(B+CONTEXT+MI)	50.13	62.26	55.54	7.69
T(B+ F_F)	46.62	62.96	53.57	5.72
T(B+CONTEX+ F_F)	55.26	67.35	60.71	12.86
T(B+MI+ F_F)	56.12	66.21	60.75	12.90
T(B+CONTEXT+MI+ F_F)	59.82	70.06	64.54	16.69
T(B+CONTEXT+MI+ F_F +RULE)	61.78	73.68	67.20	19.85

Through the experimental results it can be seen, along with the word feature added elements of Chinese new word identification precision and recall rates have increased, this several word internal characteristics of properties on the new word identification has contribution, but also can be observed when joining MI, relative to the base results in a 15.20% increase, there are other MI tests increase rate of more than 15.20%, which indicates that the MI on this experiment has an important role for Chinese new word identification. Additional rules, new words recognition also has been increasing in a certain.

Considering the different kernel functions for new word recognition results, choose three kinds of different kernel functions and using all words characteristic experiment, results were obtained as follows:

Table 5. Different kernel function the experimental results of statistical table

kernel	Penalty factor	P	R
RBF KERNEL FUNCTION	C+=0.0001 C-=0.3	61.78	72.68
POLYNOMIAL KERNEL FUNCTION	C+=0.0001 C-=0.3	43	41.93
SIGMOID KERNEL FUNCTION	C+=0.0001 C-=0.3	37	32.15

The experiment found that the use of RBF kernel function when new words recognition recalling rate and correct rate.

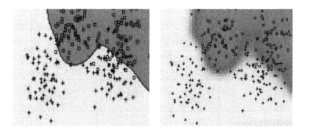

Fig. 1. Classification image of T(B) and T(B+Context+MI+ F_F +Rule)

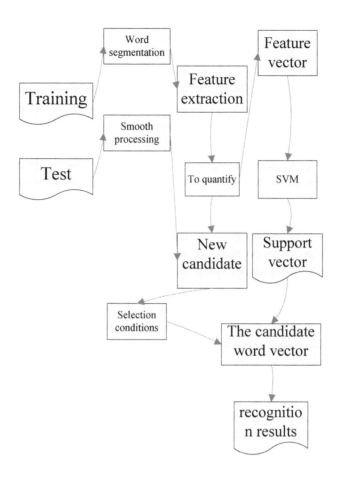

Fig. 2. The flow chart of the system

4   Conclusion

This article proposed one kind based on the SVM and word features a method of Chinese new word identification, by modifying the experimental conditions, different experimental conditions the results show, this method can improve the correct rate of word recognition and recall rate, but there are still some deficiencies, such as for string comparison long new word the new part of the false identification of words into new surrounding words affect the calculation, future work can be added to the training algorithm analysis to identify the long string and improve word recognition accuracy.

References

1. Chen, K., Bai, M.H.: Unknown word detection for Chinese by a corpus- based learning method. Computational Linguistics and Chinese Language Processing 3(1), 27–44 (1998)
2. Ning, S.: Based on word features and search engine for Chinese new word identification. Journal of Wuhan University (Science Edition) 56(6), 704–710 (2010)
3. Qian, Q., Zhang, Z.: A method based on multiple SVM classification method of relevance feedback image retrieval. Computer Technology and Development 19(8), 66–69 (2009)
4. Huang, X., Wang, Y.: SVM in unbalanced data set. Computer Technology and Development 19(6), 190–193 (2009)
5. Yong, F., Hua, L.: Based on Adaptive Chinese word segmentation and approximation of SVM text classification algorithm. Computer Science 37, 251–254, 293 (2010)
6. Cao, B., Han, Z.: ASP.NET database system project development practice. Science Press, Beijing (2005)
7. Wang, B.: Database access technology based on ASP.NET. Computer Application and Software 21(2), 120–122 (2004)
8. Jeroslow, R., Wang, J.: Solving propositional satisfiability problems. In: Annals of Mat Hematics and Artificial intelligence. Springer (1990)
9. Nie, J.-Y.: Unknown Word Detection and Segmentation of Chinese using Statistical and-heuristic Knowledge. Communications of COLIPS 5(I&2), 47–57 (2008)
10. Luo, Z., Song, R.: The adaptive method for Chinese new word identification based on multiple feature. Journal of Beijing University of Technology 23(7), 718–725 (2007)
11. Li, Y., Wang, H.: Intelligent computer assisted instruction system of knowledge ambiguity elimination. Computer Technology and Development 19(4), 220–223 (2009)

A Flexible Framework for Representations of Entities in the Internet of Things

Yu Haining, Zhang Hongli, and Yu Xingzhan

Research Center of Computer Network and Information Security Technology,
Harbin Institute of Technology, Harbin, China
yuhaining83@gmail.com

Abstract. The ultimate goal of the internet of things is to integrate virtual world and physical world seamlessly. The first and basic issue is how to represent an entity comprehensively and exactly in the virtual. To address this issue, we first clarify the concepts related to physical entities in the internet of things, and their relationships. Then, we propose a flexible framework, whose core part is a metadata model of entities, to describe entities at syntactic and semantic level, respectively. Based on the framework, the machine-readable syntactic representations are generated to support data repository and exchange for entities. In order to support automated large scale application scenarios, the terms in metadata model have to refer to several popular vocabularies, standards or ontologies to achieve the machine-interpretable and machine-processible semantic representations.

Keywords: Internet of Things, Entity, Resource, Service, Syntactic representations, Semantic representations.

1 Introduction

The Internet of Things (IoT) is a scenario where physical entities are seamlessly integrated into the virtual world, and where the physical entities can become active participants in business processes [1]. Services are available to interact with these 'smart objects' over the Internet, query their state and any information resource associated with them, taking into account security and privacy issues.

Through the IoT, everyday entities, such as cars, refrigerators, persons, etc. as well as more advanced, computer and information servers will be integrated into IoT and be able to interact and communicate. The problem has been raised that the IoT is merely a leaky concept, considering that the Internet, mobile devices and data carriers exist for quite some time. There are a lot of definitions of IoT from divergent points of view, which contains various terms. In older to make meanings of overall terms clearly, we have to achieve a common understanding of the components and concepts that constitute the IoT.

The first and the most important aspect is about 'things' in the IoT, more specifically, what are things? How to classify things? How to identify and describe the things? What are the representations of things? These problems are addressed with

Y. Yuan, X. Wu, and Y. Lu (Eds.): ISCTCS 2012, CCIS 320, pp. 295–302, 2013.

different approaches by different people, but the mechanisms of those approaches are often overlapped and redundancy and the terminology of those approaches are often mixed up, leading to confusion and hindering scientific discourse. A uniform framework for representation of thing is required. The goal of this paper is to bring some clarity into these approaches. First, we distinguish heterogeneous things in the physical world. Then, we propose a classification for overall things in an applications scenario. Finally, a uniform framework used for describing things is built, which not only refer to syntactic representation, but also semantic representation of things. The core part of the framework is a metadata model used to describe general aspects of things whose terms are defined by formalized ontologies associated with things.

2   Entity, Resource and Service

Things in the IoT almost covers every object in physical world, such as a human, animal, car, store or logistic chain item, electronic appliance or a closed or open environment like buildings, rooms, rivers and glaciers. These physical entities with telecommunication capabilities by a hardware component are the mediators to integrate the physical world with the virtual world of the Internet. We call this kind of entity device, which enable to access to the IoT directly. Actually, devices are just a small subset of entities in the IoT. Most entities are not smart, i.e., they cannot telecommunicate with other device by a hardware component. However, devices can be either attached to or embedded in these 'not smart' entities, even they can be installed in the environment of 'not smart' entities so it can monitor them. Generally, physical entities can be divided into three categories: device, attached/embedded entity and monitored entity. Device can be further divided into two categories: attached/embedded device bounded to attached/embedded entities statically or pseudostatically; environmental device related to monitored entities dynamically. The type of entity depends on the target user and application scenario heavily, it cannot be decided only by whether it accesses to the IoT directly.

Actually, the users (may be other device, applications or human beings) concern the software component on the entity, such as the information about entities and the capabilities provided by device, because software component can represent an entity in the virtual world which can be accessed to in the internet. The actual software component that provides computational elements on the entity or enables controlling of the device, is a 'resource'. Access to these resources from the outside world finally happens through service interfaces directly, or services inside the network act as proxies for the actual resources, possibly providing additional levels of aggregation and abstraction. A 'service' provides a well-defined and standardised interface, offering all necessary functionalities for interacting with entities and related processes to collect data about entities they are related to or manipulate attributions of their related entities. The relations between services and entities are modeled as associations mediating by device. These associations could be static, e.g. in case the entity is an attached/embedded entity; they could also be dynamic, e.g., if the entity is a mobile monitored entity. These identified concepts of the IoT domain and the relations between them are depicted in Figure 1.

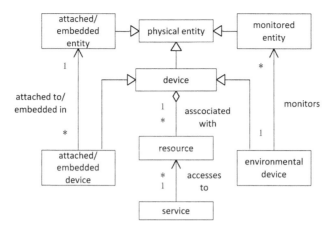

Fig. 1. Relationship between entity, devices, resources and services

3   The Framework for Representation of Entity

Based on the type of an entity, we propose a framework for representation of the entity, as shown in figure 2. This framework describes an entity at three disjoint levels, namely, from the bottom to the top, primitive, syntactic and semantic level. The core of this framework is a metadata model of entity presented at syntactic and semantic level.

3.1   Metadata Model of Entity

Physical entities need a mechanism to describe themselves, their hosted resources and related services in a format that provides interoperable and automated human and machine interpretable representations. The representations of entities are used for users to discovery and understand this entity. There are three groups of representations: unstructured, semi-structured and structured representations. Unstructured representations are text description about entities understandable to human reader, but for machine processability, they are only strings without any concrete meanings and structures. We call this content primitive representation of entity. Semi-structured and structured representations are the refinements of primitive description. They refer to metadata to describe, summarize and structure primitive description of entities in an intensional manner. Metadata is defined as data or information about data, which is used to represent and describe attributions of or relationships between entities of heterogeneous types. The function of metadata in semi-structured or structured representations is twofold:

- To enable the abstraction of representational details such as the format and organization of primitive description, and capture the information content of the underlying primitive description independent of representational details.

- To enable representation of domain knowledge describing the information domain to which the underlying primitive description belongs.

Hence, we propose a general tree-based metadata model for entities to construct their semi-structured and structured representations. The model should cover the concepts given in section 2. As shown in Figure 3, the metadata model contains the most important elements of the description of entities required for their discovery and interoperation. We describe an entity along three clusters of information:

- Resource information used to describe product attributions that contain descriptions of what the entity is, such as its URI identifier, name and owner, domain data metadata that are sensed or gather from the state of itself or the entities which it is attached to, embedded in or monitor, such as source and format of sensed data. The domain data metadata can further be dived to two groups according to whether the metadata describes the content of domain data: content-independent metadata and content-based metadata.
- Service information used to describe the service that installed on or associated with the entity. Resources are accessed by services which have capabilities to collect data about entities they are related to or modify the physical state of their related to entities. There are three different types of metadata that can be identified for a service, namely: (i) functional(describing what a service can do), (ii) behavioral(describing how the functionality of the service can be achieved) and (iii) non-functional attributions(capturing constraints over the previous two types of attributions).
- Context information used to describe both the physical and virtual surrounding facts of the entity. Typical examples of physical context are location and time, and bandwidth of the communications channel and latency are representative virtual context.

Note that the service attributions and its sub-attributions are denoted as dotted boxes. It means that the association between entities and services are optional and dynamic. Having separate associations provides a higher level of flexibility. A service may be associated with multiple entities at the same time, and at next time, there may be no entity associated with this service. This case may be caused by mobility of entities. The metadata model cannot enumerate all possible attributes for every entity, it just a general model for important attributes of most entity. Moreover, it is tree-based topological structure. When used to describe graph-based information, it may be need to add more links between various metadata. Therefore, in specific applications, the model can be modified and extended according to requirements. We can achieve a semi-structured or structured representation of an entity by fulfilling the metadata model with its primitive representation, then this observation maybe formalized with the following equation:

$$representation = metadata\ model + primitive\ description$$

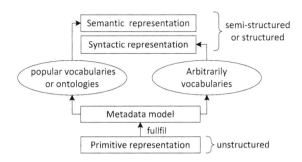

Fig. 2. The framework for representation of entity

3.2   Syntactic Representation

Semi-structured or structured representations have to employ a serialization format that typically provides a meta-language and syntactic constructs for encoding metadata model descriptions about attributions of an entity to achieve the syntactic representation of the entity at syntactic level. Typical serialization formats are HTML, XML and JSON. Note that the service attribution of an entity is more special and complex, their metadata model is well-defined at syntactic level by several standards, such as WSDL, WADL and hRESTs. The syntactic representation is machine-readable, i.e., machines can separate metadata from description of entity, and hold the structure of the representation. It is the basis of representations repository and exchange. However, machines know nothing about the meanings underlying the metadata model. The freedom of reference terms for metadata model hinds almost all meanings of syntactic representations, thus, it is hard to discover interested entities automatically and interoperate between huge heterogeneous entities intelligently.

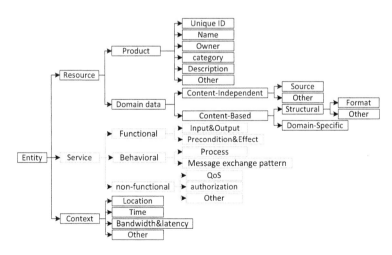

Fig. 3. General tree-based metadata model of entity

3.3   Semantic Representation

Current serialization format standards around HTML, XML, JSON, WSDL and WADL operate at the syntactic level. Therefore, although they support interoperability between the many diverse entities through pre-determined negotiation about scheme, such as XMLS and JSONS, between each other, they still require human interaction to a large extent: the human programmer has to manually analyse representations to understand them by referring to the behavior that some real or virtual procedure (or program, or machine) will exhibit on them, in addition he need to integrate every pair heterogeneous entities in order to support interoperation. Having a human programmer in the loop that needs to take care of various entity related tasks limits the scalability and greatly curtails the added economic value of envisioned with the advent of the IoT. It lacks a proper support to machine to find, access, combine and control entities automatically and intelligently. In order to automate and intelligentize tasks such as entities discovery and interoperation, we must describe entities in a machine-accessible and machine-processable formalization at semantic level.

There are two crucial aspects to create a metadata model describing an entity: a vocabulary used to create them and topological structure of the vocabulary. The key to utilizing the knowledge of an application domain related to entities is identifying the basic vocabulary consisting of terms or concepts. The topological structure is decided at syntactic level, e.g. XML and JSON use tree model, RDF uses Graph model. However, the expressiveness of diverse topological structures is different. The topological structure that has weak expressiveness may be lost some semantics from the graph-based description of entity.

Several popular vocabularies and standards are provided for describing Web resources, such as DCMI(Dublin Core Metadata Initiative),FOAF(Friend-Of-A-Friend), SKOS(Simple Knowledge Organisation System). The terms for metadata model can refer to them to assign a well-known semantics. Schema.org provides a collection of schemas, i.e., html tags, that webmasters can use to markup their pages in ways recognized by major search providers. Search engines including Bing, Google and Yahoo! rely on this markup to improve the display of search results, making it easier for people to find the right web pages of entities.

However, the semantic expressiveness of a vocabulary is very finite. A more refined concept model, namely ontology that has the formal sophistication and logical underpinnings, is required to provide formalization descriptions for entities. An ontology represents explicit specification of conceptualisation and representational vocabulary human shared understanding of specific domains which may include definitions of classes, relations, functions and other objects. Actually, an ontology of entity can be regarded as a metadata model which describe the entity more comprehensively but a vocabulary. Accordingly, the semantic representation can be considered as an instance of several related ontologies. At present, lots of ontologies for physical entities involving several aspects of entity. Generally, each of these ontologies is mainly consisted of one or more sub-ontology shown as follow: entity ontology, system ontology, capability ontology, resource ontology, service ontology, context ontology, observation & measurement ontology, domain ontology. These ontologies need to be formalized by an ontology language, such as RDFS, OWL, SWSL and WSML, thus, machines can read, understand and process the representations of entities automatically.

4   Related Work

Many popular existing vocabularies can be reused to describe entities, such as BFO, Cyc&OpenCyc, DOLCE, SUMO, DC metadata, FOAF, GeoRSS, OWL-Time, WordNet, SensorML. There have been some works focusing on representation models for sensor using ontologies as reviewed in [4]. Generally, representation models for sensor can be divided to two groups: (1) Sensor-centric ontologies, such as Onto-Sensor [5], CESN [6]. (2) Observation-centirc ontologies, such as SemSOS [7],OOSTethys [8]. SSN [9] describes sensor devices, observation and measurement data and the platform aspects. The article [10] creates ontological models describing connected objects in the IoT in order to make them "speak the same language". DoG [11] is proposed an ontology that allows a vendor-independent representation of a domotic system. Furthermore, several service description frameworks that provide both rich expressive descriptions and well-defined semantics are presented to describe services related to entities, such as OWL-S, SWSF and WSMO. These works described above always focus on description about a special kind of entities in the IoT, or only provide a partial representation of entities. There lacks a common and flexible framework for representations of entities in the IoT. This work aims to to fill this gap, it defines the main abstractions and concepts that underlie the IoT domain to reach the representations of entities in the IoT.

5   Conclusions

In this paper, we have explained and clarified the most important concepts with regard to the IoT, namely, the entities, devices, resources and services, and the relationships between them. Moreover, we argue that an absolute, clear-cut categorization isn't possible. Rather, it depends on the target user and application scenario. In order to represent entities in virtual world, we propose a framework whose core part is a metadata model of entities to describe entities at syntactic and semantic level, respectively. The metadata model covers general attributions of an entity involving resources hosted on the entity, services accessing to the resources and the context the entity located in. Future work will involve development of a resolution framework that can generate the semantic representation semi-automatically or automatically according to the requirement of user.

Acknowledgements. The work is supported by the National Natural Science Foundation of China (No.61073194) and   the National Natural Science Foundation of China (Grant No.61173144).

References

1. Atzori, L., Iera, A., Morabito, G.: The Internet of Things: A survey. Computer Networks 54(15), 2787–2805 (2010)
2. Vasseur, J.P., Dunkels, A.: Interconnecting smart objects with IP: the next internet. Morgan Kaufmann Publishers Inc. (2010)
3. Herzog, A., Jacobi, D., Buchmann, A.: Predefinned classification for mixed mode environments. Technical report, TU Darmstadt (2009)
4. Compton, M., Henson, C., Neuhaus, H., et al.: A Survey of the Semantic Specification of Sensors. In: Proceedings of the 8th International Semantic Web Conference (2009)
5. Goodwin, J.C., Russomanno, D.J.: Survey of semantic extensions to UDDI: implications for sensor services. In: Proceedings of the International Conference on Semantic Web and Web Services, pp. 16–22 (2007)
6. Calder, M., Morris, R.A., Peri, F.: Machine reasoning about anomalous sensor data. Ecological Informatics 5(1), 9–18 (2010)
7. Henson, C.A., Pschorr, J.K., Sheth, A.P., et al.: SemSOS: Semantic sensor Observation Service. In: 2009 International Symposium on Collaborative Technologies and Systems, pp. 44–53 (2009)
8. Bermudez, L.: OGC Ocean Science Interoperability Experiment Phase II Report. OGC Engineering Report Open Geospatial Consortium (2010)
9. W3C Semantic Sensor Network Incubator Group. Semantic Sensor Network Final Report (June 28, 2011), http://www.w3.org/2005/Incubator/ssn/XGR-ssn-20110628/
10. Christophe, B., Verdot, V., Toubiana, V.: Searching the 'Web of Things'. In: Proceedings of the 15th IEEE International Conference on Semantic Computing, pp. 308–315 (2011)
11. Bonino, D., Castellina, E., Corno, F.: Dog: An ontology-powered osgi domotic gateway. In: Proceedings on the 20th IEEE International Conference on Tools with Artificial Intelligence, pp. 157–160 (2008)

Community Detection Based
on Robust Label Propagation Algorithm

Bingying Xu, Zheng Liang, Yan Jia, and Bin Zhou

School of Computer Science, National University of Defense Technology, Hunan, China
bingyingxu@gmail.com, {zliang,jiayan,bin.zhou.cn}@nudt.edu.cn

Abstract. Label propagation algorithm has been proved to be an effective method for community detection in large-scale complex networks. Though many effects have been devoted to improve the original label propagation algorithm, its robustness has still not been well addressed. The random update strategy of node's label not only affects the robustness of the algorithm, but also the stability and consistency of community discovery. In this paper, we propose a robust label propagation algorithm to overcome this defect and apply it to community detection by modify update policy. As the experimental results on the real social network indicated, besides maintaining the simplicity of the original algorithm, the proposed algorithm also improves its stability and performance. The results on Sina-Microblog data set have verified that structural features of online social network have close relationship with its semantic features.

Keywords: label propagation algorithm, stability, social network, Sina-Microblog, community detection.

1 Introduction

Information networks, carrying the complex relationship among persons, have become the significant research object of the academic circles and business world. Community analysis of the information network can help us not only in the evaluation of its social nature, but also in the research of the composition form of users who are interested in some particular aspect. In recent years, there have been a large number of literatures on the method of community discovery,such as graph partition algorithm, hierarchical clustering method[1], method based on the modularity optimization [2][3] and method based on spectrum[4][5]. However,for the reason of stability, only a small part of algorithms are fit to the community discovery in the large-scale network with millions of nodes.

Adopting Label propagation to the community division in complex network is proposed by Raghavan and others [6]. Every node in network has its unique community label initially, and the label of node needing update is determined by labels with the biggest frequency of appearance in the label set of its neighbors. Being a linear method of community structure discovery, it is one of the fastest community detection algorithms.Tibely and Kertesz[7] prove that the label propagation algorithm equals the zero-temperature kinetic Potts model. Based on modularity constraint, Barber and

Y. Yuan, X. Wu, and Y. Lu (Eds.): ISCTCS 2012, CCIS 320, pp. 303–310, 2013.
© Springer-Verlag Berlin Heidelberg 2013

Clark [8] introduce a new label propagation algorithm by comparison and combination of the origin label propagation algorithm and modularity maximization methods. Leung et al. [9] introduce the concepts of Hip top and Node preference to promote the reliability of algorithm. LovroŠubel et al. makes a further improvement on the reliability of algorithm through the so-called community expansion and community defense[10].

Although so many improvements have been made on the original label propagation algorithm, an important problem still remains unsolved. This paper improves stability of the method by changing update strategy of the algorithm.Experiment results show that the stability of the algorithm gains a big increase, and the effect of community division is analyzed in a topic propagation network of Sina-Microblog. It verifies that structural features of topic propagation network have close relationship with its semantic features.

The structure of the paper is as follows: the second part is the literature review of related research on community detection methods which are based on label propagation algorithm and the summarization of existing problems. Robust label propagation based community detection will be introduced in the third part, and detailed assessment and discussion will be elaborate respectively in the fourth and fifth part.

2   Related Work

The main steps of the original label propagation algorithm can be described as follows:

1. Initialize the community label of nodes. Index of node can be adopted as the initial community label.
2. Assign a random process order for nodes in network, and then process corresponding nodes taken out according to the order.
3. For each node n, its new label value in t cycles is :

$$c_n(t) = f\big(c_1(t), \dots, c_m(t), c_{m+1}(t - 1), \dots, c_k(t - 1)\big) \tag{1}$$

$c_n(t)$ sends back labels with the most frequency in the neighbor nodes of n which server as the new label value in the circle.

$$c_n(t) = argmax_l|N^l(n)| \tag{2}$$

If there is more than one label that appears most frequently, we can randomly select any one of them to be the newlabel of the updating node.

4. When label values of all nodes change no longer, the algorithm ends. Otherwise, the algorithm will begin the circle numbered t+1, and step 2 and 3 will be carried out.

Label propagation is a heuristic algorithm which derives from the concept of "flow". The time complexity of algorithm proves to be linearly with the scale of network. It is difficult to predict the number of iteration, but in general, after 5 iterations, 95%

nodes in network will reach equilibrium [6].The result and quality of community division has close relationship with the sequence of random process. Even the termination conditions are the same, structures of community division may be different.

Leung [9] makes a deeper analysis on the basic label propagation algorithm. By comparison of respective effects of synchronous update and asynchronous update to the result of algorithm, he finds that more iterations are required in the process of asynchronous update, leading to a more stable result. The algorithm also introduces the concept node preference to modify the update rules of node label.

$$c_n(t) = argmax_l \sum_{m \in N^l(n)} p_m w_{nm} \tag{3}$$

Where p_n is the preference of node n. The degree of node or clustering coefficient of node can be taken as a basis for node preference, and according to the theory, algorithm [11] improves fatherly.

The work in [11] finds that the node which updates previous owns stronger propagation preference. As for the stability of algorithm, the concept of node balance factors is introduced, in which the position of the update sequence of node is taken as a parameter of the balancing factor. The more forward the position is, the smaller the propagation preference is. In fact, the parameter selection of the algorithm is difficult.Another attempt is to determine the update sequence of node's label by ordering nodes. The paper [11] analyzes the methods, finding that its effect is not desirable, and the order of node preference increases the execution time of the algorithm.

3   The Proposed Algorithm

Based on the comprehensive analysis of existed improved methods, we bring the situation of updating node itself and the importance of nodes into the statistics of the biggest frequency label of neighbors. Then we adopt different frequencies statistical method and keep the updating node's label unchanged if necessary. In this way, the node preference and the accomplishment of update strategy are actually implicitly used to solve the update sequence of node labels. The update sequence is impacted by the definition of the node preference, with no computing and time complexity increased.

The node preference can be any measure of degree characterizing importance of nodes in network, which can be degree, clustering coefficient, characteristic center and so on.In this paper, we adopt the degree of node only to measure the preferences of nodes.

In the original label update policy, the label of current node is replaced by the label with the most frequent appearance in the neighbor node. When there are several such labels, random selection is used. In this paper, the update rule of the current node label is modified. Labels which can be renewed can be defined as follows:

$$\Phi = \{l | argmax_l \sum_{m \in N^l(n)} p_m w_{nm}\} \tag{4}$$

Where p_m is the degree of node m, w_{nm} is the weight of edge nm. It is Clear that: $|\Phi| \geq 1$.If $|\Phi| = 1$, then $c_n = l, l \in \Phi$. If $|\Phi| > 1$, then

$$\Gamma = \left\{ l \middle| \mathrm{argmax}_{l \, \Sigma_{m \in N^l(x)} \, w_{nm}} \right\} \tag{5}$$

And if$|\Gamma| = 1$, then $c_n = l, l \in \Gamma$. If $|\Gamma| \geq 1$, then the current node maintains the original tags, with corresponding marks.

Γ indicates the collection of community labels, which appear most frequently in neighbor nodes, is consistent with the version of the original label propagation algorithm.In practical calculations, we make the node as one neighbor node of itself, that is:$n \in N(n)$.The modified algorithm is named RLAP, which shows the specific algorithm description in Algorithm 1.

```
Algorithm 1. RLPA
1:Input: the social network G= (N, E).
2: Output: Node-Community pairs.
3: Stage1: initialization
4: for i do 1: n
5:   Cluster[i] =i;
6: end for
7: Stage2: Label Propagation
8: Update = true;
9: While (Update)
10:       Nodes.shuffleOrder();
11:       Update = false;
12:       for i do 1:n
13:           initialize Φ,Γ,cpref[],cnopref[];
14:             for j do 1: Neighbor[i].length
15:               cpref[Cluster[j]]=+pref[j]*weight[i][j];
16:             cnopref[Cluster[j]]=+ weight[i][j];
```
17:$\Phi = \{l | argmax_l \; \mathrm{cpref}[l]\}$;
18:     $\Gamma = \{l | argmax_l \; \mathrm{cnopref}[l]\}$;
19:     if $|\Phi| = 1$ and Cluster$[i] \neq l \in \Phi$ then
20:          Cluster$[i]=l \in \Phi$,Update = true;
21:     else
22:          if $\Gamma = 1$ and Cluster$[i] \neq l \in \Gamma$ then
23:              Cluster$[i]=l \in \Gamma$, Update = true;
24:          end if
25:     end if
26:   end for
27: end While
28: Stage3: post-processing
29: Update Nodes label which has the same label but not
    in one connected graph.

The termination condition of the algorithm, in the previous literature, is generally established that the proportion of nodes which update no longer reaches to a certain threshold, or achieves by the pre-set number of iterations of the algorithm. In this paper, as we implicitly modify the update order and rule of the algorithm, the algorithm must reach a balance in a limited time or iterations. Therefore, the termination condition of the algorithm can be set as that no node's label will change.

4   Experiment Analysis

4.1   The Measure Standard and the Data Set

The significant measures of community structure which widely accepted is modularity Q.Q is larger, the better [12].As to the network which known community structure, normal mutual information is used to measure the accuracy of community discovery. Its value is between 0 and 1. On the basis of NMI, we adopt the measurement for the stability of the algorithm in paper [11].

$$S = \frac{\sum_{i,j} NMI_{i,j}}{n*(n-1)} \tag{6}$$

In thepaper, Karate club data setis used to verify the correct of the algorithm [13].Another data set is Tsina_lianghuiwhich contains 310 thousand of Sina-Microblogposts related to Lianghui (a general term about NPC and CPPCC in china) from March 5, 2011 to March 14, 2011 and 210 thousand of corresponding users have been obtained by the search function of Sina-Microblog. We construct the propagation network using the method in [14].

4.2   Experiment Analysis

Based on the accuracy of algorithm, algorithm LPA, LPAA ([11]) and RLPA will be made a comparison between each other. After 1000 times of executions of each algorithm (all kinds of parameters hereinafter are obtained after average 1000 times of execution), the result of community discovery which appears frequently will be taken as the final division result of the algorithm in the network. 1 shows that RLPA is most effective, with its result consistent with the division result.

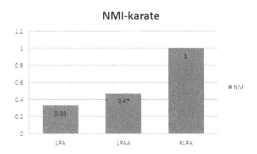

Fig. 1. Comparison of correctness of the three algorithms

Numbers of iteration needed before the end of algorithm indicate the algorithm's efficiency. Figure 2 shows the average numbers of iterations respectively required of the three algorithms in two data sets. It is clear that LPAA has the lowest efficiency. The reason may be relevant to the algorithm's preference of balancing the node importance and the node update sequence, which leads to the time required to balance the algorithm more than that of the original LPA, but its result is more accuracy than that of LPA. RLPA has the highest efficiency, with the average numbers of iteration 8.63.

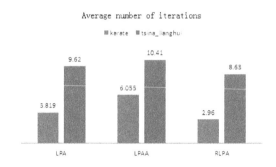

Fig. 2. Comparison of efficiency of the three algorithms

Table 1 show stability indexes of each algorithm obtain after 1000 times of executions in different networks, in which RLPA is the most stable. With the improvement of the scale of network, stability of the three algorithms gains a relatively increase. The increase of LPA and LPAA is the most obvious, while RLAP with its respective value of 0.955 and 0.959, remains a high value no matter the network is big or small.

Table 1. Evaluation of stability of the three algorithms

	Karate	Tsina_lianghui
LPA	0.626	0.803
LPAA	0.622	0.835
RLPA	0.955	0.959

Word frequency statistics is carried out from posts published from the all nodes in the same community. As shown in table 2, wherein the brackets is the number scale of the current community. For example, the first column 3 (12031) represents community with number 3 and 12031 members, which is the largest community. After removal of stop words, words with high frequency in every community are screened, such as

"CPPCC", "member", "represent", "bill" and so on. Result shows that different communities can discuss the same topic as well as different topics, and as the scale of community increases, the semantic feature of community will become more and fuzzier. Just as the first column shows, although the topic of the community is also about people's livelihood, its semantic feature is less obvious than that of community 49 which discusses the live problem of migrant workers and 59 which is about election system of representatives of people. The semantic analysis on results of algorithm further proves that there are strong relevance between structural features and semantic features in the social network, and that the algorithm is effective for data of Sina-Microblog.

Table 2. Semantic analysis of communities in Sina-Microblog

3 (12031)	11 (6849)	93 (3508)	93 (321)	7 (491)	53 (740)	49 (581)
努力	努力	经典	贯彻	最近	举行	贫富
成本	地铁	回归	保护法	悲剧	大事	体系
最近	成本	妇女节	访谈	教育	推进	领导人
压力	最近	春暖花开	贫富	离岗	反映	理解
歧视	富豪	图片	压力	民办	选举	努力
用工	反映	节目	创造	以为	围观	农民工
居然	困难	事实	努力	节目	人性	悲剧
困难	房地产	心声	领导人	贫苦	自由	限制
吃饭	贫富	努力	纳税人	代课	人民代表	心声
财政	悲剧	推进	执法	推进	权力	执法
经典	吃饭	人民代表	本来	失望	咆哮	酱油
执法	失望	可爱	权利	困难	费用	最近
人民代表	压力	科学	经典	目标	历史	压力

5   Conclusion

Label propagation algorithm is usually used on the community discovery in large-scale network for its simplicity and high efficiency. As for the unstable problem of label propagation algorithm, we introduce a more robust method for community discovery by modifying the update rule of nodes in label community, which improves the stability and efficiency of the algorithm. The accuracy and efficiency of the algorithm are verified in real social network.

Acknowledgements. The research was supported in part by Chinese National Science Foundation: No.6093305, The national science and technology support program: No.2012BAH38B04, The national 242 information security program: No.2011A010 and the National High-tech R\&D Program of China: No.2010AA012505, No.2011AA010702, NO.2012AA01A401, and NO.2011AA01A402.Thanks Liu Xinwang, Xu Yi for their constructive and insightful comments.

References

1. Han, J.W., Kamber, M., Pei, J.: Data Mining: Concepts and Techniques, 2nd edn. Morgan Kaufmann Publishers, San Francisco (2005)
2. Clauset, A., Newman, M.E.J., Moore, C.: Finding community structure in very large networks. Phys. Rev. E 70(6) (2004)
3. Blondel, V.D., Guillaume, J.-L., Lambiotte, R.: Fast unfolding of community hierarchies in large networks. Journal of Statistical Mechanics: Theory and Experiment 10(10008) (2008)
4. Boccaletti, S., Ivanchenko, M., Latora, V.: Detecting complex network modularity by dynamic clustering. Phys. Rev. E 75(4) (2007)
5. Donetti, L., Muñoz, M.A.: Detecting network communities: a new systematic and efficient algorithm (2009), http://arxiv.org/abs/conmat/0404652
6. Raghavan, U.N., Albert, R., Kumara, S.: Near linear time algorithm to detect community structures in large-scale networks. Physical Review E 76(036106) (2007)
7. Tibely, G., Kertesz, J.: Note on the equivalence of the label propagation method of community detection and a potts model approach. Physical Review E (0803.2804) (2008)
8. Barber, M., Clark, J.W.: Detecting network communities by propagation labels under constrains. Physical Review E 80(026129) (2009)
9. Leung, I.X.Y., Hui, P., Li, P., Crowcroft, J.: Towards real-time community detection in large network. Phys. Rev. E (79066107) (2009)
10. Šubel, L., Bajec, M.: Unfolding communities in large complex networks combining defensive and offensive label propagation. In: Proceeding of the ECML PKDD Workshop on the Analysis of Complex Networks, pp. 87–104 (2011)
11. Šubel, L., Bajec, M.: Robust network community detection using balanced propagation.CoRR abs/1106.5524 (2011)
12. Newman, M.E.J., Girvan, M.: Finding and evaluation community structure in networks. Phys. Rev. E 69 (2004)
13. Manning, C.D., Raghavan, P., Schutze, H.: Introduction to information retrieval. Cambridge University Press (2008)
14. Fan, P., Li, P., Jiang, Z., Li, W., Wang, H.: Measurement and analysis of topology and information propagation on sina-mircoblog. In: The 3rd International Workshop on Social Computing (2011)

Clock Synchronization Algorithm
for Distributed Video Surveillance Based on PTP

Liu Xuehai and Tang Jin

Key Laboratory of Trustworthy Distributed Computing and Service (BUPT)
Ministry of Education, Automation School, Beijing University of Posts
and Telecommunications, Beijing, China
lxh6680@163.com, tangjin@bupt.edu.cn

Abstract. In a distributed network, the clock synchronization accuracy is an important factor that affects the real-time performance of the network. In order to meet the requirements of high-precision of network clock synchronization, this paper conducts the research to the Precision Time Protocols (PTP), and elaborates the principle of the high-precision synchronization. A simulation was done for distributed video surveillance star network.The simulation results verified the correctness of the algorithm, at the same time, combined with the PTP, the simulation results were analyzed, a conclusion that path symmetry is a statistical concept was gotten and the star network time synchronization offset range was also obtained.

Keywords: distributed systems, clock synchronization, PTP, path symmetry, synchronization offset.

1 Background

With the development of the computer network, more and more industrial areas put forward higher demands of the clock synchronization accuracy, especially in the distributed control system[1], which have more stringent requirements of the time unified because it takes real-time scheduling and controlling into account. The existing technology provides a variety of network clock synchronization protocols, such as Network Time Protocol(NTP)[2], Simple Network Time Protocol (SNTP)[3].There is a common drawback of these network clock synchronization protocols that is the low precision of clock synchronization, usually millisecond, which can't meet the application requirement of the distributed control system. ThePrecision Time Protocol(PTP) [4] defines a precise time synchronization protocol that has something with the network communication, local address and distribution of objects in test and control networks. The protocol supports system-wide clock synchronization and can achieve microsecond time synchronization accuracy[5]. Due to its high synchronization accuracy, low cost and other advantages, the PTP synchronization algorithm has been widely used in industrial control, network communication and distributed network.

Y. Yuan, X. Wu, and Y. Lu (Eds.): ISCTCS 2012, CCIS 320, pp. 311–316, 2013.

2   The Synchronization Principle of PTP

The basic principle of PTP: The synchronization messages are sent between the master clock and slave clock interactively, and eachof the messages' sending and receiving time is also recorded.Bycalculating time difference of timestamps, the total time delay between the master clock and slave clock is obtained.Becauseof the symmetryof the network, one-way delay is half of the total delay, and the offset between the master clock and slave clock can be calculated, and thenthe slave clock adjusts its local time by the offset. Similarly, the rest slave clocks can also be synchronized.

IEEE 1588 defined four kinds of message, they are Synchronization information (Sync), the FollowUp information (Follow_Up), Delay Request (Delay_Rep), and Delay Response (Delay_Resp), these messages are shown in Figure 1.

The implementation process of PTP is as follows:

1. The master clock sends Sync message to a slave clock and records the sending time t_1, after receiving the Sync message , the slave clock records the receiving time t_2;
2. The master clock sends Follow_Up message which carries the timestamp t_1 following the Sync message;
3. The slave clock sends Delay_Req message which is used to calculate the time of reverse transmission and records the timestamp t_3; after receiving the Delay_Req message, the master clock records the timestamp t_4;
4. The master clock replies a Delay_Resp packet that carries the timestamp t_4 after receiving the Delay_Rep message.

At this point, the slave clock has obtained four timestamps, from t1 to t4. From process 1and 2, formula (1) can be gotten

$$t_2 - t_1 = Delay + Offset \qquad (1)$$

In formula(1), *Delay*represents one-way transmission delay time,*Offset*represents time offset between master clock and slave clock.

From process 3 and 4, formula (2) can be gotten

$$t_4 - t_3 = Delay - Offset \qquad (2)$$

Delay and *Offset*in formula (2) are the same meaning of those in formula (1).

Then the total transmission delay $[(t_2 - t_1) + (t_4 - t_3)]$can be gotten by adding formula(1) and formula(2). Because of the symmetry of the network, we can get formula (3), which is one-way transmission delay.

$$Delay = [(t_2 - t_1) + (t_4 - t_3)]/2 \qquad (3)$$

$$Offset = t_2 - t_1 - Delay \qquad (4)$$

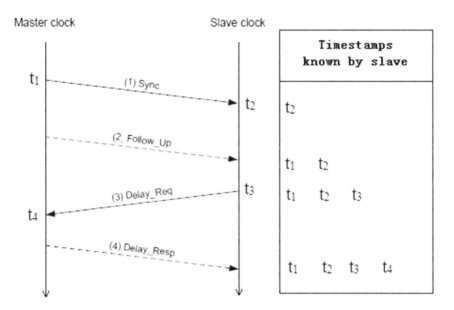

Fig. 1. PTP synchronization process

From the formula (3) and (4), the general time synchronization formula (5) can be gotten

$$Offset_k = Ts_k - Tm_k - Delay \tag{5}$$

In formula (5), the Ts_k and Tm_k represent the k-th synchronization timestamps that recorded by the slave clock and the master clock. $Offset_k$ represents the k-th calculated synchronization time offset between the slave clock and the master clock, $Delay$ represents the k-th one-way transmission time delay. Let Ts be the slave's local time, after the k-th synchronization, the slave's local time will be $Ts' = Ts - Offset$.

3   Clock Synchronization Algorithm Simulation and Analysis

In order to verify the performance of the PTP for clock synchronization, using MATLAB a simulation of slave clock deviation was done for distributed video surveillance system star network. In the simulation, the master clock node launches once clock synchronization every 1 second based on its local time, totally 10 times. The results are shown as the Figure 2.

In figure 2, it shows that the slave local clock fluctuates between two clock synchronization, but the fluctuation range is not very big, which is caused by the clockdrift.

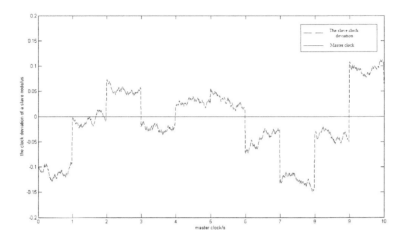

Fig. 2. The slave clock deviation

In figure 2,it also shows that not all synchronization points of slave node have reached the zerodeviation, however, from the formula (5), the PTP system master-slave clock deviation should be approximate zero after each synchronization in theory. The reason why there are still deviations between the master and slave clock in the synchronization moment is that the one-way time delay is not calculated accuracy enough. From figure 1 we can get the transmission delay from master clock to the slave clock:

$$SM\_Delay=t2-t1-Offset \quad (6)$$

And the transmission delay from the slave clock to the master clock:

$$MS\_Delay=t4-t3+Offset \quad (7)$$

The PTP principle acts on the premise that the network transmission path must be symmetrical[6]. In order to endure the accuracy of synchronization, the SM_Delay must be equal to MS_Delay. It is almost impossible for every synchronizationdue to one-way transmission time delay has to satisfy the inequality:

$$Tr\_Max \geq Tr\_delay \geq Tr\_Min \quad (8)$$

In the inequality, the Tr_Max represents the maximum one-way transmission delay time, the Tr_Min represents the minimum one-way transmission delay time, Tr_Delay represents one-way transmission delay time. So the transmission path symmetry in PTP synchronization protocol is in terms of a number of times synchronization, it is a statistical concept. Figure 3 is the simulation results of a slave clock that synchronized 1000 times.

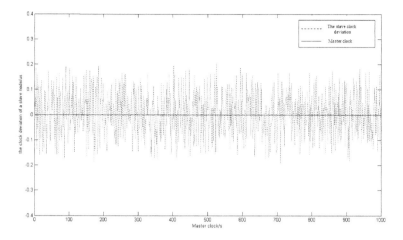

Fig. 3. The clock deviation of 1000 times synchronization

The average of the 1000 times synchronization clock offset is 0.0022us, approximately zero.

In figure 2, it last shows that even last synchronization close to zero, the next synchronization is still possible to deviate from zero, which is caused by the uncertainty of transmission time. But the deviation will not exceed a certain range, the range is:

$$-(Tr\_Max\text{-}Tr\_Min)/2 \leqslant Tm\text{-}Ts \leqslant (Tr\_Max\text{-}Tr\_Min)/2 \qquad (9)$$

4   Conclusion

On the basis of the research of the PTP, a simulation on the clock synchronization algorithm was done for the distributed video surveillance system star network. The simulation results verified the correctness of the PTP, at the same,a conclusion that symmetry of the transmissionpath in PTP is a statistical concept, which is not suitable for single synchronization and the star network time synchronization offset range were obtained. For multi-hop network, this algorithm may make cumulative error, which would cause oversized clock synchronization offset.

References

1. Chong, L., Li, G.: Application in Distributed Systems Based on IEEE 1588 Clock Synchronization Technology. Electronic Design Engineering (December 2009)
2. Mills, D.L.: Network Time Protocol (version 3) Specification,Implementation and Analysis [NetworkWorking Group Report RFC-1305] (1992)
3. David, L.M.: Simple Network Time Protocol(SNTP)Version 4 for IPv4, IPv6 and OSI[EB/OL] (January 10, 2007)

4. IEEE Std 1588-2002, IEEE Standard for a Precision Clock Synchronization Protocol for Networked Measurement and Control System. The Institute Electrical and Electronics Engineers, New York (2002)
5. Eidson, J.C., Hamilton, B.: IEEE-1588 Node SynchronizationImprovement by High Stability Oscillator. In: Workshop onIEEE 1588, Standard for a Precision Clock SynchronizationProtocol for Networked Measurement and Control Systems (2003)
6. Shi, Y., Zhao, J., Fang, H.: IEEE 1588 analysis and application of synchronous clock. Instrument Technology (September 2007)

A Low-Complexity Vector Perturbation Precoding Approach Based on Reactive Tabu Search for Large Multiuser MIMO Systems

Wei Ding[1,2], Tiejun Lv[1,2], and Yueming Lu[1,2]

[1] School of Information and Communication Engineering, Beijing University of Posts and Telecommunications, Beijing, China
[2] Key Laboratory of Trustworthy Distributed Computing and Service (BUPT), Ministry of Education
Wayne_Ding@live.cn, {lvtiejun ymlu}@bupt.edu.cn

Abstract. In this paper, we proposed a vector perturbation precoding approach based on reactive tabu search (RTS) for large multiuser MIMO (MU-MIMO) systems, where 'large' means tens to hundreds of transmit antennas (N_t) at base station simultaneously serving almost the same number of user terminals (UTs) (N_u). By exploiting RTS, contrast to the conventional algorithm, the proposed approach can efficiently escape from poor local minima and has the relatively low complexity. Additionally, for the error bit rate (BER), this proposed approach also has the diversity increasing with N_t and N_u, thus making it suitable for large MU-MIMO systems both in terms of complexity and performance.

Keywords: Vector Perturbation Precoding, Low-complexity, Reactive Tabu Search, Large Multiuser MIMO.

1   Introduction

Multiuser multi-input mulit-output (MU-MIMO) systems with very large antenna arrays at the base station (BS) have attracted much attention for some time now as large antenna arrays can bring many benefits such as increased capacities, higher spectrum efficiency and lower power consumption [1], [2]. Here, by saying 'large', we mean that tens to hundreds of antennas at BS and simultaneously serving tens of user terminals (UTs). Researches in [2] show that sample linear precoding techniques such as normal zero-forcing (ZF) precoding become optimal when BS is equipped with large number of antennas but still serves relatively less UTs.

However, in practice, it is desired that large number of UTs should be supported simultaneously for high throughput. At this case, ZF precoding shows poor performance because the required energy increases rapidly as the number of served UTs gets close to number of transmit antennas. This results in a degradation of the receive signal-to-noise ratio (SNR). An efficient way to solve this is vector

Y. Yuan, X. Wu, and Y. Lu (Eds.): ISCTCS 2012, CCIS 320, pp. 317–324, 2013.

perturbation (VP) technique, of which the principle is to exploit perturbation vector to minimize the required energy [3]. The optimum perturbation vector can be found via searching all the possible vectors using sphere encoding (SE). But in general, this requires exponential complexity [4]. Though approximate methods (i.e., Tomlinson-Harashima precoding (THP) [5], Lenstra–Lenstra–Lovász (LLL) algorithm based lattice reduction (LR) techniques [6]) have been proposed in [7] and proven to be nice substitutions of SE, they do not scale up well for large numbers of UTs in terms of complexity, making them unavailable for large MU-MIMO systems. Although the norm descent search (NDS) proposed in [8] has a relatively low-complexity, it cannot escape from a local minimum even the local minimum is poor, which results in weak robustness.

Reactive tabu search (RTS) [9] is an iterative local neighborhood search strategy, which has been successfully applied in many areas. Our new contribution in this paper is that we propose an efficient VP precoding approach with the low-complexity for large MU-MIMO systems by combination of procoding techniques with reactive tabu search. By exploiting RTS, the proposed algorithm can achieve near-optimal performance with much lower complexity compared with the methods mentioned above. This relatively low-complexity attribute is achieved by searching in a reduced searching space and avoidance of oversearching possible solution candidates. Additionally, with the inherent attributes of RTS, the proposed approach can escape from the local minima and look for better solution, which ensures a strong robustness. Besides, in terms of the bit-error-rate (BER), the proposed approach has increasingly better performance for increasing the number of antennas at BS and UTs. Thus this proposed approach is suitable for large MU-MIMO system both in terms of complexity as well as performance.

The rest of this paper is organized as follows. In Section 2, we present the system model. The proposed search algorithm is described in details in Section 3. Simulations are presented in Section 4. Finally, we conclude this paper in Section 5.

Notations: Throughout this paper, vectors are denoted and matrices by boldface lowercase letters. $(\cdot)^*$, $(\cdot)^\dagger$, $\Re[\cdot]$, $\Im[\cdot]$ and $E[\cdot]$ denote the conjugate, Hermitian operation, pseudo-inverse, the real part and the expectation respectively. The n-dimension identity matrix is denoted as I_n.

2   System Model

Consider a single cell MU-MIMO system, where a base station serves N_u single antenna users on the downlink. The base station employs N_t transmit antennas with $N_t \geq N_u$. Let $\mathbf{u} \in C^{N_u \times 1}$ denote the complex information vector. $\mathbf{x} \in C^{N_t \times 1}$ is the precoded complex transmit vector. Thus the received data $\mathbf{y}$ for all the N_u can be written as

$$\mathbf{y} = \mathbf{Hx} + \mathbf{n}, \tag{1}$$

where $\mathbf{H} \in C^{N_u \times N_t}$ is the channel matrix and $\mathbf{n} \in C^{N_u \times 1}$ denotes the Gaussian noise which is independently identically distributed as $CN\left(0, \sigma_n^2\right)$. Notice that a large MU-MIMO system is assumed, $\mathbf{H}$ can be modeled as i.i.d and $CN(0,1)$.

2.1 Vector Perturbation

The equivalent system model with power constraint can be written as

$$\mathbf{y} = \Delta\left(\mathbf{HGu} + \mathbf{n}\right) = \mathbf{HGu} + \Delta\mathbf{n}, \tag{2}$$

where $\Delta = \| \mathbf{G}_{ZF}\tilde{\mathbf{u}}\|$ is the power constraint factor and assumed to be known and compensated at the receiver. Clearly, Δ scales up the noise, which will degrade the received SNR. Additionally, in the terms of ZF precoding, namely, $\mathbf{G}_{ZF} = \mathbf{H}^{\dagger} = \mathbf{H}^H\left(\mathbf{HH}^H\right)^{-1}, \mathbf{G}_{ZF} \in C^{N_t \times N_u}$,

$$\Delta = \sqrt{\mathrm{tr}\left(\mathrm{E}_u\left[\mathbf{G}_{ZF}\mathbf{uu}^H\mathbf{G}_{ZF}^H\right]\right)} = \sqrt{\sigma_s^2 \mathrm{tr}\left\{\left(\mathbf{HH}^H\right)^{-1}\right\}} = \sqrt{\frac{\sigma_s^2}{\alpha - 1}}, \tag{3}$$

where $\alpha = N_t / N_u$ is a constant and $\mathrm{E}_u\left[\mathbf{uu}^H\right] = \sigma_s^2 \mathbf{I}_{N_u}$ for the simplicity. The last term is according to Marčenko-Pastur law when $N_t, N_u \to \infty$ [10]. This equation explains why ZF precoding show poor performance in the case of N_t and N_u getting close.

Vector perturbation is designed to solve (5) by perturbing the information vector $\mathbf{u}$ to minimize Δ. Specifically, we can define the perturbed vector $\tilde{\mathbf{u}}$ as

$$\tilde{\mathbf{u}} = \mathbf{u} + \tau\mathbf{p} \tag{4}$$

where $\mathbf{p} \in C^{N_u \times 1}$ is the perturbation vector whose coordinates are Gaussian integers set $\mathcal{A}$ and the appropriate value of τ is given in [3]. The desired $\mathbf{p}$, denoted by p_{opt}, is obtained from the following criterion

$$\mathbf{p}_{opt} = \arg\min_{p \in \mathcal{A}} \| \mathbf{G}_{ZF}\left(\mathbf{u} + \tau\mathbf{p}\right)\|^2 = \arg\min_{p \in \mathcal{A}} \Phi(\mathbf{p}), \tag{5}$$

where $\Phi(\mathbf{p}) = \tau^2 \mathbf{p}^H \mathbf{G}_{ZF}^H \mathbf{G}_{ZF} \mathbf{p} + 2\tau\Re\left\{\mathbf{p}^H \mathbf{G}_{ZF}^H \mathbf{G}_{ZF}\mathbf{u}\right\}$. Since $\mathbf{u}$ is chosen from a finite signal constellation and $\mathbf{G}_{ZF}$ is fixed for each channel realization, we argue that $\mathbf{p}$ is taking values from a finite subset of $\mathcal{A}$, i.e., $\mathbb{A} \subset \mathcal{A}$. Thus the exact solution of (6) is obtained by searching all the point in $\mathbb{A}$ using sphere encoding, which requires exponential complexity in N_u. Our contribution here is to propose a solution with acceptable complexity, which will be presented in Section 3.

In term of detection at the receiver, let $\tilde{\mathbf{p}}$ be the approximate (or optimal) solution to (5). Then, the received data is given by

$$y = (u + \tau \tilde{p}) + \tilde{\Delta} n, \tag{6}$$

where $\tilde{\Delta} = \| G_{ZF} (u + \tau \tilde{p}) \|$. Since $\tilde{p}$ is taken from the Gaussian integers set, receivers can remove the effect of $\tilde{p}$ simply by taking modulo operation of y. The equivalent form of detected data at the receiver is

$$\hat{u} = y - \tau \left\lfloor \frac{y + \tau / 2}{\tau} \right\rfloor. \tag{7}$$

In (8), the operation is defined on each entry of the vector since each user gets only one entry of the vector.

3   Proposed Perturbation Vector Search Algorithm Using Reactive Tabu Search

In this section, some important notions will be introduced at the beginning and followed by the detailed RTS algorithm.

3.1   Some Notions

Neighborhood Definition: If the i th entry of perturbation vector p, p_i, is chosen from the set $S = \{a_1, a_2, ..., a_M\}$, the neighborhood set, $\mathcal{N}(p_i)$, is defined such that $\mathcal{N}(p_i)$ includes N nearest points of p_i. Define $N_v(p_i)$ and $p^{(m)}$ as the v th neighborhood of p_i and start vector at the m th iteration, respectively. Therefore the (u, v) th neighbor vector $z^{(m)}(u, v)$ of $p^{(m)}$ can be written as

$$z^{(m)}(u, v) = \left\{ z_1^{(m)}(u, v), z_2^{(m)}(u, v), ..., z_{N_t}^{(m)}(u, v) \right\}, \tag{8}$$

where

$$z_i^{(m)}(u, v) = \begin{cases} p_i^{(m)} & i \neq u \\ N_v \left(p_u^{(m)} \right) & i = u \end{cases}. \tag{9}$$

It is obviously that there is only one coordinate is different between $p^{(m)}$ and $z^{(m)}(u, v)$. Besides, the algorithm is making a move (u, v) if $p^{(m+1)} = z^{(m)}(u, v)$.

Tabu Matrix: A tabu matrix $T \in Z^{N_u M \times N}$ is the matrix records the current tabu period of all the possible moves with the corresponding entries. The tabu period, P, is defined such that if a move is marked as tabu in an iteration, it will remain as a tabu for P subsequent iterations unless the move results in a better solution or its corresponding tabu period is over. In other words, for a given $p^{(m)}$, all its neighbors can be found and checked in $\mathbf{T}$. The indexes of each entry of $\mathbf{T}$ corresponds to an unique move, i,e, the (r,s) th entry corresponds to the move (u,v) from $\mathbf{p}^{(m)}$ where

$$u = \left\lfloor \frac{r-1}{M} \right\rfloor + 1, v = s. \tag{10}$$

And $p_u^{(m)} = a_q$ with $q = \mathrm{mod}(r-1,M)+1$. $\mathbf{T}$ is updated in each iteration used to decide the direction in which the search proceeds.

3.2 RTS Algorithm

Let $\mathbf{g}^{(m)}$ be the least criterion cost vector (or solution vector) of m th iteration, l_{rep} be the average length between two successive occurrences of repetitions and $\mathbf{p}^{(0)}$ be the initial vector. $lflag \in \{true, false\}$ is used to indicate whether the algorithm has reached the local minimum in given iteration or not. Set $\mathbf{g}^{(0)} = \mathbf{p}^{(0)}$, $P = P_0$, $flag = false$, and $l_{rep} = 0$ for initialization. Let $\mathbf{e} = \mathbf{z}^{(m)}(u,v) - \mathbf{p}^{(m)}$, $\mathbf{R} = \mathbf{G}^H\mathbf{G}$ and $\mathbf{f}^{(m)} = \mathbf{R}\left(\mathbf{u} + \tau \mathbf{p}^{(m)}\right)$. For a given start vector $\mathbf{p}^{(m)}$, the criterion cost of its neighbor vector $\mathbf{z}^{(m)}(u,v)$ is computed as

$$\Phi\left(\mathbf{z}^{(m)}(u,v)\right) = \Phi\left(\mathbf{p}^{(m)}\right) + \underbrace{\tau^2 \mathbf{e}^H \mathbf{R} \mathbf{e} + 2\tau \Re\left\{\mathbf{e}^H \mathbf{f}^{(m)}\right\}}_{C(u,v)}. \tag{11}$$

Notice that the first item of (12) from the right hand side (RHS) is fixed during the current iteration, the solution of (6) becomes to find a move $(\tilde{u},\tilde{v})$ which satisfies

$$(\tilde{u},\tilde{v}) = \arg\min_{(u,v)} C(u,v). \tag{12}$$

The operations of each iteration can be classified into three steps as follows:

Step 1) : Find the move $(\tilde{u},\tilde{v})$ satisfies (13) and check for the acceptance by following conditions:

$$\Phi\left(\mathbf{z}^{(m)}(u,v)\right) < \Phi\left(\mathbf{g}^{(m)}\right) \quad \mathbf{T}\left((\tilde{u}-1)M + q, \tilde{v}\right) = 0, \tag{13}$$

where q is such that $p_{\tilde{u}}^{(m)} = a_q$, $a_q \in S$. If none of conditions is satisfied, the move is rejected. In this case, find another pair of $(u_1, v_1) \neq (\tilde{u}, \tilde{v})$ which satisfies (13) and check the acceptance again until find an accepted move. If after $N_u M$ moves, there is still no accepted move, all the entries of $\mathbf{T}$ are decremented by the minimum values in the tabu matrix, then repeat *Step* 1). Assuming that $(\tilde{u}, \tilde{v})$ move is accepted, let $\mathbf{p}^{(m+1)} = \mathbf{z}^{(m)}(u,v)$.

Step 2) : Update the tabu matrix T and the least criterion $\mathbf{g}^{(m+1)}$: if $\Phi\left(\mathbf{p}^{(m+1)}\right) < \Phi\left(\mathbf{g}^{(m)}\right)$, make

$$\mathrm{T}\left((\tilde{u}-1)M+q,\tilde{v}\right) = \mathrm{T}\left((\tilde{u}-1)M+q',\tilde{v}'\right) = 0 \quad \mathbf{g}^{(m+1)} = \mathbf{p}^{(m+1)} \tag{14}$$

else

$$\mathrm{T}\left((\tilde{u}-1)M+q,\tilde{v}\right) = \mathrm{T}\left((\tilde{u}-1)M+q',\tilde{v}'\right) = 0 \quad \mathbf{g}^{(m+1)} = \mathbf{g}^{(m)} \quad flag = true \tag{15}$$

In (14) and (15), $q',\tilde{v}'$ are such that $a_q = p_{\tilde{u}}^{(m)} = N_{\tilde{v}'}\left(p_{\tilde{u}}^{(m+1)}\right)$ and $a_{q'} = p_{\tilde{u}}^{(m+1)}$ respectively. Above equations means that if the move results in a better solution, it should be moved out from the tabu list, otherwise, it still should be marked as tabu. Then check $\mathbf{g}^{(m+1)}$ for repetition, if $\mathbf{g}^{(m+1)} = \mathbf{g}^{(m)}$, make $l_{rep} = l_{rep} + 1$, $P = P + 1$. If P exceeds βl_{rep} for a fixed $\beta > 0$, $P = \max(1, P-1)$.

Step 3) : Update the tabu matrix and $\mathbf{f}^{(m)}$ by

$$\mathrm{T}(r,s) = \max\left\{\mathrm{T}(r,s)-1,0\right\} \text{ for each } (r,s), \quad \mathbf{f}^{(m+1)} = \mathbf{f}^{(m)} + \mathbf{R}_{\tilde{u}}\left(p_{\tilde{u}}^{(m+1)} - p_{\tilde{u}}^{(m)}\right), \tag{16}$$

where $\mathbf{R}_{\tilde{u}}$ is $\tilde{u}$ th column of $\mathbf{R}$. The algorithm terminates in *Step* 3) if the following stopping criterion is satisfied, else it goes back to *Step* 1) and begins the next iteration.

Stopping Criterion: Recall that our purpose is to decrease Δ, so for a given $0 < \gamma < 1$, we can terminate the algorithm if *flag* = *true* and

$$\frac{\Phi\left(\mathbf{p}^{(m)}\right) + \mathbf{u}^H \mathbf{R} \mathbf{u}}{\mathbf{u}^H \mathbf{R} \mathbf{u}} \leq \gamma. \tag{17}$$

In addition, the algorithm will terminate whenever the number of iterations exceeds the maximum iteration numbers *Iter_* max or the number of repetitions are beyond maximum repetition number Rep_max .

3.3   Complexity of the Proposed Algorithm

The complexity of RTS part is random, its average complexity is given in [10], which is between $O(N_u N_t)$ and $O(N_u^2 N_t)$ complexity per channel use. The complexity of RTS is a little higher than norm descent search which has a complexity as $O(N_u N_t)$. That is expected, because RTS can escape from a local minimum and look for better solution. The overall complexity of RTS is dominated by $O\left(N_u^2 N_t\right)$ per channel use, which is much less since the complexity of LR aided VP is $O\left(N_u^3 N_t\right)$ per channel and even higher for THP.

4   Simulation Results

In this section, the performance is measured in terms of the uncoded bit error rate (BER) versus the average received signal-to-noise-ratio (SNR). For the sake of simplicity, we assume that the transmitted symbols are independent identically distributed with zero mean and perfect CSI at transmitter. All the simulations in this section are using zero-forcing precoding, we refer the proposed approach as RTS-ZF algorithm for simplicity. Notice that the prohibitive complexity of SE, we only evaluate the performance of the proposed algorithm and choose the BER performance of SISO AWGN (give as $Q\left(\sqrt{SNR}\right)$) as a lower bound. In Fig. [1], the BER curves of RTS ZF algorithm for different N_t and N_u are plotted. For comparison, the BER curves of ZF precoding are also plotted. The following RTS parameters are used in it for 4-QAM: $P_0 = 2$, $\beta = 0.1$, $Iter\_max = 800$ and $\gamma = 0.5$. We can clearly see that, the performance of the proposed algorithm outperform ZF precoding and increases with increasing N_t and N_u. In Fig. [2], the BER performance of NDS-ZF is plotted to compare with the proposed approach in 32×32 MU-MIMO. As shown in Fig. [2], RTS-ZF is outperforming the NDS ZF precoding, which makes the increased complexity worthwhile.

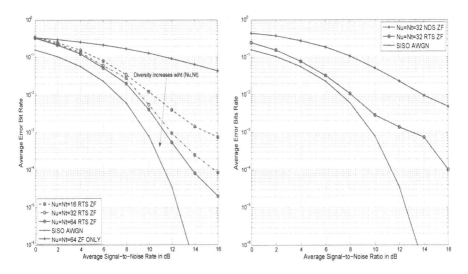

Fig. 1. Uncoded BER for different antennas   **Fig. 2.** Uncoded BER for RTS vs NDS

5   Conclusion

In this paper, we proposed a vector perturbation algorithm using reactive tabu search. This proposed algorithm is suited for large MU-MIMO system in terms of both complexity and performance. The BER performance and complexity of this algorithm are analyzed via simulations. Though there is lack of theoretical analyses of RTS, we believe that such approaches can potentially trigger wide interest in the theory and implementation of large multiuser MU-MIMO systems.

Acknowledgments. This work is financially supported by the National Natural Science Foundation of China (No. 60972075) and National 863 Project (No.2011AA01A205).

References

1. Ngo, H.Q., Larsson, E.G., Marzetta, T.L.: Energy and spectral efficiency of very large multiuser MIMO systems. arXiv: 1112.3810 (December 2011)
2. Rusek, F., Persson, D., Lau, B.K., Larsson, E.G., Marzetta, T.L., Edfors, O., Tufvesson, F.: Scaling up MIMO: opportunities and challenges with very large arrays. arXiv: 1201.3210 (January 2012)
3. Hochwald, B.M., Peel, C.B., Swindlehurst, A.L.: A vectorperturbation technique for near-capacity multiantenna multiuser communication-part II: perturbation. IEEE Transactions on Communications 53(3), 537–544 (2005)
4. Jalden, J., Ottersten, B.: An exponential lower bound on the expected complexity of sphere decoding 4, iv-393–iv-396 (2004)
5. Fischer, R.F.H., Windpassinger, C., Lampe, A., Huber, J.B.: Spacetime transmission using Tomlinson-Harashima precoding. In: ITG Fachbericht, pp. 139–148 (2002)
6. Windpassinger, C., Fischer, R.F.H., Huber, J.B.: Lattice-reductionaided broadcast precoding. IEEE Transactions on Communications 52(12), 2057–2060 (2004)
7. Seethaler, D., Matz, G.: Efficient vector perturbation in multi-antenna multi-user systems based on approximate integer relations. In: Proc. of the European Signal Proc. Conf (EUSIPCO), pp. 4–8 (2006)
8. Mohammed, S.K., Chockalingam, A., Sundar Rajan, B.: A Low-Complexity precoder for large multiuser MISO systems. In: Vehicular Technology Conference, VTC Spring 2008, pp. 797–801. IEEE (May 2008)
9. Battiti, R., Tecchiolli, G., et al.: The reactive tabu search. ORSA Journal on Computing 6, 126–126 (1994)
10. Tulino, A.M., Verdăž, S.: Random matrix theory and wireless communications, vol. 1. Now Publishers Inc. (2004)

A PSO-Based Hierarchical Resource Scheduling Strategy on Cloud Computing

Hongli Zhang, Panpan Li, Zhigang Zhou, and Xiangzhan Yu

School of Computer Science and Technology, Harbin Institute of Technology, Harbin, China
{zhanghongli,yxz}@hit.edu.cn,
{lipan,zhouzhigang}@pact518.hit.edu.cn

Abstract. Cloud computing environments facilitate applications by providing virtualized resources that can be provisioned dynamically. Computing resources are delivered by Virtual Machines (VMs). In such a scenario, resource scheduling algorithms play an important role where the aim is to schedule applications effectively so as to reduce the turn-around time and improve resource utilization. In this paper, we present a Particle Swarm Optimization (PSO) based strategy schedules applications to cloud resource taking into account both transmission cost and current load. In addition, a novel inertia weight was introduced in order to get the global search and local search effectively and avoid plunging into the local optimum. Finally, we experiment with application workflows by varying its performance and convergence analysis.

Keywords: PSO, resource scheduling, cloud computing.

1 Introduction

Cloud computing technologies are developing greatly and have gained popularity, providing resources of compute and store supporting the use of large scale Internet services for the remote construction of applications [2, 4].

Resource scheduling strategy in cloud environment is thus an important issue affecting not only the performance of cloud but also the turnaround time experienced by its clients and the prices paid by them. Cloud computing environment, as fully distributed architecture is hard to management, monitoring and pricing. Clients are interested in completing their applications in the least possible time with the least possible total cost which is the amount of money they pay the cloud for the resources used. The cloud providers, on the other hand, are interested in maximizing the resource utilization of the cloud and thus its revenue. These result in unintended client-client and client-provider interactions which are not captured by existing pricing and resource allocation mechanisms [5].

In this paper, we propose a novel modeling for optimal user application allocation to the cloud computing that takes both load balancing and the support for minimizing inter-network cost into consideration by providing a hierarchical PSO-based application scheduling algorithm with a novel inertia weight strategy.

Y. Yuan, X. Wu, and Y. Lu (Eds.): ISCTCS 2012, CCIS 320, pp. 325–332, 2013.

2   Problem Statement

2.1   Cloud Resource Scheduling Model

From the systemic viewpoint, we can treat the cloud computing environment as a huge server with unlimited resource. It means the system will allocate a bundle of resource to a specific task according to user's requirement. By virtualization technology, VM can be used as resource provider node in cloud. Generally, from the scheduler view, network of cloud computing represented with ADS (Autonomous Domain Set), where $ADS=\{AD_1,AD_2,...,AD_r\}$, and AD denotes an autonomous domain. Every AD has multiple VMs, shown as in figure 1. Cloud maps user's applications to the VM layer, through AD layers by implementing the user's applications, so the resource scheduling of cloud environment should achieve by AD layers and VM layers.

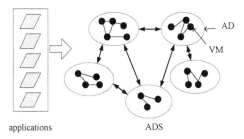

applications   ADS

Fig. 1. Application Scheduling Framework on Cloud

2.2   Standard PSO

PSO initializes particles of population randomly. Each particle changed its searching direction based on two best values or experiences in each interaction. The first one is the best searching experience of individual so far and is called *pBest*. The other one is the best result obtained so far by all particles in the population and is called *gBest*.

$$v_{id}^{t+1} = \omega v_{id}^{t} + c_1 r_1 \times \left(p_{id}^{t} - x_{id}^{t} \right) + c_2 r_2 \times \left(p_{gd}^{t} - x_{id}^{t} \right) \qquad (1)$$

$$x_{id}^{t+1} = x_{id}^{t} + v_{id}^{t+1} \qquad (2)$$

In the above equations, $v_i = (v_{i1}, v_{i2}, ..., v_{iD})'$ is the original velocity of $i-th$ particle, v_{id}^{t+1} is the new velocity of $i-th$ particle, ω is the inertia weight, c_1 and c_2 are the acceleration constants, $x_i = (x_{i1}, x_{i2}, ..., x_{iD})'$ is the original position of $i-th$ particle, x_{id}^{t+1} is the new position of $i-th$ particle, r_1 and r_2 are the random number ranging between 0 and 1. p_{id}^t is the best position of particle and p_{gd}^t is the best position of the whole particles in the population [1].

3   Scheduling Algorithms

3.1   Proposed PSO

The original PSO algorithm was inspired by the social behavior of biological organisms. First, the algorithm starts with swarm initialization using GRASP (Greedy Randomized Adaptive Search Procedure) to ensure each particle in the initial swarm is a feasible and efficient solution. The algorithm is dynamic as it updates the communication costs (based on average communication time between resources) in every scheduling loop. It also re-computes the application-resource mapping so that it optimizes the cost of computation, based on the current network and resource conditions.

For every resource request, the cloud will generates a mapping scheme randomly. As in cloud computing resource scheduling model, the application flows will be allocated to VM through AD layers. In order to get the whole cloud system load balance, we focus not only the load balance between ADs but also between the VMs in the same AD.

Main Swarm Evolutionary Process

There are several objectives can be measured for the performance and efficiency of resource scheduling to distributed system services. In the cloud computing environment, computation cost is usually the user's another concern. So, we focus not only on minimizing the cost but also on minimizing the total make span of the application flow [6].

Definition 1: N applications to be distributed, which will be divided into $|ADS|$ subswarm, and sub-swarm denoted as $AD_i(i=1,2,...,|ADS|)$.

Cloud computing environment enables the sharing of various heterogeneous resources and coordinated working of geographically distributed resources. In huge, distributed and heterogeneous computing environment, communication cost among the ADs great effect the performance of cloud. Therefore, the goal of this evolutionary must focus on the network load balancing among ADs. The initial step is to compute the mapping of all applications in the workflow to ADs. This mapping optimizes the whole cost of communication the workflow application. As the communication costs would have changed, we would re-compute the PSO mapping scheme.

$Comm(AD_{ij})$ denotes the total communication cost between application assigned to AD_i and AD_j.

$$Min\left(Comm(AD_{ij})\right)\left(i\,,j\in|ADS|,i\neq j\right) \tag{3}$$

Formula 3 ensures that all the application mapping to ADs with a low communication cost between each other. By taking formula 3 as fitness value, we only consider the communication cost between every ADs. After this evolutionary process, the main particle swarm is divided into sub-swarms close to the center of the swarm with the best fitness value by number of ADs judged by the formula 3. So, based on this thought, in our strategy, we define the best searching experience of individual in AD layer is called $pBest_{AD}$, and the best searching experience of individual in ADs is called $gBest_{AD}$. Therefore, the formula of updating particle's velocity in evolutionary process is also modified, as shown in formula 4.

$$v_{id}^{t+1} = \omega v_{id}^t + c_1 r_1 \times \left(pBestp_{AD}^t - x_{id}^t \right) + c_2 r_2 \times \left(gBest_{AD}^t - x_{id}^t \right) \tag{4}$$

Sub-swarm Evolutionary Process

After completing the above steps, there will be |ADS| VM-swarms which will be evolved respectively by same fitness value, just shown as below. In the evolutionary process of every VM-swarm, we suppose $pBest_{VM}$ is the best position of particle and $gBest_{VM}$ is the best position of the whole particles in the population. When a particle gets its $gBest$ in VMs population, this $gBest_{VM}$ must be the best position on the ADs population. Information sharing method between particles influences the convergence rate and global search capability in PSO algorithm. Therefore, the next step we will use this $gBest_{VM}$ to update $gBest_{AD}$. Those processes are shown as formula 5 and 6.

$$v_{id}^{t+1} = \omega v_{id}^t + c_1 r_1 \times \left(pBest_{VM}^t - x_{id}^t \right) + c_2 r_2 \times \left(gBest_{VM}^t - x_{id}^t \right) \tag{5}$$

$$gBest_{AD}^t = gBest_{VM}^t \tag{6}$$

Form AD layer perspective, we can see that the AD-swarm and VM-swarm share the same position when every particle gets its best position after first round of evolution. However, this step only divided AD-swarm into some VM-swarms, just taking the communication cost among ADs as fitness value without considering the load balance of every VM in the same AD. Actually in every AD, each particle also has the respective best position by taking computing load balance as fitness value.

As discussed above, the major goal for our application level scheduling is to decrease the computation on the condition of satisfying the deadline of cloud workflow application by dynamically optimizing the Application-to-Resource assignment in this step. Let's $Comput(VM_l)$ to be the total computation cost of application assign to VM_l in AD_k. And let $AveCom(AD_k)$ to be the average computation load of VM in AD_k.

$$AveCom\left(AD_k\right) = \frac{\sum Comput\left(VM_l\right)}{|AD_k|}\left(l = 1, 2, .., |AD_k|, VM_l \in AD_k\right) \tag{7}$$

$$Min\left|Comput\left(VM_l\right) - AveCom\left(AD_k\right)\right|\left(l = 1, 2, .., |AD_k|, VM_l \in AD_k\right) \tag{8}$$

Inertia Weight Strategy

Inertia weight is an important parameter in PSO, and it can control the algorithm's exploitation ability and exploration ability. Therefore, inertia weight is very crucial to the performance of PSO. So, the inertia weight should be determined by current system workload. And inertia weight can also be modified by introducing a dependence on the current system load. As the system load is heavy, high velocity of particle has good search ability on the global solution space and a fast convergence speed by a sample. On the other hand, the rework amount of an application decreased as the increase of iteration times.

$$\omega(t) = \omega_{start} - \frac{\omega_{start} - \omega_{end}}{t_{max}} \times t \tag{9}$$

where W_{start} expresses the initial value of inertia weight, W_{end} means inertia weight when iterations are completed.

Linear PSO algorithm which makes the inertia weight reduction linearly often fails to reflect the actual optimized search process. Thus, the standard PSO algorithm usually sinks into the local optimal search space at the later stage of the particles' evolution. To solve this problem, aiming at the shortcoming of inertia weight of standard PSO which is slow convergence rate at ending and easily plunging into the local optimum, a new inertia weight is proposed just shown as following formula.

$$\omega(t) = -2\left(\frac{t}{t_{max}}\right)^2 + 2\left(\frac{t}{t_{max}}\right) + \frac{4}{10} \tag{10}$$

where t_{max} denotes maximum number of iterations in evolutionary process. Inertia weight keeps increasing in the initial stage, but maintaining a downward trend as the increase of iteration times. Along with evolution, interactive abilities between particle decrease gradually. This strategy not only solves the premature convergence problem, but also avoids the slow convergence in the later convergence phase.

3.2   Information Sharing

In the course of evolution, particle not only exchanges information with other particles in the same sub-swarm but also is influenced by other sub-swarms. That is to say, the strategy based on local and global combined search will be more efficient within the process of searching.

From what is mention above, the particle swarm was divided into some subswarms. All those sub-swarms associate with particle swarm by information sharing between those. In order to get the whole system load balance, we need to build efficient way to get information sharing. Algorithm 1 shows a pseudo-code of the proposed PSO resource scheduling algorithm. The algorithm includes three main steps. Line 1-2 initializes the swarm. Based on the communication optimization, line

3-8 illustrates the evolutionary course of N particles into sub-swarm. Line 8-12 express the evolutionary process of every sub-swarm by load balancing of VMs optimization strategy.

Algorithm 1. Proposed PSO scheduling algorithm
1.   Initialize the Particle Swarms;
2.   Swarm initialization with GRASP;
3.   For swarm, calculate its fitness value in formula 3;
4.   If the fitness value is better than the previous best pBest$_{AD}$, set the current fitness value as the new pBest$_{AD}$;
5.   After Steps 3 and 4 for all particles in a swarm, select the best particle as gBest$_{AD}$;
6.   For all particles, calculate velocity using formula 10, 4 and update their positions using formula 2;
7.   If the stopping criteria or maximum iteration is not satisfied, repeat from Step 3;
8.   For each sub particles, calculate its fitness value in formula 8;
9.   If the fitness value is better than the previous best pBest$_{VM}$, set the current fitness value as the new pBest$_{VM}$;
10.   After Steps 8 and 9 for all particles in a vm-swarm, select the best particle as gBest$_{VM}$;
11.   For all particles, calculate velocity using formula 10, 5, 4 and update their positions using formula 2;
12.   If the stopping criteria or maximum iteration is not satisfied, repeat from Step 8.

4   Evaluation

In this part, we focus on the optimization degree of application delivery on Cloud. We rewrite DataCernerBroker, Cloudlet functional modules of Cloudsim which schedules answers for the allocation and execution of applications by proposed PSO algorithm [3]. The modified Cloudsim is deployed on a PC with Intel T5500, 2G RAM and 7200 RPM hard-disk, which contains 10 VMs in it.

$$ADS = \{AD_{01} = \{VM_{01}, VM_{02}, VM_{03}\}, AD_{02} = \{VM_{04}, VM_{05}, VM_{06}\},$$
$$AD_{03} = \{VM_{07}, VM_{08}, VM_{09}, VM_{10}\}\}$$

As for proposed PSO, the settings for parameters are: population size n=50; the constriction factor $\lambda=2, c_1 = c_2 = 1.5$.

Scheduling Cost

In our first experiment, we varied the size of total data processed by the workflow in the range from 30 to 90.The total costs for different data sets are compared in figure 2.

From figure 2, the total application assigning time cost by proposed PSO based application scheduling scheme increases much lower than the standard PSO and Best Resource Selection (BRS) algorithm. And the reason is that the character of modified inertia weight obtains the global optimum, not the local optimum. Thus it may induce the iteration times enormously.

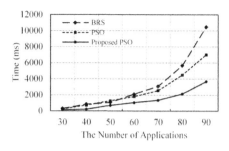

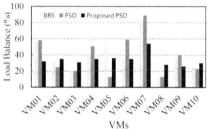

Fig. 2. Application Assigning Cost   **Fig. 3.** The Resources Load on 10 Vms

Load Balance

In order to verify the load balance of cloud environment, we choose 90 users and 10 VMs, by counting and monitoring the load of every VM, to verify the load balancing performance of three scheduling algorithms as shown in figure 3.

The result shows that proposed PSO algorithm has lower cost of execution as compared with BRS and standard PSO algorithm. One of the reasons for this is that PSO algorithm only considers "ready" applications during scheduling iteration without considering the communication cost between every ADs and cannot get the global optimal solution. However, proposed PSO scheme gets better cost value than standard PSO algorithm in evolutionary process.

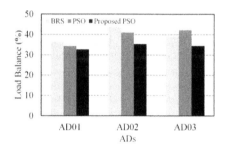

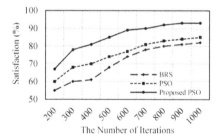

Fig. 4. The Load Conditions on 3 ADs   **Fig. 5.** The Performance Satisfaction on Different Iterations Processing

Figure 4 shows the load balance of every AD in our experiment. From this figure, we can see that the load is comparative averagely distributed to each AD in proposed PSO algorithm. However, the other two algorithms do not obtain load balancing on each AD. There are two reasons for this situation. First, proposed PSO algorithm considers the communication cost and tries to reduce it while scheduling applications to VMs. The second reason is that the novel inertia weight strategy optimizes the communication cost between every AD.

Convergence Analysis

In order to further study the optimization ability among the mentioned three algorithms, more complex workflow applications are involved. We compare constringency speed of 3 resource scheduling algorithm by creating 1024 virtual machine nodes and 600 applications. Figure 5 shows the satisfaction of all VMs on the CloudSim.

Figure 5 plots the performance satisfaction of three algorithms over the number of iterations for different sizes of total data processed by the applications workflow. We can see the proposed PSO gets convergence after integrating 700 time, however, BSO and standard POS only after 850 times. This demonstrates that proposed PSO can find global optimal solution quickly. It has been validated experimentally that the proposed algorithm is superior to the BSO and standard PSO algorithm in terms of convergence.

5   Conclusion

As cloud computing is primarily driven by its cost effectiveness and as the scheduling of composite service applications. This paper presents a PSO-based hierarchical resource scheduling algorithm to optimize the schedules of workflow application in cloud environment. In addition, a novel inertia weight strategy was introduced in order to get the global search and local search effectively and avoid plunging into the local optimum. Based on the simulation results, the proposed algorithm yields efficient performance on scheduling applications in cloud.

Acknowledgment . This work is supported by the project of National Natural Science Foundation of China (60903166, 61100188, 61173144), National Basic Research Program (973 Program) of China (2011CB302605, 2007CB311101) and National High Technology Research and Development Program (863 Program) of China (2010AA012504). We thank the anonymous reviewers for their helpful feedback and suggestions.

References

1. Shi, Y., Eberhart, R.C.: A modified particle swarm optimizer. In: Proceedings of IEEE International Conference on Evolutionary Computation, Anchorage, AK (1998)
2. Zavala, A.E.M., Aguirre, A.H., Villa Diharce, E.R., Rionda, S.B.: Constrained Optimization with an Improved Particle Swarm Optimization Algorithm. International Journal of Intelligent Computing and Cybernetics (2008)
3. Cloudsim, http://www.cloudbus.org/cloudsim
4. Wu, Z., Liu, X., Ni, Z., Yuan, D., Yang, Y.: A market-oriented Hierarchical Scheduling Strategy in Cloud Workflow Systems. The Journal of Supercomputing (2011)
5. Iosup, A., Ostermann, S., Yigitbasi, N., Prodan, R., Fahringer, T., Epema, D.: Performance Analysis of Cloud Computing Services for Many-tasks Scientific Computing. IEEE Transactions on Parallel and Distributed System (2010)
6. Lee, Z.Y., Wang, Y.: A Dynamic Priority Scheduling Algorithm on Service Request Scheduling in Cloud Computing. In: Proceeding of the 2011 International Conference on Electronic and Mechanical Engineering and Information Technology (2011)

Hiding Signatures in Variable Names

Yinjie Su, Jiahui Liu, and Dong Li

School of Computer Science and Technology, Harbin Institute of Technology, Harbin, China
{suyinjie2011,hitljh}@pact518.hit.edu.cn, lee@hit.edu.cn

Abstract. With the development of software technology, the copyright of the software is increasingly important. One aspect is the copyright of the source code. This paper proposed a new algorithm named HSVN (hiding signatures in variable names) to hide the copyright signature or watermark in the source code. It belongs to the static watermark. The basic idea of HSVN algorithm is adding signature bytes into the variable names which are located by random sequence, and the difference between the alongside two chars of the specific variable name is the hidden signature byte. HSVN Algorithm can hide the signature more easily and more invisibly. Moreover, it can hide a large amount of information with little redundancy added to the program.

Keywords: watermark, signature, random sequence, variable name.

1   Introduction

In recent years, many products spread on the Internet in the form of electronic version, such as sound, images, documents and software. The copyright protection of these digital products becomes one research focus. Several digital watermarking techniques were studied to solve this problem for the past several years [1]. When used in software field (such as source code, middle code, executable file, etc.), digital watermark is called software watermark [2]. As the important property of the Software corporations, protecting the source code and proving its copyright are essential. Software watermark technique provides the guarantee [3,4,5,6].

According to the embedded position and method, software watermark is divided into static software watermark and dynamic software watermark. Static watermark is embedding the authentication information into the code. Most of the source code watermarking technique is static. Dynamic software watermark isembedding the authentication information in the execution state of the program. We can extract the dynamic software watermark by tracking the software's running process [7].

In the premise of keeping a consistent feature of the software before and after embedding the watermark, we use the following criteria to evaluate the watermarking techniques:

(1) *stealth*. This criterion expresses the invisibility of the embedded watermark for the observer.

(2) *robustness*. A robust software watermark can still be extracted correctly though suffering a strong attack.

(3) *redundancy*. It refers to the modification to the source code.

Y. Yuan, X. Wu, and Y. Lu (Eds.): ISCTCS 2012, CCIS 320, pp. 333–340, 2013.

Based on the above criteria, we proposed the HSVN algorithm to protect the copyright of the source code. It belongs to the static software watermark. With the implementation of the algorithm, we can randomly embed the authentication information into the name of the specified function's local variables. Our algorithm can achieve a good performance on stealth, robustness and redundancy. To the best of our acknowledgement, HSVN algorithm and its extensions mentioned later are all first proposed in this paper.

The paper is organized as follows. The next Section describes the previous related work in software watermarking. In Section 3 we describe our method and present the overview of the implementation process, and in Section 4 we analyze the performance of this method and mention its extension. This paper concludes in Section 5.

2   Related Works

Davidson and Myhrvold proposed the first software watermarking algorithm [8]. By reordering the basic blocks of the program, this algorithm can embed a watermark into a program. At that time, some patented software watermarking algorithms [9, 10] were studied based on the idea of code replacement which can replace a predetermined portion of code or data in a program with the watermark value.

Later, the watermarking algorithms based on register allocation were proposed. The watermarking algorithm proposed by Qu and Potkonjak in [11] (QP algorithm) is one of these algorithms which can be applied to a graph coloring register allocator. The basic idea of QP is that edges are added between chosen vertices in a register allocation graph based on the watermark sequence. In[12]Myles and Collberg indicated that, under this algorithm, a graph embedded in a different bit sequence may produce the same results, which can lead to a wrong extraction of the watermark. They also proposed an improved algorithm named QPS(QP for SandMark) to correct this error. They analyzed that the inaccurate message recovery is due to the unpredictability of the coloring of the vertices. So QPS places additional constraints on which vertices can be selected for a triple. Using the QPS algorithm, the selected triples are isolated units so that they will not affect other vertices in the graph.

Watermarking technique based on graph theory is also an important research direction. Collberg and Thomborson proposed a new software watermarking technique in [13] (CT Algorithm) in which a dynamic graphic watermark is stored in the execution state of a program.CT algorithm uses the topology of the graph to represent a large integer N which can be split into the multiplication of two large prime integers. When embedding, N is coded into a graph G according to the special encoding algorithm. Then split G into several sub-graphs embedded into the program. But the graph detection of this algorithm needs to run the entire program. So it is fragile to the module removal attack [14]. The first static graph watermarking scheme Graph Theoretic Watermarking (GTW)was proposed by Venkatesan et al. [15]. The basic idea is to encode a watermark value in a reducible permutation graph and convert it into a control flow graph, which is then merged with the program control flow graph by adding control flow edges between the two. But Collberg et al. [16] found that watermarks of up to 150 bits increased program size by between 40% and 75%, while performance decreased by between 0% and 36%.

Based on equation reordering, Mohammad and Sajad proposed an algorithm [17] which has a very small modification to the source code and has no negative effect on the running of the program. The main idea of this algorithm is to reorder the instructions that can be swapped with each other while preserve the original functionality of the program. The authentication sequence is embedded into these swapped instructions. The weakness of this method is that it can hide a small amount of information.

3   HSVN Algorithm

The main idea of our method is that: According to the theory of large integer decomposition difficult question, we choose a large natural number N and embed it into the program. Due to N can be decomposed to two primes P and Q which are large enough, only the legal owner can extract N from the program and provide the two large prime factors.

3.1   Asmuth-Bloom Lemma

Key cryptography share idea is dividing the key K into n parts, and t $(t \leqslant n)$ parts of them can recover K.

C. Asmuth and J. Bloom proposed a method based on the Chinese remainder theorem in 1983 to implement that idea [18].

Assume that $q, d_1, d_2, ..., d_n$, $p > K$, and satisfy the following conditions:

$$\begin{cases} d_1 < d_2 < d_3 < ... < d_n \\ i, j \in \{1, 2, ..., n\}, \forall i, \gcd(p, d_i) = 1, \forall i \neq j, \gcd(d_i, d_j) = 1 \\ d_1 \times d_2 \times d_3 ... \times d_t > p \times d_{n-t+2} \times d_{n-t+3} ... \times d_n \end{cases} \quad (1)$$

Let

$$N = d_1 \times d_2 \times d_3 ... \times d_t \quad (2)$$

So N/p is greater than the product of $t-1$ pieces of d_i. Randomly select an integer r satisfying $0 \leqslant r \leqslant N/p-1$, calculate

$$k^{'} = K + r \times p \quad (3)$$

So the i-th share k_i is:

$$k_i = k^{'} \bmod d_i, i = 1, 2, ..., n \quad (4)$$

$k_1, k_2, ..., k_n$ is the n parts of K.

Now we recover K through t pieces of k_i. First use the Chinese remainder theorem to solve the t congruence equations:

$$k_{i_j} \equiv k' \bmod d_{i_j}, 1 \le i \le n, j = 1, 2, ..., t \tag{5}$$

This congruence equations has a unique solution x in the range of $\left[0, d_{i_1} \times d_{i_2} \times ... d_{i_t} \right]$. Since $d_{i_1} \times d_{i_2} \times ... d_{i_t} \ge N$, we can uniquely identify k' where $k' = x \bmod N$. Then we can recover K from the Eq. (6).

$$K = k' - r \times p \tag{6}$$

This method is called Asumth-Bloom lemma.

3.2   Watermark Embedding Algorithm

In order to enhance the robustness of the watermark to resist the watermark removal attack [19], HSVN adopts Asmuth-Bloom lemma to divide the watermark, and keep p, d_i as the copyright evidence. Watermark embedding process is as follows:

(1) Select the appropriate natural number N.

(2) Convert N into n parts using the Asmuth-Bloom method. Record the digits of each part with a vector $V=(v_1, v_2, ..., v_n)$. Such as 100 is 3-digits, and 1000 is 4-digits. Connect the n parts of N into a string, and transform this string into a binary sequence M with 4-bits per digit. Such as, the 4-bits binary sequence 0010 represents the digit 2. If M has d bytes, we can divide M into $2d$ sub-watermarks $m_0, m_1, m_2, ..., m_{2d-1}$, with 4-bits per sub-watermark. An example is presented in Fig. 1, if the n parts of N are 24,25,100,4,89,2 and 2000.

(3) According to the definition order in the source file, we assign a serial number to all the functions. For example, the total number of functions is C, then the serial numbers are $0, 1, ..., C-1$. Using random number generator and seed k, produce the random sequence $p_0, p_1, ..., p_{2d-1}$, and $p_i \in \{0, 1, ..., C-1\}$. If $p_i = s$, we embed m_i in the function that has the serial number s. Embedding method is as follows.

According to the definition order, find the first local variable in this function. If there is no variable, then add one as the chosen variable. If this is the first appearance of p_i in the random sequence (the random sequence may have repeated numbers), we add one character behind the first character of the chosen variable name. Due to m_i is a 4-bits binary data, it ranges from 0 to 15. The added character can be calculated through looking up the Table 1 and Table 2. For example if we want to add character behind 'Y' and the sub-watermark m_i is 0010, the added character is 'a'; if we want to add character behind 'x' and the sub-watermark m_i is 0011, the added character is 'A'. If this is the second appearance of p_i in random sequence, we add one character behind the second character of the chosen variable name, and if this is the j-th appearance of p_i in random sequence, we add one character behind the j-th character of the chosen variable name. Then according to this way, modify the names of all the appearances of this variable in this function.

(4) After all the embedding processes, keep k, C, V and d as the key of this source code.

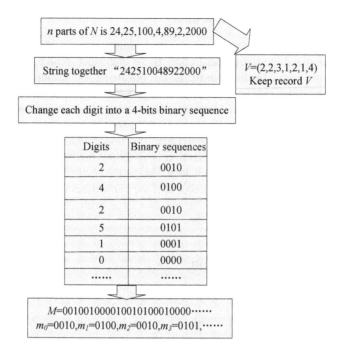

Fig. 1. The process of n parts <24,25,100,4,89,2,2000> of N

Table 1. Serial number and the character

Serial number	Character
0	A
1	B
2	C
...	...
25	Z
26	a
27	b
28	c
...	...
51	z

Table 2. Adding character behind$R$

m_i	The serial number of the added character
0000	R
0001	$(R+1)$ mod 52
0010	$(R+2)$ mod 52
0011	$(R+3)$ mod 52
...	...
1100	$(R+12)$ mod 52
1101	$(R+13)$ mod 52
1110	$(R+14)$ mod 52
1111	$(R+15)$ mod 52

The adding character is chosen this way: The character α is added behind the letter β which has serial number R. The embedded sub-watermark is m_i. First, getα's serial number through Table 2, and then translate it into character by looking up Table 1.

3.3   Watermark Extracting Algorithm

The extracting process is similar to the embedding process: First, contrast the embedded source code to the original code. If the embedded source code lack some functions, add the empty functions at the lacked positions; if it has the extra functions, just delete them. With the known number C, generate the same random sequence $p_0, p_1, ..., p_{2d-1}$ again using the seed k and the same random generator. Find the function that located by p_i, and find out its first variable. Under the rules described in the embedding process, look up Table 1 and Table 2 to find the hiding sub-watermark m_i in the name of this variable. If this function is an empty function, the extracted sub-watermark m_i is none. With the help of V we can get the divided parts of N. According to the Asmuth-Bloom lemma proved above, if we can extract at least r parts, we can restore N, and only the owner can give the two large prime factors of N which can prove the ownership of this source code.

4   Evaluation and Extension

We evaluate the performance of HSVN algorithm through the following criteria.

(1) *Redundancy*. Our method is embedding the watermark through modifying the name of some variables. The modification to the source code is very little. There is no extra overhead to the running of the source code.

(2) *Stealth*. We embed the watermark in the name of the variables which are the very common and important part of the source code. It is very hard for the attacker to find the embedding positions through observation or control flow analysis.

(3) *Robustness*. Because we adopt the Asmuth-Bloom lemma, HSVN can defend the function removal attack. Due to the use of the original source code when extracting the watermark, function adding attack doesn't affect the extracting result. Semantic keeping attack is adjusting the order of the instructions while not changing the functionality. Since our watermark is embedded in the name of the variables, this attack is useless, too. The first letter in the chosen variable name is random, so it is also very hard to crack our watermark through collusion attack which is trying to find the embedding watermark through comparing two or more embedded source codes.

Table 3. Performance comparison of several software watermarking algorithms

Algorithm	Invisibility	Robustness	Modification	Datarate	Impact on performance
HSVN	+	+	+	+	+
GWT	+	+	-	-	-
Equation reordering	+	+	+	-	+
Code replacement	-	-	-	+	+

In Table 3 we contrast the performance of several software watermarking algorithms that can be used in source code copyright protection. '+' means a good performance in that criteria and '-' means a bad performance.

Our method has a good scalability. After a slight change, it can be used in other forms of the software products and improved in the effectiveness. The algorithm mentioned above is embedding the watermark in the name of the variables. We can alsoembed the watermark in the name of the functions or the name of the formal parameters of the function using the same method. By combining the three methods together, we can increase the difficulty of cracking the watermark and data amountthat can be embedded in the source code. If we choose the variables in the same way, embed the sub-watermarks in the initial values of them rather than the names, and assign the real value to them before they are first used, we can extract the watermark from an execution of the program by tracking the initial value after the variable is defined. This extension of the algorithm can be used in the copyright protection of the executable file.

5   Conclusion

In this paper, we presented a software watermarking algorithm HSVN based on the name of the variables to protect the copyright of the source code. This algorithm can lead to a little redundancy, good stealth and strong robustness of the watermarked source code. And it can easily turn into other watermarking algorithms through a slight change, which can increase the confusion of the watermark. So it is very difficult for the attacker to find the real watermark and the actual watermark algorithm. Through this algorithm and its extensions, we can obtain the software watermarking idea that where there is the code, there is the place to embed the watermark.

Acknowledgment. This work is partially supported by the High-Tech Research and Development Plan ofChina (Grant No. 2010AA012504,2011AA010705); the National Natural Science Foundation of China (Grant No.61173145); National Grand FundamentalResearch 973 Program of China (Grant No. 2011CB302605).

References

1. Swanson, M.D., Kobayashi, M., Tewfik, A.H.: Multimedia Data-embedding and Watermarking Technologies. Proc. of the IEEE 86(6), 1054–1087 (1998)
2. Collberg, C.S., Thomborson, C.: Watermarking,Tamper-proofing, and Obfuscation-tools for Software Protection. IEEE Transactions on Software Engineering 28, 735–746 (2002)
3. Hamilton, J., Danicic, S.: A Survey of Static Software Watermarking. In: Internet Security, pp. 100–107 (2011)
4. Dai, P., Wang, C., Yu, Z., Yue, Y., Wang, J.: A Software Watermark Based Architecture for Cloud Security. In: Sheng, Q.Z., Wang, G., Jensen, C.S., Xu, G. (eds.) APWeb 2012. LNCS, vol. 7235, pp. 270–281. Springer, Heidelberg (2012)

5. Chroni, M., Nikolopoulos, S.D.: Encoding Watermark Numbers as Cographs using Self-inverting Permutations. In: 12th International Conference on Computer Systems and Technologies, pp. 142–148 (2011)
6. Zhang, S., Zhu, G., Wang, Y.: A Strategy of Software Protection based on Multi-watermarking Embedding. In: 2nd International Conference on Control, Instrumentation and Automation, pp. 444–447 (2011)
7. Collberg, C.S., Thomborson, C.: On the Limits of Software Watermarking. Technical Report. 164 (August 1998)
8. Davidson, R.I., Myhrvold, N.: Method and System for Generating and Auditing a Signature for a Computer Program (September 1996)
9. Holmes, K.: Computer Software Protection. International Business Machines Corporation (February 1994)
10. Samson, P.R.: Apparatus and Method for Serializing and Validating Copies of Computer Software (February 1994)
11. Qu, G., Potkonjak, M.: Analysis of Watermarking Techniques for Graph Coloring Problem. In: Proceedings of the 1998 IEEE/ACM International Conference on Computer-aided Design, pp. 190–193 (1998)
12. Myles, G., Collberg, C.S.: Software Watermarking Through Register Allocation: Implementation, Analysis, and Attacks. In: Lim, J.-I., Lee, D.-H. (eds.) ICISC 2003. LNCS, vol. 2971, pp. 274–293. Springer, Heidelberg (2004)
13. Collberg, C.S., Thomborson, C.: Software Watermarking: Models and Dynamic Embeddings. In: Conference Record of the Annual ACM Symposium on Principles of Programming Languages, pp. 311–324 (1999)
14. Collberg, C.S., Huntwork, A., Carter, E., Townsend, G.: Graph Theoretic Software Watermarks: Implementation, Analysis, and Attacks. In: Fridrich, J. (ed.) IH 2004. LNCS, vol. 3200, pp. 192–207. Springer, Heidelberg (2004)
15. Venkatesan, R., Vazirani, V.V., Sinha, S.: A Graph Theoretic Approach to Software Watermarking. In: Moskowitz, I.S. (ed.) IH 2001. LNCS, vol. 2137, pp. 157–168. Springer, Heidelberg (2001)
16. Collberg, C.S., Huntwork, A., Carter, E., Townsend, G.: Graph Theoretic Software Watermarks: Implementation, Analysis, and Attacks. In: Fridrich, J. (ed.) IH 2004. LNCS, vol. 3200, pp. 192–207. Springer, Heidelberg (2004)
17. Shirali-Shahreza, M., Shirali-Shahreza, S.: Software Watermarking by Equation Reordering. In: 3rd International Conference on Information and Communication Technologies: From Theory to Applications, ICTTA (2008)
18. Asmuth, C., Bloom, J.: AModular Approach to Key Safeguarding. IEEE Transactions on Information Theory IT-29, 208–210 (1983)
19. Myers, A.C., Liskow, B.: Protecting Privacy Using the Decentralized Label Model. ACM Transactions on Software Engineering and Methodology 9(4), 410–442 (2000)

Chinese New Words Detection Using Mutual Information

Zheng Liang[1,*], Bingying Xu[1], Jie Zhao[2], Yan Jia[1], and Bin Zhou[1]

[1] Institute of Software, Department of Computer, National University of Defense Technology, Changsha, China
{zliang,bingyingxu,yanjia,binzhou}@nudt.edu.cn
[2] Electromagnetic Spectrum Management Center of Nanjing Military Region, Nanjing, China
jiezhao@nudt.edu.cn

Abstract. New words detection is one of the most important problems in Chinese information processing. Especial in the application of new event detection, new words show the current trend of hot event and public opinion. With the fast development of Internet, the existing work based on lexicon will not be capable for the effectiveness and efficiency. In this paper, we proposed a novel method to detect new words in domain-specific fields based on Mutual Information. Firstly, the framework of detecting new word is introduced based on the mathematical feature of Mutual Information. Then, we propose a new method for measuring the distance of Mutual Information by word instead of character. Comprehensive experimental studies on People's Daily corpus show that our approach well matches the practice.

Keywords: new word detection, mutual information, measure metric, natural language.

1   Introduction

In the age of information explosion, the rapid developments of internet induce fast growing of new words. New words detection is one of the most important tasks in Chinese information processing. Firstly, the new words occur constantly. According to the report published by Thesaurus Research Center of Commercial Press, more than thousands of new words emerge and these new words mostly domain-specific technical terms (such as 'skyline 天际线') or time-sensitive political/entertainment terms (such as '科学发展观 Scientific Outlook on Development'). Secondly, different with English and other western languages, lots of Asian languages such as Chinese, Japanese, and Thai, do not delimit words by white-space. It is a challenge task for Chinese word segmentation to deal with the unknown words in Chinese natural language processing [1, 2]. Furthermore, in the application of new event detection, the new word created by users to denote the point or current trend of public opinion.

Recent studies have shown that the methods based on rule could not be applied directly to different domain fields and [3]. In hence, how to identify new words from internet text data is still extremely urgent for Chinese natural language processing.

---

* Corresponding author.

Y. Yuan, X. Wu, and Y. Lu (Eds.): ISCTCS 2012, CCIS 320, pp. 341–348, 2013.
© Springer-Verlag Berlin Heidelberg 2013

Most of previous works are either based on rule and statistics. The rule-based methods focus on the knowledge of nature language, such as the part of speech and construct the semantic lexicon [4]. Chen [5] build common rule using the knowledge of word constructions. The experiment result of their work show high precision in certain domain fields. To solve the dynamic text stream, Li [6] propose a model based on VSM (Vector Space Model) and recognize new words according to similarity of Vector Space. The key point of VSM-based work is feature selection for the corpus, which is easy to introduce some noises. Other kinds of works in new words detection is based on statistics, such as Mutual Information [7], Maximum Entropy [8] and so on. Different with the model based on rule, the statistics–based methods are not only used for domain-special, but it is constrained by the size of the data [9, 10].

As mention above, most of existing work focus on either rule-based inner feature or statistics-based extern feature, but do not simultaneously consider combining both features. With this aim in mind, we propose a novel model based on Mutual Information, which combines inner feature and extern feature, to improve the performance of new word detection. Fires of all, we introduce the framework and detection process. Next, two types of measure metric for Mutual Information using inner pattern are proposed. Finally, comprehensive experiments with bench data set are conducted to verify the effectiveness of the proposed framework.

2   New Word Detection Based on Mutual Information

This section first describes the basic principles of information recognition method based on mutual information, and then introduced the measure Metric of New word recognition .Finally, a specific algorithm is proposed.

2.1   Basic Principle

In the statistical model, Mutual information (MI) [4] is the common parameters to measure the correlation between two random variables, such as X and Y. It reflects the tightness of the combination between the two variables, which is estimated by equation (1):

$$\text{MI(x,y)} = \log \frac{p(x, y)}{p(x) \bullet p(y)} \tag{1}$$

In Eq. (1), we use $p(x, y)$ to represents co-occurrence probability of random variables x and y. the independent probability are indicated by $p(x)$ and $p(y)$. If the mutual information $MI (x, y)$ is very large, it indicates that they are close binary with relations. The greater $MI (x, y)$ is, the more closely between x and y is in a word. If the $MI (x, y)$ approximately equal to zero, indicating no obvious relationship between x and y, both appear merely by chance. If the $MI (x, y)$ is much smaller than zero, there is no combination relation between the x and y in most of text. Intuitively, we can filter the candidate binary word string which composed by two words phrase according to the values of the mutual information. That is to say, if the mutual information *MI (x, y)* close to or less than zero, binary string words will be filtered out. According to the above ideas, the model to identify new words based on mutual information can be estimated as follows. In this model, xy represents binary string word which means two consecutive words in the corpus. Moreover, $n(xy)$ represents the number of the co-occurrence and $n(y)$ indicates the word occurrences of word y. At last, $n(w)$ denotes the total number of words in the corpus.

$$\begin{cases} p(x, y) = \dfrac{n(xy)}{n(w)} \\ \quad p(x) = \dfrac{n(x)}{n(w)} \\ \quad p(y) = \dfrac{n(y)}{n(w)} \end{cases} \tag{2}$$

2.2   Measure Metric of Mutual Information

The new word is composed of a single word or multiple words and there are different kinds of word construction mode [11, 12]. According to the word construction mode, Chinese words can be divided into two categories. One category is composed of only one word and cannot be further decomposed into smaller lexical unit vocabulary, which are called unit words or single words. Another category is a combination of multi-unit word. As the statistical result of our experiment shown, more than 52.8 percent of the words from People's Daily corpus in January 1998 are binary words. In hence, we take the binary words of Chinese words as example and descript the measure process in detail as followed.

According the difference of Chinese word construction mode, all of binary words can be divided into six types, including '1+1', '1+2', '1+3', '2+1','2+2', '3+1'. For instance, the word '艰苦奋斗 working hard' is made of two words '艰苦 hard' and '奋斗 work' which both contain two characters, so it belongs to '2+2'. Another example is the word '犀利哥 Handsome Man' , which is composed of two character words '犀利Handsome' and '哥 Man' , belongs the type '2+1'. Based mentioned above, there are two ways to measure of mutual information, if the phrases which are made of more than two binary words. For example, the phrases 'W1W2W3W4' is made up of two binary words 'W1W2' and 'W3W4'. The definitions of these ways are as followed.

- Measuring using words: the way consider binary words 'W1W2' and 'W3W4' as one single unit for mutual information. For example, the word '艰苦奋斗 working hard', it view the words '艰苦 hard' and '奋斗 working' as two single unit and denoted as the symbols *x* and *y* in equation (2).
- Measuring using characters: this way only measure the mutual information of the characters between binary words. Take the binary word '艰苦奋斗 working hard' for instance; we measure the mutual information between the characters '苦' and '

奋'. In this way, the symbols x and y of $n(xy)$ in equation (2) are denoted with the characters between binary words but in the calculation of $p(x)$ and $p(y)$ still be denoted by the words '艰苦 hard' and '奋斗 working'.

The performance of these two kinds of measure ways is different with the composition of the words in corpus. In our experiment, we compare the performance between two measure ways for measuring mutual information to determine the appropriate measure metric.

2.3   Detection Algorithm

This subsection descripts the measure process of detection using mutual information. Our work validates the effectiveness of the proposed method by comparing the difference of ranking between frequency and MI. Assume that the original corpus A contains only Chinese characters. Firstly, all the documents of corpus are preprocessed by word segmentation and removing de-tagging. Next, we calculate the frequency of different category of Chinese word. One issue need to be mentioned is that this article only describes the analysis process of binary word for most of Chinese words are belong to binary word, and the analysis process of other types of word is similar to it.

We use A_N to represent the binary word whose frequency more than N and decompose all the words in corpus A_N into two units words to create corpus B. Then, corpus B_M is created by the binary words of which word frequency are more than M in corpus. Given the minimum threshold of mutual information, corpus B_M is divided into different subsets $B_Z \subset B_M$. The new words which are indicated as C can be recognized by the ranking by mutual information. So far, the proposed model can be summarized as in Algorithm 1.

```
Algorithm 1 New Word Detection based on Mutual Informa-
tion
Input: A, Z, N, M
Output: C
Begin
1: Rank the words in corpus A by frequency of appear-
ance.
2: Calculate the frequency of different category
of Chinese word
3: Create candidate new words with single words by dif-
ferent word construction mode.
5. Recognize new words by the ranking by mutual informa-
tion
End
```

3   Experiments

In this section, we show the effectiveness of our model with experiments on real data. First of all, we describe our data set and experiment setup. Next, validity evaluation of our model and detection performance comparison is conducted on the baselines and our proposed models.

3.1   Data Set and Evaluation Metrics

Our experimental corpus comes from People's Daily corpus in January 1998. There are 849660 characters, 467221 words in the corpus. The distribution of different kinds of words with different numbers of characters is shown in Fig. 1. As shown in Fig. 1, more than 52.8 percent of the words from People's Daily corpus in January 1998 are a binary word, which indicates that the major of words in this corpus are binary words.

We employ the Precision (P), Recall (R) and F value as evaluation metrics, which are defined as followed.

$$\begin{cases} \text{Precision=} \dfrac{n(w|w \in A_N \cap w \in B_Z)}{n(B_Z)} \\[4mm] \text{Recall=} \dfrac{n(w|w \in A_N \cap w \in B_Z)}{n(w \mid w \in A_N)} \\[4mm] \text{F=} 2 \times \text{Precision} \times \dfrac{\text{Re} call}{(\text{Re} call + \text{Pr} ecision)} \end{cases} \quad (3)$$

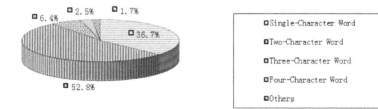

Fig. 1. Distribution of Different Kinds of Chinese Words

3.2   Validity Evaluation and Detection Result

This subsection compares the performance between two measure ways for measuring mutual information. Fig 2 shows the process of validity evaluation. In Fig 2, the words of left list are old words, and the right list is made up of the candidate new words created by the ways mentioned above.   With those two lists which are ranked by the frequency of occurrence, we validate the effectiveness of the proposed method by improved performance using mutual information. Based on the process mentioned in section 2, the results of both measuring ways are showed in Table 1 and Table 2.

The result implies the measure way for mutual information using words is better than the way using characters.

Next, we detected the new words in our data set by proposed method and show the result in Table 3. As showed in Table 3, the words of left list are the Top 15 words which are made up of old binary words and ranked by the frequency of word appearance and the right list are ranked by the mutual information. Based on two ranked list, we claim that the proposed methods can detect new words in our data set effective and efficiently.

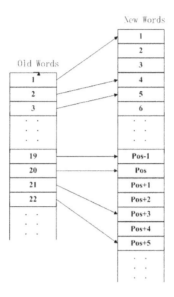

Fig. 2. The Process of Validity Evaluation

Table 1. The Result for Mutual Information using Words

MI / Mode	−1	−0.5	0	0.5	1	1.5	2	2.5	3	3.5	4	4.5
(1+2)	0.227	0.227	0.238	0.253	0.344	0.416	0.588	0.500	0.538	0.545	0.470	0.571
(1+3)	0.095	0.096	0.103	0.117	0.132	0.125	0.148	0.152	0.129	0.157	0.062	0.000
(2+1)	0.526	0.526	0.526	0.526	0.571	0.645	0.645	0.551	0.538	0.636	0.533	0.461
(2+2)	0.833	0.833	0.833	0.833	0.833	0.833	0.782	0.727	0.700	0.666	0.307	0.307
(3+1)	0.363	0.363	0.363	0.363	0.370	0.370	0.400	0.425	0.487	0.571	0.000	0.000

Table 2. The Result for Mutual Information Using Characters

MI / Mode	−1	−0.5	0	0.5	1	1.5	2	2.5	3	3.5	4	4.5
(1+2)	0.259	0.259	0.259	0.273	0.303	0.357	0.416	0.625	0.620	0.642	0.608	0.600
(1+3)	0.095	0.095	0.096	0.097	0.099	0.106	0.114	0.121	0.129	0.144	0.157	0.186
(2+1)	0.714	0.714	0.714	0.714	0.740	0.869	0.869	0.869	0.909	0.952	0.705	0.625
(2+2)	0.909	0.909	0.909	0.909	0.909	0.909	0.909	0.909	0.909	0.909	0.909	0.900
(3+1)	0.487	0.487	0.487	0.487	0.487	0.487	0.487	0.487	0.500	0.486	0.222	0.095

Table 3. The Comparison between MI and Frequency

Ranked by Frequency of Word			Ranked by Mutual Information		
Candidate Words	MI	Frequency	Candidate Words	MI	Frequency
的一	0.228	674	三优一满意	10.657	10
7年	3.215	521	轮值主席国	10.347	11
没有	4.128	494	彩虹花园	10.110	10
国的	0.174	460	配电变压器	10.096	15
新的	0.797	425	无绳电话机	10.059	12
了一	1.238	413	美容美发	10.053	17
大的	0.130	396	大红灯笼	9.946	10
是一	1.194	378	神奇旅游年	9.729	11
年的	0.060	368	防盗报警器	9.722	15
这一	1.746	367	无产阶级革命家	9.706	17
一步	3.053	365	犹太人定居点	9.705	12
可以	3.680	347	约旦河西岸	9.528	21
一年	1.116	340	刘伯承元帅	9.510	13
年来	2.173	325	防汛抗旱	9.505	10
国有	1.055	321	纪检监察	9.471	12

4   Conclusions

The identification of new words is a basic research in the field of natural language processing, information retrieval and machine translation. In this paper, based on Existing methods we proposed a new word recognition method based on mutual information for binary new words. How to make better use of mutual information to identify the effect of new words, two kinds of ways for measure mutual information are introduced and compared on true data set. The experimental results on People's Daily corpus show that our method is feasible and efficient.

Acknowledgment. The research in this paper is supported by the National High-tech R&D Program of China (No.2011AA012505, 2011AA010702, 2012AA01A401 and 2012AA01A402), Chinese National Science Foundation (No.60933005, 91124002), National Technology Support Foundation (No.2012BAH38B04) and National 242 Foundation (No.2011A010).

References

1. Sun, X., Huang, D.G., Song, H.Y., et al.: Chinese new word identification: a latent discriminative model with global features. Journal of Computer Science and Technology 26(1), 14–24 (2011)
2. Peng, F., Feng, F., Mccallum, A.: Chinese segmentation and new word detection using conditional random fields. In: Proceedings of the 20th International Conference on Computational Linguistics, p. 562 (2004)

3. Li, D., Tu, W., Shi, L.: Chinese New Word Identification Using N-Gram and PPM Models. Applied Mechanics and Materials 109, 612–616 (2012)
4. Zhang, H.J., Shi, S.M., Feng, C., et al.: A method of Part-Of-Speech guessing of Chinese Unknown Words based on combined features. In: 2009 International Conference on Machine Learning and Cybernetics, pp. 328–332 (2009)
5. Chen, K.J., Bai, M.H.: Unknown word detection for Chinese by a corpus-based learning method. International Journal of Computational Linguistics and Chinese Language Processing 3(1), 27–44 (1998)
6. Li, H., Huang, C.N., Gao, J., et al.: The use of SVM for Chinese new word identification. Natural Language Processing–IJCNLP 2005, 723–732 (2004)
7. Battiti, R.: Using mutual information for selecting features in supervised neural net learning. IEEE Transactions on Neural Networks 5(4), 537–550 (1994)
8. Phillips, S.J., Anderson, R.P., Schapire, R.E.: Maximum entropy modeling of species geographic distributions. Ecological Modeling 190(3), 23–259 (2006)
9. Nie, J.Y., Hannan, M.L., Jin, W.: Unknown word detection and segmentation of Chinese using statistical and heuristic knowledge. Communications of COLIPS 5(1), 47–57 (1995)
10. Chen, K.J., Bai, M.H.: Unknown word detection for Chinese by a corpus-based learning method. International Journal of Computational Linguistics and Chinese Language Processing 3(1), 27–44 (1998)
11. Zheng, Y., Liu, Z., Sun, M., et al.: Incorporating user behaviors in new word detection. In: Proceedings of the 21st International Joint Conference on Artificial Intelligence, pp. 2101–2106 (2009)
12. Wang, M.C., Huang, C.R., Chen, K.J.: The Identification and classification of Unknown Words in Chinese: A N-gram-Based Approach. Festschrift for Professor Akira Ikeya, 113–123 (1995)

An Efficient Parallel String Matching Algorithm Based on DFA

Yujian Fan, Hongli Zhang, Jiahui Liu, and Dongliang Xu

School of Computer Science and Technology, Harbin Institute of Technology, Harbin, China
`fanyujian2011@pact518.hit.edu.cn,`
`zhanghongli@hit.edu.cn,`
`{hitljh,xudongliang}@pact518.hit.edu.cn`

Abstract. The classical string matching algorithms are facing a great challenge on speed due to the rapid growth of information on Internet. Meanwhile, multi-core CPU has been widespread on computers. But classical string matching algorithms does not apply to multi-core CPU flexibly. It not only affects the run-time speed, but also makes a waste of the resource on CPU. In this paper, we proposed a parallel string matching algorithm based on DFA, it solved the problem effectively. By classification on the first letter of each pattern, all CPU cores could work at the same time, which do not conflict. Experiments demonstrate whether the hit rate is high or low, the algorithm has an ideal performance.

Keywords: string matching, parallel algorithm, DFA.

1 Introduction

The string matching algorithm has been a classic problem in computer science, and it is an important part in many fields, such as pattern recognition, virus scanning, content filtering, search engine, and network intrusion detection system (NIDS). In many systems, the speed of string matching algorithm has become the bottleneck. For example, in NIDS, pattern matching is the most time-consuming part. The role of pattern matching part is detecting attacks through comparing the patterns in rules with the network traffic. The paper [1] shows that the time spent on pattern matching accounted for 30% of the NIDS, and the consumption of time could increase up to 80% under intensive traffic. Thus, how to improve the speed of string matching algorithm has become a key issue to improve the performance of these systems.

Meanwhile the multi-core CPU has been increasing popularity, that each core has a separate cache and they share the memory. But traditional string matching algorithm does not give full play to the performance of the multi-core CPU, which not only affects the run-time speed, but also makes a waste of resource on CPU. In this paper, we proposed a parallel string matching algorithm based on deterministic finite automaton (DFA) which using the first letter of the pattern to classify the patterns set, and

Y. Yuan, X. Wu, and Y. Lu (Eds.): ISCTCS 2012, CCIS 320, pp. 349–356, 2013.
© Springer-Verlag Berlin Heidelberg 2013

it builds the automations that coexisted in memory. All CPU cores could work independently and collaboratively.

The rest of the paper is organized as follows. In Section 2, we summarize the related work of string matching. In Section 3, we give the description of our parallel string matching algorithm, and the method to compress the memory. The experimental results of our algorithm compared with AC algorithm are presented in Section 4. Finally, we will give a conclusion of this paper in Section 5.

2   Related Work

The problem of string matching is to find out the times of each pattern appears in text T. Throughout the paper, $P=\{P_1, P_2,...,P_k\}$ denotes the patterns set, k acts as the number of patterns.

According to the different ways of matching, Navarro *et al.* [2] divided string matching algorithms into three categories: algorithms based on prefix matching, algorithms based on suffix matching, and algorithms based on substring matching. As following it describes three representative algorithms.

1. AC algorithm [3] based on prefix. AC algorithm puts all patterns in P into an automatic machine, and utilizes it to scan the text T. The scanning process starts from the initial state, transfers to the next state according to the character read in next and the current state. It determines whether a match occurs when reaches a new state.
2. Wu-Manber algorithm [4] based on the suffix. Wu-Manber algorithm is based on the thought of BM [5] algorithm and the biggest feature of it is jumping. It creates a scan window whose length is equal to the length of the shortest pattern. Within the window, the scan direction is from right to left. It searches the longest common suffix of the window and the text T. It could jump over portions of text while meeting bad characters, thus improving the scanning speed.
3. SBOM algorithm [6] based on the substring. The scan window of SBOM algorithm is similar to the one of WM. In the window, the scan direction is also from right to left. But it searches whether there is a substring of patterns in the text T, using Factor Oracle data structure.

There also have been many parallel string matching methods in recent years besides these traditional string matching algorithms above. The main kinds are as follows.

1. *Cut the Text.* The text T is divided into $T=\{T_1,T_2,...,T_N\}$ in accordance with the number of CPU cores, and each part assigned to each core to match, then summarize the results. But this may generate some problems. Such as:
   (a) It may lose match or generate duplicate match in the intersection of two sections of text, resulting in inaccurate results.
   (b) If hit rate is higher in some sections of the text, while in others is lower, the running time will depends on the longest time, and it destroys the balance of parallel.

2. *Classify Patterns Set P.* According to the characteristic of patterns set *P*, such as the first letter of each pattern, establish classification. Each core processes the same text *T* with different patterns, and the matching results are summarized in the end. It still may have some troubles. For example, if the patterns are classified by the first letter, it may produce 26 categories, but the number of CPU cores is 2 or 4 in common, the number of classification is far greater than cores which would result in each core requires repeating many times to search the same text *T* with the different patterns classification.
3. *Choose Different Algorithms for Different Patterns.* The paper [7] maintains that the speed of string matching algorithm mainly depends on the number and minimal length of patterns. They proposed a heuristic algorithm using dynamic programming and the greedy algorithm techniques, to divide patterns set and choose an optimal string matching algorithm for them. It keeps balance of the running time on each core, to minimize total time.
4. *Rely on the Hardware.* Due to the structure of these devices, such as field programmable gate array (FPGA) [8] or graphics processing unit (GPU) [9], it can make parallel string matching algorithm run on it. However, the hardware resource is limited, so the application scenarios are restricted.

We develop a parallel string matching algorithm extended from the approaches above.

3 Parallel String Matching Algorithm Based on DFA

In this section, we will present our parallel string matching algorithm based on DFA (PSMBD). We first outline a classic string matching algorithm using DFA in sub-section 3.1. We will introduce PSMBD algorithm in detail in sub-section 3.2. Theoretical analysis is presented in sub-section 3.3. Finally, we will give a method to compress the memory in sub-section 3.4.

3.1 Description of String Matching Algorithm Using DFA

Among string matching algorithms using DFA, AC algorithm is the most classic. In pre-processing phase of AC algorithm, the patterns set *P* is converted into a definite state automata, each state with a number indicates, the input is text *T* and patterns set *P*, the output is the times of each pattern occurs. The matching process is as follows: read text *T* in order, and transfer to the next state from the initial state based on the current state and current input character with the state automata. Then check whether there is a match and make record.

This is the procedure of AC algorithm. From that we could realize when read a character in text *T*, the location in the automaton is uncertain, which led each core could not process text in parallel. Our algorithm has solved this problem.

3.2   PSMBD Algorithm

The main idea of PSMBD algorithm is to classify the patterns set by the first letter, put the patterns whose first letters are same into one DFA. These DFAs coexist in memory so that all CPU cores could access them independently. In matching process, each core enters the corresponding DFA according to the character it read. The main processes are as follows:

Pre-processing phase: read the patterns and insert them into different DFAs by the difference of first letters. The automata could use matrix to store. The difference with AC automaton is this process does not need to consider whether a pattern is prefix or suffix or substring of another. It would avoid these situations in the matching process, and save the time of pre-processing. After completing this process, the number of DFAs is same to the kinds of first letters, and these DFAs coexist in memory so that each CPU core could access them independently.

Matching process: each CPU core reads the text T in order, the character read in is regarded as the initial character, enters the corresponding DFA according to it. Within the DFA, it transfers from the initial state to the next according to the characters read in next. When reaches a state, it requires checking whether a match occurs, then makes record. One searching process will not complete until reaching the initial state or the times of transferring exceeds the maximum length of all patterns in patterns set.

3.3   Theoretical Analysis

Lemma 1. When each CPU core enters the corresponding DFA according to the character read in, all patterns led by this character existed on current location of the text T would be found.

Proof. In the matching process, after each CPU core entering the corresponding DFA according to the character read in, it will transfers to the next state according to the character read in next. After each transferring, it requires checking whether a match occurs. The searching process in DFA will not be finished until reaching the initial state which refers to matching fail, or the times of transferring exceeds the maximum length of all patterns in patterns set which means matching fail because there can be no pattern whose length is more than the maximum length of all patterns. After this search process, all patterns led by this character existed on current location of the text T will be found.

Lemma 2. Every character in the text T would enter the corresponding DFA as the initial character.

Proof. In the matching process, each CPU core reads the text T in order, and then enters the corresponding DFA. After one search process is complete, the cores will also read the rest of text T in order, which ensures that every character in the text T would enter the corresponding DFA as the initial character.

Lemma 3. In the parallel environment, this algorithm would not produce duplicate match or lost match.

Proof. Every character in text T would enter the DFA as the initial character of patterns only by one time, so it will not produce duplicate match. Each CPU core only read a single character and search for all patterns led by this character in one process of searching, so it will not lose match.

Theorem 1. All patterns existed in the text T would be found.

Proof. According to Lemma 1, Lemma 2 and Lemma 3, every character in the text T would enter the DFA as the initial letter only by one time, and within the DFA, all patterns led by this character would be found. Therefore, all patterns with different first letters may exist in the text T would be found in matching process.

3.4   Compress Transition Matrix

PSMBD algorithm uses matrix data structure to store the DFAs, so there may be many zero-states in the state table, which means jumping to initial state. This sparse matrix wasted a lot of space. Because the data structure used in PSMBD is similar to that used in AC algorithm, the method of compressing memory for AC algorithm can be used to compress transition matrix of PSMBD.

Norton proposed a format for matrix to reduce the storage space named banded-row [10]. It deletes unnecessary space at both ends of rows, and allows us to access to the valid data randomly.

Before compression: 0 0 0 2 4 0 0 0 6 0 7 0 0 0 0 0 0 0 0 0

Banded-Row Format
Number of Items: 8
Start Index: 4
Valid Values: 2 4 0 0 0 6 0 7

After compression: 8 4 2 4 0 0 0 6 0 7

Fig. 1. Banded-Row Format

The banded-row format stores the elements from the first non-zero value to the last non-zero value. To keep accessing to the data randomly we need to record the number of data elements and the starting index of the data. It is shown in Figure 1.

Before the compression, the number of items is 20. After converting to banded-row format, the number is half, so it decreases the required memory. By recording the number of data elements and the starting index, we still could access to valid data randomly. This adjustment should be applied to each row in the transition matrix, and it will greatly reduce the total storage space that occupied.

4   Experimental Results

In the experiment, the text and patterns are generated randomly. The length of the input text is 10 MB and the numbers of pattern are {10000, 20000, 40000, 80000}. The operating system is Windows 7. CPU is Intel i5-2300, which has fore cores. The RAM is 4G, and the compiler is Visual Studio 2008. We compared PSMBD algorithm with AC algorithm.

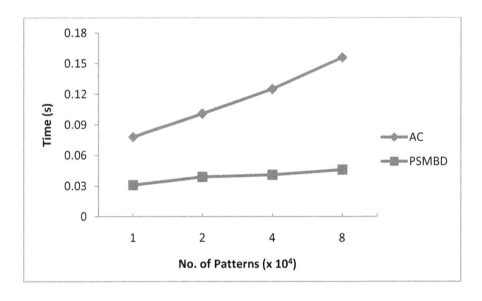

Fig. 2. Comparison on a higher hit rate

The Figure 2 shows that in the case of a higher hit rate, with the size of patterns set increases, the growth rate of time of PSMBD algorithm is less than the AC algorithm, and the time is far lower than the AC algorithm. This experiment suggests that in the case of a higher hit rate the highest speed of PSMBD algorithm is more than three times of the AC algorithm.

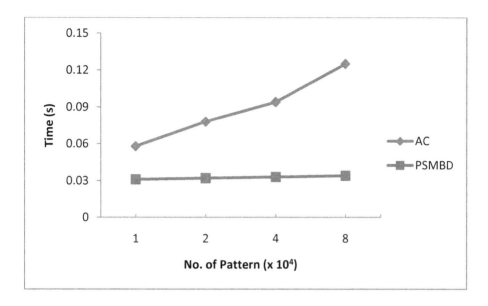

Fig. 3. Comparison on a lower hit rate

The Figure 3 shows that in the case of a lower hit rate, with the size of patterns set increases, the time that PSMBD algorithm spent is basically in a flat, and is far lower than AC algorithm. For AC algorithm, along with the size of patterns set increases, the time ascends gradually. This experiment suggests that in the case of a lower hit rate the highest speed of PSMBD is more than three times of the AC algorithm.

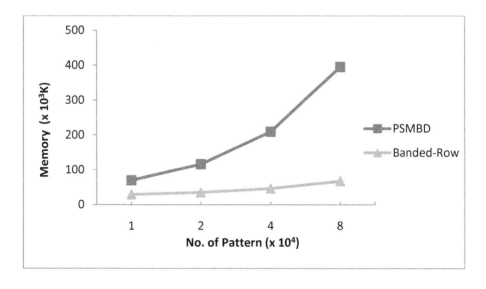

Fig. 4. Comparison between the original PSMBD and the one with Banded-Row

The Figure 4 shows that, with the size of patterns set increases, the memory PSMBD algorithm occupied increases by a big margin. While the data structures applied with banded-row format, the memory occupied by the algorithm is obvious lower. It has a less increment, and the growth rate is gentler.

5   Conclusion

We proposed a parallel string matching algorithm for multi-core CPU. It inserts patterns into different DFAs by the difference of the first letters, these DFAs coexist in the memory so that each CPU core can work independently and does not conflict. Each CPU core enters the corresponding automata according to the character it read to complete matching. Experiments show that in the same condition, whether the hit rate is high or low, the fastest speed of PSMBD algorithm could reach more than three times of AC algorithm.

Acknowledgment. This work is partially supported by the National Grand Fundamental Research 973 Program of China (Grant No. 2011CB302605), High-Tech Research and Development Plan of China (Grant No. 2010AA012504, 2011AA010705), and the National Natural Science Foundation of China (Grant No. 61173145).

References

1. Fisk, M., Varghese, G.: An Analysis of Fast String Matching Applied to Content-based Forwarding and Intrusion Detection, Technical Report CS2001-0670. University of California, San Diego (2002)
2. Navarro, G., Raffinot, M.: Flexible Pattern Matching in Strings: Practical on-line Search Algorithms or Texts and Biological Sequences. Cambridge University Press (2002)
3. Aho, A.V., Corasick, M.J.: Efficient String Matching: An Aid to Bibliographic Search. Communications of the ACM 18(6), 333–340 (1975)
4. Wu, S., Manber, U.: A Fast Algorithm For Multi-pattern Searching. Technical Report TR-94-17 (1994)
5. Boyer, R.S., Moore, J.S.: A Fast String Searching Algorithm. Communications of the ACM 10(10), 762–772 (1977)
6. Beate, C.W.: A String Matching Algorithm Fast on the Average. In: Proc. the 6th Colloquium on Automata, Languages and Programming, Graz, Austria, pp. 118–132 (1979)
7. Tan, G., et al.: Revisiting Multiple Pattern Matching Algorithms for Multi-core Architecture. Journal of Computer Science and Technology 26(5), 866–874 (2011)
8. Sidhu, R., Prasanna, V.K.: Fast Regular Expression Matching using FPGAs. In: Proc. the 9th Ann. IEEE Symp. Field-Programmable Custom Computing Machines, Rohnert, USA, pp. 227–238 (2001)
9. Qiao, G., et al.: A Graphics Processing Unit Based Multi-string Matching Algorithm for Anti-virus Systems. Energy Systems and Electrical Power, 8864–8868 (2011)
10. Norton, M.: Optimizing Pattern Matching for Intrusion Detection (2004), http://docs.idsresearch.org/OptimizingPatternMatchingForIDS.pdf

A Ciphertext Data Retrieval Method Based
on Cloud Storage

Shuo Zheng, Siyang Wang, and Cong Wang

Key Laboratory of Trustworthy Distributed Computing and Service (BUPT),
Ministry of Education, Beijing, China
{zhengshuo,xuanxuan,wangc}@bupt.edu.cn

Abstract. For the problem of mass data encryption retrieval in the cloud storage system, a three-step ciphertext data retrieval method is proposed. In this method, we introduce inverted index as the index structure, adopt the fully homomorphic and privacy homomorphism encryption algorithm and design a three-step retrieval strategy. The first step matches on the ciphertext index precisely, and the other two extend the word into other forms and correct the wrong word to query again. The latter two steps will be executed under the circumstance that the returned result is lower than the pre-set threshold. This ciphertext data retrieval method based on cloud storage improve the privacy of stored data and makes every effort to render users obtain the result they expect. The proof shows it is effective.

Keywords: inverted index, metadata, encryption algorithm.

1 Introduction

Recently, with the development of cloud computing, a lot of new applications are extended, such as Internet of Things, cloud security and cloud storage. Cloud storage is a system that varieties of storage devices work together through network applications to provide data storage and download functions to users. [1]

Since plenty of data need to be stored, and cloud storage has the advantages of low-cost, extensibility, high capacity and independence of physical storage devices [2], data storage on the cloud computing system is growing exponentially. So cloud storage security issues are concerned. To ensure data security in cloud computing, cloud server-side must provide certification services, data encryption storage, security management, security logs and data recovery, backing up for disaster recovery [3]. To encrypt stored data is one of the core functionality in the cloud storage service.

Encrypted storage means that data in the cloud computing system is encrypted and non-identifiable. The order of plaintext and ciphertext is different, thus encrypted data retrieval has difficulties. Therefore, encryption retrieval problems must be overcome.

In order to solve the problems stated above, a ciphertext data retrieval method is proposed. It could retrieve ciphertext data with high efficiency and good performance. However, problems such as the implementation of encryption algorithm in database, the key management and distribution still exist, these need to be solved in the future.

Y. Yuan, X. Wu, and Y. Lu (Eds.): ISCTCS 2012, CCIS 320, pp. 357–364, 2013.
© Springer-Verlag Berlin Heidelberg 2013

2   Related Work

For the research about retrieving the encrypted information, main algorithms include linear search algorithm [4], public key encryption with keyword search algorithm [5], security index algorithm [6] etc. Above methods will produce mass data with high cost, in addition, the sorting of relevant documents is another problem. These two problems are expected to be solved under the cloud storage environment.

Ligang Guo, et al. [7] proposes a method that creates the plaintext inverted index file based on the plaintext database, and then encrypt the plaintext inverted index file into that of a ciphertext. More concretely, they create ciphertext database table according to the plaintext table, encrypt all fields except the primary key (DocID) and finally delete the plaintext table.

Yu Liang, et al. [8] proposes a vague-keyword search under encrypted environment in cloud computing. This method generates a fuzzy set of keywords based on the k-gram index and can ensure data privacy.

Compared with the work above, our retrieval method has several advantages. First, to extract and encrypt the index information at local database can avoid the cloud server touch with the plaintext information and will improve the security and privacy of user data. Besides, the design of simplified index structure not only ensures the highly efficient retrieval, but also reduces the pressure of storage in encrypted database. Furthermore, the combination of storage structure and encryption sort algorithm enable users get the high correlation data first and at the same time, the three-step retrieval strategy makes every effort to render users obtain the result they expect.

3   The Framework of System

3.1   Files Uploading by User

Previously, users are concerned if the data files can be safely stored on the server side, which means except for the server and the user who uploads the file, the file is confidential to a third party. In our system model, we assume that the cloud server side is not credible, which means the server cannot contact the plaintext information. Therefore, in the process of uploading the files to the server, the encrypted index documents must be established at local database, rather thanat server side directly.

The process that users upload the files to the server database is as follow:

(1) Authorized uploader applies to upload files, then cloud server distributes uploader a file id (DocID). After that,the uploader uploads the plaintext file and the ciphertext file to the local database.
(2) Local database extracts keywords and creates an index file. Then it uploads the encrypted index file and the ciphertext file to the cloud encrypted database.
(3) Encrypted database sends the encrypted file to the cloud storage system.

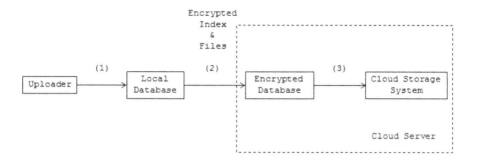

Fig. 1. The process that user uploads a file

3.2   The Establishment of the Index File

Under the environment of cloud computing, the server will store large amounts of data for authorized users, so the storage of index file will be a large resource-cost. In view of this mass storage, the structure of index file should be simplified, this would not only ensure a rapid retrieval, but also mitigate the pressure of the index server.

Here, we build an index called "inverted index". It consists of two parts:

(1) Index table: the index table is a collection of different index keywords, and the keyword id is set for the primary key.
(2)Record table: the record table records the documents that contain the index words and some information about these documents. DocID is the primary key.

The structure of the inverted index file is shown as follows:

Table 1. Index table

WordID	Word	NDocs	Offset
N1	W1	d1	a1

Table 2. Record table

DocID	Nhits
Doc1	h1

In order to simplify the storage structure, thereby reducing the overhead of the index server, the index table contains keyword id (WordID), keyword (Word), the number of documents that contain one specific keyword (NDocs) and the offset field (Offset). Offset field is actually a pointer that points to the record table so as to record the location of documents in the record table that contain the keyword. The record table only contains file id (DocID), as well as the number of one specific word in a document (NHits).NHits is used for sorting the files so that highly relevant documents are returned to the users first. Of course, in order to improve the record of document information, the index server can store other specific fields to meet the user's needs.

3.3   Encryption Method

Some parts that need to be encrypted when users upload files throughout the process are as follows:

First, ciphertext file that user uploads need to be encryptedwith symmetric encryption algorithmusing the user's secret key. After the file encryption, uploader needs to submit the key K and DocID to the trusted third party. In order to protect the security of key K, the trusted third party can take a public key encryption method to encrypt K to generate K'. In order to obtain the key K to decrypt the file, the uploader needs to use the private key to decrypt the key K' first, and the private key is included in the certificate of the authorized user.

Second, the established ciphertext index also needs to be encrypted. The usual ways of database encryption are encryption of the field, record, and attributing as the smallest unit [10]. In order to make the query more efficient, we adopt fine-grained encryption, which means encryption with field classification.

In the index table, WordID field does not require encryption and the Offset field response mapping of the two tables, which cannot be encrypted. The Word field is generated by the keyword after the process of one-way trap door. nDocs require frequent changes, so it needs to be encrypted by privacy homomorphism technology[11], which can guarantee to operate directly on the basis of the ciphertext, and this would not affect the decrypted result.

In the record table, Frequency (NHits) needs to be encrypted. This field is related to the final document relevance ranking, so it needs to use a special encryption method. Swaminathan et al. [12] proposed an encryption sort search algorithm. This algorithm can sort the document corresponding to the frequency of word that is encrypted by an isotonic algorithm and return the highly relevant documents. However, this algorithm is only suitable for a single keyword search. So in order to solve this problem, Gentry [13] proposed a fully homomorphic encryption algorithm to encrypt the word frequency information and this algorithm can sort the documents of multi-keyword search.

4   Design of Query Method

The basis of retrieval is to extract keywords by using word segmentation, which allows the user to do an exact search with keywords after a one-way trapdoor function processing.

The retrieval process is as follows:

(1) The users submit search terms to the server.
(2) Keywords are generated after the metadata processes the search terms, and then cloud server system uses MD5 algorithm to compute the hash value of keywords.

(3) The Encrypted database finds matching Word, and uses the Offset pointer to find the corresponding DocID.

(4) The cloud storage system finds the appropriate ciphertext documents based on the DocID, sends the documents and their information back to the user.

(5) If the returned result is unable to meet the needs of users, the index word will be re-processed by the metadataand retrieve again.

(6) If the result meets the requirements, the authorized user submits DocID to the Key Management Center(KMC).

(7) The authorized user will obtain the key to decrypt the document from KMC according to DocID and then decrypt the documents.

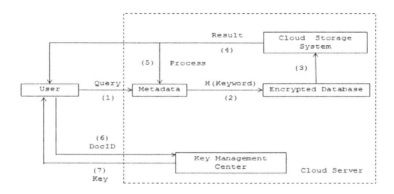

Fig. 2. The process of retrieval

Here metadata is a set of transformational rules. It involves three steps of processing strategy:

Step 1. User inputs the query words and metadata can search directly with the hash value of index keyword without doing any operations.

Step 2. The index keyword will be refined if the number of documents returned in step 1 is less than a preset threshold. Considering the different forms of the same word (eg., book, books) have a total different hash value,it is quite possible that if the user enters the word "book" and also wants to get the articles that contain the keyword "books", thus the Rule Set must be able to deal with this kind of search. Common processing includes the word case conversion, the conversion of singular and plural nouns, verb tenses transform and part-of-speech transform. Herewe take verb tenses transform as an example to explain the Rule Set processing. Verbs have four forms, namely present tense, past tense, present participle and past participle. The suffix of the past participle and past tense is the same and can be classified as a same class. In this way, the Rule Set can firstly determine the state that the retrieval word belongs to, and then the verb is converted to the other two kinds of tense, calculating hash value, and searching in index table again.

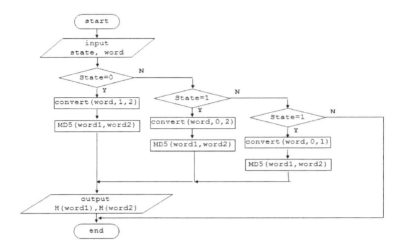

Fig. 3. The algorithm of converting one verb into other tenses

In the algorithm, *state* presents the form of the each word, *H(word)* refers the hash value of word, *convert* is a function that changes the word into the other two forms, and *MD5* is also a function that calculates hash value.

Step 3. If the result afterprocessing in step 2 still fails to meet the requirements, we will consider that the input of search terms are misspelled. In order to solve the error of keywords spelling, we introduce the concept of edit distance[16].

With the edit distance, a spell checking method is proposed [14]. Given a string s, we are trying to find the correction c, out of all possible corrections, that maximizes the probability of c to s, it could be written as $argmax_c P(c|s)$. Here, $P(c|s)$ represents the probability that user input an s while actually he wants to input c, $argmax_c$ represents the feasible c that has the maximum probability.

According to Bayes' Theorem, the expression above could convert to $argmax_c P(s|c)P(c)/P(s)$. We might ignore $P(s)$ since it is the same for every possible c. So the expression could be written as $argmax_c P(s|c)P(c)$.

In our view, when the metadata discovers a user's wrong keywords, it should be able to give the corresponding change strategy quickly. It does not have to elect one with the maximum possibility, $argmax_c$, but should sort every possible correct words based on $P(s|c)P(c)$. The metadata returns the corrected words in order and the user selects the word that he want. This would involve the issue of how to sort these words. Our schema is that we give different weightiness to different edit distances, namely the shorter the edit distance is, the bigger the $P(s|c)$ is, and $P(c)$ could be figured out in advance, so the value of $P(s|c)P(c)$ is determined.

After the spelling correction stated above, the corrected keywords will be searched again and then the user can decrypt the result with the appropriate key. .

At the same time, the proposed retrieval method can satisfy the Boolean query. For example, if a user enterstwo words (hello, world), then they will be queried respectively.Finally, the systemwill do Boolean operations to the results so as to obtain documents that meet the user's requirements.

5   Evaluation

In order to test for the efficiency and effectiveness of this three-step ciphertext data retrieval method, we rewrited Nutch-an open source platform- as our testing tool.We changed the index structure of it and stored the index words in MD5 hash value. Besides, a spell checking method was used, which is described above.

During the experiment, we set the threshold to 500, namely that the retrieval strategy will continue to be executed if the number of returned result is lower than 500. Meanwhile, we chose fifty words as our test samples. These words contained both correct words and incorrect words, because we want to make sure that all three steps will be executed at least one time.

The result of experiment is shown as follows:

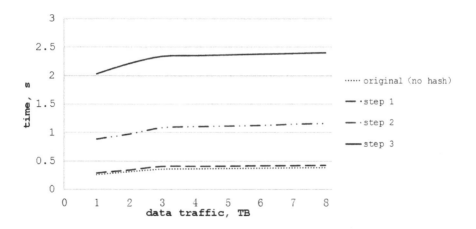

Fig. 4. The retrieval time after processing of each step

Here we only considered the situation of a single query word. From the result, we could see that after the index words processed by MD5, the efficiency of step 1 didn't drop obviously. However, the retrieval time is greatly increased after processing by step 2 and step 3, which is mainly because there is at least three retrieval times in step 2 and step 3.Also, the correction of wrong wordsand the tense conversion of words need time. For the word whose edit distance is longer than three, we didn't take them into consider, because the existence of these words will greatly affect the retrieval efficiency. In short, the result we obtained revealed that the efficiency and effectiveness of this ciphertext retrieval method is satisfactory.

6   Conclusion

The widespread use of cloud storage system brings a lot convenience to the data storage and transmission,meanwhile, the security of data storage in cloud storage system has become a hot topic. Here, we propose athree-step ciphertext data retrieval method, which could ensure the data security on the cloud storage system. Furthermore, we introduce the concrete strategy that lets the metadata deal with user input words, which could enable data retrieval to become user-friendlier. Our future work will focus on analyzing the elements that restrict the performance and efficiency of ciphertext data retrieval.

Acknowledgements. We are very grateful to Dr. Wong Kee Hau and Dr. Yao Wenbin for their careful revision to the manuscript.

References

1. Cloud Storage, http://en.wikipedia.org/wiki/Cloud_storage
2. Shen, J.: Research of Cloud Storage and Its Security. J. Computer Knowledge and Technology 7, 3829–3832 (2011)
3. Huang, Y., Zhang, J., Li, X.: Encrypted Storage and Its Retrieval in Cloud Storage Applications. J. ZTE Communication 16, 33–35 (2010)
4. Song, D., Wagner, D., Perrig, A.: Practical Techniques for Searches on Encrypted Data. In: The IEEE Symposium on Security and Privacy(S&P 2000), pp. 44–55. IEEE, Piscataway (2000)
5. Boneh, D., Di Crescenzo, G., Ostrovsky, R., Persiano, G.: Public Key Encryption with Keyword Search. In: Cachin, C., Camenisch, J.L. (eds.) EUROCRYPT 2004. LNCS, vol. 3027, pp. 506–522. Springer, Heidelberg (2004)
6. Park, D.J., Kim, K., Lee, P.J.: Public Key Encryption with Conjunctive Field Keyword Search. In: Lim, C.H., Yung, M. (eds.) WISA 2004. LNCS, vol. 3325, pp. 73–86. Springer, Heidelberg (2005)
7. Guo, L., Yao, H.: Research on Encrypted Database Search Method based on Inverted Index. J. Computer Science 9, 13–15 (2010)
8. Liang, Y., Lu, J., Liu, L., Zhang, C.: Vague-keyword Search under Encrypted Environment in Cloud Computing. J. Computer Science 38, 99–100 (2011)
9. Zhao, X., Ye, Z.: Research and Comparison of Several Database Encryption Technologies. J. Computer Technology and Development 17, 219–222 (2007)
10. Dai, Y., Shang, J., Su, Z.: Quick Index on Encrypted Database. J. Journal of Tsinghua University (Sci. & Tech.) 37, 24–27 (1997)
11. Rivest, R.L., Adleman, L., Dertouzos, M.L.: On Data Banks and Privacy Homomorphism. In: DeMillo, R.D. (ed.) Foundations of Secure Computations, pp. 169–177. Academic Press (1978)
12. Swaminathan, A., Mao, Y., Su, G.M., et al.: Confidentiality-Preserving Rank-Ordered Search. In: The 2007 ACM Workshop on Storage Security and Survivability (StorageSS 2007), pp. 7–12. ACM, New York (2007)
13. Gentry, C.: Fully Homomorphic Encryption Using Ideal Lattices. In: The 41st Annual ACM Symposium on Theory of Computing (STOC 2009), pp. 169–178. ACM, New York (2009)
14. Norvig, P.: How to Write a Spelling Corrector, http://norvig.com/spell-correct.html
15. Wang, X., Shangping, W., Qin, B.: Research on Database Encrypt ion and Verification Methods. Journal of Xi'an University of Technology 18, 263–268 (2002)
16. Levenshtein: О границах для упаковок в п-мерном евклидовом пространстве. Doklady Akademii Nauk SSR 245, 1299–1303 (1979)

A Multi-phase *k*-anonymity Algorithm
Based on Clustering Techniques

Fei Liu, Yan Jia, and Weihong Han

School of Computer Science, National University of Defense Technology, Changsha, China
1986figo@163.com

Abstract. We proposed a new *k*-anonymity algorithm to publish datasets with privacy protection. We improved clustering techniquesto lower data distort and enhance diversity of sensitive attributes values. Our algorithm includes four phases. Tuples are distributed to several groups in phase one. Tuples in a group own same sensitive value. In phase two, groups smaller than the threshold merge and then they are partitioned into several clusters according to quasi-identifier attributes. Each cluster would become an equivalence class. In phase three, remainder tuples are distributed to clusters evenly to satisfy L-diversity. Finally, quasi-identifier attributes values in each cluster are generalized to satisfy *k*-anonymity. We used OCC dataset to compare our algorithm with classic method based on clustering. Empirical results showed that our algorithm could be used to publish datasets with high security and limited information loss.

Keywords: privacy protection, k-anonymity, cluster, L-diversity.

1 Introduction

In modern society, a vast amount of data and information has been stored by different organizations. Most of the data would be published for research and other purposes. However, some sensitive information even person details could be disclosed in this process.This motived us to propose an effective method to protect privacy information while publishing datasets.

Data publication with privacy preservation has received considerable attention from information security community and *k*-anonymity [1] has been an effective method. Quasi-identify (QI) attributes are used to identify a person and generalized to shield sensitive information. Tuples in dataset published are requested to be confused among at least k tuples. These k tuples own same quasi-identifier attributes valuesand form an equivalence class. Sensitive attribute value of a tuple can't be distinguished from others in the equivalence class.Although generalization improved security of dataset, QI attribute values are distorted andmuchuseful information is destroyed.In order to solve this problem, researchers introducedclustering techniques in *k*-anonymityalgorithm [2,3].Tuples close with each other in the space of QI attributes are distributed into a cluster. Every cluster is an equivalence-class. QI attributes values change little in generalization, but these methods focused on numerical attributes.Jiuyong

Y. Yuan, X. Wu, and Y. Lu (Eds.): ISCTCS 2012, CCIS 320, pp. 365–372, 2013.
© Springer-Verlag Berlin Heidelberg 2013

Li et al.[4]introduced Hierarchical Taxonomy Tree. They used k-anonymityon different types of data, including numerical and categorical ones.They also defined distance
in different attributes values.Md. EnamulKabir et al. [5] proposed a kind of clustering
technology, but it needs sorting first.Ji-Won Byun et al. [6] proved that it's NP-hard to
find best clusters.They proposed clustering techniquesbased on greedy algorithm.

Methods above paid little attention on security of dataset against information
losses.This made dataset suffer homogeneity attack easily[7].Machanavajjhala, A. et
al. [7] proposed the idea of L-diversity .There must be L different values of sensitive
attribute at least and no proportion of value exceeds the threshold.L-diversity improved security of dataset. We improved k-anonymity algorithm by integrating clustering techniques and L-diversity to improve security of dataset while lowering
information loss.

2   The Proposed Algorithm

We distributed tuples into different groups by sensitive attribute values.Then we
merged groups who were smaller than the threshold into one group.The group was
partitioned into clusters using method proposed in reference [6].Each cluster would
become an equivalence class.Tuple in groups whose size are higher than the threshold
would be distributed into equivalence classes evenly.Finally we generalized QI
attributes values according to Hierarchical Taxonomy Trees of every attributeequiva-
lence classes. Our algorithm works on datasets with one sensitive attribute.

2.1   Preliminary Definitions

Our work bases on classic definitions of k-anonymity[1] such asQuasi-identifier
Attributes, Sensitive Attribute and Equivalence Class.The anonymity techniques proposed focus on both numerical and categorical attributes. We used Hierarchical
Taxonomy Tree[7] to describe every attribute. Besides that we introduce some new
definitions.

- *Definition 1.(DistancetoAncestor)*. In Hierarchical Taxonomy Tree of an arbitrary
  attribute, we defined Improved Weighted Hierarchical Distance (IWHD)analogous
  with WHD [8].For node a_i , Distance from a_i to its ancestor a_j is as
  lows: IWHD$(a_i, a_j) = \sum_{k=i}^{j+1} w_{k,k-1} / \sum_{k=n}^{2} w_{k,k-1}$, where $\{a_i, a_{i+1} \ldots \ldots a_j\}$ are a
  serial of nodes from a_i to a_j in the tree. $\{i, i+1, \ldots \ldots j\}$are level numbers of
  nodes. Level number of root node is 1. $w_{k,k-1}$is the weight between level k and
  level $k-1$ in the tree.$w_{k,k-1}$is determined by the amount of nodes in level k and
  $k-1$:$w_{k,k-1} = n_k/n_{k-1}$, where n_k is the amount of nodes in level k. More
  nodes in one level, higher differentiation degree of the attribute and more importance of the level. As shown in Fig 1.$w_{2,1} = 2/1 = 2$, $w_{3,2} = 4/2 = 2$, distance
  from node "heart disease" to "disease" is $2/(2+2) = 1/2$, distance from node
  "gastric cancer" to "disease" is $(2+2)/(2+2) = 1$.

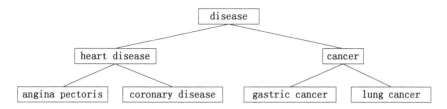

Fig. 1. Hierarchical Taxonomy Tree

- *Definition2.(Distancebetween Two Values).*The distance between two arbitrary values of an attribute is the mean value of distances to their nearest common ancestor in the Hierarchical Taxonomy Tree.Formallya_i and a_k are two nodes in the HierarchicalTaxonomy Tree of an attribute andIWHD$(a_i, a_k) = ($IWHD$(a_i, a_j) + $IWHD$(a_k, a_j))/2$, where a_j is the nearest ancestor of a_i and a_k.As shown in Fig 1, Distance between "heart disease" and "gastric cancer"is $(1/2 + 1)/2 = 3/4$.
- *Definition3.(Distancebetween Two Tuples).* Distance between two arbitrary tuples is the sum of distances betweenQI attributes values.
- *Definition4.(Information Loss).*For arbitrary tuple t, t' is the tuple after generalization of t.The information loss of t' is the distance from $t$to t'.Information loss of an equivalence class is the sum of all tuples' information loss.The mean information loss of a dataset is the mean value of all equivalence classes' information loss.Formally for an set of tuples G (it could be a cluster or an equivalence class),$\{Q_1, Q_2 \dots Q_N\}$ are QI attributes in G. $N$is the amount of QI attributes. $\{t_1, t_2 \dots t_n\}$are tuples in G.$n$is the amount of tuples. Information loss of Gafter generalization is:

$$D(G) = \sum_{i=1}^n \left(\sum_{j=1}^N IWHD\left(a_{t_iQ_j}, a_{Q_j}\right)\right) \tag{1}$$

$a_{t_iQ_j}$isthe original value of t_i in attribute Q_j, a_{Q_j} is the value after generalization.

- *Definition5.(Diversity).*We use the definition of Entropy L-Diversity to calculate information entropy of every security attribute value.Larger information entropy value means higher diversity value.For an equivalence class q its information entropyis $-\sum_{s\in S} p(q,s) \log(p(q,s))$, where S is the set of sensitive attribute values and $p(q,s) = \frac{n(q,s)}{\sum_{s'\in S} n(q,s')}$.Mean diversity is the mean value of all equivalence classes' diversity values.

2.2   Details of Algorithm

In our new algorithm, Hierarchical Taxonomy Trees must be constructed first. The algorithm can be dividedinto four phases that isgrouping, clustering, distribution and generalization. $\{Q_1, Q_2 \dots Q_N\}$ are QI attributes in G. N is the amount of QI attributes.$A$is the sensitive attribute.

Phase 1. Grouping
Every tuple in dataset is put in a group. Tuples in a group own same sensitive value.We can get a set groups of tuples: $G = \{G_1, G_2 \dots G_M\}$. Sizes of groups are$\{Size(G_1), Size(G_1) \dots Size(G_M)\}$.

Phase 2. Clustering
In practical application, sizes of groups are imbalance.Amount of tuples with some sensitive attribute value maybe much larger than others'.Besides that, tuples' sensitive attribute values could be similar with each other if their QI attributes values are close to each other.For example, most people from 30 to 40 years old often have a good income but people from 20 to 30 years old always own a lower one.If we cluster all tuples according to QI attributes values, tuples in an equivalence class may have same sensitive attribute value. Attacker can guess the sensitive attribute value of a tuple and the dataset published suffer homogeneity attack easily.

H_{Size}, threshold of every group's proportion in the entire dataset is set in advance by user.Groups smaller than H_{Size} are mergedinto one group.Greedy k-member algorithm is used to partition the group into clusters.Details of the algorithm can be found in reference [6]. The algorithm uses greedy technique to construct clusters one by one.The key of the algorithm is to put the best tuple into a cluster. If putting a tuple into a cluster produces least information loss, the tuple is the best one.We use formula (1) to replace Information Loss Function $IL(e)$in*greedy_k_member _clustering*[6]algorithm and construct and *improved_greedy_k_member_clustering algorithm*.New algorithm produces a set of clusters C. Every cluster is an equivalence class in dataset published.

```
Function:clustering(G_big,G_small,G_i,H_size,N_t)
Input: a set of groupsG={G_1,G_2…G_M }, a threshold valueH_size,
    a set of groups G_big ,a set of tuples G_small and the
    amount of tuples N_t.
Output: a set of clusters/equivalence classes each of
    witch contains no less than k tuples.

1. G_big=Φ;G_small=Φ;
2. for (i=1…M)
3.    if Size(G_i)>H_size·N_t
4. G_big=G_bigU{G_i};
5. G_small=G_smallUG_i;
6.    end if;
7. end for;
8. C=improved_greedy_k_member_clustering(G_small,k);
9. return C;

End;
```

Phase 3.Distribution
We distribute tuples in $G_{i=1\dots\dots M \wedge G_i \in G_{big}}$ into equivalence classes $C_k(k = 1 \dots N_e)$in C. $N_e$is the amount of equivalence classes in C. $N_{G_i}$is the amount of tuples in G_i. Amount of tuples distributed from G_i to C_k is $\lfloor Size(G_i)/N_e \rfloor$ or$\lceil Size(G_i)/N_e \rceil$. For a tuple to be distributed, we look for the best equivalence class. When the tuple is

distributed to the best equivalence class, it causes least information loss. For an arbitrary equivalence class, if there are too many tuples coming from the same group with the tuple being distributed, it would be skipped.Details can be found in function $distribution(C, G_{big})$, where function $find\_best\_EC(C, G_i, t_j, h)$ is used to find the best equivalence class.

```
Function: distribution(C,G_big)
Input: a set of clusters/equivalence classesC, a set of
    groups G_big and a set of groups of tuples G={G_1,G_2...G_M }.

  1. for (i=1...M)
  2.    if G_i∈G_big
  3.        for (j=1...N_Gi)
  4. C_k=find_best_EC(C,G_i,t_j,(⌊Size(G_i))/N_e⌋);
  5. C_k=C_kU{t_j };
  6. G_i=G_i-{t_j };
  7.        end for;
  8. if size(G_i)>0
  9. for (j=1...N_Gi)
 10. C_k=find_best_EC(C,G_i,t_j,(⌊Size(G_i))/N_e⌋);
 11. C_k=C_kU{t_j};
 12. G_i=G_i-{t_j};
 13.          end for;
 14.        end if;
 15.    end if;
 16. end for;

 End;


Function: find_best_EC(C,G_i,t_j,h)
Input: a set of clusters/equivalence classesC, a groupG_i,
    a tuple t_j and a threshold value h
Output: a cluster/equivalence class C_k

  1. min=∞, best=null
  2. for (k=1...N_e)
  3.    if less than h tuples in C_k came from G_i
  4.       ΔD=D(C_kU{t_j})-D(C_k);
  5. if  ΔD<min
  6. min=ΔD;
  7. best=C_k;
  8.       end if;
  9.    end if;
 10. end for;
 11. return C_k;

End;
```

Phase 4.Generalization
Every QI attribute value is generalized to its nearest ancestor in the equivalence class.

3   Experiments

We performed experiments on real dataset OCC[9]. Each data set contains 600K tuples from American census data. OCC data set has a sensitive attribute Occupation, in addition to four QI attributes, Age, Gender, Education and Birthplace. All attribute values are discrete[10]. We used part of the dataset in our experiments.We compared our new algorithm and *greedy_k_member_clustering* (k-memberin short) algorithm intime cost, mean information loss and mean diversity.We did our experiments on a Intel(R) Core(TM)2 duo computer with two 2.66 GHz processors and 1.98 GB RAM running Windows XP.We coded algorithms in Java.

Experiment 1.We compared our new algorithm with*k-member* algorithm in time costwith$k = 100$and $k = 500$respectively.New algorithms with threshold H_{Size} (h in short) value 0.01 and 0.001weretested.Size of dataset was changed from 5k to 50k. As shown in Fig 2,time cost of *k-member* is much higher than new algorithms. When h is 0.01, time cost of new algorithm falls 22.3% than that of*k-member* in average.When h is 0.001,time cost of new algorithm is only about 7.9% of *k-member*'s.We can find that parameter k takes little effect on time cost in algorithms and smaller H_{Size} value brings lower time cost.

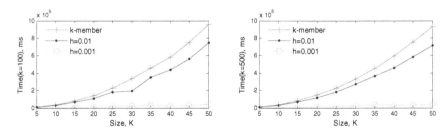

Fig. 2. Comparing of time cost among algorithms with k=100 (L) and k=500 (R)

Experiment2.We compared our new algorithm with*k-member* algorithm in mean information loss with $k = 100$and $k = 500$respectively.New algorithms with threshold H_{Size} (h in short) value 0.01 and 0.001 were tested. Size of dataset was changed from 5k to 50k. As shown in Fig 3, new algorithm causes more information loss than *k-member*. When H_{Size} is 0.01, mean information loss of new algorithm is similar with *k-member*. When H_{Size} changes to 0.001, information loss rises.When k is 100 and h is 0.01, mean information loss of new algorithm is no more than 1. When k is 100 and h is 0.001, mean information loss of new algorithm is between 2.1 and 2.7.When k is 500 and h is 0.01, mean information loss of new algorithm decreases from 1.731 to 0.961 with the increase of dataset's size.When k is 500 and h is 0.001, mean information loss of new algorithm is between 2.748 and 3.481.

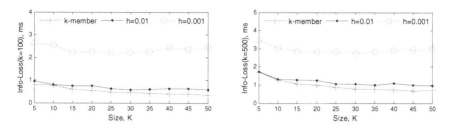

Fig. 3. Comparing of mean information loss among algorithms with k=100 (L) and k=500 (R)

Experiment 3.We compared our new algorithm with*k-member* algorithm in mean diversity with $k = 100$and $k = 500$respectively.New algorithms with threshold H_{Size} (*h* in short) value 0.01 and 0.001 were tested. Size of dataset was changed from 5k to 50k. We can findresult in Fig 4 that diversity of dataset produced by *k-member* is poor and it is no correlated with size of dataset.When k is 100, diversity of *k-member* is about 4.6, diversity of new algorithm with h=0.01 is about 4.7.When H_{Size} declines, diversity rises.Diversity of new algorithm with h=0.001 is no less than 5.7. When k is 500, diversities of all algorithms increase. Diversity of *k-member* is about 6.2. New algorithm's diversity with h=0.01 is about 6.4. When h is 0.001, diversity is no less than 7.58.

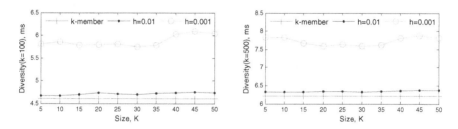

Fig. 4. Comparing of mean diversity among algorithms with k=100 (L) and k=500 (R)

4   Conclusion

In this paper, we did researchon techniques towards privacy protecting datasets publication.We proposed a new *k*-anonymity algorithm.It improves diversity of sensitive attribute values while limiting information loss in generalization.Experiments resultsshow thatour new algorithm can improve security of datasets in different degrees with different parameters values.But it's at the cost of some information loss.The new algorithm is suitable for areas with high security requirement.

Acknowledgement. The authors work was sponsoredby 863, The National High Technology Research and Development Program of China (2010AA012505, 2011AA010702, 2012AA01A401, 2012AA01A402), the Nature Science Foundation of China   (60933005), Support Science and Technology Project of China (2012BAH38B04) and Information Safety Plan of China 242.

The authors would like to thank Steven Ruggles, J. Trent Alexander, Katie Gena-dek, Ronald Goeken, Matthew B. Schroeder, and Matthew Sobek for the Integrated Public Use Microdata Series: Version 5.0 [Ma-chine-readable database]. Minneapolis: University of Minnesota, 2010.

References

1. Sweeney, L.: k-anonymity: a model for protecting privacy. Int. J. Uncertain. Fuzziness and Knowledge-based Systems 10(5), 557–570 (2002)
2. Aggarwal, C.C.: On k-anonymity and the curse of dimensionality. In: VLDB 2005, pp. 901–909 (2005)
3. Aggarwal, G., Feder, T., Kenthapadi, K., Zhu, A., Panigrahy, R., Thomas, D.: Achieving anonymity via clustering in a metric space. In: PODS, pp. 153–162 (2006)
4. Li, J., Wong, R.C.-W., Fu, A.W.-c., Pei, J.: Achieving k-Anonymity by Clustering in Attribute Hierarchical Structures. In: Tjoa, A.M., Trujillo, J. (eds.) DaWaK 2006. LNCS, vol. 4081, pp. 405–416. Springer, Heidelberg (2006)
5. EnamulKabir, M., Wang, H., Bertino, E.: Efficient Systematic Clustering Method for k-Anonymization. ActaInformatic 48(1), 51–66 (2011)
6. Byun, J.-W., Kamra, A., Bertino, E., Li, N.: Efficient k-Anonymization Using Clustering Techniques. In: Kotagiri, R., Radha Krishna, P., Mohania, M., Nantajeewarawat, E. (eds.) DASFAA 2007. LNCS, vol. 4443, pp. 188–200. Springer, Heidelberg (2007)
7. Machanavajjhala, A., Kifer, D., Gehrke, J., Venkitasubramaniam, M.: L-diversity: Privacy beyond k-anonymity. In: ICDE, p. 24 (2006)
8. Li, J., Wong, R.C.-W., Fu, A.W.-C., Pei, J.: Anonymisation by Local Recoding in Data with Attribute Hierarchical Taxonomies. IEEE Transactions on Knowledge and Data Engineering 20, 1181–1194 (2008)
9. MPC Data Projects, http://ipums.org
10. He, Y., Barman, S., Naughton, J.F.: Preventing Equivalence Attacks in Updated,Anonymized Data. In: ICDE, pp. 529–540 (2011)

A P2P Reputation Model Based on P2P File-Sharing Behavioral Characteristics

Chao Xin, Hui-jun Han, Xiu-qin Lin, and Geng-yu Wei

Lab of Computer Network and Information Security, BUPT, Beijing, China
Key Laboratory of Trustworthy Distributed Computing and Service (BUPT),
Ministry of Education, Beijing, China
{xinchao,weigengyu}@bupt.edu.cn

Abstract. In recent years, P2P networks have become a focus in the industry. The P2P network is open and anonymous, providing the opportunity for false documents, malicious attacks and other malicious acts, so its trust and security issues have emerged. Building reputation model in the P2P network environment is an effective way to solve these problems, but traditional reputation model neglect the difference of pollution files. The more popular of pollution file, the more damage it will bring to P2P network. Tosolve this problem, a P2P reputation model based on P2P file-sharing behavioral characteristics is proposed. By analyzing the P2P file-sharing behavioral characteristics, determine the file's propagation degree. Usethe file's propagation degreeto calculate the files'evaluation value and nodes' reputation value.By this means, increase the reliability of the reputation model, so as toimprove the P2P network security.

Keywords: P2P network, reputation model, file-sharing behavioral characteristics, network security.

1 Introduction

Due to P2P network's anonymity and open characteristics, it's difficult to find an effective and feasiblemethod tosolvethe P2P network securityissues. Traditional network security technologies are also difficult to apply to the P2Pnetwork. How to establish a reasonable and effective reputation mechanism in P2P networks become a hotresearch scholars [1].

Traditional P2P reputationmodeltendto onlyconsider the quality of the documents (authenticity / contaminated) and quality of service, while neglecting the influence of pollution files. This paper proposed a P2P reputation model based on the user file-sharing behaviorcharacteristics. According to analyze the downloading features ofP2P network users, we combine the evaluation value of single file and the propagation degree to determine the node's reputation value. If sharing a pollution file and this kind of files is very popular in P2P network then this node's reputation value will decrease sharply.

2 Analysis of Users' File-Sharing Behavior Characteristics

In order to analyze users' file-sharing behavioral characteristics,we have collected some download information from some main download tools' operator in some large city .The download information includes users' download time, download files'

Y. Yuan, X. Wu, and Y. Lu (Eds.): ISCTCS 2012, CCIS 320, pp. 373–379, 2013.
© Springer-Verlag Berlin Heidelberg 2013

information, the users' IP information. Based on these users' download information, it is helpful to analyze the P2P network users'file-sharingbehavior characteristics [2, 3] and thereby define a file's propagation influence degree.

2.1   Time Characteristics of Users' File-Sharing Behavior

First, we analyze the relationshipbetweenthe download requests number of P2P network usersand the download time. Results as shown in Figure 1:

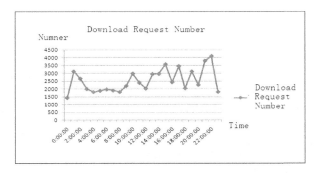

Fig. 1. Download Request Number inDifferent Time

According to the results, we can clearly see that the users' downloads number is in the day of the cycle fluctuation model. Download request number reach a peak at 21: 00 to 23: 00, accounted for 13% of the daily download share.Download request numbermeet the minimum at 00:00.From 03: 00 to 08: 00 users' download request number is relatively stable, fluctuating gently.

2.2   Type Characteristic of Users' File-Sharing Behavior

The file types including executable files, audio files, video files, document files, graphic file and compressed files. According to the statistics of user download data, the file type distribution is shown in figure 2.

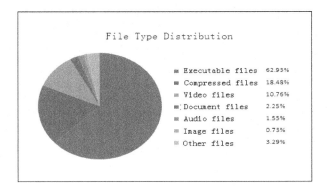

Fig. 2. File Type Distribution

Executable files including EXE file. Compressed file including RAR and ZIP files. Video fileincluding RMVB, AVI, WMV, and RMfiles. Document file including PDF, DOC and TXT files.Audio file including MP3 and WMA files. Image files including JPG and PNG files. It can be seen from Figure 2, the executable file downloads accounted for 62.93% of the total download number.

3 Reputation Model Based on the Users' File-Sharing Behavior Characteristics

This paper presents a P2P network reputation model based on users'file-sharingbehavioral characteristics, including file evaluation value and node reputation value measurement and maintenance. File evaluation value depends on thefile's propagationinfluence degree (i.e.higherfile's propagation influence degree means user will download this file more times).

3.1   Measure of File Evaluation Value and Node Reputation Value

In the traditional model of reputation, the node's reputation value was based on the history score of their servicesquality. In order to gain higher credit, node may share multiple files.A high reputation node can use only onepollution file to undermine P2P network security.In order to reduce this inconsistency behavior, a file's evaluation values will be independent of each files' evaluation values.A file's evaluation value will notbe affected by other files. The node's reputation value is determined by all the files' evaluation values in this node.

The File's Propagationinfluence Degree
Each file has its own files spread influence degree. Files'propagation influence degree can reflect the files' transmission level. After collectinga period of time of users'downloaddata,wecansummarize the characteristics of the user file-sharing behavior for this period of time, then obtained various types of file download ratio and the user downloadsratio in each period of time. Combining these two factors cancalculate the file's propagation influence degree.

Assume that a period of time P2P network users to share files collection isfile={f1 , f2 ,…,fm}, Type (k) representation of the file K's type,| Type (k) | means the download number of this type. Time (k) represents the file K's download request timestamp, | Time (k)| means the download number in this timestamp hour. Then through the statistics of the file type download radioand the filerequest time download radio to determine the file's propagation influence degree β.

The formula is as follows:

$$\beta = \frac{|\text{Type(k)}|}{|\text{File}|} * \frac{|\text{Time(k)}|}{|\text{File}|} * 100 \tag{1}$$

The Measurement of Node's Reputation Value

In each interaction request,request node will score eachserver node. Evaluation score is defined in [-1,1]. It contains the request node's judgments of file'sauthenticity, and satisfaction with the quality of service. A higher value indicates the file's authenticity higher and the higher satisfaction of service. When a node i in a P2P network share a new file j, the initial evaluation valueof this documentis $0: T_i^0(j) = 0$.File evaluation value is updated periodically, if in the nth cycle, the nodes, which downloaded this file, are C^1, C^2,....,C^n, and$S_i^n = \{C^k, 1 \leq k \leq n\}$,then evaluation value of the file:

$$T_i^n(j) \begin{cases} \alpha T_i^{n-1}(j) + (1 - \alpha) \dfrac{\Sigma_{k \in S_i^n} Score_k(j)}{|S_i^n|} \beta, \ n > 1 \\ \dfrac{\Sigma_{k \in S_i^n} Score_k(j)}{|S_i^n|}, n = 1 \end{cases} \tag{2}$$

In the formula,$T_i^{n-1}(j)$ is the evaluation value in the N-1 cycle,α is attenuation factor, and $\alpha \in (0, 1)$. The smaller theαvalue means this file draw more attention. Use attenuation factorcan prevent the node received in advance to use the real file and thenspread the pollution file.β is the f file's propagation influence degree. In the end of the nth cycle, the evaluation value of file j in node ii$sT_i^n(j)$.

The Measurement of Node Reputation Value

Any two files' evaluation values are independent of each other. Node credit (Rep) must reflect this node's contribution degree to the whole network. This includes: shared file number, service number, the authenticity of the files,quality of services, and whether the node's service is consistent. In this paper, the initial reputation of the node is defined as $Rep_{init} = 0$, Assuming that node i shared file collection for $File_i = \{f^1, f^2, ..., f^m\}$,$DL_i(k)$ is download number of the file K. Node i current reputation value calculation formula is as follows:

$$Rep_i = \begin{cases} \Sigma_{k \in File_i}(T_i(k) * DL_i(k)), |File_i| > 1 \\ T_i * DL_i, otherwise \end{cases} \tag{3}$$

3.2   Maintenance and Update of the File Evaluation Value and Node's Reputation Value

The Query of Document Evaluation Value and Node Reputation Value

When a node i requests a file K, assuming that node j1, j2,...,jm provides this file's download service. This node will broadcast the file K's evaluation value query request <"request"||IDi|k|ID1|ID2|...|IDm|>, and nodej1, j2,...,jm will respond to this message <"Reply"||IDj|k|Tj(k)|>after received the request, and then node i will sort the service node according to the service node evaluation value, choose the higher file's evaluation value of n nodes to download.

The Update of Document Evaluation Value and Node Reputation Value Update
Assume that node I download a file k from node j, the requesting node i will broadcast filescore information <"score"|IDi|IDj|socorej(k)>, aftermaintenance node of node j receives this information it will update the corresponding document evaluating value and node reputation value.

4   Simulation Results

We use two kind of P2P reputation model and compare the pollution files' propagation to verify the results. One reputation model is based on the P2P file-sharingbehavioral characteristics and the other one is based on trust and recommendation [4, 5]. To verify the Simulation results, we using Java to build an unstructuredP2P simulation platform.

The initial condition of Simulation: there are 1000 nodes in P2P network, each node store 1 to 5 files. In these files, some files are randomly marked to represent pollution files, so as to observe these pollution files' propagation.

4.1   The Compare of Pollution Files' Propagation Degree

We observed the files' propagation in 100 round of simulation. We assume that the number of nodes which have pollution files is 10.each round we let 1 to 9 nodes to try downloading that pollution file.

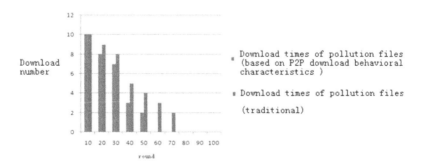

Fig. 3. Compare of pollution files' propagation degree

Figure 3 shows that the download number of pollution files in two kinds of reputation model. We can clearly see that the download number of pollution files in our reputation model (blue bar) is significantly less than traditional reputation model (red bar). That means the pollution files' propagation has been inhibited.

4.2   The Compare of Node's Successful Download Radio

A successful download means this node download a healthy file. We compare the successful download radio in each reputation model to verify the reliability of the reputation model.

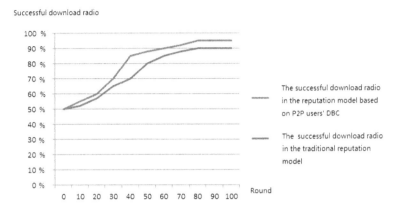

Fig. 4. Compare of node's successful download radio

Figure 4 shows that the successful download radio in our reputation model is higher than traditional reputation model. That means the successful download radio has been improved. Users are more likely to download healthy files.

4.3   Result analysis

Form figure 3 and figure 4, we can see that the pollution files' propagation has been inhibited and the successful download radio has been improved. Because the reputation model based on P2P file-sharingbehavioral characteristics use the files'propagation degree to determine the files'evaluation value. That makes the node's reputation value sharply decrease when this node share a popular pollution file. In that way, we can improve the reliability of the reputation model.

5   Conclusion

The reputation model based on the P2P file-sharingbehavioral characteristicscombines the files'evaluation value in server node and the files'propagation influence degree to choose whether download from this sever node. Thehigherpollution files'propagation influence degree, the more nodes' reputation value and files' evaluation value will be decreased. By this way, thispollution file's propagation will be inhibited and the P2P network security will be improved.

References

1. Kui, L., Dong, L.S.: Studies on Reputation Model in P2P Networks, pp. 1–2 (2008)
2. Chen, B.-G., Xu, Y., Hu, J.-L., Zhang, L.: Researchon User Behavior Characteristics of P2P File Sharing Systems. Computer Science 34(12), 122–142 (2007)
3. Huang, Z.-H., Lu, S.-N.: Peer to Peer Model Based on User Behavior. Computer Engineering 37(11) (2011)
4. Xi, J., Wang, Y., Lu, J.-D.: P2P Reputation Model Basedon Trust and Recommendation. Computer Engineering 35(4), 143–145 (2009)
5. Cornelli, F., Damiani, E., Capitani, S.D.: Choosing Reputable Serversin a P2P Network. In: Proc. of the 11th International World Wide Web Conference, Honolulu, Hawaii, USA: [s.n] (2002)

Unobservable Rendezvous Negotiation in P2P Networks

Fanwen Xu[1,4], Qingfeng Tan[2,3], Jinqiao Shi[2,3], and Li Guo[2,3]

[1] Department of Computer Science, Beijing University of Posts and Telecommunications,
Beijing, China
nbsxufanwen@bupt.edu.cn
[2] Chinese National Engineering Laboratory for Information Security Technologies,
Beijing, China
[3] Institute of Information Engineering, Chinese Academy of Sciences, Beijing, China
[4] Key Laboratory of Trustworthy Distributed Computing and Service (BUPT),
Ministry of Education, Beijing, China
{tanqingfeng,shijinqiao}@iie.ac.cn

Abstract. Internet has been the most popular platform for individuals to communicate and share ideas. With increasing threats against network privacy, anonymous and covert communication technology is becoming more and more important. In this paper, an unobservable rendezvous negotiation protocol is proposed based on P2P architecture, which establishes a covert channel leveraging an existing DHT to hide communicating behaviors and utilizes a tagging mechanism to ensure an indirect identification and mutual authentication. Experiments indicate that performance of the protocol is acceptable, and security analysis shows that the protocol can resist various threats.

Keywords: rendezvous negotiation, covert channel, P2P.

1   Introduction

Nowadays, Internet has become a primary facilitator for individualsto share information with each other all over the world. Information security especially privacy on the Internet isa critical issue, as personal behaviors and communications on the Internet may be sometimes monitored and analyzed by intentional people. For this reason, finding an unobservableway of sharing secrets is more important for the users who care about their privacy.

Anunobservablerendezvous can be used in many situations: an anonymous organization,with good willing for free exchange of ideas, news, and other information, can deliver startup messagesto initiate and manipulate an overlay networkscircumventingInternet censorship; a malicious botnet can regard the protocol as a covert channel of publishing commands; an agent under a comprehensive surveillance, as describing in a representative espionage scenario,can pass important information to a contact person who he has never seen before and to retrieve commands from the contact person.No matterwhether the usersare good or evil, we only concern about the conspiring meeting problem itself.

Y. Yuan, X. Wu, and Y. Lu (Eds.): ISCTCS 2012, CCIS 320, pp. 380–387, 2013.

Previous works concentrate on anonymous and covert communication technology under traditional web services. In this paper we focus on the unobservablerendezvous problem in the context of peer-to-peer (P2P) networks, for P2P have been one of the most popular research areas due to their distributed architectures, high scalabilities and especially peer to peer features.Traditional P2P networks provide a self-organization, high performance, and worldwide content sharing platforms, such as Emule [6], Vuze, and BitTorrent. However, a conspiring peer can be easily suspected if his behaviors are different from normal users. Consequently, anonymous P2P networksare presented to protect nodes and users from being linked to the content they share, such as Freenet [1], Tor [2], and Oneswarm [3]. While anonymous P2P networks are of great benefit, the fact that a useris using these technologiesmay expose the intention of exchanging secret information. So leverage existing infrastructures andhiding exchanging process are the key points.

In order to address these issues, we proposean unobservablerendezvous negotiation protocol using DHTsas cover traffics. For the participants who join the negotiating of rendezvous, they can exchange information withmutual authenticationand without direct contact. From the perspective of a surveillance entity, a participantappearsto be a regular P2P peer, while the participant isactually communicating with another one.

The remainder of this paper is organized as follows:Section 2defines our goalsand threat models; Section 3 presents the design detailsof our protocol; Section 4 reports the experimentalresults;Section 5 analyzes the security issues;Section 6 presents a concise review of related works;the final section presents a conclusion witha discussion on further work.

2   Problem Definition

Given a P2P network, which consists of a set P of $|P| = n$ peers. A user s of P, the Sender, wants transmit information to another user r also of P, the Receiver (Figure 1). The Sender s does not want to expose his real location, such as IP address. So s publishes the information on the public DHT of P2P network or somewhere else. Where to get the information should be decided by both sender and receiver, because receiver also does not want to expose his real location if the place where stores the information iselaborately select by the sender. We call the place the *Unobservable-Rendezvous* and call the negotiating process the *Unobservable Rendezvous Negotiation Protocol* (URNP, discussed in Section 3).Our goals are

- **Unobservablity:** the sender and receiver seem to be normal peers of a P2P network in daily life.
- **Mutual Authentication:** the sender and receiver verify each other and determine a meeting point together.
- **Indirect Contact:**the sender and receiver could not directly connect to each other with real location, such as IP address.
- **Easy Deployment:**the sender and receiver must leverage existing infrastructures and could not build an externaldedicated server.

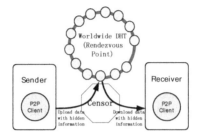

Fig. 1. General Scenario, Characters and Interactions

Threat Models. The above list the protocol goals withoutthe presence of an adversary. We now enumeratethe various types of potential adversaries (more detail security analysis in Section 5) against the URNP:

— *Individual Monitor:*a passive adversary who can monitor an individual's traffic without the capability ofcorrelating the traffic gathered at different individuals.
— *Partial Monitor:*a passive adversary who has the ability of monitoring k peers of Pand may also correlate the traffic.In particular, if the k increases to n, the complete network is monitored.
— *DHT-Integrated Adversary:*an active adversary who integrateshimself into the DHT, so he can recordall data that is asked tostore and search.
— *Compromised Participant:* an active adversary who can act as a sender or receiver by getting information from a compromised sender or receiver.

3   URNP: Unobservable Rendezvous NegotiationProtocol

In this section, we propose the *Unobservable Rendezvous Negotiation Protocol*: an invisible tagguarantees that only the receiver can identify a tagged item while regular peers cannot; without direct contact, the sender and receiverauthenticate each otherand negotiate anunobservablerendezvousbased onDiffie-Hellmankey exchange.

a)   DHT Network

A hash table with key-value pairs in all peers helps them efficiently publish and retrieve the value associated with a given key. The key-value infrastructure, called DHT in P2P, is originallya free lookup service. Every regular peer who is going to share a file publishes the file information into the DHT, so that the other peers can know where to get the file by searching the DHT.

We generalize DHT implements so as to generate a more universal put/get interface for reading and writing data in DHT networks like KAD, Khashmir and Vuze, which is implemented by two operations: get and store. In fact, normal peers frequently invoke the two operations. In our solution, the sender lookup the right peers and then stores the key and the value with tag (Section 3.2) into the hash tables of those peers; the receiver get the value with tag from them.

b) Tagging

Our tags must beindistinguishable from a uniformly random string to anyone without the private key. Someonewiththe private key should be able to examine whether the tag ispresent; if so, he can also publish another random-like tagged string for key exchange.In order to keep the tags short enough to replace some random-like field (such as the hash of file) in the value and secure enough to avoid attack,we chooseElliptic Curve Cryptography (ECC) as our public key cryptosystem. The Diffie-Hellman-like tagging process is describing as follow.

Given the key cryptosystem G (g, r, x, H), where:
        g: a generator of a group of prime order
        r: the primary private key
        $\mathbf{x= g^r}$:the public key.
        H: a hash function

The sender, who knows g, x, and H, picks a random private key s and computes g^s and $x^s = g^{rs}$. Then the tag is $g^s \| H(g^{rs}\|k)$,where k is the key of DHT store operation and $\|$ denotes concatenation.The receiver, who knows g, r, and H, searches the same key to getmany values with a list of candidate tags. Thanks to the constant lengths, he divides the tag intotwo parts: y and h.If the tag is present by the sender, y will be g^s and h will be $H(g^{ks}\|k)$, or y and h will both be random. So the receiver can computes $h' = H(x^r\|k)$, and check whether h' and h is equal to verify the tag.

c) Protocol Design

The sender and receiver negotiateameeting point through URNP. The Figure 2 provides an outline of URNP.

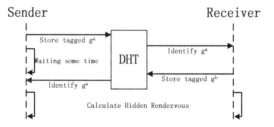

Fig. 2. URNPSequence

The tagging mechanism ensures that the receiver identifies the sender. For the sake of mutual authentication, the receiver should contribute to the key exchange. A simple way is that the sender and receiver share the same private key, so the sender can identify the receiver's tag after the receiver temporarilychange his role to a sender. But the shortcoming is obvious: a dangerous receiver can pretend to be the sender and send fake message to the other receivers of the sender.

For a safer mutual authentication, we generate two instancesof the key cryptosystem G. The sender uses G (g, r, x, H) signs the tag and the receiver uses G' (g, r', x', H).The sender holds g, r', x, and H, while the receiver holds g, r, x', and H.We can simply consider that each user has two keys: a public key x for tagging and private key r for identifying.The details of the algorithm are presented below:

```
Algorithm1 - Unobservable Rendezvous Negotiation
Sender:                          Receiver:
a := random()                    dountil return
v:= gᵃ||H(xᵃ||k)                   list V := get(k)
store(k,v)                         for v in V
sleep(t)                             y,h := divide(v)
list V := get(k)                     h':= H(yʳ||k)
for v in V                           if h' == hthen
  y,h := divide(v)                     b := random()
  h':= H(yʳ||k)                        v:= gᵇ||H(x'ᵇ||k)
  if h' == hthen                       store(k,v)
    returnyᵃ                           return
```

On one hand, the sender picks random a, computes the tag, and store the tag according to a pre-defined key selecting scheme. Both sides should get the key easily and publicly. For example, they can obtain the key from the top search key words ongoogle trends. After random time waiting for the receiver, the sender also searches the key to get a list of candidate tags and check for a valid tag tagged by receiver. On the other hand, the receiver searches the key. When he finds a valid tag, he picks random b and stores his tag. Now, both sides can calculate the same value g^{ab}. The *Hidden Rendezvous*could be simple a key valued $H'(g^{ab})$ where H' is also a hash function.

4   Implementation and Performance

There are many DHT implements at present. KADis one implementation of the Kaemlia DHT used by several P2P applications: eMule andaMule.We modifythe aMulesources[4] in order to implement the URNP.It is possible to store a random-like hashand the other meta-data (defined in FileTags.h) of a specific file.In our experiment, we used a 160-bit elliptic curve randomly generated by OPENSSL and set H to be the first 32bits of a MD5 output.

A store oprationSTOREKEYWORD ends with two conditions: the number of the peers shoring the pair is more than 10 initially; the time of the store operation exceeds the maximum time limit which is 140s. We modified the publishing parallel number from default 3 to 10. Figure 3(a) shows that the practical time is fast than theoretical time for it ends up with first condition.

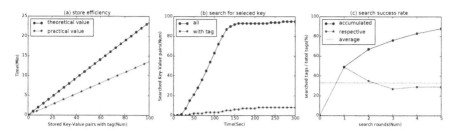

Fig. 3. Performance of Store and Search

In order to test the search efficiency for the tags stored withthe same key, we stored 20 different tags and choseto waitup to 300s (default is 45s) for the get operation. Figure 3(b) shows the result: the key has 8 tagged contents in almost 90 contents.

As formeasuring the search success rate, we modified search time back to 45s and stored 450 tags with different keys. For the first round, we searched the 450 keys to find tags. When a tag is valid, we remove the corresponding keys from key list. Then we continued to search the keys of key list. With 5 rounds, the result is shown in Figure 3(c). We can see that the accumulated success rate is 88% and average rate is 33%. It is noteworthy that the success rate of the first round is 48% whichcorresponds to the 8 searched tags among 20 total tags.

In our implementation, the sender stores 5 tags and the receiver searchers 2times. Every tag can be found with the probability of 67% after 2 times searching. So the probability that all the 5 tags are unfound is $(1-67\%)5 = 0.39\%$.Considering our protocol has two storing operations and two search operations,the sender and receiver can achieve a successful negotiation with the probabilityof $(1 C 0.0039)2 = 99.22\%$.

5   Security Analysis

This section we will analyze the security of URNP based on the potential adversariesdescribed in Section 2. The former two are passive attackers, while the other two are active attackers.

5.1   Passive Attackers

An Individual Monitor can monitor an individual's traffic and analysis his behaviors. Our protocol uses the normal DHT operations. The Individual Monitor cannot easily determine whether he is an abnormal user. One main problem may be that the frequency of DHT operations: if a person calls store and get operations so many times in a period of time. We can simply change our strategy by adding a time controller to reduce the frequency to normal level.

Let us consider a *Partial Monitor*. If the sender and the receiver are both in the k monitored peers and the key for storing and searching is unpopular (only the sender stores it and only the receiver searches it), the monitor may suspect the two peers. Note that forreal life situation, the number of nodes n can be as high as millions.The probability that both sender and receiver are in the k peers is p:

$$p = \frac{C_{n-2}^{k-2}}{C_n^k} = \frac{k*(k-1)}{n*(n-1)} \xrightarrow{k \ll n} \frac{k^2}{n^2}$$

p, depending on the monitored proportion, is small enough to be neglected, as the n is at the level of million. If the adversary increases k to be comparable with n, the calculating pressure is too high to bear. If the adversary is very strong, the key can be chose from the popular ones (eg. top words of google trends) to mitigatesuspicion.

5.2   Active Attackers

An active*DHT-Integrated Adversary*also uses a modified P2P client to record all store or search requests and analysis the records. It appears to be the same ability of a *Partial Monitor*. But the active adversary can also modify the packet. The attacker cannot arbitrarilymodify a tag to another valid tag without the public key. Though modification can attack the availability, it may also obstruct a regular user.

The Compromised Participantis a kind of inside attacker. As the receiverdoes not know the real location of the sender according to URNP, the attacker acting the receiver will not know either. Furthermore, more sophisticated overlapnetworks based on URNP can be established in future work.

6   Related Work

One research area related to our workisanonymity in networks. Thoughanonymity have been a design goals of manyP2P systems (e.g., Freenet [1], TOR [2]),they areself-built networks only used by special users.There has been little researchon anonymity in the context of exiting worldwide P2P networks. Liin [5] hides information in torrent files. In contrast to his work which is limited to a particulartorrent-basednetwork, we do not need the torrent filewhich is not exit in many P2Ps (e.g., Emule [6] and Vuze) so that we can expand our protocol to many other P2Ps.

Another related research area is covert channel. Infranet [7] attempts to disguise traffic by asymmetric communication: a client uses a sequence of HTTP requests to communicate truedestination; the proxy then fetches thedata and serves back by usingimage steganography. However, it relies on an extra proxy server. Collage [8] uses sites that share user-generated content (e.g., Flickr) to improveunobservability.An existing problem is that a UGC sites may compress the original pictures (e.g. Sina-Weibo in China) and retrospect the suspicious user, which leads to unavailability.

Related research onsecret handshakes was much more like our work in the purpose. Tsudik [9] discusses a flexible framework that allowing the participants toestablish a secure and anonymouschannel. It changes the original traffic to satisfy handshake. Raphael in [10] proposes distributed and efficient algorithmsthat transmit hidden information by varying the block requestsequence meaningfully in P2P network, in which a conspirer can broadcast amessage secretly to all fellow conspirers. But the conspiring peers may expose real locations of peerswith directly contacts.

7   Conclusion and Future Work

Many Internet users need a safe, private way for communication. We disclosed a covertchannelinP2Pnetworks and successfully exploited them to achieve an unobservable rendezvousnegotiation protocol.A novelaspect of our approach is the leveraging of the existing modern P2P systems. Furthermore, the communication entries possess the capability of tag-based mutual authentication without direct contact.

Our experiments alsoshowthe feasibility and desirableperformance of storing and getting tag from KAD. Security analysis demonstrate that the design of our protocol is able to resist varies types of adversariesto some extent.Our future work lies in improving the protocol by using more complex time mechanism, adding more negotiation participators,and deploying the protocol in more DHTs.

Acknowledgments. This work is supported by National Natural Science Foundation of China (No.6100174), National High Technology Research and Development Program of China, 863 Program (No.2011AA010701 and 2011AA01A103), and Strategic Priority Research Program of the Chinese Academy of Sciences (Grant No. XDA06030200).

References

1. Clarke, I., Sandberg, O., Wiley, B., Hong, T.W.: Freenet: a distributed anonymousinformation storage and retrieval system. In: International workshop on Designingprivacy Enhancing Technologies: Design Issues in Anonymity and Unobservability, pp. 46–66. Springer-Verlag New York, Inc., New York (2001)
2. Dingledine, R., Mathewson, N., Syverson, P.: Tor: the second-generation onionrouter. In: Proceedings of the 13th Conference on USENIX Security Symposium, SSYM 2004, vol. 13, p. 21. USENIX Association, Berkeley (2004)
3. Isdal, T., Piatek, M., Krishnamurthy, A., Anderson, T.: Privacy-preserving p2pdata sharing with oneswarm. SIGCOMM Comput. Commun. Rev. 40(4), 111–122 (2010)
4. Amule, http://www.amule.org/
5. Li, Z., Sun, X., Wang, B., Wang, X.: A steganography scheme in p2p network. In: Proceedings of the 2008 International Conference on Intelligent Information Hiding and Multimedia Signal Processing, IIH-MSP 2008, pp. 20–24. IEEE Computer Society, Washington, DC (2008)
6. Emule, http://www.emule-project.net/
7. Feamster, N., Balazinska, M., Harfst, G., Balakrishnan, H., Karger, D.: Infranet:Circumventing web censorship and surveillance. In: Proceedings of the 11th USENIX Security Symposium, pp. 247–262. USENIX Association, Berkeley (2002)
8. Burnett, S., Feamster, N., Vempala, S.: Chipping away at censorship firewalls withusergenerated content. In: Proceedings of the 19th USENIX Conference on Security, USENIX Security 2010, p. 29. USENIX Association, Berkeley (2010)
9. Tsudik, G., Xu, S.: A Flexible Framework for Secret Handshakes. In: Danezis, G., Golle, P. (eds.) PET 2006. LNCS, vol. 4258, pp. 295–315. Springer, Heidelberg (2006)
10. Eidenbenz, R., Locher, T., Wattenhofer, R.: Hidden communication in p2p net-works steganographic handshake and broadcast. In: 2011 Proceedings IEEE, INFOCOM, pp. 954–962 (April 2011)

A Hierarchical Method for Clustering Binary Text Image

Yiguo Pu[1,2,3], Jinqiao Shi[1,3], and Li Guo[1,3]

[1] Institute of Information Engineering, CAS, China
[2] Graduate University, CAS, China
[3] Chinese National Engineering Laboratory for Information Security Technologies
puyiguo10@mails.gucas.ac.cn, {shijinqiao,guoli}@iie.ac.cn

Abstract. Image clustering is a crucial task in image retrieving, filtering and organizing. Most of recent work focuses on dealing with color images or gray scale images with features extracted from text content, annotation or image content. This paper aims at binary text images and proposes a novel clustering method that can be used for automatic image procession in digital library and automatic office. The method is divided into three main steps. Firstly images are preprocessed to denoise, correct orientation and produce coarse classes. Secondly, features are extracted and similar images are grouped into new classes with hierarchical clustering algorithm. At last new classes are combined to the nearest old ones under distance condition. To speed clustering Local Sensitive Hash algorithm is imported for boosting merging procedure. Experiments show that this method is faster and efficient compared with the basic clustering method.

Keywords: binary text image, hierarchical cluster, LSH.

1 Introduction

With the development of multi-media and computing technology, more and more documents are stored as digital images. A lot of attention has been drawn to digital image procession in recent years [1]. In application of recognition and retrieving digital images, grouping similar images together become one of the key issues. For example, librarians can delete duplicate images from database. Different from common continuous tone images, binary text images only consist of characters, spreadsheets and some pictures in black or white colors. Cluster methods used for colorful images or gray scale images may not be suitable for binary text images. We propose a special method to extract features and classify binary text images.

The problem discussed in this paper can be described as follows. Given a set of text image I= {I_1, I_2, I_3, …, I_t}, we need to group similar text images together. The similarity can be measured by the layout of the images. As we know, it is possible to bring bit flips, paper tilt and scale during scanning. We first preprocess the images to remove noise, and adjust inclined images. Then features are extracted and cluster method is applied. As images are inputted as a stream, we need find the correct cluster that images belong in real-time.

Y. Yuan, X. Wu, and Y. Lu (Eds.): ISCTCS 2012, CCIS 320, pp. 388–396, 2013.

In clustering a number of features to compute similarity always cost a lot of time during clustering, a.k.a., the curse of dimension. To boost clustering procedure, a random algorithm (LSH is imported, which provides a high probability guarantee that it will return the correct answer or one close to it. Experiments reveal that the method is more efficient and faster than basic method.

The rest of paper is organized as follows. Section 2 illustrates the related work of image clustering. The detail of cluster procedure is described in section 3. We do some experiments in section 4. At last, we discuss some future work and draw a conclusion in section 5.

2   Related Work

Image clustering has broad application domain. In medical science doctors can find and classify diseases by clustering images [2], while the control personnel recognize and classify suspicious objects. In automatic office and digital library, it can also do a big favor for procession images.

Three main methods can be used in image clustering. The first is to cluster the images by the text content. Features are extracted from the text and words recognized by OCR (Optical Character Recognition) system [3]. But it always takes too much time to recognize and may contain some errors. The second method is based on the annotations words for each image [4]. However, there is no efficient way to annotate images except human recognizing and tagging them. Another reason may be that a few words can't describe an image in detail. The last method is based on image content. These methods always extract feature from images, such as color, texture and so on. Some methods focus on entire document feature, such density [5], color distribution [6], while others focus on detail features, such as character size, the number of connected components [7]. In fact, in order to well describe an image, both color feature and position feature (local and global) should be considered. Although methods above achieve good performance in common images, binary text images which have only two kinds of colors, i.e. black and white, need some special methods to extract features and cluster.

3   Cluster Procedure

Figure 1 shows the cluster procedure that is divided three main steps. In first step, we preprocess the images to extract feature easily. We also cluster images to lighten the computing workload later. In the second step, features are extracted and we apply hierarchical cluster algorithm to produce new classes. In the last round, we use LSH algorithm to merge new classes to old ones.

3.1   Preprocess

Preprocessing pays a great influence on later cluster. Sometimes cluster has no cluster efficiency just because not well preprocessed. The work before cluster contains three steps described as following.

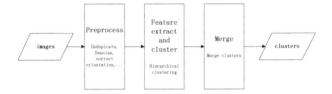

Fig. 1. The clustering procedure

Remove Same Image

The first step of preprocess is to find the complete same images and delete from the images set. In order to process a great amount of images in a short time, we choose signature-based method. If 1) the signatures of two images are identical and 2) the width and length of the images are the same, the two images are thought as two copies of a same text image. Because MD5 algorithm is independent on length and content of input, we first compute MD5 digests of all images and then delete images that have same MD5, width and length. The rest images are all different in content.

Denoising

During scanning, it is possible to bring some noise in the image. Most of noises are Gaussian noise and impulse noise [8]. [8] proposes an algorithm that first classifies the pixels into two classes, one is the pixels which are corrupted by Gauss noise and the other is the pixels corrupted by impulse noise and then average filter is used for the pixels corrupted by Gauss noise and median filter is used for the pixels corrupted by impulse noise. After that, this method scans from four margins of the image (up, down, left and right) to get text area. Figure 2 shows the effect of denoising method.

Fig. 2. The effect of denoising

Correct Tilt Images

If the paper is not well aligned the scanner, the text image is skewed. We need to correct the direction of the image before grouping similar images. Many algorithms are put forward to find the correct orientation of the images [9-11]. For an example, Hough transforming has good precisian [9], but it takes too much time to find the correct angle. Projection algorithm is a good option too, but it need try many directions to find the most accurate one [10]. What is more, it needs to scan the whole image whenever it tries a direction. [11] proposes a regression method which is proved efficient and accurate. This method first finds the line of the text in an image. Then a series of points along the line are found. We can fit the line by regression. The gradient of the line equation represents the tilt angle. To ensure the angle is accurate, it finds enough lines and calculates several slopes. The final angle is the average of all the slopes. This method is suit for text images because they have few pictures. Figure 3 shows the image corrected by the method.

Fig. 3. The effect of correcting tilt image

Cluster by Length and Width

If the difference of width and length between two images is great, we can be sure that the two images belong to different classes. So we cluster images into several classes. Each class has images with similar length and width. This can save a lot computation in hierarchical clustering.

3.2   Feature Extraction and Clustering

Binary image has less color information than gray scale images to get more detail features. But we still can get features from the shape of the text area in the image. The image preprocessed can be treated as a matrix M, with pixel in row i and column j $M(i, j) \in \{0,1\}$. [5] proposes an easy method to extract feature of binary text images by dividing the image into several blocks. The rate of number of black pixels versus the number of total pixels in each block is defined as density. At first, we divide the image M*N blocks, i.e. N blocks in each row and M blocks in each column, and calculates the density of every block as first level of feature. After that, we divide the image 2M*2N blocks and calculate the densities again as the second level of feature. We can repeat the procedure k times. The k-th density matrix is as following:

$$\begin{bmatrix} d_k(1,1) & d_k(1,2) & ... & d_k(1,2^k N) \\ d_k(2,1) & d_k(2,2) & ... & d_k(2,2^k N) \\ ... & ... & ... & ... \\ d_k(2^k M,1) & d_k(2^k M,2) & ... & d_k(2^k M,2^k N) \end{bmatrix}.$$

We can see that the higher level, the more features are extracted, and the better the image is described. If two images are the similar, they are not only similar in low level, but also are similar in high level. Every level of feature matrix can be treated as one dimension feature vector during clustering.

Because text images are input as a stream, we cannot cluster all images at one time. So we come up a two-step way to accomplish cluster task, i.e. 1) receiving enough images to produce new classes and 2) combining new classes and old classes.

To find similar images that belong to the same class, several cluster algorithms can be used, for example, k-means. However, k-means need set the number of classes before it working, and that number is always beyond known. So we choose a hierarchical algorithm as our solution.

Suppose all images are divided K times. And the distance threshold is set Δ. Initially, t image are in same set I= {I_1, I_2, I_3,...,I_t}. The cluster algorithm is as following:

1) set l=1;
2) if l>K+1, terminate cluster procedure;
3) compute the distance of two images

$$D = \sum_{i=1, j=1}^{2^l M, 2^l N} [d_k(i, j) - d'_k(i, j)]^2$$

,

where $d_k(i,j)$ is density of i row j column of the first image, and $d_k'(i,j)$ is density of i row j column of the second image. If D<Δ*4^(l-1), then the two images are grouped into one class. The result set may be a new set I'= {{ I_1, I_2}, { I_3},...,{ I_t }};
4) If any class contains more one images, set l=l+1 and go to step 1) continuing to cluster in that class.

The final classes are as the new clusters. In each class, one image that is the nearest to other images is selected as center image representing the class.

The time complexity of producing new classes is $T = O((4^{k+1} - 1)/3 L^2 MN) = O(L^2 MN)$.

3.3   Boost with Local Sensitive Hash

Each time new classes are generated, we need to find whether the new classes are similar to old classes. As there may be a lot of old classes and many features, it will cost too much time to search the most similar class. So we choose Local Sensitive Hash (LSH) [12] to increase the speed of searching the target class.

LSH is based on the simple idea that, if two points are close together, then after a "projection" operation these two points will remain close together. By sacrifice accuracy of &, LSH can speed up finding the target class greatly. It tries to map a high-dimension feature vector to HASH table, where the probability of collision is in negative correlation to the distance between the two classes. So the nearer the two classes are, the more probable they collide in hash table. It generate more than one hash table to increase the probability of collision. The definition of LSH function is as following:

h : R_n->R, satisfies:
If ||p_1-p_2||<||p_3-p_4||, then Pr[h(p_1)=h(p_2)] > Pr[h(p_3)=h(p_4)],

where p_1, p_2, p_3 and p_4 are n-dimension vector. For example, $h_{a,b}(v) = \lfloor \frac{av + b}{w} \rfloor$, is a LSH function, where a is random vector following Gaussian distribution, b is a random variable uniformly distributed between 0 and w. The probability of collision of vector p_1 and p_2 is

$$p(c) = \mathrm{Pr}_{a,b}\left[h_{a,b}(p1) = h_{a,b}(p2)\right] = \int_0^w \frac{1}{c} f(\frac{x}{c})(1-\frac{x}{w})dx$$

Where c=||p1-p2||, and f is a probability density function under Gaussian distribution. To increase the probability of collision, we create S different hash function,

$$H_i:R_n \text{->} R_t, \quad i=1,2,\ldots,S.\ H_i=\{h_{a1,b1},h_{a2,b2},\ldots,h_{at,bt}\}.$$

H_i is a function vector containing t different LSH function. So we transfer 2kM*2kN dimensions vector to St dimensions vector. Suppose we try to find the target class with the probability of 1-&, then S,t satisfy following condition:

$$S \ge \frac{\log \delta}{\log(1-p(1)^t)}$$

To locate the hash bucket easily, we generate one hash table for each Hi. Two hash value g1 and g2 are generated for each feature vector, where g1 is to index the bucket, g2 as the finger print of the vector. The structure of the hash table is as following:

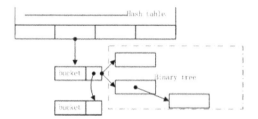

Fig. 4. The structure of the hash table

In figure 3, every hash element points to a list of bucket which contains all vectors that have the same g1 value, and every bucket is a binary tree, each element in which has the same g2 value. In experiment, we choose last level of density as the feature vector because it describes the image in more detail than other level features. The procedure of merging new classes and old classes is as following:

1)compute $Hi(d_k(1,1),\ d_k(1,2),\ldots,\ d_k(2^kM,2^kN))$, i=1,2,..,S, and get s vector of t dimensions.
2)Compute g1(v_i),g2(v_i), i=1,2,\ldots,t, and find the class that is nearest to the new class center image.
3) If the nearest distance is less than Δ, then they are merged to old class. Otherwise, the new class is not similar to any old class.

4   Experiments

In experiments 1, we examine the accuracy of the method. We use f-measure to evaluate the result of clustering [13]. F measure of the result is defined as following:

$$F = \sum_i \frac{|i| \times F_i}{\sum_i |i|}$$

Where F_i is f measure of the i-th class and defined as following:

$$F_i = \frac{2 P_i R_i}{P_i + R_i}.$$

P_i is precision and R_i is the recall.

In experiment we develop the hierarchical clustering software. We set M=N=8, L=2, Δ=0.075. So the number of feature dimensions is 256. There are 373 binary text images in the image dataset, but 11 of them are too small to extract features. So we get 362 images to experiment. We create three datasets like this: dataset 1 is made up of 362 original images. Dataset 2 contains 724 images in which half of the images are original images and the other half are original images tilting to +1 degree. Dataset 3 is made up with 1086 images----all images in the dataset 2 and 362 original images tilting to -1 degree. Because in preprocessing there are errors in the tilt angle found, the corrected images are slightly different the original ones. Table 1 lists the results of the experiment. There are 4 images that misclassified. Two of them are blank or have a few pixels to extract features and are clustered into one class. And the other two images are upside down, so they are separated in two clusters. F-measure shows that the hierarchical method is efficient enough to satisfy practical needs.

In experiment 2, we set &=0.1, W=4.0 and try to find how much time LSH algorithm takes. To prove the high speed of merging, we develop two merging methods. The basic method just searches the nearest class one by one and the LSH method use LSH algorithm to speed. As LSH always eats much memory to construct hash table, we develop a LSH module that can swap its hash nodes with disk. Figure 4(a) illustrates the LSH method speed vs. the basic method speed and Figure 4(b) compares the F1-measure of the two methods.

In this experiment, we see that by LSH, some clusters are misclassified, but the time decreases. If the number of features increases, the time saved will be more. It shows LSH can be applied to clustering application where speed is more important than accuracy.

Table 1. The result of experiment 1

The number of images	The number clusters	The number of Misclassified images	The number of misclassified clusters	F-measure
362	348	4	3	0.996
724	348	8	3	0.996
1086	348	12	3	0.996

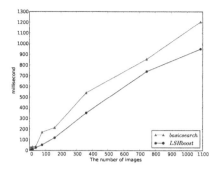

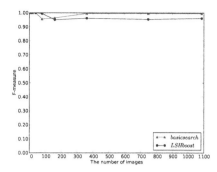

Fig. 4. (a) the speed of basic merging method vs. the speed of the LSH method

Fig. 4. (b) the F-measure of basic merging method vs. the F-measure of the LSH method

5   Conclusion and Future Work

This paper proposes the binary text image cluster method. It mainly contains three steps: preprocessing, clustering and merging. In experiments, it shows that hierarchical cluster method is efficient and LSH algorithm can be used to boost the merging procedure. The method proposed is efficient and accuracy so it can take on an important role in practice.

In experiments, we found that some images are reversed that lead to misclassify, i.e., image is up-side down. More orientation detection is needed before clustering. The cluster method described in this paper is more based on global features, so we can add some local features to enhance the clustering result in the future work.

Acknowledgements. This work is supported by National High Technology Research and Development Program of China, 863 Program (Grant No.2011AA010701 and 2011AA01A103) and National Key Technology R&D Program (Grant No.2012BAH37B04).

References

1. Xiang, Y.-J., Xie, S.-L.: Survey of image retrieving techniques. Journal of Chongqing University of Posts and Telecommunications (Natural Science) 18(3) (2006)
2. Song, Y., et al.: Research on medical image clustering Based on Approximate density Function. Journal of Computer Research and Development 43(11), 1947–1952 (2006)
3. Chang, F.: Retrieving Information from Document Images: Problem and Solution. International Journal on Document Analysis and Recognition 4(1), 46–55 (2001)
4. Yu, L.-S., Zhang, T.-W.: Image Clustering Based on Correlation Between Visual Features and Annotations. Actael Ectronica Sinica 34(7) (2006)
5. Hu, Z., Lin, X., Yan, H.: Document image retrieval based on multi-density features. Journal of Tsinghua Univ (Sci. & Tech.) 46(7) (2006)

6. Liu, Z., Zhuang, Y.: A Comparative and Analysis Study of Ten color Feature—based Image Retrieval Algorithms. Signal Processing 16(1) (2000)

7. Wang, C., Chen, T., Chan, Y., Hwang, R., Huang, W.: Chinese document image retrieval system based on proportion of black pixel area in a character image. In: Proc. 6th ICACT, pp. 25–29 (2004)

8. Guan, X.-P., Zhao, L.-X., Tang, Y.-G.: Mixed Filter for Image Denoising. Journal of Image and Graphics 10(3) (2005)

9. Qu, Y., Yang, L.-P.: Hough Transform OCR Image Slant Correction Method. Journal Of Image and Graphics 6(A)(2) (2001)

10. Lu, X.-B., Bao, M., Huang, W.: Projection Based Skew Detection of Vehicle License Plate. Journal of Transportation Engineering and Information 2(4) (2004)

11. Wang, T., Zhu, Y., Wang, H.: Document Images Skew Correction Based on Run-length Smoothing. Computer Engineering 30(1) (2004)

12. Andoni, A., Indyk, P.: E2LSH 0.1 User Manual (2006)

13. Yang, Y., Jin, F., Kamel, M.: Survey of clustering validity evaluation. Application Research of Computers 25(6) (2008)

Search Results Evaluation Based on User Behavior

Jinxiu Yu[1,2], Yueming Lu[1,2], Songlin Sun[1,2], and Fangwei Zhang[3]

[1] School of Information and Communication Engineering, Beijing University of Posts and
Telecommunications, Beijing, China
[2] Key Laboratory of Trustworthy Distributed Computing and Service (BUPT),
Ministry of Education, Beijing, China
{jxyu,ymlu,slsun}@bupt.edu.cn
[3]School of Humanities, Beijing University of Posts and Telecommunications, Beijing, China
zhangfangwei@bupt.edu.cn

Abstract. The evaluation of search results for improving the precious rank of search engines is a challenge. This paper proposes a new method of search results evaluation based on user behavior. The method includes the information extraction technology, the calculation of weight and the evaluation of results. It enhances the accuracy of corresponding answer annotation. The experimental results show that the method achieves a more precious search results rank than the way using click-through data only.

Keywords: search engine evaluation, click-through data, human factors, weight calculation.

1   Introduction

The rational evaluation of search engine is not only beneficial to the user's choice and use, but also very helpful for its improvement and development. The best search engine is accurate to give users access to the information they need. Evaluation of search engine has been studied for over 20 years. Find out the standard answer sets automatically to compare with the result lists returned by search engine is the most prevailing challenge.

Kent et al. [1] was the first to propose the criterion of relevance and the measures of precision and recall for evaluating IR (information retrieval) systems. While most current IR evaluation researches, including the famous workshop TREC (Text Retrieval Conference), are based on the Cranfield methodology, which was comprised of query sets, corresponding answer sets and metrics. And the acquisition of answer sets is usually the most difficult part.

There are numerous previous studies focused on finding the standard answer sets. At early stage, the query sets and answer sets used in evaluation were both generated by experts, it's such a time-consuming work and the result was undesirability. Later researchers paid attentions to user behavior especially click-through data. Oard and Kim [2] were among the first to model Web users' information acquisition process by behavior analysis. Joachims et al. [3] pointed out that clicks reflect relative relevance of queries and results.

Y. Yuan, X. Wu, and Y. Lu (Eds.): ISCTCS 2012, CCIS 320, pp. 397–403, 2013.
© Springer-Verlag Berlin Heidelberg 2013

Moreover Himanshu Sharma et al. [4] captured user relevance judgments actions such as print, save and bookmark, these implicit feedback interactions . Dou et al. [5] studied the problem of using aggregate click-through logs, and found that the aggregation of a large number of user clicks provided a valuable indicator of relevance preference. Later, Yiqun Liu et al.[6] proposed a performance evaluation method that fully automatically generates large scale Web search topics and answer sets under Cranfield framework.

Different from previous studies [7, 8] which generate corresponding answers automatically based on click-through data only, they consider that the relevant precision of pairs with large CTR (Click-through Rate) values higher than the ones with lower CTR values. However, the click-through data doesn't mean everything, since user click on a result page just indicate that this page was perceived relevance rather than actual relevance. We added several other user behaviors such as the dwell time to enhance the precision.

2   Search Results Evaluation Method

As outlined in the introduction, we proposed a modified metric based on Cranfield methodology. The Cranfiled-like approach was first proposed by Cranfield UniversityZ in 1950s. This evaluation system consists of three components: a query set, corresponding answers and the integrated evaluation scheme composed by metrics. Queries in the query set are processed by an IR system. Then results are compared with corresponding answers using evaluation metrics. Finally, the performance of the IR system is represented in the value of the relevance metrics.

The framework of our method shows in Fig.1. First, we extract some useful information from click-through logs. Then use two different methods to annotate the corresponding query, one is that based on click-through data only. The other is adding new features to answer set annotation. Finally, traditional Web IR evaluation metrics are used to compare the result lists and judge which one is better.

3   Information Extraction

We extract several user-behavior features from the Web search logs, including user id, queries, clicked pages and corresponding dwell time, order of click, actions such as scrolling, saving, printing, bookmarking, adding to favorites and copying.

According to Broder [9] and Rose [10] et al., there are three major types of Web search queries: navigational, informational and transactional. Yiqun [11] at al. proposed a classification method based on user click-through logs, and the decision tree learning algorithm was adopted to identify the types of queries automatically. The annotation of navigational queries was very simple compared to informational ones since there was only one specific page in the answer set.

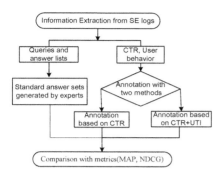

Fig.1. The framework of modified method

Table 1. The judge matrix and relevant eigenvector

A	A1	A2	A3	W
A1	1	4	5	0.67
A2	1/4	1	3	0.22
A3	1/5	1/3	1	0.11

In order to ensure the correctness of experimental results, we selected all kinds of queries, high frequency and low frequency, long and short, single item or multiple items and so on. And we choose these queries based on a certain proportion. Besides we collected other user feedback and recorded using binary judgment, either user has these behaviors or not.

Regard to the dwell time on a page, we measure it using UTI (utility). We suppose that the user kept clicking on results until she collected enough utility. Every result she clicked contributed a certain amount of utility toward satisfying her need. We assume that the more time a user spends on a search result, the more utility she gains from it. Hence the utility gain from a particular click is proportional to its dwell time.

$$\text{Util}(u_i) = \frac{T_i}{\sum_{j=1}^{n} T_j} \tag{1}$$

4   The Calculation of Weight for Each Measure

The evaluation based on CTR was not accurate enough. The position of document in the ranking would heavily skew user decisions. Besides spammers who intentionally advertise one content and deliver another, not all document snippets reflect accurately the document content. There were several user actions such as the dwell time on a result page and some user feedback interactions. They were as significant as CTR under certain circumstance. So we consider the measures comprehensively, and use a judge matrix to calculate the corresponding weight.

As mentioned in the previous literature[12], we defined the number of clicks on result d for query q, N(d|q), and the probability that d is relevant to q, P(d is relevant to q), then we normalize N(d|q) as CTR(d|q):

$$\text{CTR}(d|q) = \frac{N(d|q)}{\sum_{d_i} N(d_i|q)} \tag{2}$$

We consider the following measures: feedback interaction, dwell time and click-through rate, they were represented by A1, A2, A3. First we assignment for each measure relative significance, we use the number 1~5 and their reciprocal to represent the importance degree. A_{ij} in Table.1 means the proportion of importance between A_i and A_j. For example $A_{12} = 4$ means the dwell time was obviously important than CTR. W was the relevant eigenvector, the value represented the weight of corresponding measure. We can use this value to reset the relevance score of result lists, and then compared with the one ranking by CTR only.

5   Comparison of Result Lists

A lot of metrics were adopted to compare the relevance between query and result lists, such as Precision-recall, P@N, MRR, MAP and NDCG. These metrics have been used for many years, and was still employed by SE corporations. In this paper, we use MAP and NDCG to compare the two result lists generated by the method proposed before.

MAP(Mean Average Precision) defined to calculate the mean of the average of each relevant document's precision. It reflects the single performance value of the whole relevant documents in the system. The higher rank of the relevant document, the higher of the MAP was.

NDCG (Normalize Discounted cumulative gain) measures the performance of search engine by the relevant degree of each document, and integrate the position factor. Usually, we adopted classification of five degrees: very good, good, fair, bad, very bad.

6   Experiments and Results

The goal of the experiment is to prove that our method adding new features allowed us to improve the estimation of document relevance.

6.1   Design of Experiment

Research shows that 85% of the users will only check the first 10 results returned by search engine. So analyze the top 10 results and their sequence has an important meaning. It's very helpful for users get their information from thousands of retrieval results quickly and accurately, save time and improve efficiency.

For this experiment, we need to prepare some queries, search engines and some participants to perform. As mentioned above, we collected queries and user feedback form plentiful Web search logs. And search engines we use Baidu, Google andSougou. Besides we invited many experts to rank the documents according to queries and provided the standard answer sets. The experts were familiar with search engine products and were able to estimate user information needs according to context of queries.

For each query, we compare the similarity of the following three result lists:

The result list ranking by the experts (assessors);
The results ranking based on click-through data only;
The results ranking based on our method.

The first result list was considered as the standard answer, this experiment will prove that the result list ranking by our method was more accurate than that based on click-through data only.

6.2   Experimental Results

We first record the number of clicks of the top 10 pages returned by search engines for each query. Fig. 2 shows the click distribution for each query. We can know that the results at top positions have more chance to be viewed and clicked. In previous studies, they have the intuitive idea that one result with a large number of clicks might be more relevant to the query than the one with fewer clicks probabilistically. They annotate the corresponding answer using click-through data, ranking the result by CTR of each page. Nevertheless, interpreting click-through data for use in optimizing search engines was not sufficient. We draw conclusions on document relevance by observing the user behavior after she examined the document rather than based on whether a user clicks or not a document URL. On that basis, we added some user feedbacks to score the pages again.We classify the result pages for 5 levels: very good, good, fair, bad, very bad. The corresponding score was 5, 4, 3, 2, and 1. The following chart shows the comparison among three ranking methods.

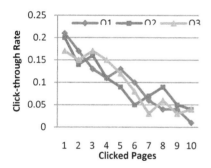
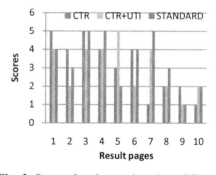

Fig. 2. Click distributions of the three queries   **Fig. 3.** Score of each page based on different measures

We can see from the Fig.3 that our method has better performance than the one based on CTR only. Our score was more close to the standard one. With the query set and corresponding answer described in the previous section, we consider the two document lists as the result returned from different search engines, the "search engine" performance was evaluated with traditional IR metrics: MAP, NDCG. The result shows in Fig.4.

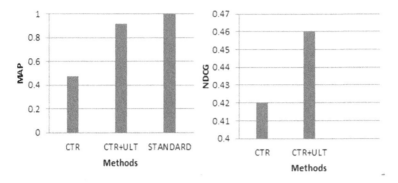

Fig. 4. MAP and NDCG improvement when adding utility feature

The experiment results show that our methods avoid the disadvantage of click-through data and allowed us to improve the estimation of document relevance. It's very useful to enhance the accuracy of corresponding answer annotation for automatic search engine performance evaluation.

7   Conclusion

In this paper, we introduced a modified method for the annotation of answer sets based on Cranfield framework. It involves a statistically significant number of users for unbiased assessment. And add several user feedbacks such as the dwell time on documents to generate corresponding answer sets automatically.

Experimental results show that our method has better performance than the one based on CTR only. Future study will focus on how to improve the evaluation reliability adding the notion of user effort. Another direction of future work is to improve the relevance estimation of result pages by using different ways that are more sensitive to user behavior.

Acknowledgments. This research was supported in part by National 863 Program (No. 2011AA01A204), National 973 Program (No. 2011CB302702), P. R. China. Thanks for the great help.

References

1. Kent, A., Berry, M., Leuhrs, F.U., Perry, J.W.: Machine literature searching VIII. Operational criteria for designing information retrieval systems. American Documentation 6(2), 93–101 (1955)
2. Oard, D.W., Kim, J.: Modeling information content using observable behavior. In: Proc. of ASIST 2001, Washington, D.C., USA, pp. 38–45 (2001)

3. Joachims, T., Granka, L., Pan, B., Hembrooke, H., Gay, G.: Accurately interpreting click-through data as implicit feedback. In: SIGIR 2005, pp. 154–161. ACM, New York (2005)
4. Sharma, H.: Automated Evaluation of Search Engine Performance via Implicit User Feedback. In: SIGIR 2005, August 15-19 (2005)
5. Dou, Z., Song, R., Yuan, X., Wen, J.R.: Are click-through data adequate for learning web search rankings? In: CIKM 2008, New York, pp. 73–82 (2008)
6. Cen, R., Liu, Y., Zhang, M., Ru, L., Ma, S.: Automatic Search Engine Performance Evaluation with the Wisdom of Crowds. In: Lee, G.G., Song, D., Lin, C.-Y., Aizawa, A., Kuriyama, K., Yoshioka, M., Sakai, T. (eds.) AIRS 2009. LNCS, vol. 5839, pp. 351–362. Springer, Heidelberg (2009)
7. Goutam, R.K., Dwivedi, S.K.: Search Engines Evaluation Using Users Efforts. In: International Conference on Computer & Communication Technology, ICCCT (2011)
8. Joachims, T.: Large-Scale Validation and Analysis of Interleaved Search Evaluation. ACM Transactions on Information Systems 30(1), Article 6 (February 2012)
9. Broder, A.: A taxonomy of web search. SIGIR Forum 36(2), 3–10 (2002)
10. Rose, D.E., Levinson, D.: Understanding user goals in web search. In: Proc. of WWW 2004, pp. 13–19. ACM, New York (2004)
11. Liu, Y., Zhang, M., Ru, L., Ma, S.: Automatic Query Type Identification Based on Click Through Information. In: Ng, H.T., Leong, M.-K., Kan, M.-Y., Ji, D. (eds.) AIRS 2006. LNCS, vol. 4182, pp. 593–600. Springer, Heidelberg (2006)
12. Hassan, A., Song, Y., He, L.: A Task Level Metric for Measuring Web Search Satisfaction and its Application on Improving Relevance Estimation. In: CIKM 2011, Glasgow, Scotland, UK, October 24-28 (2011)
13. Ali, R., Sufyan Beg, M.M.: An overview of Web search evaluation methods. Computers and Electrical Engineering 37, 835–848 (2011)
14. Cen, R., Liu, Y., Zhang, M., Ru, L., Ma, S.: Automatic Search Engine Performance Evaluation with the Wisdom of Crowds. In: Lee, G.G., Song, D., Lin, C.-Y., Aizawa, A., Kuriyama, K., Yoshioka, M., Sakai, T. (eds.) AIRS 2009. LNCS, vol. 5839, pp. 351–362. Springer, Heidelberg (2009)

Classification Research on SSL Encrypted Application

Peipei Fu[1,5], Li Guo[2], Gang Xiong[2,3,4], and Jiao Meng[3,4]

[1] Beijing University of Posts and Telecommunications, Beijing, China
[2] Institute of Information Engineering, Chinese Academy of Science, Beijing, China
[3] Institute of Computing Technology, Chinese Academy of Science, Beijing, China
[4] Graduate University of Chinese Academy of Science, Beijing, China
[5] Key Laboratory of Trustworthy Distributed Computing and Service (BUPT),
Ministry of Education, Beijing, China
mfupeipei@bupt.edu.cn

Abstract. With the rapid development of computer and communication technology, people are increasingly dependent on computers, Internet and other infrastructures. At the same time, they also bear the risks and hazards of various kinds of security incidents. Secure Sockets Layer (SSL) is used to encrypt the information on the Internet so that data can be transferred safely. This paper focuses on the study of SSL encrypted traffic and Google is chosen as an example. First, some SSL encrypted applications are studied through SSL certificates, and then we apply the C4.5 machine learning algorithm to the classification of SSL encrypted applications, using packet length, packet inter-arrival time, and the direction of a flow as features. Our classification method yields a high precision and recall rate.

Keywords: encrypted traffic, SSL protocol, traffic classification, machine learning, C4.5.

1 Introduction

With the continuous development of information technology and computer networks, the security of communication systems is facing enormous challenges, so encryption technology has been applied to a variety of applications and become an effective method to protect network security.

With a wide range of application of cryptographic protocols, encrypted traffic takes an absolute advantage in the network traffic, and will continue to increase. Accurate detection and identification of the encrypted business flow is the premise and key to fine-grained management and control of network.

Nowadays, research on encrypted traffic is mostly at the coarse-grained level, and there is little fine-grained research on encrypted traffic and SSL encrypted traffic. In this paper, we study SSL encrypted traffic at fine-grained level. We choose Google as our research object. First, we analyze different Google applications from SSL certificates, and then we make use of machine learning approach to identify encrypted applications of Google. Using C4.5 method, we select the packet length, interval,

Y. Yuan, X. Wu, and Y. Lu (Eds.): ISCTCS 2012, CCIS 320, pp. 404–411, 2013.

direction and other characteristics to identify eight kinds of applications of Google, and reach high recognition rate efficiently.

2   Evaluation Metrics

A common way to characterize a classifier's accuracy is through metrics known as False Positives, False Negatives, True Positives and True Negatives.

Table 1 illustrates the relationships between FN, FP, TP and TN.

Table 1. Evaluation Metrics

Classified as →	A	$\overline{A}$
A	TP	FN
$\overline{A}$	FP	TN

The traffic identification technology based on machine learning algorithms use recall and precision indicators to evaluate the recognition results. They defined as follows:

Recall: recall=TP/ (TP+FN).Percentage of members of class A correctly classified as belonging to class A.

Precision: precision=TP/ (TP+FP).Percentage of those instances that truly have class A, among all those classified as class A.

3   Related Work

At present, the classification of network traffic includes four types: port-based classification, payload-based classification, host behavior based classification, and machine learning classification method. But port-based and payload-based classification methods are helpless for encrypted traffic.

The identification method based on the behavioral characteristics is use of characteristic of the behavior expressed by applications to classify traffic. In [1], Karagianms et al. introduces the BLINC method to analyze the behavior of network applications in the network transport layer flow.

Machine learning identification methods are based on statistical characteristics, machine learning methods includes supervised and unsupervised method. In [2], Al-shammari et al. studied the robustness of the machine learning methods for identification of encrypted traffic.

Though extensive research has focused on encrypted traffic classification, only a comparably tiny portion has studied methods for dissecting SSL encrypted application traffic. Next, we introduce some innovation about our work.

In [3], Archibald et al. focused on disambiguating HTTP and investigated representatives of classes of applications, namely social networking (Facebook), web-mail (Gmail), and streaming video applications (YouTube), all of which communicate via the HTTP protocol. Actually, the research is on HTTPS protocol, because the three applications all support encryption access. They used SVM method, choosing packet size and time-interval as their identification feature. In our work, the innovation of our research is that it is a fine-grained classification of SSL encrypted applications based on a particular platform (like, Google). We study certificates and use the C4.5 decision tree method and use the statistical characteristics of the flow: the packet length, the time interval and direction.

In [4], Schatzmann et al. focused on the in-depth research on HTTPS and separate webmail traffic from other HTTPS traffic. They leveraged correlations across (related) protocols and exploited timing characteristics of webmail applications. SVM method was used to discriminate between the two class mail and non-mail. Our work differs in several respects from this article. First, we study the HTTPS traffic at the fine-grained level, and distinguish the types of SSL encrypted application (such as Google reader, Google news and so on). Second, we analyze SSL encrypted applications based on their certificates. Third, we use C4.5 decision tree method for classification.

4   Research on SSL Encrypted Application

4.1   SSL Application Background

SSL was designed to provide application-independent transaction security for the Internet. It allows protocols such as HTTP, FTP, and Telnet to be layered on top of it transparently. The most commonly used is HTTP over SSL, namely HTTPS, it uses port 443. It is the main research of this paper.

In addition to the HTTPS protocol, SSL also can be applied to some other protocol to ensure safety. Table 2 lists some protocol based on SSL.

Table 2. Protocol based on SSL

Common Protocol	Protocol based on SSL	Port number
FTP	FTPS-data/FTPS	989/990
IMAP4	IMAPS	993
LDAP	LDAPS	636
NNTP	NNTPS	563
POP3	POP3S	995
SMTP	SMTPS	465
Telnet	Telnets	992

4.2   SSL Protocol Introduction

Secure Sockets Layer (SSL) is a system to encrypt information transmitted on the Internet so that security of data transmission may be accomplished. SSL protocol maintains the security and integrity of the transmission channel by using encryption, authentication and message authentication codes.

The SSL protocol is located between in the TCP / IP protocol and a variety of application layer protocol, it provide security support for data communications. The SSL protocol can be divided into the following two layers. The SSL record protocol: It is built on a reliable transport protocol (TCP), and provides data encapsulation, compression, encryption and other basic functions support for high-level protocol. SSL handshake protocol: it is built on top of the SSL Record Protocol, and used before the start of the actual data transmission, and to authenticate, negotiate the encryption algorithm and exchange encryption keys between the communicating parties.

SSL handshake protocol is encapsulated in the record protocol, the protocol allows the server and client authenticate each other before the application to transmit and receive data, to negotiate an encryption algorithm and key. Establishing an SSL connection for the first time, it needs to exchange a series of messages on server and client. The process of SSL handshake is shown in Fig.1, the * transmission are optional, indicate packets do not always send.

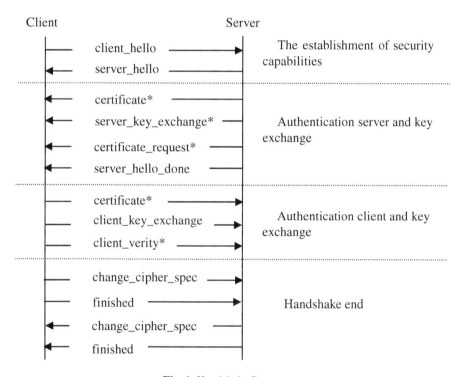

Fig. 1. Handshake Process

4.3   SSL Certificate Analysis of Google Encrypted Application

SSL protocol itself provides some information for the study of identification and analysis of cryptographic applications. The following introduced were the analysis of SSL encrypted application from the certificate.

When establishing an SSL connection, certificate will be send between client and server to verify the identity, and verify the legitimacy of the certificate. We conducted a statistical analysis of data obtained within one month from March 2012 to April 2012 in actual campus network, we get almost 250 kinds of certificates in total , a higher frequency of the certificates are shown in Table 3.

Table 3. Google Encryption Certificate

Number	Certificate
1	*.google.com
2	www.google.com
3	*.googleapis.com
4	*.googleusercontent.com
5	*.gstatic.com
6	*.google.com.hk
7	mail.google.com
8	*.g.doubleclick.net
9	accounts.google.com
10	*.mail.google.com
11	*.googlecode.com
12	*.google-analytics.com
13	talk.google.com
14	www.gmail.com
15	*.googleadservices.com
16	*.doubleclick.net

By observing these certificates, we can roughly determine which kind of Google applications the user is currently using. For example, we can roughly know that the users are using Gmail from certificate mail.google.com and *.mail.google.com. From *.doubleclick.net, we can roughly determine that the users are using Google advertising application. However, there is the situation that one application uses a variety of certificates or more applications with only one certificate, such as certificate *.google.com and www.google.com. So, it is difficult for us to separate Google applications simply according to the certificates, but it still provides a certain amount of information to analyze SSL encrypted applications.

4.4   Google Encrypted Application Research Based on Machine Learning Method

Though we can obtain some useful information from the certificates to study Google encrypted applications, but due to the complexity of actual network traffic, these analysis can't be effective to distinguish Google encrypted applications, and therefore we need to seek effective traffic classification methods to identify them.

Machine learning method is commonly used in traffic classification and it is an effective way for encrypted traffic. It depends on the statistical characteristics of data streams. WEKA is an open data mining workbench, a collection of machine learning algorithms are able to take data mining tasks, including data preprocessing, classification, regression, clustering, association rules and visualization in a new interactive interface. We use WEKA tool in our experiment.

Early in the experiment, we use WEKA to contrast the two kinds of machine learning methods, namely Libsvm (selection of the RBF kernel function) and C4.5. We use these two methods to identify four kinds of Google encrypted application, that is, Google image, Google reader, Google news and Google maps. The training number for each application is 800 traffic records and the test number is 600 traffic records. We analyze the first 6,8,10,12,15 packets of a flow respectively, and use packet length, time interval and direction as features, use 10-fold cross validation, the identification results of two machine learning methods show in Fig. 2.

It can be seen from the experimental results that C4.5 is better than Libsvm in classification rate. Therefore, we select the C4.5 method as our ultimate identification method.

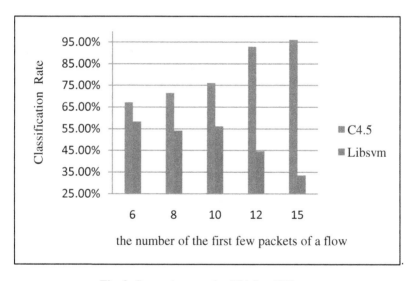

Fig. 2. Comparison result of C4.5 and Libsvm

In order to increase the classification rate, we try to increase the average of packet size and the average of time interval as our feature. Through experiments, we found no significant difference in the recognition result.

So, we only use packet length, packet arrival time interval, and the flow direction to classify eight kinds of Google applications, the classification rate reach 95.39%. Fig.3. shows the recall rate and precision of Google eight kinds of encrypted applications.

Google Application	Recall	Precision
Google image	0.955	0.986
Google reader	0.975	0.975
Google news	0.945	0.953
Google maps	0.937	0.937
Google+	0.93	0.932
Gmail	0.947	0.936
Google docs	0.957	0.947
Google video	0.987	0.967

Fig. 1. Recall and Precision of eight kinds of Google Applications

5   Conclusion and Future Work

The widespread use of encryption makes it quite difficult to carry out network management, so the study of cryptographic protocols and the recognition of the encrypted traffic has become very important.

In this paper, we analyze and study SSL encrypted traffic and Google is chosen as an example of SSL encrypted applications. First, we analyze the Google applications from the SSL certificates. Then we compare the effectiveness of C4.5 and Libsvm method. Finally, we choose packet length, packet inter-arrival time, and the flow direction as our recognition features, and use the C4.5 method to identify the types of Google applications. Experiment results show that a good identification rate is obtained by our method.

The next phase of our work should include the following aspects: First, it is necessary to use C4.5 method in the actual network environment. Second, we should be able to find new methods and features to identify more encrypted applications based on SSL protocol.

Acknowledgements. This work is supported by the "Strategic Priority Research Program" of the Chinese Academy of Sciences (Grant No. XDA06030200), the National High-Tech Research and Development Plan "863" of China (Grant No. 2011AA010703) and the National Natural Science Foundation (Grant No. 61070184).

References

1. Karagiannis, T., Papagiannaki, K., Faoutsos, M.: BLINC: multilevel traffic classification in the dark. In: ACM SIGCOMM, Philadelphia, USA (2005)
2. Alshammari, R., Zincir-Heywood, A.N.: Machine Learning Based Encrypted Traffic Classification: Identifying SSH and Skype. In: Proceedings of the 2009 IEEE Symposium on Computation Intelligence in Security and Defense Applications, Ottawa, pp. 1–8 (2009)

3. Archibald, R., Liu, Y., Corbett, C., Ghosal, D.: Disambiguating HTTP: Classifying Web Applications. In: 2011 7th International on Wireless Communications and Mobile Computing Conference (IWCMC), Istanbul, pp. 1808–1813 (2011)
4. Schatzmann, D., Mühlbauer, W.: Digging into HTTPS: Flow-Based Classification of Webmail Traffic. In: ACM SIGCOMM, New York, USA, pp. 322–327 (2010)
5. Okada, Y., Ata, S., Nakamura, N., Nakahira, Y., Oka, I.: Comparisons of Machine Learning Algorithms for Application Identification of Encrypted Traffic. In: International Conference on Machine Learning and Applications, Honolulu, Hi, pp. 358–361 (2011)
6. Hirvonen, M., Sailio, M.: Two-Phased Method for Identifying SSH Encrypted Application Flows. In: 2011 7th International on Wireless Communications and Mobile Computing Conference (IWCMC), Istanbul, pp. 1033–1038 (2011)
7. Zander, S., Nguyen, T., Armitage, G.: Automated traffic classification and application identification using machine learning. In: IEEE 30th Conference on Local Computer Networks (LCN 2005), Sydney, Australia (2005)
8. Nguyen, T.T.T., Armitage, G.: A Survey of techniques for Internet Traffic Classification using Machine Learning. IEEE Communications Surveys & Tutorials 10(4), 56–76 (2008)
9. Park, B., Hong, J.W., Won, Y.J.: Toward Fine-Grained Traffic Classification. IEEE Communications Magazine, 104–111 (2011)
10. Liu, C., Shen, B., Hu, N.: Analysis the trusted computing technology and its development. Information Security and Technology (2012) (in Chinese)
11. WEKA, http://www.cs.waikato.ac.nz/ml/weka/

S-URL Flux: A Novel C&C Protocol for Mobile Botnets

Wang Shuai[1,2], Cui Xiang[2], Liao Peng[2], and Li Dan[3,4]

[1] Institute of Information Engineering，Chinese Academy of Sciences, Beijing, China
[2] Institute of Computing Technology, Chinese Academy of Sciences, Beijing, China
[3] Beijing University of Posts and Telecommunications, Beijing, China
[4] Key Laboratory of Trustworthy Distributed Computing and Service (BUPT),
Ministry of Education, Beijing, China
pingpangtu@gmail.com

Abstract. The rapid development of 3G/WiFi network and Smartphone has greatly stimulated the evolution of mobile botnets. Mobile botnets have attracted extensive attentions from the academic community. In this paper, we introduce our design of an advanced mobile botnet called SUbot which exploits a novel command and control (C&C) strategy named Shorten-URL Flux (short for S-URL Flux). The proposed SUbot would have desirable features including being stealthy, resilient and low-cost (i.e., low battery power consumption, low traffic consumption and low money cost).This paper focuses on the design principle of the mobile botnet. In comparison to traditional mobile botnet, SUbot has stronger adaptability and stability. It's of great significance to research and defend against such kind of advance mobile botnet.

Keywords: Shorten URL, S-URL Flux, mobile botnet, C&C.

1 Introduction

With the rapid development of the smartphones, it greatly promotes the development of mobile network. Many new security problems have cropped up at the same time, especially mobile botnets. The term mobile botnets refers to a group of compromised smartphones that are remotely controlled by botmasters via C&C channels. PC-based botnets, what we called traditional botnets, have become one of the most serious threats to Internet. Compared to traditional botnets, the development of mobile botnets is at the beginning stage, and corresponding research on them are very limited. A number of factors restrict the development of mobile botnets. Such as limited battery power, limited network traffic, no fixed IP, etc. With the increasing number of the smartphones, we have to pay more attention to the security of them. Compared with PC, mobile phones tend to store more personal information, such as a lot of messages, contacts, etc. The emergence of open-source smartphone platforms such as Android and third-party applications made available to the public also provides more opportunities for malware creators. Therefore, smartphones have become one of the most attractive targets for hackers. Since the appearance of Cabir, the first mobile worm (which was introduced in 2004), we have witnessed a significant evolution in mobile

Y. Yuan, X. Wu, and Y. Lu (Eds.): ISCTCS 2012, CCIS 320, pp. 412–419, 2013.

malware. Although the number of mobile malware has been growing steadily, their functionalities have remained simple until the development of the first mobile botnet in 2009. The mobile botnet, SymbOS.Yxes [2], targets Symbian and exploits a simple HTTP-based C&C. Later the same year, Ikee.B [3], which targets jailbroken iPhones and has a C&C mechanism similar to SymbOS.Yxes, was released. In December 2010, the first Android botnet, Geinimi, broke out mainly in China, still using similar HTTP-based C&C. Although advanced mobile botnets have not been witnessed in the main population of smartphones, we believe it is just a matter of time. Mobile botnets are presently posing serious threats for both end users and cellular networks [4]. Consequently, investigations into how mobile botnets work, as well as how they may be developed and stopped, represents an important area of research.

In this paper, we propose a design method of a mobile botnet, which based on the HTTP protocol and the S-URL Flux. We called the botnet running on the mobile based on the method SUbot. SUbot is the expansion and improvement of Andbot [1].It adds the Shorten-URL Flux method to the design of the C&C. With the method, we can access one network server to get the command, instead of two network servers accessed in the Andbot.

The rest of the paper is organized as follows. Section 2 introduces related studies. Section 3 discusses the overview of SUbot. Section 4 introduces the design of SUbot. In Section 5, we compare SUbot and Andbot to prove the advantage of our design.In Section 6,we give an experiment to prove the advantages of our design. Then We introduce possible defense in Section 7. We give the conclusion in Section 8.

2   Related Work

Botnets have been an active research topic in recent years. Current research on botnets is focused primarily on detection, measurement, tracking, mitigation, and future botnet prediction. Our research belongs to the last category.

There are several differences between smartphones and PCs. These differences lead to a number of challenges in the construction of mobile botnets [4, 9]. (1). the battery power is rather limited on smartphones when compared with PCs. (2). the cost of smartphones is an extremely sensitive area for many users. (3). if C&C consumes an abnormal amount of network traffic, the abnormity is likely to be noticed. (4). the absence of public IP addresses and a constant change in network connectivity makes the robust P2P-based C&C in PC-based botnets impractical, and potentially impossible, in smartphones.

Considering the above challenges faced by botmasters, Mulliner et al. [4, 5] proposed a SMS-HTTP hybrid C&C. The main idea of the hybrid is to split the communication into a HTTP and a SMS part. The encrypted and signed commands file is uploaded to a website and the corresponding URL is distributed via SMS. But there are two defects in this structure: (1). The SMS-based C&C (especially P2P topology) will inescapably cause excessive fees to users which lead to detection; and (2). The simple HTTP-based C&C scheme suffers a single-point-failure. Based on the above shortcomings, Cui Xiang et al. proposed a botnet structure based on the HTTP protocol and URL FLUX, and implemented Andbot on android system[1]. Andbot uses of the network server to store command pictures and publish these pictures' address. It has the advantage of high controllability and low-cost. But it also has a shortcoming in this structure: When trying to get the command from the network, Andbot needs to access the micro-blogging server to get the URL of the command JPG file firstly. Then it uses the URL to access the JPG file. So each command needs to visit two servers.

3   Overview of SUbot

To outline the rough sketch of the complete C&C procedures of SUbot, the following list provides the sequence of operations for both botmaster and SUbot in Fig. 1.

① Botmaster encrypts and signs the commands to be issued then binds the ciphertext with a small JPG file.
② Botmaster uploads the JPG file to a Blog, then gets the URL of the picture.
③ Botmaster translates the URL which gets from ② to specified URL like http://tinyurl.com/t10000000 with the help of some websites, such as http://tinyurl.com.
④ SUbot visits the URLs which generated by Shorten-URL FLUX (S-URL FLUX) one by one until finding the useful JPG file.
⑤ SUbot download the JPG file.
⑥ SUbot recovers plaintext commands from the JPG.
⑦ SUbot executes commands.

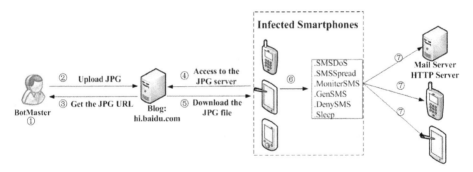

Fig. 1. The C&C Architecture of SUbot

4   SUbot Command and Control Design

Like many other botnets [6], SUbot also uses RSA to authenticate commands, so botnet hijacking is not a major problem. To obtain the capability described above, we design the C&C of SUbot sensitively and thoroughly. This chapter mainly describes the design of the SUbot, including uploading JPG file and downloading the command file.

4.1   Upload the JPG File

In the first step, a botmaster encrypts the commands to be published using RC4 then signs it using her private key which is corresponding to the public key hard-coded in SUbot. Second, the botmaster appends the ciphertext and its length to the end of a JPG file.

After generating the special JPG file, the botmaster uploads it to a public website, such as a blog or picture-hosting site. Then the botmaster compress the raw URL using popular services such as bit.ly and tinyurl.com to generate the specified URL. For example: botmaster will convert http://hiphotos.baidu.com/%D2%BB%BD%A3%B0%C1%D1%AA/abpic/item/e162 175c352ac65c318934d1fbf2b21191138af2.jpg to http://tinyurl.com/t10000000, and t10000000 will be generated in the SUbot Automatically.

4.2   Get Commands

How to get commands from website is one of the most important parts in the design of SUbot. It's also the main difference between SUbot and Andbot.

- **Uses Shorten-URL FLUX (S-URL FLUX) to generate URLs directly:** SUbot hard-codes one or more abbreviated address websites, such as http://tinyurl.com/, and a Domain Generation Algorithm (DGA). SUbot first uses DGA to generate a list of domains, such as q97415023151, et. Then uses S-URL FLUX to combine abbreviated address websites and domains, such as http://tinyurl.com/q97415023151,et. The S-URL FLUX Algorithm is shown in Fig. 2.
- **Visits the URLs generated by S-URL FLUX one by one:** In order to find commands, SUbot tries to visit the URLs generated by S-URL FLUX, one by one. If the visited URL exists, downloads the command file. If not, SUbot will try to visit another URL in the list.
- **Verifies the JPG file and decrypted the message:** SUbot will verify the JPG file using a hard-coded public key and decrypted the message using its RC4 symmetric key.
- **Executes the plaintext commands:** If obtains the commands, SUbot will execute the plaintext commands as the way we defined.

4.3   Security Mechanisms

A significant rise of the phone bill, traffic, or excessive consumption of battery power will lead to investigation of the cause, and thus may lead to bot detection. Thus, several methods were designed to minimize the consumption of the above resources.

- **Shorten-URL Flux:** S-URL FLUX is the most import point in our paper. Using this method, we can generate the URLs of the command JPG files directly. Then we can download the command JPG file from the server. Compared to Andbot, SUbot can get the command from one server, other than two. It not only reduces network traffic, but the dependence of the network server.

● **URL Caching:** Usually the command JPG file will be saved on the server for a period of time. Once one authorized URL, which points to correctly signed commands, is found, SUbot will cache it in its period of validity. When needs to get the commands, SUbot will use the caching URL first. URL Caching can reduce the network traffic and accelerates the speed of execution of the bot.

Algorithm 1. SURL FLUX Algorithm

```
1 //Q is the queue to save the URL prefix we hard-code
in 2 the SUbot
3 SURLFLUX(Queue Q)
4 {
5 Queue URL; //save the urls we will access to
6 String full_url;//save one of the urls,such as
7 http://tinyurl.com/t10000000
8 while(Q.next())
9 {
10    results = DGA(current_time);//use current time to
11    generate a list of domains,such as t10000000
12    for(result in results)
13    {
14      full_url = Q.element+result;//such as
15      http://tinyurl.com/t10000000
16      URL.add(full_url);
17    }
18 }
19 }
20 /*
21 generate a list of domains,such as t10000000
22 */
23 DGA(current_time)
24 {
25  return a list of domains
26 }
```

---

5   Andbot VS SUbot

We will compare SUbot and Andbot from the way they work below:

● **Andbot:** When trying to get the command from the network, Andbot needs to access the micro-blogging server to get the URL of the command JPG file first, then it uses the URL to access the command picture. So each command needs to visit two servers. During this period, it has to download many useless xml files.

- **SUbot:** Using of the S-URL FLUX, SUbot can generate the URL of the command JPG file in the program. It accesses and downloads the JPG file from the JPG server directly.
- **Advantage of SUbot:** For security reasons, fewer and fewer micro-blogging sites provide the interface to be accessed by users without authentication. It's difficult to find a suitable micro-blogging site for Andbot. SUbot does not need the micro-blogging server, so SUbot has a better network adaptability than Andbot. Comparison of Figures. 4 and Figures. 5, it's easy to see that SUbot is easier to be achieved than Andbot. With less network access, SUbot consumes less network traffic than Andbot.

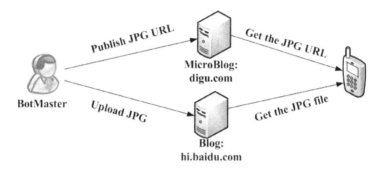

Fig. 2. URL Flux-based C&C

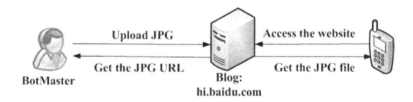

Fig. 3. Short URL Flux-based C&C

6   Evaluation of SUbot

To evaluate the functions and performance of SUbot, we've conducted preliminary experiments. We firstly convert http://hiphotos.baidu.com/%D 2%BB%BD%A3%B0%C1%D1%AA/abpic/item/e162175c352ac65c318934d1fbf2b2 1191138af2.jpg to http://is.gd/paqs28422339. We use SUbot and Andbot to obtain the same command from the website. Results are shown in Table 1 and Table 2. Comparing Table 1 and Table 2, we can find that SUbot can only visit one server(hi.baidu.com) to get the command , but Andbot needs two(hi.baidu.com and zuosa.com).What's more, SUbot requires less network traffic and less access time.

Table 1. The data of SUbot

URL	Exist	Time(second)	Size(Byte)	Result
http://is.gd/6110504 12256	No	3s	2682	No
http://is.gd/opodcm0 22192	No	4s	2682	No
http://is.gd/paqs2842 2339	Yes	5s	2318	.SendSMS#1#H ello

Table 2. The data of Andbot

URL	Exist	Time(second)	Size(Byte)	Result
http://zuosa.com/rss/ user/122621219359	No	4s	3715	No
http://zuosa.com/rss/ user/611050412256	No	4s	3715	No
http://zuosa.com/rss/ user/opodcm022192	Yes	6s	4123	http://is.gd/paqs2 8422339
http://is.gd/paqs2842 2339	Yes	4s	2318	.SendSMS#1#He llo

7   Defense against SUbot

We introduce possible defense in two ways. First, an internationally coordinated co-operation channel should be set up quickly to identify and defend against this technology; second, we should pay more attention to the URLs which start with a specific string, such as http://tinyurl/com/.

- **Building International Coordinated Mechanism:** The C&C of SUbot relies on Web 2.0 Services. For this reason, defenders should focus their defense effort on publicly available Web 2.0 services such as Microblog, blog, Google App Engine, etc. This effort can prevent these services from being abused.
- **Pay more attention to the URLs which start with a specific string:** SUbot lies on the internal auto-generated URLs to access the JPG files. In our design, all the URLs start with a common prefix. If we could prevent the phone to access these specific URLs, the bot will not get the command.

8   Conclusion

As smartphones continue to gain more capabilities, they become attractive targets to hackers. To be well prepared for the promise attack, we, as defenders, should study mobile botnets attacking techniques that are likely to be developed by botmasters in the near future. In this paper, we presented the design of a stealthy, resilient, and low cost mobile botnet called SUbot. SUbot is more suitable for the mobile platform. We believe that this architecture botnet will outbreak soon. Therefore, research on SUbot is very important. By understanding its structure, we can make the best defensive measures.

References

1. Cui, X., Fang, B., Yin, L., Liu, X.: Andbot: Towards Advanced Mobile Botnets. In: Proc. of the 4th USENIX Workshop on Large-scale Exploits and Emergent Threats (LEET 2011) (2011)
2. Apvrille, A.: Symbian worm Yxes Towards mobile botnets,
   http://www.fortiguard.com/papers/EICAR2010_
   Symbian-Yxes_Towards-Mobile-Botnets.pdf
3. Porras, P.A., Saidi, H., Yegneswaran, V.: An Analysis of the iKee.B iPhone Botnet. In: Proceedings of the 2nd International ICST Conference on Security and Privacy on Mobile Information and Communications Systems (May 2010)
4. Mulliner, C.: Fuzzing the Phone in your Phone,
   http://www.mulliner.org/security/sms/feed/smsfuzz_26c3.pdf
5. Mulliner, C., SeifertIn, J.P.: Rise of the iBots: Owning a telco network. In: The Proceedings of the 5th IEEE International Conference on Malicious and Unwanted Software (Malware)Nancy, France, October 19-20 (2010)
6. Wang, P., Sparks, S., et al.: An advanced hybrid peer to peer botnet. In: Proc. of the HotBots 2007, First Workshop on Hot Topics in Understanding Botnets, Cambridge, MA (2007)
7. Singh, K., Sangal, S., Jain, N., Traynor, P., Lee, W.: Evaluating Bluetooth as a Medium for Botnet Command and Control. In: Kreibich, C., Jahnke, M. (eds.) DIMVA 2010. LNCS, vol. 6201, pp. 61–80. Springer, Heidelberg (2010)
8. Mulliner, C.: Fuzzing the Phone in your Phone,
   http://www.mulliner.org/security/sms/feed/smsfuzz_26c3.pdf
9. Traynor, P., Lin, M., Ongtang, M., Rao, V., Jaeger, T., La Porta, T., McDaniel, P.: On Cellular Botnets:Measuring the Impact of Malicious Devices on a Cellular Network Core. In: ACM Conference on Computer and Communications Security (CCS) (November 2009)
10. Nash, D.C., Martin, T.L., Ha, D.S., Hsiao, M.S.: Towards an intrusion detection system for battery exhaustion attacks on mobile computing devices. In: Proceedings of the Third IEEEInternational Conference on Pervasive Computing and Communications Workshops, PERCOMW 2005, pp. 141–145. IEEE Computer Society, Washington, DC (2005)
11. Kim, H., Smith, J., Shin, K.G.: Detecting energygreedy anomalies and mobile malware variants. In: MobiSys (2008)
12. Davis, N.: Battery-based intrusion detection. In: Proceedings of the Global Telecommunications Conference (2004)

An Efficient Ellipse-Shaped Blobs Detection Algorithm
for Breaking Facebook CAPTCHA

Peipeng Liu[1,2,3], Jinqiao Shi[3], Lihong Wang[4], and Li Guo[3]

[1] Institute of Computing Technology, CAS, China
[2] Graduate University, CAS, China
[3] Institute of Information Engineering, CAS, China
{liupeipeng,shijinqiao,guoli}@software.ict.ac.cn
[4] National Computer Network Emergency Response Technical Team/Coordination
Center of China
wlh@isc.org.cn

Abstract. A CAPTCHA is a test designed to distinguish computer programs from human beings, in order to prevent the abuse of network resources. And nowadays, academic researches on CAPTCHA, including designing friendly but secure CAPTCHA systems and breaking existing CAPTCHA systems, are becoming a more and more hot topic. Breaking an existing CAPTCHA system can help to perfect its designs and therefore to improve its security. In this paper, ESBDA, an Ellipse-Shaped Blobs Detection Algorithm, is proposed to detect the ellipse-shaped blobs used in Facebook CAPTCHA scheme, which can be used to break the Facebook CAPTCHA system. The approach is based on detecting the contour of the ellipse-shaped blobs on the basis of erosion and dilation technologies. And the experimental results show that ESBDA can effectively remove the noised ellipse-shaped blobs in the Facebook CPATCHA scheme.

Keywords: CAPTCHA Breaking, Facebook, Ellipse-Shaped blobs.

1   Introduction

A CAPTCHA (Completely Automated Public Turing Test to Tell Computers and Humans Apart) is a program that generates and grades tests that are human solvable, but intend to be beyond the capabilities of current computer programs [1]. Nowadays, CAPTCHA is becoming a more and more important security technology for defeating those undesirable or malicious Internet bot programs, such as those registering thousands of free SNS accounts instantly. And it has found widespread application on numerous commercial web sites including Google, Youtube and Facebook.

With the development of CAPTCHA, academic researches on it are becoming a more and more hot topic.   These researches include both designing friendly but secure CAPTCHA systems and breaking existing CAPTCHA systems. It seems that CAPTCHA will go through the same process of evolutionary development as cryptography, digital watermarking and the like, with an iterative process in which successful attacks lead to the development of more robust systems [5, 10].

Y. Yuan, X. Wu, and Y. Lu (Eds.): ISCTCS 2012, CCIS 320, pp. 420–428, 2013.
© Springer-Verlag Berlin Heidelberg 2013

At the moment, the most popular CAPTCHAs are text-based schemes, which rely on sophisticated distortion of text images aimed at letting them difficult to recognize for the state of the art of pattern recognition methods .However, researches suggested that computers are very good at recognizing single characters, even if they are highly distorted [2], with standard machine learning techniques such as neural networks [3, 9, 17]. But when the location of characters in a CAPTCHA challenge is not known a-priori, state of the art (including machine learning) techniques do not work well in recognizing them. So, the state of the art of CAPTCHA design suggests that the robustness of text-based schemes should rely on the difficulty of finding where the character is rather than which character it is [3,4].

As a result, more and more well-known web sites, such as Youtube, Facebook and CNN, begin to employ novel technologies to increase the difficulty of locating where the character is in a CAPTCHA challenge. And it becomes more and more difficult to break a CAPTCHA system.

In this paper, focusing on Facebook CAPTCHA scheme, ESBDA, an Ellipse-Shaped Blobs Detection Algorithm, is proposed to detect and remove the ellipse-shaped blobs used in Facebook CAPTCHA scheme. And it proves that, with a novel algorithm, an attacker can effectively eliminate the ellipse-shaped blobs so as to use traditional segmentation and recognition algorithms to break the Facebook CAPTCHA, and the Facebook CAPTCHA scheme designers should take some measures to improve their security.

The experiments have achieved a satisfactory effect in eliminating the ellipse-shaped blobs used in Facebook CAPTCHA scheme. And it believes that, by attacking well-designed, deployed CAPTCHA, we can learn how they could fail and could be improved. Overall, this paper contributes to immediate improvement of the security of the CAPTCHA that were widely deployed by Facebook, as well as other schemes exhibiting similar weaknesses.

The remainder of this paper is organized as follows. Section 2 discusses related works. Section 3 reviews the Facebook CAPTCHA scheme .Section 4 and section 5 detail the algorithm and its results respectively. Section 6 summarizes this paper, discusses future works and offers conclusions.

2   Related Works

With the development of CPATCHAs, more and more researchers begin to pay attentions to it, including both the ones who want to improve the security of CAPTCHA and the ones who try to break them.

Nowadays, almost all of the popular CAPTCHA schemes focus their challenges on the difficulty of segmenting characters. For example, Youtube CAPTCHA adopts "crowding characters together" mechanism to make it very hard to separate two adjacent characters (see Fig.1 (a)). CNN CAPTCHA adds irregular noise lines which pass through the characters so that it is difficult to distinguish the characters and the noise lines (see Fig.1 (c)). Differently, the Facebook CAPTCHA adds two ellipse-shaped blobs, inside of which the color is inverted, into its CAPTCHA images making it very hard to distinguish the background and the foreground (see Fig.1 (b)).

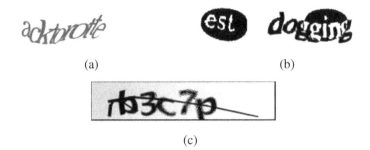

(a)   (b)

(c)

Fig. 1. (a) The Youtube CAPTCHA scheme (b) The Facebook CAPTCHA scheme (c) The CNN CAPTCHA scheme

A survey on CAPTCHA research (including the design of most early notable schemes) can be found in [11], and the limitations of defending against bots with CAPTCHA (including protocol-level attacks) were discussed in [13].

In [5], Jeff Yan detailed the Microsoft's CAPTCHA scheme and designed a special algorithm to break it, and his algorithm achieved a high success rate. Huang SY proposed special breaking algorithms against MSN and YAHOO CAPTCHA schemes in [15] and experiments showed that his algorithms worked well.

It seems that, a specific CAPTCHA breaking algorithm is only for a certain type of CAPTCHA scheme, and there is not a general algorithm for all types of CAPTCHA schemes. In this paper, focusing on Facebook CAPTCHA scheme, ESBDA is proposed to detect and remove the ellipse-shaped blobs used in Facebook CAPTCHA scheme, making it possible for an attacker to break it.

3   The Facebook CAPTCHA Scheme

Some more sample challenges generated by the Facebook CAPTCHA scheme are shown in Fig. 2. We have no access to the codebase of the Facebook scheme, so we collected from Facebook website random samples that were generated in real time online. By studying the samples we collected, we observed that the Facebook CAPTCHA scheme has the following characteristics.

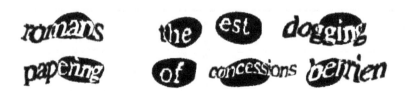

Fig. 2. The Facebook CAPTCHA: 4 sample challenges

- Two words are used in each CAPTCHA , and there is a white space between them
- Warping   is used for character distortion
- Each word has an ellipse-shaped blob. Outside of the ellipse-shaped blobs, the foreground is dark grey and background is light grey. While inside of   the ellipse-shaped blobs , the colors are inverted

Warping is commonly used for distortion in text-based CAPTCHA. However, ellipse-shaped blobs are added as clutters in the Facebook CAPTCHA scheme. The rationale was as follows. These ellipse-shaped blobs make it hard to separate the foreground color and the background color, and as a result, it is very difficult to know which pixels are used to form the words. The included ellipse-shaped blobs would confuse the state of the art segmentation methods, providing strong segmentation resistance.

4   Ellipse-Shaped Blobs Detection Algorithm

We have developed a low-cost and efficient algorithm that can effectively detect and remove the ellipse-shaped blobs generated by the Facebook CAPTCHA scheme. Specifically, the algorithm achieves the followings:

- Separate the two words in the challenges
- Detect and remove the ellipse-shaped blob in each word

The algorithm is built on observing and analyzing the random samples we collected. And the algorithm involves 5 consecutive steps [see Fig. 3], each of which is detailed in the following sections.

Fig. 3. The steps of the algorithm

4.1   Pre-processing

Firstly, we convert a rich-color CAPTCHA image to a black-white image using a threshold method: pixels with intensity higher than a threshold value are converted to white, and those with a lower intensity to black (see Fig. 4 (a) and (b)). The threshold was manually determined by analyzing the sample CAPTCHA challenges.

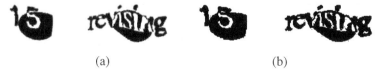

(a)   (b)

Fig. 4. Pre-processing. (a)   Original image, (b) Binarized image.

The second step of pre-processing is to separate the two words in a CAPTCHA. We project the binarized image to the x-axis, and get those areas which do not contain black pixels which we marked as white area [15]. At last, we use the second white area as a boundary to separate the CAPTCHA into two parts each containing a word (see Fig. 5).

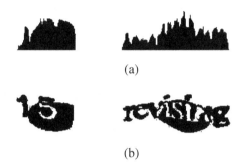

(a)

(b)

Fig. 5. (a) The result of projection (b) The result of words-separation

4.2   Remove Small White Connected-Components

In this step, an algorithm is applied to each part separated in the previous step to turn the small white connected-components to black. The basic idea of this algorithm is to detect every connected white component, and turn the small ones to black .The algorithm works as follow. First, detect a white pixel, and then trace all its white neighbors until all pixels in this connected component are traversed. Next, the algorithm locates a white pixel outside of the detected ones, and start another traversal process to identify a next component. This process continues until all white connected components are located .And at last, after we get all the white connected-components, the algorithm turn the white connected-components, except for the largest one, to black (see Fig. 6).

Fig. 6. Remove small white connected-components

4.3   Erosion

Erosion is applied in this step to eliminate the small irregular apophysises in the images obtained by previous steps. The erosion process works as follows. First we find all the black pixels in the image, and then for each black pixel, we check whether it has a white neighbor, if it has, we turn it to white, otherwise it remains unchanged. Then we repeatedly use the erosion process, and leave only a few black connected-components left in the image. The number of erosion iterations is manually determined by analyzing the sample CAPTCHA challenges. And at last, we remove the little black connected-components which have significantly less pixels than others. Finally, we get Fig. 7.

Fig. 7. The result of Erosion

4.4   Dilation

After erosion, an immediate step is to dilation .The dilation algorithm aims to recover the ellipse as much as possible. In contrast to erosion, the dilation process adds black pixels to the image. The first step of dilation is to find all white pixels in the image ,and then for each white pixel ,the algorithm check all of its neighbors to determine whether it has a black neighbor , and depending on the determination ,the algorithm decide to turn the white pixel to black or not. The number of   dilation iterations is same to the erosion process. And after adopting the dilation algorithm, the images become like Fig. 8.

Fig. 8. The result of Dilation

4.5   Eliminate Ellipse-Shaped blobs

After the previous steps, an elimination algorithm is applied with Fig. 5 and Fig. 8 as inputs to remove the ellipse-shaped blobs. This elimination algorithm is simple and it acts like this. For each pixel in Fig. 5, the algorithm checks the corresponding pixel with the same coordinates in Fig. 8, and if the pixel in Fig. 8 is black, the algorithm changes the corresponding pixel in Fig. 5 to its opposite color; otherwise the color of the pixel in Fig. 5 remains unchanged. After applying the elimination algorithm, the algorithm process is finished, and the final effects are shown in Fig. 9.

Fig. 9. The final results of the algorithm

5   Results

The images after pre-process and the images after eliminating ellipse-shaped blobs are shown in Table 1. We use visual effects to express the quality of the results. Obviously, ESBDA has got satisfactory results, and it effectively removed the noised ellipse-shaped blobs, making it possible to break the Facebook CPATCHAs, since without the color-inverted blobs, it becomes easier to segment the characters in the CAPTCHA images and recognize them with current image processing technologies and machine learning technologies [3, 9, and 17].

Table 1. Experiment results

The images after pre-process	The images after eliminating ellipse-shaped blobs	Visual effects
of understood	of un terstood	poor
men extends	men extends	satisfactory
15 revising	15 revising	good
of papering	of papering	good
est dogging	est dogging	satisfactory

6   Conclusions and Future Works

This paper has shown that although the Facebook CAPTCHA scheme intentionally bases its robustness on ellipse-shaped blobs, a simple and low-cost algorithm can effectively remove the ellipse-shaped noised blobs. Our algorithm has achieved a satisfactory effect and it applies that it is possible for an attacker to break the Facebook CAPTCHA. Therefore, it shows that the Facebook CAPTCHA scheme   provides a false sense of security.

Besides, we analyzed all cases of failures of the algorithm, and found that the main reason which leads to failures is the inaccuracy of the erosion and dilation processes. We are now trying to overcome this problem, and we have already got several ideas. Firstly, after adopting the erosion algorithm, we can use the histogram technology to remove those very narrow apophysises. Secondly, when adopting the dilation algorithm, we should detect the large right angles and change them to arcs which are similar to part of an elliptic curve. Both of the methods will help to improve the accuracy of the noised blobs detection and therefore improve the effect of the algorithm.

Overall, all these contribute to furthering current understandings of the design of better CAPTCHAs, in particular the design and implementation of segmentation resistance mechanisms. Designing a CAPTCHA that exhibits both good robustness and usability is much harder that it might appear to be [12]. And the experience suggests that CAPTCHA will go through the same process of evolutionary development as cryptography, digital watermarking and the like, with an iterative process in which successful attacks lead to the development of more robust systems [5, 10].

Acknowledgements. This work is supported by National Natural Science Foundation of China (Grant No.6100174 and Grant No.61170230), National Key Technology R&D Program (Grant No.2012BAH37B04), National High-Tech Research and Development Plan of China (Grant No.2012AA011002) and Strategic Priority Research Program of the Chinese Academy of Sciences (Grant No.XDA06030200).

References

1. von Ahn, L., Blum, M., Langford, J.: Telling Humans and Computer Apart Automatically. CACM 47(2) (2004)
2. Chellapilla, K., Larson, K., Simard, P., Czerwinski, M.: Computers beat humans at single character recognition in reading-based Human Interaction Proofs. In: 2nd Conference on Email and Anti-Spam, CEAS (2005)
3. Simard, P., Steinkraus, D., Platt, J.: Best Practice for Convolutional Neural Networks Applied to Visual Document Analysis. In: International Conference on Document Analysis and Recognition (ICDAR), pp. 958–962. IEEE Computer Society, Los Alamitos (2003)
4. Simard, P., Szeliski, R., Benaloh, J., Couvreur, J., Calinov, I.: Using character recognition and segmentation to tell computers from humans. In: International Conference on Document Analysis and Recognition, ICDAR (2003)
5. Yan, J., El Ahmad, A.S.: A Low-cost Attack on a Microsoft CAPTCHA (2008)
6. Huang, S.-Y., Lee, Y.-K., Bell, G., Ou, Z.-H.: An efficient segmentation algorithm for CAPTCHA with line cluttering and character warping (2009)
7. Yan, J., El Ahmad, A.S.: Breaking Visual CAPTCHA with Naïve Pattern Recognition Algorithms (2007)
8. von Ahn, L., Blum, M., Langford, J.: Telling Humans and Computer Apart Automatically. CACM 47(2) (2004)
9. Chellapilla, K., Simard, P.: Using Machine Learning to Break Visual Human Interaction Proofs. In: Neural Information Processing Systems (NIPS). MIT Press (2004)
10. Yan, J., El Ahmad, A.S.: A Low-cost Attack on a Microsoft CAPTCHA. School of Computing Science Technical Report, Newcastle University, England (2008)
11. Pope, C., Kaur, K.: Is It Human or Computer? Defending E-Commerce with CAPTCHA. IEEE IT Professional, pp. 43–49 (March 2005)
12. Yan, J., El Ahmad, A.S.: Usability of CAPTCHAs - Or,Usability issues in CAPTCHA design. In: The Fourth Symposium on Usable Privacy and Security, Pittsburgh, USA (July 2008)
13. Yan, J.: Bot, Cyborg and Automated Turing Test. In: The Fourteenth International Workshop on Security Protocols, Cambridge, UK (March 2006)

14. Baird, H.S., Bentley, J.L.: Implicit CAPTCHAs. In: Proceedings of Document Recognition an Retrieval XII, pp. 191–196 (2005)
15. Huang, S.Y., Lee, Y.K., Bell, G., Ou, Z.H.: A projection-based segmentation algorithm for breaking MSN and YAHOO CAPTCHAs. In: Proceedings of the 2008 International Conference of Signal and Image Engineering (ICSIE 2008), London, UK (2008)
16. Moy, G., Jones, N., Harkless, C., Potter, R.: Distortion estimation techniques in solving visual CAPTCHAs. In: Proceedings of the 2004 IEEE Computer Society Conference on Computer Vision and Pattern Recognition, vol. 2, pp. 23–28 (2004)
17. Chellapilla, K., Simard, P.: Using machine learning to break visual human interaction proofs (HIPs). In: Saul, L.K., Weiss, Y., Bottou, L. (eds.) Advances in Neural Information Processing Systems 17, pp. 265–272. MIT, Cambridge (2005)

Security and Cost Analyses of DNSSEC Protocol

Yao Yao[1,2], Longtao He[1], and Gang Xiong[1,2,3]

[1] Institute of Computing Technology, Chinese Academy of Sciences, Beijing, China
yaoyao@software.ict.ac.cn
[2] Graduate University of Chinese Academy of Sciences, Beijing, China
[3] Institute of Information Engineering, Chinese Academy of Sciences, Beijing, China

Abstract. Domain Name System Security Extensions (DNSSEC) is a security extension to DNS protocol, which has many security issues and is vulnerable to attacks. By using digital signature technology, DNSSEC provides data origin authentication and integrity. However, designed as the substitute to DNS, the deployment of DNSSEC doesn't go well as predicted. In this paper, we will first present some security issues of DNSSEC in its practical application, and then analyze the computational and bandwidth costs of those resolvers and authoritative name servers that have been deployed with DNSSEC, through which we try to explain the current difficulties in DNSSEC deployment.

Keywords: DNSSEC, DNSSEC deployment, protocol security.

1 Introduction

As one of the most widely used application layer protocol, the security issue of DNS is of great importance, but as security factor had not been taken into consideration early in the design process of DNS, it is now extremely vulnerable to a range of attacks, such as data tampering, man in the middle attack, cache poisoning, etc. The root of these troubles is that DNS lacks a mechanism to data origin authentication and integrity. DNSSEC solves these problems by introducing the digital signature technology, a resolver deployed with DNSSEC (security-aware resolver) is able to check if the information it receives is originated form a legitimated server and identical to the data on the authoritative server.

In recent years, The Internet Corporation for Assigned Names and Numbers (ICCAN) has been working on pushing the deployment of DNSSEC worldwide. However, up to now, except the root zone and some top-level domains (TLDs), few companies have announced their authoritative name server supporting DNSSEC, including those leading corporations in IT industry such as Google and Microsoft, which is definitely an adverse situation to the spread of DNSSEC.

We believe this slowness of deployment of DNSSEC is partly due to the following weaknesses of DNSSEC: 1) DNSSEC still suffers from some security flaws in practice which we will discuss in detail later; 2) by using digital signature technology to

Y. Yuan, X. Wu, and Y. Lu (Eds.): ISCTCS 2012, CCIS 320, pp. 429–435, 2013.

enhance its security, DNSSEC also bring further computational and bandwidth cost to both the security-aware resolver and the authoritative name server. We analyze the costs on a security-aware resolver in our experimental environment and compare them with those on a normal DNS resolver, and then shed light on the security issue concomitant to these additional costs. The work of Ariyapperuma et al. [4] and Kolkman [5] are the pioneers of our study.

The rest of the paper is organized as follows. In Section 2 we explore the security flaws of DNSSEC in practice and how we may deal with them. In 3 we present the computational and bandwidth costs brought by DNSSEC and discuss their impact. In 4 we conclude the paper.

2   Vulnerability in Practice

2.1   Most Vulnerable Spot Remains Unprotected

In most current realistic environment, a DNSSEC client depends on its security-aware recursive resolver to do all the queries and the validations of digital signatures in responses from security-aware authoritative name servers. In other words, the recursive resolver takes full responsibility for its validation result, if it successfully validates an answer by checking the digital signature, the resolver sends the result to the client who initiate this query with the message header bit Authenticated Data (AD) set, which is reserved in the DNS protocol for future use, to indicate that the result is verified. The client, after receiving an answer with AD set from the resolver it trusts, takes it as a verified answer and will not do any further check. However, the communication channel between the client and the trusted resolver is not protected by DNSSEC itself (see Figure 1). The lack of security protection in this section makes DNSSEC almost as vulnerable to attacks as DNS is, even though it provides data origin authentication and data integrity from the root zone to the security-aware recursive resolver, because many resolvers are located in the same local area network with the client, which is the most probable location that a man in the middle attack would happen. So it seems that the most vulnerable spot in DNS is still unprotected in nowadays practical application of DNSSEC.

An IPsec tunnel is suggested in [1] as an additional mechanism to provide channel security between clients and the recursive resolver, but this suggestion has not been widely adopted by most implementations of DNSSEC application, maybe due to the complexity of IPsec itself.

2.2   Unsigned Resource Records (RRs)

In our experiment, we find another potential operational flaw in the responses from the root and some top-level domain name servers. Usually when receives a DNSSEC query message, for example a query for the IPv4 address of the domain "baidu.com", a root server will not give a direct answer to this question. Instead, it will give the requester the IP address of the authoritative name server of the domain of "com", with the NS and A type Resource Records (RRs) in its response to that requester. However, as far as we know, none of the NS and A RRs in these responses have been digitally signed, which they should have been to prevent possible data tampering attack. Although an attack based on these unsigned RRs can be detected by an security-aware resolver, by checking the Delegation Signer (DS) type RR [1][2] to the domain "com" from the root server, such kind of operation of the root name server will at least cause confusion to the administrator of the security-aware resolver: he cannot pinpoint the message that comes from the attacker, because both the message from root server and that from the "com" server might be tampered.

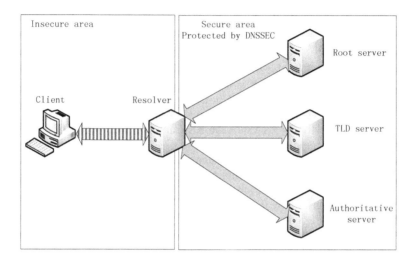

Fig. 1. Vulnerable channel of DNSSEC in practice

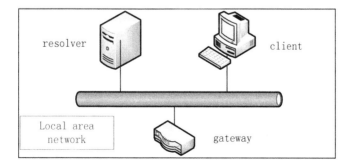

Fig. 2. Experimental environment

3   Costs

3.1   Dataset & Experimental Environment

Dataset. We use a dataset with 10000 queries to those domains whose authoritative name servers have been deployed with DNSSEC to measure the computational and bandwidth load on a security-aware recursive resolver.

Experimental Environment. Our experimental environment is shown in Figure 2. The client and the resolver are in the same local area network and are connected to the gateway to the Internet through a switch. We have a high-bandwidth network of 300Mbps to the Internet. The resolver is loaded with a 2.2GHz dual-core processor and 4GB of memory. For this experiment, the resolver runs BIND, the most widely used DNS software on the Internet. The version of BIND we use is 9.7.3, which supports the full DNSSEC standard.

3.2   Computational Cost

A key signing key (KSK) and a zone signing key (ZSK) [1] [2] are used by a zone in DNSSEC to sign its RRs. The ZSK is used to sign all the RRs in this zone except the DNSKEY type RR [1] [2], while KSK is used to sign DNSKEY RR only. Because KSK is critical to the security of the zone, the KSK length should be relatively longer. A combination of a 2048 bits RSASHA256 KSK and two 1024 bits ZSK for a zone in DNSSEC is the most common case.

Since all the digital signatures are pre-signed, DNSSEC will not cause a sharp rise of the computing resources of the authoritative name servers. However, the computational cost of a security-aware resolver is bound to soar, as all the digitally signed messages should be verified by the security-aware resolver. Sending the query dataset mentioned above at different rates from the client, we compare the computational load of our recursive resolver when it is configured as a security-aware resolver (verify digital signature) with when it is not. We find that the computational load doubles when the recursive resolver is configured to be security-aware (see Figure 3).

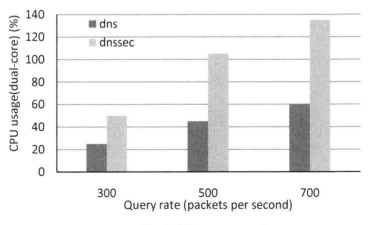

Fig. 3. CPU usage on resolver

3.3   Bandwidth Cost

With one or more digital signatures or several public keys in the packet, most DNSSEC response packets have a load length of 400~800 bytes, whereas most DNS response packets only have a load length less than 300 bytes (see Figure 4) [6] [7]. Thus, bandwidth load is surely to increase for those servers supporting DNSSEC standard. To affirm this, we analyze the bandwidth load of our recursive resolver still using our dataset. In order to reflect the bandwidth load accurately, we send those queries in our dataset to the resolver slowly enough to ensure that the denial of service issue will not happen during the test. We find that, when configured to be security-aware, the resolver generates about 32MB (22MB from authoritative name servers) network traffic to resolve those 10000 DNSSEC queries recursively. Comparatively, only about 13MB (9MB from authoritative name servers) network traffic is generated when those queries are sent to the resolver with normal DNS message format and the resolver is not configured to be security-aware meanwhile (see Figure 5).

We also measure the proportion of queries that can be successfully answered by the recursive resolver at different query rates, the result is shown in Figure 6. This result indicates that a security-aware resolver is absolutely more vulnerable to the DDoS attacks.

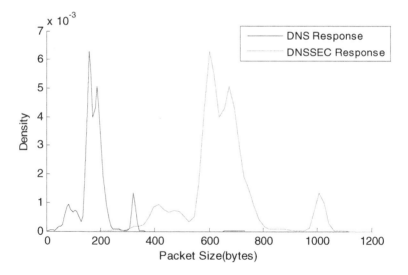

Fig. 4. Packet size distribution

3.4   Impact of Cost on Deployment of DNSSEC

All these additional computational and bandwidth costs will undoubtedly adversely affect the deployment of DNSSEC, because they not only mean that a considerable

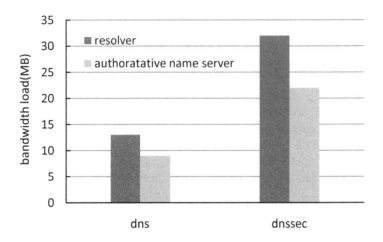

Fig. 5. Bandwidth load of 10000 queries

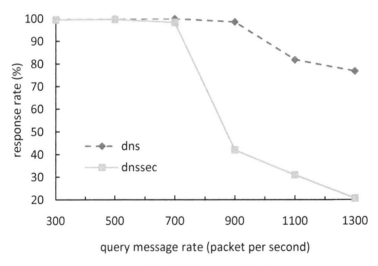

Fig. 6. Tolerance to DDoS

amount of hardware in current domain name systems be replaced to support
DNSSEC, but also make the security-aware name servers and resolvers more vulnerable to DDoS attacks. In our experiment, we find that the memory overhead is always
low whether the resolver is security-aware or not, with less than 100MB memory
consumed. This feature we believe can be used to reduce the computational and
bandwidth load with more information cached longer in the resolver's memory, thus
to some extent solve the problem of hardware update.

4   Conclusion

In this paper, we present some security vulnerabilities of DNSSEC that can be exploited by attackers in its practical application, and analyze the computational and bandwidth cost of those resolver that have been deployed with DNSSEC. We believe these vulnerabilities and the high costs in current DNSSEC implementation are the main reasons why DNSSEC is not widely used. Suggestions are made in this paper to ease these problems such as a tradeoff between memory overhead and computational and bandwidth load.

Acknowledgement. This work is supported by the "Strategic Priority Research Program" of the Chinese Academy of Sciences (Grant No. XDA06030200), the National High-Tech Research and Development Plan "863" of China (Grant No. 2011AA010703) and the National Natural Science Foundation (Grant No. 61070184).

References

1. Arends, R., Austein, R., Larson, M., Massey, D., Rose, S.: DNS Security Introduction and Requirements. RFC 4033 (Proposed Standard) (March 2005)
2. Arends, R., Austein, R., Larson, M., Massey, D., Rose, S.: Resource Records for the DNS Security Extensions. RFC 4034 (Proposed Standard) (March 2005)
3. Arends, R., Austein, R., Larson, M., Massey, D., Rose, S.: Protocol Modifications for the DNS Security Extensions. RFC 4035 (Proposed Standard) (March 2005)
4. Ariyapperuma, S., Mitchell, C.J.: Security vulnerabilities in DNS and DNSSEC. In: IEEE ARES (2007)
5. Kolkman, O.M.: Measuring the resource requirements of DNSSEC. Technical report, RIPE NCC / NLnet Labs (October 2005)
6. Jansen, J.: Measuring the effects of DNSSEC deployment on query load. NLnet Labs (May 2006)
7. Ager, B., Dreger, H., Feldmann, A.: Exploring the Overhead of DNSSEC (April 2005)

An Automatic Approach to Detect Anti-debugging in Malware Analysis

Peidai Xie, Xicheng Lu, Yongjun Wang, Jinshu Su, and Meijian Li

[1] School of Computer, National University of Defense Technology, Changsha, China
`peidaixie@gmail.com, xclluu@163.com, wwyyjj1971@126.com`

Abstract. Anti-debugging techniques are broadly used by malware authors to prevent security researchers from reversing engineering their created malware samples. However, the countermeasures to identify anti-debugging code patterns are insufficient, and mainly manual, which is an expensive, time-consuming, and error-prone process. There are no automatic approaches which can be used to detect anti-debugging code patterns in malware samples effectively. In this paper, we present an approach, based on instruction traces derived from dynamic malware analysis and an instruction-based pattern matching method, to detect anti-debugging tricks automatically. We evaluate this approach with a large number of malware samples collected in the wild. The experience shows that our proposed approach is effective and about 40% of malware samples in our experimental data set has been embedded anti-debugging code.

Keywords: malware analysis, anti-debugging, instruction trace, obfuscation, dynamic analysis.

1 Introduction

Malicious software (malware) is a generic term to denote all kinds of unwanted software that fulfills the deliberately harmful intent of attackers. Terms such as viruses, worms, Trojan horses, spywares or bots are used to describe malware samples that exhibit some specific malicious behavior[1]. Attackers create malware in order to infiltrate computer systems, collect users' private-sensitive information and attack internet infrastructures. To gain financial benefits is their ultimate goal, and the financial loss caused by malware can be billions of dollars in a year[2]. Nowadays, the sheer number of unique malware samples grows exponentially every year[2] and poses a major security threat to internet.

To detect and mitigate malware effectively, the first step is the dissection of the target, means to extract malicious behavior patterns of malware accurately, a process of malware analysis[3]. There are two major approaches which have been established: *static analysis* and *dynamic analysis*. Static analysis techniques, when used for malware, have several weaknesses, such as it is time-consuming, reliant on disassembling heavily and vulnerable to code obfuscations, and the code being analyzed is possible not the code executed actually, etc.

Y. Yuan, X. Wu, and Y. Lu (Eds.): ISCTCS 2012, CCIS 320, pp. 436–442, 2013.

Dynamic malware analysis techniques are proposed to gain a briefly understanding of malware sample, and at the same time, the syntactic signatures are extracted for malware detection. Several specific debuggers, such as WinDBG[4], OllyDBG[5], etc., are playing a significant role as restricted environments for dynamic malware analysis.

However, malware authors use anti-analysis techniques broadly to impede reversing engineering of their creations in order to evade analysis and detection. If a malware sample is aware of an unreal environment in which it is running, it will quit or suspend running to avert exposure of its malicious behavior. In this paper, we focus on anti-debugging techniques. Lots of tricks can be played by a malware sample to detect if the running is in debug-mode. When a huge number of malware samples use anti-debugging techniques, the effectiveness of impeding malware analysis cannot be undervalued.

The existing countermeasures proposed in literatures are insufficient. For example, some plugins for OllyDBG are developed in [5] to tackle the problem of debugger detection, but they can only detect whether a Windows API IsDebuggerPresent() is invoked. A stealthy debugger based on Virtual Machine environment or a hardware-level emulator such as QEMU[6] can avoid debugger detection, but the dynamic analysis tool aims at the effects performed by the sample under analysis on operation system resources (e.g., which files or register hives are created or modified). There is not a general method for detecting the anti-debugging code fragments automatically and efficiently.

In this paper, we present an automatic approach, named as ITPM, to detect anti-debugging in malware samples. This approach is based on *Instruction Trace* derived from a dynamic analysis tool and *Pattern Matching* algorithm between the instruction trace and predefined rules which is configured into a database to describe the anti-debugging code patterns. We implement a prototype to demonstrate its effectiveness and the experiment shows that more than 40% of malware samples use anti-debugging techniques even though the packers are broadly used.

This paper makes the following contributions:

- ITPM, an approach based on instruction trace and pattern matching technique, is proposed for identifying automatically anti-debugging in malware samples. The instruction trace is derived from a dynamic analysis tool implemented by ourselves and the patterns of anti-debugging code are in the form of predefined rules configured into a database. ITPM is scalable for new form of anti-debugging patterns.
- A prototype system is designed and implemented to demonstrate ITPM's effectiveness. The dynamic analysis tool used for generation of instruction trace is built on top of QEMU.

The remainder of this paper is structured as follows. In section 2, we introduce related work of detection methods of anti-debugging in malware analysis. In section 3, we describe detailed ITPM, including rule generation, the instruction tracer, the trace refiner, and an instruction-based matching algorithm. Section 4 evaluates our detection approach. Finally, section 5 concludes this paper.

2   Related Work

In this section, we briefly explain previous studies related to detection methods of anti-debugging in malware analysis. A malware analyst usually removes anti-debugging code manually depending on the reverse engineering experience during analyzing a malware sample in a debugger. It is time-consuming and error-prone, and special skills of malware analysis in a certain level are required[7].

Kawakoya[8] implemented a stealthy debugger for automatically unpacking. A stealthy debugger is a debugger which uses original debugging functionalities embedded in a virtual machine monitor in order to hide from the malware running on a guest OS. This method is effective but cannot known what anti-debugging techniques are used in malware samples.

3   The ITPM Approach

In this section, we describe our proposed approach, ITPM, in detail. The work flow of ITPM approach is shown in Fig. 1. The rules of anti-debugging code patterns are generated from corresponding code fragments identified by experts. Instruction traces are recorded from a dynamic analysis tool and be deobfuscated to match with the predefined rules. One instruction trace should be matched with all rules.

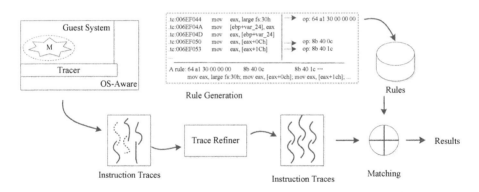

Fig. 1. The work flow of ITPM approach

3.1   Rule Generation

In order to detect the anti-debugging in malware samples, patterns of anti-debugging code fragment should be known as a prior knowledge. All rules are generated from well-known code fragments implemented for anti-debugging by malware authors.

A rule used in ITPM is defined as <*id, I, D, desc*>. The *id* is an identification of a rule; the *I* is an instruction sequence i_1; i_2; i_3..., a set of instructions; the *D* is the binary data corresponding instructions, printed with hex value if needed; the last *desc* is a description of the rule.

When generating a rule with a code pattern of anti-debugging techniques, it is necessary to get rid of uncorrelated instructions imbedded in the code fragment. Uncorrelated instructions include obfuscation code, some redundant branch instructions and so on. It is very difficult to refine a pattern of anti-debugging code fragment as more or less instructions in a rule are all not expected for pattern matching.

As anti-debugging code pattern is varied, the form of rules can be upgrade to deal with corresponding scenarios.

3.2 Instruction Tracer

The tracer implemented in host OS is responsible for recording the instructions executed in the process of a malware sample. It is a dynamic analysis tool for malware analysis built on top of QEMU, an open source CPU emulator, that there are several features due to the hardware-level implementation which are exceeding appropriate for malware analysis. Certainly, there is a semantic gap between guest OS and host OS. In instruction tracer, we bridge the semantic gap by installing a kernel module in the guest OS, a very common solution.

Given the OS semantic information, the tracer reads 15 bytes to a buffer from the EIP in memory when CPU executes an instruction which belongs to a thread whose process is under monitoring. A third party open source library is used to disassemble data in the buffer. And then the EIP, the binary data according to length of current instruction and the instruction denotation are logged as a single line. The instruction trace only includes instructions which belong to the executable under analysis. If the running jumps to a DLL module, all instructions will be omitted.

A timeout interval is set for each analysis. The process which is still running when the interval elapsed will be killed. A clean snapshot of guest OS is loaded for next analysis.

3.3 The Trace Refiner

Code obfuscation techniques are heavily applied in malware samples for evading analysis and detection. If a sample under analysis is obfuscated with syntactic transformation, the trace is too rough to match rules which ought to be matched[9].

On the other side, a trace may include a large number of loops unfolded during actually execution. Those instructions are redundant and should be removed.

The trace refiner is responsible for trimming instruction traces by deobfuscation[10] and loop identification algorithm[11]. Two obfuscations, i.e. code reordering and junk code insertion[12], are detected and replaced by NOP instruction. Loops are pruned to one loop iteration.

3.4 Instruction-Based Matching Algorithm

The last step of ITPM is matching the trimmed instruction traces with rules. We present an instruction-based matching algorithm, as is show in Table 1.

Table 1. Instruction-based Matching Algorithm

Algorithm 1: Instruction-based matching.	
Input: The rule set R and a trimmed instruction trace T.	
Output: A set O, the element of which is $<r, p>$, r is a matched rule and p is value of EIP.	

Begin	**if** $i_j == t_k$ **then**
while R is not empty **do**	**if** i_j is the last instruction of I_r **then**
Let r is one element of R	$O \leftarrow O \cup <r, EIP_T>$
$R \leftarrow R\backslash r$	**break**
$j\leftarrow0, k\leftarrow0$	**else** $j\leftarrow j+1$
Foreach $i_j \in I_r$ and $t_k \in T$ **do**	**else** $j\leftarrow0$
if t_k is NOP **then**	$k\leftarrow k+1$
$k\leftarrow k+1$	**return** O
continue	**End**

In the instruction-based matching algorithm, the instruction in a rule and an instruction trace is compared one by one. We do not use the corresponding bytes. Although the comparison between instructions is more cost than bytes, the number of comparison operation is reduced by a great amount. Instruction-based matching algorithm is effective according to the experiment shown in next section.

4   Experiment

In this section, we present the results of the experiment to demonstrate that the ITPM approach to detect anti-debugging is effectiveness. We conducted the experiment as follows. First, we generate a set of rules according prior studies and our experience, as is shown in Table 2. To demonstrate its effectiveness, we develop a set of experimental tiny programs of which each one has a form of anti-debugging code pattern which is corresponding a rule. After compiled into binaries and obfuscated using well-known packers, we evaluate the ITPM approach. The result shows that all anti-debugging code patterns are detected.

Second, a set of malware samples are collected from Internet, as is shown in Table 3, and marked using Kaspersky, an excellent commercial anti-virus product. We run each sample in the dynamic analysis tool to record an instruction trace with 5 minutes of a timeout interval. And then we trim the set of traces. The length of several traces after trimmed is too short to be discarded.

Table 2. The rule set for anti-debugging detection

Categories	The Mechanism	#Rules	Average of #Instructions
C1	Windows API	12	9
C2	Flags in windows data structure	6	6
C3	Magic strings of debuggers	5	7
C4	Others	2	7

Third, the instruction-based matching algorithm is performed to generate the results. In Table 3, the row #R (Repeated) denotes that some samples have more than one category of anti-debugging code pattern.

Table 3. The malware samples and detection results of ITPM approach

Categories	#	#Trace	Results						
			C1	C2	C3	C4	#Total	#R	%
Bot	331	328	56	41	35	13	131	14	39.6
Worm	296	290	61	39	23	7	118	22	39.9
Trojan	121	117	34	0	22	5	43	18	35.5
Unknown	20	20	3	2	2	0	7	0	35.0
sum	768	755	154	82	82	25	299	54	**38.9**

Table 3 shows that about 40% of malware samples have the ability of anti-debugging. We conclude that Trojan is less to use C2 anti-debugging tricks.

5   Conclusion

Anti-debugging techniques are broadly used by malware authors to prevent security researchers from reversing engineering their creations, means malware. In this paper, we present ITPM, an automatic approach to detect anti-analysis tricks in order to make an automated process of malware analysis. The experiment shows that ITPM is effective and about 40% of malware in the wild have anti-debugging function.

Acknowledgment. This work was partially supported by the National Natural Science Foundation of China under Grant No. 61003303 and No. 60873215, Hunan Provincial Natural Science Foundation of China No.s2010J5050 and 11jj7003, the PCSIRT (NO.IRT1012), and the Aid Program for Science and Technology Innovative Research Team in Higher Educational Institutions of Hunan Province "network technology".

References

1. Egele, M., Scholte, T., Kirda, E., Kruegel, C.: A Survey on Automated Dynamic Malware Analysis Techniques and Tools. J. ACM Computing Surveys, 1–49 (2010)
2. Internet Security Threat Report, vol. 16. Symantec Corporation (January 2012), http://www.symantec.com/business/threatreport/
3. Moser, A., Kruegel, C., Kirda, E.: Exploring Multiple Execution Paths for Malware Analysis. In: IEEE Symposium on Security and Privacy, Oakland, pp. 231–245 (2007)
4. Sreedhar, V.C., Gao, G.R., Lee, Y.F.: Identifying loops using DJ graphs (1995)
5. Yuschuk, O.: OllyDbg
6. Bellard, F.: Qemu: A Fast and Portable Dynamic Translator. In: The USENIX Annual Technical Conference (2005)

7. Chen, X., Andersen, J., Mao, Z., Bailey, M., Nazario, J.: Towards an Understanding of Anti-virtualization and Anti-debugging Behavior in Modern Malware. In: IEEE International Conference on Dependable Systems and Networks With FTCS and DCC (DSN 2008), pp. 177–186 (2008)
8. Kawakoya, Y., Iwamura, M., Itoh, M.: Memory Behavior-Based Automatic Malware Unpacking in Stealth Debugging Environment. In: Proceeding of the 5th International Conference on Malicious and Unwanted Software (2010)
9. Santos, I., Ugarte-Pedrero, X., Sanz, B.: Collective Classification for Packed Executable Identification. In: Proceedings of the 8th Annual Collaboration, Electronic Messaging, AntiAbuse and Spam Conference (CEAS 2011), pp. 231–238 (2011)
10. Yoann Guillot, A.G.: Automatic Binary Deobfuscation (2009)
11. Wei, T., Mao, J., Zou, W., Chen, Y.: A New Algorithm for Identifying Loops in Decompilation. In: Riis Nielson, H., Filé, G. (eds.) SAS 2007. LNCS, vol. 4634, pp. 170–183. Springer, Heidelberg (2007)
12. Christodorescu, M., Kinder, J., Jha, S., Katzenbeisser, S., Veith, H.: Malware Normalization. Tech. Report, No.1539, University of Wisconsin, Madison, Wisconsin, USA (2005)

OpenVPN Traffic Identification Using Traffic Fingerprints and Statistical Characteristics

Yi Pang[1, 2], Shuyuan Jin[1], Shicong Li[1, 2], Jilei Li[1,2], and Hao Ren[2]

[1] Institute of Computing Technology, Chinese Academy of Sciences, Beijing, China
[2] Graduate University of Chinese Academy of Sciences (GUCAS), Beijing, China
{pangyi,lishicong,lijilei,renhao}@software.ict.ac.cn,
jinshuyuan@ict.ac.cn

Abstract. OpenVPN is a user-space SSL-based VPN, which doesn't use fixed port and communication contents are encrypted after the establishment of handshake process. Therefore, traditional port-based or payload-based identification methods are not applicable for OpenVPN traffic identification. In this paper we introduce OpenVPN communication mechanism in detail, and give an analysis of its packets and traffic behavior. We propose a model which can recognize the OpenVPN tunnel in the early period by combining traffic fingerprints method and statistical characteristics technique. Evaluation shows that this model is effective and highly accurate.

Keywords: traffic identification, OpenVPN, network security.

1 Introduction

VPN stands for Virtual Private Network which creates an encrypted tunnel over the public network between two private machines or networks. With the extensive use of VPN, a variety of tunneling protocols are emerging, such as IPSec/OpenVPN[1]. OpenVPN is a user-space SSL-based VPN that implements SSL VPN simply while providing functions and protection equivalent, and in some cases superior to other VPN protocols [2]. OpenVPN uses TCP or UDP network protocols and provides the source code freely, making it the ideal alternative of IPSec and other VPN protocols, especially in the case of ISPs filtering some VPN protocol. With OpenVPN popularly and widely applied, its traffic identification becomes more important and urgent for us to improve Quality of Service, control network bandwidth and ensure network security.

Although IANA (Internet Assigned Numbers Authority) assigns default port number 1194 to OpenVPN, OpenVPN can change any port number while communication and commonly do not use port 1194. So it is impossible for port-based identification technology to find OpenVPN tunnel accurately. Furthermore most communication contents are encrypted after the establishment of handshake process, which make it more difficult and complicated for DPI (Deep Packet Inspection) method. But DPI makes itself outstanding with the high accuracy and low false positive rate in traffic

Y. Yuan, X. Wu, and Y. Lu (Eds.): ISCTCS 2012, CCIS 320, pp. 443–449, 2013.
© Springer-Verlag Berlin Heidelberg 2013

identification technologies. And many companies choose DPI as basic algorithms to develop their traffic identification equipments [3]. We definitely take this advantage into consideration when compose our model accurately.

The limitations of port-based and payload-based methods have motivated use of statistical methodology for traffic identification. These identification techniques rely on the fact that different applications typically have distinct behavior patterns when communicating on a network [4]. Most of the proposed mechanisms perform traffic classification using flow statistics such as duration, number of packets, mean packet size, or inter-arrival time. In fact, recognizing traffic identification as soon as possible is very practically needed in the real network management. Unfortunately, these techniques are not appropriate for early traffic identification as they only classify a flow after it is finished [5]. So when building our model to recognize OpenVPN traffic, we refer to the view in [6] which performs traffic classification based on the first few packets of a TCP connection. And what's more, UDP is commonly used in OpenVPN. We must explore this idea and make it suitable for OpenVPN.

In this paper, we propose a model by combining traffic fingerprints method and statistical characteristics technique. We just choose the first few bits of each packet payload as the fingerprints to make our model be more effective and practical if we are not allowed to get the complete packets because of privacy and security reasons and unable to capture the whole packets in the high-speed backbone network. And we also take the first few packets of a communication as statistical characteristics to recognize the OpenVPN tunnel in the early period.

The remainder of this paper is arranged as follows. The different Internet traffic classification methods are reviewed in Section 2. Section 3 we introduce the OpenVPN communication mechanism in detail. Section 4 and Section 5 respectively outlines our methodology and demonstrates our experimental evaluation. Section 6 presents our conclusions.

2   Related Work

Although [6] is the first to design an application-recognition mechanism for encrypted traffic and test it on real SSL traffic, we specify this problem for OpenVPN and consider its characteristics to make model higher accuracy. However [6] just analyzes the second data packet in the connection ("Server Hello"). If they do not get this packet, which situation may happen owing to high-speed network and the limitation of equipment, then they will miss the traffic tunnel with high false negative rate. And they also select more bits of payload as the fingerprints which seem not effective or practical if not allowed to get much more packet payload because of privacy, security and speed reasons. Referring to their idea, we make the model more suitable for OpenVPN.

3   OpenVPN Communication Mechanism

OpenVPN is an open source software solution that implements VPN (Virtual Private Network) methods based on SSLv3/TLSv1. OpenVPN applies encryption, authentication and integrity using the OpenSSL library [7] in conjunction with a virtual network interface, the TUN/TAP device [8] which is used for injecting network packets into the operating system.

OpenVPN is developed by James Yonan and is able to create encrypted tunnels over the Internet or other network. Unlike many other VPN implementations, OpenVPN does not use the IPsec protocol to secure the data transfers. Moreover, the application distinguishes itself with other VPN solutions with the fact it is a user space implementation of a VPN [9-11].

Figure 1 shows the difference of OpenVPN packet formats when it uses TCP or UDP protocol. Note that when -tls-auth function is opened up, all message types are protected with an HMAC (16 bytes or 20 bytes) signature, even the initial packets of the TLS handshake. And there are still packet id (4 bytes) and timestamp (4 bytes) written into packets.

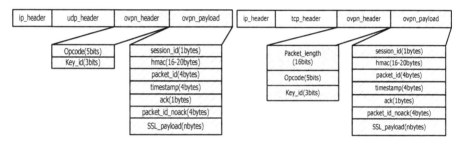

Fig. 1. OpenVPN Packet Format (the left for UDP and the right for TCP)

As shown above, different Opcodes stand for different functions of OpenVPN packets in different communication stages. And it plays an important role in our model to identify the OpenVPN traffic what we will demonstrate in detail later. Opcode takes 5 bits and ranges from 1 to 8 and their meanings are explained in Table 1.

Table 1. Description of Opcode

Opcode	Value	Description
P_CONTROL_HARD_RESET_CLIENT_V1	1	Key method 1, initial key from client, forget previous state
P_CONTROL_HARD_RESET_SERVER_V1	2	Key method 1, initial key from server, forget previous state
P_CONTROL_SOFT_RESET_V1	3	New key
P_CONTROL_V1	4	Control channel packet (usually TLS ciphertext).
P_ACK_V1	5	Acknowledgement for P_CONTROL packets received.
P_DATA_V1	6	Data channel packet containing tunnel data ciphertext.
P_CONTROL_HARD_RESET_CLIENT_V2	7	Key method 2, initial key from client, forget previous state
P_CONTROL_HARD_RESET_SERVER_V2	8	Key method 2, initial key from server, forget previous state

OpenVPN establishment process can be reached by four stages [11-12] shown by Figure 2. Stage-1 proceeds OpenVPN connection initialization and server sets up the data structure for a new connection from client. And then Stage-2 is SSL/TSL handshake process and the detail of handshake process has been presented in [2]. At the end of Stage-2 an encrypted tunnel is set up and Stage 3-4 client and server use this encrypted tunnel to negotiate and exchange their session key for OpenVPN record protocol. And our model can identify the OpenVPN traffic in the early period of establishment process during Stage 1 and Stage 2.

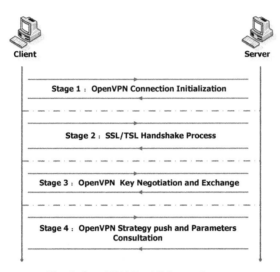

Fig. 2. OpenVPN Establishment Process

4   Feature and Model

4.1   Notation Description

We define some basic notations, which are illustrated in Table 2, to conveniently describe our method and statistical characteristics of packets later.

Table 2. Notation Description

Notation	Description
F	the flow whose series of packets sharing the same five-tuple (source IP, source port, destination IP, source port, protocol) or reverse direction traffic
F_o	the OpenVPN flow whose series of packets sharing the same five-tuple (source IP, source port, destination IP, source port, protocol) or reverse direction traffic
P	all of packets in F
n_1	the number of packets of which opcode beyond the range of 1-8 in P
n_2	the number of packets of which opcode is P_CONTROL_HARD_RESET_CLIENT_V2 in P
n_3	the number of packets of which opcode is P_CONTROL_HARD_RESET_ SERVER _V2 in P
n_4	the number of packets of which opcode is P_ACK_V1 in P
n_5	the number of packets of which opcode is P_CONTROL_V1 in P
len_2	the length of packet of which opcode is P_CONTROL_HARD_RESET_CLIENT_V2
len_3	the length of packet of which opcode is P_CONTROL_HARD_RESET_ SERVER _V2

4.2   Feature Selection

Different Opcodes, taking 5 bits and ranging from 1 to 8, stand for different functions of OpenVPN packets in different communication stages. And it plays an important role in our model to identify the OpenVPN traffic.

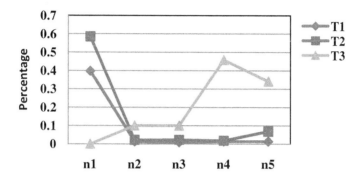

Fig. 3. The percentage of packets in different types

We collect three datasets T1, T2 and T3 manually and the percentage of F_o in each are 0.009%, 0.022% and 100% .To observe the statistical characters of OpenVPN traffic, we respectively analyze the percentage of n1-5 in the first ten packets of F. Note that we ignore the TCP handshake packets and ACK packets made by TCP protocol itself when we count the first ten packets of F. And this is not happened in UDP protocol. The result of calculation is shown in Finger 3. Then we will found the significant difference between OpenVPN packets and other traffic packets. n1 is equal to 0.00% in T3 while higher than 40% in T1 and T2. This conclusion applies to n4 and n5 . There n4 and n5 is greater than 33% in T3 but both below 10% in T1 and T2. According to the OpenVPN mechanism, the opcodes of the first two packets are 7 and 8. That is why n2 and n3 both definitely equal 10% in T3.

As mentioned in Section 3 when -tls-auth is used, all message types are protected with an HMAC signature. We observe the packets of OpenVPN finding that len_2 and len_3 have the fixed values. When using UDP protocol and no HMAC, len_2 equals 0x2a and len_3 equals 0x36. While using TCP protocol and no HMAC, len_2 equals 0x38, len_3 equals 0x44. We can use len_2 and len_3 to distinguish whether OpenVPN open up -tls-auth or not.

4.3   Model

We demonstrate our OpenVPN traffic identification model in Figure 4. The model inputs are packets in the real network. When a new packet comes, the Packet Analysis Processor classifys the packet into n1-5 .check whether F the packet belonging to has been in Flow Records. If F has been here, then get the old record and renew the value of n1-5 and other values of this data entry. If F is not here, the set up a new data entry and record all the values it needs.

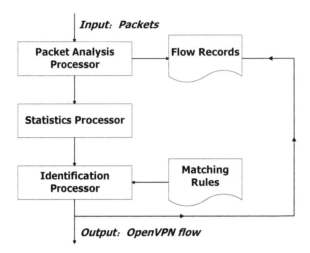

Fig. 4. The Identification Model

When the model collects the first ten packets of F, Statistics Processor will handle all the values of this data entry and transfer the result to Identification Processor. Identification Processor evaluate F, to decide whether it belong to F_o or not, according to the rules in Matching Rules module. If F is F_o, it will be written into Flow Records.

5   Evaluation

We make known number of computers use OpenVPN traffic in the experimental network in different time of a day and other computers traffic with any protocol but not OpenVPN. Then we get the three traces T4, T5 and T6 manually. We choose the 5 bits of each packet payload as the traffic fingerprints to classify packets into five types .And set the matching rule as $\{n_1=0, n_2=1, n_3=1, n_4>3, n_5>2\}$ in the first 10 packets of one F.

After applying our identification mechanism to T4, T5 and T6, the results of experiment are shown in Table 3. We can see that our method is valuable and useful with accuracy higher than 99.988%, false positive rate lower than 0.012% and false negative rate closing to 0.

Table 3. The Experiment Result

Trace	Bytes	F	F_0	Accuracy	False Positive rate	False Negative rate
T4	769,660,960	90268	7	99.995%	0.003%	0.000%
T5	2,619,414,770	125189	24	99.991%	0.007%	0.000%
T6	2,129,534,812	112893	76	99.988%	0.012%	0.000%

6   Conclusion and Future Work

We choose the 5 bits of opcode in each packet as the traffic fingerprints to classify five types of packet and take the first 10 packets of a communication as statistical characteristics to recognize the OpenVPN tunnel in the early period. Based on this, we construct our model to identification OpenVPN traffic. Though the experiment, we receive the results with accuracy higher than 99.988%, false positive rate lower than 0.012% and false negative rate closing to 0. And it proves that our model is effective and precise to identify OpenVPN traffic.

Our future work lies in extending our model to identify more types of VPN and detect the specific content of packets for network security.

References

1. Yang, F., Zhang, Z.-Q.: Research of Application Protocol Identification System Based DPI and DFI. In: Qian, Z., Cao, L., Su, W., Wang, T., Yang, H. (eds.) Recent Advances in CSIE 2011. LNEE, vol. 127, pp. 305–310. Springer, Heidelberg (2012)
2. Hosner, C.: OpenVPN and the SSL VPN Revolution. SANS Institute (2004)
3. Chen, L., Gong, J., Xu, X.: A Survey of Application-Level Protocol Identification Algorithm. Computer Science 34(7), 73–75 (2007)
4. Erman, J., Arlitt, M., Mahanti, A.: Traffic classification using clustering algorithms. In: Proceedings of the 2006 SIGCOMM Workshop on Mining Network Data, MineNet 2006, pp. 281–286. ACM Press, New York (2006)
5. Bernaille, L., Teixeira, R., Salamatian, K.: Early application identification. In: Proceedings of the Second ACM Conference on Emerging Network Experiments and Technologies (CoNEXT 2006), pp. 1–12 (2006)
6. Bernaille, L., Teixeira, R.: Early Recognition of Encrypted Applications. In: Passive and ActiveMeasurement Conference (PAM), Louvain-la-neuve, Belgium (April 2007)
7. The OpenSSL Project: The open source toolkit for ssl/tls, http://www.openssl.org (consulted on June 20, 2011)
8. Krasnyansky, M., Clark, B.: tun/tap devices, http://vtun.sourceforge.net/tun/ (consulted on June 23, 2011)
9. Hoekstra, B., Musulin, D.: Comparing TCP performance of tunneled and non-tunneled traffic using OpenVPN (2011), http://staff.science.uva.nl/~delaat/rp/2010-2011/p09/report.pdf
10. Guo, X.-C., Zhai, Z.-J.: Investigation on Security of OpenVPN Architecture. Science Technology and Engineering 7(8), 1743–1744 (2007)
11. http://openvpn.net/index.php/open-source/documentation.html
12. http://blog.csdn.net/dog250/article/details/6990814

An Intent-Driven Masquerader Detection Framework Based on Data Fusion

Chen Xiaojun[1,2,3], Shi Jinqiao[2,3], Pu Yiguo[1,2], and Zhang Haoliang[2,3]

[1] Institute of Computing Technology, Chinese Academy of Sciences
[2] Institute of Information Engineering, Chinese Academy of Sciences
[3] Chinese National Engineering Laboratory of Information Security Technologies
(Chenxiaojun,Shijinqiao)@iie.ac.cn

Abstract. Different from outside attacks, malicious insiders steal sensitive data or sabotage information systems through misuse of privilege or identity theft (masquerader). These attacks, which are very hard to detect, can cause considerable damages to the organization. Most previous detection methods are based on single observable, which can find insider attacks to some extent; as for intent analysis, their usage seems to be limited. In this paper, we monitor users' various observables on host, and then build a new framework based on data fusion technique to locate this situation. Our framework is more precise for masquerader detection and capable of analyzing attack intents.

Keywords: insider threats, data fusion, attack intents.

1 Introduction

Recent newspapers have reported many events of insider attack. In July 25. 2010, WikiLeaks released a document set called "the Afghan War Diary" that includes over 91,000 reports covering the war in Afghanistan from 2004 to 2010[1]. After investigation, Bradley Manning – a United State Army soldier – was accused of leakage of hundreds and thousands of top-secret documents while serving as an Army intelligence analyst. This event triggered an earthquake in the whole world and internal-security attracted more and more attentions from security researchers. The Cyber Insider Threat (CINDER) program, supported by DARPA in 2010, is "to develop novel approaches to the detection of activities within military-interest networks that are consistent with the activities of cyber espionage."[2]

Masquerader is one kind of malicious insider who commits a penetration to an organization's network, system or data through identity theft. One most common scenario is that the legal user leaves for dinner without locking his computer and one of his colleagues enters his computer with the owner's access privilege to steal confidential business documents or personal privacy information. More complicated attacks may be conducted by installing back-door software on the victim's computer for further attacks.

Y. Yuan, X. Wu, and Y. Lu (Eds.): ISCTCS 2012, CCIS 320, pp. 450–457, 2013.
© Springer-Verlag Berlin Heidelberg 2013

Masquerader is very hard to detect because they are behaving with a legitimate access privilege. Many researches on masquerader detection have focused on the identity theft by the detection of deviation from normal user behavior profile. They used human-computer interaction (HCI) based biometric and other observables such as commands and file access records to build user's normal profile [3] [4].

Although these methods mentioned above can detect abnormal behavior of identity theft, they do few things to reveal the attacker's intent. For example, system administrator's computer maintenance process will be regarded as a masquerade attack because the behavior is far away from normal behavior profile. To solve this problem, firstly we add attack intent analysis into taxonomy of masquerader. As we will show in section 3, we give an initiatory attack intent classification that includes *confidential document theft*, *personal privacy stealing* and *installing of back door software etc.* Secondly, we propose an approach based on data fusion to correlate abnormal behavior and attack intent.

Data fusion technique are widely applied to analyze correlation of alerts from different sensors in intrusion detection system[5]. In addition to the statistical advantage gained by combining same-source data, the use of multiple types of sensors may increases the accuracy with which a quantity can be observed and correlates several alerts into one multi-stages attack to understand attacker's intent. The advantage of data fusion can be used for masquerader detection.

The main purpose of this paper is to improve the masquerader detection capabilities, such as the accuracy and analysis of attack intent. Specifically speaking, the contributions are:

- Taxonomy of masquerader to deeply understand masquerader attacks especially from attack intent and system consequence.
- A feature fusion framework with capability of attack intent analysis.

The following sections are organized as this: Section 2 describes our taxonomy of masquerader from three dimensions and gives some cases to illustrate the usefulness of our taxonomy. In section 3 we describe our sensors implement and the approach to fuse multi-source feature set. We discuss related work in the area of masquerader detection and data fusion in section 4 and then conclude the paper and provide future work in section 5.

2 Analysis of Masquerader's Attack

Several models of insider threats exist. CMO model is the first model to understand insider attacks. CMO postulates that to commit an attack, the malicious user must have the Capability, Motive to do so and Opportunity to commit the attack. Many other models are derived from this framework. Parker[6] presents a model based on similar but not identical factors – Skills, Knowledge, Resources, Authority and Motives – and applies it to all computer crimes included insider or outsider attacks. These models above point out some elemental factors to understand insider attack, but they are far away from implementing a feasible approach or a practical system to detect malicious insider.

Margklaras's model[7] move forward a step to understand the harm of inside misuser. The model contributes all misuse accidents into three dimensions – system role, reasons of misuse and system consequences. System role of the user can be system master, advanced user or application user. Reasons of misuse can be intentional or accidental. Intentional misuses include data theft or deliberate ignorance of rules; accidental misuses include cases of inadequate system knowledge, stress, etc. System consequence is the response or result of misuse event and that can be divided into three level, O/S based, network data or hardware. Margklaras's model firstly introduced system consequence into the taxonomy of insider threat, which helps researchers understand how to detect insider threats from information monitoring system.

Our model refer to Margklaras's work but is more meticulous to analyze another important kind of insider threat – masquerader attack. We give a masquerader analysis framework (Figure 1) from three dimensions that include:

- *User role*: The system role or organization role of current logined user. The system role of user decide user's access control on system resources and that can be administrator, common user or remote user etc.
- *Attack intent*: Attack intent describe the masquerader's intents that are important indicators for building detection tools. We group intents into two categories: Malicous goals and Other goals. One kind of users who are going to matain customer's computer or do some other operation due to work cooperation could be define as a masquerader witch other goals. Other users are targeting some maclicous goals such as confidential document theft, personal privacy stealing or installing of back door software in the aimed-system for futhure attacks.
- *System consequence*: We describe the system consequence from host and network levels. A masquerader intrused into a personal computer would behave differently from the original user in keyborad hitting, mouse moving, applications lunching and file system accesses. These operation sequences can result in different system logs, such as application log, security log etc. These events can be observed by our system monitors. In network level, a masquerader may leak data on mail transferring or covert channels that can be capture by other network monitors.

3   Detection Framework

We hope to design an approach to detect masquerader behavior and find attacker's intent. To achieve this goal, firstly we propose design of several sensors which capture system consequence, such as key-hit, mouse-move, application-run, file access event etc. And then, we describe our algorithm to extract aggregative features vector and fuse them together. We apply Principle component analysis (PCA) to reduce dimensions of features vector and use Support Vector Machine to find masquerader with different attack intent from normal behavior base.

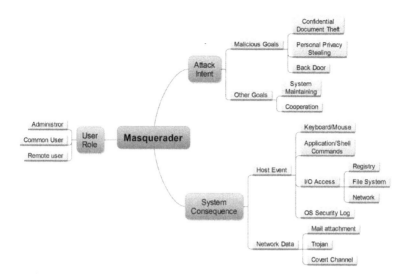

Fig. 1. Taxonomy of Masquerader Attacks

3.1 Sensors and Basic Features

According to our taxonomy of masquerader, we classify system consequence into host events and network data. In our framework, we just focus on host events, especially on personal computers installed with Windows-OSs. We chose four types of observables generated by four sensors which are Key-Sensor, Mice-Sensor, App-Sensor and I/O-Sensor.

Key-Sensor: Key-Sensor registers a hook function in OS and capture keystroke events. All events are grouped by two arrays. The first array is a transfer matrix that records average time interval from one kind of keys to another kind of keys. For example, the time interval you hit a number-key '9' after hitting an alpha-key 'o'. All keys are divided into seven groups. That are Number-keys, Alpha-keys, Sign-keys(shift + num), Ctrl-keys(ctrl, alt etc.), Fun-key (F1,F2…), Dir-keys(->, <- etc.), ESC-key. So the first array has forty-nine elements. The second array record the key hit duration from down to up. These records cover all important keys on the keyboard. All data are mean values among a fixed time window which is changeable before the monitor is run.

Mice-Sensor: Mice-Sensor captures mainly mouse move events and click events. We divide the direction of mouse move into eight directions (Figure 2) and then record down the mean value and variance of distance and speed of mouse move in every direction. Mice Sensor also records duration of clicks events including left-click, right click and double click. We monitor up to 50 features of mouse during one time window.

App-Sensor and I/O-Sensor: We use process monitor to monitor process activities and I/O accesses. Process monitor is an excellent process monitor tool for Windows that show real-time file system, registry and network activity. Detail description about process monitor can be got from its website[8].

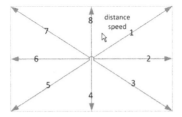

Fig. 2. Mouse move direction

3.2   Data Fusion

Data fusion is a bottom-up style solution for problems. For identity fusion, there are three types of architecture which can be used: 1) data level fusion, 2) feature level fusion, 3) decision level fusion. We employ the second architecture – feature fusion – to solve masquerader detection problem because of two reasons: 1) our data sources are not homogeneous but relevant with each other; 2) our goal is to detect masquerader behavior and analyze attacker's intent. We define input and output of our algorithm framework at first and then describe process steps.

Input <K, M, A, IO>: The input is a quad-tuple vector. K, M, A and IO represent feature sets collected by Key-Sensor, Mice-Sensor, App-Sensor and I/O-Sensor respectively. In particular, *IO* is a triple which can be decomposed into <Reg, File, Net>, that respectively means operation features on registry, file system and network.

Output <Result>: The output *<Result>* of algorithm is a flag of current events which should be labeled as 'normal' or one type of attack intents.

The procedure of algorithm is composited of three steps:

Feature_Fusion: If we expand *IO* feature set, there are six types of feature sets which are key, mouse, application, registry, file, and network. We design two joint operators to mix them together. Firstly, *JOINT_BY_PID* connect four feature sets – application, registry, file and network – with same PID into a vector P <App, Reg, File, Net>. Secondly, *JOINT_BY_INTERVAL* generates a full feature vector < K, M, P1, P2, P3, P4, P5> every time interval from Key-features, Mouse-features and P-Features sets. There are so many active processes in OS at the same time, so we divide them into 5 groups denoted as <P1, P2, P3, P4, P5> by their utilities and frequency of utilization.

At last we get a fused feature vector as shown in Table 1:

Table 1. Final Fused Features

Time Interval	Key		Mouse				P1			
	Duration	Transfer	Move	Clicks	**App**	**Reg**	**File**		**Net**	
	Alpha	A->N	direction	Left	type	Reg_num	File_num	TCP	UDP	
	Number	N->A	distance	right	name	Oper_num	Oper_num	connect	session	
	Fun	A->Fun	speed	double	path	Read	Open	accept	send	
	Ctrl	Fun->A	mean	drag	command	Write	Read	send	receive	
	SIGN	N->Fun	variance	scroll	CPU	Create	Write	receive	...	
	...	...	...	...	memory	Delete	Query	close	...	
					...	...	Set	...	...	

Noted: P2, P3, P4, P5 are omitted due to space cause.

PCA_Procedure: After feature fusion process, we get a final feature vector with high dimension. The final feature vector is about 200-dimensional, which includes 50-dimensional key features, 44-dimensional mouse features, 5 type application feature sets with 20-dimensional features per set. Too high dimensional data will give rise of over-fitting problem in practical computing. Principal component analysis is a mathematical procedure which uses an orthogonal transformation to covert a set of observations of possibly correlated variable into a set of values of linearly uncorrelated variables.

Classifier: We use a common implement of LibSVM as our classifier to detect masquerader.

3.3   Analysis of Framework

Accuracy and speed of masquerader detection: In principle, fusion of multi-sensor data show significant advantages over single source data. For our framework, we select four sensors and fuse the monitored features. Every type of feature has been proven to be good indicator of re-authentication. So, our framework is expected to obtain better accuracy than single-source approach. In addition, PCA is employed to reduce fused feature set, which can fasten our training and testing phase.

Capability of attack intent analysis: In four sensors, key and mouse events have been used for masquerader detection and showed high degree of distinction to different personal behavior. And application and I/O events are regarded as good observables related with attack intent. For example, a confidential document thief will probably search sensitive data by using Explore.exe or Google desktop searching tool. These programs will generate a lot of file access records. So a lot of file access records may be related with document searching. If the monitor has identified an abnormal mouse or key event at the same time, a confidential document theft event will be detected. So our framework used multiple different sensors is deemed to fulfill the capability of attack intent analysis.

4   Related Work

Human computer interaction based biometric approaches are widely used in re-authentication. Keystroke feature are based on time durations between the keystroke inter-key stroke and dwell time. Dowland [9] combined keystroke feature and application information to make a distinction between different users and their experiment showed 60% accuracy with eight users data. In a mouse re-authentication system implemented by Pusara [10], they applied a supervised learning algorithm on mouse move data from eight users working with Internet Explore. Their result showed they can obtain a false positive rate of 0.43%, and false negative rate of 1.75%. These work based HCI biometric showed good experiment results but their experiment just get enough good result in specified scenarios such as in workspace of Word, Power Point or Internet Explore. That limits the use of their methods.

In the cyber domain, data fusion has been paid closely attentions. Bass, in his paper published in 2000[11], advocates the need of information fusion to fill the void of intrusion detection. Since then, much work, e.g., [12], has been devoted to correlate Intrusion Detection System (IDS) alerts, so as to provide better situation awareness of cyber-attacks. Correlating alerts provides the network security analysts a view of the attacks, instead of a view containing an enormous volume of alerts, many of which could be irrelevant. Yang et cl. [13] assumes well administered networks and many of the security components are in place, so that even sophisticated attackers will need to execute multiple operations before reaching critical files or compromising core network operation. Based on such premise, their work identifies the roles of information fusion for cyber security, and focuses on the lacking components – tracking and projection of multistage cyber-attacks.

Some research of insider threats also mentioned data fusion. Matzner,Feng et cl.[14, 15] advocated to use data fusion to discover evidence of malicious activity by correlating and analyze a variety of low-level data. Maybury [16] et cl. also provided a framework that fused multiple indicators that were related by IP, user name, etc. into one single indicator and allowed customer selectable weights for each element in the observable taxonomy. These works above just propose a framework of using data fusion to detect insider threat but are lack of detail of algorithm and practical system. Tang [17] et cl. in their paper gave a   detail description of one data fusion algorithm based on Dynamic Bayesian Network. Tang's work still is a theoretical work and lack of support from practical data.

5   Conclusion

The purpose of this research is to detect masquerader with higher accuracy and analysis of intent. For this purpose, we adds attack intents in the taxonomy of masquerader and analyzed some host behavior events related to detection system; And then we build a framework based on data fusion to detect masquerader from multi-sensor data.

However, our taxonomy of masquerader is still limited by our knowledge about insider threats. A complete and consistent taxonomy needs number of investigations on real attack cases. That's one of our future work. Another limit of our approach is that all sensors are running on host, which may make us miss some observables which are related to some important attack intents. Previous work also mentioned that all alerts from host monitors, network monitors and honeypot should be fused for anomaly detection. However, concrete approaches and practical systems are still rare. Our future work will fill the void of practical systems for masquerader detection from multi-sensors.

Acknowledgements. This work is supported by National High Technology Research and Development Program of China, 863 Program (Grant No.2011AA010701 and 2011AA01A103) and National Key Technology R&D Program (Grant No.2012BAH37B04).

References

1. Afghan War Diary, 2004-2010 (July 2010),
   `http://wikileaks.org/wiki/Afghan_War_Diary,_2004-2010`
2. Cyber-Insider Threat (CINDER) (2010), `http://www.darpa.mil/Our_Work/I2O/Programs/Cyber-Insider_Threat_(CINDER).aspx`
3. Yampolskiy, R.V.: Human computer interaction based intrusion detection. IEEE (2007)
4. Salem, M., Stolfo, S.: Modeling user search behavior for masquerade detection. Springer (2011)
5. Hall, D.L., Llinas, J.: An introduction to multisensor data fusion. Proceedings of the IEEE 85(1), 6–23 (1997)
6. Parker, D.B.: Fighting computer crime: A new framework for protecting information. John Wiley & Sons, Inc. (1998)
7. Magklaras, G., Furnell, S.: Insider threat prediction tool: Evaluating the probability of IT misuse. Computers & Security 21(1), 62–73 (2001)
8. Process Monitor v3.01 (2012), `http://technet.microsoft.com/en-us/sysinternals/bb896645.aspx`
9. Dowland, P., Furnell, S., Papadaki, M.: Keystroke analysis as a method of advanced user authentication and response. Kluwer, BV (2002)
10. Pusara, M., Brodley, C.E.: User re-authentication via mouse movements. ACM (2004)
11. Bass, T.: Intrusion detection systems and multisensor data fusion. Communications of the ACM 43(4), 99–105 (2000)
12. Ning, P., Cui, Y., Reeves, D.S.: Constructing attack scenarios through correlation of intrusion alerts. ACM (2002)
13. Yang, S.J., et al.: High level information fusion for tracking and projection of multistage cyber attacks. Information Fusion 10(1), 107–121 (2009)
14. Matzner, S.N.: Approaches to Insider Threat Mitigation. ISSA Journal, 6–8 (2004)
15. Feng, Z.N.D.: Situation Assessment and Threat Assessment Technique in Data Fusion. Electronic Warfare 1 (2007)
16. Maybury, M.: Analysis and detection of malicious insiders. DTIC Document (2005)
17. Tang, K., Zhao, M., Zhou, M.: Cyber Insider Threats Situation Awareness Using Game Theory and Information Fusion-based User Behavior Predicting Algorithm. Journal of Information & Computational Science 8(3), 529–545 (2011)

An Integration of Several Different Data Flow Analysis Techniques

Yuchen Xing, Hanfei Wang, and Jianhua Zhao

Department of Computer Science and Technology, Nanjing University, Nanjing, China
{xingyuchen,wanghanfei1988}@seg.nju.edu.cn, zhaojh@nju.edu.cn

Abstract. This paper describes a tool which integrates three different kinds of data flow analysis techniques: null pointer dereference analysis, integer variables differences analysis and single linked list analysis. Each one of them can share and exchange program information with the other two. And also users can add properties manually to enhance the processing capabilities. Through the demonstration in the case study section, we can see that our tool achieves the goal to connect these three analysis techniques and can explore more insightful program information with the artificial help.

Keywords: data flow analysis, program analysis, null pointer dereference.

1   Introduction

As an important static program analysis technique, data-flow analysis [1, 2] gathers run-time information of the possible sets of values which are extracted from various points in a program. Such information is often used in compiler optimization, program verification, debugging, testing, etc.

Our work integrates three different data flow analysis techniques and makes the results of each analysis can be used by the other two techniques. Also we allow users to add new information manually in order to improve the information mining capabilities. After several iterations of the cross-analysis and manual improvement, users can achieve more program information than they achieve when these techniques are used separately. Our technique can be used in program verification or some other areas that require a deeper level of program information.

2   Solution Framework

We designed three different data flow analysis techniques -- null pointer dereference analysis, integer variables differences analysis and single linked list analysis -- as the automated analysis part of our tool. And we also allow users to add some key information manually to improve the automated analysis capabilities. The program information can be picked from or stored into the program information management platform by all the analysis techniques and users. Therefore, we can achieve the purpose of information-sharing.

Y. Yuan, X. Wu, and Y. Lu (Eds.): ISCTCS 2012, CCIS 320, pp. 458–465, 2013.

Fig. 1. An overview of the solution framework

The syntax of the simple program language we dealt with is a subset of the C language's syntax. The specific differences are: for the loop statement we only accept *while*; for the branch statement we only accept *if-else*; the *break* and *continue* statements are not accepted; and the addressing operator & is removed to avoid complex address dependencies.

2.1   Program Information Management Platform

The program information management platform is used to store and share the variable information and function definitions. It connects three analysis techniques and the tool user. Finally, an analysis result will be generated from it.

After opening a program, we will insert a function definition point in the very beginning of the code, and insert several nodes storing variable information at every program points.

At the function definition point, user can define functions to describe some properties of variables. Like the *isSList* function shown in subsection 2.4, if this statement *isSList(first)* is established at some program point, it means that the property *"first == null?true:((first isIn nodeSet(first->next)) && isSList(first->next))"* is satisfied in that program point. The function definitions inserted in this point are used to simplify the description of properties, especially the recursive properties of variables, and make it easy to be used by automated analysis techniques.

The property of a variable is presented as a boolean-typed expression which is called *formula* in our tool. Formulas are stored in the program point nodes. It has four attributes: id, statement, status and proved-by-info. The status of formula is PROVED or UNPROVED. The proved-by-info stores the dependent formula ids. A formula establishes only when the status is PROVED and all of its dependent formulas are established.

By allowing automated analysis techniques and users to insert or modify formulas in program points, the program information management platform becomes an interactive media of variable information.

2.2   Null Pointer Dereference Analysis

The null pointer dereference analysis is to find whether a null-pointer variable is dereferenced somewhere in the program. This analysis technique has become one of the typical dataflow analyses techniques.

In our tool, the specific analysis algorithm [3, 4] is as follows. First, get all pointer-typed variables definition from code. Second, gather the assignment information of these variables from the statements of the program and the variable properties from every program points. Third, do the kill/propagate/meet operations of data flow analysis iteratively. At last, all the new properties of these variables will be written into the program points as formulas.

There are four statuses of pointer variable: UNKNOWN, NULL, NOT_NULL, EITHER. UNKNOWN is the initial status of a pointer variable. NULL and NOT_NULL mean the variable is known as null or not-null specifically. The statement of EITHER is defined as the condition that the variable can be either null or not-null. The specific status can only be determined in runtime executions. The EITHER status is generated by the meet operation or a complex right value of an assignment.

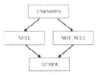

Fig. 2. The meeting lattice for the null pointer dereference analysis

The meet [5,6] strategy: properties will meet when branch and loop statements are used in the program. The lattice [4,7] in discrete mathematics is used here to calculate the new properties of variables. As shown in Fig. 2. The new status of variable is the greatest lower bound. In other words, we get the weakest status when two statuses meet.

In our tool, we concentrate on the assignments of the following forms:

```
p = q; p = null; p = alloc(); p = ...
```

In the program points, we concentrate the properties generated by other analysis of the following forms.

```
p == q; p == null; p != null;
```

The assignment "p = ..." means that the right-hand of this assignment is complex and cannot be analyzed automatically. We will set the status of p as EITHER in the point after this assignment.

2.3   Integer Variables Differences Analysis

Typically, when using arrays in their programs, programmers often needs to increase/decrease arrays' index or compare the index with another integer. By analyzing the differences between integer-typed variables, we can extract some formulas to describe the range of the differences between them. Usually, these formulas can be used to prove some other formulas.

The basic algorithm is just same as the one which we have explained in the previous subsection. But the representation method, meet lattice and meet/kill strategy are different.

We use a matrix to represent the differences between every two integer variables or between one integer variable and the integer zero. As the matrix shown in Fig. 3, the values in the matrix show the value that the landscape orientation variables minus the portrait orientation variables.

	V_1	V_2	...	V_n	0
V_1		-3		1	
V_2	3				2
!					
V_n		6			
0					

Fig. 3. The matrix to represent the integer variables differences

The lattice is quite different from the one in null pointer analysis. The height of this lattice is infinite. The values are UNKNOWN, $-\infty$, ... ,-2,-1,0,1,2,...,$+\infty$. As shown in Fig. 4.

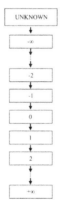

Fig. 4. The meeting lattice for integer variables differences analysis

When two properties meet, we keep the greater value as the value of the difference of these two variables. But it is different when we deal with the meet operation of the formulas before loop and the formulas in the last program point in the loop. When the value decreases after the first time of iterate, we keep the value calculated by the lattice as the new value. Obviously, it's the same value as the one in the previous properties before current loop. But if the value increases after the first time try of iteration, it means that the value may not convergent as the iteration deepening in. So the new value of the difference of these two variables will be set as $+\infty$.

In our tool, we concentrate on the assignments of the following forms:

```
i = 2; i = j; i = i ± 1; i = j ± 1; i = ...
```

And the properties of the following form in the program points:

```
i == 2; i == j; i == j ± 1; i > 1; (<、>=、<=);
i > j ± i; (<、>=、<=);
```

The right-hand of the assignment "i = ..." is a complex expression that cannot be deal with automatically. We will set the difference between i and other variables as "+∞". This kind of treatment influences the precision, but not the correctness of the analysis.

2.4   Single Linked List Analysis

Single linked list is a common data structures in C programs. The node adding and removing operations are commonly used by programmers. Our single linked list analysis is designed to find whether a pointer variable points to a single linked list. These two kinds of properties can be described by recursive functions in our tool. The general definitions are:

```
bool isSList(EdgeNode *first;) := first ==
    null?true:(not(first isIn nodeSet(first->next)) &&
        isSList(first->next))
bool isSListSeg(EdgeNode *first;EdgeNode *end;) :=
    (first == end) || (first != null &&
                        isSListSeg(first->next,end))
```

	V₁	V₂	...	Vₙ	NULL
V₁		Y			
V₂	Y				Y
⋮					
Vₙ	Y				

Fig. 5. The matrix to represent the linked status of single linked list

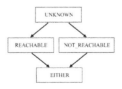

Fig. 6. The meeting lattice for single linked list analysis

The point-to information of single linked list node pointer variables are described in matrix(Fig. 5) too, basically as the way used in the integer variable difference analysis. The values in the matrix mean the reachability status from the landscape orientation variables to the portrait orientation variables. The NULL value is set as the last column in the matrix. A pointer can reach NULL means that it points to a single linked list.

There are four statuses of the reachability properties: UNKNOWN, REACHABLE, NOT_REACHABLE, EITHER. The lattice of these four statuses is shown in Fig. 6.

The meet strategy is basically same as the one used in the null pointer dereference analysis. The lowest upper bound in the lattice is used as the new status when two variables meet.

After the single linked list analysis, the formulas will be written back into program points using the *isSList* and *isSListSeg* functions above. When a variable A can reach NULL through the link, it will described as *isSList(A)*. When a variable A can reach another variable B, it will described as *isSListSeg(A,B)*.

In our tool, we concentrate on the assignments of the following forms:

```
p = q; p = q->next; p = p->next; p = null; p = alloc;
p->next = q; p->next = p; p = ...; p->next = ...;
```

And the formulas of the following form in program points:

```
isSList(p); isSListSeg(p,q);
```

2.5   User Improvement

Users can define functions, modify or insert formulas in order to give new program information to the automated analysis techniques. Then users can use the analysis techniques to extract more information automatically. Therefore, we can make better use of the automated analysis techniques to simplify some analysis procedure and at the same time guarantee the correctness.

3   Case Study

In order to evaluate the capabilities of our tool, we propose an example to demonstrate. The input program is depth-first traversal algorithm of adjacency list graph, shown in Fig. 7.

After opening the program, the function definition point and program points has been inserted into the abstract syntax tree, as shown in Fig. 8.

By using the single linked list analysis, we can get that the variable *stack_temp* at the program node from A11 to A30 is a single linked list, the *stack_ first* at the program node from A12 to A30 is a single linked list; the list from *stack_first* to *stack_temp* becomes a segment of single linked list in the program node from A12 to A30. The formulas of *isStackSList(stack_first)* and *isStackSListSeg(stack_first, stack_temp)* are inserted into these program points.

After proving $k{\geq}0$ and $k{\leq}9$ in the program point A19 manually, we can use integer variables differences analysis to prove these two properties in the program points from A20 to A29. The manual prove procedure is easy for users, because " $\forall i \in [0,9]$ $\rightarrow (AdjList[i] \rightarrow adjvex \in [0,9])$ " is a pre-condition of the program.

The properties $k{\geq}0$ and $k{\leq}9$ can be used to manually prove the *VertexNode* index pushed into/poped from the stack is between 0 and 9. Thereby in A15, *isS-List(temp_first)* can be proved. Then we can use single linked list analysis again to prove *isSList(temp_first)* in the program points from A15 to A30.

```
typedef struct {int adjvex;   EdgeNode *next;} EdgeNode;
typedef struct {char vertex; EdgeNode *firstedge;} VertexNode;
typedef struct {int vNodeIndex; VertexNodeStack *next;} VertexNodeS-
tack;
VertexNode AdjList[10];
int visited[10];
int i;
int k;
int nodeCount;
VertexNodeStack *stack_first;
VertexNodeStack *stack_temp;
EdgeNode *p;
EdgeNode *temp_first;

i = 0;
nodeCount = 10;

while(i < nodeCount)
{
    visited[i] = 0;
    i = i + 1;
}
i = 0;

stack_temp = alloc(VertexNodeStack);
stack_temp->vNodeIndex = 0;
stack_temp->next = null;
stack_first = stack_temp;
visited[0] = 1;

while(stack_first != null)
{
    temp_first = AdjList[stack_first -> vNodeIndex] . firstedge;
    p = temp_first;
                    stack_first = stack_first -> next;
    while(p != null)
    {
        k = p->adjvex;
        if(visited[k] == 0)
        {
            visited[k] = 1;
            stack_temp = alloc(VertexNodeStack);
            stack_temp->vNodeIndex = k;
            stack_temp->next = stack_first;
            stack_first = stack_temp;
        }
        else
        {
            skip;
        }
        p = p->next;
    }
}
```

Fig. 7. A program of adjacency list graph depth-first traversal algorithm

```
typedef struct {int adjvex; EdgeNode *next;} EdgeNode;        Assert 13,A13
typedef struct {char vertex; EdgeNode *firstedge;} VertexNode;  while(stack_first != null)
typedef struct {int vNodeIndex; VertexNodeStack *next;} VertexNodeStack;   Assert 14,A14
VertexNode AdjList[10];                                            temp_first = AdjList[stack_first -> vNodeIndex] . firstedge;
int visited[10];                                                   Assert 15,A15
int i;                                                             p = temp_first;
int k;                                                            Assert 16,A16
int nodeCount;                                                     stack_first = stack_first -> next;
VertexNodeStack *stack_first;                                     Assert 17,A17
VertexNodeStack *stack_temp;                                       while(p != null)
EdgeNode *p;                                                          Assert 18,A18
EdgeNode *temp_first;                                                 k = p->adjvex;
Function Definition(8)                                               Assert 19,A19
Assert 1,A1                                                           if(visited[k] == 0)
i = 0;                                                                     then
Assert 2,A2                                                                   Assert 20,A20
nodeCount = 10;                                                               visited[k] = 1;
Assert 3,A3                                                                   Assert 21,A21
while(i < nodeCount)                                                          stack_temp = alloc(VertexNodeStack);
    Assert 4,A4                                                               Assert 22,A22
    visited[i] = 0;                                                           stack_temp->vNodeIndex = k;
    Assert 5,A5                                                               Assert 23,A23
    i = i + 1;                                                                stack_temp->next = stack_first;
    Assert 6,A6                                                               Assert 24,A24
Assert 7,A7                                                                   stack_first = stack_temp;
i = 0;                                                                        Assert 25,A25
Assert 8,A8                                                                else
stack_temp = alloc(VertexNodeStack);                                         Assert 26,A26
Assert 9,A9                                                                   skip;
stack_temp->vNodeIndex = 0;                                                   Assert 27,A27
Assert 10,A10                                                             p = p->next;
stack_temp->next = null;                                                 Assert 28,A28
Assert 11,A11                                                             Assert 29,A29
stack_first = stack_temp;                                            Assert 30,A30
Assert 12,A12                                                     Assert 31,A31
visited[0] = 1;
```

Fig. 8. After opening the program in our tool

Generally, there will be some unproved dependent formulas like *stack_first != null* for pointer variables after a few operations of analysis, for example the *stack_first != null* in A16. At such times, we can use null pointer dereference analysis. In most cases, this analysis technique can determine whether a pointer variable is null or not-null.

4   Conclusion

Each data flow analysis technique has its own advantages and limitations for specific scenarios and data structures. And due to the diversity and complexity of data flow, some key information may not be extracted by algorithms automatically. They can be added and proved manually by users. We believe that our tool can use different features and capabilities of every data flow analysis more efficiently; by combining with ability to add manual proved information, our tool can avoid some limitations of automated analysis capabilities; and finally, for the reasons above, we will get more program information in the analysis results.

At present, the data structures our tool can deal with are relatively simple (only single linked analysis); the supported branch and loop program structures are also very limited. In the future, we will concentrate on supporting the entire C language's syntax and more common data structures.

Acknowledgments. This work is supported by the National Natural Science Foundation of China (No.91118002).

References

1. Aho, A.V., Sethi, R., Ullman, J.D.: Compilers-Principles, Techniques and Tools, 2nd edn. Addison Wesley (2007)
2. Khedker, U.P., Sanyal, A., Karkare, B.: Data Flow Analysis Theory and Practice. CRC Press (2009)
3. Allen, F.E., Cocke, J.: A program data flow analysis procedure. Communication of the ACM 19(3), 137–147 (1976)
4. Kildall, G.A.: A unified approach to global program optimization. In: Record of the ACM Symposium on Principles of Programming Languages, New York, pp. 194–206 (1973)
5. Hsieh, C.S.: A fine- grained data- flow analysis framework. Acta Informatica 34(9), 653–665 (1997)
6. Khedler, U.P., Dhamdhere, D.M.: A generalized theory of bit vector data flow analysis. ACM TOPLAS 16(5), 1472–1511 (1994)
7. Liu, X., Wu, Y., Li, M., Zeng, X.: A Study of Data- flow Analysis Framework Based on Lattice. Computer Engineering and Applications 21(1), 48–51 (2006)

Specifying and Detecting Behavioral Changes in Source Code Using Abstract Syntax Tree Differencing

Yuankui Li and Linzhang Wang

State Key Lab. for Novel Software Technology, Nanjing University, Nanjing, China
Department of Computer Science and Technology, Nanjing University, Nanjing, China
lyk@seg.nju.edu.cn, lzwang@nju.edu.cn

Abstract. During the development of a software, its source code is continuously being modified. Even after the deployment, the maintenance work still involves changing the source code. Some of the modification performed on the source code is rather meaningless, while others might cause some critical behavioral changes. To help understand the modification, we can distinguish the behavioral changes and ease the tedious work. Our approach focuses on eliminating two kinds of changes: the unessential changes and the behavioral-unrelated changes, to achieve a better change detection result.

Keywords: change detection, source code analysis, behavioral change.

1 Introduction

Change detection is a very common task, even in our daily life. Likewise, change detection is also an important task. When a new version of a software is released, people would ask, what has changed? When some source code files get modified, fellow programmers and coders would concern the changed part most. And when environment is different, concentrating on the changed area is the best way to help you get adapted.

When softwares are been developed, the processes involve a lot of workers, who will collaborate with each other and cooperate to make things done. As artifacts which are brought into existence by human intellectual activities, softwares are designed by designers, and implemented by coders. And finally after the deployment, people still have to take care of them, which is called the maintenance. From the coding phase to the maintenance phase, the source codes of softwares never cease to get modified.

Since the source codes are modified iteratively, they are usually managed with version control systems such as CVS, SVN, GIT, Mercurial and so on. When someone get two different versions of source codes, he might wonder what are the differences between them. The ancient diff tool, which is embedded in UNIX distributions, aimed to solve the problem. By performing line-to-line text-matching while locating the longest common string (LCS) between the versions, *diff* could isolate the different lines, which are usually the changed parts.

Y. Yuan, X. Wu, and Y. Lu (Eds.): ISCTCS 2012, CCIS 320, pp. 466–473, 2013.

However, the *diff* tool might give meaningless results.   For example, sometimes a mismatch may happen while calculating the LCS. Moreover, the changes about white spaces might also be included not only for the white space sensitive programming language such as Python, but also for the insensitive languages such as Java, C++. In these situations, the output of diff failed to capture the changes between the two versions. It seemed, that introducing a white-space-ignoring feature could make up the latter drawback of diff. Still, the mismatch problems are not solved.

In this paper, we propose a new way to detect the specified changes between the original code and the modified code. The source code are transformed to abstract syntax tree(AST), which is a compiling intermediate representation, and the differencing algorithm is performed on the ASTs. The differencing information between the source codes are also represented as trees, which are formally defined and could be used to perform more analysis. The transformation from source codes to ASTs in our study are performed by a configured compiler generated by ANTLR[4], however, the idea is applicable to any parser-generator.

A compiler generator generates a compiler which could recognize and process a certain language which are specified with grammar or syntax. A set of grammar describes the structure and components of a language, it tells the compiler generator what a language is like. We use the tree grammar to describe the ASTs to be generated, which is a domain specific language used by ANTLR.

In most compiler-related work, the ASTs are used only as a intermediate representation, to retain the useful information of the source codes, as a result, they are usually stored in memories.   In our case, we store ASTs in extendable markup language (XML) files. The advantage is that the change info can be used for further analysis.

2   Related Work

In this paper, we are addressing this problem:

> "When a software is under iteratively development, sometimes a version of source code is structurally changed, while sometimes it's behaviorally changed. However, to different people focus different sort of changes, for example, a testing engineering dealing with regression testing would concentrate on the behavioral changes. Be behavioral changes, we mean the changes that influence the control flow of a program.   Here is the problem: with the source code files as input, how to find out the behavioral changes only."

In most computer programming languages, source code files are written by programmers or coders to describe the structural details and behaviors of a designed software. Take the most popular one, Java, as an example, usually programmers write declarations and specifications of classes in *java* files, including the members such as *field*s and *method*s.   Among the members of a class, *fields* are usually a static picture of the class, while the *method*s specify what the class would do, i.e., its possible behaviors.

Sometimes the behavioral parts are more critical for a process, a program or a software, and they might be the focus of related workers.   Look at code snippet Listing 1.1. People wouldn't care if the String typed field *hello* gets renamed as long as its value remains correctly referenced, which is actually a structural information. But if the method main does any different things, causing some changes in code behaviors, they'd want to know.   For those people, they need a code comparing and differencing tool, which could neglect any changes except the behavioral changes. But how to specify the behavioral changes and detect such changes only?

Listing 1.1. Example java code: HelloWorld.java

```
public class HelloWorld
{
  static private String hello = "hello";
  static private String world = "world";
  static public void main( String args [ ] )
  {
    System.out.println(hello + " " + world + "!");
  }
}
```

To judge if a phrase is behavioral or structural, the semantics of the phrase must be clear, and by analyzing its semantics, the phrase could be grouped into categories. However, since the common differencing tools does little semantics analysis to the code, it could be boldly presumed that such functionality is beyond the ability of the *diff* utility as well as any text-based change-detection technique. So, there are two obstacles to tackle, the **unrelated changes** and the **unessential changes**. Unessential changes are those changes that have no essential effect on the semantics of a program, such as reformatting of the code structure, reordering of some sibling fields, and in most programming languages(except Python, Haskell, etc.), white space elimination and addition. Unrelated changes are those changes which have no direct effect on the behavior of a program, i.e., the structural changes such as the definition of a local variable or a field member, the rename of some variables.Solving the problem in a compiling way.

2.1   The Whole Picture

A source file is filled with programs or program entities which constitute programs, which is visually lines of code, assimilating to raw text files.   The most distinguishing feature of source file is that the text in a source file must conform to a set of language syntaxes, which are usually well-defined.   The syntax of a language defines the necessary structure of a language which could make any sense.   Usually, the basic unit in a language is tokens. And the tokens constitute the language constructions in a way as the bricks constitute the walls.

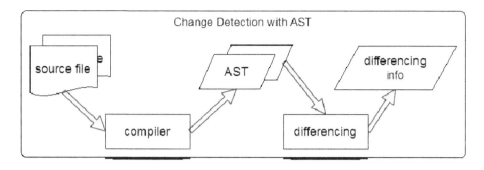

Fig. 1. Change detection on AST

Listing 1.2. Example syntax definition: java.g

```
tokens {
// operators and other special chars
    LPAREN = '(' ;
    RPAREN = ')' ; SEMI = ';' ;
// keywords
    FOR = 'for' ;
// tokens for imaginary nodes
    FOR_CONDITION; FOR_EACH; FOR_INIT; FOR_UPDATE;
forStatement
    : FOR LPAREN forInit SEMI forCondition SEMI forUpdater
RPAREN statement
        -> ^(FOR forInit forCondition forUpdater statement )
    ;
forInit
    : localVariableDeclaration -> ^(FOR_INIT localVariab-
leDeclaration )
    | expressionList -> ^(FOR_INIT expressionList )
        -> ^(FOR_INIT) ;
forCondition : expression?
    -> ^(FOR_CONDITION expression ?) ;
forUpdater : expressionList?
    -> ^(FOR_UPDATE expressionList ?) ;
...
```

For example, the grammar for Java language in List 1.2 consists of two parts, the tokens and the BNFs, a.k.a. grammar rules. The tokens are defined with regular expressions and referenced in BNFs. The specification of a language are written in a pre-defined Domain Specific Language. With grammatical structure, the source code are more than common texts, but something more normalized. To figure out the meaning of source codes, they are processed with compilers, usually transformed to a intermediate structure called Abstract Syntax Tree. An AST retains all the useful information conveyed in its original source code, while neglecting the coding format styles, such as the position of a brace for an *if* statement, or the number of white spaces, which contribute nothing in the final execution of programs.

Listing 1.3. Reformatted example java code: HelloWorld.java

```
public class HelloWorld{
static private String hello = "hello";
static private String world = "world" ;
static public void main( String args [ ] ) {
System . out . println ( hello +"" + world + "!");;}
}
```

It is AST that could reflect the semantical information of a source file, and it is the changes on ASTs that could reflect the essential changes of a source file. For example, the Java code in List 1.2 are modified to List 1.3. It's doubtless to say that by text matching, these two snippets are obviously different. And the *diff* utility and any mechanically similar tools would detect many changes, though human programmers who may be concerned will regard them as false alarms. However, when those code snippets are compiled, their ASTs are identical, which is agreeable to programmers' intuition.

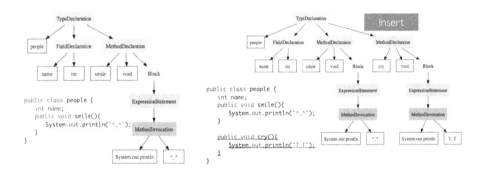

Fig. 2. When source code changes, its AST might change

As is shown above, if we detect changes from ASTs of different versions of source codes, we can exclude the **Unessential Changes**, thus getting a better result than detecting the raw text of source codes.

2.2   Picking Certain Nodes from a Whole AST

As described in previous part, in some situation, people want to concentrate on certain sorts of changes, for example, the changes happened to the code which describes the behavior of a programs might be more important, while the structural changes could be neglected as long as they are consistent. An AST reflects the structure of its original source code, and the components of the language are organized as layered nodes in AST. Each node has its semantical functionality, for instance, the **forInit** nodes in List 1.2 represent the initial statement of a *for* statement. With this observation, we can pick up certain behavioral parts in a complete AST and construct a minified AST which consists the information we care only. To pick up the nodes, we'd recognize the named tree nodes and describe the behavioral patterns.

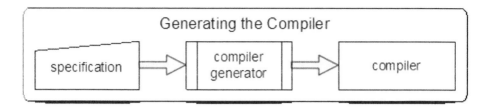

Fig. 3. Generating the compiler to pick nodes

During the development of compilers, many useful tools have emerged, most of them are compiler generators. Actually, compiler generators are compilers, too. They take Domain Specific Language like List 1.2 as input, which describes a language and specifies how to recognize the language, and generate a compiler front-end as output. If we want to pick behavioral nodes from a complete AST, we could feed our specification to a compiler generator and the rest work will be done automatically. As is illustrated in Figure 3, we specify our requirement of picking certain nodes in the form of DSL for a compiler generator. To sum up, the specification mainly covers up such details: *Class Declaration*, *Method Declaration*, *While Statement*, *If Statement*, *Method Invocation* and other properties which are related to those mentioned nodes.

When the user-defined special compiler is ready, the source code could be processed to get its corresponding AST, which is minified to reduce the size. Similar to any compiling process, the source code must be stored in a source file, and it must conform to the grammar. Then it is parsed by the compiler, however, the parsing stage is unusual, the compiler will generate an AST with limited node types and store it in an xml file.

2.3   Comparing the ASTs

The AST is a tree structure, so the change detection of AST is different from the lines-of-text situation and a little more complicated, so comparing the tree structured data is by no means easy [1]. Many algorithms have been devised [5]. To detect the difference in two ASTs, we must notice that the AST's nodes, though stored in a xml file, are ordered. Since in our method, all the ASTs are stored in xml files, we could deploy an xml file-differencing algorithm to detect and output the Edit Script. After comparison, we adopted the algorithm by [6]. This algorithm supports three kinds of change rules: *change* the attributes of a node, *delete* a sub-node and *insert* a new node. More change patterns such as *move* some nodes or *reorder* the sibling nodes could be considered, however, in reaching for a compromise, we've decided to work with a smaller change vocabulary.

3   Case Study

In this section, we will give an example to illustrate the effectiveness of our approach.

Listing 1.4. Java code snippet from: demo.java

```
public void storyOfSisyphus (){
  boolean notDetached=true ;
  int years ;
  divulgeTheScandalOfZeus () ;
  while ( notDetached ){
    rollingStone () ;
    rest () ;
    years++;
  }
  free () ;
}
```

Listing 1.5. AST of demo.java : demo.xml

```
<method name=" storyOfSisyphus ">
  <call name=" divulgeTheScandalOfZeus " />
  <whiles cond=" [ notDetached ] ">
    <then>
      <call name="rollingStone"/>
      <call name="rest"/>
    </then>
  </ whiles>
  <call name=" free" />
</method>
```

If the code in Listing 1.4 is modified, then comparing the minified ASTs of each version, a change report as Listing 1.6 will be generated.

Listing 1.6. Differencing Info : DiffResult.xml

```
<treediff>
  <changeattr xpath="/type/method[1]/ whiles [1]">
    <attribute name="cond" newvalue="[notDetached]" oldva-
lue="[true]"/>
  </changeattr>
  <addsubtree insertOrder="2" xpathleftsibl-
ing="/type/method[1]/whiles[1]/then[1]/call[1]" xpathpa-
rent="/type/method[1]/whiles[1]/then[1]">
    <call name="rest"/>
  </addsubtree>
  <addsubtree insertOrder="2" xpathleftsibl-
ing="/type/method[1]/ whiles [1]">
    <call name="free"/>
  </addsubtree>
</treediff>
```

As is shown above, our change detection method could efficiently distill the changes between two versions of source code.

4   Related Work

Yu and his coworkers also addressed the problem of eliminate the **Unessential Changes** [7], which used a special language to specify the transformation to be performed on the source code. After that, they adopt clone detection and elimination to isolate the meaningful changes. Some work else has used the idea of comparing AST to detect the changes in version history [2][3]. These work emphasized the accuracy of change detection by AST matching and comparing.

5   Conclusion and Future Work

This approach is effective to detect the behavioral changes, i.e., the changes of control flow in a program.   The differencing info would be valuable to conduct the regression testing because it all about the modified parts of the execution branches.

Acknowledgment. This work is supported by the National Natural Science Foundation of China (No.91118002).

References

1. Chawathe, S., Rajaraman, A., Garcia-Molina, H., Widom, J.: Change detection in hierarchically structured information. ACM SIGMOD Record 25, 493–504 (1996)
2. Fluri, B., Wursch, M., PInzger, M., Gall, H.: Change distilling: Tree differenc- ing for fine-grained source code change extraction. IEEE Transactions on Software Engineering 33(11), 725–743 (2007)
3. Neamtiu, I., Foster, J., Hicks, M.: Understanding source code evolution using abstract syntax tree matching. ACM SIGSOFT Software Engineering Notes 30, 1–5 (2005)
4. Parr, T., Quong, R.: Antlr: A predicated-ll (k) parser generator. Software: Practice and Experience 25(7), 789–810 (1995)
5. Peters, L.: Changedetectioninxmltrees:asurvey. In: 3rd Twente Student Conference on IT (2005)
6. Wang, Y., DeWitt, D., Cai, J.: X-diff: An effective change detection algorithm for xml documents. In: Proceedings of the 19th International Conference on Data Engineering, pp. 519–530. IEEE (2003)
7. Yu, Y., Bandara, A., Tun, T., Nuseibeh, B.: Towards learning to detect meaningful changes in software. In: Proceedings of the International Workshop on Machine Learning Technologies in Software Engineering, pp. 51–54. ACM (2011)

Timing Aspects Construction
Using UML-MARTE Profile

Qingqing Sun, Xiaopu Huang, Jiangwei Li, and Tian Zhang[*]

State Key Lab. for Novel Software Technology, Nanjing University, Nanjing, China
Department of Computer Science and Technology, Nanjing University, Nanjing, China
{sunqq,hxp,ljw}@seg.nju.edu.cn, ztluck@nju.edu.cn

Abstract. Modern real time embedded systems are typically composed of multiple functional and nonfunctional concerns with nonfunctional concerns affect the former in many aspects. MARTE, an extension profile of UML2, aims to be the unified standard language for real time and embedded systems. Aspect-Oriented technology, as a complement to Object-Oriented technique, decomposes systems into distinct features by separating and modularizing crosscutting concerns. In this article, we illustrate how to use plenty of time modeling elements in MARTE profile to support comprehensive modeling of RTES. Similar to general crosscutting concerns, time concerns are often triggered at multiple concerns and tangled with other requirements. We try to deal with time as typically crosscutting concerns by AO technology. We practice these thoughts by means of examples and seek to explore an effective modeling mechanism using of both Aspect-Oriented methods and MARTE profile.

Keywords: MARTE, time, modeling, Aspect-Oriented technology, RTES.

1   Introduction

UML profile for MARTE (Modeling and Analysis of Real-Time and Embedded Systems) [1] is a new UML specification which adds capabilities for model-driven development of Real-Time Embedded Systems (RTES). This extension provides support for specification, design, and verification stages and intends to replace the existing UML profile for SPT. With plenty of time modeling elements, MARTE provides comprehensive support for modeling time of RTES.

The evolving cognitive complexity of large computer systems is a topic of utmost concern, and then the efforts on simplicity are required. In academic research, lots of specific approaches and architectures have already emerged, such as object oriented technology, design patterns and aspect-oriented techniques [2]. Each new methodology has presented new ways to decompose problems and concerns and allowed a more natural mapping from system requirements to programming constructs. But as complexity grew, either these methods had some limitations or raised new problems [3]. Theme approach is a typically aspect-oriented method. It performs well in modeling

---

[*] Corresponding author.

Y. Yuan, X. Wu, and Y. Lu (Eds.): ISCTCS 2012, CCIS 320, pp. 474–481, 2013.

the crosscutting concerns of RTES. In our opinions, modeling the time as an aspect with Theme approach and describing the details in MARTE will be a necessary step towards an appropriate way for modeling RTESs.

The rest of this article is structured as follows. Section 2 describes time relevant concepts in MARTE profile. Section 3 presents an aspect-oriented design approach: Theme approach. Section 4 illustrates how MARTE can aid time modeling how to model time concerns in embedded systems as aspects, while Section 5 concludes the article and outlines plans for future work.

2   The MARTE Time Structure

As a successor of SPT, MARTE must align with the new version UML2 which added many new meta-classes to represent time, duration and some forms of time constraints.

2.1   Time Structure and Accesses to Time

Time structure is well defined in the specification [1]. It can be viewed as the combination of a set of time bases and time structure relations. A time structure contains a tree of multiple time bases. A MultipleTimeBase consists of one or more time bases.

Clocks are usual devices to measure time in real world. In MARTE we adopt a more general point of view: a clock is a model element giving accesses to time, be it physical or logical. LogicalClock and ChronometricClock are two concrete subclasses of Clock. In the time domain view, the corresponding concepts in the UML view are ClockType and TimedDomain. Figure 1 shows their relationships.

2.2   Time Related Entities

TimeRelatedEntities package contains multiple entities such as TimedObservation and TimedProcessing. A TimedObservation is made in the runtime context of a (sub) system behavior execution. TimedProcessing is a generic concept for modeling activities that have known start and finish times, or a known duration, and whose instants and durations are explicitly bounded to Clocks.

3   Theme Approach

Aspect-Oriented Modeling (AOM) is an emerging solution for handling complexity of software models and application code [4] in which a system is viewed as a set of concerns. Recent work in AO design: [5], [6] and [7] have demonstrated the need to deploy this technology early in the software life cycle in order to utilize the technology to its full potential.

Theme approach is an approach for aspect-oriented analysis and design. It provides support for aspect-oriented development at two levels. At the requirements level, Theme/Doc provides views of requirements specification text. At the design level, Theme/UML allows to model features and aspects of a system, and specifies how they should be combined [8].

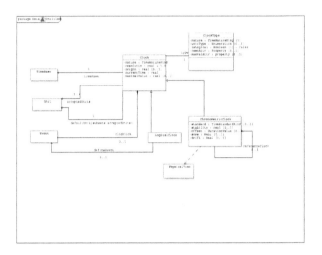

Fig. 1. The ClockType

3.1   Theme/Doc

Theme/Doc deals with the requirements specification in the following steps:

● To identify main themes in the system
● Ascertain whether a theme is an aspect or not

When ascertaining the aspects, there are many features that need to be considered such as whether we can split the requirements and estimate the triggers.

3.2   Theme/UML

For every identified theme, Theme/UML allows the developer to design them respectively in UML style. Base themes are designed in traditional UML style and aspect themes are designed by Theme/UML method. Besides, Theme/UML provides a template and binding paradigm to illustrate their relationships. We present an example of log behavior in figure 2 and figure 3.

Log file is a special in many systems, and log actions are trigged by many behaviors. Those triggers are modeled as LoggedClasses and they cooperate with log file. Figure 3 illustrates the binding mechanism.

4   MARTE Modeling with Timing Aspects

Theme approach handles system evolution which is common but important in software engineering effectively by the definition of themes. Traditional Object Oriented can hardly manage it properly. A theme is designed closed focusing only on its directly related entities. Then the system evolution is viewed just as new themes composing to the primary themes. These compositions are easy to achieve with respect to the unknown relationships brought by uncertain new entities and behaviors in OO technique.

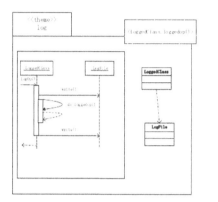

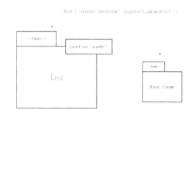

Fig. 2. Thelog theme   **Fig. 3.** The Aspect Theme

In RTESs, time concerns are common but also the key points. AO usually handles crosscutting requirements as aspect themes separating them at point cuts and weaving at join points. Time related requirements can also be treated like this. Time related entities are modeled as TimedClass and behaviors modeled as trigger actions of Timer class in Theme approach. After implementing separately, designers weave these themes to form systems.

MARTE offers the possibility to precisely describe RTES by means of its different and useful components [10]. Moreover, MARTE profile provides multiple time elements to make up existed UML2 profile. To model time concerns, we must first model time accesses: Clock. According to the system requirements, we set different precision clock using IdealClock and LogicalClock elements. We present the proposing phases in figure 4.

4.1   MARTE Clock Modeling

MARTE aims to be the unified standard language for RTES and provides support for specification, design and verification/validation stages for it. It extends the semantics of UML model by several kernel concepts of ClockType, Clock and TimeBase. Among these concepts, MultipleTimeBase are introduced to depict multiple types of clock and Clock to use to define synchronization and priority.

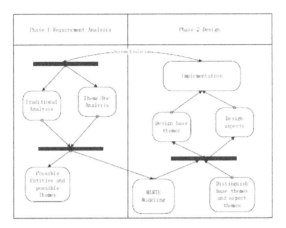

Fig. 4. Phases in MARTE Modeling with Theme process

4.1.1   Modeling Examples

Train-Bridge system, a typical real time and embedded system, is a classic example used in UPPAAL which is a model checker tool for Timed Automata. The bridge in this system likes a critical region in operating system. It has multiple pathways but only one bridge allowing a single train to get through at the same time. The requirements are illustrated in figure 5.

- A train must notice the controller in advance when it is approaching the bridge.
- Controller decides whether to let it go through or wait.
- Receiving the let go signal, a train must pass the bridge in 10 min and inform the controller.
- Receiving wait signal, a train must stop in 5 min.
- Other requirements about response time constraints of hardware.

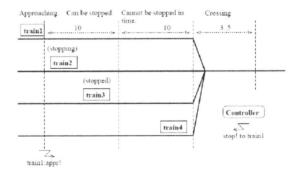

Fig. 5. Train − Bridge Requirements

Considering the accuracy of the system demands, we set two chronometric clocks clk1 and clk2 using the Clock stereotype in MARTE. clk1 is to model the time constraints of passing the bridge and stopping the train, and clk2 is used to model strict time constraints of hardware. These clocks are instances of the Chronometric which applies the ClockType stereotype. Using MARTE time modeling elements, figure 6 shows the final time model of the system.

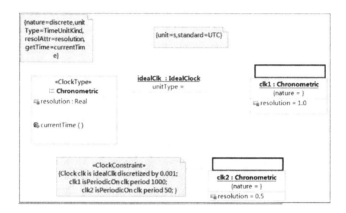

Fig. 6. Time model of Train – Bridge System

Clock clk is an idealClock discretized by 0.001. Clock clk1 is periodic on clk period 1000 which means this clock is triggered one time every minute and it will be used to measure train's approach and leave behaviors. clk2 is periodic on clk period 50 as noted in the ClockConstraints. It means clk2 ticks twice every one second and it will be used as reference of response time constraints. With these clocks, modeling of time related behaviors is possible.

4.2   Timing Aspects

Aspect-Oriented software development is a separation of concerns technique that decomposes systems into distinct features with minimal overlap [9]. Focusing on separating of crosscutting concerns and uncoupling base modules with core modules leads to high reliability and maintenance of a system and make evolution simple to deal with. Time is the decisive concern in RTES and it will be an effective way to manage it as crosscutting concerns and aspect themes.

Train-Bridge system contains several time related classes such as the controller, train and signal sender. Their behaviors are time constrained. With this resemblance, they are abstracted as TimedClass in figure 7 and the corresponding operations are just expressed as an abstract operation op (). When this operation comes, firstly it will invoke the timer or check its time constraints. After this, it returns to its own executing thread. At the end of the operation, it will cancel the timer. Then, all the time related behaviors are modeled as cooperation with Timer (fig.8).

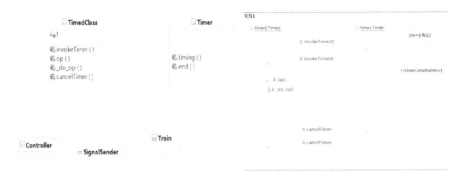

Fig. 7. Timed Class   **Fig. 8.** Aspect Theme

Train-Bridge system contains several time related classes such as the controller, train and signal sender. Their behaviors are time constrained. With this resemblance, they are abstracted as TimedClass in figure 7 and the corresponding operations are just expressed as an abstract operation op (). When this operation comes, firstly it will invoke the timer or check its time constraints. After this, it returns to its own executing thread. At the end of the operation, it will cancel the timer. Then, all the time related behaviors are modeled as cooperation with Timer (fig.8).

4.3   System Modeling

Modeling necessary clocks with MARTE profile after traditional requirement analysis provides basic access to system time. Design processes consists base theme design and aspect theme design inside which modeling time as aspect theme. When system evolves or requirement changes, designers may back to first process to check new themes. System modeling in this way helps resolve code tangling and code scattering problems and explores an effective modeling mechanism making use of Aspect-Oriented methods and MARTE profile.

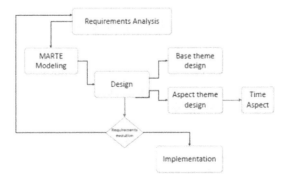

Fig. 9. Process Of system modeling

5   Conclusion and Future Work

In this article, we have presented our thoughts about Timing Aspects Construction using UML-MARTE profile. We illustrated the outline of aspect-oriented technique and useful timed elements in MARTE. We followed that by describing how MARTE facilitates the time modeling with Theme approach. In a Train-Bridge system, we have demonstrated how to describe the time by MARTE profile and model them as aspect themes. System modeling is then regulated as requirement analysis, MARTE modeling and design processes.

However, the current version of this method has some limitations, some of which have already been identified throughout this article. Our method does not capture all real-time and embedded systems concerns and provides little support for synchronization. We are currently investigating a more mature framework about this thought by experimenting on more complex RTES and dealing with more complicated time constraints. Besides, we are exploring a useful and efficient tool for both Theme approach and MARTE profile.

Acknowledgment. This work is supported by the National Natural Science Foundation of China (No.61003025, 91118002), and by the Jiangsu Province Research Foundation (BK2010170).

References

1. OMG, Inc. UML Profile for MARTE: Modeling and Analysis of Real-Time and Embedded systems, Tech. rep. formal/2009-11-02, Object Management Group (2009)
2. Laddad, R.: I want my AOP! Java World (2002), http://www.javaworld.com/javaworld/jw-01-2002/jw-0118-aspect.html
3. Clarke, S., Baniassas, E.: Aspect-Oriented Analysis and Design: The Theme Approach
4. Nouh, M., Ziarati, R., Mouhed, D., Alhadidi, D., Debbabi, M., Wang, L., Pourzandi, M.: Aspect Weaver: a model transformation approach for UML Models
5. Clarket, S., Walker, R.J.: Composition Patterns: An Approach to Designing Reusable Aspects
6. Gray, J., Bapty, T., Neema, S., Tuck, J.: Handling Crosscutting Constraints in Domain-Specific Modeling
7. Elrad, T., Aldawud, O., Bader, A.: Aspect-Oriented Modeling: Bridging the Gap between Implementation and Design. Computer Science, 189–201 (2002)
8. Baniassas, E., Clarke, S.: Theme: An Approach for Aspect-Oriented Analysis and Design. In: Proceedings of the 26th International Conference on Software Engineering, ICSE 2004 (2004)
9. Driver, C., Reilly, S., Linahan, É, Cahill, V.: Managing Embedded Systems Complexity with Aspect-Oriented Model-Driven Engineering
10. Marcello, M., Lius, G.M., Mauro, P.: Model-based Design Space Exploration for RTES with SysML and MARTE

An Overtime-Detection Model-Checking Technique for Interrupt Processing Systems

Xiaoyu Zhou and Jianhua Zhao

State Key Laboratory of Novel Software Technology, Nanjing University, Nanjing, China
Dept. of Computer Sci. and Tech. Nanjing University, Nanjing, China
sandzhou@seg.nju.edu.cn, zhaojh@nju.edu.cn

Abstract. This paper presents an overtime-detection model-checking technique for interrupt processing systems. It is very important to verify real-time properties of such systems because many of them are safety-critical. This paper gives a method to check that critical interrupts can be handled within their timeout periods. Interrupt processing systems are modeled as extended timed automata. Our technique checks whether the system under check can handle critical interrupts in time using symbolic model-checking techniques. Taking an aerospace control system as an example, we show that our technique can find time-scheduling problems in interrupt processing systems.

Keywords: interrupt processing system, overtime detection, model checking.

1 Introduction

Nowadays, real-time embedded systems are widely used in safety-critical systems, such as flight control, railway signaling, health care and so on. Interrupt processing systems play important roles in such safety-critical systems.

In interrupt processing systems [1, 2], it is vital to handle interrupts within given time limits. Fully testing these systems is unrealistic because of the randomly-arrived interrupt sequence, the varying interrupt processing period, and the complexity of both hardware and software systems. For such systems, testing is expensive and low-efficient. Test can only cover a small fraction of state space of the interrupt processing systems under test. Model checking [3] has been introduced as a promising tool to analysis and verify (the models) of interrupt processing systems. It is possible to check whether the specified deadline for the interrupt-handling could be met by exhaustive exploration of the state-spaces of system models [4].

In this paper, we present a new approach to model interrupt processing systems and to detect the overtime situation of interrupt-handling by exhaustively exploring the state spaces of interrupt processing systems.

2 Preliminary

Many existing formal models can be used to model real-time interrupt processing systems, for example, timed automata [5] or hybrid automata [6]. In this paper, we extend timed automata to model such systems.

Y. Yuan, X. Wu, and Y. Lu (Eds.): ISCTCS 2012, CCIS 320, pp. 482–489, 2013.
© Springer-Verlag Berlin Heidelberg 2013

2.1 Timed Automata

Timed automata can be used to simulate time behaviors of real-time systems by adding a finite set of real-valued clocks and time guards to conventional finite-state automata.

Let $\mathcal{C}$ be a set of clock variables. A clock valuation u over $\mathcal{C}$ is a map from $\mathcal{C}$ to $\mathbb{R}$. For $\in \mathbb{R}$, $u + t$ is also a map. It maps each x in $\mathcal{C}$ to $u(x) + t$. We use $\mathcal{G}(\mathcal{C})$ to stand for time guards over $\mathcal{C}$, which is a conjunction of atomic formulas of the form $x \sim n$, where $x \in \mathcal{C}$, $\sim \in \{\leq, <, =, >, \geq\}$ and n is an integer.

A timed automaton $\mathcal{A}$ is a tuple $< L, l_0, \mathcal{C}, \Sigma, E, F >$, where L is a finite set of locations; $l_0 \in L$ is the initial location; $\mathcal{C}$ is a finite set of clocks; $\Sigma \subseteq \mathcal{G}(\mathcal{C}) \times 2^{\mathcal{C}}$ is a finite set of transitions, i.e. a transition e in Σ is a tuple $e = (g, r)$, where $g \subseteq \mathcal{G}(\mathcal{C})$ is the time guard of e and $r \subseteq \mathcal{C}$ is the set of clocks reset by e; $E \subseteq L \times \Sigma \times L$ is a finite set of edges; $F \subseteq L$ is the set of acceptance locations.

We write $l \xrightarrow{\ e\ } l'$ if $(l, e, l') \in E$. We also use $enable(l)$ to denote the transition set $\{e \mid l \xrightarrow{\ e\ } l'$ for some $l'\}$. We say e is enabled at l if $e \in enable(l)$.

A concrete state of this timed automaton is a tuple (l, u), where $l \in L$ and u is a clock valuation over $\mathcal{C}$. A timed automaton may evolve by either time-elapsing or concrete transitions.

- Time-elapsing: $(l, u) \xrightarrow{\ t\ } (l, u + t)$.

- Concrete transition: $(l, u) \xrightarrow{\ e\ } (l', u')$ where $e = (g, r)$ if following conditions hold:

  - $(l, e, l') \in E$;
  - For each time guard $x \sim n$ in g, $u(x) \sim n$;
  - For each clock $x \in r$, $u'(x) = 0$; and for each $x \in \mathcal{C} - r$, $u'(x) = u(x)$.

The basic reachability analysis calculates symbolic successors of every enabled transition at each reachable state till no more new state can be generated [7].

3   Modeling Interrupt Processing Systems

3.1 Modeling Interrupt Sources

In an interrupt processing system, there are usually two kinds of interrupt sources: regular interrupts which occur repeatedly with fixed time intervals; and contingency interrupts which occur randomly. Each interrupt source is assigned with a unique priority.

Regular interrupts are spontaneous activities which are issued every 0.5s, 1s, 2s and 4s respectively. Regular interrupts are usually used to maintain the system state. It includes routine tasks such as information backup, time-triggered communications, etc. Each regular interrupt is assigned a fixed priority in direct proportion to its frequency. So, the assigned priority of 0.5s-interrupts is higher than that of 1s-, 2s- and 4s-interrupts and so on.

Contingency interrupts are used to dealing with events that happen randomly, for example, start or shut-down of the engine, adjusting the direction of the aircraft. The occurrence frequency of the contingency interrupt is unpredictable. Generally, the priority of a contingency interrupt is higher than that of regular interrupts.

Fig. 1. The timed automata model of interrupt sources

In Figure 1, we use timed automata to model two kinds of interrupt sources. The automata modeling a regular interrupt consists of a local clock x and a self-loop state. Supposing the interval of the regular interrupt source is 2s, c_1 and c_2 are set to 0 and 2000 respectively.

3.2   Modeling the Interrupt Vector Table

The interrupt vector table in an interrupt processing system is a table of interrupt descriptors that associates an interrupt handler with an interrupt request in a machine-specific way. In our work, we simplify this concept and use a table, denoted as $InterruptVector$, to map interrupt sources to corresponding interrupt procedures. The elements in this table are sorted by interrupt priorities. Given an interrupt source with the priority p_i the mapping relation in the $InterruptVector$ points out the corresponding interrupt handler,

$$InterruptVector[p_i] = InterruptHandler_{id}.$$

3.3   Modeling Interrupt Handlers

In response to each interrupt source, we abstract the interrupt handler, denoted as $InterruptHandler$, as a list of to-do tasks with upper and lower execution time bounds. Each task in the to-do list is viewed as an atomic transaction which takes some time units to execute. Let the $InterruptHandler_i$ contains n tasks: $task_1$, $task_2, \ldots, task_n$, where $task_k$ takes t_k time units to be accomplished. There exists a time constraint as follow.

$$lowerBound(InterruptHandler_i) \leq \sum_{j=1}^{n} t_j \leq upperBound(InterruptHandler_i)$$

4 Deadline Detection

4.1 Simulating the Interrupt Processing

In our algorithm, a stack is used to model the state of interrupt processing. The stack is a snapshot of the current system context. Figure 2 shows the overall organization of the interrupt processing model.

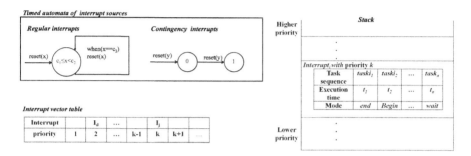

Fig. 2. The organization of our model system

A stack member keeps the information of an *InterruptHandler* and records the details of execution situation of the task sequence. Each task of the *InterruptHandler* in the stack has three modes: wait to be executed, begin to execute and finish the execution. The priority of stack member increases from bottom to top such that the *InterruptHandler* at the top of the stack has the highest priority, while the *InterruptHandler* at the bottom of the stack has the lowest priority.

4.2 Calculating Symbolic Successor of Interrupt Processing Systems

A global state of an interrupt processing system is consists of three components:

- the state (l, D) of timed automata modeling interrupt sources;
- an interrupt vector table *InterruptVector*   to record interrupt requests;
- a *stack*   contains runtime context of involved interrupt handles.

Let *topPRIvector* and *topPRIstack* be the current highest priority respectively in the *InterruptVector* and the *stack*. The set of enabled events of the global state *globalstate* = < (l, D), *InterruptVector*, *stack* > is calculated by the following algorithm enabled(globalState). The successor of *globalstate* is calculated according to different kinds of enabled events.

```
for each edge leaving e from (l,D)
    add e to globalState.enabledEvents;
if ( topPRIvector > topPRIstack)
    add topPRIvector to globalState.enabledEvents;
else if(topPRIvector <= topPRIstack)
    add stack to globalState.enabledEvents;
```

For a transition e leaving from a state (l, D) of the interrupt source model, the successor is calculated by the following algorithm successorOf-TA(globalState).

```
Let e_i be an enabled transition at (l,D)
(l',D') = sp((l,D),e_i);
if (D' ≠ EMPTYSET)
p:= the priority of the corresponding TA;
InterruptVector[p]:= InterruptHandler_i;
return <(l',D'), InterruptVector, stack>;
```

The operator sp is used to calculate the symbolic successor of a symbolic state (l, D). $sp((l, D), e)$ represents the set:

$$\{(l', u') \mid \exists (l, u) \in (l, D) \cdot ((l, u) \xrightarrow{e} (l', u'))$$

Using the data structure DBM [8] to represent the symbolic state, the operator sp can be evaluated effectively.

For the enabled event *InterruptVector*, the successor of *globalstate* is calculated by the algorithm successorOfIV(globalState). The *Interrupt-Seq* is a record of the interrupt sequence being added into or removed from the stack. We use the *InterruptSeq* to record the execution order of tasks in the stack.

```
InterruptHandler_i := InterruptVector[p];
Create a stack member stMember of InterruptHandler_i;
Push stMember into the stack;
topPRIstack := the priority of InterruptHandler_i;
Execute the first task of InterruptHandler_i;
Record information of task_1 in InterruptHandler_i to
InterruptSeq;
return <(l,D), InterruptVector, stack>;
```

For an enabled event corresponding to a task of the interrupt handler in the stack, the successor w.r.t. the interrupt handler is calculated by the following algorithm successorOfStack(globalState).

```
InterruptHandler_i:= the top member of the stack;
TASK_k := the current task in InterruptHandler_i;
if (the mode of TASK_k is wait)
{   change the mode of TASK_k to begin;
    record new TASK_k to InterruptSeq;
} else if (the mode of TASK_k is begin)
{   Change the mode of TASK_k to end;
    Record new TASK_k to   InterruptSeq;
    if (TASK_k is not the last task in
            InterruptHandler_i)
    { Set the current task be the one next to TASK_k;
```

```
        Set the mode of the current task to wait;
      } else
      { Remove InterruptHandler_i from the stack; }
    }
    return <(l,D), InterruptVector, stack>;
```

4.3   The Model Checking Algorithm

The model-checking algorithm exhaustively explores the state space of the interrupt processing system, using the depth first search method. Initially, the *InterruptVector* and *stack* are empty, the initial global state is $globalstate_0 = <$ $(l_0, D_0), InterruptVector, stack >$. This method guarantees that all permutation of occurrence sequences of interrupt sources are considered.

```
Unexplored :={globalState0}
while (Unexplored ≠ NULL) do
{   select a  global state curState from Unexplored;
    remove curState from Unexplored;
    for each event e in enabled(curState)
    { if (e is an edge leaving from curState)
        add successorOfTA(curState) to Unexplored;
      else if (event is InterruptVector)
        add successorOfIV(curState) to Unexplored;
      else if (event is stack)
        add successorOfStack(curState) to Unexplored;
    }
}
```

We only record generated symbolic states into the reachability graph when the stack is idle. When removing *InterruptHandler* from the *stack* by the algorithm `successorOfStack(globalState)`, we retrieve the execution order of tasks occurred in the *stack* from *InterruptSeq*, and check whether every interrupt has been processed within its timeout period using the linear programming technique. If so, we determine the containment relation and record the symbolic state into the reachability graph if necessary. Otherwise, a counter example of overtime schedule can be retrieved from *InterruptSeq*. The following algorithm clarifies this method.

```
Let GRAPH be the generated reachability graph;
Let the current global state be
 <(l,D), InterruptVector, stack> with InterruptSeq;
if(stack is empty)
{ Retrieve a task execution sequence from InterruptSeq;
  for each InterruptHandler_i occurs in InterruptSeq
  {   executionTime:=sumOf(taskExecutionTime);
      if(lowerBound(InterruptHandler_i)≤executionTime
          ≤higherBound(InterruptHandler_i))
```

```
{    if (there exist a node (l,D') in GRAPH such
            that (l,D)⊆(l,D'))
        { add InterruptSeq to (l,D') in GRAPH;}
        else
        { add (l,D) with InterruptSeq  to GRAPH;}
    }else
        report InterruptSeq as a counter example;
}
}
```

However, the state-space may be infinite. We solve this problem based on the following observation. An interrupt processing system contains several regular interrupt sources with different frequencies. It implies that there exists a periodical interrupt sequence of these regular interrupts. As the priorities of regular interrupts are lower than that of contingency interrupts, to guarantee that these regular interrupts are handled in time, all the interrupts in the *stack* must be finished within some time period. This period is proportional to the maximal interval of the regular interrupts. If the stack keeps busy for a time period longer than this period, we can already conclude that the system under-check is unable to handle all interrupts within time limits. When the stack becomes idle, the symbolic system state is just a state for timed automata. There are finite number of such states if an appropriate equivalence relation is applied. We add an auxiliary timer to check whether the stack is always busy. The termination of our algorithm is guaranteed.

5   Examples

Here, we present a simplified example taken from an aerospace control system. It has two regular interrupt sources: the 2s-interrupt for the satellite-ground communication and the 0.5s-interrupt for the system information backup. It also has two contingency interrupt sources: the navigation interrupt and the mode-switch interrupt with the highest priority. The corresponding timed automata model of these interrupt sources is shown in Figure 3.

Fig. 3. The timed automata model

Each interrupt contains several to-do tasks. The maximum execution-time of these interrupt-handlers are $500ms$, $250ms$, $100ms$, and $100ms$ respectively. The system requires that each regular interrupt must be handled within 80 percent of its time period. Our algorithm checks this model by exploring the state-space exhaustively. The algorithm finds that when an execution of the regular interrupt handler is nested by two contingency interrupts continuously, it cannot be finished before the time deadline.

We also checked that if the execution time upper-bound of the second interrupt handler is $200ms$, all interrupts could be accomplished within its time limits.

6   Conclusion

In this paper, we present a technique to model and check interrupt processing systems using extended timed automata. The state space of the model system can be explored exhaustively to check whether the schedule of interrupt processing can meet the time requirements. A simplified real example is used to demonstrate how our method works.

Acknowledgment. This work is supported by the National Natural Science Foundation of China (No.91118002).

References

1. Silberschatz, A., Galvin, P.B.: Operating System Concepts (1998)
2. Walker, W., Cragon, H.G.: Interrupt Processing in Concurrent Processors. IEEE Computer 28(6), 36–46 (1995)
3. Clarke, E., Grumberg, O., Peled, D.: Model Checking. MIT Press, Cambridge (2000)
4. Brylow, D., Palsberg, J.: Deadline Analysis of Interrupt-driven Software (2003)
5. Alur, R., Dill, D.: A Theroy of Timed Automata. Theoretical Computer Science 126, 183–235 (1994)
6. Henzinger, T.A.: The Theory of Hybrid Automata. LICS, 278–292 (1996)
7. Zhao, J., Li, X., Zheng, T., Zheng, G.: Removing Irrelevant Atomic Formulas for Checking Timed Automata Efficiently. In: Larsen, K.G., Niebert, P. (eds.) FORMATS 2003. LNCS, vol. 2791, pp. 34–45. Springer, Heidelberg (2004)
8. Dill, D.L.: Timing Assumptions and Verification of Finite-state Concurrent Systems. In: Sifakis, J. (ed.) CAV 1989. LNCS, vol. 407, pp. 197–212. Springer, Heidelberg (1990)

MDE-Based Verification of SysML State Machine Diagram by UPPAAL

Xiaopu Huang, Qingqing Sun, Jiangwei Li, and Tian Zhang

State Key Lab. for Novel Software Technology, Nanjing University, Nanjing, China
Department of Computer Science and Technology, Nanjing University, Nanjing, China
{hxp,sunqq,ljw}@seg.nju.edu.cn, ztluck@nju.edu.cn

Abstract. State Machine Diagram (SMD) is one of the SysML behavior diagrams, but it is a kind of semi-formal model language. As a consequence, models can not be verified conveniently and efficiently, especially in real-time embedded system (RTES) field as there are no descriptions of time and probability in SMD. To address these problems, we extend SMD with time and probability elements extracted from MARTE and propose a transformation algorithm based on MDE. With the algorithm, we transform the extended SMD to timed automata (TA) and then analyze and verify the transformation result using existing tools. So at the very beginning of system design, errors and deficiencies can be found. At last, we construct an instance to illustrate the validity of our approach.

Keywords: SysML SMD, MDE, timed automata, MARTE, model transformation.

1 Introduction

Nowadays real-time embedded systems (RTES) are widely used in the fields of manufacturing industries, communications, automotive, aerospace and so on. Real-time embedded system is a computer system which can perform a calculation or transaction and respond to external events in a determined period of time.

The development of real-time embedded system is usually very complex. So building an appropriate model abstraction early in the development of the entire system will control the system complexity.

SysML (Systems Modeling Language) [1] is an object-oriented standard system modeling language and SysML state machine diagram is very convenient for describing states and behaviors in system. But SMD is lack of standardized description of time in real-time system. However, OMG proposed UML MARTE (Modeling and Analysis of Real-Time and Embedded Systems) [2] specifically for the modeling of real-time embedded systems in 2007. We make it more convenient for modeling by extending SMD with time and probability elements in MARTE, which enables SMD both the standardization of time and the characteristics of probability when modeling real-time systems.

Y. Yuan, X. Wu, and Y. Lu (Eds.): ISCTCS 2012, CCIS 320, pp. 490–497, 2013.

For real-time systems, correctness and security of the system is of vital importance. However, SysML SMD is a kind of semi-formal model and existing tools don't support analyzation and verification of design models. To solve this problem, we first transform the existing semi-formal design models to formal models taking advantage of MDE (Model Driven Engineering), and then use existing model checker to check the corresponding properties. In this way, the original design models are indirectly verified.

The transformation between models has been the focus of both academia and industry. Traditional solutions are mostly ad-hoc style. But it gradually exposed a lot of problems in this way. For example, the mixing of semantic matching and syntax mapping, difficulties in reusing existing models.

MDE is an emerging software development mode in the field of software engineering and the primary software products are models. It can give a better solution to solve these problems.

The contributions of this paper can be summarized as follows.

— We extend SysML SMD with time and probability elements in MARTE and standardize the usage of time and probability in SMD.
— We construct the transformation rules from SMD to TA and implement the whole process based on MDE which is a real-time system model transformation method based on meta-modeling.
— We are indirectly able to simulate the operations and verify the propertiesof the semi-formal design models.

2   Related Work

Most of the traditional transformations are ad-hoc style, for example, SMV to PVS transformation and Automata to Petri Net transformation as mentioned in literature [16], as well as in literature [17]. Many verification experience, for example [12], have been conducted on the model checker Uppaal and they are proved to be effective. MDE-based modeling and model transformation is a new field in the development of software engineering, and some work have already been done [7]. In [7], the author builds two meta models of MARTE and FIACRE, and gives the mapping rules between these two meta models. MARTE is a new UML Profile and it is released as the new UML formal specification in real-time and embedded system modeling. Some work have been done using MARTE in RTES [15]. Literature [8] [9] transform petri-net to TA.

We re-examine the model transformation from MDE perspective on the basis of problems of traditional work and conduct a case study of transformation from semi-formal SMD models to formal TA models in the thoughts of MDE. Through the case study, we think our method is effective in separation of syntax and semantic transformation.

3   Background

3.1   SysML SMD

SysML is an object-oriented standard system modeling language. SMD is one of the SysML behavior diagrams and it is very convenient and clear for describing state transition and dynamic behavior changes in system. But SMD is a kind of semi-formal model and lack of standardized description of time in real-time system.

3.2   MARTE

MARTE (Modeling and Analysis of Real-Time and Embedded Systems) is released as a new UML Profile by OMG at the end of 2007 to replace SPT (UML Pro-file for Schedulability, Performance and Time) as the new UML formal specification in real-time and embedded system modeling.

There is a complete set of definitions about models of time in MARTE. Time structure consists of *TimeBases*, *MultipleTimeBases*, *Instants* and so on. While time access mainly consists of *Clocks*.

3.3   Timed Automata and Uppaal

A timed automaton is a standard finite state automaton extended with a finite collection of real-valued clocks. The vertices of the automaton are called locations, and the edges are called switches. While switches are instaneous, time can elapse in a location. More details in [4].

Uppaal is an integrated tool environment for modeling, validation and verification of real-time systems modeled as networks of timed automata, extended with data types (bounded integers, arrays, etc.). It is based on the theory of timed automata.

4   Verification of SysML State Machine Diagram

In this section, we will show an MDE-based transformation approach from SysML SMD to TA based on our algorithm. Then, we can verify the properties in Uppaal.

4.1   MDE-Based Modeling and Model Transformation.

The process of MDE-based software development is actually the process building the model and transforming the model. Model Transformation is one of the most important parts in MDE. ATL [3] [13] is a model transformation language and toolkit. ATL provides ways to produce a set of target models from a set of source models and is inspired by the OMG QVT requirements [5] and builds upon the OCL formalism [6].

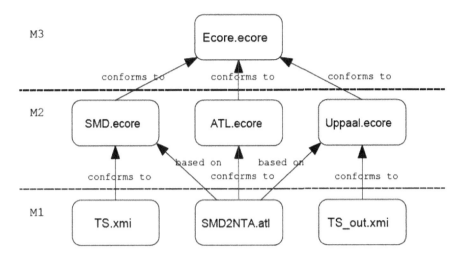

Fig. 1. An overview of ATL model transformation process

Figure 1 summarizes our full model transformation process. A SysML SMD model TS.xmi, conforming to its meta-model SMD.ecore, is here transformed into a Uppaal model TS out.xmi that conforms to its meta-model Uppaal.ecore. The transformation is defined by SMD2NTA.atl which itself conforms to its meta-model ATL.ecore. ATL.ecore meta-model, along with SMD.ecore and Uppaal.ecore meta-models, has to conform to a meta-meta-model Ecore.ecore.

4.2   Meta-model

Based on the MDE-based Model transformation process, we need to construct the SMD meta-model and TA meta-model to achieve the transformation and then we also need to construct the elements and semantic mapping rules implementing by ATL between two meta-models.

Figure 2 is the simplified SMD meta-model and we have extended the SMD with time and probability. The property on in Region is the clock this region depends on and the clock itself is constructed in MARTE. The properties lb and up in Invariant are the minimum and maximum time the system can stay in this state. Exponentialrate, isBranchPoint and prob are probability related elements.

4.3   Mapping from SMD to TA

After the building of two meta-models, we construct, between two meta-models, a series of mapping rules. Table 1 shows the main mapping rules from SMD to TA and we have implemented these rules in ATL.

5   Case Study

In this section, we will give an example to illustrate the effectiveness of our approach.

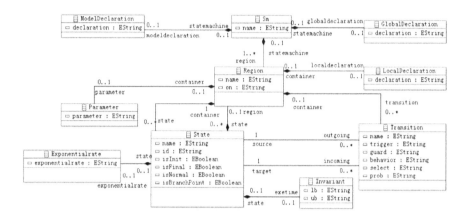

Fig. 2. Simplified SMD meta-model extended with time and probability in MARTE

Table 1. Main mapping rules from SMD to TA

Elements in SMD	Elements in TA
SMD	NTA
region	TA
state	location, branchpoint
init	location.initial
end	location
transition	transition
trigger	transition.label.kind.synchronization
guard	transition.label.kind.guard
behavior	transition.label.kind.assignment
prob	transition.label.kind.probability, transition.label.kind.exponentialrate
invariant	location.label.kind.invariant, location.urgent, location.commted
region.on	clock

The actual system we will model is called Railway-Control System (RCS). It is a railway control system which controls access to a bridge for several trains. The bridge is a critical shared resource that may be accessed only by one train at the same time. The system is defined as a number of trains (assume 2 for this example) and a controller. A train can not stop instantly and restarting also takes time. Therefore,

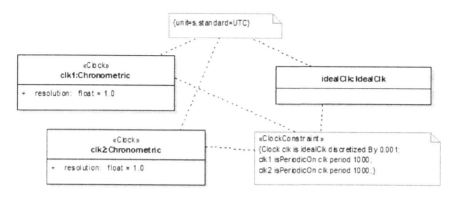

Fig. 3. Two clock instances in RCS

there are timing constraints on the trains before entering the bridge. When approaching, a train sends an *appr* signal. Thereafter, it has 10 time units to receive a *stop* signal. This allows it to stop safely before the bridge. After these 10 time units, it takes further 10 time units to reach the bridge if the train didn't stop. If a train stops, it resumes its course when the controller sends a *go* signal to it after a previous train has left the bridge and sent a *leave* signal.

Because there is time constraints in the system, we first need to model the time and define a discrete clock type named *Chronometric*. As RCS needs clocks to count the time, we build two instances of *Chronometric*: *clk1* and *clk2* (Frigure 3). *idealClock* is an instance of *IdealClock* which is pre-defined in the library of MARTE. *idealClock* represents the real physical clock and it is continuous.*clk1* is achieved by time constrain language on *idealClock*. First, we get *clk* by 0.001-discretization on *idealClock*. Then, we get *clk1* by sampling once every 1000 cycles of *clk*.

Then, we construct the SMD model of the system and add time constraints in MARTE on the model states and transitions. The left part of Figure 4 is the train model of RCS modeling in SysML SMD with MARTE.

Then we transform the RCS model to the corresponding TA by ATL (right part in Figure 4). Taking the results of transformation as input of UPPAAL, we can simulate and verify the RCS model indirectly.

The main verification is whether the model is satisfied with liveness and safety properties. UPPAAL uses simplified CTL to express the properties of system.

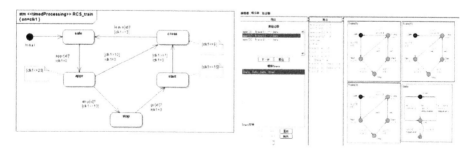

Fig. 4. Train models of RCS

— Liveness:

E<> Train(1).Cross

Description: Train 1 can cross the bridge.

Verification result: property satisfies.

Train(1).Stop→Train(1).Start

Description: The train can restart sometime after stopping.

Verification result: property satisfies.

— Safety:

A[] not deadlock

Description: check whether there's deadlock existing in the system.

Verification result: property satisfies.

A[] Train(0).Cross imply Train(0).clk1≤5

Description: Train 0 should cross the bridge in 5 time units.

Verification result: property satisfies.

6   Conclusion

In this paper, we briefly introduce MARTE and extend the SysML SMD with time and probability elements in MARTE. After extension, SysML SMD is more capable of describing of time and probability in a system.

Moreover, we give an MDE-based model transformation method to solve, to some degree, the problems and deficiencies exist in traditional solutions. Based on MDE thoughts, we propose a set of transformation rules. With these rules, we transform extended SMD to TA and then verify the transformation result using existing tools. So at the very beginning of system design, errors and deficiencies can be found in the design models making a better and faster system development.

Now we are thinking about the solution to concurrency if existing in SMD and come up with an idea. In the next, we intend to implement this idea, also deal with nested state. Meanwhile, we also consider the formalization of other SysML behavior diagrams.

Acknowledgments. This work is supported by the National Natural Science Foundation of China (No.61003025, 91118002), and by the Jiangsu Province Research Foundation(BK2010170).

References

1. OMG: Systems Modeling Language. Formal/2010-06-01 (2010),
   http://www.omg.org/spec/SysML/1.2
2. OMG: UML Profile for MARTE: Modeling and Analysis of Real-Time Embedded systems. Formal/2011-06-02 (2011), http://www.omg.org/spec/MARTE/1.1

3. ATLAS Team. ATLAS Transformation Language (ATL) Home Page,
   http://www.eclipse.org/gmt/atl/
4. Alur, R., Dill, D.L.: A Theory of Timed Automata. Theoretical Computer Science 126(2),
   183–236 (1994)
5. OMG/RFP/QVT MOF 2.0 query/views/transformations RFP. Formal/2011-01-01 (2011),
   http://www.omg.org/spec/QVT/1.1
6. OMG: Object Constraint Language. Formal/2006-05-01 (2006),
   http://www.omg.org/spec/OCL/2.0
7. Zhang, T., Jouault, F., Attiogb, C., Li, X.D.: MDE-based mode transformation: from
   MARTE model to FIACRE model. Journal of Software 20(2), 214–233 (2009)
8. Gu, Z.H., Shin, K.G.: An Integrated Approach to Modeling and Analysis of Embedded
   Real-Time Systems Based on Timed Petri Nets. In: Proceedings of Distributed Computing
   Systems, pp. 350–359 (2003)
9. Cortés, L.A., Eles, P., Peng, Z.B.: Verification of embedded systems using a petri net
   based representation. In: Proceedings of the 13th International Symposium on System
   Synthesis, ISSS (2000)
10. Behrmann, G., David, A., Larsen, K.G.: A Tutorial on UPPAAL. In: Bernardo, M.,
    Corradini, F. (eds.) SFM-RT 2004. LNCS, vol. 3185, pp. 200–236. Springer, Heidelberg
    (2004)
11. Bengtsson, J.E., Yi, W.: Timed Automata: Semantics, Algorithms and Tools. In: Desel, J.,
    Reisig, W., Rozenberg, G. (eds.) ACPN 2003. LNCS, vol. 3098, pp. 87–124. Springer,
    Heidelberg (2004)
12. Havelund, K., Skou, A., Larsen, K.G., Lund, K.: Formal Modelling and Analysis of an
    Audio/Video Protocol: An Industrial Case Study Using Uppaal. In: Proceedings of the
    18th IEEE Real-Time Systems Symposium, pp. 2–13 (1997)
13. ATLAS group LINA and INRIA.: ATL: Atlas Transformation Language (2006)
14. Budinsky, F., Steinberg, D., Merks, E., Ellersick, R., Timothy, J.: Eclipse Modeling
    Framework: A Developer's Guide, p. 704. Addison-Wesley Professional (2003)
15. Tan, H.B., Yao, S.Z., Li, W.Y.: Modeling Time-Triggered Mechanisms using MARTE. In:
    Information Science and Engineering (ICISE), pp. 4590–4593 (2010)
16. Katz, S., Grumberg, O.: A Framework for Translating Models and Specifications. In:
    Butler, M., Petre, L., Sere, K. (eds.) IFM 2002. LNCS, vol. 2335, pp. 145–164. Springer,
    Heidelberg (2002)
17. Cui, K.L., Yang, Z.Y., Xie, J.K., Wan, K.Y.: Unifying Modeling and Simulation Based on
    UML Timing Diagram and UPPAAL. In: Proceedings of ICCMS (2010)

CppIns: A Source Query Language for Instrumentation

Ying He, Yongjing Tao, and Tian Zhang

State Key Laboratory for Novel Software Technology, Nanjing University, Nanjing, China
Department of Computer Science and Technology, Nanjing University, Nanjing, China
{hy,tyj}@seg.nju.edu.cn, ztluck@nju.edu.cn

Abstract. Source instrumentation is one of the most common tasks used in software testing and dynamic program analysis. However, instrumentation fragments containing contextual information are scattered in source code and hard to be maintained. To generate and manager instrumentation codes, we divide the source instrumentation task into two parts, searching the instrumentation points where code fragments should be planted and generating the code fragments according to the contextual variables. Following such idea, we present a query-based method locating points where codes to be planted and collecting contextual information so that generated codes could contain variables around the points. The CppIns language provided by our method is aimed to specify instrumentation rules for C++ source, which is constructed following a SQL-like style and easily understood. We evaluate the method in terms of the reduced complexity of query specifications with several common instrumentation tasks.

Keywords: instrumentation, query, predicate logic, context-sensitive grammar.

1 Introduction

Most of the dynamic program analysis requires some preparation work, which usually is to insert the necessary code fragment into the analyzed program, and this code fragment is called instrumentation. The instrumentation can be done in two ways, either by modifying the binary code or by modifying the source code.

(1)The binary code instrumentation requires programmers to understand the underlying implementation details, such as focusing on the offset of methods and data in binary code, and their relocating offsets after the instrumentation. And this way is mostly used in practice, especially in memory monitoring software, as the binary code format is only related to the operating system instead of a specific programming language. However, due to the lack of information of syntax, semantic, and high requirements of code lexical syntax analysis, some testing tools based on path coverage use source code instrumentation.

(2) The source code instrumentation is usually based on the complete lexical and syntax analysis of the source file, which guarantees the high accuracy and relevance of source code instrumentation. However, it may result in more work because of the need to reach to the source code, and the modifications of the coding language and version.

Y. Yuan, X. Wu, and Y. Lu (Eds.): ISCTCS 2012, CCIS 320, pp. 498–505, 2013.

By source code instrumentation additional code fragments are directly inserted into the program's source code. With the diversity and complexity of the information in the running application, it is hard to guarantee the correctness and effectiveness of the program by manually direct code fragment instrumentation into the source code. If the user can describe formally instrumentation demand, automatic batch instrumentation method can solve the above difficulty. With our study, existing methods of source code instrumentation are usually based on some simple rules, and these rules are not flexible to describe all of the requirements and cannot supply the instrumented statements which are tailored depending on the program context.

In order to solve such restrictions, a query-based source code instrumentation is offered and a language called CppIns is defined to allow users to describe the content and location of the insert statement flexibly and accurately. This language is similar to simplified SQL statement. And the preferred steps will be carried out code query process, when the query process is completed, instrumentation statement will be constructed with the specific context information obtained in the query process and user-defined template, then the statement will be inserted into location which has been queried. Based on this approach this paper supply a prototype, and it is developed based on eclipse plug-in for the C++ language.

The main contributions of this paper are as follows:

— **Instrumentation language is definition and expansion.** This article defines the instrumentation language which describes complex query rules by predicate logic expressions, and makes it more appropriate for C++ language query.
— **Instrumentation is fine-grained and context-sensitive.** This instrumentation language allows users to define statement template with parameters, the template parameter value will be replaced by some matching results after the query process, the same with the place the instrumentation to be located. This strategy ensures that the flexibility and fine-grained (statement level or expression level) instrumentation location while the query results are used to construct context-sensitive instrumented statement.

The rest of this paper is organized as follows: Sections 2 respectively introduces the features of the query and the instrumentation parts of the CppIns language. Section 3 details the implementation of the CppIns language and Section 4 introduces the case study. We evaluate the CppIns and compare it with related work in Section 5, and finally Section 6 draws conclusions and plans the future work.

2   The CppIns Approach

Usually Instrumentation process can be divided in two steps:

(1) Locating the point the instrumented statement to be inserted;
(2) Constructing the instrumented statement by the context and some template.

Code query is a means of locating the point of the instrumented statement.

2.1   Code Query

Code query technology takes an important position in software design. And there exist more and more code query tools designed to help programmers understand large number of frequently changing and complex relationship in programs. At present, the code query technique has been widely used and plays an important role in software analysis and testing work. And in areas such as software architecture, reverse engineering, consistency verification and code review, it is also widely used. On the other hand, code query has been extended to the system framework error detection, reconstruction recognition, project defects locating, crosscutting checking, development process monitoring, design evaluating, redundant conditions tracking and so on.

In order to describe the user's query needs accurately, we designed a query language. It requires the users to specify the type of program elements they want to query such as a *variable*, a *statement*, a *function*, a *class*, an *expression*, or an *operator*, and the query conditions the target element should satisfy. In order to construct query conditions it may also need to introduce other program elements to help describe the target element to be queried. The query conditions CppIns supports may include two categories: property conditions and relations conditions, and through logical conjunction (&&, | |, !) and quantifiers (*exist*, *all*) several conditions can be combined together. Next, we will describe the query language syntax in detail, as well as the definition of attributes and the relationship between elements.

The query command *S* entered by the user should follow the syntax rules as follows:

```
S => find Id: T satisfying CS
T => variable| statement| function| class| expression|
operator
CS => {exist Id: T} {all Id: T} where CE
CE =>CE && CE
    | CE || CE
    | ! CE
    | ( CE )
    | Id.Att = 'value'
    | Id Rel Id
Att => vName| vDataType| vAttr| sType| fName| fReturnType
     | fParamsType| fAttr| cName| eContext| eType| oType
Rel => extend | use | change | in | call
```

As defined above, the attribute information *Att* need to be specific explained. Among it, *vName* and *vDataType* means the name and type of *variable*; *vAttr* represents the declaring type of a *variable*, such as *'field'*, *'global'*, *'parameter'*, *'static'*; *sType* means the type of *statement*, such as *'single'*, *'for'*, *'while'*; *eType* is the operator of an *expression*, such as '++', '-', '='.

2.2   Instrumentation

As what has been mentioned above which provides a method to locate the position of instrumentation, we expand the definition of the code query language. The extended query language can locate the instrumentation location and construct instrumentation statement by the information we obtained from code query.

With the results obtained in the query process is a set of program elements which meet what the user has described, a corresponding set would be created for each program elements defined in the predicate. And the reason why we expand the language is that we can use information obtained in the code query to help us complete the implement of instrumentation.

Based on the grammar rules defined above, we offer a new extended grammar for instrumentation:

```
S => find Id: T satisfying CS IS
IS => insert before Id IN IS
    | insert after Id IN IS
    | NULL
IN =>'STR'
STR => String STR
     | %Id.Att%STR
     | String
     | %Id.Att%
```

One of the advantages of this extended syntax is that we provide a consistent user interface with code query so that users do not need to learn extra knowledge. From a technical point, the user can use the information by code query to construct instrumentation statement directly. And in this way it would help us not only to avoid the possibility of invalid code instrumentation, but also to generate corresponding and distinguish instrumented code in different instrumentation places.

3   Implementation

Now we come up with a prototype tool called CppIns for C++ language. And this tool is accomplished based on eclipse extension mechanism. It works on the eclipse CDT[1] framework to help us analyze the C++ source file.

Our prototype tool is mainly divided into four parts: the information collection of source code, code query, instrumented code customization and instrumentation.

3.1   Code Information Collection

The collection of code information is based on the abstract syntax trees (AST) provided by CDT. In this step, we need to collect all the information of elements such as *variable*, *statement*, *function*, *class*, *expression* and *operator* from the AST of the source code. The information mentioned here includes both attribute and relationship information of program elements. In addition, the tool also records the location information of each element in the source file, in order to facilitate positioning of elements in the result collection.

To this end, we designed an element collector *EC* used to collect all the information we need in the source code. Specific process for program elements information gathering is just as follows: Firstly, the tool generates AST for all of the source files. Then while AST is scanned, if the current node corresponds to the program elements we are concerned about, the tool will create an appropriate data structure to save the information.

3.2   Code Query

In this section we will describe the process of code element retrieval: First, the tool reads the query command *S*, and validate it to see whether it satisfies the proposed grammar rules; then parsing will be done to get the information of the command, and the query conditions will be converted into a binary tree, where attribute and relation conditional expression are regarded as the atomic node. While the tool goes through all the information collected by *EC*, this binary tree will be recursively computed. And if all of the query conditions are matched, this group of elements would be added to the result set.

3.3   Instrumented Code Customization

When the step of code query is completed, we could generate the corresponding instrumented statement with the custom template. Through the running of the algorithm above, we will get the final result set *RS* which includes all the program elements satisfying all the conditions, we customize instrumented statement by replacing the symbol with value get from code query. The replaced string is what we need to insert into the source code.

3.4   Instrumentation

Then we use the marker mechanism of the eclipse to add the appropriate tag in the source file, which specifies the location of the instrumentation. So the user can determine whether the inserted content is expected firstly. And if it meets the requirements, instrumentation would be done. It is repeated until all the instrumentation is done.

4   Case Study

A prototype tool is developed according to the above method, and it provides two basic functions: query and instrumentation. The entire tool is appeared in the form of eclipse plugin.

Now, if we want to find all the statements which call the function *add* and print the function's name after the statements, we can act as the following steps:

Firstly, enter the next command in the dialog box:

```
find s :statement satisfying f : function
where f.vName =' add' && s call f
insert after s 'cout << "have execute function
%f.vName%";'
```

Then click the button ok, the program will show all the positions for instrumentation to the user by the eclipse viewer. And while the viewer displays the corresponding location information, the tool also adds markers to the source file and gives the content to be instrumented. At last, source code instrumentation could be executed, when the information is checked to be correct by users. Figure 1 shows this process.

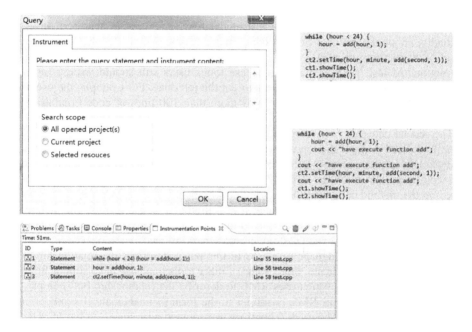

Fig. 1. Process of Instrumentation

Nowdays, there exist many instrumentation tools, but little for source code instrumentation in C++ language. CPPX/FETCH[8] is one of the few methods for C++ source code instrumentation, but it's mainly used for reverse engineering, and uses an chain of number of other tools, which may require users to spend much time learning these tools and API.

The main advantage of this tool CppIns we proposed is to help describe the instrumentation needs by very simple syntax, and automatically generate the instrumented points, which may make it easier to do source code instrumentation automatically.

5   Related Work

At present, there are many tools for users to do instrumentation. But most of them can be attributed to two categories. One is based on the underlying target code, and the other is based on the specific points of the program.

The former way is supported by a lot of tools, such as Valgrind[7], Pin[4], and BCEL[3]. Their common features are to operate on underlying instruction level. By this way, it has some advantages that the other does not have. For example, because of instruction level instrumentation, it can reduce the effects of time and space. However, due to operate on instruction, there exist inevitable defects. First of all, we cannot identify whether a *loop* instruction is corresponding to a *while* statement, *for* statement, or *do-while* statement; at the same time, the instruction *GOTO* also cannot be determined that it is translated by the statement of *continue* or *break*. Such defects result in that users are unable to do instrumentation accurately at statement level. Secondly, although a number of tools have shielded some operate details, such as the offset of instructions, users still need to master some specific details of the underlying instruction. At last, instrumentation by these tools, users still should write a lot of code to locate the instrumentation points to get the job done. For example, the use of BCEL to rewrite the field of a class needs more than 100 lines of code in addition, and use of Valgrind may need much more code.

The second category is instrumentation by using some specific points which have been predefined. One of the representations of such tools is AspectJ[2]. AspectJ is a heavyweight implementation of AOP[6]. If we use it for instrumentation, program crosscutting points should be defined firstly. And the crosscutting in AspectJ is focused on the method call, variable read/write, if branch. It is convenient to help users use custom behaviors, on the other hand, it also limits the scope for instrumentation. Although methods of this kind have solved the defects mentioned in the above paragraph, in the process of instrumentation, programmers still need additional code.

The instrumentation language proposed in this paper describes the relationship of program elements by predicate logic, Some of other tools may also have similar function, such as CrocoPat[5] which uses RML to describe the relationship between program elements. However as RML is similar to the form of mathematical symbols, it also becomes a burden to the users. Therefore, we adopted a language similar to SQL, called CppIns.

At present, almost all of the instrumentation tools are aimed at providing more powerful, more flexible and more efficient API, but dealing with how to describe the instrumentation location and how to customize the instrumented content becomes the work of users, which leads that even a very simple instrumentation also requires the user to look over dozens of pages of technical documentation. Our work is aimed to provide users the most simple, flexible and efficient interface and command.

6   Conclusions and Future Work

In this paper, we have supplied a new method for source code instrumentation, which can find the location of instrumentation by code query based on first order predicate logic and make flexible instrumentation customization using the query results.

Our future work will be commenced in the following areas: We will optimize the search algorithms, to obtain higher efficiency. And this instrumentation language can be expanded to provide more descriptive ability. What's more, we can also consider customizing a series of templates for the users of this tool.

Acknowledgment. This work is supported by the National Natural Science Foundation of China (No.61003025, 91118002), and by the Jiangsu Province Research Foundation (BK2010170).

References

1. CDT project website, http://www.eclipse.org/cdt/
2. AspectJ project website, http://eclipse.org/aspectj/
3. BCEL(Byte-Code Engineering Library) website, http://jakarta.apache.org/bcel/
4. Luk, C.-K., Cohn, R., Muth, R., Patil, H., Klauser, A., Lowney, G., Wallace, S., Reddi, V.J., Hazelwood, K.: Pin: Building Customized Program Analysis Tools with Dynamic Instrumentation. In: Proceedings of the 2007 ACM SIGPLAN Conference on Programming Language Design and Implementation (PLDI 2005), pp. 190–200 (2005)
5. Beyer, D., Lewerentz, C.: CrocoPat: Efficient Pattern Analysis in Object-Oriented Programs. In: Proceedings of the 11 th IEEE International Workshop on Program Comprehension (IWPC 2003), pp. 807–810. ACM, New York (2003)
6. Kiczales, G., Lamping, J., Mendhekar, A., Maeda, C., Lopes, C., Loingtier, J.-M., Irwin, J.: Aspect-oriented Programming. In: Aksit, M., Auletta, V. (eds.) ECOOP 1997. LNCS, vol. 1241, pp. 220–242. Springer, Heidelberg (1997)
7. Nethecote, N., Seward, U.: Valgrind: A Framework for Heavyweight Dynamic Binary Instrumentation. In: Proceedings of the 2007 ACM SIGPLAN Conference on Programming Language Design and Implementation (PLDI 2007), pp. 89–100 (2007)
8. Du Bois, B., Van Rompaey, B., Meijfroidt, K., Suijs, E.: Supporting reengineering scenarios with FETCH: an experience report. In: Proc. of the 3rd International ERCIM Workshop on Software Evolution, ICSM, Paris, France, pp. 69–82 (October 2007)

An UML Model Query Method Based on Structure Pattern Matching

Xuelin Zhang, Huajie Chen, and Tian Zhang

State Key Laboratory for Novel Software Technology, Nanjing University, Nanjing, China
Department of Computer Science and Technology, Nanjing University, Nanjing, China
{zhangxl,chenhj}@seg.nju.edu.cn, ztluck@nju.edu.cn

Abstract. UML has been widely used for modeling, and models are becoming increasingly important in the software development process. As a consequence, the number of models being used is increasing. Comprehending and reusing models face a real challenge. So, it is necessary to get efficient methods to query models. In this paper, we propose an UML model query method which is based on structure pattern matching. This paper will show how to extract the structure information of UML model from the textual model file. Then, a model query language and the matching algorithm will be detailed described. After that a case study is presented, which proves the effectiveness of our query method.

Keywords: model query, structure pattern matching, query language.

1 Introduction

UML is the OMG's standard for object oriented modeling and has quickly become the de facto standard for specifying OO systems[1]. UML has been widely used for modeling at different phases of a system. With model-driven development (MDD) gaining importance, an increasingly large number of models are being produced and used by software organizations. The model repository becomes so large that it is too difficult to be comprehended. Moreover, the reuse problem is extended to models in addition to code and other artifacts[2], because of that the difficulties in finding reusable models are greater. So, it is necessary to get efficient methods to query models in large repositories. Querying models can not only help to comprehend and reuse models of the system but also have an important educational benefit for students and teachers, allowing learners to find good or bad examples that can then be used to improve the acquisition of knowledge and provide hints at solutions[2].

UML sustains many aspects of software engineering. However, it does not provide an explicit facility for writing queries[1][10]. The Object Constraint Language (OCL) is a precise text language that provides constraints and object query expressions on UML model that cannot otherwise be expressed by diagrammatic notation[9]. Since the specification of the OCL mentions "query language" as one of its possible applications, lots of researchers try to form a query language based on OCL and

Y. Yuan, X. Wu, and Y. Lu (Eds.): ISCTCS 2012, CCIS 320, pp. 506–513, 2013.

extensions to it[3][4][5][6][7]. Querying models with OCL query language, which will generate very complex query statements[5] and with poor efficiency, is not a good choice. The developers must be skilled in OCL programming before they can query models with OCL language. What's more, OCL was originally designed specifically for expressing constraints about a UML model, it is not a specialized language for querying[7][9]. Hence, the query expressions formed with OCL even don't have the same expression power as those formed with relational algebra[1].

The OMG defines a standard document type definition (DTD)[11] for the UML model file. So, the UML model can be described in a XMI type document, which follows the DTD standard. In this way, many tools of the UML can exchange data easily with the common DTD standard. Because of this, we can get the model information from the exported XMI model file. Then, some query work can be done with the model information without OCL. In this paper, we proposed a method of UML model query, which is based on structure pattern matching. A target model pattern and the system UML model are needed before querying. Then, after parsing the target model, it will be matched with the system UML model using a specialized algorithm. In addition, the target model pattern is described with a query language in a textual file, which is defined by us. The framework of model query is showed as figure 1.

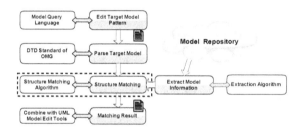

Fig. 1. Framework of Model Query

The rest of this paper is organized as follows: Section 2 discusses the method of extracting the structure information of UML model. In section 3 a model query language will be described. Section 4 discusses the algorithm of model query and its implementation. Section 5 shows a case study of our model query. Section 6 concludes the paper and presents our plans for future work.

2   Extraction of Model Information

The system UML model is described in a XMI type document. However, if you attempt to read the model file line by line, you will find that it isn't practical to comprehend the whole structure of the system model because of its complex document structure. The model file consists of very abundant contents, which contain lots of information that we don't need. As the model file is a XML type document follows the DTD standard, we chose a XML parser that based on SAX[12] to parse the model file according to the DTD standard. The major advantage of the XML parser is that it is based on the streaming media technique, we can only extract the information that we want, with fewer resources and be faster. The DTD definition of the model element and the method of extraction will be described below.

2.1   DTD Definition of Classifier

The element of the UML model is very abundant, such as *Attribute, Operation, Class, Generalization, Realization*, etc. They can be classified into two categories, classifiers and relations between classes. Before parsing the model file, we should know how these elements are generated in the model file with the DTD standard.

Classifier is one of the elements that declared in the namespace of UML DTD definition. It is also the super class of *Class, Interface* and *DataType*, these three model elements have the similar definition in UML. The detailed definition of *Classifier* is showed in figure 2.

```
<!-- ========= UML:Classifier ========= -->
<!ELEMENT UML:Classifier.feature (UML:Feature|
UML:StructuralFeature|UML:Attribute|
UML:BehavioralFeature|UML:Operation|
UML:Method|UML:Reception)*>
<!ELEMENT UML:Classifier.powertypeRange (UML:
Generalization)*>
<!ENTITY % UML:ClassifierFeatures '%UML:Gener-
alizableElementFeatures;|UML:Namespace.owned
Element|UML:Classifier.feature|
UML:Classifier.powertypeRange'>
......
```

```
<UML:Class xmi.id = '-76--47-6--73--236f8c30:136c018605a:
  -8000:000000000000096E' name = 'SpecializedAbstraction'
  visibility = 'public' isSpecification = 'false' isRoot = 'false'
  isLeaf = 'false' isAbstract = 'false' isActive = 'false'>
<UML:GeneralizableElement.generalization>
    <UML:Generalization xmi.idref = '-76--47-6--73--236f8
c30:136c018605a:-8000:000000000000096F'/>
</UML:GeneralizableElement.generalization>
....
</UML:Class>
```

Fig. 2. DTD Definition of Classifier   **Fig. 3.** Class Structure in Model File

As we can see from figure 2, *Attribute* and *Operation* are two main elements of *Classifier* in the element of *Classifier.feature*. Another important element *Parameter* always appears in the element of *Operation*. It is necessary to mention that the *Parameter kind* is distinguished by different keywords, such as *in, out* and *inout*. These elements are all have detailed definitions in the DTD standard of UML, which mainly describes the inner elements and structure of the model element. We will not describe them one by one here.

2.2   Algorithm of Classifier Extraction

Algorithm 1. Algorithm of Class Extraction

1. **function** classExtraction(*tagName : String*, ...)
2.   **if** *tagName* == *"UML:Class"* **then**
3.   *currentClass* = New Class(...);
4.   **if** *currentClass* is legal **then**
5.   Add the *currentClass* into the class list;
6.   **end if**
7.   **end if**
8.   Update references of parent class(package) and the current class(package);
9. **end function**

We take *Class* the sub-class of *Classifier* as an example to describe the extraction algorithm. Figure 3 shows the structure of *Class* in the model file. As shown in figure 3, the element *UML:Class* corresponds to *Class* consists of some sub-elements and lots of specific feature values, such as *xmi.id, name, visibility*, etc.

In view of the structure of *Class* in model file, the algorithm of extraction is designed as **Algorithm 1**, combined with the technique of streaming media in XML. Due to the nested structure of *Class* and *Package*, it is necessary to hold references of the parent *Class (Package)* and current *Class (Package)*.

2.3   Relations Extraction

Another category of UML model elements is relations between *Classes*, such as *Generalization, Realization, Dependency*, etc. At the same time, their structures in the DTD definition are much similar. The general structure of them is made up of a supplier and a client.

The structure of *Relations* in the model file is much simpler than *Classifiers*. During extracting, we just need to recognize the element like *UML:Dependency* corresponds to *Dependency* and two sub-elements: *UML:Dependency.client* and *UML:Dependency.supplier*. So, the relation extract algorithm isn't necessary to be described in detail here.

3   Model Query Language

```
<Class> ::= [<name>][<visibility>][<isAbstract>]
        {<Attribute>}{<Operation>}
<Attribute>  ::= [<name>][<visibility>][<type>]
        [<ownerScope>][<targetScope>][<multiplicity.range.lower>]
        [<multiplicity.range.upper>][<initialValue>]
<Operation> ::= [<name>][<visibility>][<ownerScope>]
        [<isQuery>][<concurrency>][<isAbstract>]{<Parameter>}
<Parameter> ::= <name> <kind> <type>
<Abstraction> ::= <name><client><client.type><supplier>
        <supplier.type>
<Generalization> ::= <child><child.type><parent><parent.type>
<Dependency> ::= <client><client.type><supplier><supplier.type>
```

```
[Class]
c1:
        id = '$$001'
        name = 'MAX_LIFE_MS'
        visibility = 'public'
        isAbstract = 'false'

[Attribute]
a1:
        name = 'MAX_LIFE_MS'
        visibility = 'public'
        type = 'int'
        ownerScope = 'classifier'
        targetScope = 'instance'
... ...
```

Fig. 4. Syntax Segment   **Fig. 5.** Example of Model Query Language

In order to describe the query model pattern better, a model query language is designed by us, which is described in a textual document. The class diagram will be taken as an example to describe it. Two types of information can be obtained from the UML class diagram, inner nested elements and relations between each element. The inner nested elements are defined as elements in *Class*: *Attributes, Operations* and *Inner Classes*, and the nested structure is described as relations between them in order to avoid the deep nested structure in class and improve the readability of query language.

The syntax definition of the model query language is showed as figure 4. For example, the *Class* consists of some feature values like *name, visibility* and so on, and zero or more *Attributes* and *Operations*. Only thing to note here is that the elements in square brackets([]) are not indispensable, and the number of elements in braces({}) may be zero or more just like *Attributes* in *Class*, others are absolutely necessary.

An example of textual model query language is showed in figure 5, which describes a class and one of its attributes. The inner nested structure of class is described in the indented form, such as the *Attribute a1* is nested in the *Class c1*. Corresponding to the syntax definition, *Class* consists of its *id, name, visibility, type, isAbstract, attributes and operations*. The relations will be defined after all the classes of the class diagram have been defined. As shown above, the textual model query language is so concise that the model structure is very obvious.

4   Structure Matching

In order to query the target model, a rough target model pattern should be given, then match it with the models in the system model repository through the specialized algorithm. The kernel of the algorithm must be the structure matching. However, two types of information, structure of model and feature values of each model element, should be matched with the model pattern. The structure of models is mainly about the relations between classes. And feature values of each element in the model need to be checked first.

Before matching, the target model pattern will be cut into various patterns, which are stringed with each element's id. The id here is the same with the xmi.id in the model file. Need to mention that it isn't necessary to match the id during the matching process. The id just works as the index of each model element, which makes it more convenient to find the model element we need.

Algorithm 2. Matching Algorithm
___

1. **function** MATCH(*queryPattern*: *list, depth*: *int*)
2.   **if** *depth == queryPattern.Size()* **then**
3.   Add matching result into the result map;
4.   **end if**
5.   **for all** pattern in query patterns **do**
6.   **for all** element matches the pattern **do**
7.   %The element here can be a *Class pattern , Dependency pattern, Generalization pattern* and so on.%
8.   Add the id mapping of the pattern and model element into result set;
9.   MATCH(*queryPattern, depth+1*);
10.   Remove the id mapping from result set;
11.   **end for**
12.   **end for**
13. **end function**
___

During the process of matching, one of the query patterns may be selected, then the adjacency list of that pattern will be checked whether the list contains the unknown pattern's id or not. If it doesn't contain, next pattern will be selected to do the same process. Otherwise, the unknown pattern should be checked whether it matches or not. The algorithm will recursively do this until it reaches the depth of the model pattern, which indicates the end of the pattern matching.

4.1   Class Structure Matching

Two types of patterns can be obtained in the model patterns, *Class* corresponds to the *Class Pattern*. As the syntax definition of the *Class*, it contains some general information, *Attributes* list and *Operations* list. During matching, these elements will be mainly matched with the model pattern. However, feature values of *Class* which the model pattern offered is not very comprehensive. Before matching, it is necessary to check whether the *Class* of the model pattern contains all the features that will be matched or not. Only the features contained by the *Class* of the model pattern will be checked while matching. The fact is that there are different types of feature values, some feature values are enumerated type and some are string type. There are different match approaches for different types. For the enumerated type, match the value directly. However, the string values, we take advantage of regular expression to do the matching.

During the process of the class structure matching, the general information of *Class* should be checked first whether it matches or not. If it returns false, the matching algorithm will be stopped as the negative conclusion. After that, the *Attributes* and *Operations* will be matched one by one. Once all the elements are corrected matched, the algorithm will return true, which means that the *Class Structure* matched success.

4.2   Relation Structure Matching

Another type of pattern is *Relation Pattern*. The *Relation Pattern* is much more important during matching, because the structure of the model is mainly depended on the relations between classes. They make up the skeleton of model. However, relations are various, such as *Generalization*, *Dependency*, *Realization* and so on. But, the structure of relations is much similar. So, it simplifies the problem more or less. During matching, we just need to check all the feature values of each *Relation Pattern*. If that all matched, the *Relation Pattern* matches successfully.

4.3   Priority of Matching

Different model elements and feature values have different discrimination of models, which depends on the frequency of usage in the model, that means using different model elements and feature values to match will get different results of matching. Some elements or feature values can filter lots of model elements that don't match, others are not. For this reason, we introduce two basic concepts: rare feature value and rare model element. For example, the feature value *isAbstract* is a rare feature value, because of that abstract *Class* is very few in the model. If we match this feature value first, lots of unnecessary matching can be avoided. By this way, the efficiency of the matching algorithm will be greatly improved.

5   Case Study

In order to verify that the query method based on structure pattern matching is effective, vast of experiments have been done. We also do experiments on some open source projects, like *Vuze*, which is the most powerful bittorrent app on earth. However, the model scale of *Vuze* project is so large that it is not convenient to demonstrate whole of it here. We just take one of the segments as an example to show the experiment (see figure 6).

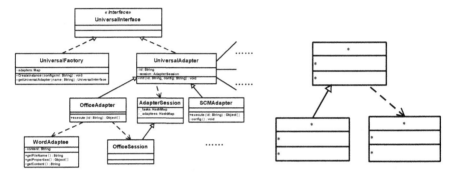

Fig. 6. System Model Segmen   **Fig. 7.** Query Model Pattern

Now a query model pattern has been provided as figure 7, which will be queried in the system model segment. As we can see, the query pattern doesn't have any feature value, it is just a pure structure of the *Adapter* design pattern. Due to the system model segment isn't very complex, it is obvious that the query pattern exists in it, and two results should be matched, one is *UniversalAdapter OfficeAdapter* and *AdapterSession*, the other one is *UniversalAdapter AdapterSession* and *SCMAdapter*. The result of our experiment is right that, and the result we returned is a mapping of model element's id, which maps the model element's id in the query pattern to that in the system model. A graphical demo of the results will be better, which must combine with UML model tools, because of that it is difficult and not realistic to read or comprehend the results in a textual document directly.

Although the experiment we showed is very simple, it proves the effectiveness of our query method more or less. When the model repository is large enough, it is not so easy to find the result by manual work, the true worth of the model query will be demonstrated incisively and vividly then.

6   Conclusion

In this paper, we proposed a UML model query method, which is based on structure pattern matching. Firstly, we introduced how to extract structure information of UML model from the model file. Then, a model query language was described succinctly.

After that, we described our algorithm of structure pattern matching. And we pointed out the influence of the priority of matching to the efficiency of the matching algorithm in brief. At last, a case study was presented to show the effectiveness of our model query method. The major advantage of our model query method is that it can support for both key words and pure structure query. It is a very general method for UML model query.

As the efficiency of our matching algorithm depends on the scale of the model repository, if the model repository's scale is too massive that it will cost a long time to get the final query result, so a higher efficient algorithm is needed. It needs much more effort to improve the algorithm. Now, the query pattern is described with a textual query language, which needs to edit by manual work. While a graphical user interface for model input is much better, like OOQBE[8] which are based on the ideas of Zloof's Query-By-Example. That will be more user-friendly and convenient. So, all the work mentioned above may be done in the future.

Acknowledgment. This work is supported by the National Natural Science Foundation of China (No.61003025, 91118002), and by the Jiangsu Province Research Foundation (BK2010170).

References

1. Akehurst, D.H., Bordbar, B.: On Querying UML Data Models with OCL. The Unified Modeling Language - UML, 91–103 (2001)
2. Lucrédio, D., de M. Fortes, R.P., Whittle, J.: MOOGLE: a metamodel-based model search engine. Software and System Modeling - SOSYM 9(3), 1–26 (2010)
3. Habela, P., Kaczmarski, K., Stencel, K., Subieta, K.: OCL as the Query Language for UML Model Execution. In: International Conference on Computational Science - ICCS, pp. 311–320 (2008)
4. Grinev, M., Kuznetsov, S.D.: UQL: A UML-based Query Language for Integrated Data. Programming and Computer Software 28(4), 189–196 (2002)
5. Stein, D., Hanenberg, S., Unland, R.: Query Models. The Unified Modeling Language - UML, 98–112 (2004)
6. Mandel, L., Cengarle, M.V.: On the Expressive Power of OCL. In: Wing, J.M., Woodcock, J. (eds.) FM 1999. LNCS, vol. 1708, pp. 854–874. Springer, Heidelberg (1999)
7. Gaafar, A., Sakr, S.: Towards a Framework for Mapping Between UML/OCL and XML/XQuery. The Unified Modeling Language - UML, 241–259 (2004)
8. Staes, F., Tarantino, L.: OOQBE: An Intuitive Graphical Query Language with Recursion. In: Human-Computer Interaction - HCI, pp. 603–608 (1993)
9. Object Management Group: Object Constraint Language version 2.0 (May 2006), http://www.omg.org/cgi-bin/doc?formal/2006-05-01
10. Object Management Group: Unified Modeling Language Specification, version 1.3, formal/2001-09-67, http://www.omg.org/spec/UML/1.3/PDF
11. Object Management Group: XML Metadata Interchange, XMI 1.1 RTF UML DTD, http://www.omg.org/cgi-bin/doc?ad/99-10-05
12. Simple API for XML: SAX 2.0.1, http://www.saxproject.org/

A Lightweight Type Enforcement Access Control Approach with Role Based Authorization

Yan Ding, Hongyi Fu, Lifeng Wei, Lianyue He, Huadong Daib, and Qingbo Wu

School of Computer Science, National University of Defense Technology, Changsha, China
{yanding,hongyifu,lifengwei,lianyuehe,huadongdai,
qingbowu}@nudt.edu.cn

Abstract. Type Enforcement (TE) and Role-Based Access Control (RBAC) are both applied widely in operating system security. Addressing the complexity of security configuration caused by the combination of TE and RBAC, this paper proposes a TE access control model featuring loose-coupled role authorization, named as RS-TEAC. In the model, the role-relevant subject domain transition is exploited to enable subjects with different roles entering their corresponding security domain. Hence the access control based on role authorization is achieved. The RS-TEAC model is implemented in Linux, and its effectiveness and performance are tested through a series of applications and experiments.

Keywords: secure OS, MAC, TE, RBAC, domain transition.

1   Introduction

In this network age, information is processed in ever open environment, which brings great security risks. The security of operating system provides the basis of the information system security. As an important access control policy in operating system, Type Enforcement (TE) policy categorizes objects in the operating system according to their security attributes, by which the access privileges can be established for every attribute. Such an access control scheme is fine-grained, and the configuration of access control rules is flexible. So it can be easily used to achieve application-based operation security domain isolation. However in practice, TE itself is not able to differentiate users with different roles. So, the control based on user's role is needed. SELinux combines Role Based Access Control (RBAC) with TE in hierarchy model, which assigns TE domains as authorization of roles. But in SELinux, policy analysis needs to guarantee the correctness of authorization both on two different levels. Furthermore, this combination mode causes that altering users dynamically will influence TE rules configuration greatly. Since the grammar and syntax of policy description language may be complex, it is difficult to manage rules. So automation or semi-automation analysis tools of SELinux security policy configuration are now high-lightened by researchers [5]-[11]. And other studies focus on simplifying the security configuration of access control model and improve the system efficiency. RDTEAC model [12] inherits the advantages of RBAC96,

Y. Yuan, X. Wu, and Y. Lu (Eds.): ISCTCS 2012, CCIS 320, pp. 514–521, 2013.

meanwhile embeds the security principal of DTE, and makes the implementation of DTE easily, but the policy configuration is complicated. J. He and etc. presented implementation of Clark-Wilson model based on TE [13], the model can be used to protect the integrity of military and business systems, but not in operating system access control.

In secure operating systems, RBAC are commonly used regarding privilege differentiating for users who have special application requests. Users with different roles generally can only access authorized applications. And, these applications barely overlap, so the roles in system are almost independent to each other. If distinguishing different roles with their actual functions is needed, every one of these roles may be restricted in a very certain of applications. In practice, the combination of TE policy and role authorization can be performed by using TE as the basic policy to control accessing in the system, and role based controlling only guiding the process to enter specific application domain. So, it's necessary to seek a loose coupled combination of role authorization and TE policy. This paper proposes a light-weight type enforcement access control method that supports role privilege separation, combining role authorization with TE in subject domain transition stage. So different roles enter respective domains and role based privilege differentiating access control is achieved. In this method, configuration of a role is done only in its relevant security domain, without modifying other TE security configurations in operating system.

The paper is organized as follows. Section 2 presents the role privilege differentiating supported type enforcement access control model, named RS-TEAC; section 3 introduces an implementation of RS-TEAC model in Linux system; section 4 shows the performance of RSTE Linux by benchmark test. Finally a conclusion is given.

2   Type Enforcement Access Control That Supports Role Based Privilege Differentiating

2.1   Role Supported Type Enforcement Access Control (RS-TEAC)

RS-TEAC is created based on classic TE model, with extending of role based privilege differentiating. The definitions are given in following:

Def. 1: (The RS-TEAC Model). RS-TEAC model = { *USERS* (set of users), *ROLES* (set of roles), *TYPES* (set of types), *OPS* (set of operations), *DOMAINS* (set of subject domains), *TYPE_DEF* (set of default security types), *u_roles* (user-role assignment), *UR* (set of user-role assigning rules), *ac_perms* (access control permissions), *AC_RULES* (set of access controls rules), *d_trans* (plain subject domain transition), *TR_RULES* (set of plain subject domain transition rules), *rd_trans* (role-relevant subject domain transition), *RTR_RULES* (set of role-relevant subject domain transition rules), *o_trans* (object type transition), *OTR_RULES* (set of object type transition rules) }. And,

— **The sets of users, roles, types, access operations** are presented as *USERS*, *ROLES*, *TYPES*, *OPS*. *DOMAIN* is the set of subjects in system, and $DOMAINS \subset TYPES$

— **The set of default security types in system**, TYPE_DEF = { *PROC_ROOT_T*, *UNLABELED_T*, *WILDCARD_T* }, and $TYPE\_DEF \subset TYPES$. $PROC\_ROOT\_T \in DOAMINS$, it is the default type of a process in system. In other words, it is the type that a process will be when the user login. $UNLABELED\_T \in TYPES$, it is the default type of objects. All security attributes of an object that have not been explicitly set by the administrator will have the type of *UNLABELED_T*. $WILDCARD\_T \in TYPES$, it is a wildcard type in system, and presents for any security types.

— **The user-role assignment**, $u\_roles: USERS \rightarrow ROLES$, is a mapping from users to their corresponding roles. All assignment of users to roles form a set named *UR*, and $UR \subseteq USERS \times ROLES$. In RS-TEAC, using and managing roles shall be as simple as possible. In practice, roles management can be extended in adapting to the environment.

— **The access control permission**, $ac\_perms: DOMAINS \times TYPES \rightarrow 2^{OPS}$, is a set of mapping relations between the combination of subject domains and object types to those operations that are allowed. Access control rules, denoted as *ac_rules*, are used to specify which access operations will be allowed when a certain subject accessing a certain object. $ac\_rules = (d, t, p), d \in DOMAINS, t \in TYPES, p \in 2^{OPS}$, it is a triplet comprised of subject domain, type, and subsets of operation set. The triplet must meet: $p = ac\_perms(d, t)$. The set of access control rules, $AC\_RULES \subseteq DOMAINS \times TYPES \times 2^{OPS}$, is a set containing several *ac_rules*.

— **The plain subject domain transition**, $d_{trans}: DOMAINS \times TYPES \rightarrow (DOMAINS - \{PROC\_ROOT\_T\})$, is the mapping relationship to specify what domain to transit when subject is executing a certain type of object. Plain subject domain transition rules are used to specify the new types subjects will transit to, when they are executing certain security types of objects. It is denoted by *tr_rules*. $tr\_rules = (d\_old, t, d\_new), d\_old \in DOMAINS, t \in TYPES, d\_new \in (DOMAINS - \{PROC\_ROOT\_T\})$. The triplet of plain subject domain transition rules is demanded to meet: $d\_new = d\_trans(d\_old, d\_new)$. The set of these rules is denoted as $TR\_RULES \subseteq DOMAINS \times TYPES \times (DOMAINS - \{PROC\_ROOT\_T\})$, is a set consists of numbers of . RS-TEAC demands that once subject domains transit out of *PROC_ROOT_T*, no further transitions back to *PROC_ROOT_T* are permitted. So, the result set of mapping *d_trans* is DOMAINS-{*PROC_ROOT_T*}.

— **The role-relevant subject domain transition**, $rd\_trans: ROLES \times TYPES \rightarrow (DOMAINS - \{PROC\_ROOT\_T\})$, is the mapping presents what the subject domains with certain roles will transit to by executing certain types of objects. The role-relevant subject domain transition rules, denoted by *rtr_rules*, are used to specify the target new domain according to the current role, when subjects with PROC_ROOT_T as their domain are executing certain objects. $rtr\_rules = (r, t, d\_new), r \in ROLES, t \in ROLES, t \in TYPES, d\_new \in DOMAINS - \{PROC\_ROOT\_T\}$. This triplet shall meet $d\_new = rd\_trans(r, t)$. The set of role-relevant subject domain transition rules, $RTR\_RULES \subseteq ROLES \times TYPES \times (DOMAINS - \{PROC\_ROOT\_T\})$, is consist of a number of rtr_rules.

— **The object type transition**, $o\_trans: DOMAIN \times TYPES \rightarrow TYPES$, is the security type transition of new objects that created by subject domains in the directories of certain object types. The object type transition rules are used to specify the security type of the new objects created by specified subjects in the directories of certain types. It is denoted as otr_rules. $otr\_rules = (d, t\_dir, t\_new), d \in DOMAINS, t\_dir \in TYPES, t\_new \in TYPES$. The triplet is required to meet $t\_new = o\_trans(r, t\_dir)$. The set of object type transition rules, $OTR\_RULES \subseteq DOMAINS \times TYPES \times TYPES$, is consist of many otr_rules.

Beyond the definitions above, RS-TEAC performs two kinds of security management, access control and type transition. Regarding these the following decision principles are defined:

Def. 2 (The Access Control Permission Decision Making Principle). Assume that subject S has access on object O, with operation type of op; the security type of S is t_s, and $t\_s \in DOMAINS$; the security type of O is t_o, and $t\_o \in TYPES$, $op \in OPS$. If $\exists rule \in AC\_RULES$, so that $op \in ac\_perms(t\_s, t\_o)$, the operations is allowed. Or, it is disallowed.

Def. 3 (The Plain Subject Domain Transition Decision Making Principle). Assume that a subject S issues "execve" operation on an object O, the security type of S is t_s, and $t\_s \in DOMAINS$; the security type of O is t_o, and $t\_o \in TYPE$. If $\exists rule \in TR\_RULES$, so that $d\_trans(t\_s, t\_o) \in (DOMAINS - \{PROC\_ROOT\_T\})$, the new type of the object is $d\_trans(t\_s, t\_o)$. Or, its type is still t_s.

Def. 4 (The Role-relevant Subject Domain Transition Decision Making Principle). When subject S issue "execve" operation on an object O, the current role is $r \in ROLES$, the security type of S is $PROC\_ROOT\_T$, and the security type of O is $t\_o \in TYPES$. If $\exists rule \in RTR\_RULES$, so that $rd\_trans(r, t\_o) \in (DOMAINS - \{PROC\_ROOT\_T\})$, the new type transition of the subject is $rd\_trans(t\_s, t\_o)$. Or, its type is still $PROC\_ROOT\_T$.

Def. 5 (The Object Type Transition Decision Making Principle). Assume that a subject S creates new subjects in specific directories, the security type of S is t_s, and $t\_s \in DOMAINS$; the security type of O is t_o, and $t\_o \in TYPE$. If $\exists rule \in OTR\_RULES$, so that $o\_trans(t\_s, t\_o) \in TYPES$, the new type of the object is $o\_trans(t\_s, t\_o)$. Or, it gets its father directory's type t_o.

2.2 The Subject Domain Transition Decision Making Scheme with Role Privilege Distinguishing Support

RS-TEAC is designed to directly define user roles during the subject domain transition. To assign different access privileges to different roles, firstly when subjects with different roles are executing RS-TEAC the same object, RS-TEAC enforces controls upon the procedure to make their subject domains transit differently. Then the access control privileges are configured according to the subject domains of new processes, so that subjects with their own roles can enter their respective security domains. Accordingly, the access privileges upon objects are differentiated.

As shown in Fig. 1, the plain subject domain transition decides transition result only based on the current domains of subjects and the types of objects being executed. While, role relevant subject domain transition needs to check the current roles in further. If the roles of the subjects differ from each other, their subject domains might transit differently, even though they are executing the same type of objects.

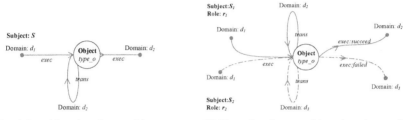

(a) The plain subject domain transition   (b) The role relevant subject domain transition

Fig. 1. The illustration of a subject domain transition

In practice, to avoid role checking at every time that subjects alter their images, RS-TEAC sets implicit conditions for role relevant subject domains. That is, role relevant transition is granted only in the case that the current subject domain is *PROC_ROOT_T*, i. e., the subject domain never transited. This makes sure that all subjects who have ever entered some applications' security domain do not get back to the original status, and consequently enter other security domain, so subjects is not able to reveal information using the privileges of the original security domain *PROC_ROOT_T*.

3   Implementing RS-TEAC in Linux

Based on RS-TEAC discussed above, and taking Linux as a foundation, we implemented a secure operating system named RSTE-Linux, which supports administrator privilege differentiating and type enforcement access control. RSTE-Linux has been practically used. Its subsystem of security is shown as Fig. 2, from which we can see, that the core of security subsystem is a RSTE security module implemented using RS-TEAC. The module is loaded in Linux LSM access control framework. It gets access operation information through the object manager in LSM framework, concludes the security decision, and finally enforces the decision through the object manager.

RSTE security model includes the following 5 parts, policy initializing, subject security domain transition, object security type transition, access permission checking, policy rules configuration and management. Policy initializing is responsible for registering security module to access control framework, and for initializing the system security policy configuration and system initial security type setting. After initialization, system receives request from the access control framework. Specifically, access permission checks whether an access is allowed or not, according to security labels of subjects and objects provided by the access control framework, as well the types of access operations. Subject security type transition decides if transition shall happen when a user process changes its executing image. Object security type transition concludes the security types of new objects created when users create new file objects. In addition, user can use policy rule configuration module to modify the configuration of policies.

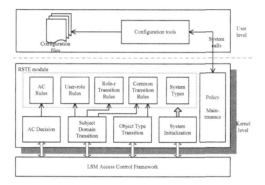

Fig. 2. The security subsystem using RS-TEAC in RSTE-Linux

4   Experimental Evaluation

This section evaluates the performance of RSTE-Linux. Overhead of low-level system operations is measured using benchmark UnixBench and lmbench. In both cases, two different kernel configurations are used. Base kernel, which is based on unmodified Linux 2.6.18 kernel, serves as a basis of performance for benchmark tests. RSTE-Linux kernel uses RSTE Linux 2.6.18 kernel, its performance is compared with base kernel to illustrate the overhead. The experimental set up is as follows: CPU is Intel(R) Xeon(R) E5540 2.53GHz dual cores, Memory size is 3GB. And the benchmark versions are UnixBench 5.1.2 and Lmbech 3.0.a9.

4.1   UnixBench

The experimental data of UnixBench is shown in Table 1. The unit of the test data of Shell Script is loop iterations per millisecond, the unit of File Copy is kilobytes per second, and the unit of remaining data is loop iterations per microsecond.

Table 1. Experimental data of UnixBench test

MicroBenchmark	Base	RSTE	Expense
Process Creation	11460.5	11458.2	**0.02%**
Execl Throughput	4776.7	4753.3	**0.49%**
Shell Scripts (1 concurrent)	5807.8	5482	**5.61%**
Shell Scripts(8 concurrent)	1561.4	1545.5	**1.02%**
File Copy 256	119092.6	109741	**7.85%**
File Copy 1024	361192.9	340559.9	**5.71%**
File Copy 4096	773301	748456.2	**3.21%**
Pipe Throughput	749623.4	629529.2	**16.02%**
Pipe-based Context Switching	257281.9	219385.9	**14.73%**

4.2   lmbench

The experimental result of lmbench is shown in Table 2. The unit of test data is millisecond.

Table 2. Experimental data of lmbench test

MicroBenchmark	Base	RSTE	Expense
null I/O	0.5	0.64	**28.00%**
stat	2.8	3.64	**30.00%**
open close	4.14	5.18	**25.12%**
fork proc	88.07	89.3	**1.40%**
exec proc	286.67	289.33	**0.93%**
sh proc	1234.67	1267.67	**2.67%**
0K File Create	69.5	80.2	**15.40%**
0K File Delete	12.83	14.23	**10.91%**

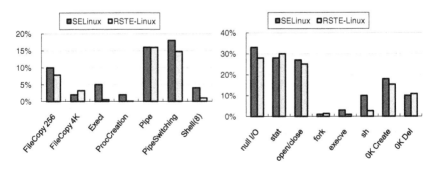

Fig. 3. Performance comparison between RSTE-Linux and SELinux

Fig. 3 shows the performance comparison between RSTE-Linux and SELinux[2]. From the figures we can see that RSTE-Linux has better performance than SELinux in processes related operations. As for file and pipe access operations, RSTE-Linux shows comparable performance to SELinux.

5   Conclusion

The current dominant RBAC and TE policies combined in hierarchy, to provide flexibility of system management, but meanwhile induce tight coupling of roles and types, which makes difficult to do policy configuration. In this paper, a light type enforcement access control scheme with role privilege differentiating supporting is proposed. Through role relevant subject domain transition, role based authorization is achieved. It keeps the flexibility of system security management, meanwhile simplifies the security policy configuration, and improves the performance.

Acknowledgements. This work was supported by HGJ Major Project 2012ZX01040-001.

References

1. Badger, L., Sterne, D.F., Sherman, D.L., Walker, K.M.: A domain and type enforcement UNIX prototype. Usenix Computing Systems 9(1), 47–83 (1996)
2. Loscocco, P., Smalley, S.: Integrating flexible support for security policies into the Linux operating system. NSA Technical Report (2001)
3. Loscocco, P.A., Smalley, S.D.: Meeting Critical Security Objectives with Security-Enhanced Linux. In: Proceedings of the 2001 Ottawa Linux Symposium (2001)
4. Sarna-starosta, B., Stoller, S.D.: Policy analysis for security enhanced Linux. In: Proceedings of the Workshop on Issues in the Theory of Security (WITS) (2004)
5. Jaeger, T., Zhang, X., Edwards, A.: Policy management using access control spaces. CM Transactions on Information and System Security (TISSEC) 6(3), 327–364 (2003)
6. Kuliniewicz, P.: SENG:An Enhanced Policy Language for SELinux. In: SELinux Symposium (2006)
7. Jaeger, T., Sailer, R., Zhang, X.: Analyzing Integrity Protection in the SELinux Example Policy. In: Proceedings of the 12th USENIX Security Symposium, SSYM (2003)
8. Zanin, G., Mancini, L.V.: Towards a Formal Model for Security Policies Specification and Validation in the SELinux System. In: Proceedings of the Ninth ACM Symposium on Access Control Models and Technologies (SACMAT) (2004)
9. Guttman Joshua, D., Herzog Amy, L., Ramsdell John, D.: SLAT:Information flow in security enhanced Linux (2005), http://www.nsa.gov/SELinux
10. Yang, Z.: A Information-Flow-Based Verification Solution with Security Sensitivity to Check Security Policy of SELinux. Chinese Journal of Computers 32(4), 709–720 (2008)
11. Wu, Y., Zhao, C.: Research on Role-Permission Assignment in SELinux. Journal of Computer Research and Development, Z2 (2006)
12. Zhao, Q., Sun, Y., Zhang, X.: Research and Implementation of Role-Based Domain and Type Enforcement Access Control Model. Acta Electronica Sinica 31(6), 842–846 (2003)
13. He, J., Guo, X., Qin, S.: An Approach to Enforcing Clark-Wilson Model Based on type Enforcement. Acta Electronica Sinica 36(2), 216–223 (2008)

Composition of AADL Components by Transformation to Interface Automata

Jiangwei Li[1,2], Jizhou Zhao[1,2], Qingqing Sun[1,2], Xiaopu Huang[1,2], Yan Zhang[3], and Tian Zhang[1,2]

[1] State Key Laboratory for Novel Software Technology, Nanjing University
[2] Department of Computer Science and Technology, Nanjing University, Nanjing, P.R. China
{ljw,zjz,sunqq,hxp}@seg.nju.edu.cn,
ztluck@nju.edu.cn
[3] Department of Computer Science and Technology, Beijing Electronic Science and Technology Institute, Beijing, P.R. China
zhangyan@besti.edu.cn

Abstract. AADL, an industrial standard in embedded field, is a component-based semi-formal modeling language. Incompatibility of behaviors is a problem that we must face up with when the AADL components composite, because the sequence of some interactive activities may not match with each other. Shielding the incompatible behavior and reusing the compatibly behavior maximally are main problems to increase the reusability of AADL components. This paper proposes an MDE based method to implement the transformation from AADL to IA using the heterogeneous model transformation framework. Then we can use the IA model to derive available behavior all out from incompatible component compositions through construct the environment, and now the environment maps back to AADL component to solve the AADL components composition problems we proposed.

Keywords: AADL, Interface Automata, components composition, model transformation.

1 Introduction

With the development of embedded system, the complexity of embedded software continuously increases. The traditional development method cannot adapt to the requirement. MDE [1], proposed by OMG, is a software development framework, which highlights the usage of models. MDE technology have been introduced to the embedded software development, so the developers have to consider the correctness of the software model, and then lots of problems will be found and solved at the early stage of software development. Then the development cycle will be shortened and development cost will be reduced.

SAE (Society of Automotive Engineers) presented the real time embedded system model language---AADL (Architecture Analysis and Design Language) [4] at 2004

Y. Yuan, X. Wu, and Y. Lu (Eds.): ISCTCS 2012, CCIS 320, pp. 522–529, 2013.
© Springer-Verlag Berlin Heidelberg 2013

and it was released as SAE AS5506 Standard. AADL, a component-based semi-formal modeling language, supports software model, hardware model and NFP (non-function property) analysis. Because of simple grammar and extensible annex, AADL has been supported by many organizations. At 2006 and 2011, SAE released AS5506/1[5] and AS5506/2[6] AADL annex to complement AADL specification. The AADL components behavior description was presented in the AS5506/2.

As a components-based model language, AADL has to face the components composition problem which decides whether the components can be composited or not. Many ideas to solve this problem are to give up the incompatible components or to construct the interface wrapper for them; however, these ideas will bring the development cost increasing and development cycle extending problems. IA (Interface Automata)[7] is proposed to solve these problems. As a formal modeling language, IA uses an optimistic approach to solve components composition problems. In our early study [2], we had given an IA-based method to utmost reuse the available behavior of two incompatible components by constructing an environment for them.

In this paper, components are described by AADL, and we transform AADL models to IA models using ATL (Atlanmod Transformation Language) [8, 9]; IA is used to verify the components composition problems, and then we use the method given in[2] to construct an environment for two incompatible IA. Finally, the environment is mapped back to AADL models, and then the AADL components composition problems and components behavior compatibility problems are solved.

The paper is structured as follows: Section 2 introduces the AADL and Interface Automata simply. Section 3 describes the approach of transforming AADL components models to IA models. In Section 4, we present a case study on the approach. The concluding remarks are shown in Section 5.

2   Background

2.1   AADL

Architecture Analysis and Design Language (AADL) is a kind of architecture design language based on MDA. AADL can be applied in the field of embedded software system.

There are three kinds of components in AADL: software components, execution platform components and system components. Components are defined through type and implementation declarations. A component type declaration defined a component's interface elements and externally observable attributes. A component implementation declaration defines a component's internal structure in terms of sub-components, subcomponent connections, subprogram call sequences, modes, flow implementations and properties.

In the AS5506/2 annex, the behavior specification of components is presented for the first time. The behavior specifications can be attached to any AADL components types and components implementations using an annex subclause. When defined within component type specifications, it represents behavior common to all the associated implementations. If a component type or implementation is extended, behavior annex subclause defined in the ancestor are applied to the descendent except if the later defines its own behavior annex subclause.

The detailed description and examples of the AADL behavior have been provided in the AS5506/2 annex, so we will not provide in this paper.

2.2   Interface Automata

[7] presents the Interface Automata which was a new theory to describe interface at 2001. It is different from other theories. There are two main features, one is optimistic approach and the other is game thinking. The former feature is used to solve the problem of interface compatibility, the latter feature to describe the semantics of this problem. The theorems and definition of IA will not be shown in this paper because IA has been explained in detail in [7].

3   AADL2IA Transformation

In the practical application, components composition problems are ubiquitous. If we can find out and solve the components composition problems in the modeling stage of software development, the development time and cost will be reduced. AADL is components-based modeling language; however, it is not a formal modeling language. To solve the components composition problems of AADL, we transform AADL models to the IA models which are easy to verify the components compatibility.

3.1   Transformation Framework

The transformation framework is described in Fig.1 [10]. It shows the general model transformation process [3]: from the source model Ma, conform to the MMa (meta model of the Ma), then conform to the MMM (meta-meta model of the Ma). In the M3 level, we use the ecore as the meta-meta modeling language to describe the AADL meta-model and IA meta-model, and then we use the mapping rules to complete the transformation.

3.2   AADL and IA Meta-model

We adopt the AADL meta-model given by AS5506/1 annex, since it has contained all the AADL components. The meta model of IA in Fig.2, is designed by ourselves using EMF (Eclipse Modeling Framework).

3.3   Transformation Mapping Rules

To complete transformation from AADL models to IA models, Table 1 has given the main mapping rules from AADL to IA.

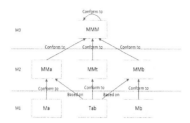

Fig. 1. Model Transformation Framework

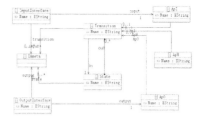

Fig. 2. IA meta-model

4   Case Study

4.1   Scenarios Description

We illustrate the feasible of the proposed rules with an example which describes the preparation work of docking of spaceship and space station simply.

Table 1. Transformation Mapping Rules

AADL components info	IA info
single component	an interface automaton
component features	IA ports
component states	IA state set V_P
component transitions	IA transition setT_P
component transitions Guard	IA input action set A_P^I
component transitions Action	IA output action set A_P^O
......	......

4.2   Model with AADL

To model this system easily, we consider the space station as *Space* thread, spaceship as *Ship* thread components, the *Space* thread and the *Ship* thread composite the process A. In the model, some components declarations have been removed due to space limitations.

The Model of The System.

```
thread Ship
  features
    msg: in event data port ;
    ack: in event port;
    nack: in event port;
    send: out event data port;
    ok: out event port;
```

```
    fail: out event port;
  --Snip
end Ship;

thread implementation Ship.impl
  annex behavior_specification {**
   states
  0:initial complete final state;
  2,3:complete state;
  1,4: state;
   transitions
  0-[on dispatch,msg]->1;
  1-[]->2{send!("send")};
  2-[on dispatch,ack]->3;
  2-[on dispatch,nack]->4;
  3-[]->0{ok!("ok")};
  4-[]->0{fail!("fail")};
  **};
  --Snip
end Ship.impl;

thread implementation Space.impl
  annex behavior_specification {**
   states
  v0:initial final state;
  v1:complete state;
   transitions{**
  v0-[]->v1{msg!("msg")};
  v1-[on dispatch,ok]->v0;
  **};
  --Snip
end Space.impl;

process implementation A.impl
  subcomponents
    SpaceA: thread Space.impl;
    ShipA: thread Ship.impl;
  connections
    A1: event port        ShipA.ok -> SpaceA.ok;
    A2: event port        ShipA.fail -> SpaceA.fail;
    A3: event data port   SpaceA.msg -> ShipA.msg;
  --Snip
end A.impl;
```

4.3   Model Transformation to IA

The AADL models we have created can transform to the IA models according to the transformation mapping rules. We get the IA models of *Ship* and *Space* in Fig.3 finally.

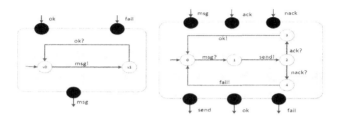

Fig. 3. Space station and spaceship IA models

4.4   Verification and Environment Construction

According to the interface automata composition definition [7], we can give the interface automaton C (Fig.4) which is the composition of the *Ship* and *Space* interface automata. In the Fig.4, there is an illegal state $(v_1, 4)$ can be reached, according to the interface automata compatibility definition [2], the interface automata *Ship* and *Space* are incompatible. This problem has been solved in our early research [2], and then we can use this method directly.

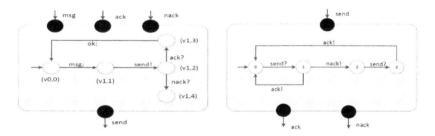

Fig. 4. Maximum legal environment user   **Fig. 5.** Interface Automaton C

According to the construction algorithm of maximum legal environment shown in [2], we can construct maximum legal environment of the interface automata *Ship* and *Space*, named *User* in Fig.5.

The interface automaton space $\otimes$ ship $\otimes$ user is closed, definite and nonblocking in Fig.6. In other words, the behavior incompatible components spaceship and space station can work compatibly in the environment user.

Finally, the environment user maps back to AADL thread component which make the behavior incompatible AADL components spaceship and space station can work compatibly. This process is implemented according to some mapping strategies. Parts of the rules are listed as follows.

Rule 1.
An Interface Automaton → AADL Component..

Rule 2.
The Interface Automaton Port Set → The Feature of AADL Component.

Rule 3.
The Interface Automaton State Set → The States of AADL Component.

Rule 4.
The Interface Automaton Input Action → The Guard of AADL Component Transition.

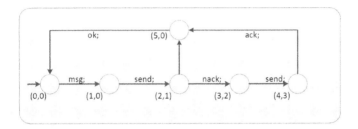

Fig. 6. Space ⊗ ship ⊗ user

5   Related Work

There have been many works about AADL behavior and IA component composition. Reference [11] proposed a formal semantics for the AADL behavior annex using Timed Abstract State Machine (TASM), and used UPPAAL [12] by mapping TASM to timed automata to verify the AADL behavior models. Bernard Berthomieu [13] mapped AADL models into the Fiacre language, which contains assignments, conditionals, while loops and sequential composition constructs. In [14], R.Passerone has developed a game-theoretical approach to find out whether incompatible component interfaces can be made compatible by inserting a converter between them which satisfies specified requirements.

In summary, there are few works on the problems of AADL components composition which are important, and interface automata have been widely used to solve components composition problem. Therefore, it is a new attempt to use IA to solve the AADL components composition problems.

6   Conclusion

Although AADL is a widely used component-based model language, it cannot solve the component composition problems expediently. On the other hand, IA is a formal model for describing software components behavior and it uses the optimistic approach to solve the components composition problems effectively. We study the transformation from AADL model to IA through ATL heterogeneous model transformation framework, present the meta-model of interface automata and propose a series of transformation rules. IA can be used to verify the behavior compatible of components and construct the compatible working environment. The environment can be mapped back to AADL components which make the behavior incompatible components can work together. In the future, we plan to analyze the semantics of AADL behavior in detail, try to verify the AADL components behavior compatibly and construct the environment which makes the behavior incompatible components can work together on the AADL directly.

Acknowledgment. This work is supported by the National Natural Science Foundation of China (No.61003025, 91118002), and by the Jiangsu Province Research Foundation (BK2010170).

References

1. OMG, Inc. Model Driven Architecture (MDA), `http://www.omg.org/gov`
2. Zhang, Y., Hu, J., Yu, X.F., Zhang, T., Li, X.D., Zheng, G.L.: Deriving available behavior all out from incompatible component compositions. In: Liu, Z., Barbosa, L. (eds.) Proc.of the 2nd Int'l Workshop on Formal Aspects of Component Software (FACS 2005). ENTCS, vol. 160, pp. 349–361. Elsevier, Netherlands (2006)
3. Zhang, T., Jouault, F., Attiogb, C., Li, X.D.: MDE-based model transformation: from MARTE model to FIACRE model. Journal of Software 20(2), 214–233 (2009)
4. SAE Aerospace. SAE AS5506: Architecture Analysis and Design Language (AADL), Version 1.0 (2004)
5. SAE Aerospace. SAE AS5506/1: Architecture Analysis and Design Language (AADL) Annex vol.1 (2006)
6. SAE Aerospace. SAE AS5506/2: Architecture Analysis and Design Language (AADL) Annex vol. 2 (2011)
7. de Alfaro, L., Henzinger, T.A.: Interface Automata. ACM Sigsoft Software Engineering Notes 26(5), 109–120 (2001)
8. The ATL Model Transformation Language, `http://www.emn.fr/z-info/atlanmod/index.php/Model_Transformation`
9. ATLAS group LINA and INRIA.: ATL: Atlas Transformation Language (2006)
10. Jouault, F., Allilaire, F., Bézivin, J., Kurtev, I.: ATL: A model transformation tool. Science of Computer Programming 72(1/2), 31–39 (2008)
11. Yang, Z., Hu, K., Ma, D., Pi, L.: Towards a formal semantics for the AADL behavior annex. In: Proc. DATE 2009. IEEE, Los Alamitos (2009)
12. UPPAAL, `http://www.uppaal.org/`
13. Berthomieu, B., Bodeveix, J.-P., Chaudet, C., Dal Zilio, S., Filali, M., Vernadat, F.: Formal Verification of AADL Specifications in the Topcased Environment. In: Kordon, F., Kermarrec, Y. (eds.) Ada-Europe 2009. LNCS, vol. 5570, pp. 207–221. Springer, Heidelberg (2009)
14. Passerone, R., de Alfaro, L., Henzinger, T., Sangiovanni-Vincentelli, A.L.: Convertibility Verification and Converter Synthesis: Two Faces of the Same Coin. In: Proceedings of the International Conference on Computer Aided Design, ICCAD 2002 (2002)

Finding δ-Closure Property of BitTorrent System and Applications Based on This Property

Wang Kun[1,2,3], Sha Ying[2], Tan Jian-long[2], Guo Li[2], and Li yang[2]

[1] School of Computer Science, Beijing University of Post and Telecommunication,
Beijing, China
[2] Institute of Computing Technology, Institute of Information Engineering,
National Engineering Laboratory for Information Security Technologies Beijing, China
[3] Key Laboratory of Trustworthy Distributed Computing and Service (BUPT),
Ministry of Education, Beijing, China
wangkunbupt@gmail.com

Abstract. In the Peer-to-peer (P2P) field, a basic problem is to build a model which can exactly represent the behaviors of peers. According to the protocols of BitTorrent (BT) system, participating peers are selected randomly when downloading some content. However, by using the connection model gathered during a one-month period, we found that the BT peers are subject to the δ-closure property, which is that the content in one δ-closure tends to spread inside this δ-closure. In this paper, we defined δ-closure according to the complex network theory. Then we tried to design algorithm to attain δ -closure. By gathered dataset, we verified the existing of δ-closure in BT system. Finally, we proposed possible applications based on this property.

Keywords: BitTorrent, δ- closure, behavior model.

1 Introduction

With the features of openness, high dynamics, self-organization, large-scale and node heterogeneity, the security of network application systems presents new characteristics and needs. One of the main reason is the behavior models of peers in P2P networks is very different from the traditional model. Therefore, building a model which can accurately represent the behaviors of peers becomes fundamental problem for the research in P2P networks.

Only by understanding the characteristics of the behavior of peers in P2P network systems, we can obtain the attack methods against the characteristics of behavior model in P2P network, and propose corresponding defending methods.

There are lots of researches on the features and behaviors model of P2P networks. Some of them derive network features and characteristics of the behaviors of peers by direct measurement [1、2、3].Iosup[5] observed a BT network for several months and analyzed the location, time model and relationship between users, and data demonstrated that BT shared content shows multi-level local characteristics. Others studied P2P network attacks, taking advantage of the infectious disease mode. Lee[4]

Y. Yuan, X. Wu, and Y. Lu (Eds.): ISCTCS 2012, CCIS 320, pp. 530–538, 2013.
© Springer-Verlag Berlin Heidelberg 2013

analyzed the transmission patterns of a single version file, and derived "exit rate" threshold guaranteeing successful transmission.

The behavior model of P2P nodes is the basic work in the field of P2P networks. Establishing a model which accurately describes the intent and implication of the node's behavior is extremely important for the in-depth research of P2P network. Previous papers concentrated on the behavior of the nodes in a single torrent or multiple torrents environment using; the theories of small world, points and cut vertical to describe the interaction characteristics between nodes. However, when a certain number of nodes participate in downloading the shared content, it also contains the semantic understanding in shared content for each node.

By using the connection model collected during a one-month period, we found that the BT peers are subject to the δ-closure property, which is that the content in one δ-closure tends to spread inside this δ-closure. In this paper, we defined δ-closure according to the complex network theory. Then we tried to design algorithm to attain δ-closure. By collected actual data, we verified the existing of δ-closure in BT system. Finally, we proposed possible applications based on this property.

This paper is organized as follows: Section 2 gives the definition and extraction algorithm of δ-closure; Section 3 verifies the existence of δ-closure property in BT network by analyzing experiment data; Section 4 shows the possible applications of δ-closure property in P2P network security; Section 5 summarizes this paper and proposes future research.

2   Definition of δ-Closure and Extraction Algorithm

2.1   Peer Network G

The δ-closure is defined upon the abstract weighted undirected peer network G = (V 、 Q、 E、 P), where V is the set of peers, each peer has a weight which form the vector Q; E is the set of edges, the weight of edges forms vector P.

A swarm forms a group downloading the same content, while all the swarms constitute the entire P2P network. The calculation of the edge weight indicates that these two peers not only appear in the same swarm at the same time, but also indicates the occurrence interaction between corresponding to edge weight add 1.The process above can be summarized as δ-closure network statistical algorithms, shown in Algorithm 1.

- **Normalization of Q :** Let the sum of all peers' weight be 1, which is given by:

$$\sum_{i=1}^{|V|} Q_i = 1 \tag{1}$$

- **Normalization of P :** Let the sum of the weight of all the edges starting from each peer be 1, which can be expressed as::

$$\sum_{j=1}^{|V|} P_{ij} = 1, \quad i = 1,2,\cdots,|V| \tag{2}$$

Table 1. Statistic algorithms of node network G

	statistic algorithms of node network G
Data preparation:	First, build BitTorrent network distributed crawling system. For each swarm, acquire corresponding peers and the connections between these peers.
input	The peers and the connections between these peers in multi swarms.
output	Peer network G=(V,Q,E,P)
steps:	1. Set V and E null, reset the elements in Q and P
	2. Read a swarm from the input and get the peers inside,which are denoted as V=(V$_1$,V$_2$,...,V$_n$),Mark q_i as the appearance number of V$_i$
	3. $V \cup v \rightarrow V$
	4. $Q(v_i) + q_i \rightarrow Q(v_i)$ $i = 1,2,\cdots,n$
	5. Obtain edge e in this swarm. Let p_{ij} be the appearance number of e_{ij}
	6. $E \cup e \rightarrow E$
	7. $P(v_i,v_j) + p_{ij} \rightarrow P(v_i,v_j) \rightarrow P(v_j,v_i)$ $1 \le i < j \le n$
	8. If the input is null, outputing G; otherwise go to step 2.

2.2 The Definition of δ-Closure

In node network G, P defines a Markov process on a V, that is, the probability from node V$_i$ to node V$_j$ (i.e., conditional probability) is denoted by P $_{Vi-Vj}$, it can be expressed formally as:

$$P_{v_i \rightarrow v_j} = P(v_j | v_i) = P_{ij} \tag{3}$$

According to matrix multiplication, the transferred probability from node V$_i$ to V$_j$ after t steps is P$^t_{ij}$, that is:

$$P^t_{v_i \rightarrow v_j} = P^t_{ij} \tag{4}$$

The δ-closure is a subset of V named S, S has the following properties: (1) it should be sparse between two δ-closures; (2) it should be compact inside one δ-closure.

The node in S should meet certain tightness, which can be characterized by the random walk in P. Specifically, starting from any node in S; the probability of backing S after t steps is not less than δ. While describing this kind of tightness, we should take into account of the size of δ-closure, namely this kind of tightness surpassing it in random network.

Assume that the network G is random, then any transition probability between two any nodes is $\frac{1}{|V|}$, the δ-closure in such networks should be inconspicuous. For a subset of V which named S, it should be more tight than random network to be a δ-closure. Note start from any node in S, the probability of backing S after t steps is not less than δ$_1$, if the node network is random network , note it be δ$_2$,then δ$_1$-δ$_2$ should be larger than δ given.

Definition 1: （δ-closure） δ-closure in node network G is the non-null subset of V named S which meet the following function:

$$P^t_{u \to S} - \frac{|S|}{|V|} \geq \delta \quad \forall u \in S \tag{5}$$

$P^t_{u \to S}$ is the transition probability starting from u to the set S after t steps, calculated by the following function:

$$P^t_{u \to S} = P(S/u) = \sum_{v \in S} P(v/u) = \sum_{v \in S} P^t_{u \to v} \tag{6}$$

$P^t_{u \to v}$ is defined in formula 4. Parameter δ determines the tightness of δ-closure-The larger δ is, the tighter δ-closure will be. The size of δ can be adjusted according to actual situation. T is the number of transfer steps, usually subject to discrete distribution, then

$$P^t_{u \to v} = \sum_{k} P(t = k) P^k_{u \to v} \tag{7}$$

Where t is a random variable, k is non-negative integer.

2.3   Extraction Algorithm of δ- Closure

According to definition (1), we can define a 0-1 program to attain maximal δ- closure

$$\max \sum_{i=1}^{|V|} x_i$$

$$\text{s.t} \begin{cases} \sum_{j=1}^{|V|} x_j P^t_{ij} - \frac{1}{|V|} \sum_{j=1}^{|V|} x_j \geq (\delta + 1) x_i - 1 & i = 1, 2, \cdots, |V| \\ x_i \in (0, 1) \end{cases} \tag{8}$$

By solving (8), the maximum δ- closure in node network G can be calculated. After all the nodes in the current δ- closure are obtained, these nodes can be removed from the network. Then all the δ- closure can be obtained by solving (8) iteratively. The methods of removing all the nodes in existing δ- closure can be either removing directly or removing indirectly by adding constraints to the optimization problem.

Table 2. Extraction algorithm of δ- closure

	extraction algorithm of δ- closure
input :	Node network G= （V,Q,E,P）,parameter δ, distribution t
output :	S (all δ- closure)
steps :	1. Obtain transition probability matrix P in distribution t by formula 7
	2. By solving 0-1 program 8, attain s(δ- closure).If δ- closure is null, exit and output S.
	3. $S \cup \{s\} \rightarrow S$, remove s from G,go to step 2

The 0-1 programming (7) is NP-complete. The GLPK package can solve the problem but the efficiency is low. There is lots of community discovery algorithms in complex network theory, whose function is similar to the derivation of δ- closure. Therefore, δ- closure algorithm can be replaced by community discovery algorithms temporarily.

In community discovery, it usually use community module index Q as the parameters to describe the strength of community characteristics, which can be defined as blows [10]:

$$Q = \frac{1}{2m} \sum_{ij} \left(A_{ij} - \frac{k_i k_j}{2m} \right) \delta(C_i, C_j) \qquad (9)$$

Where k_i and k_j is the degree of nodes, C_i is the community which i belongs to, m is the total number of edges in network. If $C_i=C_j, \delta(C_i,C_j)=1$ otherwise $C_i=C_j, \delta(C_i,C_j)=0$. The value of Q is between 0 and 1, generally taking Q=0.3 as the lower bound for community structure exist in a network.

The modularity optimization is a NP difficulty, the time complexity of its specific algorithm is relatively high. Now there are lots of improvement algorithms based on modularization. For example, [11] proposed an algorithm named BGLL which can detect hierarchical community structure.

The basic methods of BGLL is : firstly make each node as an independent community, and then calculate the module gain of corresponding community when one node join the neighbors' community, selecting the maximum gains community to join, otherwise remain in the initial community. Repeat this procedure to divide first level community. And then construct a new network, the nodes of this network is in the first level community, then divide the network by the algorithm in stage 1. By that analogy, algorithm BGLL generate a hierarchical community structure

BGLL has the following characteristics: high speed, suitable for large-scale weighted network; bottom-up approach, never miss small-scale community.

3   The δ- Closure Property in BT Network

By the BT network data collected in one-month period, we obtain the connections from about 11,376 BT nodes. We research the BT δ- closure property using this information, what is that the node in one δ- closure tends to connect to the nodes inside this δ- closure rather than external nodes. We found that this property is formatted naturally. It indicates nodes group has the common interest to the shared content.

3.1 Data Set

The data set is obtained by collecting the BT nodes in November 2010 in a period of one-month, which is distinguished by the IP. The information collected includes node IP, connections information between nodes, the connection holding time and so on. According to the BT protocol, two nodes connected means they have the common interest content, but this data set does not include shared content between nodes.

A total number of11376 nodes were noted in the data set, an average of 2987 nodes and 11,076 connections online daily, as shown in Figure1:

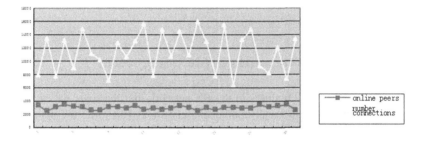

Fig. 1. The average nodes and connections online on observation days

3.2 The Extraction of δ- Closure

Usually, in Social networks (such as facebook, kaixin, etc.), it is up on the individual to decide whom to be connect. Therefore, the individuals often form community according to adjacent location in the past or now, or belonging to the same organization because of their common interest. In the network, it shows as the interconnections between the nodes of the same community is much more intensive than the random connections. [9,10]

Compared to social networks, many nodes in P2P network, including BT system, rely on the fixed protocol to establish connections, usually randomly selecting nodes from a certain number of qualified node pools. This feature may lead people misunderstand that the δ- closure property in P2P network is not significant. However, similar to social networks, the connection established in two nodes in P2P networks means they have the common interest. Particularly in BT, the connection established in two nodes proved these nodes at least interest in one shared content.

Using the extraction algorithm described in section 2, according to the roughly partition in current P2P shared file downloading methods-we extract about 10 δ- closure. It shows that the roughly common interest in downloading is sufficient to the

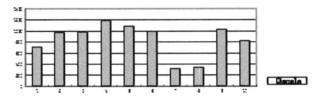

Fig. 2. The scale of 10 δ- closure on one day

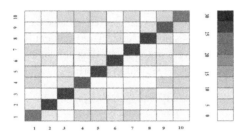

Fig. 3. The comparison of the connection density

formation of the δ- closure features in the BT network, but the scale for each δ- clo-sure is very different, the minimal number is only about 100 while the maximal can reach thousands. Figure 2 shows the scale of these 10 δ- closure on a day.

Using the data collected during the 3rd week, the δ- closure inside can be ex-tracted. Figure 3 shows the differences in connection density between the nodes inside the same δ- closure and in different δ- closure. From Figure 3, we know that the connection density in the nodes inside the same δ- closure is much higher than it in different δ- closure. It means some kind of common interest in downloading is suffi-cient to form powerful δ- closure property. It also proved the semantic information included in shared downloading content in δ- closure.

4   The Security Applications Based on δ- Closure Property

This paper provides a theoretical basis for the relevant attack. By extracting and analyzing the δ-closure property in BT network. It indicates that a strong correlation between nodes exists by the common interest in shared content, which can be de-scribed accurately by δ- closure.

The δ-closure property accurately depicts the dynamic feature in interaction between the nodes in P2P network, reflecting the evolution process of BT network. Based on δ- closure property, it is more precise to determine the coverage rate, the life cycle and the expansion of the resources.

The δ-closure property makes it more targeted to the pollution attack on P2P network. Based on δ-closure property, the pollution attack to some resources or themes can be achieved. Moreover, it can provide theoretical support to prove the effects of pollution spreading as well as the effects of preventing the spread.

With δ-closure theory, it is known that some content spread between some relatively fixed nodes with a great probability. It constitutes community which similar to the social network community between these nodes. If the connection between this δ-closure and the δ-closure outside can be cut off, the corresponding content can be restricted in a certain area and prevent its further spread, through the density comparison between the connections inside the δ-closure and outside above, we know this method is feasible. It belongs to P2P network division attack.

5   Conclusion

A model which can describe the behavior between nodes accurately is crucial in the research on P2P networks. According to the BitTorrent protocol, participating peers are selected randomly when downloading shared content. However, by observing the BitTorrent networks during a one-month period, we found that the BT peers are subject to the δ -closure property, which is that the content in one δ -closure tends to spread inside this δ -closure. The definition of δ -closure and the extraction algorithm is given. And the experimental data support the result of theoretical analysis: basically δ -closure can associate with some content or some kind of content, reflecting the common interest and behavioral characteristics of nodes while downloading.

Future work lines in: 1.Currently, the extraction algorithm for δ-closure is dividing, there is no overlap between δ-closure. The overlap between δ-closure reflects some semantic cross in different content. 2. The information of torrent seeds turned into the form of δ-closure. By matching to the δ-closure, we can query the content and participate nodes directly.

Acknowledgements. This research was supported by The National Natural   Science Foundation of China(61070184), the   "Strat egic Priority Research Program" of the Chinese Academy of Sciences，Grant No.XDA06030200,and National High Technology Research   and Development Program 863 No. 2011AA010705.

References

1. Choffnes, D.R., Bustamante, F.E.: Taming the torrent: A practical approach to reducing cross-ISP traffic in peer-to-peer systems. In: Proc. of ACM SIGCOMM (August 2008)
2. Gummadi, K.P., Dunn, R.J., Saroiu, S., Gribble, S.D., Levy, H.M., Zahorjan, J.: Measurement, modeling, and analysis of a peer-to-peer file-sharing workload. In: Proc. of the ACM (SOSP 2003), pp. 314–329 (2003)
3. Piatek, M., Isdal, T., Anderson, T., Krishanamurthy, A., Venkataramani, A.: Do incentives build robustness in bittorrent. In: Proc. of USENIX NSDI (April 2007)
4. Lee, U., Choi, M., Cho, J., Sanadidi, M.Y., Gerla, M.: Understanding Pollution Dynamics in P2P File Sharing. In: Proc. of IPTPS 2006 (February 2006)
5. Iosup, A., Garbacki, P., Pouwelse, J.A., Epema, D.H.J.: Analyzing BitTorrent: Three Lessons from One Peer-Level View, PeerLevel View. In: Proc. 11 th ASCI Conf.

6. Qiu, D., Srikant, R.: Modeling and performance analysis of BitTorrent-like peer-to-peer networks. In: ACM SIGCOMM Conference 2004, Portland, Oregon, USA, pp. 367–378 (2004)
7. Guo, L., Chen, S., Xiao, Z., Tan, E., Ding, X., Zhang, X.: A performance study of BitTorrent-like peer-to-peer systems. IEEE Journal on Seclected Areas in Communications 25(1) (January 2007)
8. Arenas, A., Danon, L., Dfaz-Guilera, A., Gleiser, P.M., Guimera, R.: Community analysis in social networks. Eur: Phys. J. B 38, 373–380 (2004)
9. Wasserman, S., Faust, K.: Social Network Analysis. Cambridge University Press, Cambridge (1994)
10. Newman, M.E.J., Girvan, M.: Finding and evaluating community structure in networks. Phys. Rev. E 69(2), 026113 (2004)
11. Blondel, V.D., Guillaume, J.L., Lambiotte, R., et al.: Fast unfolding of community hierarchies in large networks. Journal of Statistical Mechanics: Theory and Experiment 10, 10008 (2008)

A Tool to Construct One Comprehensive Legal Environment for Behavioral Incompatible Components

Jizhou Zhao[1,2], Jiangwei Li[1,2], Yan Zhang[3], and Tian Zhang[1,2]

[1] State Key Laboratory for Novel Software Technology, Nanjing University, Najing, China
[2] Department of Computer Science and Technology, Nanjing University,
Nanjing, China
{ljw,zjz}@seg.nju.edu.cn, ztluck@nju.edu.cn
[3] Department of Computer Science and Technology,
Beijing Electronic Science and Technology Institute, Beijing, China
zhangyan@besti.edu.cn

Abstract. Behavioral incompatibility in component compositions is an important problem in the field of component-based software development. To solve this problem, one approach is to construct an environment in which the incompatible components can work together. So we write this tool, which uses the interface automata to model the behavior of components, to derive available behaviors all out from two incompatible component compositions and construct a comprehensive legal environment for them. This paper presents all the details of our tool, including the main steps, the core algorithm and the analysis of efficiency. A case-study is also illustrated showing the validity and practicability of our tool.

Keywords: components composition, behavioral incompatibility, interface automata, comprehensive legal environment.

1   Introduction

Component[9-11] reuse is commonly known as a valid and practicable measure to efficiently develop high quality software at a low cost [1]. By using components as reusable building blocks, we can rapidly and economically attain reliable, flexible, extensible and evolvable systems [2].

Component composition is one of the major problems of component-based software development [7-8]. Behavioral incompatibility, related to the problem we concern in this paper, is one issue of component composition. The meaning of behavioral incompatibility is that between two composed components no message will ever be sent by one, whose reception hasn't been anticipated in the design of the other [3].

We developed this tool to solve the behavioral incompatibility problem, in the approach of constructing one environment for the incompatible components, in which they can work together without any error. In detail, firstly we compose two incompatible components together. Secondly, the valid transition set is derived. Thirdly, according to the valid transition set, we construct one comprehensive legal

Y. Yuan, X. Wu, and Y. Lu (Eds.): ISCTCS 2012, CCIS 320, pp. 539–546, 2013.

environment, such that two incompatible components can work together and the behaviors of their composition can be preserved as much as possible.

We use interface automata [4] to model the behavior of components, and the products of the interface automata to represent the compositions of components, as the optimistic approach in the interface automata theory suits to our problem to be solved. The optimistic approach [5] here, different from the pessimistic approach [6], means that two components are seen as compatible if there exist an environment for them to work together without any error. Based on the optimistic approach, interface automata make the problem easier [3].

Although we have settled the behavioral incompatibility problem to some extent, this tool is not able to model the behavior of components into interface automata by itself. Likewise, the comprehensive legal environment we get from the tool cannot be mapped to the original component automatically. In other words, the support offered by our tool to derive available behaviors is limited to the operations on the interface automata modeling the behavior of original components.

This tool is developed in the language of JAVA with Eclipse and has to run under the environment of JVM.

2   Overview

Our tool is consisted of four modules as followed: the Input Module, which allows user to import two interface automata. The Compose Module, which composes the two interface automata together. The Delete Module, which deletes the illegal states and derives the valid transition set. The Environment Module, which deals with the transitions of the valid transition set and constructs one comprehensive legal environment.

Only thing for user to do is to input their interface automata, the tool will handle the rest. Click the output button and the results are already there to be seen.

Figure 1 shows the interaction of four main modules. The arrows in the figure show how the data go.

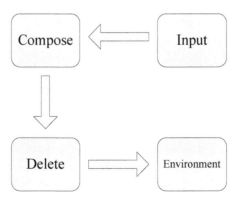

Fig. 1. The interaction of four main modules

3   Approach

In this section, most of concepts about interface automata refer to [4] and the main algorithm refers to [3].

We view the interface automata as a graph to simplify the operation and make it easier to be understood. To express the graph, we choose adjacency list as the main data structure. Each state of the interface automata corresponds to a vertex of the graph. Each transition of the interface automaton corresponds to an edge of the graph. The action of each transition corresponds to the weight of the related edge of the graph.

As is mentioned above, four modules build up the main part of our tool. In this section, we will discuss the details of Compose Module, Delete Module and Environment Module.

3.1   The Compose Module

After getting the two input automata, we can start to compose. Before that, whether the two automata can be composed or not should be taken into consideration. Two interface automata are composable only if they don't share the same input action or output action and any internal action of one automaton cannot be the action of another one. We write a method named "canBeComposed" to determine.

If the two interface automata are composable, the next step we do is to calculate their product, which seems to be the composed interface automata. However, the product is not the final result that we want. In order to facilitate the operation later, only states that can be reached from the initial state are valid. To pick out the valid states, we put the transitions of the product into an array-list. Then start from the initial state, we traverse the array-list through every possible path that can be reached. Those paths can be split into the valid transitions of the composed interface automaton.

With the valid transitions, we can rebuild the composed interface automaton in adjacency list. The states of the composed interface automaton are the states that valid transitions go through. The actions of the composed interface automaton are the actions of valid transitions plus the non-enabled actions of the original two interface automata.

3.2   The Delete Module

The Compose Module already gives out the composed interface automaton of the two input interface automata in the form of adjacency list. The next step is to derive the valid transition set. In the Delete Module, we will handle this problem.

First of all, we should try to find all the illegal states. Suppose there are two interface automata P and Q. In their composition P×Q, illegal states are those at which one interface automaton cannot accept the input action provided by the other interface automaton. We write a method named "findIllegalStates" to do this job. As long as those illegal states exist, the two interface automata are behaviorally compatible. Our target in this module is to remove the illegal states.

The composed interface automaton is expressed by adjacency list. For the purpose of convenience, first we should transform adjacency list into inverse adjacency list. The method "list2inlist" is designed for the transaction. Then we start from one illegal state, along output actions and internal actions, find all the states that can be arrived. Delete those states as well as the path related. Keep repeating until there is no illegal state left. Use method "list2inlist" to transform the inverse adjacency list left into adjacency-list form, which is the valid transition set we need.

3.3   The Environment Module

To complete transformation from AADL models to IA models, Table 1 has given the main mapping rules from AADL to IA.

Having derived the valid transition set, the last and the most complicated step is to deal with the transactions of the valid transition set and to construct the comprehensive legal environment.

If the valid state transition is empty, we can say that the comprehensive legal environment doesn't exist. Else, according to the algorithm referring to [4], there are four rules to construct the transitions of the comprehensive legal environment.

Suppose transition T starts from state X and ends in state Y along with the action A.

Rule 1: if X and Y is one same state, the corresponding transition of the comprehensive legal environment shall start from one state and end in the same state, too.

Rule 2: if there exists one path which starts from Y, ends in the initial state and each action is an internal action, then the corresponding state of Y shall be the initial state in the comprehensive legal environment.

Rule 3: if the corresponding state of Y in the comprehensive legal environment doesn't exist, create a new state and make it be the corresponding state of Y.

Rule 4: if the action A is an internal action, the corresponding transition shall be changed into one single state.

We traverse the transitions of the valid transition set in the way of depth-first and construct corresponding transition according to the rules mentioned above. All the corresponding transitions constitute the comprehensive legal environment.

4   Case Study

This section presents a case study of the construction of two interface automata from [3].

First we open the input interface and import two interface automata. Figure 2 shows the illustration of the interface automaton Comp and Figure 3   shows its adjacency list.

Suppose there are two sides named A and B. The interface automaton Comp describes a component behavior, which receives a message from side A (msg) and then sends the message to side B (send). If the first trial is failed, send again. After sending the message up to twice, a confirmation from B will be received. If the confirmation is "ack", which means B has received the message successfully, a new action "ok" will send information to A to announce the success. If the confirmation is "nack", which means B fails to receive the message, a new action "fail" will send information to A to announce the failure.

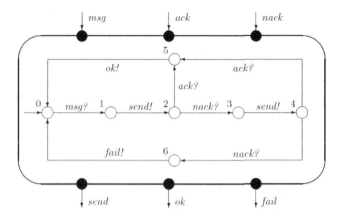

Fig. 2. The Comp in the IA form

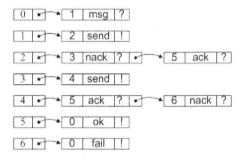

Fig. 3. The Comp in the adjacency-list form

Figure 4 shows the illustration of the interface automaton Client as well as its adjacency list.

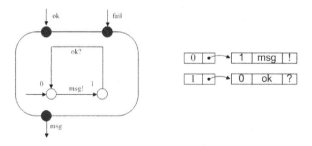

Fig. 4. The Client

The interface automaton Client uses the Comp to send messages to one side and always expects a successful transmission, which means the Client only deals with the information send by the "ok" action announcing success and ignores the other action. It is obvious that the action "fail" is not enabled on the state 1, so the two interface automata are behavioral incompatible.

After the operation of composition, we can get a new interface automaton. Figure 5 shows the illustration of the composed automaton.

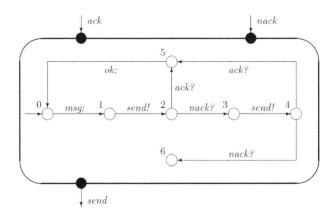

Fig. 5. The composition of Client and Comp in the IA form

We can see that the state 6 is an illegal state, since the action "fail" is not enabled on the state 1 in the Client. In the valid state set, we delete the state 6 and the paths leading to it.

It is easy to tell that there exists a comprehensive legal environment for the composed interface automaton of the Client and the Comp as the valid transition set is not empty. So we can start to traverse the transitions of the valid transition set in the way of depth-first. The first transition is (0, msg, 1). According to rule 3, we create a state 0 in the comprehensive legal environment to correspond state 0 and state 1. Then we come to the second transition (1, send, 2). According to rule 1, we create a corresponding transition (0, send, 1) in the comprehensive legal environment. The third transition is (2, nack, 3). According to rule 1, we create a corresponding transition (1, nack, 2). Similarly, the transition (3, send, 4) corresponds to the transition (2, send, 3) in the comprehensive legal environment. When it comes to transition (4, ack, 5), we use rule 2 to create the corresponding transition (3, ack, 4). And so we can construct the comprehensive legal environment little by little.

Figure 6 shows the illustration of the comprehensive legal environment we construct as well as its adjacency list.

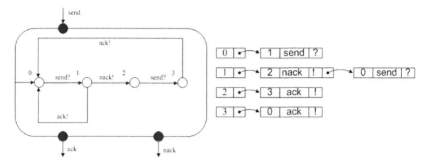

Fig. 6. The environment

Figure 7 shows the interface of the tool when we are running the case mentioned above.

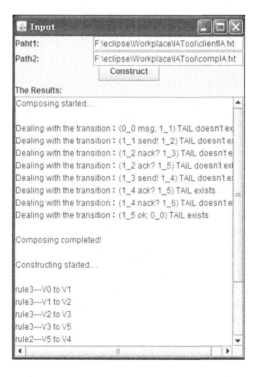

Fig. 7. The interface of the tool

5   Analysis

In this section we will discuss the efficiency of the main algorithm.

Suppose there is one interface automaton R. The amount of states of R is Vr and the amount of transitions of R is Tr.

The time complexity of deriving the states of the valid state set is apparently $O(Vr)$. And the time complexity of deleting related paths to get the valid transition is $O(Tr)$. The time complexity of constructing the comprehensive legal environment is proportional to the square of Vr. However, in most situations, there will not be a transition between every two states. So the time complexity of constructing the comprehensive legal environment can be $O(Tr)$.

So the time complexity of the whole algorithm is $O(Vr+2Tr)$. Normally Vr is far less than Tr so the time complexity can be $O(Tr)$.

Acknowledgment. This work is supported by the National Natural Science Foundation of China (No.61003025, 91118002), and by the Jiangsu Province Research Foundation (BK2010170).

References

1. Yang, F., Zhu, B., Mei, H.: Sofeware Resuse. Journal of Sofeware 6(9), 525–533 (1995)
2. Heineman, G.T., Councill, W.T.: Componet-Based Software Engineering: Putting the Pieces Together. Addison-Wesley, Boston (2001)
3. Zhang, Y., Hu, J., Yu, X., Zhang, T., Li, X., Zheng, G.: Deriving Available Behavior All Out from Incompatible Component Compositions. In: Proceedings of the 2nd International Workshop on Formal Aspects of Component Software (FACS 2005). Electronic Notes in Theoretical Computer Science, vol. 160, pp. 349–361. Elsevier (2006)
4. de Alfaro, L., Henzinger, T.A.: Interface Automata. In: Proceedings of 9th Annual ACM Symposium on Foundations of Software Engineering (FSE 2001), pp. 109–120. ACM Press, New York (2001)
5. de Alfaro, L., Henzinger, T.A.: Interface Automata. In: Proceedings of the 9th Annual ACM Symposium on Foundations of Software Engineering (FSE 2001), pp. 109–120. ACM Press, New York (2001)
6. Allen, R., Garlan, D.: A Formal Basis for Architectural Connection. ACM Transactions on Software Engineering and Methodology 6, 69–90 (1997)
7. Pfleeger, S.L.: Software Engineering: Theory and Practice, 2nd edn. Pearson Prentice Hall, Upper Saddle River (2001)
8. Pressman, R.S.: Software Engineering: A Practitioner's Approach, 5th edn. McGraw-Hill, New York (2001)
9. Councill, B., Heineman, G.T.: Definition of a Software Component and Its Elements. In: Componet-Based Software Engineering: Putting the Pieces Together, pp. 5–19
10. Szyperski, C.: Component Software and the Way Ahead. In: Foundations of Component-based Systems, pp. 1–20
11. Pfister, C., Szyperski, C.: Why Object Are Not Enough. In: Jell, T. (ed.) Proceedings of the 1st International Component Users Conference, pp. 141–147. Cambridge University Press, Cambridge (1998)

Research of Security Relationship Based on Social Networks

Li Yang[1,2,3,4], Wang Xiaoyan[4], Sha Ying[4], and Tan Jian-long[4]

[1] Institute of Computing Technology, Chinese Academy of Sciences, Beijing, China
[2] Graduate School of Chinese Academy of Sciences, Beijing, China
[3] College of Computer Science and Information Engineering, Central South University
of Forestry and Technology, Changsha, China
[4] Institute of Information Engineering, National Engineering Laboratory for Information
Security Technologies, Chinese Academy of Sciences, Beijing, China
leoncs2000@gmail.com

Abstract. This paper introduces the security problems of social networks and the research topics of core nodes, relationship, structures of social network, and so on. This paper discusses the importance of "security relationship" in social networks, analyzes the relevance between security risks and events, and adopts the qualitative and quantitative mechanism based on grade partition, numerical measure, polymorphic data fusion, and the logical relevance. Based on Bayesian network, this paper proposes a kind of assessment model for the situation of security relationship in social networks so as to provide theoretical bases for the perception and prediction of security situation in social networks.

Keywords: social networks, security relationship, situation assessment, Bayesian network.

1   Introduction

With the rapid development of newer media and its applications, people have took part in the abundant social affairs increasingly through internet, for example, people pay attention to the latest information of their friends from Twitter and Sina weibo, or making good friends and playing interactive games on Facebook or Renren. In recent years, the growth trend of users in social networks is shown in Table 1.

Table 1. Growth Trend of Users in Social Network

	2009	2010	2011	2012
Twitter	0.058billion	0.175billion	0.415billion	0.5billion
Facebook	0.34billion	0.6billion	0.845billion	1billion
Weibo	0.075billion	0.1billion	0.25billion	0.3billion
RenRen	0.08billion	0.117billion	0.137billion	0.16billion

Y. Yuan, X. Wu, and Y. Lu (Eds.): ISCTCS 2012, CCIS 320, pp. 547–554, 2013.
© Springer-Verlag Berlin Heidelberg 2013

(1)Current Security Problems

Currently a large number of researchers, although sufficient analysis and re-searches of social network, have got a lot of beneficial results, the following serious security problems still exist.

①Internet Fraud: Based on the increasing risks of social network phishing fraud, according to the 360 anti-phishing system sampling survey[1] : 2011, the ratio of the fishing websites that make use of social networks has reached 15.7%.

② Privacy Leak: As for the privacy issues behind the social networks, according to the latest survey from the security software company Webroot [2], the users of social networks suffer security threats more easily, such as the loss of financial infor-mation, the stealing of identity information, the infection of malware and so on.

③ The Dissemination of Malicious Information (Rumors): Rumors have existed since ancient times, but networks has changed the spreading ecological of rumors, from "circulate erroneous reports" to "well-founded facts", from "mouth-to-mouth" to "spreading as virus", all kinds of Internet rumors emerge and spread rapidly, such as "the salt robbing disturbance" during the period of the earthquake in Japan, they spread rapidly in the way of geometric explosion.

④ Group events on Networks: Through the application of the prominent mobiliza-tion function of social networks, it is easy to cause malignant group events. With strong properties of new media, social networking sites, micro-blog and social com-munication business, are easy to be used by evildoer, spread false information, and incite malignant group events.

(2)The Source of the Threat to Social Security

At present, the social security threat origins from three aspects [1]: ① The large num-ber of users. ②The development of social business. ③Friends-trusting relationship.

This paper is organized as follows: it introduces the current security problems of the social networks in Chapter1, and the Chapter2 focuses on what the security relation-ship face; in Chapter3 it describes the cur-rent research situation of the relationship between social networks; the Chapter4 puts forward the assessment of framework based on the social network security; and the Chapter5 is a summary of the full text.

2   The Problems of Security Relationship in Social Networks

For the problems resulting from the security of social networks, based on the impor-tant role as a bridge that the friend relationship plays, but at present the researches on security are lack of the following considerations.

(1) Security Relationship in Social Networks

The social networks are developing rapidly, bringing many security problems, such as the fraud on networks, privacy protection, information theft, the dissemination of garbage information, phishing, worm attack and so on. These security problems emerge constantly. The researches always focus mainly on the mining and utilization of friends, colleagues, cooperation in the aspect of economy, but still lack of the in-fluence of security relationship in social networks.

(2) "Sub-Security State" of Current Network Structure

The node with a large number of followers (fans) in personal accounts in social networks is called the core node, which tends to be an opinion leader. Whether the frame relationship of links or the dissemination relationship of a specific topic, the core node with high authority influences the fans node strongly, and to some extent, it stands for security risks; When these key nodes are involved in the information-security problems intentionally or unintentionally, such as some internet fraud, privacy leak, malicious information and so on, the rapid dissemination of great influence and the cascading effect of key nodes is likely to lead to unexpected events, that is to say the social networks made up from these key nodes are in a certain extent of sub-security state.

(3) Security Assessment base on Quantitative and Qualitative Mechanism

Along with the deeply research of social network, it is also shortage of security assessment based on quantitative and qualitative mechanism. Although there are some local analysis, it is shortage of association between security risk and generated event, we can't establish an global probabilistic security assessment relying on the grade classification, numerical measure, multi-mode data integration, logical associations (non-mutual independence), and so on, which will cause us not to take measures timely to manage the emergency based on the security risk.

3   Research Status of Relationship in Social Network

This chapter deeply introduces the research status from the progressive view, contains the node relationship, strength relationship, structure relationship of communities and so on. Finally based on the formed structure relationship, we analyze the key nodes and its influence scale.

(1) Research of Nodes Relationship

In the social network, there are few friends one often interacts in the buddy list, and these points affect each other and connect with each other closely, this bi-directional group has the smallest percentage in the web social network, but it is a stable core contact group in the community. While the one-way contact and passive contact accounts for from 2/3 to 3/4 of the total contact, and such contact is mostly established accidentally and is very unstable [3].

(2) Research of Social Network Relationship

The social network can be divide into two parts based the strength of the relationship: ①Strong relationship: such as Facebook, Renren, kaixin001, LinkedIn, Pengyou. ② Weak relationship: such as Twitter, Sina Weibo.

(3) Research of Structure Relationship in Social Network

The important character of web social networks is the community structure of the network, this structure can be denoted a social network with weighted graph. Therefore we introduce some chief algorithms as follow: ①graph partition method[4-7], ②sociology method, ③divided method[8],④overlapping community detection[9].

(4) Research of Key Nodes and Its Influence Scale

①Find the Key Nodes: The early authority node discovery and links are the Page-Rank [11] and the HITS [12]. At present, the core node of networks is mainly found in the following ways: measuring the importance of nodes based on the static parameter of social network analysis[13], and GBMFS [14], SPLINE[15], LeaderRank [16].

②Dissemination Scale of Node's Influence: The problem of dissemination scale in the social network need to depend on the corresponding dissemination model, the mainly dissemination models are the linear threshold model and independent cascade model[17][18]. There are other models such as: Comprehensive cascade diffuse model[19], SIR model[20], Bass model[21], Vote model[22], and so on.

4   Assessment Model of Security Relationship Based on Social Network

This chapter can be divided two parts. One part is the qualitative analysis of security and association analysis with the event tracing, another is based on the quantitative research of the security relationship, and the multi-mode system probabilistic security assessment model based on Bayesian network.

4.1   Security Risk Research and Event Tracing Analysis

In the research of social network's relationship, by distinguishing the security relationship, we develop the hierarchical and numerical measure for the security risk from the node relationship and structure relationship.

(1)Analysis of the Security Relationship among the Nodes:
As for the security relationship, that is to say the events generated or associated by two nodes, which can be taken into account from two points: one is the node, another is the edge. We mainly focus the two kinds of nodes: hidden danger node and dangerous node. We collectively called "Key node", the hidden danger node is the node which hasn't the association with the security problems but holding the great influence, as soon as which take part in the internet fraud, privacy leaks and spam dissemination, the destructive power is very maximum; the dangerous node is the node which have different scales influence, but associate with security problems closely. The edge can be used to describe the associated events, one is the general event, another is the security event (grade classification). Then the edge associated the events and the key nodes can constitute the important "security relationship" for us to research. As for the key nodes and constructed social network with its neighbor nodes, which can generate the security behavior by edge and disseminate its influence by the network, and finally bring great detriment to the security of social network.

(2)Structure Relationship Constituted by Social network
The nodes of social network can constitute the different communities, that is to say the entire network is constituted by the divers communities. We plan to adopt the agglomerative hierarchical clustering method to find the multi-scale communities in the social network, combine the hidden danger nodes and dangerous nodes, analyze the communities and security of the social network.

(3)Find Key Nodes

The discrepancy and influence among with the nodes in social net-work is the focus of our research, which is the status of node in the network. We plan to adopt the assessment rule of combining the influence measure and associated information, search Top-k Key nodes by virtue of greedy algorithm.

(4)Dissemination Scale of Key Nodes

Based on the main dissemination models: linear threshold model and independent cascade model, we can compute the dissemination scale of the hidden danger node and dangerous node in the social net-work.

(5)Tracing of Key Node based on Security

As for the special security problem in social network, we can grade the extent of security problem, with the help of the path tracing, find the associated nodes on this trace, till we find the source node. Then by combining the key nodes, we can make a study of the grade, influence, dissemination scale and special behavior information among with these nodes.

4.2   Computation, Assessment and Analysis of the Situation on the Security Relationship

In the research of the assessment mechanism of security relationship in social networks, we primarily construct the logical associations among many factors which can influence the security relationship.

(1)Determine Objects Set and Factors Set

The objects set of influencing the security relationship situation=$\{F1, F2, F3, F4\}$=(Key nodes, community structure, dissemination scale, Keywords). As for the each object($F1$, $F2$, $F3$, $F4$),which can be assessed by the factor Xij from the next level, i=1, 2, 3, 4; j=1, 2, …, z; , z represents the amount of the next level of Fi. In this model:

$F1$=$\{X11$, $X12$, $X13$, $X14$, $X15\}$=$\{$degree, neighbor node, multi-channel association, security grade of hidden danger node, security grade of dangerous node$\}$;

$F2$=$\{X21$, $X22$, $X23$, $X24$, $X25$, $X26\}$=$\{$security grade of hidden danger node, security grade of dangerous node, amount of nodes, average path length, cluster coefficient, degree and degree distribution$\}$;

$F3$=$\{X31$, $X32$, $X33$, $X34$, $X35$, $X36\}$=$\{$security grade of hidden danger node, security grade of dangerous node, grade of influence scale, timeliness, IC model, LT model$\}$;

$F4$=$\{X41$, $X42$, $X43$, $X44$, $X45$, $X46$, $X47$, $X48$, $X49\}$=$\{$security grade of hidden danger node from tracing, security grade of dangerous node from tracing, amount of tracing nodes, grade of influence scale, amount of keywords, grade of sensibility, grade of tendentiousness, amount of retransmission, amount of review$\}$.

(2) Determine the Assessment set

As for the security assessment of key nodes in social networks, we strive to make the quantitative measurement on the basis of the integral security situation, therefore we can determine the five awareness levels of security (such as: green, blue, yellow, orange, red), as well as the corresponding score.

In this model, Assessment Set A=(A5，A4，A3，A2，A1)={Security, Inferior Security, Critical Value, Inferior Danger, Danger}={2，1，0，-1，-2}. As shown in table 2:

Table 2. Table of Assessment Grade

Grade of Security	Assessment	Measure
Green	Security	2
Blue	Inferior Security	1
Yellow	Critical Value	0
Orange	Inferior Danger	-1
Red	Danger	-2

Aiming at the five dangerous levels of table 2, we should be on guard against the latter levels.

(3)Determine the Weight of Assessment Index

This paper adopts the analytic hierarchy process based on the qualitative and quantitative mechanism so that we can determine the weight of each assessment index, the steps are as follows: establish hierarchy structure model, construct comparative matrix in pairs, compute the weight vector and consistency test, computer the combined weight vector and consistency test.

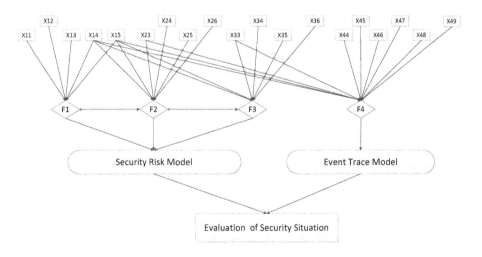

Fig. 1. A Security Relationship's Situation Assessment Model in Social Network based on Bayesian Network

(4)Establish the Multi-mode Systematic Probabilistic Security Assessment Model based on Bayesian Network

In this part, on the basis of Bayesian network, we can establish the model from the above information so as to assess the security situation from the following steps:

> Determine the nodes: Bayesian network is constituted by nodes, the nodes corresponds with different events, which are the Objects Set and Factors Set. That is to say it is the combination between the security risk model and the event-tracing model.
> Determine the relationship between nodes: after determining the content of node, we should determine the causative relationship and correlative relationship among the events so as to determine the structure of Bayesian network.
> Probability allocation: by measuring the factors of different events from analytic hierarchy process, we can allocate the probability on the basis of the weight influence, the causative relationship and the correlative relationship.
> Establish the probabilistic security assessment model based on the Bayesian network. (As shown in Fig 1)

Therefore, through the result from the probabilistic security assessment model and the relation of the table of assessment grade, we can judge the security grade of some community in social networks; Afterwards, by focusing on the specific security problems(such as internet fraud, privacy leaks and malicious information dissemination), we can find the key nodes or communities so as to take appropriate measures for the guarantee of the security of social networks.

5   Conclusion

This paper analyzes the security problems of social networks and the thinking and measurement based on security relationship, introduces the history and current situation of social networks, proposes a kind of assessment model for the situation of security relationship in social networks based on Bayesian network. Combining the qualitative with the quantitative mechanism, we compute, assess and analyze the security situation of social networks by researching on the security risks of the relationship in social networks and analyzing the relevance of the origins of events, which can provide theoretical bases and reference in reality for us to manage the security problems in social networks better.

Acknowledgements. This research was supported by The National Natural Science Foundation of China (61070184), the "Strategic Priority Research Program" of the Chinese Academy of Sciences , Grant No.XDA06030200, and National High Technology Research and Development Program 863 No. 2011AA010705.

References

1. 360 Internet Security College, Internet Security Report in China from 2011 to 2012:11-12 (in Chinese)
2. Kong, Q.: Research of Privacy Protection for Personal Information and Relationship of the Social Network, pp. 8–9. Zhejiang University of Technology (2011) (in Chinese)

3. Lei, W.: The Study of Community Discovery Method on Large-scale Social Network, pp. 17–18. Soochow University (2009) (in Chinese)

4. Kernighan, B.W., Lin, S.: An efficient heuristic procedure for partitioning graphs. Bell System Tech. J. 49(2), 291–307 (1970)

5. Barnes, E.R.: An algorithm for partitioning the nodes of a graph. SIAM J. Alg. Disc. Meth. 3(4), 541–550 (1982)

6. Flake, G.W., Lawrence, S., Giles, C.L.: Efficient identification of Web communities. In: Proceedings of the Sixth ACM International Conference on Knowledge Discovery and Data Mining, SIGKDD 2000, pp. 150–160. ACM, New York (2000)

7. Flake, G.W., Lawrence, S., Giles, C.L., Coetzee, F.M.: Self-organization and identification of Web communities. IEEE Computer 35(3), 66–70 (2002)

8. Girvan, M., Newman, M.E.J.: Community structure in social and biological net-works. Proc. Natl. Acad. Sci. 9(12), 7821–7826 (2002)

9. Palla, G., Derenyi, I., Farkas, I., Vicsek, T.: Uncovering the overlapping community structure of complex networks in nature and society. Nature 435(7043), 814–818 (2005)

10. Palla, G., Barabasi, A.-L., Vicsek, T.: Quantifying social group evolution. Nature 446(7316), 664–667 (2007)

11. Brin, S., Page, L.: The anatomy of a large-scale hypertextual Web-search engine. In: Proc 7th International World Wide Web Conference, pp. 146–164. SIGIR, Brisbane (1998)

12. Kleinberg, J.: Authoritative sources in a hyperlinked environment. In: Proceedings of the 9th ACM-SIAM Symposium on Discrete Algorithms, pp. 668–677. ACM, New York (1998)

13. Freeman, L.C.: Centrality in social networks: Conceptual clarification. Social Networks 1(3), 215–239 (1979)

14. Song, W., Liu, H., Wang, C., Xie, J.: Core nodes detection based on frequent itemsets of graph. Journal of Frontiers of Computer Science and Technology 04(01), 84–86 (2010) (in Chinese)

15. Tang, C., Liu, W., Wen, F., Qiao, S.: Three probes into the social network and Consortium Information Mining. Journal of Computer Applications 26(9), 2020–2023 (2006) (in Chinese)

16. Lu, L., Zhang, Y.-C., Yeung, C.H., Zhou, T.: Leaders in social networks, the delicious case. PLoS ONE 6(6), e21202 (2011)

17. Kempe, D., Kleinberg, J.M., Tardos, E.: Maximizing the spread of influence through a social network. In: The 9th ACM SIGKDD Conference on Knowledge Discovery and Data Mining, pp. 137–146. ACM, New York (2003)

18. Watts, D.: A simple model of global cascades in random networks. Proc. Natl. Acad. Sci. 99(9), 5766–5771 (2002)

19. Ji, J., Han, X., Wang, Z.: Community Influence Maximizing Based on Comprehensive Cascade Diffuse Model. Journal of Jilin University (Science Edition) 47(5), 1032–1035 (2009) (in Chinese)

20. Wang, X., Li, X., et al.: Theory and Application of Complex Network, pp. 72–98. Tsinghua University Press, Beijing (2006) (in Chinese)

21. Mahajan, V., Muller, E., Bass, F.: New Product Diffusion Models in Marketing: A Review and Directions for Research. Journal of Marketing 54(l), l–26 (1990)

22. Even-Dar, E., Shapira, A.: A Note on Maximizing the Spread of Influence in Social Networks. In: Deng, X., Graham, F.C. (eds.) WINE 2007. LNCS, vol. 4858, pp. 281–286. Springer, Heidelberg (2007)

Vulnerability Evaluating Based on Attack Graph

Chunlu Wang[1,2], Yu Bao[1,2], Xuesen Liang[1,2], and Tianle Zhang[1,2]

[1] School of Computer Science and Technology, Beijing University of Posts
and Telecommunications, Beijing, China
[2] Key Laboratory of Trustworthy Distributed Computing and Service (BUPT),
Ministry of Education, Beijing, China
wangcl@bupt.edu.cn

Abstract. Networked hosts are facing more and more threats due to software vulnerabilities. Every year, there are an increasing number of security vulnerabilities discovered in software. It is impractical that we patch all the vulnerabilities because of the high cost of patching procedure. In this paper, we propose a user environments based scoring method. We analyze vulnerability impact from three aspects: confidentiality, integrity and availability. The score is customized to reflect the vulnerability's risk under certain security request by assigning the weight on the three aspects according to the host's function in an organization. We use attack graph to analyze the relationships among vulnerabilities in a host, and calculate on the context to get each vulnerability's threat. The experimental results indicate that our scoring method can better reflect the real situation.

Keywords: vulnerability, network security, risk assessment.

1 Introduction

Over the past decade, we have seen an ever-increasing number of security incidents reported as well as the vulnerabilities discovered in software. As described by CVE [1] official web site, a vulnerability is "a mistake in software that can be directly used by a hacker to gain access to a system". According to the statistics published by CERT [2], the number of vulnerabilities has grown in the last five years as shown in Fig. 1.

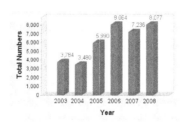

Fig. 1. Reported vulnerabilities from 2003 to 2008

One may consider the system is secure from attacks after all vulnerabilities are patched, but for many organizations, keeping each vulnerability patched is unrealistic

Y. Yuan, X. Wu, and Y. Lu (Eds.): ISCTCS 2012, CCIS 320, pp. 555–563, 2013.
© Springer-Verlag Berlin Heidelberg 2013

and sometimes undesirable. Firstly, there are so many new vulnerabilities discovered each year. Existing scanners can find the latest vulnerability by keeping them update, but for some vulnerabilities, they only provide the characteristics but no solutions. System managers are also incompetent to solve these problems. Secondly, unconfirmed patches may bring the system into instability and introduce more bugs. Thirdly, patching on OS kernel level often needs to be rebooted, and some organizations are intolerant of availability being affected.

In order to keep the organizations safe, the security managers must have a clear image of which hosts are most critical and execute system security checks when new vulnerabilities are published or when new hosts are installed in strict rotation. Security manager has to ensure that any un-patched vulnerabilities will not be exploited, or would not cause much cost even exploited. Since it's not practical that we patch all discovered vulnerabilities, we have to face the following problem: Which vulnerability needs to be patched first? To answer this question, the managers need to understand the risk and potential damage of each vulnerability to the hosts. Such an understanding is hard to achieve only by reading daily vulnerability reports from various sources even from the automated security tools. Modern sophisticated intrusions usually consist of multi-stage attacks which combine multiple vulnerabilities, while most security tools typically focus on identifying individual vulnerabilities, and have no clue about which and how vulnerabilities can be combined for an attack.

This paper introduces a way to analyze vulnerabilities based on the host's customizable security request of Confidentiality (C), Integrity (I) and Availability (A) and the combined effect of vulnerabilities. We calculate the threat of individual vulnerabilities to certain host by using the context provided by the attack graph, and then prioritize them and give advice to the manager. The rest of the paper is organized as follows. In section 2, related work of this paper is discussed. In Section 3, we present how we evaluate the vulnerabilities and explain the related concepts. The calculations of analysis using attack graphs are given in section 4. Section 5 shows the detail of the method a through an experiment. Conclude in Section 6.

2   Related Work

When analyzing the system risk, we can get the information about vulnerabilities from various vulnerability databases, for example OSVDB [5], Security Focus's vulnerability database [9], and Public Cooperative Vulnerability Database [6]. But until the creation of CVE which is a common identifier, it is hard to share data across separate databases. Now CVE Identifiers are frequently used and are easily cross-linking with other repositories that also use CVE identifiers. In our work, attack graph will be talked about. Phillips and Swiler first proposed the method that uses attack graphs for analyzing network security [8]. In the graph, nodes represent network states, and its edges represent the application of an exploit. The path is a series of exploits leading to the goal of an attacker. Since this method can not automatically generate attack graph, it can not be used in large-scale network security analysis. Ritchey and Ammann [9] first used model checker to analyze network vulnerabilities. The advantage of using model-checking approach is that we can use existing model checkers rather than write an analysis engine. A model checker can check the model against a security formula, and then a counterexample shows the attack path that leads to the violation of the security property. In Ritchey's method it can only give one counterexample. Sheyner [10] improves the model checker which can give all the counterexamples. However, in model checking, most state transition sequences are unnecessary for network security analysis and lead to combinatorial explosion. In order to cut down the space and time complexity, the monotonicity is proposed. It states that gaining more privileges can only help the attacker in further compromising the system and there is no need for backtracking. Based on the monotonicity, Ammann, et al. proposed an approach where dependencies among exploits are modeled in a graph structure [11]. The method described in this paper assumes the same monotonicity property, and is compatible with other attack graph generation method.

3   Evaluating Aindividle Vulnerability

There are many vulnerability "scoring" systems, for example, CERT/CC [2], SANS [12], Microsoft's proprietary scoring system [13] and CVSS [4], each of which has its metrics and vulnerability database. Organizations use different labels to index the vulnerabilities. In this paper we choose CVSS as our vulnerability scoring system, which is designed to provide an open and standardized method for rating IT vulnerabilities. The National Vulnerability Database [3] (NVD) provides CVSS metrics for almost all known vulnerabilities, e.g. Fig. 2.

Vulnerability: CVE-2007-3168
Access Vector: Network exploitable
Access Complexity: Low
Authentication: Not required to exploit

Fig. 2. A vulnerability example

An attack scenario is a series of vulnerability exploitation with the attacker's privilege escalated. Detailed privilege classification method was determined by operating systems. In order to eliminate the diversity of privilege levels, most vulnerability databases only provide three levels: admin, user and other. The risk levels are in a decreasing order of admin > user > other. We think that the actual situation could not be properly described only by privilege and it may lead to an underestimation of potential risk. Instead of privilege, our method divides vulnerability impact into three aspects: C, I and A, and uses a three-dimensional vector(x_1, x_2, x_3) to characterize vulnerability's degree of loss on C, I and A. Each component has three levels of degree: None (N), Partial (P), and Complete (C). The corresponding values are listed in Table 1.

$$v = (x_1, x_2, x_3); x_{1,2,3} \in \{N, P, C\} \tag{1}$$

Table 1. Impact degrees and values

Level	Value
N	0
P	0.275
C	0.660

When a vulnerability cause complete loss of confidentiality, integrity, and availability, it equals to providing a root privilege, while vulnerabilities that give user privilege can be represented with only partial loss of C, I and A. Let Impact (v) denotes the impact value of v, and the formula is:

$$\text{Impact}(v) = 1 - (1 - x_1) \times (1 - x_2) \times (1 - x_3) \qquad (2)$$

The above formula came from CVSS equations, and we made little change. A ratio that makes a score rang from 1 to 10 was removed from the old equations. Because we think it is unnecessary in our model and doesn't affect the relationship of vulnerabilities.

Modern enterprise network consists of many computers and other equipments, which take different responsibility. For example, some are running a HTTP server, and some have databases installed for confidential information storage. For the web server, availability is more important than confidentiality; while for a database server, quite contrary. Thus availability volatized vulnerability will not have the same effect on these hosts, but get a same score. More importantly, sometimes sensitive information can be obtained by an attacker without privilege escalation. So to make a rational evaluation, both the vulnerabilities and host's security requirement should be taken into consideration. A Weight Group (W) can be assigned to customize the security requirement on CIA of a certain host by the system administrator.

$$W = (\alpha, \beta, \gamma), 0 \le \alpha, \beta, \gamma \le 1; \alpha + \beta + \gamma = 1 \qquad (3)$$

α, β and γ are preference weights for C, I and A respectively. These weights enable the manager to customize the way we evaluate vulnerabilities depending on the function of the host to a user's organization. That is, if a host is used to store confidential document for which confidentiality is most important, the manager should assign a higher weights to α, relative to β and γ.

Given a host with specific security requirement, we assign the W. Risk is the weighted impact of a vulnerability.

$$\text{Risk}(W, v) = 1 - (1 - \alpha x_1) \times (1 - \beta x_2) \times (1 - \gamma x_3) \qquad (4)$$

4   Calculation on Attack Graphs

When analyzing sophisticated intrusions, we find that multiple vulnerabilities can be combined together for reaching a goal. During the attack, vulnerability may be a step stone of others and can still keep its effect after the exploitation. In this paper, we use attack graph to help analyze the threat of a host instead of a large network. After reducing the scale of problem the attack graph analysis can be done in desirable time. By using the context provided by the attack graph, we calculate each vulnerability's contribution to the system's compromise and get the ranked list of all vulnerabilities to help the administrator make priority remediation. Another weakness of many previous approaches is that information used to build the graph is usually freely formatted, which requires extensive manual analysis of vulnerabilities and attacks. Our approach extracts most information from NVD, where well-formed data can be easily accessed. We try to make our method more compatible with different design and easier to implement. Because the attack in a host is monotonic, the attack graph is a Directed Acyclic Graph (DAG) or an attack tree. Each node is a vulnerability and the edges mean the exploitations. A path from root to leaf indicates a successful attack.

Fig. 3. Attack graph

Fig. 4. Attack tree

The root of the tree v_0 represents a start point which contains no vulnerability information.

A. **Attack Complexity(AC)**

AC measures the complexity of the vulnerability required to be exploited once the conditions are complied. It can be regard as the likelihood of a successful attack. In CVSS [4], AC is a variable that has three values: 0.31(H), 0.61(M) and 0.71(L). Let **AC**(v) be the function to get the AC of v.

B. **Base Score(BS)**

BS is an overall score of a vulnerability ranging from 0 to 10. A vulnerability scored 10 is one of the most critical vulnerabilities. We define a function **BS**(v) to achieve the base score of v from the databases. Once we give a list of vulnerabilities to **BS**(*vulnerability list*) it returns the sum of each vulnerability's base score.

Next, we define two functions to manipulate the attack tree:

a)   **Father**(v_i) returns the father of the node v_i on the tree. Take the example of Fig.3, **Father**(v_2)= v_0, Father(v_0)= Ø.

b)   **Children**(v_i) is a node list of v_i's direct children, for example, in Fig.3. **Children**(v_0)=**V**=(v_1, v_2, v_3), **Children**(v_1)= Ø

C. **Attack Factor(AF)**

AF describes how likely an attacker is going to exploit each vulnerability under a certain condition. When building the attack tree the vulnerabilities which have been exploited together with the ones providing less privilege than current one will not be the next target. Attack factor of v depends on the proportion of $\mathbf{BS}(v)$ among all reachable vulnerabilities.

$$AF(v) = \frac{BS(v)}{BS(Children(Father(v)))} \tag{5}$$

D. Success Probability(Prob)

Success probability measures the likelihood of a vulnerability to be successfully exploited. The Prob of v to be exploited equals is the product of the probability of its conditions to be met and the probability to be chosen multiplying the attack complexity. So the formula goes like:

$$\text{Prob}(v) = \text{Prob}(Father(v)) * AF(v) * AC(v) \tag{6}$$

and we set $\mathbf{Prob}(v_0)$ equals to one.

E. Threat

Threat is an overall score of vulnerability in its host. It integrates the possible harm and successful probability.

$$Threat(v) = Risk(W, v) * Prob(v) \tag{7}$$

5   The Experiment

In this section, we perform an experiment based on real situation. A server runs Serv-U under Windows XP to provide a FTP service. In order to make our demonstration short and clear, all the operating system vulnerabilities have been patched. After a full vulnerability scan is done, five Serv-U vulnerabilities are found: CVE-1999-0219, CVE-2000-1033, CVE-2001-0054, CVE-2005-3467 and CVE-2004-2111. There are many vulnerability scanners available such as Nessus and OVAL Scanner, the usage will not be elaborated here. Here we use v_1 to v_5 to represent these vulnerabilities. Some characteristic are listed in the Table 2.

Table 2. Sample vulnerabilities' characteristic

Node	CVE-ID	Privi-lege	Impact on C, I, A	Description
v_1	1999-0219	/	(N,N,C)	Buffer overflow caused dos
v_2	2000-1033	user	(P,P,P)	Unrestricted brut forcing of user accounts.
v_3	2001-0054	/	(P,N,N)	Directory traversal
v_4	2005-3467	/	(N,N,P)	Denial of service
v_5	2004-2111	admin	(C,C,C)	Stack-based buffer overflow

v_1 is a buffer overflow vulnerability that could allow a remote attacker to create a denial of service, causing a complete loss of availability on the host. v_2 allows remote attackers to guess the passwords of other users. v_3 can cheat the server into allowing a remote attacker access to any directory on the FTP server's disk partition by a command containing specially crafted hexadecimal encoding, causing a partial loss of confidentiality. v_4 is an unspecified Denial of Service vulnerability. v_5 could be exploited by a remote authorized attacker to ultimately execute instructions with the privileges of the Serv-U server process, typical administrator or system. It could possibly be exploited by the use of the booty of v_2.

A simple attack graph is generated, as shown in Fig. 4.

Here we consider a normal attacker who has neither privilege nor any authorized account. And there are no firewalls between the FTP server and the attacker. This server is used to store and share public business data. If this server can not provide stable service, it will affect daily work. So the administrator set the security request a higher weight on availability rather than on confidentiality and integrity, the value of w is (0.2, 0.2, 0.6). First of all, we calculate each vulnerability's impact score and risk score based on (2) and (4), the base score of vulnerability (defined by CVSS) is also listed in Table 3.

Table 3. Sample vulnerabilities' scores

Node	Base Score	Impact score	Risk score
v_1	7.8	0.6600	0.3960
v_2	7.5	0.6189	0.2543
v_3	5.0	0.2750	0.0550
v_4	5.0	0.2750	0.1650
v_5	8.5	0.9607	0.5449

The outcome clearly shows the improvement after we introduced the weight group based on the user environment. v_4's risk is three times higher than v_3's risk. Thus vulnerability's risk is no longer constant, but changeable under different security requests. This enables the analysis closer to our actual situation. Then the correlations of the vulnerabilities are calculated by formulas (5), (6), (7).

Table 4. Sample vulnerabilities' prob

Node	Attack complexity	Attack factor	Prob(Fther(V_i))	Prob
v_1	Low (0.71)	0.3084	1.0000	0.2190
v_2	Low (0.71)	0.2964	1.0000	0.2104
v_3	Low (0.71)	0.1976	1.0000	0.1403
v_4	Low (0.71)	0.1976	1.0000	0.1403
v_5	Medium (0.61)	1.0000	0.2104	0.1283

Table 5. Threat of each vulnerability

Node	Threat
v_1	0.0867
v_2	0.0535
v_3	0.0077
v_4	0.0232
v_5	0.0699

Finally we calculate threats from v_1 to v_5, ranked as $v_1 > v_5 > v_2 > v_4 > v_3$.

6   Conclusion

In this paper, a new methodology for vulnerability analysis has been presented. This methodology correlates the vulnerabilities and the possibility of successful attacks and the security requests of certain asset. In order to make our method widely applicable, we describe our work at an abstract level. The risk of a particular vulnerability was analyzed based on user environment, and the threat was calculated according to the context of attack graph. Other methods can be compatible too if essential information can be provided. Vulnerability databases can be changed dynamically. In our method, the thread of a vulnerability is getting high either its risk is high or the total vulnerability number is small. Our task is to provide a priority remediation list, only used for host patch up.

Acknowledgements. The research is supported by China Natural Science Foundation (60973009) and China Postdoctoral Science Foundation(20100470256).

References

1. CVE, http://cve.mitre.org/
2. CERT/CC,CERT/CC Statistics (2004-2008),
   http://www.cert.org/stats/cert_stats.html/
3. NVD, http://nvd.nist.gov/
4. CVSS, http://www.first.org/cvss/
5. Open Source Vulnerability Database (OSVDB), http://osvdb.org/
6. Public Cooperative Vulnerability Database,
   https://cirdb.cerias.purdue.edu/coopvdb/public/
7. Security Focus Vulnerability Database,
   http://www.securityfocus.com/vulnerabilities
8. Phillips, C., Swiler, L.: A graph-based system for network-vulnerability analysis. In: Proceedings of the New Security Paradigms Workshop, NSPW 1998 (1998)
9. Ritchey, R.W., Ammann, P.: Using model checking to analyze network vulnerabilities. In: Proceedings of the IEEE Symposium on Security and Privacy, pp. 156–165 (2001)

10. Sheyner, Haines, J., Jha, S., Lippmann, R.: Automated generation and analysis of attack graphs. In: Proceedings of the 2002 IEEE Symposium on Security and Privacy, pp. 254–265 (2002)
11. Ammann, P., Wijesekera, D., Kaushik, S.: Scalable, graph-based network vulnerability analysis. In: Proceedings of the 9th ACM Conference on Computer and Communications Security, Washington, DC, USA, pp. 217–224 (2002)
12. SANS Institute. SANS Critical Vulnerability Analysis Archive. Undated (cited March 16, 2007)
13. Microsoft Corporation. Microsoft Security Response Center Security Bulletin Severity Rating System (November 2002) (cited March 16, 2007)
14. Sheyner, O., Wing, J.: Tools for Generating and Analyzing Attack Graphs. In: Proc. of Workshop on Formal Methods for Comp. and Objects, pp. 344–371 (2004)
15. Jha, S., Sheyner, O., Wing, J.: Two formal analyses of attack graphs. In: Proceedings of the 15th IEEE Computer Security Foundations Workshop, pp. 49–63 (2002)
16. Ingols, K., Lippmann, R., Piwowarski, K.: Practical Attack Graph Generation for Network Defense. In: Proc.of Comp. Sec. App. Conf., pp. 121–130 (2006)
17. Noel, S., Jacobs, M., Kalapa, P.: Multiple Coordinated Views for Network Attack Graphs. In: Workshop on Visualization for Computer Security, Minneapolis, MN, USA, October 26, pp. 99–106 (2005)
18. Dawkins, J., Hale, J.: A Systematic Approach to Multi-Stage Network Attack Analysis. In: Proceedings of the Second IEEE International Information Assurance Workshop (IWIA 2004) (2004)
19. Jajodia, S., Noel, S., O'Berry, B.: Topological analysis of network attack vulnerability. In: Kumar, V., Srivastava, J., Lazarevic, A. (eds.) Managing Cyber Threats: Issues, Approaches and Challenges. Kluwer Academic Publishers, Dordrecht (2003)
20. Wang, L., Noel, S., Jajodia, S.: Minimum-cost network hardening using attack graphs. Computer Communications 29(18), 3812–3824 (2006)

A Dynamic Strategy to Cache Out-of-Sequence Packet in DPI System

Qingyun Liu[1,2,3], Wenzhong Feng[1], and Qiong Dai[1]

[1] Institute of Information Engineering, Chinese Academy of Sciences, Beijing, China
[2] Institute of Computing Technology, Chinese Academy of Sciences, Beijing, China
[3] Graduate School of the Chinese Academy of Sciences, Beijing, China
liuqingyun@iie.ac.cn,
hectorinsane@gmail.com,
daifq@hotmail.com

Abstract. As a major approach for a network security system to discover threats or forensics, DPI (Deep Packet Inspection) technique is widely used in monitoring network flow. With the rapid development of Internet bandwidth, DPI system is facing more and more challenges on performance. One of these challenges is that out-of-sequence packets in TCP transmission will greatly affect memory consumption and data-recall. For a large scale DPI system, each DPI node has to monitor a huge amount of TCP session. It will consume too many resources to allocate plenty of space for storing all out-of-sequence packets. Meanwhile, insufficient space for buffer results in dropping packets and thus unable to reassemble network flow. We analyze the out-of-sequence characteristic of different Internet flow, and implement a dynamic strategy to cache out-of-sequence packet, which provide a more flexible way to keep track of the sessions. Experiment shows that based on the new strategy, a DPI system can greatly improve the completeness of data recall with little extra consumption of space.

Keywords: TCP out-of-sequence, out-of-sequence packet buffer, network flow identification.

1 Introduction

DPI (Deep Packet Inspection) is the technique used to detect and control on network flow of application layer, and it has a good effect in many fields, such as management on network flow, analysis on network and security, and so on. When IP packets, TCP packets or UDP packets flow through the DPI-based bandwidth management system, it will reassemble the application layer data of the OSI model by inspecting the IP packets deeply, and get the full contents of the application, and then deal the flow according to the pre-defined management policies. With the rapid development of network bandwidth, the TCP sessions processed by the DPI-based network security product also increase rapidly. Meanwhile, the out-of-sequence TCP packets become more obvious in WAN link. The process ability of DPI-based network security

Y. Yuan, X. Wu, and Y. Lu (Eds.): ISCTCS 2012, CCIS 320, pp. 564–571, 2013.

product is limited by its physical attributes (such as memory, etc.). With the rapid development of network bandwidth, DPI system is also facing more challenges. As Gilder's law points out, the growth rate of the network bandwidth is triple of that of computing power. So DPI system needs to process more and more data with limited time and memory resources.

The key point of designing the DPI system based on the content scanning is to process the out-of-sequence packet. TCP/IP are the stream-oriented protocol and provides a stable transfer mechanism, the two parties in the network check each other's response to determine whether the data is successfully transmitted. Even so, the arriving sequence of the TCP packets may be different from that of sending due to factors like delay, packet loss and different routing path. DPI system needs to cache and reassemble the out-of-sequence data, and then transfer it to pattern matching module for further processing, which greatly increased the memory burden of DPI system. Especially for the embedded device with less memory resource, it is requisite to utilize the memory more efficiently. With the rapid development of network bandwidth, DPI system needs adapt to monitor more network applications, such as scanning the compressed file, decoding and detecting the audio and video files, and so on. More and more new requirements on the performance of out-of-sequence data process are put forward for DPI system.

In summary, the out-of-sequence packet processing will be directly related to the performance of the DPI system. In order to effectively use the memory resource of the packet buffer, this work designed an adjustment mechanism for caching the out-of-sequence data. The mechanism obviously improved the recall ratio of DPI system. The remained of this paper is organized as follows:

1) Section 2: Introduce the research on the out-of-sequence data processing.
2) Section 3: Introduce the analysis on the features of the out-of-sequence data.
3) Section 4: Introduce the system architecture design of the dynamic out-of-sequence packet caching based on the application layer protocol identification.
4) Section 5: Introduce the system verification result.
5) Section 6: Summarize and evaluate on the system design.

2   Research on the Processing of the Out-of-Sequence Data

Some researchers have researched the features of the out-of-sequence TCP packet in different application scenarios. Paxson[1] tested 20000 TCP sessions, and found that about 12% sessions are out of sequence. Jasiwal[2] experimented on the Tier-1 backbone network, and the result is that about 4% data is out of sequence, the main cause is that the packet is transmitted again if it doesn't arrive at the destination correctly or the routing path is different.

There are two basic strategies on the processing of the out-of-sequence packet[3]: caching the out-of-sequence packet and discarding the out-of-sequence packet. The method of caching the out-of-sequence packet is to cache the out-of-sequence packet till the missing packet arrives. Then, re-order the packets according to the sequence number (SEQ) in the TCP header, and send it to the detection unit of upper layer. This method will occupy a large amount of buffer size in congested network. Semke[4] puts forward an automatic buffer adjustment algorithm, and as far as possible, it makes that each TCP session obtains a relatively balanced number of buffer. It creates a special buffer to cache the out-of-sequence data, and divides the buffer into N blocks. One session only use one block to cache data, this case considered the global resources. It ensures that the maximum and minimum size of available buffer used to cache the out-of-sequence is optimal, and avoids exhausting the resources. However, the defect is that it can't save the related data completely if a large amount of out-of-sequence data is transmitted. Amit[5] put forward an assignment algorithm based on probability, it checked the remained memory of the system, and when an out-of-sequence packet is received, system rejects it according to the changed probability to avoid exhausting the resources. Fisk[6] put forward an algorithm of discarding the follow-up packets whose sequence number (SEQ) order is inconsistent. Because of the TCP's retransmission timeout mechanism, the packets with the consistent logic order can be obtained finally. However, this case leads to discard a large amount of packets and also largely reduce the TCP sending windows, which result in the reducing of network throughput.

3   Analysis on the Features of the Out-of-Sequence Data

It isn't rare that the network traffic appears out-of-sequence situation[7]. Network congestion, different routing path, and so on, all possibly result in an out-of-sequence packet. As mentioned in above, DPI needs to cache the out-of-sequence TCP packet which flows through the system. Here, we define 'the maximum buffer size allocated for a TCP session S for caching the out-of-sequence packets' as the disordering tolerance of S, noted tol(S). It is to say that tol(S) is the maximum number of the system cached packets before the last packet (Pkt_n) which makes the out-of-sequence packets can be reassembled arrives. When the number of cached packets is larger than tol(S), if the packet can't be reassembled, then send all the cached data to upper layer. Later, if the packet is out-of-sequence and its sequence number equal to that of some one packet cached before, it will be discarded.

In practice, the different types of transmission data influence the DPI system in different degree. For example, during a video file transmission, if one critical packet was lost, the reassemble of the transmitted content for file decoding and detecting may become impossible; whereas, it harms rareness for an IM chat session if the same case occurred. Various protocols are designed to transmit different types of data, they show different sensitive to out-of-sequence.

To check out the size of buffer required to cache all the out-of-sequence packets, we designed and conducted the following experiments. The dataset for these experiments is composed of the traffic traces of 190 emails with audio/video attachments. The sizes of these attachments are range from 2 to 15 MB. The collected trace was fed to DPI modules repeatedly with setting various maximum buffer sizes, and we collect the number of audio/video files which are reassembled correctly.

Table 1. The number of complete audio/video flows on different tol(S)

tol(S)	5	10	20	40	60
processed audio/video flows (Bytes)	1348M	1354M	1358M	1362M	1364M
number of complete audio/video flows	1	4	21	64	171
ratio of complete audio/video flows	0.6%	2.3%	14%	37%	90%

The experiment shows that, the recall ratio of audio/video files is sensitive to tol(S) of DPI modules. The recall ratio is only 2.3% when tol(S) is 10. It also shows a dramatic promotion when tol(s) increases from 40 to 60. Finally, the recall ratio reaches a plateau at a high level as tol(S) >= 60.

In summary, we learn that the out-of-sequence of network traffic exhibits the following features:

1. Various protocols show a diverse sensitive to out-of-sequence.
2. For audio/video traffic, DPI needs a large buffer to cache all the data for reassembling.

The increasing bandwidth requires the growing memory of the out-of-sequence processing module of the DPI system. If using a memory pool to support "allocate on demand", the out-of-sequence module can manage the memory more effectively, however, it can neither handle the large volume of cached data under network congestion, nor deal with those malformed attacking packets. Whereas, on the other hand, if we manage each TCP session individually, it is hard to determine the cache size: too large size will cause resource wasting, while too small will harm the data reassembling. Consequently, under the current network environment, the DPI system needs an out-of-sequence process strategy which incorporates the merits of the above two cache managing approaches.

4   Design of the Dynamic Out-of-Sequence Packet Caching Based on the Application Layer Protocol Identification

The existing works on TCP disordered-packet-reassembling mostly focus on the factors like delay and space. They use the same reassembling strategy for all TCP packets. In this work, we propose and implement a framework which incorporates DPI technique and cache size adaptation. Thus, it can dynamically adjust the cache size for disordered packets, and get more effective memory utilization. At the meantime, based on the observation that different applications behave diversely on packets disordering, we determine the cache strategies of out-of-sequence packets for TCP sessions according to its application-layer characteristics in the management of massive TCP sessions.

The core idea of the framework is that: by feeding the output of application layer protocol identification back to the connection management module, it can assign a proper monitoring level based on the monitoring requirements. Each monitoring level has a corresponding maximum cache size for disordered packets, where the size can be adjusted according to the utilization of current cache space.

The implementation of the adjustment thread follows the following principles:

1. The adjustment thread should occupy memory and time as little as possible when collecting the information of the main program.

2. There should be a correlation between free cache size and the disordering tolerance of various monitoring levels.

3. Under the same memory occupation, the maximum number of disordered packets for each monitoring level should be consistent after a long running.

4. The tolerance variation caused by adjustment thread only affects the follow-up packets. Thus the previous session could keep untouched. It can prevent the performance loss caused by frequent interactions and lock/unlock operations, and meanwhile avoid the churn of space occupancy.

4.1   Process on Transport Layer

The transport layer handler should maintain a session table to record relevant information (including SEQ/ACK sequence number, corresponding application layer protocol, etc.) of unidirectional TCP flows. Upon a packet arrived, system looks up the session table firstly (to create it if no item exists in the table), and then compare the sequence number with the expected one to decide whether it's an out-of-sequence packet. If it is, allocate appropriate memory space to cache it and count the number. When the number of disordered packets (of a unidirectional TCP flow) exceeds tol(S), all the allocated memory should be freed, and these packets are dropped. Otherwise (not an out-of-sequence packet), send it to the upper layer for the processing, such as application layer protocol identification, and so on.

4.2   Interface of Application Layer

The transport layer handler should provide an interface to the application layer handler, by which the application layer can obtain data from transport layer, and label the corresponding protocol of the flow.

4.3   Design of Adjustment Thread

The role of adjustment thread is to adjust the disordering tolerance of different traffics according to current cache occupancy (refer to Fig. 1). In the following experiments, we define several levels of disordering tolerance and adjustment functions. According to the statistical sensitive degree of the data transmit by different protocol, we set different level for every protocol. Different type of traffic can be set as a relevant level based on the network traffic characteristics and the actual detecting requirements. After the application protocol identification module recognized the protocol,

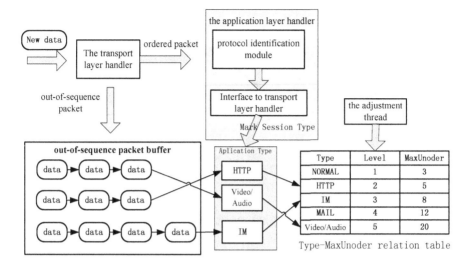

Fig. 1. The architecture of dynamic strategy to cache out-of-sequence packet

system set an appropriate tolerance level for the session. Each level has multiple thresholds of the out-of-sequence occupancy ratio, and once the actual occupancy exceeds a threshold, the tolerance of all levels will be altered. This will affect the connection management of successive packets.

Based on the above framework, we implement a timed adjustment thread. Once the thread started, will collect the cache space occupancy for disordered packets of the connection management module per second. When there is a large bulk of idle space, the adjustment thread will increase tol(S) so that each connection can cache more disordered packets. Otherwise, it decreases tol(S). The experiments show that, even though the DPI's load balance behaves normally, the cache occupancy of various threads shows a significant difference, which can up to 20% of the cache size. Thus it is requisite to individually regulate each thread's space occupancy, and make the maximum cached packets number of a connection can be adjusted at a small granularity.

5   Verification on the Effect of Dynamic Cache Adjustment

To evaluate the effect of memory adjustment thread, we configured the following experimental environment (refer to Fig. 2). It includes a node on a backbone network with 2Gbps bandwidth, a traffic replay device which can replicate the input traffic to multiple output port, and three DPI server modules. The input traffic is injected with some labeled audio/video streams[1]. The three DPI modules adopt the following three cache strategies respectively: with tol(S) = 5, 80, and a dynamic adjustment.

---

[1] Under real network environment, the interrupt of the data transportation happens easily, that is, the traffic passing through DPI module may be not a complete connection. So we inject some labeled flows into traffic to accurately detect the recall ratio of DPI system.

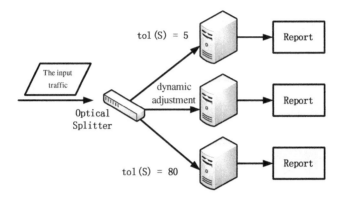

Fig. 2. The experimental environment for three cache strategies evaluate

The experiment lasted 6 hours. The DPI module will record the memory utilization during processing traffic data, and calculate the recall ratio of audio/video flows once experiment terminated.

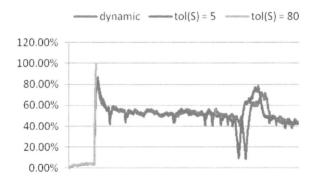

Fig. 3. The memory utilization on three cache strategies

Table 2. The number of complete audio/video flows on three cache strategies

tol(S)	5	80	dynamic
number of complete audio/video files	6	65^2	698
ratio of complete audio/video files	0.73%	9.3%	85.01%

---

[2] The fixed strategy with tol(S) = 80 will cause the buffer always full, and not out-of-sequence packets can be saved.

For the cache memory occupancy, the dynamic cache strategy behaves similar as that with a fixed number of cached packets. While for the recall ratio, dynamic strategy can achieve a higher level. The strategy of fixing large number of cached packets will casue DPI module laid off once the large cache space was exhausted, and it will affect the recall ratio.

6   Discussion and Conclusion

In this work we analyzed the difference of out-of-sequence data for various type of network traffic, and proposed a dynamic strategy for caching out-of-sequence pack-ets. The core idea is to rationally allocate the memory to various traffics for a higher recall ratio when the total memory resource is limited. This new strategy is deployed in the real network environment, and it promotes the audio/video flow recall ration by about 7% with the same cache space occupation. However, the effect of the dynamic strategy relies on the application layer protocol identification. Thus for those flows, where the application protocol was not identified even if the maximum number of cached packets arrived, cannot be recalled completely by the new strategy. The future research can focus on the TCP connection management of DPI system, such as how to use the application layer identification result to optimize the phase-out strategy of TCP connection.

Acknowledgements. Supported by the "Strategic Priority Research Program" of the Chinese Academy of Sciences (Grant No. XDA06030200) and the National High-Tech Research and Development Plan 863 of China (Grant No. 2011AA010703) and the National Natural Science Foundation (Grant No. 61070026).

References

1. Paxson, V.: Automated Packet Trace Analysis of TCP Implementations. In: Proceedings of the 1997 SIGCOMM Conference, Cannes, France, pp. 167–179 (September 1997)
2. Jaiswal, S., Iannaccone, G., Diot, C., Kurose, J., Towsley, D.: Measurement and Classifica-tion of Out-of-Sequence Packets in a Tier-1 IP Backbone. IEEE IEEE/ACM Transactions on Networking 15(1) (February 2007)
3. Xu, K., Li, Y., et al.: line speed deep packet detecting techniques on high speed link. 徐克付, 李阳等, 高速网络线速深度分组检测技术, 信息技术快报 9(3) (May 2011)
4. Semke, J., et al.: Automatic TCP Buffer Tuning
5. Amit, S., Jaggi, M.: (Sunnyvale, CA, US) , Buffer allocation using probability of dropping unordered segments
6. Fisk, M., Varghese, G.: Fast content-based packet handling for intrusion detection. Tech-nical Report CS2001-0670, Department of Computer Science, University of California, SanDiego (May)
7. Bennett, J.C.R., Partridge, C., Shectman, N.: Packet Reorder Is Not Pathological Network Behavior. IEEE/ACM Trans. Net. 7(6) (December 1999)

Speeding Up Double-Array Trie Construction for String Matching

Niu Shuai[1,3], Liu Yanbing[2], and Song Xinbo[1]

[1] Institute of Computing Technology, Chinese Academy of Sciences, Beijing, China
[2] Institute of Information Engineering, Chinese Academy of Sciences, Beijing, China
[3] Gruduate School of Chinese Academy of Sciences, Beijing, China
songxb@ict.ac.cn

Abstract. Double-Array Trie is presented as a data structure for Trie which has advantages both in the compactness and access speed. Thus Double Array Trie structure is broadly adopted by many string matching algorithms. However, the Double Array Trie construction process is faced with problems of huge temporary peak of memory consumption and low construction speed when applied to large scale sets of strings. It's hard to meet the requirement of detecting high speed network flow in real time. This paper presents two optimization strategies in the Double Array Trie construction process to avoid the temporary peak of memory consumption and reduce the construction time. The first is to generate the Trie recursively. The second is to take different methods in finding current node's base value process according to the number of child nodes. We applied the improved strategy to Aho-Corasick algorithm and tested with different large-scale sets of strings. From the results, it turned out that the space consumption and the construction time are both significantly improved on the premise of same search efficiency.

Keywords: information retrieval, Double-Array, Trie, string matching, Aho-Corasick algorithm.

1   Introduction

String matching (pattern matching) is a classic problem that has been widely studied in past decades and string matching algorithm is the heart of Intrusion Detection System(IDS). Some existing string matching algorithms (Aho-Corasick, SBOM, etc) build matching automaton during preprocess period[14]. With the rapid development of the Internet, the soaring number of pattern strings leads to huge storage to present the automaton due to the rapid growth of its states and longer construction time.

Storage requirement is the bottleneck of string matching which has millions of rules to match with. The Aho-Corasick algorithm, for example, if there is 100w pattern strings of which average length is 30, suffers about 30GB(4B*256*1000000*30) storage requirement for Aho-Corasick automaton(presented in list form). Most of small and medium equipments can't meet such huge requirement. As a result, many scholars put forward index structures to solve the problem of storage explosion. In

Y. Yuan, X. Wu, and Y. Lu (Eds.): ISCTCS 2012, CCIS 320, pp. 572–579, 2013.

this paper we focus on Double Array Trie proposed by Aoe[9][10]. It can compress the storage on the basis of assuring search efficiency.

Memory consumption and building time are crucial in systems which have both huge pattern sets and the need of updating rules frequently. In this paper, we generate the Double Array Trie recursively and take different methods in the process of finding current node's base value according to the number of child nodes to reduce the memory occupation and speed up the building process.

The aim of this paper is to present optimization strategies to reduce the memory consumption and build time in building string matching automaton presented by Double Array Trie structure. In the following sections we make such arrangement: firstly, we introduce the Double Array Trie structure. Then we introduce our optimization methods in detail. In the next we give the analysis of the experimental results. At last we make the summary.

2   Related Work

2.1   Aho-Corasick Algorithm

Aho-Corasick algorithm[4] is an exact string matching algorithm which is an extension to the KMP. This prefix algorithm scans letters one by one so it is able to search in worst-case linear time and independent of the size of the rule sets. With such capabilities to resist attacks, Aho-Corasick algorithm has been adopted by engineering widespreadly. The core of the Aho-Corasick algorithm is Aho-Corasick automaton which adds some supply links on the basis of Trie structure generated by the strings to be matched. In that way can the Aho-Corasick automaton transfer to appropriate position according to the input chars.

2.2   Double Array Trie

Trie is a kind of indexing method whose name is abbreviated from 'Retrieval'. It is an efficient structure that has a wide range of applications.

Aho put forward Triple Array Trie in order to reduce the storage consumption in his paper[8]. After that Aoe proposed an improved structure by enhancing Aho's idea. In his paper [9], Aoe posed the Double Array Trie structure to represent the Trie. And then researchers presented various methods to further compact the storage and accelerate the building process[12][13][15]. The access time of Double Array Trie is O(1) and the storage requirement is compact as a list form. That makes the worst-case time complexity for retrieving is O(n) in which n is the length of the input string. Although the update cost could be very expensive when pattern sets change (add, delete, alter). In this paper, we just consider the static case. We also do not adopt the TAIL array and two-trie structure[12] in order to ensure the search efficiency of our algorithm. It means that we represent all of the transfers in the Double Array structure.

The core idea of Double Array Trie is to use two one-dimensional arrays: Base[] and Check[] (index number of array corresponds with node number in the Trie) to represent the Trie structure. We can use the following relations to signify the transfers between nodes:

When there is a transition from state m to state n via character c, if and only if two conditions below are satisfied. (code[c] is the numerical value for character c)

$$n = Base[m] + code[c] \qquad (1)$$

$$Check[n] = m \qquad (2)$$

The Trie in Fig.1 could be represented with the Double Array Trie structure in table.2. The numerical values of transfer characters are shown in table 1.

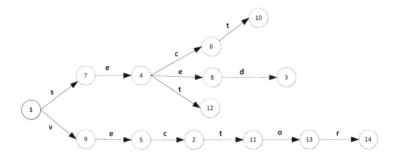

Fig. 1. Trie built by 4 patterns {sect, seed, set, vector}

Table 1. Code table for transfer characters

c	1
d	2
e	3
o	4
r	5
s	6
t	7
v	8

Table 2. Double Array structure that represent the Trie in Fig. 1

	1	2	3	4	5	6	7	8	9	10	11	12	13	14
Base	1	4	-1	5	1	3	1	1	2	-1	9	-1	9	-1
Check	0	5	8	7	9	4	1	4	1	6	2	4	11	13

3   Speeding Up Double Array Trie Construction

In this section we will focus on the application of Double Array Trie structure on large-scale pattern sets and the optimizations in the construction process. Applying to large-scale sets, string matching algorithm faces two issues of crucial importance: memory occupation and time consumption. We take optimization methods below to gain both compact storage and time efficiency.

3.1   Build Double Array Trie Recursively

There are 2 basic methods in building Double Array Trie according to given patterns:

1. Insert pattern strings into the Double Array structure one by one. This forthright method has obvious drawback that adding strings into double array structure would likely conflict with the occupied position. This method needs to change the position of nodes, base value and check value automatically. With the growth of the string number, conflicts and regularizations cause more expensive construction cost necessarily and the time efficiency is unacceptable for large-scale patterns.
2. Construct the Trie structure according to patterns then build the Double Array Trie structure from the generated Trie. This method is faster than the above, but additional memory is required for representing the Trie structure which can cause the temporary peak of memory consumption.

Each method above has its own shortcomings in different aspect. Our idea is to sort the strings in dictionary order and find the appropriate base and check values according to node's out-degree recursively since the node position is determined by its parent node's base value. Only in this way can we build the Double Array structure without any extra storage and time consumption.

Construction algorithm of the Double Array structure is as follows:

1. Init Double Array structure;
2. Sort Patterns in increasing order;
3. Call recursive function to set nodes' base and check values in each iteration;

The pseudo-code for the recursive function (named SetNode) is described in algorithm 1:

Algorithm 1. The approach to construction Double Array Trie recursively

---

1: **procedure** SetNode(root, depth, first_str, last_str)
2:        **if** first_str > last_str **then**
3:            exit(0)
4:        **end if**
5:        **if** first_str = last_str **then**
6:            Add the remains of the string to the Double Array structure from depth
7:        **end if**
8:        divide the strings between first_str and last_str into child[] (array of structs) according to string[depth]
9:            base←FindBaseValue()

10:	SetBase(root, base)
11:	**for** each struct in child array
12:	SetCheck([base+child[].char, root)
13:	**end for**
14:	**for** each struct in child array
15:	SetNode(base+child[].char, depth+1, child[].first_str, child[].last_str)
16:	**end for**
17:	**end procedure**

3.2   Optimize the Find Base Value Process

In his paper[10][11], Aoe presented an efficient implementation for finding base value process: finding and checking the unoccupied positions easily by linking the positions available bidirectionally without consuming any extra space.

We propose a block structure on the foundation of bidirectional link to represent the continuous available nodes in the rear of the Double Array structure. All we need is to record the begin position of the block as a variable named block_begin_pos which can help us to find the available nodes. Figure 2 shows a state of Double Array structure in the building period.

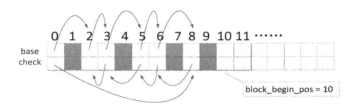

Fig. 2. A state of Double Array structure

As is shown in Figure 2, position 1, 4, 7, 9 in Double Array structure are occupied while the available nodes (2, 3, 5, 6, 8) are linked by a bidirectional link and the positions available after 10 are marked by the start position   (block_begin_pos=10).

There is a time-consuming operation in building process: FindBaseValue(in SetNode function in section 3.1). The core function of FindBaseValue is to find an appropriate value for parent node based on all of the child characters (c_1, c_2, ..., c_n). That means we should find a base value to meet the requirements that the nodes (base+c_1, base+c_2, ..., base+c_n) are all available in the Double Array structure. Traditional method is to traverse the whole bidirectional link and compute a base value (take the available node as the first child node) until find a position that meets all the requirements. The block in the rear of the Double Array should be checked if there is no such appropriate position in the links.

As is well known, the more edge characters a node has, the more conditions it should satisfy, that is to say, the greater probability of failure it will suffer when searching in bidirectional link. When checking position in available blocks, we can find the eligible base value in one trial no matter how many characters the parent node has. So our idea is to use different strategy in finding process according to the size of out-degree m:

- If m<3, as the traditional strategy, firstly traversing the whole bidirectional link to find a base value and finding in the block if that fails.
- If m>=3, finding in the block directly to get the appropriate base value at one time.

The method is illustrated as follows:

As the state of Double Array structure is shown in figure 4, assume that node 4 has 3 transfer characters{c, e, t}, now we are about to find a suitable base value for node 4.

— Traditional method:

Traverse the bidirectional link first:

node 2, base=2-code[c]=1; base+code[e]=4(occupied), skip to next node in bidirec-
            tional link.
node 3, base=3-code[c]=2; base+code[e]=5(unoccupied); base+code[t]=9(occupied),
            skip to next node in bidirectional link.
node 5, base=5-code[c]=4; base+code[e]=7(occupied), skip to next node in
            bidiretional link.
node 6, base=6-code[c]=5; base+code[e]=8(unoccupied);base+code[t]=12
            (unoccupied), all conditions are met, set 5 as the base value of node 4.

— Our improved method:

The out-degree of node 4 is 3. According to our method, we should check the position in the block directly marked by block_begin_pos to compute the base value:

pos=block_begin_pos(10); base=pos-code[c]=9, set 9 as the base value of node 4.

We can see that the failure number is brought down from 3 to 0 and our improved method is more competitive when there are a mass of nodes that have out-degree greater than 3. We can accelerate the construction speed by using our method (finding base value directly) without wasting much storage (the unoccupied nodes generated by our strategy can be accessed by node that has 1 or 2 out-degree). Furthermore, the threshold (we take 3 for example) can be changed according to specific situation.

In addition, our method includes optimizing the bidirectional link by limiting its size (take 100 for example). When the quantity is too large, we would abandon the front nodes from the link by deleting them from the link. That way can we make the best of the bidirectional link.

4   Evaluation

We realized the improved strategy into Aho-Corasick algorithm using about 500 lines of C++ and tested with different large-scale sets of patterns.

Our experiment environment is as below:

— Hardware: CPU 3.07 GHz (Inter Core i3), RAM 4GB
— Software: Windows 7 OS, Microsoft 2010 Visual Studio

We evaluated our method with several pattern sets include DNA fragments, SNORT signatures (www.snort.org), blacklist patterns (urlblacklist.com) and URL patterns (captured in actual network). In addition, blacklist patterns and URL patterns are cut into parts ranging from 2w to 10w. The pattern sets are searched against corresponding datasets separately.

We take several aspects (building time, memory consumption, failure time in FindBaseValue function, searching speed) as the evaluation indexes and the results are shown in Table 3.

Table 3. Expremental results for different pattern sets

	DNA	SNORT	BL2W	BL5W	BL10W	URL2W	URL5W	URL10W
Key number	5000	5029	20000	50000	100000	20000	50000	100000
Buildtime(s)								
Original	0.190	0.329	0.301	0.524	0.808	0.365	0.726	1.657
improved	0.128	0.201	0.187	0.329	0.669	0.220	0.470	1.024
Memory(MB)								
Original	2.674	4.868	4.867	8.597	14.12	5.906	12.432	26.995
improved	2.064	3.704	3.808	6.889	11.30	4.249	8.872	18.989
Fails in FindBaseValue								
Original	296	217	1821	2684	22783	85366	865075	1780042
improved	96	60	640	953	5640	1792	4043	6226
Searching speed(MB/s)								
Original	48.30	39.81	96.66	70.88	67.30	89.41	82.26	78.71
improved	48.94	39.65	95.27	72.08	66.95	87.65	81.05	79.55

From the results, the memory usage of our improved method is 19% to 29% less and the building time is about 32% to 39% faster (except blacklist10w, 17%) than that of the original method. The reduction of building time could be explained partly by the decline of failure time in FindBaseValue process. Our method also gains equivalent search efficiency in our experiments.

Therefore, by adopting our method, memory consumption can be about 21 percent smaller and building time can be about 30 percent shorter than that of the original method while the search speed is unaffected.

5   Conclusion

In this paper, we propose two optimization strategies in the construction period of Double Array Trie that enable us to accelerate the building speed and to avoid temporary peak of memory consumption. The first is to generate the Trie recursively after sorted the given strings; the second is to take some methods in finding base value process according to the number of child nodes. Our method includes marking the block position in order to find base value directly if the node's out-degree is over the threshold and making the limitation on the size of bidirectional link. Our experimental results show that the construction time was 17 to 39 percent lower and the storage consumption was 19 to 29 percent lower with our strategies.

The significance of this paper is to propose our strategies to reduce construction costs of Double Array structure which can be accepted in string matching algorithms such as Aho-Corasick. In particular, we can adopt the improved algorithm in: systems that have very large-scale patterns to match, systems need to update the automaton more frequently, resource sensitive equipments such as mobile phones, tablet PCs and embedded devices.

Acknowledgement. This work is partially supported by the National Science Foundation of China (NSFC) under grant No. 61070026 and the National High Technology Research and Development Program of China(863 Program) under grant No. 2011AA010703.

References

1. http://linux.thai.net/~thep/datrie/datrie.html
2. http://urlblacklist.com/
3. http://www.snort.org/
4. Aho, A., Corasick, M.: Efficient String Matching: An Aid to Bibliographic Search. Communications of the ACM 18(6), 333–340 (1975)
5. Boyer, R., Moore, J.: A fast string searching algorithm. Communications of the ACM 20(10), 761–772 (1977)
6. Morris, J.H., Knuth, D.E., Pratt, V.R.: Fast pattern matching in strings. SIAM J. Comput. 6(1), 322–350 (1977)
7. Tarjan, R.E., Yao, A.C.: Storing a Sparse Table. Communications of the ACM 22(11), 606–611 (1979)
8. Aho, A., Sethi, R., Ullman, J.: Compilers: Principles, Techniques, and Tools. Addison-Wesley (1985)
9. Aoe, J.: An Efficient Digital Search Algorithm by Using a Double-Array Structure. IEEE Transactions on Software Engineering 15(9), 1066–1077 (1989)
10. Aoe, J.: An Efficient Implementation of Static String Pattern Matching Machines. IEEE Transactions on Software Engineering 15(8), 1010–1016 (1989)
11. Aoe, J., Morimoto, K.: An Efficient Implementation of Trie Structures. Software-Practice and Experience 22(9), 695–721 (1992)
12. Aoe, J., Morimoto, K., Shishibori, M., Park, K-H.: A trie compaction algorithm for a large set of keys. IEEE Transactions on Knowledge and Data Engineering 8(3), 476–491 (1996)
13. Morita, K., Tanaka, A., Fuketa, M., Aoe, J.: Implementation of Update Algorithms for a Double-Array Structure. In: 2001 IEEE International Conference on Systems, Man, and Cybernetics, pp. 494–499 (2001)
14. Navarro, G., Raffinot, M.: Flexible Pattern Matching in Strings: Practical on-line search algorithms for texts and biological sequences (2002)
15. Tuck, N., Sherwood, T., Calder, B., Varghese, G.: Deterministic Memory-Efficient String Matching Algorithms for Intrusion Detection. In: IEEE INFOCOM (2004)

Modeling of Hierarchical Index System for Network Operation Security

Yongzheng Zhang and Xiaochun Yun

Institute of Information Engineering, Chinese Academy of Sciences, Beijing 100093, China
National Engineering Laboratory of Information Content Security Technology, Beijing 100093, China
zhangyongzheng@iie.ac.cn, yunxiaochun@cert.org.cn

Abstract. An index system of network operation security is a necessary technical means for reflecting and measuring network operation security macro-situation. On the basis of introducing a concept of network operation security index and its application senses, this paper proposes a general architecture model of security index system (MSIS) with computing ability. An instance of IP data network of China Telecommunications Corporation is given to illustrate the modeling method and process, so as to validate the feasibility and effectivity of MSIS on the level of instances. The analysis of the application instance indicates that MSIS is able to provide a uniform modeling methodology and computing standard for establishment of index system examples to meet the needs of different applications.

Keywords: Network Operation Security, Index; Index System, Modeling, Macro Situation.

1 Introduction

In recent years, most networks all over the world often suffer from malicious attacks even to collapse so that the security of network infrastructures and important information systems is being greatly compromised. These severe issues about network security have been recognized by every country such as United States, Russia, Japan and China. Most of them constitute a series of policies to promote the capability of ensuring key information systems. So under the above strong requiring background, techniques of monitoring, evaluation and prediction on network security situation are gradually becoming a research hotspot. As a basis and common problem of these techniques, how to scientifically establish an index system for network security has important theoretical and practical significances.

Security indices [1] can be divided into four layer indices of physical security, operation security, data security and content security, respectively reflecting electromagnetic equipment security, information system security, information self security and information exploiting security, where the operation security index is also regarded as network security index. Thus, this paper only discusses the conception category of network security index.

Y. Yuan, X. Wu, and Y. Lu (Eds.): ISCTCS 2012, CCIS 320, pp. 580–590, 2013.

From the literatures published, some typical study works about index or indicator system of network security mainly include:

(1) Indicator systems for security risk assessment

The literature [2] summarizes stochastic modeling and evaluating technologies for network security, concludes and proposes some evaluating indicators including reliability, availability, safety, confidentiality, and integrity. From the views of security layers, sides and dimensions, the literature [3] presents a security architecture for telecom network containing physical security, transmission network security and service network security. The literature [4] establishes an indicator system based on communication, operation, access control and assets. The literature [5] constructs an indicator system framework for telecom risk evaluation based on the probability and consequence of security events.

(2) Indicator systems for security threat assessment

The literature [6] presents an agent-based architecture for monitoring network vulnerability metrics and measures the impact of faults and attacks based on network performance indicators. For the given attacks, the literature [7] proposes some parameters for measuring network security. A model of multiple behavior information fusion and two indices of privilege validity and service availability are proposed to evaluate the impact of prevalent network intrusions on system security in the literature [8]. An indicator system for evaluating network attack effects is proposed in the literature [9].

As stated above, existing works mainly focus on subjective indicator systems for risk assessment and threat assessment, emphasizing particularly on a case of micro security events of small-scale networks. By contrast, there is little research on objective index systems based on characteristics of actual network data in operating time, especially for measuring macro security situation of large-scale networks. It is more important that existing works lack a uniform model and modeling methodology for establishing index system examples so as to always propose different approaches for different applications.

Therefore, this paper first introduces a concept of network operation security index and its application senses and then proposes a general architecture model of security index system (MSIS) with computing ability based on a hierarchical structure model (HSM). Finally, an instance of IP data network of China Telecommunications Corporation is given to illustrate the modeling method and process of applying MSIS to establish an example of S_4 so as to validate its feasibility and effectivity. The purpose of this paper is to strive for providing a uniform modeling methodology and computing standard for establishment of index system examples to meet different needs of different applications and further to reflect and measure macro situation of large-scale networks.

2   Definition of Index

Based on network security research and practical experiences and socio-economic statistic theory [10], we give a series of definitions of network operation security indicator and index as follows.

Definition 1. Network Operation Security Indicator (abbr. Security Indicator or Indicator), indicates conception and quantity of network data characteristics which are able to reflect operation security situation of network information systems. It is generally used to reflect and measure the security situation and trends in system operation. For example, a traffic indicator is based on a data characteristic of network traffic while an IP distribution indicator on IP distribution law.

Definition 2. Network Operation Security Index (abbr. Security Index or Index), indicates a relative number of variable degree of network data characteristics which are able to reflect operation security situation of network information systems. It is generally used to reflect and measure the variable quantity of security situation in system operation. For example of the above traffic characteristic, a traffic index depends on variable degree of network traffic to reflect change of security situation.

From the above definition of index and indicator, we can see that an index is a relative number of variable degree of an indicator on quantity. As a measuring approach, an index can integrate quantitative variety of heterogeneous data. Therefore, an index can be used to measure an integrated variable degree of complex data characteristics which can not be directly added.

Definition 3. Base Period and Reporting Period. An index can be usually calculated by the quantity of the corresponding indicator at a benchmark period and an investigated period, where, the specified benchmark period is named as base period and the investigated period as reporting period. Generally, a relatively stable and security period should be selected as base period.

To be convenient for understanding the concept of our proposed index, we give an instance of a traffic index and its computing formula as shown in Table 1, where a total traffic indicator is a sum of individual traffic indicators of all the network nodes and an individual traffic indicator is an average traffic during a time interval. Because the variety of total traffic depends on two factors of network scale and individual traffic and the network scale factor can not reflect the change of network data essential characteristics, the variety of individual traffic should be investigated in the same condition of network scale. Therefore, we have to use the relative number of average individual traffic indicators at reporting period and base period to calculate network traffic index *TI*. As analyzed above, a category of factors like the network node number can be generally called isometric factor due to their unified metric, while a category like the individual traffic can be named as indexation factor due to their determining the variable degree of *TI*.

As an instance of *TI* stated above, we can see that: 1) if a typical network normal period is selected as base period, the quantity of *TI* can reflect the variable degree of traffic, namely can depict security situation on traffic; 2) *TI* can measure and evaluate security influences of different events on traffic if the base period is specified as a uniform evaluating criteria; 3) *TI* can reflect macro situation of traffic and its evolution and trends over time. It may be deduced by analogy of this instance that index study has important theoretical and practical significances.

Table 1. An instance of traffic index

Index Name	TI : network traffic index
Computing Formula	Assuming: at base and reporting period, node number indicators are respectively n_b and n_r, total traffic indicators are respectively t_b and t_r. Then: $$TI = \frac{t_r}{n_r} \bigg/ \frac{t_b}{n_b}$$

3   Index System Modeling

3.1   Hierarchical Structure Model

The prime problem of index system modeling is how to formulize the system architecture. For this, we first give the definition of a hierarchical structure model.

Definition 4. Hierarchical Structure Model (HSM) $T = (H, G)$, where:

1) H is a family of element sets defined as follows:

$H = \{H^1, H^2, ..., H^n\}$, where, $H^i(i = 1 \sim n-1)$ denotes the element set at i layer as called layer element set for short, and specially, the first layer element set H^1 is also called root element set. H^n denotes base element set. The above corresponding elements are respectively called layer element, root element and base element. $n(n \geq 2)$ means HSM T has a n-layer structure and it is generally written $n-T$.

2) G is a set of mapping between layer elements defined as follows:

$G = \{g_i \mid g_i : H^i \rightarrow 2^{H^{i+1}} \wedge \bigcup_{h \in H^i} g_i(h) = H^{i+1}, i = 1 \sim n-1\}$, defines the hierar-

chical relations between layer elements so as to make all elements formed into a hierarchical structure model.

Based on Definition 4, we give the concepts of Tree-type, Forest-type and Acyclic-Digraph-type hierarchical structures.

Definition 5. Tree-type and Forest-type hierarchical structures. On the premise of the mapping set G satisfying $g_i(x) \cap g_i(y) = \Phi(\forall x \neq y \in H^i \wedge |H^i| > 1, g_i \in G, i = 1 \sim n-1)$. If $|H^1| = 1$, then model T is called Tree-type structure and if $|H^1| > 1$, then called Forest-type structure.

Definition 6. Acyclic-Digraph-type hierarchical structure. If the mapping set G satisfies $g_i(x) \cap g_i(y) \neq \Phi(\exists x \neq y \in H^i \wedge |H^i| > 1, g_i \in G, i = 1 \sim n-1)$, then model T is called Acyclic-Digraph-type hierarchical structure which is an extended structure against Tree-type and Forest-type.

To be convenient for understanding the definition of HSM, we give an instance of model $3 - T$ shown as Fig.1, where, a round denotes an element, an arrow shows a mapping relation. By the above definitions, an instance of model $3-T$ can be depicted to $T = (H, G)$, where:

$$H = (H^1, H^2, H^3) = (\{h_1^1\}, \{h_1^2, h_2^2, h_3^2\}, \{h_1^3, h_2^3, h_3^3, h_4^3, h_5^3, h_6^3, h_7^3, h_8^3\});$$

$$G = \{g_1, g_2\} = \{\quad g_1(h_1^1) = \{h_1^2, h_2^2, h_3^2\}, g_2(h_1^2) = \{h_1^3, h_2^3, h_3^3\},$$
$$g_2(h_2^2) = \{h_4^3, h_5^3, h_6^3\}, g_2(h_3^2) = \{h_7^3, h_8^3\} \quad \}$$

H^1 is a root element set, H^1 and H^2 are layer element sets, H^3 is a base element set. Obviously, model $3-T$ has a Tree-type structure.

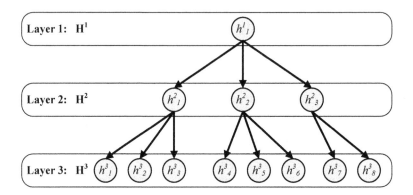

Fig. 1. An instance of model $3-T$

3.2   Index System Model

Based on HSM, we propose a hierarchical model of security index system, defined as follows:

Definition 7. Model of Security Index System (MSIS) $S = (T, F)$, where:

1) T is a HSM where index instances of root, base and layer element are respectively called root, base and layer index. T is used to define a hierarchical structure of index system including base indices and mapping relations between layer indices;

2) F is a set of index computing formulas, defined as follows:

$$F = \{f_i \mid f_i : \{g_i(h) \mid g_i \in T.G, h \in H^i \in T.H\} \to R, i = 1 \sim n - 1, R \text{ is real set}\}, \text{ is}$$

used to define computing methods and formulas between layer indices by means of applying requirements. Thus, root and layer indices can be calculated by base indices step by step.

Through analysis of the above definitions, the features of MSIS can be summarized as follows:

- As a general architecture model of index system, MSIS can provide a uniform modeling methodology for establishing different examples for different applications.

- MSIS has ability of describing multi-architectures such as Tree-type, Forest-type and Acyclic-Digraph- type. For an instance of representative Tree-type structure, each layer index set denotes an index attribute in which each layer index denotes a category of indices on the attribute and all the mapped base indices belong to this category. Moreover, there are one-to-one relations between each upper layer index and a category of lower layer indices (or base indices).
- MSIS has ability of computing indices and can provide a uniform computing method and standard.

4 Case Study on Modeling

4.1 Index, Attribute and Mapping Sets

For an instance of IP data network of China Telecommunications Corporation, this paper first respectively gives the sets of index, attribute and mapping:

(1) Index set $I = \{i_x^y \mid x \in [1,8], y \in [1,4]\}$, where, x respectively denotes 8 categories of indices, y respectively denotes Beijing, Shanghai, Guangzhou and other telecom objects, detailed definitions shown as Table 2.

Table 2. Definitions of the index set

Index Name	Computing Formula	Brief Description
Bandwidth Utilization Index i_1^y	Assuming: at base and reporting period, total bandwidth indicators of network object y are respectively b_b^y and b_r^y, total traffic indicators are respectively t_b^y and t_r^y. Then: $$i_1^y = \frac{t_r^y}{b_r^y} \Big/ \frac{t_b^y}{b_b^y}$$ where, total traffic is the sum of traffic of network nodes selected.	To reflect the variable degree of bandwidth utilization in the specified network object
Delay Index i_2^y	Assuming: at base and reporting period, the selected node number indicators of network object y are respectively n_b^y and n_r^y, total delay indicators are respectively d_b^y and d_r^y. Then: $$i_2^y = \frac{d_r^y}{n_r^y} \Big/ \frac{d_b^y}{n_b^y}$$ where, the delay time may be calculated by average interval of sampled packets in a same TCP link.	To reflect the variable degree of delay in the specified network object

Table 2. (*continued*)

Traffic Index i_3^y	Assuming: at base and reporting period, the selected node number indicators of network object y are respectively n_b^y and n_r^y, total traffic indicators are respectively t_b^y and t_r^y. Then: $$i_3^y = \frac{t_r^y}{n_r^y} \bigg/ \frac{t_b^y}{n_b^y}$$	To reflect the variable degree of traffic in the specified network object
Packet Rate Index i_4^y	Assuming: at base and reporting period, the selected node number indicators of network object y are respectively n_b^y and n_r^y, total packet rate indicators are respectively p_b^y and p_r^y. Then: $$i_4^y = \frac{p_r^y}{n_r^y} \bigg/ \frac{p_b^y}{n_b^y}$$	To reflect the variable degree of packet rate in the specified network object
IP Distribution Index i_5^y	Assuming: at base and reporting period, the selected node number indicators of network object y are respectively n_b^y and n_r^y, total IP distribution indicators are respectively s_b^y and s_r^y. Then: $$i_5^y = \frac{s_r^y}{n_r^y} \bigg/ \frac{s_b^y}{n_b^y}$$ where, the IP distribution indicator may be calculated by the method of absolute entropy.	To reflect the variable degree of IP distribution characteristic in the specified network object
Port Distribution Index i_6^y	Assuming: at base and reporting period, the selected node number indicators of network object y are respectively n_b^y and n_r^y, total port distribution indicators are respectively r_b^y and r_r^y. Then: $$i_6^y = \frac{r_r^y}{n_r^y} \bigg/ \frac{r_b^y}{n_b^y}$$ where, the port distribution indicator may be also calculated by the method of absolute entropy.	To reflect the variable degree of port distribution characteristic in the specified network object

Table 2. (*continued*)

Ineffective Packet Component Index i_7^y	Assuming: at base and reporting period, the selected node number indicators of network object y are respectively n_b^y and n_r^y, total ineffective packet component indicators are respectively e_b^y and e_r^y. Then: $$i_7^y = \frac{e_r^y}{n_r^y} \bigg/ \frac{e_b^y}{n_b^y}$$ where, the ineffective packets may include ICMP packets, TCP Syn/Ack/Rst/Fin packets, UDP packets without payloads, etc.	To reflect the variable degree of ratio of ineffective packets to total packets in the specified network object
Forged Packet Component Index i_8^y	Assuming: at base and reporting period, the selected node number indicators of network object y are respectively n_b^y and n_r^y, total forged packet component indicators are respectively f_b^y and f_r^y. Then: $$i_8^y = \frac{f_r^y}{n_r^y} \bigg/ \frac{f_b^y}{n_b^y}$$ where, the forged packets may include spoof source IP packets, etc.	To reflect the variable degree of ratio of forged packets to total packets in the specified network object

(2) Classifying attribute set $A = \{A_1, A_2\} = \{\{a_{11}, a_{12}, a_{13}, a_{14}, a_{15}\}, \{a_{21}, a_{22}, a_{23}\}\}$, where, A_1 denotes object scale attribute including total index of China telecom, class indices of Beijing, Shanghai, Guangdong and other telecom index. A_2 denotes security characteristic attribute including availability index, anomaly index and effectivity index.

Table 3. The classifying mapping δ_1 based on object scale

Mapping Rule	Index Class	Classifying Results
To reflect the variable degree of whole phenomena of China telecom	China telecom's total index: a_{11}	Φ
To reflect the variable degree of a group of phenomena of Beijing telecom	Beijing telecom's class index: a_{12}	$\{i_x^1 \mid x \in [1,8]\}$
To reflect the variable degree of a group of phenomena of Shanghai telecom	Shanghai telecom's class index: a_{13}	$\{i_x^2 \mid x \in [1,8]\}$
To reflect the variable degree of a group of phenomena of Guangdong telecom	Guangdong telecom's class index: a_{14}	$\{i_x^3 \mid x \in [1,8]\}$
To reflect the variable degree of a group of phenomena of other telecom	Other telecom's class index: a_{15}	$\{i_x^4 \mid x \in [1,8]\}$

(3) Classifying mapping set $\Delta = \{\delta_1, \delta_2, \delta_\Pi\}$, where, δ_1 and δ_2 are respectively the classifying mappings based on object scale and security characteristic, shown as Table 3 and Table 4, δ_Π is 2-dimension classifying mapping. Due to $\delta_\Pi^{-1}((x,y)) = \delta_1^{-1}(x) \cap \delta_2^{-1}(y)$ ($x \in A_1, y \in A_2$), the classifying results of δ_Π can be obtained by means of δ_1 and δ_2.

Table 4. The classifying mapping δ_2 based on security characteristic

Mapping Rule	Index Class	Classifying Results
To reflect the extent of availability on network data communication and information sharing	Availability index: a_{21}	$\{i_1^y, i_2^y \mid y \in [1,4]\}$
To reflect the extent of anomaly on network communication data characteristics caused by security threats or attacks	Anomaly index: a_{22}	$\{i_3^y, i_4^y, i_5^y, i_6^y \mid y \in [1,4]\}$
To reflect the extent of effectiveness of information load over network communication data	Effectivity index: a_{23}	$\{i_7^y, i_8^y \mid y \in [1,4]\}$

4.2   An Example of Index System Modeling

In order to illustrate the modeling method and process, we will adopt MSIS to construct an example of index system, where, element set family H in T can be established by index set I and classifying attribute set A, and mapping set G in T can be constructed by classifying mapping set Δ.

Thus, we construct an example of index system described as $S_4 = (T, F)$, where:

(1) $T = (H, G)$, where:

- $H = \{H^1, H^2, H^3, H^4\} = \{\{a_{11}\}, A_1', A_1' \times A_2, I\}$, where, $A_1' = A_1 / \{a_{11}\}$. Obviously, T is a model of $4 - T$.

- $G = \{g_1, g_2, g_3\} = \{\ g_1 : \{a_{11}\} \to 2^{A_1'}, g_2 : A_1' \to 2^{A_1' \times A_2}, g_3 : A_1' \times A_2 \to 2^I\}$
$$= \{\ g_1(a_{11}) = A_1',$$
$$g_2(x) = \{(x,y) \mid (x,y) \in A_1' \times A_2\}\quad (\forall x \in A_1'),$$
$$g_3((x,y)) = \delta_\Pi^{-1}((x,y)) = \delta_1^{-1}(x) \cap \delta_2^{-1}(y)\quad (\forall (x,y) \in A_1' \times A_2)\ \}$$

, obviously, g_i satisfies $\bigcup_{h \in H^i} g_i(h) = H^{i+1} (i=1,2,3)$. Therefore, the above construction meets Definition 4 of HSM.

Obviously, S_4 is a Tree-type structure.

(2) $F = \{f_1, f_2, f_3\}$, where, f_1 is a method for calculating total index by class indices, f_2 for calculating class indices by security characteristic indices and f_3 for calculating security characteristic indices by base indices, defined as follows:

- $f_1(A_1') = \sum_{a \in A_1} v(a)$

- $f_2(\{(x, y) \mid y \in A_2\}) = \sum_{y \in A_2} v((x, y)) \Big/ |A_2|, \forall x \in A_1'$

- $f_3(\{i_1^y, i_2^y\}) = Max\{\frac{1}{i_1^y}, \frac{1}{i_2^y}\}, \forall y \in [1,4]$

  $f_3(\{i_3^y, i_4^y, i_5^y, i_6^y\}) = Max\{i_3^y, i_4^y, i_5^y, i_6^y\}, \forall y \in [1,4]$

  $f_3(\{i_7^y, i_8^y\}) = Max\{\frac{1}{i_7^y}, \frac{1}{i_8^y}\}, \forall y \in [1,4]$

where $v(x)$ denotes the value of layer index x.

As stated above, we have constructed an index system example of S_4 with 4-layer and Tree-type structure shown as Fig.2. As can be seen from Fig.2, through calculating step by step, S_4 is able to timely reflect macro situation of China telecom and its evolution and trends over time on different levels of total index and class index and from different sides of security characteristic. Moreover, if a typical network normal activity at base period is selected as a uniform evaluating standard, then S_4 is also able to measure, compare and evaluate security situation of different network objects, different security events and different periods.

Therefore, MSIS proposed in this paper is feasible and effective.

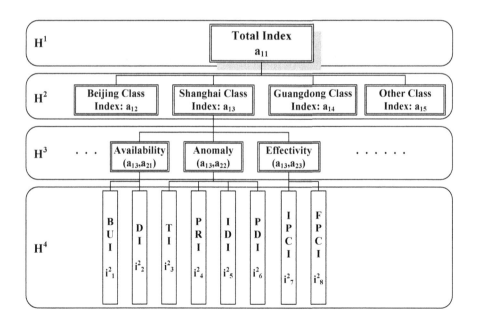

Fig. 2. The architecture of an index system example S_4

5   Conclusions

On the basis of introducing a concept of network operation security index and its application senses, this paper proposes a general architecture model of security index system (MSIS) with computing ability. An instance of IP data network of China Tele-communications Corporation is given to illustrate the modeling method and process, so as to validate the feasibility and effectivity of MSIS on the level of instances. The analysis of the application instance indicates that MSIS has ability of computing indices and describing multi-architectures such as Tree-type, Forest-type and Acyclic-Digraph-type, and is especially able to provide a uniform modeling methodology and computing standard for establishment of index system examples to meet the needs of different applications.

Acknowledgement. This research is supported by the National Natural Science Foundation of China (Grant No. 61070185), the National High Technology Research and Development Program of China (863 Program) (Grant No. 2007AA01Z444), and the Knowledge Innovation Program of the Chinese Academy of Sciences.

References

1. Fang, B.X., Yin, L.H.: Research on Information Security Definition. Information and Network Security (1) 8–10 (2008)
2. Lin, C., Wang, Y., Li, Q.L.: Stochastic Modeling and Evaluation for Network Security. Chinese Journal of Computers 28(12), 1943–1956 (2005)
3. Cheng, X.D.: Research on evaluation index system of telecommunication security. Modern Science and Technology of Telecommunications (8), 10–13 (2005)
4. Gao, H.S., Zhu, J., Li, C.C.: The analysis of uncertainty of network security risk assessment using Dempster-Shafer theory. In: Proceedings of 12th International Conference on Computer Supported Cooperative Work in Design (CSCWD 2008), Xi'an, China, pp. 754–759 (April 2008)
5. Hu, Y., Ren, D.B., Wu, S.H., et al.: Study and Application of Evaluation Index System for Telecommunication Network Risk. Telecommunications Science (5), 50–54 (2008)
6. Hariri, S., Qu, G., Dharmagadda, T., et al.: Impact analysis of faults and attacks in large-scale networks. IEEE Security & Privacy 1(5), 49–54 (2003)
7. Qu, G., Hariri, S., Zhu, X., et al.: Multivariate Statistical Online Analysis for Self Protection against Network Attacks. In: Proceedings of the IEEE International Conference on Information and Computer Science (ICICS 2004), Dhahran, Saudi Arabia (November 2004)
8. Chen, X.Z., Zheng, Q.H., Guan, X.H., et al.: Multiple behavior information fusion based quantitative threat evaluation. Computers & Security (24), 218–231 (2005)
9. Wang, S., Sun, L.C.: Research and Implementation of Evaluation System for Network Attack Effect Based on Indicator System. Computer Engineering and Applications 41(34), 149–153 (2005)
10. Su, J.H.: Social Economy Statistics Theory, 2nd edn. Lixin Accounting Publishing House (2006)

An Evaluation Framework of Coverage-Based Fault Localization for Object-Oriented Programs

Qing Xu[1], Yu Pei[2], and Linzhang Wang[1]

[1] Department of Computer Science and Technology,
Nanjing University, Nanjing, China
`xuqing@seg.nju.edu.cn`,
`lzwang@nju.edu.cn`
[2] Chair of Software Engineering,
Swiss Federal Institute of Technology, Zurich
`ypei@inf.ethz.ch`

Abstract. Fault localization is always a complex and time-consuming process. Fault localization techniques based on code coverage information have shown their inspiring ability to narrow down the range of suspicious code. In this paper, we summarize the special features of object-oriented programs, and then we propose a framework to evaluate the effectiveness of these techniques on object-oriented. In the end, a new fault localization technique for object-oriented programs would be proposed, together with a prototype tool to support it.

Keywords: fault localization, code coverage, object-oriented program, suspicious rank.

1 Introduction

Software debugging is a process of locating and correcting faulty program statements, which is usually expensive and mostly manually. To debug effectively, programmers need to identify the exact locations of the bugs. While throughout the whole process, locating faults in a program can be very time-consuming and arduous, and therefore, there is an increased demand for automated techniques that can assist in the fault localization process.

Fault localization techniques assist in software debugging by reducing the amount of code people have to inspect to pinpoint faults. Researches in recent years have confirmed that fault localization techniques based on code-coverage information could narrow down the range of suspicious code significantly. The technique of code coverage [1] has been recognized by its effectiveness in identifying suspicious statements that may contain the fault. A code coverage-based method with a family of heuristics was proposed by Eric Wong etc. in order to prioritize suspicious code according to its likelihood of containing program bugs [3].

Such researches, however, mostly focused on procedure-oriented programs: even though some of the existing work in this area used object-oriented programs in one

Y. Yuan, X. Wu, and Y. Lu (Eds.): ISCTCS 2012, CCIS 320, pp. 591–597, 2013.

way or another, the fault localization techniques in such work weren't designed, or evaluated, with the special features of object-orientation, e.g. inheritance and dynamic binding.

In this paper, we summarize the fault types of object-oriented programs, and then design a framework to evaluate existing fault localization techniques. Based on the framework we try to propose a code coverage based fault localization method for object-oriented programs. Program spectrum-based techniques record the execution information of a program with respect to each test case. We will use the combination of the executable statement hit spectrum and class information to achieve more accuracy and effectiveness of fault localization result for object-oriented programs.

The rest of this paper is organized as follows: in section 2 object-oriented fault types that may not be identified accurately by existing technologies are introduced. In section 3 we describe the framework of our work. A case study is presented in section 4. Finally, in Section 5 we offer our conclusions and future work.

2   Object-Oriented Faults

2.1   Yo-Yo Problem

The yo-yo problem occurs in an anti-pattern program whose inheritance graph is very long and complicated. To understand programs with yo-yo problem, the programmer has to keep flipping between many different class definitions in order to follow the control flow.

Class	Method A	Method B	Method C	Method D
C1	Implements Sends self to B and C			
C2		Implements Sends self to D	Implements	Implements Sends self to C
C3	Refines Sends super to A	Refines Sends super to B		
C4	Refines Sends super to A		Refines Sends super to A	
C5				Refines Sends super to A

Fig. 1. The yo-yo problem [10]

In object-oriented programs, as classes grow deeper and applications grow more complex, execution can sometimes "bounce" up and down among levels of inheritance. This execution action is just like the up-down movement of a toy yo-yo. In

1989, Taenzer et al. first proposed the conception of yo-yo problem to describe the misusing of polymorphism and method refinement in Objective-C. Along with the complexities due to method overriding and polymorphism, it creates more difficulty and required effort in software testing.

Fig.1 is an example for yo-yo problem [10]. "C1 is a super class, and C2 is its subclass, etc. In this example, the implementation of method A uses B and C; B uses D. Messages to these methods are bound according to the class hierarchy and the use of self and super."

Suppose an object of class C5 accepts message A. The trace of the yo-yo execution should be: C5.A → C4.A → C3.A → C5.B → C3.B → C2.B → C5.D → C2.D → C5.C → C4.C → C2.C. As the inheritance level increases, the complexity of execution trace grows exponentially.

2.2   Fault Patterns in OO Programs

Jeff Offutt proposed a fault model for subtype inheritance and polymorphism [5]. This model can be used to support empirical investigations of object-oriented testing techniques, to inspire further research into object oriented testing and analysis. In this model, Offutt introduces a list of object-oriented faults which can occur when inheritance and polymorphism is used. Table.1 shows the faults and anomalies due to inheritance and polymorphism.

Table 1. Transformation Mapping Rules [5]

Acronym	Fault/Anomaly
ITU	Inconsistent Type Use (context swapping)
SDA	State Definition Anomaly (possible post-condition violation)
SDIH	State Definition Inconsistency (due to state variable hiding)
SDI	State Defined Incorrectly (possible post-condition violation)
IISD	Indirect Inconsistent State Definition
ACB1	Anomalous Construction Behavior (1)
ACB2	Anomalous Construction Behavior (2)
IC	Incomplete Construction
SVA	State Visibility Anomaly

3   Framework of Fault Localization Techniques

We've designed a framework to evaluate the efficiency of existing techniques on object-oriented programs: inject faults into object methods that feature dynamic binding, apply exiting coverage-based techniques to locate the faults, and then evaluate the effectiveness and efficiency of these techniques. In this framework, code-coverage would be computed in two various settings. In a flattened setting, code-coverage is based on method definitions, i.e. disregarding the dynamic types of the objects on which the method is called; in a hierarchical setting, a method of a sub-class is considered as being different from its ancestor version in the super-class, even if the method is not redefined in the inheritance path, and therefore their code-coverage's are also different. Effectiveness and efficiency of fault localization in both settings would be evaluated and compared, as in Fig.2.

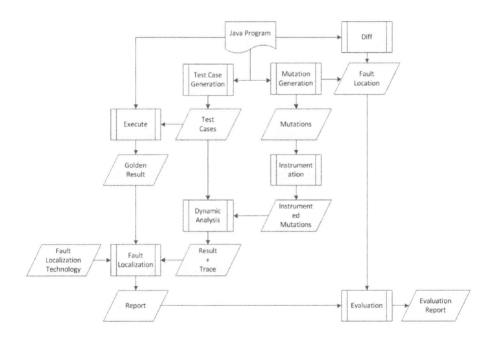

Fig. 2. The evaluation framework of fault localization

James A. Jones provided a summary of five coverage-based fault localization techniques: Tarantula, Set union, Set intersection, Nearest Neighbor, and Cause Transitions [9]. Each of these techniques provides a method to rank the suspiciousness of statements. Studies show that the Tarantula technique outperforms the other techniques both in terms of effectiveness and efficiency in fault localization.

To compare and evaluate the effectiveness and efficiency of fault localization between those coverage-based techniques mentioned above, we respectively apply them on a set of java program mutants. Test cases are run on actual projects, and Cobertura- -a Java code coverage analysis tool-- is used to get the testing result and code-coverage information. The execution results and code-coverage information are recorded for suspiciousness calculation. Considering the special features of object-orientation, the suspicious rank is not satisfactory in some situation.

To improve the effectiveness and efficiency of fault localization techniques on ob-ject-oriented programs, we introduce the java class information for suspiciousness calculation. Traditional techniques only care about the code-coverage information and execution results of test cases. In the "Instrumentation" process in Fig.2, we get class information together with execution results and executable statement hit spectrum by code instrumentation. Thus the suspiciousness rank would be more precise and con-sistent with the real fault situation. However, still much work remains to be done to get the new algorithm finalized.

4   Case Study

4.1   Inconsistent Type Use (ITU)

In this kind of fault type, the subclass does not override any super class method. Thus, there can be no polymorphic behavior. However, there exists the possibility of that the extension methods can access the methods in super class or change inherited state variables. Prog.4.1 shows an example of ITU.

Prog. 4.1 Example of ITU

```
public void removeElement(Vector v){
    v.removeElementAt(v.size() - 1);
}
public void addElement(Vector v){
    String str = "";
    v.addElement(str);
}
public void push3AndPop3(Stack s){
    String s1, s2, s3;
    push(s , s1);
    push(s , s2);
    push(s , s3);
    ...
    addElement(s);
    removeElement(s);
    ...
    pop(s);
    pop(s);
    pop(s);
}
```

It is illegal to apply the operations like removeElement(Vector) and addEle-ment(Vector) to the data constructor Stack. These operations may change the program status in an uncontrollable way and increase the complexity and difficulty in fault localization.

4.2   State Definition Inconsistency Due to State Variable Hiding (SDIH)

If a state variable defined in subclass shares the same name with the inherited state variable, the inherited variable is hidden from the scope of the descendant. Problems may occur if not all inherited methods are overridden. Here is an SDIH example, as in Prog.4.2.

*Prog.*4.2 Example of SDIH

```
public class Father {
    protected int x;
    public Father(){
        x = 0;
    }
    public void setX(){
        x = 100;
    }
    public int getX(){
        return x;
    }
}
public class Son extends Father{
    public int x;
    public Son(){
        x = 1;
    }
}
```

Execution Part:

```
Son s = new Son();
s.setX();
 System.out.println(s.x);
```

When the statements in Prog.4.2 being executed, we can never get the right value of x in subclass. Experiments in Tarantula show that the constructor method and setX() method share the high level suspiciousness, instead of the definition of x in subclass.

5   Conclusion and Future Work

This paper has presented the status quo of fault localization techniques for object-oriented programs. We have established a framework to evaluate the effectiveness and efficiency of these techniques. And a new method is proposed to improve the fault localization technique. In the future, large-scale experiments are expected, and the algorithm to calculate the suspiciousness would be finalized. Finally, a prototype tool would be proposed to support our fault localization technique, and at the same time, systematic experiments and evaluation would be carried out.

Acknowledgments. This work is supported by the National Natural Science Foundation of China (No.91118002).

References

1. Jones, J., Harrold, M.J., Stasko, J.: Visualization of Test Information to Assist Fault Localization. In: Proceedings of 24th International Conference on Software Engineering (ICSE), pp. 467–477 (2002)
2. Huang, T.-Y., Chou, P.-C., Tsai, C.-H., Chen, H.-A.: Automated Fault Localization with Statistically Suspicious Program States. In: LCTES 2007, San Diego, California, USA, June 13-15 (2007)
3. Eric Wong, W., Debroy, V., Choi, B.: A family of code coverage-based heuristics for effective fault localization. The Journal of Systems and Software 83, 188–208 (2010)
4. Nainar, P.A., Liblit, B.: Adaptive Bug Isolation. In: ICSE 2010, Cape Town, South Africa, May 2-8 (2010)
5. Offutt, J., Alexander, R., Wu, Y., Xiao, Q., Hutchinson, C.: A Fault Model for Subtype Inheritance and Polymorphism. In: ISSRE 2001, Hong Kong, PRC, pp. 84–95 (November 2001)
6. Eric Wong, W., Qi, Y., Zhao, L., Cai, K.-Y.: Effective Fault Localization using Code Coverage. In: 31st Annual International Computer Software and Applications Conference (COMPSAC 2007) (2007)
7. Eric Wong, W., Debroy, V.: Software Fault Localization. In: IEEE Reliability Society 2009 Annual Technology Report (2009)
8. Naish, L., Lee, H., Ramamohanarao, K.: A Model for Spectra-Based Software Diagnosis. ACM Transactions on Software Engineering and Methodology 20(3), Article 11 (August 2011)
9. Jones, J.A., Harrold, M.J.: Empirical Evaluation of the Tarantula Automatic Fault Localization Technique. In: The 20th IEEE/ACM international Conference on Automated Software Engineering
10. Binder, R.V.: Testing Object-Oriented Software: a Survey. Software Testing, Verification and Reliability 6, 125–252 (1996)
11. Do, H., Elbaum, S., Rothermel, G.: Supporting Controlled Experimentation with Testing Techniques: An Infrastructure and its Potential Impact. Empirical Software Engineering 10(4) (October 2005)
12. Santelices, R., Jones, J.A., Yu, Y., Harrold, M.J.: Lightweight Fault-Localization Using Multiple Coverage Types. IEEE Computer Society, Washington, DC (2009)

Research of New Words Identification in Social Network for Monitoring Public Opinion

Wang Xiaoyan[1,3], Xu Kai[1,2], Sha Ying[1], Tan Jian-long[1], and Guo Li[1]

[1] Institute of Computing Technology, Institute of Information Engineering,
National Engineering Laboratory for Information Security Technologies Beijing, China
[2] School of Computer and Information Engineering, Jiangxi Agricultural University,
Nanchang, Jiangxi, China
[3] Graduate School of Chinese Academy of Sciences, Beijing, China
wangxiaoyan@nelmail.iie.ac.cn

Abstract. With the rapid development of Internet, a large number of new words have emerged and widely been used in social network. Traditional segmentation algorithm can't identify these new words efficiently, which will greatly affect the accuracy in extracting out these hot words and keywords. Moreover, it will affect the performance of the network public opinion monitoring system. In this paper, we use tweets collected from Twitter as the experimental data-set. By calculating frequency statistics of k-gram strings, we can find out new words as candidates, and then identify new words by their practical application frequency using Twitter's search function. The experiment shows: this segmentation algorithm can effectively identify the new keywords and is more suitable for public opinion monitoring system.

Keywords: public opinion monitoring, social network, new words identification.

1 Introduction

Recently, rapid development of Internet in our country leads to a wider adoption of it. Network becomes an essential media and tool in people's information acquisition, view expressing and communication. It is not uncommon that the spread of some critical decisions, discussions of important event, and arguments of social hotspot start from these network application platforms. These moods, desires, attitudes and opinions spreading in Internet against all kinds of events related to or concerned by the holders add up to network public opinion [1].

People are more willing to express their view points, attitudes and opinions on the Internet due to the openness and freedom of it, moreover its virtual characteristic and anonymity enhance the reality and trustworthy of these opinions. In other words, these information exists in the Internet can help the government to develop a deeper understanding of the hotspot that citizens concern and act as an objective evidence in the decision making. But in the other hand, violent, reactionary, and fake information

Y. Yuan, X. Wu, and Y. Lu (Eds.): ISCTCS 2012, CCIS 320, pp. 598–603, 2013.

can be found in every corner of the Internet, and there are also many illegal behaviors like rumor making , which are definitely menaces to the national security, people's safety and reputation of enterprise. In order to maintain social peace, develop harmonious society and keep enterprise impression, data mining of public opinion is critical.

Chinese word segmentation is the basis of public opinion monitoring and its function has direct influence on the clustering procedures, while new words identification is always a difficult point in this technology. Single word, which is discovered by word splitting algorithms, is the basic unit of the vector form of texts that spiders have collected. One basic task of network public opinion monitoring is to identify new topics, hotspot topics and emergency event from large data set of network corpus [2].Yet the topic words of these new topics, hotspot topics or emergency events are most commonly new words and they are not included in the dictionary of robot, which is very limited, and thereby, they can't be recognized and will be split into single characters. Whereas, these topic words are important criteria for clustering in network public opinion monitoring system, being unable to identify these critical words can lead to problems such as poor performance in clustering and unacceptable large result set.

2   Related Work

The research of new words discovering has become a research frontier. Many researchers and institutes have proposed their own method of automatic discovering of new words and made significant progress in many fields. Traditional text corpus like People Daily text corpus, Sogo text corpus and other text corpuses are all static data sets. These data sets don't evolve with time, thereby have no timeliness. The quality of text corpuses directly impacts the performance of discovering of unrecorded words. A good text corpus for unrecorded words discovering needs some scale of data, balance of source and good timeliness. Recently, the research of text corpus of network forum and web news gains lots of interests.

[3] proposes an unrecorded word discovering method based on forum text corpus. The text corpus is initialized and updated periodically by a network spider to maintain timeliness. A constructed statistic MD is used for splitting word of the text corpus and producing a list of candidates. By comparing the candidates and the recorded words, unrecorded words will be discovered and added into the vocabulary.

Being aware of the problem that the rapid emerging of new words in Internet and the difficulties of identifying them, [4]proposes a new words identification method using improved association rule mining algorithm, noting the fact that characters in the candidate string are adjacent, ordered and frequent appearance. Those candidate strings are constructed by using the frequency of co-occurrence and the time pattern of characters. [5]identifies the new words from the collected corpus by large-scale analysis of the pages collected from the Internet, building large set of words and strings from them, applying automatically new words detection, and finally filtering the result according to word formation rules.

[6], [7] proposed a new word detection method based on the large-scale corpus. [6] firstly applies Chinese lexical segmentation on large-scale Internet raw corpus, and then finds candidates of new words according to the frequency statistics. To handle regular patterns like two-, three- or four-character new words, self-learning method is used to produce three garbage dictionaries and a affix dictionary for spam filtering on these candidates, and finally lexical category filter rules and independent word probability technique is used for further filtering.[7]uses statistics of repeating strings and language characteristic of analysis of the external environment and internal structure of each strings, judging of the context of adjacent species, probability of being a word of the first and last character and the degree of coupling for filtering and discovering of new words.

[8] notifies the new words discovering problem in the network public opinion monitoring and identifies unrecorded topic words by using the local high-frequency characteristic of unrecorded topic words in network public opinion monitoring and calculating the degree of bonding between the abnormal words and those around them.

In the existing research, there is no use of social network data as Corpus. Social network, which is a new form of information dissemination, provides a new channel for people to express their views. So it has become the focus of network public opinion monitoring. Twitter is a popular social network that enables the users to send and read short text messages (up to 140 characters), commonly known as tweets. After its launch on July 2006, Twitter users have increased rapidly，till 2011, they were estimated as 200 million worldwide with around 450 thousands new accounts per day, which makes Twitter one of the fastest growing web sites in the world [9]. Over the past few years, Twitter has become the main source on the web for users to share their thoughts. Users can absorb content from those they follow, as well as distribute content to those who follow them. The manner in which has been streamlined through the Twitter service has allowed Twitter to become a hub for such information passing activities. So we do our new words research on the data collection of Tweets from Twitter.

3   New Words Discovering Method

New words are often split into characters in traditional word splitting method. This happens in these three cases in most of cases:

1)combination of single character words, eg., "Tui Te" being split into "Tui" and "Te";

2)combination of one single character word and a multi characters word, eg., "Yao Qing Ma" being split into "Yao Qing" and "Ma";

3)combination of multi characters words, eg., "Nan Fang Zhou Mo" being split into "Nan Fang" and "Zhou Mo";

The new words we are looking for are popular and active in some period of time, so the words are suppose to show up in text corpus frequently and repeatedly, and we can expect a primary analytical result by applying statistic method of words frequency. We split tweets into strings of 2, 3, or 4 elements, and calculate the frequency of the strings, and then treat words with high frequency and out of known words as new word candidates. Finally, we utilize the search function provided by Twitter to find out the frequency of candidates in real world tweets, so to determine new words. This research is mainly about Chinese and Twitter has many non-chinese user, so we apply a pretreatment of trimming out non-chinese characters and transcoding the remain text into GB encoding on the collected data.

Let S_m is the sentence, where m is a positive integer, then the corpus to be processed can be expressed as $\{S_1, S_2, ... , S_n\}$, k is the initial value of 1.

The algorithm for dividing strings and counting words frequency describes as:

1) For k> n, then the end; otherwise using regular expressions to match S_k, all the non-Chinese characters will be removed, replaced with '/'. Treating sentence S_k = $\{p_1/p_2 / ... / p_j\}$, p_i on behalf of a phrase (i is a positive integer).

2) Using segmentation tool ICTCLAS to divide data into words. After the process, p_i in S_k can be expressed as $p_i = \{W_{i1} W_{i2} ... W_{ir}\}$, W_{it} (t is a positive integer) represents a word.

3) For k> n, then the end; otherwise using the stop word lists to remove stop words in S_k, such "De"、 "Shi". As strings maximum length of our study is 4, so if the W_{it}'s length is greater than or equal to 4, remove it.

4) For k> n, then the end; otherwise handling p_i in the S_k as follows: firstly, remove the spaces in p_i, get of p_i', divide p_i' into strings of two、 three and four words length. Then find out if p_i contains the string, if it is not an existing word, add the string into collection of the candidate strings and plus one with the number of the string, otherwise delete n strings from the collection and skip n characters in the p_i and continue the process.

Because of the flexibility of combination of words in Chinese and some defeats of the automatic word segmentation program, there are some meaningless strings in the new word candidates of frequency statistic method. The search function of Twitter API will then be used to find out the numbers of tweets which contain each candidate. This number and the frequency of the candidate will determine the final selection of new words.

4   Experiment and Results

With data collecting program developed by ourselves, we collect three different data sets with number of 140k, 1000k and 2000k. With the pretreatment of trimming out non-Chinese characters, these data sets include 100k, 500k and 1000k tweets, respectively.

Use our new words recognition method on these three corpuses. Through experiments, we found that the frequency of new words in the 100k's data set is greater than 50, to 0.5 million scale data set this frequency is 200 and to 1 million scale data set this frequency is 300. The counts of new words found in the three corpuses were 60,

120 and 150. You can see that with the doubling of the size of the data set, the count of new words did not multiply. This is due to the count of new words within a period of time will not grow freely. We can also find out that the patterns of high frequency new words of these three data sets are basically the same.

Below is the table of major high frequency new words discovered from the data set mentioned above with new word discover method we propose here.

Table 1. High-frequency new words of different data sets

Data scale:100000		Data scale: 500000		Data scale: 1000000	
Words	Frequency	Words	Frequency	Words	Frequency
TuiTe	224	WeiBo	1294	ShiMing	2015
YaoQingMa	217	ShiMing	1198	YangShi	1988
FanFou	207	YangShi	1182	BoXun	1655
WeiBo	149	DianJi	840	DianJi	1620
KuangNan	131	BoXun	837	WeiBo	1543
ShiMing	112	QiangChai	806	QiangChai	1326
NanFangZhouMo	72	BeiJu	740	BeiJu	1259
Beiju	71	GaoTie	727	GaoTie	1148
		XiNao	682	KengDie	1053
		WeiRuan	681	KeHuDuan	996
		DanDing	676	TuCao	927
		HeiMei	663	TieZi	865
				BaoLiao	754

5   Conclusion

In the paper, we propose a new words discovering method targeting at monitoring public opinion in social network by calculating the frequency of them, which makes use of the high frequency of topic words in the data-sets of social network. With the data-sets of tweets collected from Twitter, we find new word candidates by their frequency and use the search function of Twitter to get their real world frequency to finally determine new words. The result shows that this method can discover some new words out of the dictionary, which supports its effectiveness in public opinion monitoring. Yet this method has a shortcoming that some meaningless strings would appear as new word candidates. The future work will focus on eliminating this sort of strings and improving the accuracy of new words discovering.

Acknowledgements. This research was supported by The National Natural Science Foundation of China (61070184), the "Strategic Priority Research Program" of the Chinese Academy of Sciences，Grant No.XDA06030200, and National High Technology Research and Development Program 863 No. 2011AA010705.

References

1. Xu, X.-R.: Study on the Way to Solve the Paroxysmal Public Feelings on Internet. Journal of North China Electric Power University (Social Sciences) (1), 89–93 (2007) (in Chinese)
2. Wei, W., Xin, X.: Online Public Opinion Hotspot Detection and Analysis Based on Document Clustering. New Technology of Library and Information Service (3), 74–79 (2009) (in Chinese)
3. Du, J., Xiong, H.-L.: Algorithm to recognize unknown Chinese words based on BBS corpus. Computer Engineering and Design 31(3), 630–633 (2010) (in Chinese)
4. Li, D., Cao, Y.-D., Wan, Y.-L.: Internet-Oriented New Words Identification. Journal of Beijing University of Posts and Telecommunications 31(1), 26–29 (2008) (in Chinese)
5. Zou, G., Liu, Y., Liu, Q., et al.: Internet oriented Chinese New Words Detection. Journal of Chinese Information Processing 18(6), 1–9 (2004) (in Chinese)
6. Cui, S.-Q., Liu, Q., et al.: New Word Detection Based on Large- Scale Corpus. Journal of Computer Research and Development 43(5), 927–932 (2006) (in Chinese)
7. He, M., Gong, C.C., Zhang, H.-P., et al.: Method of new word identification based on larger-scale corpus. Computer Engineering and Applications 43(21), 157–159 (2007) (in Chinese)
8. Tang, J.-T., Li, F., Guo, C.S.: Research of New Word Pattern Recognization in Network Monitoring Public Opinion. Computer Technology and Development 22(1), 119–125 (2012) (in Chinese)
9. Trendistic, http://trendistic.com/

A Novel Dynamic Self-adaptive Framework
for Network Security Evaluation

Wu Jinyu[1,2,3], Yin Lihua[2], and Fang Binxing[1,3]

[1]Beijing University of Posts and Telecommunications, Beijing, China
[2]Institute of Information Engineering, Chinese Academy of Sciences, Beijing, China
[3] Key Laboratory of Trustworthy Distributed Computing and Service (BUPT),
Ministry of Education, Beijing, China
eyoudian19@gmail.com,
yinlihua@software.ict.ac.cn, fangbx@bupt.edu.cn

Abstract. Evaluating network security is vital step in risk management. However, existing evaluating methods such as using tools like attack graphs or attack trees to compute risk probabilities did not consider the concrete running environment of the target network, which may make the obtained results deviate from the true situation. In this paper, we propose a novel dynamic self-adaptive framework for network security evaluation. In addition to using Scan Tool and Attack Graph Generator to generate attack graphs, we design Audit Processor and Property Evaluator to get key information in the running environment of the target network. The major evaluation computing will be performed in Security Evaluator. We show how to use our framework to the real network. Experiment results show that our framework which capture the concrete running environment information of the network get closer result to the true situation and can dynamically adapt to changing environment.

Keywords: network security evaluation, self-adaptive framework, attack graphs, audit processor, property evaluator.

1 Introduction

Evaluating network security is vital step in risk management. It does not only uncover the security situation of the network, but also forms the basis of consequence security strategies. Many models have been proposed for performing evaluation of network security. Graphical models such as attack graphs become the main-stream approach [1], [2], [5], [7], [8], [10]. Attack graphs which capture the relationships among vulnerabilities and exploits show us all the possible attack paths that an attacker can take to intrude all the targets in the network. However, existing analysis methods [6], [11], [12] did not consider the concrete running environment of the network.

Let us look at an example shown in Fig. 1. Consider 4 running circumstances which have the same network and the same vulnerabilities in the network: (1) Web Server, FTP Server and Mail Server have about the same frequency of use by users; (2) Web Server has been heavily used, but FTP Server and Mail Server have been

Y. Yuan, X. Wu, and Y. Lu (Eds.): ISCTCS 2012, CCIS 320, pp. 604–612, 2013.

rarely used; (3) all of the data in Web Server, FTP Server and Mail Server are not important; (4) the data in FTP Server is very important and valuable, while the data in Web Server and Mail Server are not. We can easily conclude by common sense that Web Server in case 2 will be more likely attacked by intruder than that in case 1, and FTP Server in case 4 will be more likely attacked by intruder than that in case 3.

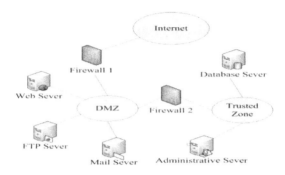

Fig. 1. An example network

Therefore, the running environment information is important for getting accurate results of security evaluation.

In this paper, we propose a novel dynamic self adaptive framework that captures the concrete running environment information for network security evaluation, which get more accurate results and can dynamically adapt to changing environment.

2   Related Works

Phillips and Swiler [2] were the first to introduce the attack graph mode and develop an attack graph generation tool [3]. Ritchey [4] used model checking to generate attack graph. Sheyner [5] improved the method of using model checking to generate attack graph, and gave some analysis method of attack graph. However, using model checking to generate attack graph exists the state explosion problem. To cope with the scalability problem of attack graph generation, Ammann [7] propose the monotonicity assumption that simplifies pre-condition checking for possible exploits and dramatically reduces the time complexity of attack graph generation from an exponential in n to $O(n^6)$. Ingols [8] reduced the size of the generated attack graph through aggregating hosts of the same reachability characteristics into one group and eliminating redundant common paths. Ou [9] proposed a logic-based network security analyzer MulVal and used it to analyze network security. Later, Ou [10] proposed the concept of logical attack graph and used MulVal to generate the logical attack graph. Ou's method has time complexity of $O(n^2)$ in the worst case, which is the lowest time complexity so far as we know.

Jha [6] used probability to analyze attack graph. He defined probabilistic attack graphs, and used Markov Decision Processes to compute the probability of the nodes in attack graph. However, Jha's method apply on the attack graph which has state explosion problem and has poor scalability. Mehta [11] used algorithm that is similar to the PageRank algorithm used by Google. YE [12] proposed a methodology for security risk analysis that is based on the model of attack graphs and the Common Vulnerability Scoring System (CVSS). He analyzed two challenging problems and gave corresponding method. Our method does not only use CVSS, but also audit information and property information to get more accurate results.

3   The Network Security Evaluation Framework

Our network security evaluation framework contains five parts: Scan Tool, Attack Graph Generator, Audit Processor, Property Evaluator and Security Evaluator. Their relationships are shown in Fig. 2.

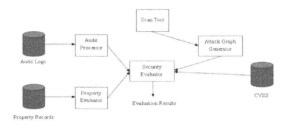

Fig. 2. The Network security Evaluation Framework

Scan Tool scans the network to find all the vulnerabilities. Attack Graph Generator uses all the vulnerabilities and the corresponding exploit information to generate the network attack graph. Audit Processor process the audit information to get the running environment threat information. Property Evaluator gets the distribution of the property values.

3.1   Scan Tool and Attack Graph Generator

Scan Tool is used to find all the vulnerabilities on the network. Lots of vulnerabilities scan tools, such as Nessus, X-Force and etc can be used as this part. After gathering all the vulnerabilities and the connection information, we use Attack Graph Generator to generator the network attack graph. Some off-the-shelf tools [7], [10] can be used as Attack Graph Generator.

Attack graph contains two kinds of nodes: condition node and exploit node. Each exploit node corresponds to each kind of vulnerabilities. Each condition node either corresponds to the pre-condition of exploiting the vulnerabilities or the post-condition of exploiting the vulnerabilities.

3.2   Audit Processor

As we see in the first example, different running environment of the network contains different threat. We can analyze the security audits to get the concrete threat of the concrete environment.

Original audit data often is "raw". Audit Processor first has to preprocess the raw data to the standard form. Here the standard form of the audit data is a 7-tuple (id, time, srcIP, srcPort, desIP, desPort, type).

After transforming the origin raw data to the standard form, we calculate the threat factor of the node in the attack graph, which we will introduce later.

3.3   Property Evaluator

Different value of property often has different attractiveness to the intruder. We assign numbers to each property in the network according to the importance of them in the network and store the numbers into the Property Records Database. Property Evaluator processes the Property Records Database and gets the attractive factor of the node in the attack graph, which we will introduce later.

3.4   Security Evaluator

The final results are got by the Security Evaluator. The input of the Security Evaluator includes: (1) Attack graph (generated by the Attack Graph Generator); (2) Threat factors (calculated by the Audit Processor); (3) Attractive factors (calculated by the Property Evaluator); (4) Difficult factors (calculated in Security Evaluator according to the CVSS).

CVSS (Common Vulnerability Scoring System) scores for all vulnerabilities provided by the National Vulnerability Database. CVSS gives the standardized metrics on the exploit difficulty of vulnerabilities. The base metric of Access Complexity (AC) in CVSS describes the complexity of exploiting the vulnerability and can take the values of "high", "medium", or "low". This metric indicates the success likelihood of an exploit when all the necessary pre-conditions are met and an attacker launches the exploit. So we can use this field to get the difficult factors of the nodes in the network attack graph.

Security Evaluator gets all the inputs and calculates the final results. We will introduce the corresponding algorithms later.

4   Algorithms

We will give the corresponding algorithms in this section.

4.1   Threat Factor Algorithm

The Threat Factor Algorithm which is executed in Audit Processor calculates the threat factors of the nodes in the attack graph.

```
Threat Factor Algorithm
Input: standard form of audit data set D;
       Attack Graph G.
Output: threat factors T.
1 Set each element of T to be zero.
2 for each d in D,
3   get the node set I of G involved with d.
4   for each i in I,
5       increase the corresponding element in T by 1.
6 Let n is the number of elements of audit data set.
7 divide each element of T by n.
8 return T.
```

In the Threat Factor Algorithm, Line 1 initiate the result array T. Line 3 gets all the nodes involved with the current record. There are two types of nodes in attack graph. We use srcIP, srcPort, desIP, desPort to get all the involved condition nodes, and use type to get all the involved exploit nodes. Line 7 normalizes the result to make sure all the element of T in the range [0, 1].

4.2   Attractive Factor Algorithm

The Attractive Factor Algorithm which is executed in Property Evaluator calculates the attractive factors of condition nodes in the attack graph.

```
Attractive Factor Algorithm
Input: property records R of the network;
       Attack Graph G.
Output: attractive factors A.
1 Set each element of A to be zero.
2 for each r in R,
3   get the condition node set I of G involved with r.
4   for each i in I,
5   add the number in r to the corresponding element in
    A.
6 Let S is the sum of numbers in R.
7 divide each element of A by S.
8 return A.
```

In the Attractive Factor Algorithm, Line 1 initiate the result array A. Line 3 gets all the condition nodes involved with the current record. Line 7 normalizes the result to make sure all the element of A in the range [0, 1].

4.3   Security Evaluation Algorithm

The Security Evaluation Algorithm which is executed in Security Evaluator calculates the final results which are the risk probabilities of all nodes in attack graph.

```
Security Evaluation Algorithm
Input: threat factors T;
       attractive factors A;
       difficult factors D;
       Attack Graph G.
Output: risk probability P of each node.
1 Set each element of P to be zero.
2 for each condition node c0 that has no income edge,
3    P[c0] = T[c0] * A[c0];
4    if P[c0] is zero, Set P[c0] to be a small value.
6    label c0 as visited.
7 while (true),
8    if exist exploit node e that is not visited and all
     of its pre-condition nodes are visited,
9       P[e] = T[e] * (1 - D[e]);
10      if P[e] is zero, Set P[e] to be a small value.
11      for each c that is pre-condition nodes of e,
12         P[e] *= P[c];
13      label e as visited.
14   if exist condition node c that is not visited and
     all of exploit nodes that result in it are visited,
15      P[c] = T[c] * A[c];
16      if P[c] is zero, Set P[c] to be a small value.
17      union = 1;
18       for each e that that is exploit node results in
         c,
19          union *= (1 - P[e]);
20      P[c] *= (1 - union);
21       label c as visited.
22   if do not exist new node which has been labeled as
     visited, break.
23 return P.
```

In the Security Evaluation Algorithm, Line 2-6 calculates the risk probability of the condition nodes which have no income edge. Line 8-13 calculates the risk probability of the exploit nodes. Line 14-21 calculates the risk probability of the condition nodes. This algorithm assumes that there is no cycles in the attack graph, and compute the risk probabilities in topological order of the attack graph.

5   Experiments

We adopt the network shown in Fig. 1 as the experiment network. We use Nessus as the Scan Tool and use the MulVAL attack graph toolkit [10] as the Attack Graph Generator.

The vulnerabilities of all hosts in the network are shown in Table 1 as follow.

Table 1. List of Vulnerabilities in the network

Host	Vulnerability	CVE number
Web Server	Local access on the server	CVE-2002-0392
FTP Server	Execute arbitrary code via an NFS packet	CVE-2002-0380
Mail Server	Remote code execution in SMTP	CVE-2004-0840
Database Server	SQL Injection	CVE-2008-5416
Administrative Server	MS SMV service Stack BOF	CVE-2008-4050

We use MulVAL to generate the attack graph. The audit logs are shown in Table 2.

Table 2. Audit Log

id	time	srcIP	srcPort	desIP	desPort	type
1	1.1	outside	trivial	Web Server	80	Buffer overrun
2	1.2	Web Server	trivial	Admin Server	trivial	Local-2-root
3	1.3	outside	trivial	Web Server	80	Buffer overrun
4	1.4	outside	trivial	FTP Server	2049	NFS shell

We replace the concrete time, IPs or Ports with descriptive characters, words or names for readability.

Table 3. Property Values

Device	Value
Web Server	5
FTP Server	3
Mail Server	2
Database Server	7
Admin Server	9

Table 3 gives the assignment property values according to the true value of the property (for example, the host containing important data has higher value), the key position of the device in the network, the importance of the device.

According to all the above information and the corresponding CVSS scores, we use the algorithms to compute the final results. The computing result of the experiment show that the Web Server in the network is more risky than FTP Server and Mail Server, and Administrative Server is more risky than Database Server.

To see if our method really catches the running environment correctly, we do 2 additional experiments: (1) We change the audit logs (adding new logs and delete logs); (2) We change some property values. The result of Additional Experiment 1 shows that the risk probabilities increase as the corresponding audit logs added and the risk probabilities decrease as the corresponding audit logs deleted. The result of Additional Experiment 2 shows that the risk probabilities increase as the corresponding property values increased and the risk probabilities decrease as the corresponding property values decreased.

Our experiment results show that our method leads to more accurate result comparing with traditional methods which do not consider the concrete running environment of the network and can dynamically adapt to changing environment.

6   Conclusions

We propose a novel dynamic self-adaptive framework for network security evaluation. In addition to the traditional tools like scan tools and attack graphs, our framework include Audit Processor and Property Evaluator which capture the concrete running environment of the network and the final results are computed in Security Evaluator. Experiment results show that our method leads to more accurate results and can dynamically adapt to changing environment.

Our further works include developing more efficient method for real time security evaluation.

References

1. Lippmann, R.P., Ingols, K.: An annotated review of past papers on attack graphs. Technical Report, ESC-TR-2005-054, MIT Lincoln Laboratory (2005)
2. Swiler, L.P., Phillips, C., Gaylor, T.: A graph-based network-vulnerability analysis system. Technical Report, SANDIA Report No. SAND 97-3010/1 (1998)
3. Swiler, L.P., Phillips, C., Ellis, D., Chakerian, S.: Computer-Attack graph generation tool. In: Proc. of the 2nd DARPA Information Survivability Conf. & Exposition, pp. 307–321. IEEE Computer Society Press, Los Alamitos (2001)
4. Ritchey, R., Ammann, P.: Using model checking to analyze network vulnerabilities. In: Proc. of the 2000 IEEE Symp. on Security and Privacy, pp. 156–165. IEEE Computer Society Press, Oakland (2000)
5. Sheyner, O., Jha, S., Wing, J.M., Lippmann, R.P., Haines, J.: Automated generation and analysis of attack graphs. In: Proc. of the IEEE Symp. on Security and Privacy, pp. 273–284. IEEE Computer Society Press, Oakland (2002)
6. Jha, S., Sheyner, O., Wing, J.: Two formal analyses of attack graphs. In: Proc. of the 15th IEEE Computer Security Foundations Workshop, pp. 49–63. IEEE Computer Society, Cape Breton (2002)
7. Ammann, P., Wijesekera, D., Kaushik, S.: Scalable, graph-based network vulnerability analysis. In: Proc. of the 9th ACM Conf. on Computer and Communications Security, pp. 217–224. ACM Press, New York (2002)

8. Ingols, K., Lippmann, R., Piwowarski, K.: Practical Attack Graph Generation for Network Defense. In: Proc. of Comp. Sec. App. Conf., pp. 121–130 (2006)
9. Qu, X.M., Govindavajhala, S., Appel, A.W.: MulVal: a logic-based network security analyzer. In: The 14th USENIX Security Symposium, pp. 113–128. ACM Press, MD (2005)
10. Ou, X.M., Boyer, W.F., McQueen, M.A.: A scalable approach to attack graph generation. In: Proc. of the 13th ACM Conf. on Computer and Communications Security, pp. 336–345. ACM Press, Alexandria (2006)
11. Mehta, V., Bartzis, C., Zhu, H., Clarke, E.: Ranking Attack Graphs. In: Zamboni, D., Kruegel, C. (eds.) RAID 2006. LNCS, vol. 4219, pp. 127–144. Springer, Heidelberg (2006)
12. Ye, Y., Xu, X.-S., Jia, Y., Qi, Z.-C.: An Attack Graph-Based Probabilistic Computing Approach of Network Security. Chinese Journal of Computers 33(10), 1987–1996 (2010)

Wireless Sensor Network MAC Protocol
Used in the City Fire

Xiaoyan Cui, Xiaoshuang Chen, Haitao Zhang, and Shizhuo Zheng

Key Laboratory of Trustworthy Distributed Computing and Service (BUPT),
Ministry of Education, Beijing, China
Automation School, Beijing University of Posts and Telecommunications, Beijing, China
d_win@163.com

Abstract. The MAC protocol of wireless sensor networks sensor nodes channel access control protocol located between the physical layer and network layer plays a vital role in data transmission. We can extend the life cycle of the sensor network with designed MAC protocol, because it can improve the channel utilization and energy efficiency of the node. Wireless sensor network is an application-oriented wireless network, MAC protocol design based on actual scenarios is reasonable, the article sets the city building fire as application background and designs a protocol based on polling of wireless sensor network MAC and the agreement of the clustering mechanism that has been improved, the key consideration of the agreement are energy efficiency and delay control indicators, and it uses NS2 simulation for the agreement analysis.

Keywords: Wireless sensor networks, forest fire, MAC protocol, clustering.

1   Introduction

Wireless sensor network, the MAC (medium access control, MAC) protocol determines the occupation of the sensor node on the wireless channel, the MAC layer in the network layer and physical layer. Characteristics of the wireless channel has broadcast a node to send data is likely to send the data somewhere and another node collision resulting in the data failed to send the sensor nodes with limited radio channel the allocation of resources becomes particularly important, wireless sensor network MAC protocol is a network protocol to solve the problem of wireless sensor network nodes access channel, a good MAC protocol can be a good use of the coordination node of the channel, as far as possible to avoid data conflicts.

Wireless sensor networks is very different to the traditional network, mainly reflected in the node itself low-cost, small size, node, carry limited energy, limited processing power and communications capability aspect, it is these limitations wireless sensor networks in the protocol design a big difference with traditional wireless networks. As the computing power and carry the energy of sensor nodes is limited, so the algorithm design of the MAC protocol of wireless sensor networks is as simple as

Y. Yuan, X. Wu, and Y. Lu (Eds.): ISCTCS 2012, CCIS 320, pp. 613–620, 2013.

possible, and energy efficiency as the paramount consideration of protocol design indicators [1].

Oriented applications are also wireless sensor networks and traditional wireless network is an important distinction, the protocol design of wireless sensor networks must be a specific application background, there is no MAC protocol to adapt to any scenario. According to the design of specific applications of wireless sensor network MAC protocol can be more efficient network channel [2] .

2   The MAC Protocol of Wireless Sensor Network Used in the City Fire

2.1   The Current Application Status

The application of wireless sensor networks in the city fire is widely used. The most typical application is to monitor the temperature and smoke concentration of urban buildings, in order to determine the fire situation, which is event detection application in a wireless sensor network. The significant features as followed are: in most of the time the nodes are in idle listening mode, a stricter real-time data transfer requirement, generally millisecond delay. Status and characteristics of wireless sensor networks in the city fire, the paper proposes a MAC protocol algorithm, the algorithm uses a virtual carrier sense mechanism and control of priority delivery mechanism to improve energy efficiency, reduce the data transmission delay.

The structure used in wireless sensor networks in the city building fire generally is the joint topology shown in Fig. 1.In this network, the ordinary nodes only can communicate with coordinator nodes, which are not only a data collector but also an action executor. Once the fire happens, the coordinator nodes will implement the control command to control the fire, such as publishing a number of instructions to control mist switch.

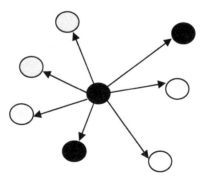

Fig. 1. Applied to the sensor network topology map of the city fire

2.2   S-MAC Protocol Research

Wei Ye puts forward a kind of S-MAC protocol applicable to wireless sensor network [3]. S-MAC protocol is specifically designed for wireless sensor networks, it uses CSMA/CA conflict avoiding mechanism which is similar to the IEEE802.11 and periodic monitor as well as sleep way to save energy. When the node does not need to send data, the node is in a suspended state and during the sleep time the collected data will be stored in the cache. When the node wakes up, random competition channel starts to send the data. But the mechanism also brings some new problems, such as sleeping lead to large time delay, early sleeping and fast consumption of boundary nodes energy. To solve the problem, we propose a MAC protocol based on polling and section 2.3 will give the specific algorithm.

2.3   MAC Protocol Algorithm Description Based on Polling

There are mainly four types of MAC frame structure in the algorithm as followed, the data frame (data), the beacon frames (beacons), the CTS frame and the poll frame (poll). Types of nodes in the network coordinator node (coordinator) and node (device), the coordination nodes and between nodes can communicate between the common node can not communicate directly [3], the data transmission between the common node to take advantage of coordination node as a route.

In the initialization of the construction of the network, the ordinary nodes send beacon frames and request to add to the coordinator node of the network and the coordinator node receives beacon frame of the ordinary node after the node is added to the polling queue (query-queue). While after the construction of the network, the coordinator node starts to transmit a poll frame to query the ordinary nodes; The coordinator node will check whether there is data to send to ordinary nodes before it sends poll frames, if the data needs to be sent to a node, the radio and CTS frames inform the other nodes in the data is sent to occupy the duration of the channel length (duration), the ordinary node receives broadcasts of coordinator nodes, the CTS frame goes to sleep mode until the data transmitting is finished. If no data is sent by the coordinator node, the coordinator node will transmit a poll frame to inquire every useable node if there is data to transmit, after the node receiving the poll frame, it should send a CTS frame which contains occupy time of the channel (duration) to response, if the node has no data to send data, the duration will be 0, the other nodes receive the CTS will go to sleep mode, sleep time is duration + period. The period is a fixed length of time, can be configured according to the specific requirements of the network.

Fig. 2 shows the algorithm flowchart of the ordinary nodes:

Ordinary nodes are mainly responsible for the execution of the field of information collection, transmission and coordination of node control information. Ordinary nodes using a portable battery-powered, so the energy problem is the protocol algorithm first thing to consider. Polling algorithm to avoid data collision, to avoid waste of energy due to collision retransmission [4] ; virtual carrier sense to avoid a string of neighbor nodes listen, to avoid the neighbor string listen not necessary waste of energy.

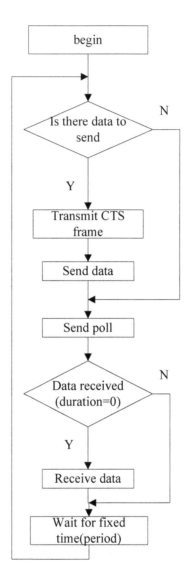

Fig. 2. Ordinary node algorithm flowchart

In the city fire applications, the coordinator node uses the wall power for wireless sensor network, so the coordinator nodes do not need to consider the issue of energy, they will send controlling information before every polling, and use a virtual carrier sense mechanism as well [5] . So that non-target receiver nodes go to sleep mode. This will ensure the coordinator node send control information priority and avoid the energy waste caused by the other nodes mistakenly to listen. This will improve the energy efficiency of the network as a whole, and to extend the network lifetime.

3   Simulation Tools

NS2, namely the Network Simulator, the Version 2, is an object-oriented of the discrete event-driven network environment simulator. The original purpose of the UC Berkeley Design NS2 is for a computer network simulation, but with the development of wireless networks, NS2 also carried out a corresponding expansion, and now also supports wireless network simulation.

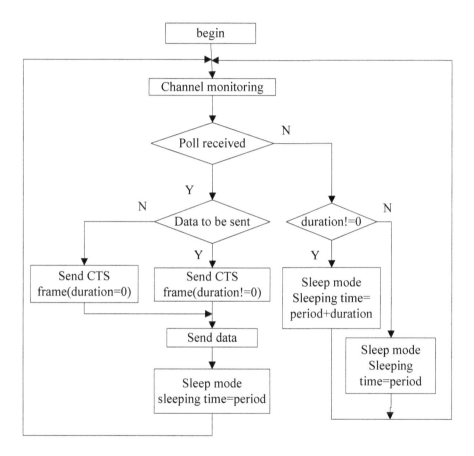

Fig. 3. The coordinator node algorithm flowchart

Fig. 3 shows the algorithm flow chart of the coordination node.

There are two programming languages in NS2, C + +and OTcl. The reason of choosing these two languages is that NS2 will implement two different things; in one hand, in some of the network underlying agreement, the algorithm needs a highly efficient system which requests programming language must effectively control the header bytes and achieve some of the complexity of the algorithm; and the execution speed is very important that these agreements do not change often, it needs compiled once can thousands of time used. Therefore, C + + language is more appropriate. On the other hand, the network needs to do some of the parameters to configure and modify the operation of these changes the simulation every time, therefore OTcl which is an object-oriented scripting language is more appropriated, the interpretation of the implementation, no compiler can perform.

In order to coordinate the C + + and OTcl, NS2 takes object-splited model, which will bind the objects, the methods and the properties of C + + and OTcl. This OTcl script can call C + + objects and C + + method calls and attribute settings. Understand the NS2 object-splited model is the key to learning NS2 [6] .

The design ideas and the open code source of NS2 made it become a popular simulation software rapidly, \the researchers can easily extend the lib of NS2, making the NS2 component library to constantly improve, NS2 now matured into the mainstream of simulation software.

4   Analysis of Simulation Results

4.1   Simulation Network Configuration

NS2 simulation environment is configured as follows: network range 100m * 100m; the number of nodes in the network is 15 besides a coordinator node; the run time of the simulation is 1000 seconds; a Poisson distribution of data streams is used in the application layer proxy (two packets generation time interval a negative exponential distribution); the packet size is 500 bytes; the transport layer uses TCP agent; routing protocol is set as DumbAgent, no routing protocols, in case it will prevent routing protocols affect the comparison of the indicators of the MAC layer; buffer area queue length is 20; priority Drop Tail queue is used; network interface is Phy/ WirelessPhy; wireless channel model is the dual-diameter ground reflection (propagation / Two Ray ground) [7]; transmission rate is 250Kbps; transmission frequency is 2.4GHz; the initial energy of the node is 10 joules; received power is 0.003 watts; transmit power is 0.005 watts; idle listening power is 0.002 watts; in the simulation sleep power is 0; fixed sleep cycle for the PCF protocol is set to 10ms, TDMA agreement in the time slot length is 5ms; the IEEE802.15.4MAC agreement beacon enabled network, BeaconOrder = 3, SuperOrder = 3.

4.2   The NS2 Simulation Results Compared

Comparison of the simulation results of the agreement, the agreement of two of the main contrast is IEEE802.15.4MAC agreements and the TDMA protocol, the contrast to the performance of energy efficiency and delay; these two indicators are used in wireless sensor networks of the city fire.

The coordination of the three protocols node delay contrast shown in Fig. 4.

The first 200 seconds before the beginning of the simulation is the data used in the simulation diagram, delay = end-start; the end is the destination that node receives the data; the start is the time of the application layer proxy generates data packet rather than the sending time; the delay includes the queuing time; and the delay is the coordinator node date delay; from the Fig. 4, we can find out that the protocol coordinator node data delay is more advantage than other protocols.

The energy efficiency of the three protocols comparison is in Fig.5.

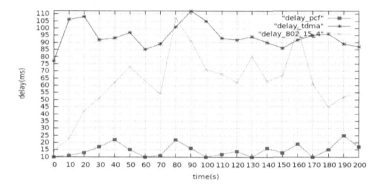

Fig. 4. Coordination node data transmission delay comparison chart

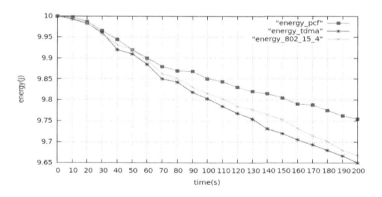

Fig. 5. Node energy consumption comparison chart

5   Conclusion

In this paper, the propose of the algorithm is based on polling of wireless sensor network MAC protocol, the protocol used in the city fire can greatly reduce the delay of information from the coordinator node to the ordinary node transmission, while it also improves the energy efficiency of the common node. As the wireless sensor network is application-oriented wireless network protocol design should be based on specific scenarios, it is unable to fully utilize the limited wireless channel.

Acknowledgements. This work was supported by 863 project NO.2009AA01A324.

References

1. Ren, F., Huang, H.: Wireless Sensor Network. Journal of Software 14(7), 1282–1291 (2003)
2. Sun, L.: Wireless Sensor Network. Tsinghua University Press, Beijing (2005)
3. IEEE Std 802.15.4 TM IEEE Standard for Information technology-Telecommunications and information exchange between systems-local and metropolitan area networks-Specific requirements-Part15.4: Wireless Medium Access Control (MAC) and Physical Layer (PHY) Specifications for Low-Rate Wireless Personal Area Networks (LR-WPANs). IEEE Press, New York (2003)
4. Ye, W., Heidemann, J., Estrin, D.: An energy-efficient MAC protocol for wireless sensor networks. In: Proc. 21st Annual Joint Conf IEEE Computer and Communications Societies (INFOCOM 2002), New York (June 2002)
5. IEEE Computer Society LAN MAN Standards Committee. IEEE Std 802.11-1999, Wireless LAN Medium Access Control (MAC) and Physical Layer (PHY) specification (1999)
6. Wang, H.: The principle and application of the network simulator, 1st edn. Northwestern University Press, Xi'an (2008)
7. Huang, H., Feng, H., Qin, L.: NS network simulation and protocol emulation, 1st edn. Posts & Telecom Press, Beijing (2010)

The Application of Robot Localization and Navigation Based on WSN in the Disaster Relief

Xiaoyan Cui, Xiaoshuang Chen, Wei Shi, and Yi Zhang

Key Laboratory of Trustworthy Distributed Computing and Service,
Automation School, BUPT
d_win@163.com

Abstract. Disasters always disturb our normal life, and the loss is immeasurable. In this paper, we intend to find a new way to reduce the harm. We select the wireless sensor network to control the robot localization and navigation in the disaster relief. This paper means to design a pre-disaster monitoring and reconstruct network with new nodes added in the network, and robot position & navigation, and also build a post-disaster history disaster mode. This paper also takes consider of the actual result of the node energy consumption. It has practical significance.

Keywords: WSN, Zigbee, Robot cloud, AP algorithm, Forest fire.

1   Introduction

All around the world, disasters such as natural disasters, terrorist activities and any other unexpected incidents occur frequently every year. It is very important to rescue in time. In addition, when a fire occurs in open areas (such as a forest fire), it often brings a lot of vegetation destruction by the impact of the ecological environment. Since we don't known about the specific topography, the disaster trend is always not very clear. And also the rescue workers have the risk to be trapped in the disaster magnification.

Traditional disaster monitoring system is useless when this type of disaster happens. The reasons are as follows: firstly, the current system can be easily damaged in the disasters. Secondly, the arrangement of traditional detector system is not enough. What's more, the cost of wiring in the open countryside is very high.

In this paper, we mainly study the open environment disaster monitor and rescue system, including monitoring network and decision-making & task-scheduling system. We choose to use AP clustering algorithm for network hierarchy clustering management, thus the response to the disaster will be quicker. In the rescue of the decision scheduling system, we combine cloud computing and physical robot to finish target research based on analysis of historical monitoring data, and build a disaster model robot scheduling. In addition, this article makes a research of wireless sensor network positioning technology and does a discussion on positioning and navigation of robots.

Y. Yuan, X. Wu, and Y. Lu (Eds.): ISCTCS 2012, CCIS 320, pp. 621–628, 2013.

2   System Overview

As shown in Fig.1, we can divide the frame structure of the system into three parts, namely, wireless sensor networks, early warning alarm system and robot cloud systems. The relationship between the various parts is under the followings:

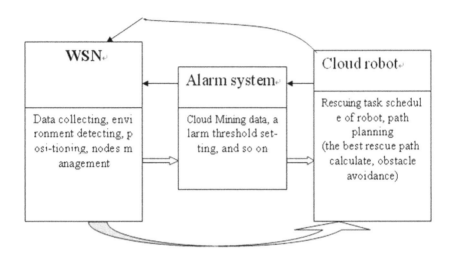

Fig. 1. The frame structure of the system

1) wireless sensor networks: on the one hand, the formation of self-organizing network that can easily expand, acquisition integration of data sent to a user, which is the source of the data of the early warning alarm system; on the other hand, after the disaster happen, the mobile robot will join to rescue. And it can provide positioning and navigation functions.

2) alarm system: on the one hand, it allows personnel to detect timing manually activate the monitoring network for data collection, and upload it to this section; on the other hand, if the alarm signal generator, alarm command is sent alarm to the robot cloud system and active scheduling decision part.

3) The robot cloud systems: on the one hand, after the disaster, the scheduling of the part of the robot or aircraft to the sensor network randomly tossed the sensor nodes to form a new network, this network structure is more fine program; the same time, the part will scheduling a number of rescue robots to the implementation of the rescue work; other hand, the alarm system to send disaster relief after the lifting of the alert command.

3   Key Technologies

3.1   Randomly Spilled Node Networking

In the monitoring of network coverage area, if any situation happens, the sensor nodes will be collected to the sink node transmission data "singular" ---- these singular values are more than what we have to determine the threshold of the system design. These values inform the user somewhere some data abnormalities, and may presage the event of a disaster. If it is determined the event of a disaster, then, in order to understand the developments of the disaster, escape and relief personnel to rescue people trapped in specified direction, just by virtue of a wide range of existing monitoring network monitoring node is not enough, there must be more the number of nodes to join, refine the segmentation of the network monitoring, but also help make up the network because of node failure and partial paralysis. These nodes can be newly added to ordinary communication distance of nodes do not need high-powered node.

In the existing monitoring network, random shed new node, and the rapid formation of a new monitoring network. In order to ensure that the newly added node locations are determined, the communication distance of the new node should monitor network communication in high-power node distance to meet a certain relationship. In this way, and then rely on the received signal strength indication [4] (the Received Signal Strength Indication, RSSI) to determine the new node location coordinates in the coordinate system. Because each new node in the network must know its own location coordinates have actual meaning, to understand its position must be known to rely on those who have position coordinates node to determine, and at least three known coordinates node of the signal can be determined.

3.2   Robot Cloud

Robot cloud parts of the system including the main function of a robot relief scheduling system, part of the robot path planning including obstacle avoidance, most several parts of the escape route calculation. The block diagram shown in Fig. 2, the whole robot cloud system has a three-tier (ie, three types of roles) structural framework. These three layers from top to bottom, respectively, is a robot cloud, cloud robot distribution center, service robots. Robot cloud center is the core of the entire robot cloud. It is responsible for handling robot cloud computing-intensive and memory-intensive tasks. A robot cloud also includes a series of cloud robot distribution center. Robot cloud requires a lot of interaction and the real world, these cloud robot distribution center will be located in different physical environments, in other words, is placed at different locations in a city. A cloud robot distribution center will have a number of service robots. It is these service robots robot cloud the perception of interaction layer.

3.3   The AP Algorithm

AP algorithm is a clustering algorithm based on neighbor of the spread of information. It is proposed by Frey and Dueck [5], In the initial stage of the AP clustering algorithm, all the sample points are considered potential clustering center. Then the sample points began sending messages between repeatedly to make the goal function maximization, until clustering center, and the corresponding cluster produce. Namely AP algorithm can find out the lower variance clustering center than getting the optimal solution of running 100 times k-means clustering. Neighbor spread method does not need to specify the cluster number, but need data similarity between matrix. the similarity between two samples can be calculated by the negative kansai.

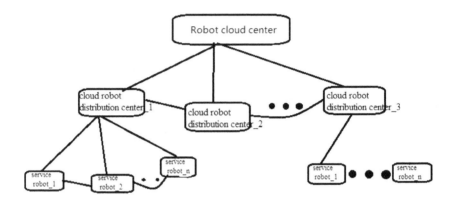

Fig. 2. Robot cloud part

Compared with the K-means clustering, the AP goal is to find the best representative point set (a representative point corresponds to a concentration of data points for the actual data, of disparate types), so that all data points to the nearest representative point of degree and the largest. From the simulation results can be seen that the AP convergence of the algorithm is better, the smaller the variance of the results obtained, and the calculation of the number of relatively small [5].

K-means clustering faults:

1) In K-means algorithm K is given in advance, the K value is very difficult to estimate.

2) In K-means algorithm, first we need to determine a initial region according to initial clustering center, and then optimize on the basis of the division. The initial clustering center choice has a great influence to the clustering results, once failed, it may not be able to get effective clustering results.

3) From K-means algorithm framework we can see, this algorithm need to constantly adjust sample classification and calculate new clustering center after the adjustment. So when there is a large amount of data, the time spending is very big.

AP clustering algorithm advantages in comparison:

1)Different with other clustering algorithms, the AP clustering needs not to specify the cluster number parameters.

2) In a clustering, the most representative point in the AP algorithm is called Examplar, and different from k-means algorithm clustering center, examplar is exactly the data point of original data, it is not clustering center calculated by average many data points.

3) Executive AP clustering algorithm many times, the results are exactly the same, that is, it doesn't need to selecte random initial value.

From the analysis of the above, it is known that in case of same number of nodes, the classification of AP algorithm is faster; and the more nodes, the more advantages of AP algorithm has.

3.4   Robot Positioning and Navigation

The robot's actions in the network based on wireless sensor networks, this system uses the RSSI to the nodes and the robot positioning. For robot navigation, using the following method.

After the disaster, we will shed to the network "backbone" of a large number of nodes, the network will be the basis of the location information, RSSI positioning method using the above-mentioned step by step to get these "new" position coordinate information so that the whole network are known in front of us. In this network, the equivalent is placed in a fixed position with a fixed node, they have been set a good location coordinates (x, y) to establish a node plot of these nodes is the network's detection range within the sensor node ---- This is the basis of the monitoring network to the robot positioning [6] and navigation. To the routing table in front of the location coordinates of each node can be easily obtained on the use of the routing table to guide how to move the node.

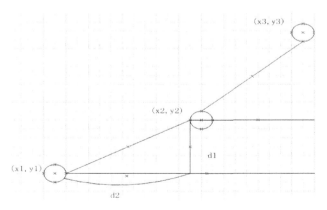

Fig. 3. Navigation calculation

Fig.3 indicates the location of several nodes in the routing table. Eventually, it passes the signal to the robots which can be identified. Then, it is transformed into the robot's operational instructions. Mobile robot can recognize the distance and direction, so we can pass a pair of data which contains the absolute distance between two points and angle deviate from the positive X axis direction. Robot starting position is located in the first node. And the location is node 3, a mobile which also need to go through an intermediate node 2. Then the robot start node 1 to node 2 executable is calculated as follows:

$$d_1 = |y_2 - y_1| \tag{1}$$

$$d_2 = |x_2 - x_1| \tag{2}$$

$$(\sqrt{d_2^2 + d_1^2}, tan^{-1}\frac{d_1}{d_2}) \tag{3}$$

It is similar to calculate the distance from node 2 to node 3. In this way, the robot gets executable command and is able to achieve the target location. However, the navigation must also be dynamic monitoring of the robot to see if the robot accurately reaches a certain point or not. Therefore we also consider the path of robot dynamic calibration. This calibration is carried out in accordance with the time we correspond. Also you can do some manual instructions to make some adjustments.

4   Data Transmission and Rescue Decision-Making

We have already mentioned in front of our disaster relief system consists of two subsystems, namely: Mitigation (disaster monitoring) and post-disaster rescue. Mitigation is mainly about the structures of the disaster monitoring system, such as: forest fires in the open forest. If we can know in time the fire situation and its trend of development, the guiding significance for the investment of human and material resources to extinguish the fire is very large [7] . Post-disaster rescue is what we do after the disaster happen, such as disaster trends forecast.

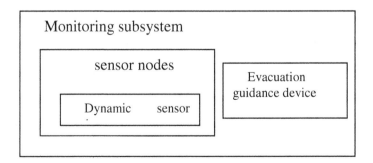

Fig. 4. Monitoring subsystem

Data collection use different sensor as it varies from disaster monitoring to environmental monitoring, such as: a building fire, you can use sensors such as temperature, smoke, and building distortion; landslides can use the tilt sensor to detect mountain change; water level monitoring and audio monitoring can be used on the ocean tsunami monitoring; mine monitoring and so on [8]. The data acquisition part of the framework structure was shown in Fig.4.

Monitoring subsystem includes wireless sensor nodes and the evacuation guidance device. Sensor nodes use random placement in the form of arrangement; guidance device uses the signal of the acousto-optic or infrared signs as guidance. Decision-making subsystem actives these signal according to the actual. This system requires a temperature sensor for temperature monitoring of the forest fire scene. All of sensor and their function are shown in Table 1.

Table 1. Sensor and its function

Type	Function
Temperature sensor	Environment temperature monitoring
Infrared sensor	Fire tendency monitoring and road monitoring
Inclination sensor	Geographical environmental change monitoring

Rescue decision-making [8] , is mainly reflected in two aspects. The personnel in the accident area can quickly evacuate and the rescue operations can work effectively. Firstly, we can use sensor networks to locate and detect adjacent nodes in accordance with the data obtained and use real-time status of the disaster to analyze the development trend of the forecast the near future disaster, considering the specific location of the relief items, to find the rescue path. Secondly, if there are persons in a fire environment, when the disaster occurs, we can make full use of the advantage of wireless sensor network technology and considerate distribution of the staff who are trapped in the accident, the direction of movement, the disaster site and its development trend, as well as real-time relief workers distribution. Then combined with the geographical environment of the disaster scene, we can generate real-time figure. In this way, the headquarters can be a good grasp of the real-time situation, the rescue center can guide disaster relief personnel or scheduling Rescue Robot on the disaster site , rescue, and be the fastest, most effective action in accordance with the master . This forms more than one object (the disaster development, escape personnel and rescue personnel) observations, coordinated decision-making system.

This system is used of the robots cloud system to complete the rescue decision-making tasks. Scheduler---task scheduling is responsible for all requests received by the robot cloud; robot management module is responsible for new registration of the robot and old robot removed, etc. It is also responsible for the mapping of the robotic missions; robot show module responds for monitoring the status of all robots, and provides the service. Also it is responsible for the analysis of the log of each robot; service agent management module is responsible for create, read, update and delete operations of the service agent.

5   Summary

This paper proposes the strategy of disaster mitigation and relief system, which effectively overcomes the defects of the traditional disaster alarm system such as the poor accuracy and the easily damaged circuit. Also the system has network self-organization, personnel location and tracking, disaster trend forecasting, rescue decision support and other functions, which will help the rescue operators effectively completing the rescue. The framework structure and the completion of the system are presented in this paper, and the further research is to improve the design and develop the hardware and software of the system.

Acknowledgements. This work was supported by 863 project, NO. 2009AA01A324.

References

1. Liu, C.: The disaster scene of body detection. Harbin engineering university degree thesis (2010)
2. Shi, W.: Wireless sensor network navigation robot localization in the rescue and relief of application. Beijing university of posts and telecommunications degree thesis (2012)
3. Qu, D.: Mobile robot path planning method research. Robot (2008)
4. Xu, B.: Based on ZigBee technology solar street lamps monitoring system. Zhongshan university degree thesis (2008)
5. Bobrowski, L., Bezedek, J.: C-means clustering with the I1 and I norms. IEEE Trans. on SMC 21(3), 545–554 (1991)
6. Lazos, L., Poovendran, R.: Rope: Robust Ppsition Estimation in Wireless Sensor Networks. EEE (2005)
7. Jin, C.: ZigBee technology base and case analysis. Defense Industry Press (2008)
8. Saha, S., Matsumoto, M.: A Framework for Disaster Management System and WSN Protocol for Rescue Operation. IEEE (2007)

Comparison and Performance Analysis
of Join Approach in MapReduce

Fuhui Wu, Qingbo Wu, and Yusong Tan

School of Computer, National University of Defense Technology, Changsha, China
{fuhui.wu,qingbo.wu,yusong.tan}@nudt.edu.cn

Abstract. MapReduce framework has become a general programming model. MapReduce proved its superiority in fields like sorting, full-text searching. However, as demands become complicated, MapReduce could not directly support relational algebra, typically as join, on heterogeneous data source. We discusses the factors that influence the performance when implementing join both in map function and in reduce function. We also conduct implementation and make analysis. Experimental result shows that the first approach wins in situation that datasets involved in join have significant difference in size and one of them is small enough. In order to get advantages of the first approach, we conduct further discuss when the smaller dataset grows and improve it.

Keywords: MapReduce, Hadoop, join process, performance, analytics.

1 Introduction

1.1 Background and Related Work

Parallelization has gradually become an important issue to consider in software design and development. MapReduce is one of parallel development framework of high performance in such a context. However, there are also dissenting voices [1]. Someone think that it gives up many experiences and lessons learned from the field of RDBMS. With the arrival of the era of big data, RDBMS meets inevitable bottleneck of scalability. MapReduce is becoming competent to increasingly complex deep-analysis problems by studying from RDBMS.

MapReduce does not provide direct support for processing heterogeneous data source with strong association right now. People must program specially or use advanced tools [2] [3] [4] to achieve the target.

Recently, [5] [6] [7] [8] [9] [10] carried out research on join in MapReduce to process heterogeneous data source. [5] add a merge phase to MapReduce; [6] conducted in-depth analysis of join in MapReduce in particular scenario of log analysis; [7],[8] take detailed analysis on join in MapReduce and propose algorithms; [9][10] conducted exploration of MapReduce in large-scale and heterogeneous datasets. In this paper, we focus on the performance of join in MapReduce from the view of the factors that affect MapReduce performance in real environment.

Y. Yuan, X. Wu, and Y. Lu (Eds.): ISCTCS 2012, CCIS 320, pp. 629–636, 2013.

1.2   Main Work

The contributions of this paper can be summarized as follows:

- Analysis of MapReduce framework, make a comparison between two different ways to implement join in MapReduce;
- Analysis of affecting factors to MapReduce, and study the new influence of these factors when implementing join in MapReduce;
- Design and implement the two approach In Hadoop [11] [12] [13], and evaluate the experimental results;
- From the experimental results, we find that the first way performs better, but it is limited by the size of data source. We propose an "Improved Map-Side Join" approach to alleviate this limit.

2   Join Approach in MapReduce

2.1   MapReduce Overview and Working Mechanism

In the paper [14], Google proposed the MapReduce parallel programming model for the first time. The idea of MapReduce can be abstracted as shown in Figure 1:

```
Map (k1, v1) ->list (k2, v2)
Reduce (k2, list (v2)) ->list (k3, v3)
```

Fig. 1.

It is simple to program with MapReduce. People need define one map and reduce function. Map function takes input data as a series of key/value pairs (k1, v1), produces intermediate key/value pairs (k2, v2); and then, intermediate results are translated into (k2, list (v2)), list (v2) is a list of values associated with k2. Reduce function produces final results of list (k3, v3). Between them there is a shuffle phase that is responsible for copying intermediate results from map nodes to reduce nodes.

2.2   Two Approach of Join in MapReduce

In this paper, we compare two basic kinds of join approach in MapReduce.

2.2.1   Map-Side Join

As the name implies, Map-Side Join is to implement join in map phase. This approach works if one dataset R is small enough to be copied to all the map nodes, and should better be stored all in memory. This approach can be abstracted as shown in Figure 2:

Join is usually based on join key from different data source. Map (k1, vl, vr) operates on records (k1, vl) and (k1, vr) of the same key k1 from different datasets L and R. This process requires a good algorithm to complete join algorithm. Because the join is completed in map phase, we can get final result in reduce phase through aggregating the intermediate results after join.

Map (k1, v_l, v_r) ->list (k2, v2)
Reduce (k2, list (v2)) ->list (k3, v3)

Fig. 2.

Map (k1, v_l) ->list (k2, $v2_l$)
Map (k1, v_r) ->list (k2, $v2_r$)
Reduce (k2, list ($v2_{l, r}$)) ->list (k3, v3)

Fig. 3.

2.2.2   Reduce-Side Join

Relative to Map-Side Join, Reduce-Side Join chooses to achieve join in reduce phase. If the sizes of L, R are both too large to be copied to all map nodes, Reduce-Side Join is a good choice. Because the inputs of mapper are records from heterogeneous data source, it requires people to design their own key and value formats. Firstly, people need to design a key partition method to guarantee that records with the same keys will be copied to the same reducer. People also need to tag values, so that reducer can identify which dataset the value belongs to. Usually, a new compare function is needed to merge and sort intermediate results in shuffle phase. This approach can be abstracted as in Figure 3:

List ($v2_{l, r}$) is a value list by merging and sorting $v2_l$ and $v2_r$ from different mapper. The join is actually calculation on this list. In this approach, since the join is completed in the reduce phase, we often need a new job to process aggregation on the results after join in the first job to get final results.

2.3   Comparison between Two Approach

There are two major differences: 1)As the map function processes records of data source in a brute way as one by one, this leads to the operation of join in map phase also in a brute-force way. But the problem does not exist in Reduce-Side Join, because the input of reduce is already sorted and merged in shuffle phase. 2)The Map-side Join retain the integrity of a MapReduce job, the results of join can be aggregated in reduce phase of the same MapReduce job, while in Reduce-Side Join, people usually need another MapReduce job to aggregate result of join from the first job's reduce phase.

In general, Map-Side Join is suitable if the sizes of input datasets are quite different. The smaller dataset is transmitted to all the map nodes. The Reduce-Side Join does not have this limit. However, as the results after join operation remain a large dataset. People need a new job to process this dataset to obtain final results.

3   Performance Analysis

3.1   Influence Factors of MapReduce

In this paper we divide all the factors into three aspects as shown in Figure 4:
(1) Node Capacity of Calculation

1. In map phase, the resolution, projection and filtering over input. 2. Sorting and partition over intermediate outputs from map phase. 3. If a combiner is assigned, the combination is also one aspect. 4. Merging and sorting the intermediate results in shuffle phase. 5. The execution of reduce function over results after shuffle phase.

(2) Network Transmission Efficiency

1. In MapReduce, there is no communication from mapper to mapper or reducer to reducer, the use of communication resource mainly occurs in data transmission between mapper to reducer.

(3) Disk I/O

We focus on the following two aspects: 1. the cache of mapper's intermediate result is a complex process, disk I/O will be triggered if the cache reaches a certain threshold. 2. In shuffle phase, if the memory is insufficient to accommodate all intermediate results, it will trigger disk I/O.

(4) Connection between Three Factors

The three factors do not influence MapReduce performance separately. Node capacity of calculation will directly influence the performance of the MapReduce. But the intermediate results from the calculation of computing node will trigger the network transmission and disk I/O effect to MapReduce.

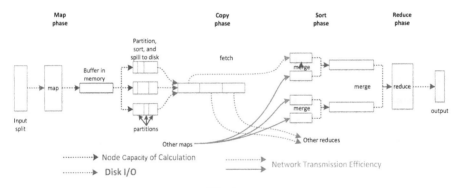

Fig. 4.

3.2   Performance Analysis of Join in MapReduce

Map-Side Join adds two additional affects: 1. the copying of smaller dataset R to map nodes increases demand for network resource. 2. The process of join in map phase increases demand of the node capacity of calculation.

Reduce-Side Join also brings two additional affects: 1. as the join finished in reduce phase, more intermediate results will be produced. This will bring in three affects: 1) the intermediate results will trigger disk I/O of the map node. 2) The transmission of intermediate results increases network resource demand. 3) In shuffle phase, a large number of intermediate results may also trigger disk I/O and demand for calculation capacity. 2. The process of join in reduce phase increases the demand for calculation capacity of reduce nodes. However, as the input of the reducer is already merged and sorted in shuffle phase, the additional demand for calculation capacity is not as obvious as Map-Side Join.

For the Map-Side Join, as the join is completed in map phase, people can get final results after aggregation in reduce phase. While the Reduce-Side Join do the join in reduce phase. The dataset need another job to do aggregation. The process of a large number of intermediate results is an important factor impacts the performance.

4   Implementation and Evaluation in Hadoop

4.1   Dataset and Environment

We generate two datasets of message L and user R. L has two key fields of username and message platform. R also has two key fields of username and gender. The experimental goal is to compute the relationship between platform-usage and gender through join the records with same username from L and R.

We used Hadoop version 1.0.0 and configured it to run up to two map tasks and two reduce tasks concurrently per node. For fault tolerance, each HDFS block was replicated two times. All our experiments were run on a cluster of 1 master node and 8 slave nodes. Each node has a single 2.93GHz Intel Core 2 Duo processor with 2GB of DRAM and one 200GB SATA disk, the network is 10-100MB/s Ethernet network.

4.2   Implementation

4.2.1   Map-Side Join

In Map-Side Join, we adopt the technology of distributed cache to copy R to map nodes. To achieve the join between L and R, we firstly index R using MapFile format, then for each record "ri" from L, search the gender information from R'.

We use two MapReduce job to complete the calculation. We setup a job to generate MapFile format user information, and then set MapFile format user information as distributed cache file. In another job, we do the join between L and R' (user information dataset of MapFile format) in map phase, and do aggregation on results from map phase to obtain the final result in reduce phase. The program runs as shown in Figure 5(a):

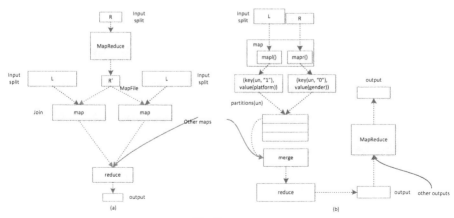

Fig. 5.

R' is user information dataset of MapFile format generated from R. It takes user-name as key, gender as value.

4.2.2   Reduce-Side Join

In Reduce-Side Join, we use MultipleInputs technology provided by Hadoop to process L and R at the same time in map phase. In order to identify intermediate results in reduce phase, we use the text pair format for the key of intermediate results. If the intermediate result is from L, the key is set as (username, "1"), and the value is set by platform. If the intermediate result is from R, the key is set as (username, "0"), and the value is set by gender. In addition, we partition the intermediate results according to first field of the key.

The above can be completed in one MapReduce job. But the output of this job is composed of pairs of platform and gender information. We need another MapReduce job to aggregate the output to obtain the final results as shown in Figure 5(b):

4.3   Evaluation

We selected two group datasets as: L: 1.79GB (25,000,000 records), R: 3.8MB (100,000 records) and L: 6.45GB (90,000,000 records), R: 30.26MB (600,000 records), the experimental results are shown as follows:

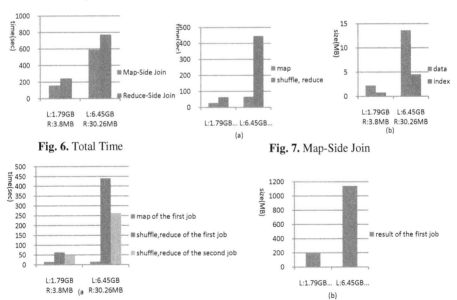

Fig. 6. Total Time   **Fig. 7.** Map-Side Join

Fig. 8. Reduce-Side Join

Figure 6 shows that Map-Side Join works better if R is small enough, and the effect is more obvious if the percentage of R to L is smaller. The main cause is that we need another job to process output from the first job in Reduce-Side Join, but the output in map phase of the first job and the output of the first job are still large datasets. To handle a large number of intermediate results in shuffle and reduce phases of the second approach affected the overall performance as in Figure 8(a).

Figure 7(a) shows that, a single map task executes for longer time corresponding to the growth of data source. This is because we add the operation of join between heterogeneous data source to the map task. However, as all map tasks execute in a parallel way, this influence is not so obvious in overall effect. Later, we can use mature technologies [15] [16] [17] in RDBMS to replace the brute join in our implementation.

Compared to the impact to Map-Side Join, the influence to Reduce-Side Join mainly manifests in the way that the results of the first job in Figure 8(b) require the second job to process. The procession increase the pressure of network resource and trigger disk I/O by intermediate results, and the pressure affects the overall performance linearly.

5   Improved Map-Side Join

From the experimental results and analysis, we can see that the first approach has certain advantages if R is small enough. We propose an Improved Map-Side Join to alleviate the limit. We choose to partition L and R according to the join key, and then conduct Map-Side Join for each partition as shown in Figure 9:

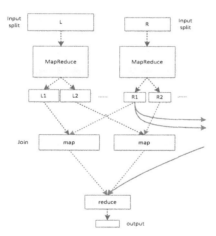

Fig. 9. Improved Map-Side Join

Improved Map-Side Join requires an efficient partition algorithm. The output R1, R2 of R might be cached to a number of nodes, this needs the partition algorithm to minimize the number of copies of the R1, R2, reducing the use of network resource. This approach retains Map-Side Join's strengths, adding a partition job to L. The research and implementation of this approach includes further works as: a new partition algorithm, improvement to distributed cache algorithm and the placement of original data sources. In our future work, we will conduct research on these aspects.

6   Conclusion

MapReduce is a successful programming framework for parallel computing, but it does not mean that MapReduce is suitable for all our works. In this paper, we divide the factors that will affect performance of MapReduce into Node Capacity of Calculation, Network Transmission Efficiency and Disk I/O. And then, we analyze the influence of these factors when implementing join in MapReduce. We also implement the two approaches in Hadoop, and make evaluation. From the analysis we get the following conclusions. First, an efficient join algorithm is needed, which is particularly important in Map-Side Join as is mentioned in section 2.2.1. Second, it is necessary to take the intermediate result into account. As we usually cannot implement join in one MapReduce job, too much intermediate result will bring network pressure and trigger frequent Disk I/O.

References

1. DeWitt, D.J., Stonebraker, M.: MapReduce: A major step backwards. Blog post at The Database Column (January 17, 2008)
2. Thusoo, A., Sarma, J.S., Jain, N., Shao, Z., Chakka, P., Anthony, S., Liu, H., Wyckoff, P., Murthy, R.: Hive – A Warehousing Solution Over a Map-Reduce Framework. In: VLDB (2009)
3. Olston, C., Reed, B., Srivastava, U., Kumar, R., Tomkins, A.: Pig latin: A not-so-foreign language for data processing. In: SIGMOD, pp. 1099–1110 (2008)
4. http://www.cascading.org/
5. Yang, H.-C., Dasdan, A., Hsiao, R.-L., Parker, D.S.: Map-reduce-merge: simplified relational data processing on large clusters. In: SIGMOD, pp. 1029–1040 (2007)
6. Blanas, S., Patel, J.M., Ercegovac, V., Rao, J.: A Comparison of Join Algorithms for Log Processing in MapReduce. In: SIGMOD (2010)
7. Vernica, R., Carey, M.J., Li, C.: Efficient parallel set-similarity joins using mapreduce. In: SIGMOD, pp. 495–506 (2010)
8. Okcan, A., Riedewald, M.: Processing Theta-Joins using MapReduce. In: SIGMOD (2011)
9. Zhang, S., Han, J., Liu, Z., Wang, K., Xu, Z.: SJMR: Parallelizing Spatial Join with MapReduce on Clusters. In: CLUSTER (2009)
10. Xu, L., Jin, K., Tian, H.: MRData: a MapReduce-Based Tool for Heterogeneous Data Integration. In: ISME (2010)
11. http://hadoop.apache.org/
12. http://hadoop.apache.org/mapreduce/
13. White, T.: Hadoop: The Definitive Guide
14. Dean, J., Ghemawat, S.: MapReduce: Simplified data processing on large clusters. In: OSDI (2004)
15. Bernstein, P.A., Goodman, N.: Full reducers for relational queries using multi-attribute semi joins. In: Symp. on Comp. Network (1979)
16. Graefe, G.: Query evaluation techniques for large databases. ACM Comput. Surv. 25(2) (1993)
17. Mishra, P., Eich, M.H.: Join processing in relational databases. ACM Comput. Surv. 24(1) (1992)

Analysis of Public Sentiment Based on SMS Content

Zhilei Wang[1, 2], Lidong Zhai[2], Yongqiang Ma[1], and Yue Li[1]

[1] School of Information Science & Technology, Southwest Jiaotong University,
Chengdu, China
{wangzhilei12,swjtuliyue}@163.com, yqma@swjtu.cn
[2] Institute of Information Engineering, Chinese Academy of Sciences, Beijing, China
zhailidong@iie.ac.cn

Abstract. Short message has become to one of the most important communication manners of our daily life. There may be some hot topics contained in short messages differing with the internet. In this paper, we present a method of analysis of public sentiment based on SMS (short message serves) content. The process of discovering short message public sentiment is introduced systematically. After a serial of preprocessing, obtained original data of short message are then used for text mining. We adopt the text mining technique based on the frequent pattern tree, aiming to find some hot topic information from the SMS content, to observe the public sentiment. Experiments show that this method is feasible to a certain degree.

Keywords: SMS, public sentiment, hot topic detection, FP-tree.

1 Introduction

Recent years, along with the increasing popularity of mobile terminals, short message serves develop rapidly. SMS has become to one of the major daily communication manners of human beings, because it has so many advantages such as brevity, convenience, high speed and efficiency. Characterized by SMS, mobile network has come to be "The fifth media" after television, newspaper, radio and the internet. More and more messages are transferred from one person to another through SMS [1]. Topic Detection is a sub-process of Topic Detection and Tracking (TDT) that attempts to identify "topics" by exploring and organizing the content of textual materials [2]. Hot topics in short messages are broadcasted in a Small World way to a certain extent, that is why short topics in short messages can broadcast rapidly and influence widely. Unlike tradition public sentiment, public sentiment in short messages covers a wide range, and transfers rapidly. Once a hot event emerge, sending a short message is the most convenient and direct means to broadcast. Therefore, to discover the hot topics in SMS content promptly and effectively has great significance.

After preprocessing like data cleansing and text format conversion, and then using the hot topic mining algorithm, this paper use the original obtained SMS data in order to find hot information from the large number of SMS data. In the end, this paper presents the experiment and result.

Y. Yuan, X. Wu, and Y. Lu (Eds.): ISCTCS 2012, CCIS 320, pp. 637–643, 2013.
© Springer-Verlag Berlin Heidelberg 2013

The motivation of this research is to mine hot topics from large datasets of SMS, grasp the public sentiment timely and accurately, in order to take appropriate measures to deal with them, minimize the social impact and reduce losses. It can be used in the relevant government departments. For the large datasets, we sample the business data of an operator from some regions and process the information under terms of strict commercial confidentiality.

Fig. 1. The overall framework

2   Short Messages Based Public Sentiment Analysis

Aiming at the SMS content, the process of public sentiment analysis is as follows: first of all is to obtain original SMS data. Secondly, do some prepossessing with them including extracting the content of short messages， filtering the useless information, text format transforming and so on. After that, short message content needs to be divided into single word which is an important and essential step. And then using hot discovery algorithm to extract the hot topics, thereby obtaining the content of the public sentiment. At last, the result of hot topic mining is being analyzed.

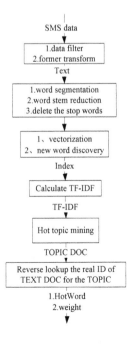

Fig. 2. The flow of public sentiment analysis

3   Key Technologies

3.1   Data Preprocessing

Information in every single short message is limited. On one hand, some data cannot represent too many information itself. On the other hand, if every single short message is processed with no selective, addition performance overhead is bound to be brought in. Thus, preprocessing to original data is necessary. Not every package contains short message text. Thereby, to these packages, first thing need to be done is to extract the content of the message, and then filter and clean up in order to meet the requirements of processing speed and precision.

After preprocessing, the SMS data are storage in the format of excel. We cannot use a excel format to do text mining directly, that means a text format transform is necessary.

3.2   Word Segmentation and TF-IDF Calculation

Word is the minimal, independent and significant part of language, but the characteristic of Chinese is that wordage rather than word is the fundamental writing unit, and there is no apparent separator between words. Therefore, before hot topic mining, short message context need to be cut up into words. Word segmentation is a vital step before mining.

Segmentation system is a major component of Chinese information processing and the most basic component of Chinese natural language understanding, literature retrieval, search engine and text mining system. This paper uses ICTCLAS [3] (the Chinese Lexical Analysis System designed by the Institute of Computing Technology Chinese Academy of Sciences) whose word segmentation accuracy can reach up to more than 98%. After word segmentation, we need to calculation the frequency of a term to measure its importance.

TF-IDF algorithm is widely used in text feature extraction, in which IDF value demonstrates the importance of a term. In a common information processing system, two factors are used to weight a term: 1) Term Frequency (TF), the frequency of the term in the text segment, and 2) Inversed Document Frequency (IDF), which is used to indicate the distinction of the term. This results in larger weights for terms that appear more frequency, and larger weights for the unusual terms.

IDF is a measurement of the general importance of a term [4]. It's based on the statistical conclusion that, the importance is offset by the frequency of the term in the collection, and it's an index reduction. It is proportional to the number of occurrences of the term in the document and inversely proportional to the number of documents that contain the term in the corpus [5]. It is computed as follows [6].

$$\mathrm{wf}_{t,d} = \begin{cases} 1 + \log \mathrm{tf}_{t,d} & \text{if } \mathrm{tf}_{t,d} > 0 \\ 0 & \text{otherwise} \end{cases} \tag{1}$$

$$\mathrm{idf}_t = \log \frac{N}{\mathrm{df}_t} \tag{2}$$

$$wf - idf = wf_{t,d} \times idf_t \tag{3}$$

Equation (1) is a variant of term frequency called sub linear term frequency scaling, where $tf_{t,d}$ stands for the number of occurrences of term t in document d. In Equation (2), N refers to the number of documents in the corpus and df_t is the number of documents containing the term t. Equation (3) is the TF-IDF value used in this research.

3.3   Hot Topic Mining: Frequent-Pattern Tree

The hot topic mining part is the key component of the whole analysis of public sentiment. All the former preprocessing to the SMS data is pave the way for this step which provides input to the hot mining algorithm. Preprocessing to data can influence the quality and efficiency of the output to a certain extent, but the design of hot topic mining algorithm plays a key role in the whole analysis of public sentiment.

Frequent-pattern tree (FP-tree) structure is an extended prefix-tree structure for storing compressed, crucial information about frequent patterns. FP-tree is first introduced by Canadian professor Jiawei Han in 2000[7-8]. Given a transaction database DB and a minimum support threshold ξ, the problem of finding the complete set of frequent patterns is called the frequent-pattern mining problem. FP-tree is used to address this kind of problem. It consists of a root node labeled as null and child nodes consisting of the item-name, support and node link. Its characteristic is to produce frequent set straightly, and does not produce selected set. Thus, we can scan the database only for 2 times that improves the efficiency greatly.

For example, the first two columns of Table 1 show the transaction database, and the minimum support threshold be 3 (i.e., ξ = 3).

Table 1. Atransaction database as running example

TID	Items bought	(Ordered)frequent items
100	f, a, c, d, g, i, m, p	f, c, a, m, p
200	a, b, c, f, l, m, o	f, c, a, b, m
300	b, f, h, j, o	f, b
400	b, c, k, s, p	c, b, p
500	a, f, c, e, l, p, m, n	f, c, a, m, p

We can construct a frequent-pattern tree as follows. First, a scan of DB derives a list of frequent items, <(f:4),(c:4),(a:3),(b:3),(m:3),(p:3)>, in which items are ordered in frequency-descending order. This ordering is important since each path of a tree will follow this order. The frequent items in each transaction are listed in this ordering in the rightmost column of Table 1. The algorithm represents a novel thought of association rule mining [9].

Secondly, the root of a tree is created and labeled with "null". The FP-tree is constructed by scanning the transaction database DB the second time. It extracts frequent items from $T_i(i = [1 \cdots n])$. Afterward, sort these items then frequent items are inserted to the tree. For tree insertion, increasing the support of the node if the node corresponds to the items name found; otherwise a new node is created and the support is set to 1. The header table keeps node-link that connects nodes with the same items name in FP-tree used in traversal the tree during mining process. After scanning all the transactions, the tree, together with the associated node-links, are shown in Fig.3.

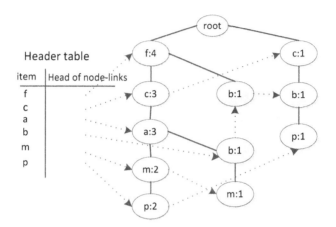

Fig. 3. The FP-tree

Afterward, FP-growth is used for mining frequent patterns. FP-growth method is efficient and scalable for mining both long and short frequent patterns, and is about an order of magnitude faster than some recently reported new frequent-pattern mining methods. It selects an item as mining target from header table. The prefix path can be found by node-link and follow the node to root to get conditional pattern base of item. Then a new FP-tree, conditional FP-tree, constructed from conditional pattern. Subsequently, recursive this mining process until an empty tree of single path is found. Then another mining target selected from header table to find all frequent items set [10].

4   Experiments and Result

In order to test the effect of the public sentiment analysis based on short message, we adopt two different SMS data sets to conduct two experiments. One of the two data sets is formal test data from Nanjing Jiangsu province, which contain 52950 items from the date 2011-12-12 7:30 to 2011-12-12 14:52. The other is group patrol test data from Guangzhou, which contain 2855 items from the date 2011-12-16 23:35 to 2011-12-17 6:00. The result is show in the following table:

Table 2. Test result

Dataset	Hot words
Guangzhou group patrol test dataset	one time 16 12 direct option remind dial key Guangdong call electrical
Nanjing formal test dataset	tunnel double south north door road conditions overhead sunny section remind peak pave cloud secretary bridge early way set transfer traffic

From the result table, we can see that the hot words in Guangzhou group patrol test dataset are majorly associated with telephone and call, while the hot words are majorly associated with in Nanjing formal test dataset traffic and road condition. It is not difficult to speculate that both of this two dataset contains a number of service information such as traffic and weather remind service messages pushed by the mobile operator.

5   Conclusion and Future Works

Compared with traditional media, short message is the most convenient and direct way for people to express their opinions. Through all kinds of short message event, we can observe a public sentiment which is more colorful and comprehensive. Therefore, mining the short message is bound to be an important way to observe the public opinion.

The major contribution and innovation of this paper lies in representing a method of public sentiment analysis based on the SMS content. Because the theme of SMS content is divergent and the dataset's duration is short, plus spam messages flood, all these reasons influence the effectiveness and accuracy of hot mining. In our future work, we will collect original SMS data continuously and extensively to provide enough information for our experiments, meanwhile improve the method of data filtering and the hot mining algorithm.

Acknowledgements. This paper is supported by National Key Technology R&D Program (No.2012BAH37B04), and 863 Program (No.2011AA01A103).

References

1. Xia, T.: Large-Scale SMS Message Mining Based on Map-Reduce. In: International Symposium on Computational Intelligence and Design (2008)
2. Allan, J., et al.: Topic Detection and Tracking Pilot Study Final Report. In: Proceedings of the DARPA Broadcast News Transcription and Understanding Workshop (February 1998)

3. Zhang, H., Yu, H., Xiong, D., Liu, Q.: HHMM-based Chinese Lexical Analyzer ICTCLAS. In: Proceedings of the Second SIGHAN Workshop on Chinese Language Processing, Sapporo, Japan, July 11-12 (2003)
4. Xu, M., He, L., Lin, X.: A Refined TF-IDF Algorithm Based on Channel Distribution Information for Web News Feature Extraction. Education Technology and Computer Science (2010)
5. Chen, Y.-H., et al.: Chinese Readability Assessment Using TF-IDF And SVM. In: Machine Learning and Cybernetics, Guilin, July 10-13 (2011)
6. Salton, G., Buckley, C.: Term-weighting approaches in automatic text retrieval. Information Processing & Management 24(5) (1988)
7. Han, J.: Mining Frequent Patterns without Candidate Generation. In: Proc. 2000 ACM-SIGMOD Int. Conf. on Management of Data (SIGMOD 2000), Dallas, TX (May 2000)
8. Han, J., Kambr, M.: DATA MINING Concepts and Techniques. Morgen Kaufmann Publishers
9. Huang, J.-H., et al.: The study of algorithm for association rule based in the frequent pattern. In: Machine Learning and Cybernetics, Guangzhou, August 18-21 (2005)
10. Zhou, J., Yu, K.-M.: Balanced Tidset-based Parallel FP-tree Algorithm for the Frequent Pattern Mining on Grid System. In: Semantics, Knowledge and Grid (2008)

Control Method of Twitter- and SMS-Based Mobile Botnet

Yue Li[1,2], Lidong Zhai[2], Zhilei Wang[1,2], and Yunlong Ren[2]

[1] School of Information Science & Technology, Southwest Jiaotong University,
Chengdu, China
swjtuliyue@163.com
[2] Institute of Information Engineering, Chinese Academy of Sciences, Beijing, China
zhailidong@iie.ac.cn

Abstract. Along with the rapid development of mobile network, the botnet is shifting from traditional network to mobile one. The mobile botnet has already become a focus of future internet security. With wide application of twitter and with its characteristics of real-time, asynchronous and loose coupling communication, the mobile internet becomes a more controllable and more concealed information platform carrier for the mobile botnet. Communication quality of the mobile network SMS service is stable with independent of the communication mechanism. SMS services can provide a stable and robust communication environment for mobile botnet. This paper puts forward a mobile botnet based upon twitter and SMS control. Based on this, the author puts forward two common algorithm for network topologies according to real application environment, and with simulation analysis, the author proves the twitter- and SMS-control-based mobile botnet is superior with its invisibility, robustness and flexibility.

Keywords: mobile botnet, twitter, SMS, mobile internet, network security.

1 Introduction

Botnet attack and defense research is always the hot issue in the field of security, the botnet was defined by professor Fang Binxing that a botnet is a collection of internet-connected computers whose security defenses have been breached and control ceded to an unknown party. [1]. In 1998 the first botnet called GTBot appeared, later appears HTTP protocol, simple P2P protocol and Fast-flux[2] technology as the representative of the Botnet in succession, in recent years the botnet development enters the phase of confrontation, Domain Flux[3], URL Flux[4] technology, Hybrid P2P[5] protocol which can improve the invisibility, robustness of the botnet. Nowadays, botnet has gradually developed into the cross domain, multiple protocol fusion zombie network [1].

This paper proposes a Control Method of Twitter- and SMS-based Mobile Botnet, aiming to strengthen the understanding of the defender of such botnets, and to response in time. The main contributions of this paper are as follows:

- Proposes a Control Method of Twitter- and SMS-based Mobile Botnet.
- Using the SMS to contact with the unreachable botnet and the collapsed Twitter network, improving robustness and channel communication quality of the botnet.

Y. Yuan, X. Wu, and Y. Lu (Eds.): ISCTCS 2012, CCIS 320, pp. 644–650, 2013.

- A method of using micro-blog to construct the logic layer structure of P2P mobile botnet. Using this method can easily combine the traditional botnet and mobile botnets into an organic one, and realize the integration of mobile botnet.
- The topology of Twitter botnet can be defined by the controller freely; the flexibility can be improved greatly.
- Analyze the botnet attack and defense, and propose the defense strategy and future research direction.

2   The Overview of the Proposed Twitter- and SMS-Based Botnet

The proposed mobile botnet control and command channels to build through Twitter server and SMS command channel. SMS as a disaster recovery channel communicate with lost bots which do not connect to twitter. The construction strategy proposed in this paper can build a mobile botnet as well as traditional ones and they can integrate with each other to build a cross-network botnet. This is because the twitter service has solved the technical problems of cross-domain and multi-protocol support heterogeneous network.

2.1   Parts of Twitter-Based Botnet

The mobile botnet with a P2P-structure topology have no centralized C&C infrastructure. Instead, commands of twitter message are injected into the botnet via any bot. These commands are signed as botmaster, which tells the bot to automatically propagate the twitter message to other bots. P2P-structure botnet are highly resilient to shut down and hijacking because they lack centralized C&C and employ multiple communication paths between bots, as is shown in Fig.1.

If we register one twitter account for each bot to set up our botnet, defenders can find out the topology of botnet and compute the relationship of bots via the list of following and followed. So we must register a pair which are independent to each other. They are

$$botAccount=<earAccount, mouthAccount>$$

Here earAccount only receives commands of twitter message and mouthAccount only sends message. The following list of earAccount save a queue of mouthAccount of others for solving this problem.

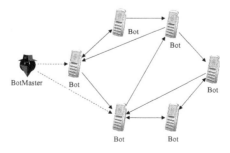

Fig. 1. Twitter-based botnet topology

Fig.2. describes the overall a new bot register procedure. First of all, the new bot register a pair of twitter accounts (botAccount) at the twitter official website. Then the new bot enerypt botAccount with public key of botmaster and send into network backup. Finally it log in the earAccount to receive the first command. Botmaster download botAccount and decrypt it with private key of itself. And then botmaster will set up the following list of the new bot with topology generating algorithm.

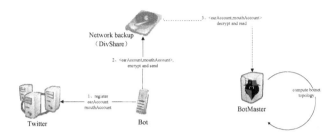

Fig. 2. Bot joins in mobile botnet

A bot in a botnet is always in two states: active and inactive. And we considered the state bots waiting for control commands the sleep state and the state response to control commands the active state. Bot node defines two states as follows:

$$state=<sleep, active>,$$

In the sleep state, the bots log in earAccount and listen to the control command. In the active state, the bot log in mouthAccount, order to execute malicious attacks and to receive the command to convert to sleep state automatically, and   then to wait for the the new command, as is shown in Fig.3.

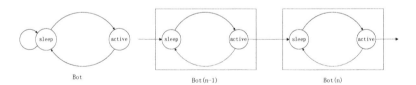

Fig. 3. Bot state

2.2   Parts of SMS-Based Botnet C&C

Control methods of twitter-based mobile botnet have some problems:

1. Botmaster can't communicate with bots, which shut down 3G/GPRS service by twitter messages.
2. Twitter's account of bots may be destroyed by twitter administrators as defender.

Those problems can be solved by using the method of SMS-based controls. Botmaster sends short message of commands to connect those disconnected bots. After the bots receives short message, they will re-open the services or log in a pair of new twitter accounts which was re-registered by botmaster or directed by executive orders (attacking action).

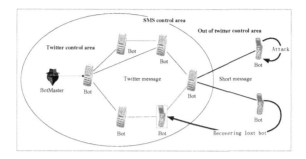

Fig. 4. SMS-based control send command messages to the closed 3G/GRRP cellphones

Fig.4. depicts the general control method of SMS-based structure for sending commands and recovering those out-of-control bots. To connect with them, which lost their twitter accounts by defenders, a bot in twitter control area can send short message of commands. There are two kinds of SMS command message that the one is send natural commands like twitter command message, and the another message contains a pair of twitter accounts and a recover commands. The former message is to overcome the first problem and the latter is to settle the second one. Thus the lost bots are likely to be re-connected .

The methods mentioned above are useful and practical for botmaster to control those lost bots. The robustness of botnet has been strengthened significantly by this method.

3   Topology Generating Algorithm Based on Simulation

The mobile botnet we proposed in this paper is P2P-structured and twitter commanded-and-controlled. A new bot can be changed into a controllable one by botmaster after registration. The advantage of the method is that the botnet topology could be preserved from defenders even if the program has been decompiled.

Topology generating algorithm of botnet is run on botmaster servers. We propose two kinds of algorithm:

- Random tree P2P-structured algorithm
- Random P2P-structured algorithm

The random tree P2P-structured algorithm is that botmaster random some mouthAccount of database and set up the following list for new bot. This algorithm is realized easily, however the front-end bots is unable to receive the twitter message of the rear-end bots as the algorithm weakness.

The random P2P-structured algorithm is that botmaster need reset all the following list of bots when a new bot coming. This algorithm is hard to realize, but all the bots are able to connect with each other.

We construct different topologies to study their different performances based on networks simulations. By doing so, we hope to find an efficient topology for the mobile botnet. The topologies can describe as

$$TOPOLOGY = \{algorithm, branch\},$$

Where algorithm is the topology generating algorithm and branch is the number of the following list of twitter. We always assume that the time-delay is one second and simulate for 10, 000 bots.

Fig.5. presents the simulation results of TOPOLOGY = {random tree, 5/10/20}. When branch=5 the maximum time of propagation is 6. When branch=20 the minimum time is 4. So the number of following twitter improved is a time-efficient way to propagate command of botnet. Meanwhile we found this graph present a S sharp and the maximal slope is at the middle of the curves. In other words, at that moment, we have the most bots receive the twitter message. Fig.6. presents the simulation results of TOPOLOGY = {random, 5/10/20}.

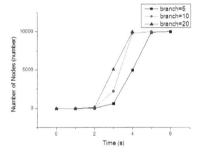

Fig. 5. TOPOLOGY = {random tree, 5/10/20}

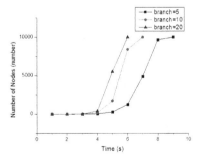

Fig. 6. TOPOLOGY = {random, 5/10/20} on the right

Fig.7. presents the simulation results of TOPOLOGY = {random tree/random, 5}. The propagation efficiency of random tree is higher than random. The random tree is perfect in propagation efficiency. However it has a weakness that bots cannot connect with each other. Therefore we cannot make sure which one is the best. To solve this problem , the botmaster should be concrete for us to analyze.

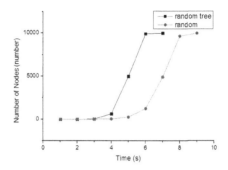

Fig. 7. TOPOLOGY = {random tree/random, 5}

4   Defense Strategies

This mobile botnet is not invulnerable. The first defender can be intercepted by the honeypot. Also, hackers can use an information hiding technique. The control command is hidden in the twitters messages or twitters multimedia files to increase the difficulty of detection. Therefore the focus to the botnet detection problem is transformed to the areas of multimedia content security.

5   Conclusion

In this article, we propose the Control Method of Twitter-and SMS-based Mobile botnets. However, this method is not limited to the mobile Internet; twitter control method is feasible to build a multi-network integration botnet. We shed light on the P2P structure of mobile botnet and recovery work.

We propose a defense strategy and make clear the direction of development. For further study, we need to continue to put forward many new botnets infection and control methods as well as to reinforce research methods of attack and defense.

Acknowledgement. This work is supported by National Natural Science Foundation of China (Grant No.6100174), Strategic Priority Research Program of the Chinese Academy of Sciences (Grant No.XDA06030200), National Key Technology R&D Program (Grant No.2012bah37B04), and 863 Program (Grant No.2011AA01A103).

References

1. Wang, P., Sparks, S., Zou, C.: An Advanced Hybrid Peer-to-peer Botnet. In: Proc. USENIX HotBots 2007, p. 2 (2007)
2. Holz, T., Gorecki, C., Rieck, C., et al.: Detection and mitigation of fast-flux service networks. In: Proc. of the 15th Annual Network and Distributed System Security Symposium. USENIX, Berkeley (2008)
3. Stone-Gross, B., Cova, M., Cavallaro, L., et al.: Your botnet is my botnet; Analysis of a botnet takeover. In: Proc. of the 16th ACM Conf on Computer and Communications Security, pp. 635–647. ACM, New York (2009)
4. Cui, X., Fang, B., Yin, L., et al.: Andbot: Towards advanced mobile botnets. In: Proc. of the 4th Usenix Workshop on Large-scale Exploits and Emergent Threats. USENIX, Berkeley (2011)
5. Geer, D.: Malicious bots threaten network security. Computer 38(1), 18–20 (2005)
6. Guo, W., Zhai, L., Guo, L., Shi, J.: Worm Propagation Control Based on Spatial Correlation in Wireless Sensor Network. In: Wang, H., Zou, L., Huang, G., He, J., Pang, C., Zhang, H.L., Zhao, D., Yi, Z. (eds.) APWeb 2012 Workshops. LNCS, vol. 7234, pp. 68–77. Springer, Heidelberg (2012)
7. Brown, J., Shipman, B., Vetter, R.: SMS: The Short Message Service. Computer 40(12), 106–110 (2007)
8. Boyd, D., Golder, S., Lotan, G.: Tweet, Tweet, Retweet: Conversational Aspects of Retweeting on Twitter. In: Proc. of 43rd Hawaii International Conference on System Sciences(HICSS), pp. 1–10 (2011)
9. Perera, R.D.W.: Twitter Analytics: Architecture, Tools and Analysis. In: Proc. of Conference on Military Communications, pp. 2186–2191 (2010)

A Cache Management Strategy
for Transparent Computing Storage System

Yuan Gao, Yaoxue Zhang, and Yuezhi Zhou

Department of Computer Science and Technology, Tsinghua University,
Beijing, China
y-g06@mails.tsinghua.edu.cn, zyx@moe.edu.cn,
zhouyz@mail.tsinghua.edu.cn

Abstract. TranStore is a transparent computing platform based on a virtual disk system that supports heterogeneous services of the operating platform and their above applications. In TranStore, OS and software which run in the client are stored on the centralized servers, while computing tasks are carried out by the clients, so the virtual disk access is the bottleneck of the system performance. In this paper, we firstly study the client and server cache access patterns in Tran-Store. LRU algorithm is used in the client-side cache. A cache management algorithm called Frequency-based Multi-Priority Queues (FMPQ) proposed in this paper is used in the server-side cache. The simulation methods are used to evaluate the FMPQ performance and compare FMPQ with some other existing cache replacement algorithms. The results show that FMPQ can adapt to different cache sizes and workloads in transparent computing environment, and the performance of FMPQ is significantly better than others.

Keywords: virtual storage system, transparent computing, cache arrangement.

1 Introduction

A new computing paradigm is proposed, namely, transparent computing [1, 2], whose core idea is to realize the "stored program concept [3]" model in the networking environment, in which the execution and the storage of programs are separated in the different computers. A typical transparent computing system is illustrated in Fig. 1. A prototype of transparent computing, TranStore [4], is implemented, which is a distributed storage system based on C/S model. In TranStore, a client is nearly a bare hardware, which is responsible for the execution of programs and the interaction with users. Most programs including OSes and applications executed on the clients are centralized on the server, which is responsible for the storage and the management. In order to fetch the remote programs and data transparently, the virtual disk system (Vdisk) in TranStore extends the local external memory to the disks and the memory on the server. Using Vdisk, TranStore can not only share the data, but also share the programs like operating systems and applications.

Y. Yuan, X. Wu, and Y. Lu (Eds.): ISCTCS 2012, CCIS 320, pp. 651–658, 2013.
© Springer-Verlag Berlin Heidelberg 2013

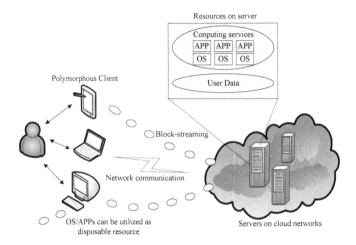

Fig. 1. The environment of Transparent Computing

The growth of disk access speed is far behind the growth of CPU and memory speed, so the access time gap between CPU and disk is widened. And when multiple users remotely access data concurrently, I/O requests arriving at the server are tens of thousands or more, resulting in the increased delay. If the I/O request delay is too long and is more than the user's patience, the quality of the user services will be affected. Cache strategies are often used in the data obtaining to shorten the speed gap between the CPU and the disks. Therefore, we set the disk block cache in both client and server to constitute a two-level cache structure. When an I/O request generated by applications on the client is met in the local cache, a network transmission can be reduced. If the request cannot be met, it will be sent to the server. If the required data is right in the server cache, a disk operation will be reduced. Therefore, the I/O latency can be reduced and the system response time is improved significantly.

In this paper, we firstly study the client and server cache access patterns in TranStore. LRU [5] algorithm is used in client-side cache. A cache management algorithm called Frequency-based Multi-Priority Queues (FMPQ) proposed in this paper is used in server-side cache. We use simulation methods to evaluate the FMPQ performance and compare FMPQ with some other existing cache replacement algorithms. The results show that FMPQ can adapt to different cache sizes and workloads in transparent computing environment, and the performance of FMPQ is significantly better than others. The remaining sections are organized as follows. The overall architecture of the TranStore system is shown in section 2. In section 3, we use real-system traces and analyze the access modes of the server cache and the client cache. FMPQ algorithm is proposed and described in section 4. In section 5, we provide the experimental results and evaluation. The conclusions and future works are discussed in section 6.

2   System Overview

TranStore system is based on C/S model, where a single server can support up to tens of clients connected in a network system. Fig.2 shows the overall architecture of a TranStore system with a server and a single client. Without the local hard disk, each client accesses the OS, software and data from the remote virtual disks which simulate the physical block-level storage devices. Vdisk, in essence, is one or more disk image files located on the server and accessed by the client remotely via Network Service Access Protocol (NSAP) [6]. TranStore server, running as an application daemon, maintains a client management process, a disk management process, and all Vdisk image files belonging to all clients in the system.

As seen from its structure in Fig.2, the Vdisk driver is composed of two parts running on the TranStore client and TranStore server, respectively. OS-Specific Driver (OSD) is mainly used to provide the interaction interface with a specific Client OS, so that Client OS may perform various operations on the virtual devices as usual. Independent Driver (ID) which runs in TransOS is used to fulfill the Vdisk functions that are irrelevant with a specific Client OS. The interface between OSD and ID is an ordinary hardware-level interface based on the I/O controller and register. Service Initiator is used to locate the TranStore server for ID and to transport the requests for Vdisk operations to relevant handling programs on the TranStore server via NSAP. Waiting for the response from the server, Service Initiator then passes the handling results to ID for further handling. Service Handler is used to receive I/O requests from the TranStore client, search relevant database, check the access authority, perform operations to the corresponding Vdisk image files and physical devices, and finally return the results to the TranStore client. NSAP communication protocol is the communication protocol to locate the TranStore server, verify relevant authorization, and transport requests and responses for various I/O operations.

As mentioned above, the Virtual I/O (VIO) path needs to go through the TranStore delivery network (a round-trip transportation) and the physical I/O operations of the TranStore server. Therefore, a complete VIO operation will take more time than commonly known I/O operations. More often than not, this makes the VIO the bottleneck of system performance. In order to enhance the access performance to VIO in the TranStore system, it is necessary to add cache modules along the VIO path through "add-in" mechanism, so as to further improve the read or write performance.

Client Cache (CC) is used to cache the requests or responses data from the Client OS and remote TranStore servers, and to reduce the I/O response time. Server Cache (SC) is added based on Service Handlers on the TranStore server. After the caching modules are added, in handling VIO requests sent from the TranStore client, the Service Handlers will first search the cache for the I/O data requested by the user using the SC. If the VIO data requested by the user is in the cache, it will directly return the I/O data to the TranStore client. Otherwise, the Service Handler will directly operate on the Vdisk image file and its corresponding physical device, acquiring the VIO data requested by the users, updating the content in the cache buffer with SC, and then sending the result to the sending queue. SC also will determine whether it is needed to pre-read some VIO data into the cache buffer, according to the specific VIO request

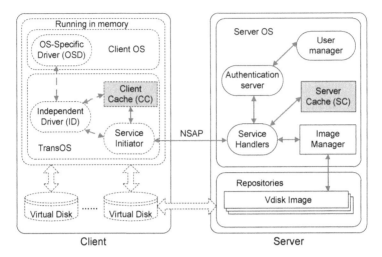

Fig. 2. Overall architecture of a TranStore system with a server and a single client

sent by the user. If it is needed, it will invoke the Service Handler to operate directly on the Vdisk image file and its corresponding physical device, so as to read the VIO data beforehand.

TranStore is designed for the special purpose, so the two-level buffer caches in TranStore have different access patterns from traditional distributed storage systems. Understanding the workload characteristics of Vdisk is a necessary prelude to improve the performance of TranStore cache mechanism. In next section, we use a trace-driven analysis method to observe I/O characteristics of Vdisk and discuss the effect of the cache on both server and client side.

3   Trace and Analysis

We study a real usage case deployed in the network and system group in Tsinghua University. The system is set up as the baseline case. The server is Dell PowerEdge 1900 machine, equipped with an Intel Xeon Quad Core 1.6 GHz CPU, 4 GB Dual DDR2 667 MHz RAM, one 160 GB Hitachi 15000rpm SATA hard disk, and a 1 Gbps on-board network card. Each client is configured as Intel Dual Core E6300 1.86GHz machines, with 512MB DDR 667 RAM and 100Mbps on-board network card. All the clients and server are connected by an Ethernet switch with 98 100Mbps interfaces and two 1Gbps interfaces. All clients run the Windows XP Professional SP3. The server runs Windows 2003 Standard SP2, with the software providing the TranStore services.

The access patterns must be defined carefully in our model. To make a reasonable definition, the characteristics of TranStore I/O are explored by a trace study on the baseline system. The I/O requests issued by the clients in the baseline system were traced in Tsinghua University for 4 weeks. There are 15 users, a professor and several graduate students, working on each client with Windows XP from 8am to 6pm. The applications used most frequently are the internet browser (IE 7.0), the text editor (Microsoft Office 2007) and the text viewer (Adobe acrobat reader 8.0). Besides, New Era English software, a multimedia application for English self-learning, is often used by students.

According to the results of our trace analysis, several key points are summarized as follows. TranStore system is configured at a saturated scenario in most of the cases. Therefore, although minimizing the remote access latency at a light load is of some value, it is much more significant to improve the performance at a heavy load. The heavy-load performance is governed by the most heavily utilized device. The disk is the primary bottleneck while the network is secondary. In a caching scheme, requested blocks are saved in the main memory so that the subsequent requests for these blocks can be satisfied without disk operations. The performance of the cache depends on the behaviors of the workload and the deployed location (client or server).

The effect of the cache at both the server and the client is analyzed. According to our observations, several conclusions can be summarized. We firstly study whether data accesses in the CC/SC cache have temporal locality characteristics. Previous studies have shown that the CC buffer cache accesses show a high degree of temporal locality [7]. LRU algorithm, which takes full advantage of temporal locality, is mainly used in CC. Those blocks which have temporal locality characteristics may remain in CC, and at the same time the block requests unmet in CC will access the SC buffer cache. Therefore, SC is a critical mechanism to improve the overall performance of TranStore. The capability of the server increases slowly along with the hit ratio when the hit ratio is at a low level. However, it increases dramatically when the hit ratio is over 30%. Since the Vdisk image is widely shared, the working set size is small enough that a reasonable large cache size achieves a high hit ratio on the server. The workload of SC is less of temporal locality, so appropriate cache algorithm which achieves a higher hit ratio can reduce the access latency.

4   Frequency-Based Multi-Priority Queues (FMPQ)

In TranStore client, the CC buffer cache has temporal locality characteristic. Therefore, some cache replacement algorithm based on the temporal locality, such as LRU can be used. We use LRU algorithm as the CC management algorithm. In the TranStore server, I/O requests accesses in SC show the characteristics, that some of the frequently accessed blocks satisfy a higher proportion of accesses, so we designed a cache replacement algorithm, namely Frequency-based Multi-Priority Queues, which is based on the access frequency priority. FMPQ gives the highest priority on the blocks which are accessed most frequently. FMPQ also gives different priorities for the blocks depending on the access frequencies, and reserves for different periods according to the priorities of the blocks in SC.

FMPQ uses more than one LRU queue (Q_0, Q_1 to Q_{w-1}) to store the different priorities of the blocks. w is an adjustable parameter. If the priority of Q_i is lower than the priority of Q_j (i < j), the life cycle of the blocks in the Q_i will be less than Q_j. FMPQ also sets up a queue Q_{off}, which records the access frequencies of the blocks which have recently been replaced. Q_{off} is a FIFO queue with a limited size, which only stores the identities and the access frequencies of the blocks.

FMPQ sets a function QCount(g) = log_2g, which puts the blocks on the proper LRU queue. g is a given frequency. When the frequency of a block is changed, the function ascends the position of the block. For example, the block P is hit in the SC buffer cache, and then P is firstly removed from the LRU queue. And according to the current access frequency of the block P, the function QCount(g) = log_2g calculates the result which is presented as d. The block is put at end of the Q_d queue. For another example, the block P is accessed eighth times, and then P will be upgraded from the Q_2 queue to the Q_3 queue. When the block P has not been hit, FMPQ selects a block which is evicted from the SC buffer cache to make a room for the block P. When the replacer is chosen, FMPQ starts to query the head of Q_0 queue. If Q_0 is an empty queue, FMPQ will query the queues from Q_1 until it finds a non-empty queue Q_i with the lowest level, and then replaces the head of the queue. If the block R is replaced, its identity and the current access frequency will be inserted into the end of the historical cache queue Q_{off}. If Q_{off} is full, the identity reserved for the longest period in Q_{off} will be deleted. If the request block P is in the Q_{off} records, P will be loaded from the hard disk into the SC buffer cache, and the value of its frequency g is set to be the record value of the access frequency in Q_{off} plus 1. If the block P is not in Q_{off}, it will be loaded into the SC buffer cache, and its frequency g is set to 1. At last, according to QCount(g), P is moved into the relevant   LRU queue.

In the SC buffer cache, FMPQ sets a failure time parameter, OverTime, for each block, which is used to drop the inactive blocks from the high priority queue to a low priority queue and is used to exceed the access count limit. "Time" here refers to the logical time, which is the access count. When a block enters a LRU queue, OverTime is set to be NowTime + DurationTime. The DurationTime is an adjustable parameter for setting the survival time of each block in a LRU queue. When an access happens, FMPQ compares OverTime of the head block of the queue with NowTime. If Over-Time is less than NowTime, the block will be moved to the end of the next level queue and the value of its OverTime will be reset.

When w is equal to 1, FMPQ is same as LRU algorithm. When w = 2, two queues and a history cache are used in FMPQ, same as 2Q [8] algorithms. However, FMPQ uses two LRU, and 2Q uses a FIFO queue and a LRU queue. In FMPQ, if the time in which the block is not accessed in Q_1 queue is more than DurationTime, the block will be downgraded from Q_1 to Q_0. 2Q does not carry out this kind of adjustment. In 2Q algorithm, when a block in Q_1 queue is replaced, it is not put into the historical buffer. FMPQ records the identity and the access frequency of the block into the historical buffer queue to record the block's access history. Similar to 2Q algorithm, FMPQ also has a time complexity O(1). Because all of the queues use the LRU list, w is usually very small. When an access happens, up to w-1 head blocks will be checked for the possible downgrade. Relative to FBR [9] or LRU algorithm, FMPQ is highly efficient and very easy to be implemented. The time complexity of those algorithms is close to O(log_2t). t is the number of entries in the cache. A binary tree data structure is usually needed to be implemented.

5   Experiment and Evaluation

We have evaluated the local algorithms for the two level buffer caches using trace-driven simulations. We used the analysis of the I/O request access patterns in the section 3 to simulate FMPQ algorithm. LRU cache replacement algorithm is used in the client's Vdisk driver, on server-side the FMPQ and three existing replacement algorithms, LRU, FBR, and 2Q, are implemented. The block size is set to 4KB. The requests have a significant temporal locality characteristic in CC, so this section will not evaluate the performance of the CC cache algorithm in TranStore client, and focus on the performance of FMPQ algorithm in SC.

In the experiments, we found that the warm blocks can be separated from other blocks by 8 LRU queues. The buffer size of the historical queue Q_{off} is set to be the eight times size of the blocks in the SC buffer cache. Because the buffer space occupied by each entry in the historical queue does not exceed 64 bytes, so the memory space required in the Q_{off} is less than 1% of the SC buffer cache. DurationTime is adjusted dynamically at the runtime. The main idea of the dynamic adjustment is the effective collection of the static information on the distribution of the temporal distance from the access history.

Table 1 shows FMPQ algorithm outperforms other algorithms in the SC buffer cache. For example, when the cache size is 256MB, the LRU hit ratio is 15.8%, the FMPQ hit ratio is 24.9%. For the same cache size, the hit ratio of FMPQ is 19% more than FBR, because the warm blocks are reserved selectively for a long time until the next request happens in FMPQ. In the trace load tests, the performance of LRU algorithm is not very good, even if it has a good performance in CC. There is no algorithm worse than LRU, because the longer minimal distance in SC cache makes the access frequency inaccurate. The performance of FBR algorithm is better than LRU, but it is always worse than FMPQ, in several cases the difference is very large. Although FBR considers the access frequency in order to overcome the defects of LRU algorithm, but it is difficult to adjust the parameters to combine the frequency and recency properly. The performance of 2Q algorithm is better than other algorithms except FMPQ. To set up a separate queue, for the blocks only accessed once, 2Q will store the blocks accessed frequently in the queue for a long time. When the SC cache size is small, 2Q hit ratio is lower than FMPQ, because the life cycle of a block in the SC buffer cache is not long enough to reserve it to be accessed in the next cycle.

Table 1. Hit Ratios of different cache algorithms

Cache Size	FMPQ	2Q	FBR	LRU
32MB	5.9	5.3	3.7	2.8
64MB	11.1	9.2	6.8	5.5
128MB	16.3	15.8	11.5	9.2
256MB	24.9	24.3	19.4	15.8
512MB	38.2	33.1	30.9	27.3

To learn more about the test results, we use the temporal distance as a measurement to analyze the performance of the algorithm. The analysis in section 3 shows that the access to the SC buffer cache mostly tends to maintain a longer temporal distance, so the performance of the SC replacement algorithm depends on the extent that it meets the survival time attribute of the block. If the temporal distance of the majority accesses is longer than S, the replacement algorithm which cannot save most of the blocks during a period that is longer than S is unlikely to have a good performance.

6   Conclusions and Future Work

TranStore is a novel pervasive computing system which allows users to download and execute heterogeneous commodity OSes and their applications on demand. This paper analyses the characteristics of its real usage workload, and studies the client and server cache access patterns in TranStore system. LRU algorithm is used in client-side cache. A cache management algorithm called Frequency-based Multi-Priority Queues proposed in this paper is used in server-side cache. We use simulation methods to evaluate the FMPQ performance and compare FMPQ with some other existing cache replacement algorithms. The results show that FMPQ can adapt to different cache sizes and workloads in transparent computing environment, and the performance of FMPQ is significantly better than others. To solve this problem, another solution is to combine the clients' cache to form a cooperative cache system. A p2p protocol should be introduced to locate and download the required blocks from other clients' memory.

References

1. Zhang, Y.: Transparent computing: Concept, architecture and example. Chinese Journal of Electronics 32(12A), 169–174 (2004)
2. Zhang, Y., Zhou, Y.-Z.: 4VP: A Novel Meta OS Approach for Streaming Programs in Ubiquitous Computing. In: 21st International Conference on Advanced Information Networking and Applications (AINA 2007), Niagara Falls, Canada, May 21-23, pp. 394–403 (2007)
3. Aspray, W.: The Stored Program Concept. IEEE Spectrum 27(9), 51–57 (1990)
4. Zhang, Y., Zhou, Y.-Z.: Separating computation and storage with storage virtualization. Computer Communications 34(13), 1539–1548 (2011)
5. Aven, I., Coffmann, E.I., Kogan, I.A.: Stochastic Analysis of Computer Storage. Reidel, Amsterdam (1987)
6. Kuang, W., Zhang, Y., Zhou, Y., et al.: NSAP—A network storage access protocol for transparent computing. Tsinghua Univ. (Sci. &Tech.) 49(1), 106–109 (2009)
7. Karedla, R., Spencer Love, J., Wherry, B.G.: Caching strategies to improve disk system performance. Computer 27(3), 38–46 (1994)
8. Johnson, T., Shasha, D.: 2Q: A Low Overhead High Performance Buffer Management Replacement Algorithm. In: Proc. Very Large Databases Conf., pp. 439–450 (1995)
9. Robinson, J., Devarakonda, M.: Data Cache Management using Frequency-Based Replacement. In: Proceedings of ACM SIGMETRICS Conf. Measurement and Modeling of Computer Systems (1990)

Network Security Situation Prediction
Based on BP and RBF Neural Network

Yaxing Zhang, Shuyuan Jin, Xiang Cui, Xi Yin, and Yi Pang

Institute of Computing Technology, Chinese Academy of Sciences, Beijing, China
zhangyaxing@software.ict.ac.cn,
{jinshuyuan,cuixiang,yinxi}@ict.ac.cn,
pangyi@software.ict.ac.cn

Abstract. With tremendous complex attacks on the network, network analysts not only need to understand but also predict the situation of network security. In the field of network security, the research on predicting network security situation has become a hot spot. The prediction of network security situation can dynamically reflect the security situation of the entire network and provide a reliable reference to ensure the network safety. This paper predicts the network security situation using the BP and the RBF neural networks, and then makes a comparison between the two methods. The results show that the effect of the model based on the BP neural network is better than that of the model based on the RBF neural network on predicting the network security situation.

Keywords: network security situation awareness, prediction of situational value, BP Neural network, RBF Neural network.

1 Introduction

As rapid development of network technology, researchers have paid more attentions to the issues of network security situation prediction. The capability of understanding the situations of network security can help network managers know whether the current network is under attack or not and if so how much the strength of attack is.

The method of neural network is widely used in the prediction of network security situation. [1] proposed a network security situational awareness model based on audit log and network security posture correction algorithm. In order to take comprehensive network security factors into consideration, [2] provided a method for network security situation assessment using Honeynet. [3] proposed a method of network security prediction based on dynamic BP neural network with covariance to resolve the limitations of depending on experts giving weights. [4] predicted the network security situation using the method of RBF neural network with hybrid hierarchy genetic algorithm. Most of work has not focused on the difference between the BP and the RBF neural networks on predicting security situation. This paper provides two methods based on the BP neural network and the RBF neural network respectively to predict the network security situation. More importantly, it compares the two methods from different aspects, for example, time, correct rate, and mean-squared error.

Y. Yuan, X. Wu, and Y. Lu (Eds.): ISCTCS 2012, CCIS 320, pp. 659–665, 2013.

2   Related Concepts

Network security situation is the macroscopic reflection of network state, reflecting the past and the present situation and then predicting the status and the trend of next phase [5]. The meaning of "network security situation" is the same as the concept of "situation" used to explain all the states of an object with complex structure. The prediction of network security situation can help decision-makers do situation awareness faster and better [6]. The value of network security situation is an important quantitative indicator to illustrate the level of the network security. The value of network security situation could manifest the operating situation of the network, varying with the frequency and quantity of security incident and the degree of threat [5]. We can use intrusion detection system or network management system to collect the original information of network security situation.

3   Artificial Neural Network Profile

Artificial Neural Network (ANN) is a kind of artificial intelligence technology, which has a rapid development in 1980s. In recent years, the neural network has made a huge breakthrough both in theory and practice [7].

The neural network is an ideal tool used to predict the network security situation. The BP and the RBF neural networks are most commonly used in information processing, pattern recognition and optimization problems [8].

4   Methods

This section shows the methods of the BP neural network and the RBF neural network used in the prediction of the network situation.

4.1   BP Neural Network Method

The BP network is a feedforward network with three or more layers, spreading error from back to front while adjusting the parameters. Generally speaking, the BP neural network contains the input layer, the hidden layer and the output layer. After our providing the network with a learning sample, the neurons' values of activated will be transferred from the input layer to the output layer. The neurons in the output layer should modify their connection weights and thresholds according to the error to minimize the mean squared error between the actual output and the desired output. In this paper we use the BP neural network with three layers which is shown in Fig. 1.

4.2   RBF Neural Network Method

A new and effective feedforward neural network with three layers called radial basis function (RBF) neural network, which has fine characteristics of approximation performance and the global optimum [3]. Generally speaking, the RBF network consists

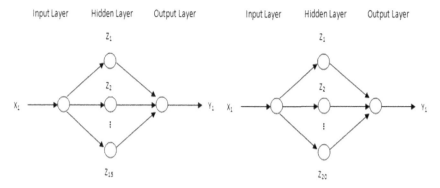

Fig. 1. BP Neural Network Structure   **Fig. 2.** RBF Neural Network Structure

of the input layer, the hidden layer and the output layer. The neurons in the input layer are only responsible for transferring the input signal to the hidden layer. In the hidden layer, we often use the radial basis function as the transfer function, while we usually adopt a simple linear function in the output layer. The RBF neural network with three layers used in the paper is shown in Fig. 2.

5   Experiment

In this paper, we use a neural network toolbox provided by MATLAB to establish the BP and the RBF neural networks.

5.1   Sample Data

The data used in the experiments is collected by "the network security situation analysis system", developed by the laboratory where the authors work. The system will give a parameter called nsas_score, which is the value of network security situation used in this paper.

The system collected data every five minutes during the dates from 2011-05-13 to 2011-05-18. During this period, the system was taken a complex artificially attack. There are 1728 sets of sample data, which is shown in table 1 (The data is too much to be shown). 864 sets are used to train the neural network models , while the others are used to test.

Table 1. Data used in the experiments

number	nsas_score	number	nsas_score	number	nsas_score
1	1.36	8	1.38	15	1.37
2	1.28	9	1.35	16	1.37
3	1.4	10	1.39	17	1.34
4	1.34	11	1.29	18	1.32
5	1.38	12	1.39	19	1.28
6	1.36	13	1.35	20	1.36
7	1.35	14	1.37	21	1.32

5.2   Pretreatment

In the neural network models, the input vector P is 1-dimensional vector, while the output vector T is 1-dimensional vector. For the collected data were not in the same order of magnitude, the data must be normalized in the pretreatment period. The normalization function used in the experiments is mapminmax.

5.3   Experimental Results Analysis and Discussion

5.3.1   BP Neural Network Model

The prediction model based on the BP neural network contains three layers: the input layer, the hidden layer and the output layer. The number of neurons in the hidden layer is set to 15, the Mean Squared Error (mse) is 0.1 according to the actual training process, the maximum number of training is 1000, and the learning function is trainlm. The error curve is shown in Fig. 3 and the fitting curves between the predicted output and the expected output is shown in Fig. 4.

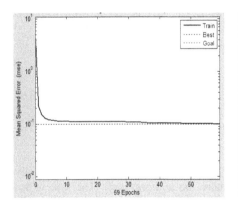 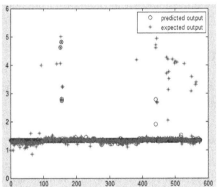

Fig. 3. Error curve in the network training

Fig. 4. Fitting curve between the predicted output and the expected output

Fig. 3 shows the error curve of the BP neural network model during the training process. In Fig. 3, the horizontal axis shows the number of training data, and the vertical axis represents the mean-squared error. The mean-squared error has the trend of becoming smaller as the growth of the number of training data. The curve shows that the learning algorithm has a fast convergence speed so that the model reaches the requirement after 59 epochs.

Fig. 4 illustrates the differences between the predicted and the expected outputs. The horizontal axis shows the number of the test data, and the vertical axis represents the predicted output and the expected output. The curve shows the fitting degree of the two kinds of output is high, and the correct rate is 85.42%.

5.3.2   RBF Neural Network Model

This paper uses the newrbe function to establish the RBF neural network model. The extension constant is set to 0.8 and the maximum number of neurons is 20. The other parameters such as the mean-squared error, the maximum number of training data, the learning function are set as the model based on the BP neural network. The error curve is shown in Fig. 5 and the fitting curves between the predicted output and the expected output is shown in Fig. 6.

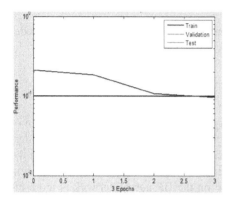
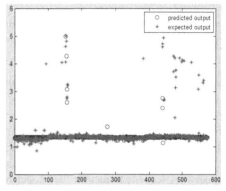

Fig. 5. Error curve in the network training

Fig. 6. Fitting curve between the predicted output and the expected output

Fig. 5 shows the error curve of the RBF neural network model during the training process. The horizontal axis in Fig. 5 shows the number of training data, the vertical axis represents the mean-squared error. The mean-squared error also becomes smaller with the growth of the number of training data. The curve shows that the learning algorithm has a faster convergence speed so that the model reaches the requirement after 3 epochs.

The fitting degree of the predicted output and the expected output is shown in Fig. 6. The horizontal axis shows the number of test data, the vertical axis represents the predicted and the expected outputs. The curve shows that the predicted output is similar to the expected output. The correct rate is 84.2%.

5.4   BP Network and RBF Network

- The time consumed by the BP neural network model is shorter than the RBF neural network model: the time used by the BP network model is less than 1 second, while the RBF network model uses 13 seconds. But the training time of the BP network is longer than that of the RBF network. This is because that the BP network reaches the goal after 59 epochs, while the RBF network makes it after 3 epochs. This shows that the test time of the BP network is less than that of the RBF network. This is partly because in the test of the RBF network, almost each sample has to be compared with the center vector of each neuron in hidden layer. This increases the time of test.

- The correct rate of the BP neural network model is higher than that of the RBF neural network model. The BP network reaches 85.42%, while the RBF network reaches 84.2%. Since the correct rate is calculated with a function, the predicted output of the RBF network may not be suitable for the processing function.
- The mean-squared error of these two methods is relatively large. The reason may be that the sample data used in the experiments is too small.

In a word, the model based on the BP neural network is more effective than the model based on the RBF neural network in the prediction of network security situation.

6   Conclusions and limitations

The prediction technology of network security situation could reflect the situation of the whole network and predict its trend. It gives network managers a better understanding of the network security situation, and effectively protects the network in the complex network environment. The experimental results show that in the prediction of network security situation, the model based on the BP neural network is more effective than the RBF neural network model. Due to the lack of the sample data and the mismatch between the test data and the training data, the mean-squared error that two networks could reach is relatively large. The performance of the experiments could be improved at this point.

References

1. Wei, Y., Lian, Y.: A Network Security Situational Awareness Model Based on Log Audit and Performance Correction. Chinese Journal of Computers 32, 763–772 (2009)
2. Xia, W., Wang, H.: Prediction model of network security situational based on regression analysis. In: 2010 IEEE International Conference on Wireless Communications, Networking and Information Security, WCNIS (2010)
3. Tang, C., Xie, Y., Qiang, B., Wang, X., Zhang, R.: Security Situation Prediction Based on Dynamic BP Neural with Covariance. In: Advanced in Control Engineering and Information Science, CEIS 2011 (2011)
4. Meng, J., Ma, C., He, J., Zhang, H.: Network Security Situation Prediction Model Based on HHGA-RBF Neural Network. Computer Science 38, 70 (2011)
5. Ren, W., Jiang, X., Sun, T.: The Prediction Method of Network Security Situation Based on RBF Neural Network. Computer Engineering and Applications 31, 136–144 (2006)
6. Xu, B.: Network Security Situation Prediction. Dalian University of Technology 1, 6–8 (2008)
7. Haykin, S.: Neural Networks, a Comprehensive Foundation, 2nd edn., pp. 161–175, 183–221,400–438. Prentice Hall (1998)
8. Xi, R., Jin, S., Yun, X., Zhang, Y.: CNSSA: A Comprehensive Network Security Situation Awareness System. In: 2011 IEEE 10th International Conference on Trust, Security and Privacy in Computing and Communications, TrustCom (2011)

 9. Onwubiko, C., Owens, T.: Situational Awareness in Computer Network Defense: Principles, Methods and Applications. Information Science Reference Press (January 2012) Ebook
10. Hu, W., Li, J., Chen, X., Jiang, X.: Network security situation prediction based on improved adaptive grey Verhulst model. Journal of Shanghai Jiaotong University (Science) 15(4), 408–413 (2010)
11. Jajodia, S.: Cyber situation awareness: issue and research (advanced in information security) (2009) Ebook

Research on Redundant Channel Model
Based on Spatial Correlation in IOT

Fangjiao Zhang[1,2,3], Wei Guo[1,2,3], Jincui Yang[2,3], Fangfang Yuan[1], and Lidong Zhai[1]

[1] Institute of Information Engineering, Chinese Academy of Sciences, Beijing, China
[2] Beijing University of Posts and Telecommunications, Beijing, China
[3] Key Laboratory of Trustworthy Distributed Computing and Service (BUPT),
Ministry of Education, Beijing, China
fangjiaozhang@126.com, guowei_apple@hotmail.com,
jincuiyang@sina.com,
{yuanfangfang,zhailidong}@iie.ac.cn

Abstract. With the widely discussion of IOT (Internet of Things) in many applications recently, more and more attentions have been paid to the security of its security. In this paper, we present a redundant channel model based on spatial correlation in IOT. The proposed model is mainly for attacks which could increase the traffic of the network such as DDos. Firstly, redundant channel is introduced systematically, including the spatial correlation. Then, a control mechanism is put forward for the model. A Matlab simulation is performed to test the availability of the model at last. And the results verify that this model is feasible to a certain degree.

Keywords: redundant channel, spatial correlation, IOT.

1   Introduction

There are many such forms of existence of IOT like RFID and WSN. Here we are mainly discussing the WSN. Wireless sensor network is exposed to the open physical environment, which is more vulnerable to malicious attackers compared to the Internet, making sensor nodes in the network are flooded by a vast number of useless requests information. It leads to the consumption of network bandwidth or system resources, resulting in the bad quality of service.

In a worst-case scenario, the network or system is so overloaded that they are paralyzed to stop the normal network services.

In order to improve the reliability of the running system, we propose a method of adding an alternate mode of operation by adding redundant channel to prevent blocking. Periodical communications testing is made to measure the system performance, which would be compared to previous system settings, thereby determining whether the redundant channel is enabled.

Therefore, the questions of "what on earth is the redundant channel?", "where we should put it?", "why is it necessary?" and "when and how to adopt it?" are raised naturally.

Y. Yuan, X. Wu, and Y. Lu (Eds.): ISCTCS 2012, CCIS 320, pp. 666–672, 2013.

The redundancy we depict in this paper refers to adding a new sensor node beside sink node in the network. How to select the sink node? We define the node of the maximum of Tsp, a parameter we raised base on spatial correlation, as the sink node, which would send the data gathered from other nodes to applications. The new-added node either takes place of the related node, or holds a portion of the responsibility of the node. In this paper, we will take the latter one. On the one hand, the channel can reduce the risk that the node is down; On the other hand, it could prolong the life of the whole network, which is critical for the WSN. We only put the redundant channel around the significant node-sink node, considering the cost of it. For when and how to enable the channel, there would be a detailed description in Section 3.

Parts of the work are discussed here, and others are left as future jobs. The rest of this paper is organized as follows. In Section 2, we give background and related work on spatial correlation and redundant channel. Section 3, present a new model to describe channel control based on spatial correlation. In Section 4, we discuss the results of simulations of redundant channel control model. We summarize our work in Section 5.

2   Related Works

The wireless sensor network is a typical ad-hoc network, where each sensor node is required to be independent and flexible to be self-organizing. Besides, an ad hoc network always requires spatially dense sensor deployment to achieve satisfying coverage [1, 2]. Just because of the high density in network topology, the transmitting among spatially proximal sensors is highly correlated [3]. Due to the nodes' interaction with multiple nodes around in high-density region, their traffic is relatively high.

There is still much work to do in despite of the many researches about spatial correlation. James O Berger et al gave four spatial correlation models, spherical, power exponential and rational quadratic in [4]. A new spatial correlation model is used by Na Li et al in [5] to analyzed data distortion in WSN. Recently, the worm propagation model in [6] is mentioned, in which the conception of spatial correlation is adopted. Our work is inspired by the model.

3   Redundant Channel Model

"Where to put the redundant channel" and "when and how to enable it" would be the crucial contents in this section.

The new argument, Tsp (Traffic State Parameter), is put forward based on the spatial correlation model in [6]. We assume that the node with maximum of Tsp becomes the sink node. In [6], we know that there are a quantity of nodes at the point of maximum Csc(Close Spatial Correlation). And once Csc of each node is fixed, it won't change any more. Here energy is taken into consideration, thus making Tsp of every node dynamic. Apparently, the node with highest Tsp varies dynamically at every moment, which means that the redundant channel is mobile. It is also the innovation of this dissertation. The next is the channel control mechanism in order to proceed with the channel appropriately and effectively. More information is detailed as follows.

3.1   Spatial Correlation Parameters

Suppose sensor nodes do not move any more once they are deployed in the wireless sensor network. In addition, all the sensor nodes in the network are the same, regardless of information sensing, transmitting and processing. All the sensor nodes have a fixed sensing radius Rs and the sensing area is valid within a circle centered by the node's spatial position [7]. At the same time all the sensor nodes have a transmitting radius Rt which is double as sensing radius Rs.

From the paper [6], we can know:

Let $\theta = 2R_s$

$$K_\theta(d) = \begin{cases} \dfrac{\theta^2 \cdot arcsin\sqrt{1-\frac{d^2}{\theta^2}} - d\cdot\sqrt{\theta^2-d^2}}{\theta^2\left(\pi - arcsin\sqrt{1-\frac{d^2}{\theta^2}}\right) + d\cdot\sqrt{\theta^2-d^2}} ; & 0 \le d \le \theta \\ 0; & d > \theta \end{cases} \tag{1}$$

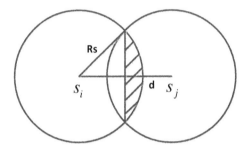

Fig. 1. Spatial correlation

Note: Rs is the sensing radius.

From the formula (2), we know $K_\theta(d)$ only represents the correlation between two nodes. Two new correlation parameters are proposed in order to describe the correlation of each node independently. Csc is the summation of one node with all the rest nodes in the WSN.

$$Csc_i = \sum_n K_\theta(d) - 1 \tag{2}$$

If one node's Csc is high, it means that there are a lot of nodes close to it. In other words, it has a high spatial correlation.

Now we take energy of each node into account. And another parameter-Tsp(Traffic State Parameter) is proposed, to visually represent the flow changes of nodes .

Tsp is defined as follows:

$$Tsp_0 = Csc \cdot E_0 \tag{3}$$

$$\Delta E(t) = \mu \cdot log2(Tsp + 1) \cdot Csc \tag{4}$$

Apparently, when Csc of a node is high, it means that there are many nodes around it, thus leading to more traffic and consuming more energy, that is $\Delta E(t) \propto Csc$ and $\Delta E(t) \propto Tsp$. At the same time, we define the relationship of Tsp(t+1) and Tsp(t) in equation (5).

$$Tsp(t+1) = Tsp(t) - \Delta E(t) \qquad (5)$$

Put the formula (4) into (5), and then obtains a new formula (6):

$$Tsp(t+1) = Tsp(t) - \mu \cdot \log2(Tsp+1) \cdot Csc \qquad (6)$$

Suppose $\mu = 0.8^t$, because as time goes on, the rate of energy reduce will be smaller. Then

$$Tsp(t+1) = Tsp(t) - 0.8^t \cdot \log2(Tsp+1) \cdot Csc \qquad (7)$$

Note: E(t) is the energy of any node at the moment t. And the initial energy of each node is equal. Tsp_0 and E_0 are initial values of the node.

What is described is the redundant channel model and we solve it by Matlab. The next following part would be the channel simulation based on the model.

3.2   Redundant Channel Control Mechanism

The flow chart about the redundant channel control mechanism is shown below.

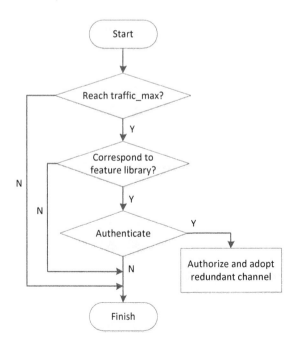

Fig. 2. Redundant channel control mechanism

We define a threshold, named traffic_max, here and don't care about the specific value. When the traffic of sink node reaches it, we easily conclude that the node may be suspicious. However, the increased traffic might not the result of hostile attacks, possibly due to transferring large files. So the packets would be checked to see whether they correspond to feature library predefined according to the attack types or not. If the node is judged suspicious, we would consider adopting the redundant channel. And yet, it has a bearing on authentication and authorization. As depicted in Fig. 3, not every node knows and could access the redundant channel. While the sink node has to enable the channel, it would inform node A that it also can communicate with node B. Node A can't access node B unless sink node offer the digital certificate or anything else of node A to prove that the node is reliable. Knowing that A is A, the channel accept the A's connections, achieving load sharing of sink node.

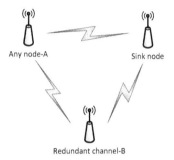

Fig. 3. Authentication and authorization

4   Simulations and Analysis

4.1   Simulation Description

The simulations are performed to prove the feasibility of redundant channel. The numerical analysis tool, Matlab, is used to derive theory results from the mathematical model we raise. In the simulations, we assume that the WSN is an Ad-hoc network, where the nodes are randomly distributed and deployed densely.

4.2   Analysis on Simulation Results

In the simulation, N=4000, S=1600*1600, Rt=100, Rs=50, to keep a high density of wireless sensor network just as depicted in [6]. In addition, the initial energy $E_0=1000$.

Fig4 and Fig5 respectively examine the nodes distribution, and if the redundant channel works or not.

Fig.4 shows the nodes distribution of spatial relation in the network. It obeys the normal distribution for the reason that nodes in the wireless network are randomly distributed.

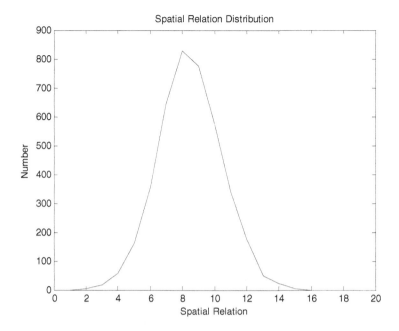

Fig. 4. Spatial Relation Distribution

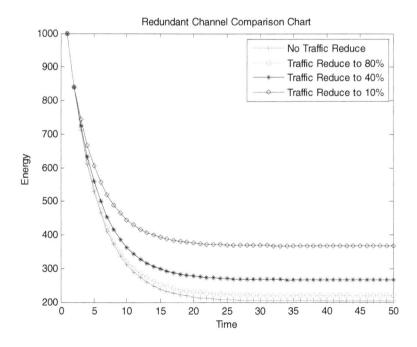

Fig. 5. Redundant Channel Comparison Chart

Fig.5 is the redundant channel comparison chart. It describes node's energy change trend. The node with the highest Tsp at t=1 is taken as an example. And we suppose that the redundant channel would be adopted at t=2.From the picture, we can conclude that the consuming energy will become smaller when the redundant channel is adopted, respectively reducing to 80 percent、 40 percent、 10 percent of the original traffic. And as time goes on, the energy consuming rate also becomes smaller. When different kinds of redundant channel are enabled, the situation of energy consumption is different. It depends on the cost could be paid. But, above all, the result proves the feasibility of the redundant channel.

5   Conclusion and Future Works

In the paper, the main contribution is to propose a new parameter -Tsp based on spatial correlation. With it, we give a redundant channel model and corresponding model control mechanism. And the simulation also proves the certain feasibility of the model.

In our future work, we will perfect the model raised above continuously and extensively, where there are still many problems existing. Meanwhile, we will improve the simulation more visually. Beyond that, the redundant channel would be practiced, researching certain attributes of it.

Acknowledgements. This paper is supported by National Key Technology R&D Program (Grant No.2012BAH37B04), and 863 Program (Grant No.2011AA01A103).

References

1. Clouqueur, T., Phipatanasuphorn, V., Ramanathan, P., Saluja, K.: Sensor deployment strategy for target detection. In: Proceedings of the ACM WSNA 2002, Atlanta, USA (September 2002)
2. Meguerdichian, S., Koushanfar, F., Potkonjak, M., Srivastava, M.B.: Coverage problems in wireless ad-hoc sensor networks. In: Proceedings of the IEEE INFOCOM 2001, Anchorage, AK (April 2001)
3. Berger, J.O., de Oliviera, V., Sanso, B.: Objective Bayesian analysis of spatially correlated data. Journal of the American Statistical Association 96, 1361–1374 (2001)
4. Li, N., Liu, Y., Wu, F., Tang, B.: WSN Data Distortion Analysis and Correlation Model Based on Spatial Locations. Journal of Networks 5 (December 2010)
5. Song, J.-G., Jung, S., Kim, J.H., Seo, D.I., Kim, S.: Research on a Denial of Service (DoS) Detection System Based on Global Interdependent Behaviors in a Sensor Network Environment. Sensors 10, 10376–10386 (2010)
6. Guo, W., Zhai, L., Guo, L., Shi, J.: Worm Propagation Control Based on Spatial Correlation in Wireless Sensor Network. In: Wang, H., Zou, L., Huang, G., He, J., Pang, C., Zhang, H.L., Zhao, D., Yi, Z. (eds.) APWeb 2012 Workshops. LNCS, vol. 7234, pp. 68–77. Springer, Heidelberg (2012)
7. Hossain, A., Biswas, P.K., Chakrabarti, S.: Sensing Models and Its Impact on Network Coverage in Wireless Sensor Network. In: IEEE Region 10 and the Third International Conference on Industrial and Information Systems (ICIIS 2008), Kharagpur, December 8-10, pp. 1–5 (2008)

Design of a Trusted File System Based on Hadoop

Songchang Jin, Shuqiang Yang, Xiang Zhu, and Hong Yin

School of Computer, National University of Defense Technology, Changsha, China
jsc04@126.com

Abstract. This paper analyses the data security issues in Hadoop platform, and proposes a design of trusted file system for Hadoop. The design uses the latest cryptography—fully homomorphic encryption technology and authentication agent technology, it ensures the reliability and safety from the three levels of hardware, data, users and operations. The homomorphic encryption technology enables the encrypted data to be operable to protect the security of the data and the efficiency of the application. The authentication agent technology offers a variety of access control rules, which are a combination of access control mechanisms, privilege separation and security audit mechanisms, to ensure the safety for the data stored in the Hadoop file system.

Keywords: fully homomorphism encryption, authentication agent, Hadoop, trusted storage.

1 Introduction

1.1 Background

With the development of computer science and technology, the Internet now is producing vast amounts of data every day. IDC's latest statistics show the growth rate of structured data in the Internet now is about 32%, and unstructured data is 63%, to 2012, the unstructured data occupies a proportion will reach more than 75% of the entire amount of data in the Internet [1]. The volume of digital content of the world grows to 2.7ZB in 2012, up 48% from 2011, rocketing toward 8ZB by 2015 [2]. A 2011 McKinsey research report points out that data have swept into every industry and business function and are now an important factor of production, and the use of big data will underpin new waves of productivity growth and consumer surplus [3].

Hadoop has become the de facto platform for large-scale data analysis in commercial applications, and increasingly so in scientific applications [4]. In fact in the next 5 years, 50 percent of Big Data projects are expected to run on Hadoop.

1.2 Hadoop Distributed File System Introduction

Hadoop is a framework written in Java for running applications on large clusters of commodity hardware. HDFS is a highly fault-tolerant Hadoop distributed file system.

Y. Yuan, X. Wu, and Y. Lu (Eds.): ISCTCS 2012, CCIS 320, pp. 673–680, 2013.
© Springer-Verlag Berlin Heidelberg 2013

MapReduce is a programming model for processing large data sets, which is typically used to as distributed computing on clusters of computers [5]. The model is inspired by the map and reduced functions commonly used in functional programming.

Files on HDFS are split into blocks and stored in a redundant fashion across multiple machines to ensure their durability to failure and high availability to very parallel applications.

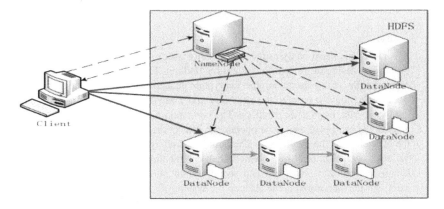

Fig. 1. HDFS architecture

A HDFS cluster has two types of node operating in a master-worker pattern: a NameNode and a numbers of DataNodes. NameNode manages the file system namespace. It maintains the file system tree and the metadata for all the files and directories in the tree. It also knows the DataNodes on which all the blocks for a given file are located. However NameNode does not store block locations persistently, since this information is reconstructed from DataNodes when the system starts.

DataNodes are the worker nodes of the file system. They store and retrieve blocks when they are told to by clients or the NameNode, and they report back to the NameNode periodically with lists of blocks that they are storing [6]. All data transfers occur directly between clients and DataNodes or between DataNodes. Communication with the NameNode only involves transfer of metadata.

1.3   HDFS Data Security Risks

HDFS uses unix 'whoami' utility to identify users, and "bash –c groups" for groups. And this is the weakest link because of which Hadoop file permissions and quota settings are for namesake. Anybody who's like to unauthorized access to the file on HDFS can write its own whoami script or group script and add it in its path to impersonate someone else including super user.

1. Hadoop services do not authenticate users or other services. As a result, Hadoop is subject to the following security risks.
   (a) A user can access an HDFS cluster as any other user.

This makes it impossible to enforce access control in an uncooperative environment. For example, file permission checking on HDFS can be easily circumvented.

(b) An attacker can masquerade as Hadoop services.

For example, user's code running on a MapReduce cluster can register itself as a new TaskTracker (a compute node similar to DataNode in HDFS cluster).

(c) Super-user can do anything without checking.

The super-user is the user with the same identity as name node process itself. If somebody started the name node, then it is the super-user. The super-user can do anything in that permissions checks never fail for the super-user. Data on HDFS is fully visible and operational for super-user.

2. DataNodes do not enforce any access control on accesses to its data blocks.

This makes it possible for an unauthorized client to read a data block as long as it can supply its block ID. It's also possible for anyone to write arbitrary data blocks to DataNodes.

3. Data faces with the issue of data encryption.

Data sets stored and derived on HDFS face with the issue of data encryption. Data aggregation on HDFS increases the risk of data leaks.

The latest Hadoop version has added the Kerberos security mechanism to ensure that the cluster is trusted on machine level. Combining with the Kerberos mechanism, we propose a design scheme for a trusted HDFS based on fully homomorphic encryption and Authorization agent technology in this paper.

2 Fully Homomorphic Encryption

Homomorphic encryption proposed by Rivest, Adleman and Dertouzos in 1978 is a form of encryption which allows specific types of computations to be carried out on ciphertext and obtain an encrypted result which is the ciphertext of the result of operations performed on the plaintext. In simple terms, homomorphic encryption has the ability to perform computations on the ciphertext without decrypting it first.

The encryption algorithm $E()$ is homomorphic if given $E(x)$ and $E(y)$, one can obtain $E(x \perp y)$ without decrypting x, y for some operation $\perp$.

There are several efficient, partially homomorphic cryptosystems such as RSA, Benaloh, and two fully homomorphic, but less efficient cryptosystems.

- RSA (Multiplicative Homomorphism)

If the RSA public key is modulus m and exponent e, then the encryption of a message x is given by $E(x) = x^e \bmod m$. The homomorphic property is then

$$E(x_1) \cdot E(x_2) = x_1^e x_2^e \bmod m = (x_1 x_2)^e \bmod m = E(x_1 \cdot x_2) \tag{1}$$

- Benaloh

In the Benaloh cryptosystem, if the public key is the modulus m and the base g with a block size of r, then the encryption of a message x is $g^x u^r \bmod m$. The homomorphic property is then

$$E(x_1) \cdot E(x_2) = (g^{x_1}u_1^r)(g^{x_2}u_2^r) = g^{x_1+x_2}(u_1u_2)^r = E(x_1 + x_2 \bmod r) \qquad (2)$$

Craig Gentry using lattice-based cryptography showed the first fully homomorphic encryption scheme on June 25, 2009. His scheme supports evaluations of arbitrary depth circuits. His construction starts from a somewhat homomorphic encryption scheme using ideal latticesthat is limited to evaluating low-degree polynomials over encrypted data.

The existence of an efficient and fully homomorphic cryptosystem would have great practical implications in the outsourcing of private computations, for instance, in the data processing of HDFS.

3   System Design

3.1   Authentication Agent Design

HDFS has a permissions model for files. There are three types of permission: read permission, write permission, and execute permission. Each file has an owner, a group, and a mode. The mode is made up of the permissions for the owner, members of the group, and the others. By default, a client's identity is determined by the username and groups of the process it is running in. This makes it possible to become an arbitrary user, simply by creating an account of that name on the remote system. Thus, permissions should be used only in a cooperative community of users, as a mechanism for sharing file system resources and for avoiding accidental data loss, and not for securing resources in a hostile environment.

We design an authentication agent to prevent unauthorized user from accessing HDFS and authorized user from unauthorized accessing. Fig.2 shows the authentication agent architecture.

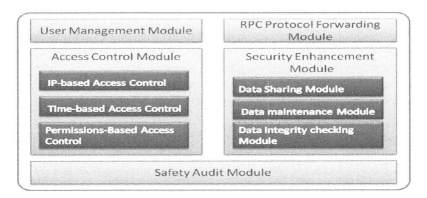

Fig. 2. Authentication Agent Architecture

User management module provides user registration interface, uses USB key and password two-factor authentication mechanism to verify the user's true identity, which can be effective in preventing unregistered users to access HDFS and the administrator of HDFS to create accounts illegally, distort authorization .etc.

Access control module checks permissions of the user who is going to access the file on HDFS and set access rules to restrict user's access. There are three main types of access control rules.

- IP-based access rule

Checking user's IP and MAC to ensure that only authorized IP/MAC address pair can access to corresponding data on HDFS. With this, we can prevent unauthorized users to access HDFS by modifying the IP address to masquerade as other users.

- Time-based access rule

Checking the access time user-initiated to ensure that user can access HDFS within the specified time interval.

- Permissions-based access rule

User should register an account on authentication agent first, the administrator then authorizes the account, and last, the authorized account is able to access the appropriate file on HDFS.

RPC protocol forwarding module is mainly forwarding the request data from users to NameNode and the response data from NameNode to users which is transferred using RPC protocol.

Security enhancement module aims to enhance the security of data on HDFS. It consists of three modules.

- Data maintenance module

Scanning the number of replications of the blocks for each file on a regular basis, and then calling the HDFS API to repair data replications in time according to the minimum safe number of replication set by user, we can improve data availability.

- Data integrity checking module

Data on HDFS is now checked with CRC32. When file created on HDFS, client computes 4 bytes checksum per 512 bytes, and DataNode stores the checksum. When read file from HDFS, client retrieves the data and checksum from DataNode and validates the checksum. if validation fails, client tries other replicas.

Safety audit module audits the behavior of the administrator. We use privilege separation strategy, and set administrator account and auditor account. Administrator takes settings of authentication agent and manages user registration and authorization. Security audit modules audits the behaviors of the administrator and generates security logs.

3.2   System Architecture

Kerberos is a computer network authentication protocol which works on the basis of "tickets" to allow nodes communicating over a non-secure network to prove their identity to one another in a secure manner. Hadoop 1.0.0 version comes with the Kerberos mechanism.

In the deployment of a HDFS cluster, it places the trusted server authentication key in each node of the cluster to achieve the reliability of the Hadoop cluster node communication, which can effectively prevent non-trusted machines posing as internal nodes registered to the NameNode and then process data on HDFS. This mechanism is used throughout the cluster. So from storage perspective, Kerberos can guarantee the credibility of the nodes in HDFS cluster.

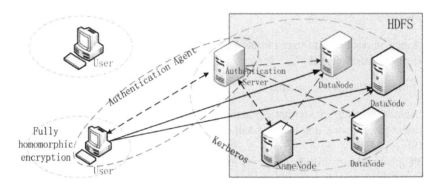

Fig. 3. Hadoop trusted storage system architecture

Fully homomorphic encryption allows multiple users to work on encrypted data in an encrypted form with any operation, but yields the same results as if the data had been unlocked. So, it can be used to encrypt the data for users, and then, the encrypted data can be uploaded to HDFS without worrying that data be stolen when transferring on the network to HDFS. After data processing with MapReduce, the result is still encrypted and safely stored on HDFS.

Authentication agent provides user registration interface, uses two-factor authentication (2FA) to ensure the user's true identity and provides three types of access control rules to restrict users' access. Enhance the security of the system with security enhancement module, and supervise administrator's behaviors by security audit module.

The system architecture is shown in Fig.3. In the system we designed, fully homomorphic encryption is used to protect user's data and make the encrypted data to be operable, so it improves the process efficiency of the encrypted data. Kerberos is used to ensure the reliability of the storage environment on machine level. Authentication agent is used to ensure the safety and legitimacy of the users and their operations.

4   Experiment and Analysis

The experiments were carried out on a Hadoop cluster which consisted of 30 Power-Leader PR2760T servers and a Cisco WS-C3750G-48TS-S switch, the client node was same to the server.

Kerberos mechanism can guarantee the credibility of the cluster and client nodes, but is provided by the latest Hadoop version, so this paper did not intend to test it. All operations on the content of a file come down to read and write operation ultimately. Therefore, a document uploading experiment was carried out to test the writing efficiency and a MapReduce program for traversing the content of a file was carried out to test the reading efficiency of the system.

File uploading test. In the experiment, users encrypted local text file with RSA segmented parallel encryption referred to in section 2 and then uploaded the file onto hdfs. In the end, all the data of users was stored in the form of ciphertext on hdfs. This didn't affect the operations on the file of the users, but led to the expansion of data size. The result is shown in Table 1.

Table 1. Time-consuming and expansion ratio of encryption operation

Data(Mb)	Encrypted data(Mb)	Time consume(min)	Data expansion ratio
200	203.4	11.3	1.017
400	406.5	22.7	1.016
600	609.7	35.1	1.016
800	813.5	47.5	1.017
1000	1017.4	59.8	1.017

The experimental results show that the data expansion rate of about 1.0, and the encryption algorithm is relatively inefficient.

File reading test. In the experiment, the MapReduce program traverse the encrypted content of the file on hdfs directly in contrast to traditional encrypted data processing including file downloads, decryption and traverse operations. The result is shown in Table 2.

Table 2. Time-consuming of fully homomorphic and traditional encrypted data processing

Encrypted data(Mb)	Time consume (min)	
	Fully homomorphic	Traditional
203.4	1.4	13.5
406.5	1.7	31.5
609.7	1.8	52.7
813.5	2.1	73.2
1017.4	2.4	103.9

Data on hdfs is split into blocks, and each MapReduce node in this experiment only need to deal with one block, so the efficiency is much higher than the traditional encrypted data processing method.

Authentication agent test is mainly to test the access control rules, user management and security enhancement modules. The results show that it can effectively control the privileges of administrator, ensure the reliability and authenticity of the users of the system and effectively control users access to the system.

5   Summary

With the rise of cloud computing, Hadoop plays an increasingly important role in the massive data storage and analysis. Due to the lack of a valid user authentication and data security defense measures, Hadoop is now facing a lot of security problems in the data storage.

We introduce the fully homomorphic encryption algorithm and design an authentication agent for Hadoop to ensure the safety and reliability of the users when accessing HDFS and the operations carried out on the data.

Currently, because of the computational complexity, data increases seriously and other reasons when using fully homomorphic encryption, it has not been put into practical use. With the development of cryptography, we believe that there will be a practical fully homomorphic algorithm program in the near future.

Acknowledgments. This work was supported by the Key Technologies R&D Program of China (No.2012BAH38B-04, 2012BAH38B06), National High-Tech R&D Program of China (No.2010AA012505, 2011AA010702), National Natural Science Foundation of China (No. 60933005).

References

1. Zhou, K.: China Internet market insight: Study of Internet Big Data Technological Innovation (2012), http://www.idc.com.cn/
2. Gens, F.: IDC Predictions 2012: Competing for 2020, http://cdn.idc.com/research/Predictions12/Main/downloads/IDCTOP10Predictions2012.pdf
3. James, M., Chui, M., Bughin, J., Brown, B., Dobbs, R., Roxburgh, C., Byers, A.H.: Big Data: The next frontier for innovation, competition, and productivity. McKinsey Global Institute (May 2011)
4. Buck, J.B., Watkins, N., LeFevre, J., Ioannidou, K., Maltzahn, C., Polyzotis, N., Brandt, S.: SciHadoop: Array-based Query Processing in Hadoop. In: Proceedings of SC (2011)
5. Dean, J., Ghemawat, S.: MapReduce: simplified data processing on large clusters. In: Proceedings of the 6th conference on Symposium on Opearting Systems Design & Implementation, San Francisco, CA, December 06-08, p. 10 (2004)
6. Chansler, R., Kuang, H., Radia, S., Shvachko, K., Srinivas, S.: The Hadoop Distributed File System, http://www.aosabook.org/en/hdfs.html

Architecting Dependable Many-Core Processors Using Core-Level Dynamic Redundancy

Wentao Jia, Chunyuan Zhang, Jian Fu, and Rui Li

School of Computer, National University of Defense Technology, Changsha, China
{wtjia,cyzhang,jianfu,lirui}@nudt.edu.cn

Abstract. Future many-core processors probably contain more than 1000 cores on a single die. But continued scaling of silicon fabrication technology make such chips orders of magnitude more vulnerable to errors. This means reliability techniques have to be an essential part of many-core processors. Redundant execution is a efficient solution to improve reliability. Present redundant execution mechanisms such an SRT,CRT,DIVA and RECVF aim to improve performance decrease using execution assistance and other speculative mechanisms. We are from another way that utilizing idle cores in may-core processors to execute redundancy. We propose core-level dynamic redundancy (CDR) which includes the following unique properties : i) eliminates restriction of hardware and supports redundancy on arbitrary core. ii) dynamically chooses core to execute redundancy on cores conditions, so effectively balance reliability, performance and power. Experimental results show the effectiveness of the pro-posed techniques.

Keywords: fault tolerance, dynamic redundancy, many-core, reliability.

1 Introduction

Nowadays, the number of transistors still doubles every two years, but no longer with significant frequency enhancements and the cost of extra power. These facts open the doors for new processors with probably more than 1000 cores and an increasing need for exploiting such large amount of resources[1].

With the ongoing decrease of the transistor size, the probability of soft errors and physical flaws on the chip, induced by voltage fluctuation, cosmic rays, thermal changes, or variability in the manufacturing process will further raise [2], making errors in many-core systems unavoidable.

Redundant execution is a efficient solution to improve reliability, which runs redundant copies of the same program and compares outputs from the redundant copies to detect faults. redundant execution can be implemented on most implementations of multithreading, such as simultaneous multithreading (SMT) or chip multi-core processors(CMP).

Present redundant execution techniques such as SRT[3], CRT[4], DIVA[5] and RECVF[6] aim to improve performance by execution assistance and other speculative mechanisms. We make another way that dynamically chose idle cores for redundant

Y. Yuan, X. Wu, and Y. Lu (Eds.): ISCTCS 2012, CCIS 320, pp. 681–688, 2013.
© Springer-Verlag Berlin Heidelberg 2013

execution based resources utilized. Core-level dynamic redundancy (CDR) is implemented on many-core processors which contain more than 1000 cores and usually leaving some of cores idle. CDR means not only to choose arbitrary core for redundancy at the beginning of redundancy but also switch to other cores at checkpoints. The most advantage of CDR is to schedule redundant execution on cores conditions, so it can effectively balance performance, reliability, power and so on.

There are two challenges for CDR: first, how to eliminate restriction of hardware and support redundancy on arbitrary core. Second, how to decrease redundant communication on networks-on-chip (NoC). Redundant execution needs special hardware such as dedicated bus, comparer, buffers and so on, which restrict redundancy across arbitrary core. Communicating over the NoC with a potentially distant core may increase in NoC traffic which could severely impact performance.

We make following solutions: i) expand local cache inside the sphere of replication, which reduce data needed to buffer and to output compared. ii) simplify hardware of reliability manager, remove dedicated bus and utilize the NoC for redundant core communication. iii) compress output compared data.

In this paper we propose CDR, a many-core processors fault-tolerance technique that utilizes idle cores in may-core processor to execute redundancy and allows arbitrary cores to verify each other's execution while requiring only a little communication channels and buffers. CDR is able to schedule redundant execution on cores conditions to effectively balance performance, reliability and power.

Our evaluation based error injection shows that CDR is capable at satisfying error coverage with a little NoC traffic, that cover 99.97% errors with 3.1% more NoC traffic and 96.8% with 0.03%.

2   Related Work

2.1   Redundant Execution

CDR falls within a class of fault tolerant architectures that use redundant execution. AR-SMT [7] and SRT [3] proposals to use SMT to detect transient faults. SRTR [8] extends SRT by adding support for recovery.

CRT [4] uses a CMP composed of processors for redundant execution. CRTR [9] extends CRT by providing recovery from transient faults. Reunion [10] is a CMP architecture that significantly reduces result forwarding bandwidth by compressing results. Sampling DMR[11] runs in DMR mode for a small percentage of each periodic execution window, which is a simple and low-overhead mechanism to detect permanent fault.

2.2   Mechanisms for Performance Improvement

Execution Assistance. Typically in redundant execution the leading core assists the trailing core in order to improve the trailing core's performance. AR-SMT forwarded branch outcomes and all values as predictions to the trailing core. Variants of this idea were also explored in DIVA   and SRT.

Speculative Mechanisms. Paceline [13] operates the leading core at higher than its nominal frequency. In effect, the leading core performs timing speculation, while the trailing core is used to detect errors. MRE[14] propose a low-overhead architectural technique that executes multiple redundant threads on a single processor core.

2.3   Fault Tolerance in Many-Core

Many-core processors differ from CMP in architecture, which i) contain more cores but less usage, ii) NOC performance   effects total chip, iii) cache coherence is hard to keep by hardware. Lei Zhang[15]propose to achieve fault tolerance by employing redundancy at the core-level instead of at the micro-architecture level and reconfigure the processor with the most effective topology when faulty cores existing on-chip in this architecture.

There are two major distinctions between previous work and CDR. first, CDR aims at utilize idle core in many-core processors rather than reduce performance loss due to redundant execution by speculative mechanisms. Second, CDR exploit architecture characters of many-core processors such as core-level redundancy, cache coherence and NoC traffic.

3   CDR Mechanism

CDR architecture shows in Figure 1. CDR employs a many-core processor with shared memory interconnected with a mesh network. For each core, we add a redundancy control module named redundancy manager (RM). RM consists of small control circuits and two FIFO buffers and the area of RMs is negligibly small compared to cores/networks. The core modifications are limited to the following mechanisms: i) generating registers update trace, ii) sym request signal, iii) stall inputs signal, and iv) transferring of the architectural state between cores. CDR uses the existing on chip networks for trace data transfer and supports input replication via a remote value queue (RVQ).

Every core in CDR may be checked core or checker core or non-redundancy core. non- redundancy cores are ones that is busying and do not need redundancy. Others are either checker cores or checker cores. In the checked core, the RM receives registers updates from the core and writes it into the sender FIFO. Typically the registers update information is register name/value pairs. The RM interfaces with NoC. RM compresses the trace data and send messages to the checker core. To reduce this inter-core communication we use parity check as fingerprinting [12].In the checker core, RM receives messages from the coupled checked core into a receiver FIFO. The checker core's RM writes its compressed registers updates   into its sender FIFO. A comparator compares elements in the two FIFOs. Any time they differ, the RM raises a redundancy error exception.

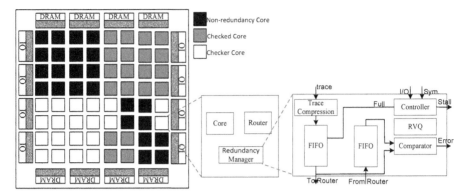

Fig. 1. CDR architecture

The controller in the RM includes a simple state-machine that stall the processor when the FIFOs become full.

3.1   Arbitrates and Schedule

Once a program starts to run, CDR arbitrates whether to redundantly execute it or not and if yes which core to execute it. CDR must consider cores, NoC state and power restriction.

If a redundancy reaches a checkpoint, CDR also arbitrates whether to continue execute the program or to schedule it. If the checker core have emergency task, CDR chooses other core to continue or simply stop the redundancy.

3.2   Synchronization

Synchronization begins once a processor receives a schedule or checkpoint request. Checkpoint synchronization is used to get correct program state, which is used to recover from error   or start for a redundancy schedule.

First of all, checked cores send checkpoint request to RM. Once RM receives the request, it checks number of instructions committed since the last checkpoint. If the number for checked core is more, RM stalls it and make the checker core commit enough instructions to synchronize. Otherwise RM stalls the checker and make the checked core commit enough instructions to synchronize. If both cores reach the checkpoint successfully, they update checkpoint and synchronization finished.

3.3   Input Replication and Output Comparison

Unlike previous work, only remote value but load value need be replicated in CDR. CDR supports input replication via RVQ. When the checked core gets a value from remote note(core or memory), it forwards the result to the checker core's RVQ. The checker core reads remote values from the RVQ rather than access to remote node.

Besides remote value, CDR also compares register update values each cycle to improve the fault coverage and delay. CDR does not compare store vales, because we assure that if a error transmits to store value ,it must transmit to registers sooner or later.

3.4   State Compression

State compression is use to reduce the bandwidth requirements of comparing state between two cores. Fingerprinting[12] proposed the use of a CRC-16 compression circuit to compress all of the register file and memory updates. We have found that CDR along with parity check (labeled parity-1) is adequate to a satisfying coverage. In order to get more effective compression, CDR merges many updates to get once parity check. Parity-1/10 means one bit parity check every ten register updates, so as parity-1/100 and parity-1/1000. Compression solutions in CDR is listing in table 1.

Table 1. compression solutions

solutions	Compression Rate (times)	Bandwidth (Bytes/Instruction)	Bandwidth Scales (%)
No compression	1	5	125
Parity-1	40	1/8	3.1
Parity-1/10	400	1/80	0.31
Parity-1/100	4000	1/800	0.031
Parity-1/1000	40000	1/8000	0.0031

The bandwidth per core in TILE64[16] is 4 bytes/cycle. We take it as reference and assume bandwidth per core in CDR is 4 bytes/instruction. The bandwidth requirements for CDR is largely depend on compression techniques. If do not compress state, bandwidth requirement is 5 bytes/instructions, which is larger than NoC bandwidth. Whereas bandwidth requirement of parity-1 is 1/8 bytes/instruction and is 3.1% of total bandwidth. bandwidth requirement in emerged   parity check is even less, which can be ignored at all.

3.5   Recovery

CDR supports recovery from both hard- and soft-errors. If error occurred, both cores rollback architectural state to their last valid checkpoint and resume execution from the checkpoint. If the fault was transient, the cores will successfully complete their next checkpoint. However, if the fault is permanent, the same checkpoint interval will repeat and CDR will starts another redundancy using anther checker core, which is able to diagnose fault core. CDR stops the fault core and migrates program to fault free cores.

4 Evaluation

4.1 Methodology

We present experimental results using openRISC 1200 cores in a Altera Stratix IV FPGA system. The applications evaluated are: MatrixMult (13M) and BubbleSort (5M). The fault model is bit-flip. The number of experiments is 20,000 (fault sites) * 5 (solutions) * 2 (applications) = 200,000.

Error injection. One register from the 32 GPRs and 6 control registers (PC, SR, EA, PICMR, PICPR and PICSR) is randomly chosen and one bit out of 32 bit locations is randomly chosen and flipped. At previous, we found the error rate is 4.6% and 8.8% for the two applications when injected 20'000 error. we found some of registers injected never manifest as error at all. we removed these registers so that error rate improved to 26.7% for MatrixMult and 39.8% for BubbleSort. So results below is based on the improved error injection.

Table 2. Classification of fault injection experiment outcomes

Outcome	MatrixMult	BubbleSort
Masking completely	48-53%	44-47%
Masking partly	17-20%	11-16%
Error detected	24-27%	33-41%
Silent data corruption	0-9%	0-4%

Table 2 summarize the outcome distribution of injected errors. About 53% of errors that injected do not impact traces at all, 20% impact traces but do not impact the application's correct behavior, about 27% impact the application and are detected, about 0~9% impact application but not are detected. This is consistent with the experimental results on other systems.

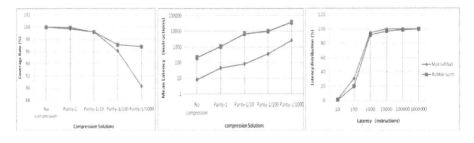

Fig. 2. results: (a)error coverage rate (b)mean detact latency (c)parity-1/100 latency distributon

4.2   Error Coverage

CDR compress traces using parity and emerged parity check to balance reliability and NoC performance. Error coverage rate is shown in fig 2(a). Comparing traces without compress can get 100% coverage. Parity-1 reduces 40 times bandwidth without lost coverage, 99.7% for MatrixMult and 99.9% for BubbleSort. Emerged parity reduce more bandwidth, while keep satisfying coverage. Coverage rate in parity-10 is 99.6% and 99.8% for the applications, while in parity-100 is 96.8% and 97.1%, even in parity-1000 is 90.1% and 96.3%.

4.3   Detection Latency

Communicating over the NoC with a distant core may incur a greater latency than to an adjacent core. The emerged parity may also lead to larger latency. However, results in fig2(b) show that detect delay in CDR is controlled.   Mean error detection latency(MEDL) without state compression is 8 and 215 instructions for the two applications. MEDL in parity-1 is 45 and 1,096, in parity-1/10 is 83 and 6,946, in parity-1/1000 is 2,680 and 37,617 instructions.

MEDL looks a little larger especially for BubbleSort, however detect latency in most case is small. Take parity-1/100 for example shown in fig2(c), MEDL is 363 for Bub-bleSort and 10,140 for BubbleSort, but the possibility that latency is below 1000 instructions is 95% and 92% for the applications. the possibility that delay is larger than 10,000 instructions is 0.2% and 3% for the applications.

5   Conclusion

We have presented core-level dynamic redundancy(CDR), an inexpensive redundancy mechanism for many-core processors, which allows arbitrary processor cores to verify each other's execution without requiring high communication cost.

Unlike previous work, CDR dynamically chosees idle cores for redundant execution based resources utilized. CDR means not only chose arbitrary core for redundancy at the beginning but also switch to other cores at checkpoints. The most advantage is to schedule redundant execution on cores conditions, so it can effectively balance per-formance, reliability, power and so on.

Our evaluation has shown that CDR is capable at perfect error coverage at little cost, that covers 99.97% error within 3.1% more commutation and 96.8% at 0.03%. The traffic of CDR is negligibly small compared to NoC bandwidth.

Overall, we have shown that flexible redundancy frameworks like CDR hold significant performance potential when confronted with the challenges of deep submicron process technologies in current and upcoming many-core processors.

Acknowledgment. The authors gratefully acknowledge supports from National Nature Science Founda-tion of China under NSFC No. 61033008, 60903041 and 61103080, Research Fund for the Doctoral Program of Higher Education of China under SRFDP No. 20104307110002.

References

1. Borkar, S.: Thousand core chips: a technology perspective. In: Proceedings of the 44th annual Design Automation Conference (June 2007)
2. Srinivasan, J., Adve, S.V., Bose, P., Rivers, J.A.: The impact of technology scaling on lifetime reliability. In: Intl. Conf. on Dependable Systems and Networks (June 2004)
3. Reinhardt, S.K., Mukherjee, S.S.: Transient fault detection via simulta-neous multithreading. In: Intl. Symp. on Computer Architecture (June 2000)
4. Mukherjee, S.S., Kontz, M., Reinhardt, S.K.: Detailed design and evaluation of redundant multithreading alternatives. In: Intl. Symp. on Computer Architecture (May 2002)
5. Austin, T.: DIVA: A Reliable Substrate For Deep Submicron Microarchitecture Design. In: Proceedings of the 32nd MICRO, pp. 196–207 (1999)
6. Subramanyan, P., Singh, V., Saluja, K.K., Larsson, E.: Energy-Efficient Fault Tolerance in Chip Multiprocessors Using Critical Value Forwarding. In: Intl. Conf. on Dependable Systems and Networks (June 2010)
7. Rotenberg, E.: AR-SMT: A microarchitectural approach to fault tolerance in microprocessors. In: Intl. Symp. on Fault-Tolerant Computing (June 1999)
8. Vijaykumar, T.N., Pomeranz, I., Cheng, K.: Transient-fault recovery using simultaneous multithreading. In: Intl. Symp. on Computer Architecture (May 2002)
9. Gomaa, M., Scarbrough, C., Vijaykumar, T.N., Pomeranz, I.: Transient-fault recovery for chip multiprocessors. In: Intl. Symp. on Computer Architecture (June 2003)
10. Smolens, J.C., Gold, B.T., Falsafi, B., Hoe, J.C.: Reunion: Complexity-effective multicore redundancy. In: Intl. Symp. on Microarchitecture (December 2006)
11. Nomura, S., Sinclair, M.D., Ho, C., Govindaraju, V., de Krujif, M., Sankaralingam, K.: Sampling + DMR: Practical and Low-overhead Permanent Fault Detection. In: Intl. Symp. on Computer Architecture (June 2011)
12. Smolens, A.C., Gold, B.T., Kim, J., Falsafi, B., Hoe, J.C., Nowatzyk, A.G.: Fingerprinting: bounding soft-error detection latency and bandwidth. In: Intl. Conf. on ASPLOS (October 2004)
13. Greskamp, B., Torrellas, J.: Paceline: Improving Single-Thread Performance in Nanoscale CMPs through Core Overclocking. In: Proceedings of the 16th PACT (September 2007)
14. Subramanyan, Singh, V., Saluja, K.K., Larsson, E.: Mulitplexed Redundant Execution: A Technique for Efficient Fault Tolerance in Chip Multiprocessors. In: Proc. of DATE (2010)
15. Zhang, L., Han, Y., Xu, Q., Li, X.: Defect tolerance in homogeneous manycore processors using core-level redundancy with unified topology. In: Proc. Design, Automation and Test in Europe, DATE 2008, pp. 891–896 (2008)
16. Wentzlaff, D., Griffin, P., Hoffmann, H., Bao, L.W., Edwards, B., Ramey, C., Mattina, M., Miao, C.C., Brown, J.F., Agarwal, A.: On-chip interconnection architecture of the tile pro-cessor. IEEE Micro 27(5), 15–31 (2007)

Study on Transformed Keywords Identification in Spam Filtering

Dapeng Xiong, Zhang Yan, and Aiping Li

Computer School, National University of Defense Technology, Changsha 410073, China
xiongdapeng1987@gmail.com

Abstract. By means of Active-Jamming, spammers deform original keywords into a variety of deformation, which can escape from the traditional filtering based on original keywords matching. In order to identify the transformed keywords, a comprehensive summary of the deformations and corresponding solutions for each case is put forward. Based on the summary, a transformed keywords identification scheme is designed specific to three broad categories. And a technique based on character co-occurrence is proposed to identify the transformed keywords in a flexible way, in which the bidirectional-ranged searching is innovatively put forward.

Keywords: Chinese Active-Jamming, transformed keywords, deformation identification, character co-occurrence, bidirectional-ranged.

1   Introduction

As the threat of spam on the Internet grows increasingly severe, a large number of approaches are put forward to restrain the spams [1], such as techniques based on domain check, content check, and open relay prohibition.

Among the masses of anti-spam technologies, anti-spam filters have become popular tool for Internet providers. To keep up with ever more sophisticated spam, filters have proposed a variety of techniques over the years [2]. Here is a bird's-eye view of some popular techniques: Keyword-based and Bayesian filters, Whitelist/verification filters, etc.

In this paper we focus on textual analysis filter based on keyword identification. Traditionally, Keyword-based filters search for original keywords hidden in the context directly [3]. This category of modeling methods works well for western languages. But the circumstance comes to complicated when applied in the Chinese context, which is a more flexible and unstructured language. Spammers transform original Chinese keywords into metamorphosed keywords by Active-Jamming, while the deformed keywords could hardly be detected. An instance is provided to explain this phenomenon.

Original	穆斯林利用儿童发起恐怖袭击
Transformed	木40利用er童发起恐&忄 布袭G

Y. Yuan, X. Wu, and Y. Lu (Eds.): ISCTCS 2012, CCIS 320, pp. 689–697, 2013.
© Springer-Verlag Berlin Heidelberg 2013

Original context contains three keywords, which can be detected by filters easily. Then, we make some changes to the keywords by means of common methods of Active-Jamming. After transforming, the source meaning of context can still be figured out by sense. While judging from the view of traditional filters, we cannot even find the keyword anymore.

A wide range of Chinese Active-Jamming methods emerge and challenge the traditional spam filter based on direct keywords identification. Spammers easily overcome the traditional detecting measures by means of Active-Jamming. The technology of deformation identification needs to be upgraded.

2   Related Works

Some woks have been done in the field of transformed Chinese keywords identification. Luo Wanwen [4] summarized the existed problems in traditional Keywords-based information filter. Ru Chen [5] proposed the solutions for 4 specific transformed patterns. Xueguang Zhou [6] introduced the method of flexible pattern matching into transformed keywords searching. Dun Li [7] put forward a way of extract new words based on association rules.

Although some solutions have been put forward oriented in some specific conditions, it not enough to deal with the tricks of Active-Jamming on keywords.

In this paper, I summarize almost all transforming methods and propose solutions for each case. Put forward a practical scheme for transformed keyword-based filter, and then propose an algorithm based on character co-occurrence.

3   Deformation of Chinese Keywords

In this section, all patterns of Active-Jamming are grouped into two categories: Displacement of Single Character and Restructure of Multi-Character word. Statistical analysis of spam indicates that almost all of the Active-Jamming approaches taken by spammers can be sorted out to either of the two categories.

3.1   Displacement of Single Character

About two thousand years ago, Xu Shen summarized the Liushu (six categories of coinage) theory [8], which is so classical that still the law of Chinese coinage. The theory of Liushu reveals the regularity of Chinese coinage, details about how to create a new character based on similar object.

Displacement of single character means to substitute a character with a similar one, which acts based on similarity between characters. Moreover Liushu is the law of Chinese coinage, which is based on relation between characters too. We conclude that it's reasonable to use the theory of Liushu to analysis the phenomenon of single character displacing. In fact, masses of practical statistics supported this conclusion.

The theory of Liushu maps all events to six categories. Go down this way, all types of single character displacement obedience to category of six classes.

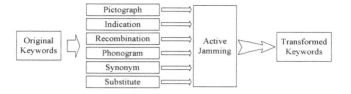

Fig. 1. Deformations of Single Character Replacement

- **Pictograph**

    Pictograph means graphic character based on similarity of direct visual illustra-tion. In Active-Jamming, a character of the original keyword might be replaced based on the relationship between the shapes of object in memory and the appearance of single character. For example,

    窘 → 囧

    Use a depressed face to express "confused".

    <u>Solution:</u> Only a few of the pictograph can be approved in Active-Jamming, unilateral announcement is meaningless. A preferable approach to pictograph re-placing is to build a expand keywords list to cover them.

- **Indication**

    Indication is similar to pictograph. The difference lies in what they focus on. Pictograph mainly acts on graphics, while indication focuses on symbols. Differ-ent from graphics, symbol is abstract and general. Comprehending of indication based on knowledge. For example,

    下流 → ↓6

    Use the down arrow symbol to express "obscene".

    <u>Solution:</u> Similar to the process of pictograph, typical transformed keywords should be preserved in the expand keywords list for directly querying.

- **Recombination**

    Recombination is originally refers to join two or more sole characters together into a compound character. It's a rather common used measure in Active-Jamming, in which recombination has more abundant circumstances.

    Category A: The first circumstance is to assemble two or more sole characters into a new compound character. For example:

    王八 → 天

    Two normal characters assemble into a slang word.

    Category B: The second circumstance is to split one compound character into individual characters according to the rules of radicals. For example:

    炸弹 → 火乍弓单

    The original keyword is split into 4 single characters, which means bomb.

Solution: For category A, a combined character can be approved and spread only if it is supported by the input method and sensitive to spam, which leads to its small-scale. So we can add them to the list of original keywords list when necessary. For category B, we should split all common recombination Chinese characters into sole characters forwardly, and then we can identify recombination-transformed keywords just like the original ones.

- **Phonogram**

  Phonogram means to transform a character to a similar one according to the pronunciation. There are some types of deformation of this kind.

    Category A: replace with a homophone, For example:

    法轮功 → 发仓攻

  They sound the same with the each other, which means a CULT.

    Category B: replace the original simplified Chinese character with its complex form. Both are of the same pronunciation. For example:

    袭击 → 襲擊

  They sound the same with the each other, which means assault.

    Category C: replace with a near-homophone, For example:

    本拉登 → 本拉丹

  They sound similar but not the same to each other, which mean Bin Laden.

  Solution: For category A and B, a pinyin entry list of all common used Chinese characters should be built forwardly. Then translate the context and all original keywords into pinyin, and seek for pinyin-formed keywords instead of original keywords. For category C, We can seek the head of the pinyin instead of the whole pinyin.

- **Synonym**

  Synonym means two characters are of the same meaning and similar annunciation. The model of synonym is called interchangeable words in Chinese. For example:

    焰 → 炎

  They can be exchanged with each other, which mean fire.

  Solution: The issued list of interchangeable words covers the majority of synonyms. In most cases, synonyms can be treated as each other in the filter.

- **Substitute**

  Substitute is a common phenomenon in dialect: the character exists only in spoken language. The model of substitute is to represent it with a similar character based on its pronunciation or typeface of dialect. For example:

    可能 → 扩冷

  South Chinese dialect means possible.

Solution: Substitute is a flexible method of transforming, but uncommon used in Active-Jamming. Sometimes they vary greatly in pronunciation or typeface. So what we can do is to add it to the lexicon if it is widely used.

3.2   Restructure of Multi-character Word

Commonly spam filters acts on the intact keywords, whose single characters are close to each other in order. Chinese Active-Jamming restructures the primary single characters of the original keywords, which confuses the rigid filters. Some typical deformations based on restructure are presented as follows.

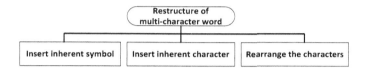

Fig. 2. Typical Deformation of Word Restructure

Take this original keyword for example: 恐怖袭击

- **Insert inherent symbol**

    Some inherent symbols like letters and digits are inserted into the original key-word, shaped like "恐1怖￥袭&击". Such symbols like letters and digits have nothing to do with the meaning of original keyword, but it is fatal to the rigid original keywords-based spam filters.
    Solution: Weed out all symbols from the context. Spam filters acts on keywords without any inherent symbol.

- **Insert inherent character**

    Similar to however more complex than the previous case, shaped like "恐怖布袭儿击". This situation is more difficult to be perceived and deal with. It's hard to judge whether the character is intentionally inserted to the keyword, or justly the junction of two words.
    Solution: An effective method is proposed to solve it in section 4.2.

- **Rearrange the characters**

    Sequence of characters in the original keyword is intentionally disrupted, shaped like "怖恐袭击". It will certainly be ignored by the traditional filters, which match patterns towards a fixed direction.
    Solution: An effective method is proposed to solve it in section 4.2.

4   Countermeasure of Transformed Keywords

Comprehensively considering of all deformations and corresponding solutions, this work provides a systematic scheme from the engineered standpoint.

4.1   Practical Scheme for Identification

Deformation of Active-Jamming can be summarized as pronunciation-based, appearance-based and some accustomed situations. Naturally, corresponding countermeasure of Transformed Keywords are put forward.

- **Pronunciation-based Identification**

    Pronunciation-based Identification is proposed to solve these forms of transformation: homophone replacing, complex form of simplify character replacing, pinyin replacing, and inherent symbols inserting.

    Implementation:
    Step 1: Create a pinyin library for all common Chinese characters. Each character should be mapped to the only corresponding pinyin.
    Step 2: Translate original context T into text of pinyin P literatim. Discard the inherent symbol which is non-Chinese and non-Latin.
    Step 3: Translate all original keywords to the form of pinyin K. Then use the technique of pattern matching to seek for keyword K in context P.

- **Appearance-based Identification**

    Appearance-based Identification is proposed to solve these forms of transformation: Recombination and Pictograph.

    Implementation:
    Step 1: Split common recombination Chinese characters into corresponding sole characters forwardly, and then create a library of split keywords.
    Step 2: Split each recombination Chinese character of the original keywords into single characters. Considering the conditions of partially transformed, we should seek for each spilled recombination character (some single characters) in the original context character by character.

4.2   Algorithm Based on Character Co-occurrence

Measures proposed previously are particularly effective when targeted the specific deformation. However, the deformations are usually hybrid in the real world. Single detect model demonstrate to be high accuracy rate, while its cost is equally outstanding. A more flexible algorithm is proposed in response to most types of deformation without discrimination. The algorithm relies on character co-occurrence, which means all characters of one original keyword could be found within a limited range in a sentence. Centered in the current character, we can find the next character within a certain range.

Fig. 3. Traditional Pattern Matching

The figure draw that: the traditional pattern matching can be characterized as unidirectional and step-by-step. When facing to transformed keywords, rapid failure of the traditional pattern matching is inevitable.

In the new algorithm based on character co-occurrence, bidirectional-ranged searching is innovative proposed.

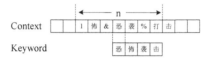

Fig. 4. Improved Algorithm Based on Character Co-occurrence

Step 1: Determine a limited range n, and then search for the first character of the original keyword in the original context. Jump to Step2 if success.

Step 2: Shift the center to current character. Search for the next character of the original keyword forward and backward in the predetermined range. Repeat Step2 until reach the end of original keyword. Return False if failed.

This algorithm does not conflict with the provided scheme. They can be united used in the flittering system.

5   Experiment

Spam data used in the experiment is collected from the Internet, which is in small-scale for the convenience of artificial verification. A typical original keywords library is artificially picked out in advance. The spam contains 87 original keywords and 490 corresponding transformed keywords.

In the proving experiment, traditional spam filter identifies 87 original keywords and 0 corresponding transformed keywords. As a comparison, the new algorithm is separately combined with the Pronunciation-based Identification and the Appearance-based Identification. After two rounds of identifying, the filter system returned 459 search hits, of which 385 keywords are correctly judged.

Table 1. Result of Experiment

	Transformed Keywords	Inherent Keywords
Identification	385	74
Un-Identification	105	unknown

Performance of the system can be evaluated with two indicators: Recall rate and Precision rate. Recall rate assess the performance of comprehensively identifying of all transformed keywords. Precision rate assess the performance of correctly identifying of all transformed keywords.

Recall rate of the system is 78.6%. Analysis of the result shows that, some types of deformation mentioned previously avoid from being detected. The specialized solutions relevant to these cases have been proposed. But the system focuses on common types of deformation, and simplified the process in consideration of the efficiency and availability.

Precision rate of the system is 83.9%. Analysis of the result shows that, erroneous judgment exists in the system. A sample like "方法：轮询；功效：" misstated lead to an identification of "法轮功". In order to improve precision, we should verify the preliminary result with the technique of word-splitting.

6   Conclusion

This paper summarized the deformation of Chinese keywords in the view point of two aspects, Displacement of Single Character and Restructure of Multi-character Word. And then put forward solutions for each case. Based on the summary of deformation, a practical scheme is designed to separately achieve Pronunciation-based identification and Appearance-based Identification. In the end, an efficient algorithm based on character co-occurrence is proposed to identify the transformed keywords in a flexible way. The experiments show that the summary of deformation is comprehensive. And the filter system combined with the new algorithm is practical and effective in contrast with the traditional spam filter.

Acknowledgement. The authors acknowledge the financial support by National Key Technology R&D Program (No. 2012BAH38B -04), "863" program (No. 2010AA012505, 2011AA010702) and NSFC (No. 60933005) The author is grateful to the anonymous referee for a careful checking and for helpful comments that improved this paper.

References

1. Fumera, G., Pillai, I., Roli, F.: Spam Filtering Based on the Analysis of Text Information Embedded Into Images. Journal of Machine Learning Research (2006)
2. Subramaniam, T., Jalab, H.A., Taqa, A.Y.: Overview of textual anti-spam filtering techniques. International Journal of the Physical Sciences 5(12), 1869–1882 (2010) (in Chinese)
3. Beik, A.J.G., Abadi, A.H.: Anti-Spam Filtering keyword-based and multi agent method with personal E-mail messages on the basis of interests of user. Canadian Journal on Artificial Intelligence, Machine Learning and Pattern Recognition 2(4) (May 2011)
4. Luo, W., Gao, F., Zhou, X.: Summary of Chinese Anti-Active-Jamming Filters. Journal of Jishou University (Natural Science Edition) (May 2011) (in Chinese)

5. Chen, R., Zhang, Y., Liu, T.: Information Filtering for Modified Specific Chinese Information. High Technology Letters (2005) (in Chinese)
6. Zhou, X., Zhang, H.: Flexible Pattern Matching Algorithm for Anti-Active-Jamming in Chinese String. J. Wuhan Univ. (Nat. Sci. Ed.) 55(1) (2009) (in Chinese)
7. Shuai, Z., Zhou, X.: Research and Implementation of Content Flexible Filter in Chinese Webpage. Computer & Digital Engineer 37(11) (2009) (in Chinese)
8. Shen, X.: Preface of Shuowen. Han Dynasty 100 AD (in Chinese)

Preliminary Study of Enhanced Collaborative Information Extracting and Sharing System

Mingfei Wu, Yi Han, Bin Zhou, and Aiping Li

School of Computer, National University of Defense Technology, Changsha, China
wumingfeixing@163.com

Abstract. Web search has been studied extensively in recent years. To meet the demand for searching needed information rapidly over internet of users, searchers and commercial companies at home and abroad had built various search engines. To improve the search efficiency and find needed information more comprehensively, more accurately, more rapidly, searchers and commercial companies had designed and developed a series of collaborative search systems and some collaborative algorithms. Unfortunately, it's difficult for us to compare these systems in a meaningful way because different searchers defined collaboration in different ways. In this paper we try to define a relatively practicable and unified collaboration model. This model contains these following six dimensions: intent of collaborator, geographical distribution of collaborator, concurrency of collaboration, relationship of collaborator, collaboration tactics and collaboration devices. Based on this model, we will make an objective comparison to these systems, and then come up with a prototype of Group Search system, which is an enhanced collaborative information extract system we are researching.

Keywords: collaboration, information extracting and sharing, comparison, dimensions, model, Group Search.

1 Introduction

With the development of Internet technology, amount of data in the cyberspace is great many and continuously growing. People find that it's more and more difficult to find target information in the vast cyberspace. The birth of the search engine provides a convenience for users to find the needed information quickly, but it's notoriously that, the existing search engines ae designed for a single user, and even the most advanced search engine cannot surely provide search results that absolutely in line with users' needs. Many people have experiences like these: (1)Users search information with one or more keywords by search engines, but they can't find satisfied information in the result pages. This is mainly caused by two reasons: the first, users often cannot express their information needs in the form of query keywords accurately; secondly, the responses of the search engines for fuzzy query keywords are very vague [1]. (2) The returned result pages , from different search engines with the same query keywords, are greatly different, and sometimes, some information can be found

Y. Yuan, X. Wu, and Y. Lu (Eds.): ISCTCS 2012, CCIS 320, pp. 698–705, 2013.

with search engine *A* but cannot with search engine *B*. Data comes from BaiGoogledu reveals that: the result links returned by the same query keyword are not the same at the percent of 85% between Google and Baidu[2].

To solve the second problem, some researchers and commercial companies have developed many kinds of integrated search engines and Meta search engines. To solve the first problem, some researchers and commercial companies have designed and developed many kinds of collaborative search systems. All of these collaborative search systems can be divided into four types : 1 network service, as TeamSearch and I-SPY; 2 browser plug – ins, as SearchTogether and HeyStacks; 3 mobile terminal client, as CoSearch and iBingo; 4 software, as Cerchiamo and S^3 system.

2   Related Works

Although the collaborative search systems mentioned above are different in form and usage purposes, the researchers regard them all as collaborative search systems. From this we can see that, definition of collaboration is not the same by different research-ers. Therefore, we cannot judge exactly which one is better, nor do a meaningful comparison among them without practicable and unified collaboration model. In the following section, we will define and analyze the model: this model includes these following six dimensions: intention of the collaborators, collaborators geographical distribution, and concurrency of collaboration, relationship among collaborators, col-laborative tactics and collaboration devices [3].

2.1   Intention of Collaborators: Explicit vs. Implicit

According to whether the users have the intention of collaboration in the Web search process, we can divide collaborative systems into two types: explicit vs. implicit [3][4].

Explicit collaborative search systems often provide the function of exchanges among users, assignment of search tasks etc. Allow users to interact with each other directly or indirectly via specific work environment or open network community. In which a group of people search for pages to meet a same information need. The need may change over time, but through-out a search session that need is shared by all team members and it determines their search activities. The most important feature of such collaborative search system is to provide a range of functions for user groups with the same search interest or purpose to support collaborative search behavior.

Implicit collaborative search systems capture the query words and collect other in-formation related to the search for each user, then find other users' relative search information which related with one or a group of users by certain methods and recommend these relative search information to the users or use them to optimize the users' search results. Such cooperative search system is the further development of personalized Web search and social Web search and the use of collaborative intelligence.

2.2   Collaborators Geographical Distribution: Co-located vs. Distributed

Co-located collaborative search systems provide collaborative search experience for multiple users in a particular place, usually through a PC, some through computing devices which are easy to provide such collaborative services. For example, the TableTop[5] interactive environment, using smart screen computer in the same table for collaborative web search. The advantages of such systems is achieved more direct cooperative search through face-to-face interaction.

Distributed collaborative search system allows multiple users to complete their tasks in different locations. Such as S^3 system introduced in literature [6], SearchTogether in literature [7], HeyStaks in literature [8]. The advantages of such collaborative search systems is provided more users the opportunity to cooperative search. But, Distributed collaboration implies the need for additional channels to coordinate searchers' activities. Such channels may include chat, voice, or audio conferencing [3].

2.3   Concurrency of Collaboration: Synchronous vs. Asynchronous

Synchronous collaborative search means spreading the search request out, requiring specified participants completed a well-defined search tasks within the prescribed time. Group members are actively involved in various subtasks of information seeking activity at the same time. They may complete their subtasks in any manner supported by the tools they use. The key factor is that each team member's actions can influence other team members. For example, the iBingo collaborative video search system for mobile devices described in literature [9].

Asynchronous collaborative search means various collaborators make their own contribution for the evolving search session in a very long time span. In which collaborators do not work at the same time, those who search later can benefit from the work of earlier collaborators, but the earlier ones did not benefit from contributions of subsequent collaborators [3]. For example, the S^3 system described in literature [6] and the I-SPY described in literature [13].

This dimension reflects the flow of influence among members of a collaborating group. If search activity by more than one person occurs at the same time, it is possible for influence to flow between members during a search session [3].

2.4   Relationship among Collaborators: Equal vs. Unequal

Collaboration may occur among people, among people and equipments, among equipments. Either people or equipment, will inevitably play a certain role in the process of cooperative search, the relationship between roles may include equal, hierarchical, split or compositional [11]. We believe that dualizing relationship between the collaborators is inappropriate, but in order to facilitate the classification, we tentatively classified hierarchical, split and compositional as unequal relationship. Besides, we regard those systems which face to specific users as unequal systems.

First, we illustrate the unequal relationship of collaborators. For those collaborative search systems which collaborators are hierarchical, relationship between the task initiator and the task participants is subordinate. For example, relationship between collaborators in Cerchiamo system is Prospector and Miner [12]. For those collaborative search systems which collaborators are split, collaborators are designated as a fixed role and complete the assigned task by the system. Such as in the Split Search mode of SearchTogether system [7]. For those collaborative search systems which collaborators are compositional, the task initiator assigns to the task participants some resources and certain tasks, Such as in the Multi-engine Search mode of SearchTogether system.

Then, we define an equal collaborative relationship: For users, each collaborator can either be task initiator or be participants, they can freely select the task, free select work space, search manner. All users in the collaborative process are independent of one another but also mutually supporting. Devices, whether mobile devices or PCs, are independent of each other, there is no control relationship among them.

2.5   Collaboration Tactics: UI-Only Mediation vs. Deeper Algorithmic Mediation

Coordinating collaboration between users includes two ways: UI mediation and deeper algorithmic mediation. The series of collaborative search systems referred to in the first part of this paper, all are UI mediation system except for Cerchiamo and Split Search mode of SearchTogther. In addition, collaborative filtering and recommendation systems are also coordinated by the underlying algorithm. Distinction between UI-only mediation and deeper algorithmic mediation is whether the system can clearly reflect the contribution of the different users for a collaborative search session [3].

2.6   Collaboration Devices: Mobile Devices vs. PC

For the collaborative devices, collaboration includes cooperation among PCs, among mobile devices, among PCs and mobile devices. However, the existing collaborative search systems mainly include two types: cooperation among PCs and cooperation among PCs and mobile devices. In the domain of distributed computing based on mobile agent, interaction between mobile devices is common. But in collaborative search domain, due to defects of the performance of mobile devices, there are no research and product about collaborative search based on mobile devices. The series of collaborative search systems referred to in the first part of this paper, collaboration of CoSearch [10]and iBingo belongs to cooperation among Mobile Devices and PCs, collaboration of the other systems belongs to cooperation among PCs.

3   Group Search Proto-Type

In the following parts, we will show you the architecture of Group Search system, and then, make a comparison with other collaborative systems.

Group Search employed the C / S structure. Client is directly user-oriented work interface, user registration, log in, creating tasks, selecting tasks, selecting the search engines, searching and extracting information, submiting information are all done on the client; The server is the link which connecting user, the information released by each user (including the extracted target information, instant conversation message) stored on the server and then broadcasted to each collaborator by the server. In addition, the server also responsible to divide search tasks and summarize search results. *Group Search* system includes three layers: user interface layer, formalizer layer and algorithm layer. Seen from Figure 1.

3.1   User Interface Layer

User interface of the Group Search system includes three parts: Creation UI, Processing UI and Browsing UI. Creation UI is designed to issue search tasks for users. Once the search task is initialized, it will be submitted to server, anyone who login the system can view the tasks and choose one to take part in. The initiator can set permissions for the task or invite participators and select the task division method. Processing UI is designed for each users (include initiator) to take part in task and to search for target information peer to peer. If the initiator specified a task division method, users just responsible for completing their subtask or just searching for target information in specified channel(s). Browsing UI is designed to act as browser and provide an integrated working environment for users to search. It's realized by calling the browser of local PC and embedding to the Group Search system client.

3.2   Formalizer Layer

Formalizer layer is mainly responsible to facilitate the users to submit the archived target information and instant messaging to server in accordance with the uniform format. Formalizer layer includes three modules: Session Module, Processing Module and Storing & Sharing Module. In Session Module, we pre-defined some search task template, such as person, event, plan, etc, and each task template includes various subtask as well. User can choose default task template according to their information needs and modify subtasks, can also create a new task template and its corresponding sub-tasks; Processing Module provide the tools to users for searching, reviewing, extracting and submitting the target information to server. User can select a variety of information channels, as various search engines and varied website to search. Storing and Sharing Module responsible to broadcast collaborative search developments and results.

3.3   Algorithm Layer

Specifying search channels and/or sub task, the function of divide task in Group Search system, is realized on algorithm layer. What's more, the collaborative filtering function of search engines is reserved. Thus allows the user to reduce the review of the duplicate pages and promotes division of labor between users. Formalizer layer and Algorithm layer prompt Group Search system implemented both UI mediation and Algorithm mediation function and make Group Search system has efficient collaborative effect.

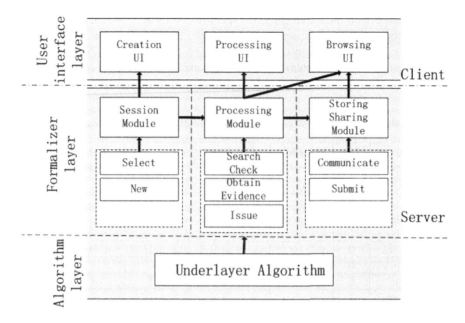

Fig. 1. Group Search System Architecture

4   Comparison

In the above part of this paper, we defined the six dimensions of the collaborative search system and analyzed each dimension from two aspects respectively. Next, we will make a comparison among the systems mentioned in the first part of this paper, then come up with the design goal of our Group Search system. Before that, we first simplify the six dimensions respectively as: Intent, distribution, concurrency, tactics, relationship, devices, and then signify two aspects of each dimension by 1 and 0.Seen in Table 1.

Table 1. Evaluate each side of six dimensions

Dimensions	Sides	Values
Intent	Explicit	1
	Implicit	0
Distribution	Distributed	1
	Co-located	0
Concurrency	Synchronous	1
	Asynchronous	0
Tactics	Algorithmic mediation	1
	UI-only mediation	0
Relationship	Equal	1
	Unequal	0
Devices	Mobile Devices	1
	PC	0

In accordance with measurement value specified in Table 1, we make a comparison among those collaborative search systems, seen in Table 2. Values displayed in italics in the last column representation the design goals of Group Search. It's an equal collaborative search system that supporting explicit, co-located and distributed, synchronous and asynchronous, UI-only mediation and deeper algorithmic mediation.

Table 2. Comparison of exist systems and design goals of Group Search

Dimensions / Systems	Intent	Distribution	Concurrency	Tactics	Relationship	Devices
TeaSearch	1	0	1	0	1	0
I-SPY	0	1	1	1	0	0
Search-Together	1	1	1	0	0	0
HeyStacks	0	1	1	1	0	0
CoSearch	0	0	1	0	1	1
iBingo	0	0	1	1	1	1
Cerchiamo	1	1	1	1	0	0
S^3 system	0	1	0	1	0	0
Group Search	*1*	*1|0*	*1|0*	*1|0*	*1*	*0*

5   Conclusion

In this paper we analyzed and summarized amount of research reports and almost all exist collaborative search system. Based on this, we defined the six dimensions of the collaborative search system and analyzed each dimension from two aspects respectively. Then we made a comparison among the systems mentioned in the first part of this paper and came up with the design goal of our Group Search system. Finally, we described the system architecture of Group Search system and analyzed the function of each layer respectively.

Acknowledgement. The authors acknowledge the financial support by National Key Technology R&D Program (No. 2012BAH38B -04), "863" program (No.2010AA012505, 2011AA010702) and NSFC(No.60933005). The author is grateful to the anonymous referee for a careful checking of the details and for helpful comments that improved this paper.

References

1. Smyth, B., Balfe, E., Briggs, P., Coyle, M., et al.: Collaborative Web Search. In: Proceedings of the 18th International Joint Conference on Artificial intelligence, pp. 1417–1419
2. Website, http://www.baigoogledu.com

3. Golovchinsky, G., Pickens, J., Back, M., et al.: A Taxonomy of Collaboration in Online Information Seeking. Presented at 1st Intl Workshop on Collaborative Information Seeking (2008)
4. Sun, J.-Y., Chen, J.-J., Yu, X.-L., Li, X.-H.: A Survey of Collaborative Web Search. College of Computer Science and Technology. Taiyuan University of Technology
5. Smeaton, A.F., Lee, H., Foley, C., et al.: Collaborative video searching on a tabletop. Multimedia System 12(4-5), 375–391 (2007)
6. Morris, M.R., Horvitz, E.: S^3: Storable, Shareable Search. In: Baranauskas, C., Abascal, J., Barbosa, S.D.J. (eds.) INTERACT 2007. LNCS, vol. 4662, pp. 120–123. Springer, Heidelberg (2007)
7. Morris, M.R., Horvitz, E.: SeachTogether: an interface for collaborative web search. In: Proceedings of the 20th ACM UIST Conference, pp. 3–12. ACM Press, New York (2007)
8. Smyth, B., Champin, P.A.: The experiences web: a case based reasoning perspective. In: Proceedings of Grand Challenged for Reasoning from Experiences, Workshop at UCAI 2009, Pasadena, California [s.n.], pp. 1–6 (2009)
9. Smeaton, A.F., Foley, C., Byrne, D., et al.: iBingo mobile collaborative search. In: Proceedings of the 2008 International Conference on Content-based Image and Video Retrieval, pp. 547–548. ACM Press, New York (2008)
10. Amershi, S., Morris, M.R.: Cosearch: a system for co-located collaborative web search. In: Proceedings of the 26th Annual SIGGH Conference on Human Factors in Computing Systems, pp. 1647–1656. ACM Press, New York (2008)
11. Pickens, J., Golovchinsky, G., Shah, C., et al.: Algorithmic Mediation for Collaborative Exploratory Search. In: Proceedings of the 31st Annual International ACM SIGIR Conference on Research and Development in Information Retrieval
12. Golovchinsky, G., Adcock, J., Pickens, J., et al.: Cerchiamo: a collaborative exploratory search tool. In: Proceedings of CSCW. San Diego [s.n.], pp. 8–12 (2008)
13. Smyth, B., Freyne, J., Coyle, M., Briggs, P.: I-SPY: Anonymous, Community-Based Personalization by Collaborative Meta-Search. In: Proceedings of the 23rd SGAI International Conference on Innovative Techniques and Applications of Artificial Intelligence

A Compatible and Graphical Modeling Approach for Earth System Model

Taiping Guo and Zhongzhi Luan

Sino-German Joint Software Institute, Beihang University, Beijing, China
taiping.guo@gmail.com

Abstract. The emergence of Earth System Modeling Framework (ESMF) provides convenience for ESM code developers using component modeling method to make the code segments loose coupled and reusable. This approach, however, may not be appropriate for ESM domain researchers, who pay more attention on constructing an ESM application using existing components in minimal time and do not care about the implementation details of each component. This paper proposes CMS, a compatible modeling standard that provides: (1) semantics for describing components, (2) adapters which support data transmission between components wrapped by distinct frameworks, (3) extensible interface for bringing other frameworks later. At the same time, an eclipse-based ESM tool suite is designed to help researchers create application by dragging encapsulated components. We are particularly concerned with simplifying development and increasing efficiency. Initial results from ongoing development demonstrate that this approach significantly reduces the time required to develop ESM applications.

Keywords: Compatible Modeling Standard (CMS), Graphical Component-based Modeling Approach (GCMA), ESM Tool Suite.

1 Introduction

In recent years, earth system science development quickly extended to the hydrosphere (oceans, sea, and ice). Simultaneously, the study expands from atmosphere to geosphere (lithosphere, mantle, and core) and the biosphere (including humans). As a result, the structure of ESM application becomes tremendous and complex; in addition, there are some reusable code segments in the process of development.

NASA with other research institutions has built Earth System Modeling Framework (ESMF) [7], which defines a component-based architecture and aims to reduce the coupling between each module and increase Earth System Modeling software reusability. It is almost the most universal framework in the field of earth system model.

We also take research on Flexible Modeling System (FMS)[4], another widely-used ESM framework developed by GFDL. [1]FMS maintains high-level code structure needed to harness component models and representations of climate subsystems developed by independent groups of researchers.

Y. Yuan, X. Wu, and Y. Lu (Eds.): ISCTCS 2012, CCIS 320, pp. 706–713, 2013.
© Springer-Verlag Berlin Heidelberg 2013

To some extent, the two frameworks mentioned above provide convenience for junior code developers. However, each of them has advantages and drawbacks: the ESMF is clear-structured but its parallel ability needs to be improved; FMS is superior in parallel but its data transfer mode is complex. Furthermore, it may be insufficient for ESM researchers to study only one framework, they pay much attention on collecting existing components together to develop a new application rapidly then run it to obtain new results, instead of focusing on the implementing details of components, it is hard to realize data transfer between ESMF-component and FMS-component.

In order to solve these problems, this paper firstly introduces the Compatible Modeling Standard (CMS). CMS can describe not only simple ESMF-component, but also the whole ESM application structure including the data transfer among components. Moreover, based on this standard we develop an ESM tool suite which contains components which meet the criterion of ESMF in the CMS library. Researchers can simply use these components to form an application in minimal time, then compile and run it.

The remainder of the paper is organized as follows. Section 2 gives a short introduction to the ESMF. The syntax structure of the CMS is presented in Section 3. In section 4, we demonstrate the Graphical Component-based Modeling Approach (GCMA). Section 5 introduces a CMS-based ESM tool suite. In section 6, we demonstrate how the ESM tool suite assists the researchers and the junior developers in developing ESM components as well as the whole ESM application with a case study of Hurricane Model. Finally, we conclude with Section 7.

2   ESMF Overview

As illustrated in Figure 1, the ESMF comprises a superstructure and an infrastructure. The role of the superstructure layer is to provide a shell that encompasses user code and a context for interconnecting input and output data streams between components. Classes called gridded components, coupler components, and states are used in the superstructure layer to achieve this objective [8]. The infrastructure layer provides a standard support library that researchers can use to speed up construction of components and ensure consistent, guaranteed component behavior. It contains a set of data classes such as Array, Field, and utility classes (including Time, Config). [2]

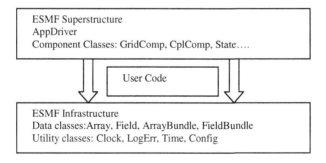

Fig. 1. Architecture of the ESMF

3   The CMS

In this section we will make rules for the coding behavior of users before introducing the CMS, which simplify the complexity and is also beneficial to the realization of CMS. (1)All the components, based on CMS, should contain at least three subroutines of the three CMS type: CMS_SETINIT, CMS_SETRUN, and CMS_SETFINAL. (2)Each State object created in the parent Gridded Component is associated with only one child Gridded Component. It means if one Import State object is passed to any method of one child Gridded Component as parameter, another child Gridded Component couldn't take in it as input.(3)The name of Registration method, if exists, adopts uniform format "*_setServices", which can be identified by tool. State object (import or export) can only be added into the same type of State object. (4)For CMS Adapter, the INF subroutines contain the data type conversion process.

We adopt XML instead of other textual, graphical or binary formats to define CMS standard, since it has many advantages such as scalability, platform-independence and readability. The Compatible Modeling Standard composes two parts as following.

CMS Component

Init denotes CMS component initializes its arguments and apply for resources. InitializeComp indicates that this Gridded Component will initialize its subcomponents. StateAdd and AttributeSet indicate that the Gridded Component creates data and adds them into state object.

Run consists of four subelements: RunComp, StateGet, AttributeGet and AttributeSet. RunComp indicates that this Gridded Component will run its subcomponent. StateGet and AttributeGet indicate that the CMS Component needs the data which is necessary to execute.

Restart denotes CMS component reloads its configuration and writes files. RestartComp indicates that CMS Component will restart its subcomponents.

Final denotes CMS component flushes its configuration and releases resources.FinalizeComp indicates that CMS Component will finalize its subcomponents

CMSGrid donates the subcomponent of CMS component. For purpose of describing this relationship, each component element has childName, type and moduleName property.

CMS Adapter

CMS Adapter is designed to deal with data type conversion between Esm frameworks contained in CMS. It consists of 4 parts below:

Registration: CMS Adapter registers all CMSINF (CMSInit, CMSRun, and CMSFinal) methods which can be multi-phase and create all sub-components and States.

CMSInit denotes CMS Adapter registers a CMS_SETINIT type of method in the *_SetSevice subroutine. DataTypeConversion indicates that CMS Adapter complete the data type conversion between two CMS components. InitializeComp indicates that this CMS Adapter will initialize the CMSComp below CMS Adapter.

CMSRun denotes CMS Adapter registers a CMS_SETRUN type of method in the *_SetService subroutine. DataTypeConversion indicates that CMS Adapter complete the data type conversion between two CMS components. RunComp indicates that this CMS Adapter will run the CMSComp below CMS Adapter.

CMSFinal denotes CMS Adapter registers a CMS_SETFINAL type of method in the *_SetSevice subroutine. DataTypeConversion indicates that CMS Adapter complete the data type conversion between between two CMS components. FinalizeComp indicates that this CMS Adapter will finalize the CMSComp below CMS Adapter.

4   The Graphical Component-Based Modeling Approach

The CMS standard helps ESM researchers and developers with compatible and concise code architecture. To improve the efficiency, we also put forward a new modeling method called graphical component-based modeling approach (GCMA).

The traditional component-based method[5] used in ESM field is low efficient, using GCMA, researchers or developers can simply create an earth system model by dragging icons representing physical modules from our CMS library, instead of copying and pasting code segments, which is low efficient and easy to make error.

Using the component-based method, we separate the earth system model into several components which are loose coupled and have little data exchange. Specific example will be narrated in section 6.

As shown in Table 1, we define 9 icons to represent the necessary elements for an earth system model.

Table 1. Graphical earth system model elements

Element	Icon		
AppDriver			
CMSComponent			
AppRoot			
GridChild			
Subroutine		CMSInit	
		CMSRun	
		CMSRestart	
		CMSFinal	

5 The ESM Tools Suite

To uniformly build, share components and templates, we created a graphical development tool. This tool is based on CMS and GCMA which consists of graphical modeling, components publishing and sharing, code generating and data validation. It is built on the Eclipse platform [3] and adopts Photran [9], GMF [10] plug-in technology to strengthen the extensibility. The system is composed of five parts.

CMS library: It consists of three parts: templates、components and tools. It is used to manage ESM templates and components and CMS adapters as well as corresponding CMS interface files published by different researchers, including registering, deleting, searching and other functions. The principle that issued once and used many times is followed to provide component providers and consumers with a uniform platform, which make their sharing model code convenient and flexible.

Graphical editor: In the Graphical editor, researchers and developers can do the following things. (1)Build an ESM application by dragging CMS components and CMS adapters from the CMS components library, and generating code automatically. (2)Building an ESM application by simply checking out an ESM template from the CMS templates library, then generating application code.(3) Create a CMS code frame by dragging and dropping tools from the CMS tools library and configuring them using the Properties view, then generating CMS code frame automatically. After compiling and running an ESM application successfully, researchers and developers can extend the CMS templates or components library by adding this application to the CMS templates library and its components to the CMS components library.

Code editor: It contains some IDE features such as syntax-highlighting, content assisting, file comparing, vi supporting and so on.

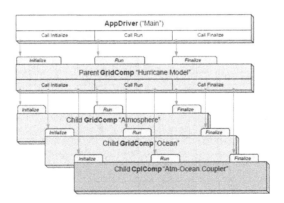

Fig. 2. The Structure of Hurricane Model

Terminals: After building the integrated application code according to the above steps, researchers can use the Terminals view to compile and run the application. This part also provides the feature of error locating when encountering troubles during the compile process, which guides the researchers locating the compile error in the graphical editor as well as the code editor. Researchers can modify code or configuration, and then recompile the application until passing the compile process.

Version control: This part is developed for maintaining the code version developed by different researchers in different time, which helps the collaborative development.

6   Case Study

To show how to use our graphical ESM Tool Suite to realize the functions above mentioned in session IV, we now give a complete example, Hurricane Model, one of the most simple and representative models in ESM field. Figure 3 displays the structure of HM bringing in superstructure and infrastructure for ESMF. As is shown in Figure 4, the component-based Hurricane Model is composed of a parent GridComp with two child GridComps and one CouplerComp which is designed for the data exchange and data type transmission using algorithms such as interpolation. AppDriver is the entry point of the application.

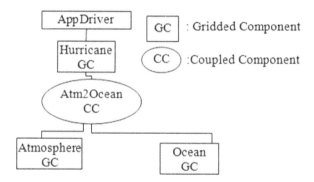

Fig. 3. The component-based Structure of Hurricane Model

As illustrated in Figure 5 we demonstrate how to create, run and publish the Hurricane model via our graphical ESM tool suite.

First of all, we create an ESM diagram into a FORTRAN project, drag an appDriver from the CMS Tools library to the diagram editor, configure its name using the Properties view. Then drag and drop 3 GridComp and one CplComp one by one, including Hurricane GC, Atmsphere GC, Ocean GC, Atm2Ocean CC. Afterwards, we link the AppDriver and the 4 components in the graphical editor. Lastly, we configure the importState and the exportState using the Properties view. a) Set the states of Hurricane GC as s1, s2, s3, s4. b) Set the importState of Atmsphere GC as s1 and exportState as s2 using the drop-down list; Set the importState of Ocean GC as s3 and exportState as s4. c) Set the importState of Atm2Ocean CC as s2 and exportState as s3.Through the above steps, the Hurricane Model diagram will be created. We add this Hurricane Model diagram into our CMS templates lib. We then generate the ESMF code frame for this model using the customized menu. We finish the necessary logical code for every component to build the Hurricane Model. Once we have the whole application code, we use the Terminals view to compile the application, no error occurs, we proceed running the application, also no error occurs. This time we add the four components with correct code into our CMS components lib using the customized wizard.

The modeling method illustrated above probably suits junior ESM developers more than ESM researchers, who care little about the implementation details of every component. They may be much interested in the function of creating a model by only checking out an existing template from the CMS templates lib and generating model code directly. To realize this function, we do like this:1)Create a Fortran project; 2)Create a ESM template existing in the templates lib;3)Generate model code using the menu "Generate Application Code " .4)Compile and run application code using the Terminal view.

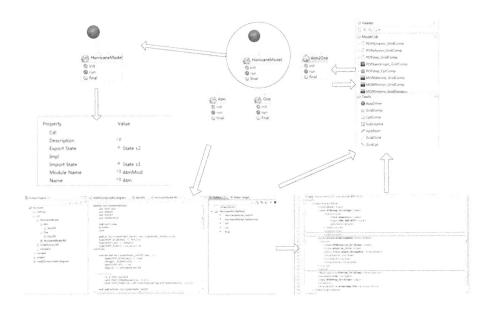

Fig. 4. The Structure of Hurricane Model

7   Conclusion

This paper proposes a Compatible Modeling Standard and Graphical Component-based Modeling Approach, then based on this standard and approach introduces a graphical development tool which has been widely used by the earth system researchers in China. We have presented a case study that demonstrates the process of creating one earth system model application by using our graphical development tool. We conclude that the graphical development tool not only improves development efficiency for ESM application but also accumulates plenty of reused components and templates which will offer help to other researchers.

In the future, we will continue our research in the following directions: 1) improving the performance of the component-based earth system model by introducing the parallel technology; 2) expanding the CMS to describe more ESM frameworks; 3) applying the CMS and the tool to other earth system models to cumulate much more reusable components into our component library.

Acknowledgement. This paper is supported by the 863 project of China under the grant No. 2010AA012404, the China International Science and Technology Cooperation Program from the Ministry of Science and Technology of China under the grant No. 2009DFA12110.

References

1. Dunlap, R., Rugaber, S., Mark, L.: A Feature Model of Coupling Technologies for Earth System Models. Technical Report GT-CS-10-18 (2011) (revised)
2. Hill, C., DeLuca, C., Balaji, V., Suarez, M., DaSilva, A.: The architecture of the earth system modeling framework. Computing in Science and Engineering 6(1), 18–28 (2004), doi:10.1109/MCISE.2004.1255817
3. Eclipse (2011), http://www.eclipse.org
4. Balaji, V.: FMS: the GFDL Flexible Modeling System. Princeton, NJ (2004)
5. Whittle, Ratcliffe, M.: Software Component Interface Description for Reuse. IEEE BCS Software Engineering Journal 8(6), 307–318 (1993)
6. Balaji, V.: PRISM-ESMF Collaboration. ESMF Inter-Agency Meeting (2004)
7. DeLuca, C., and the ESMF Joint Specification Team:The Earth System Modeling Framework and the Earth System Curator(2006)
8. Earth System Modeling Framework Reference Manual for Fortran Version 5.2 (2011), http://www.earthsystemmodeling.org
9. Photran (2011), http://www.eclipse.org/photran/
10. GMF (2010), http://www.eclipse.org/modeling/gmp/

Who Can Haul the ANDON-CORD in the Software Development Process

Liu Yinglian[1,2], Jørgen Bøegh[1,2], and Sun Qi[3]

[1] Beijing University of Posts and Telecommunications, School of Software Engineering
[2] Key Laboratory of Trustworthy Distributed Computing and Services (BUPT),
Ministry of Education, China
[3] School of Computer Science and Technology, Southwest University for Nationalities,
Chengdu, China
{Yinglianliu,Jorgen}@bupt.edu.cn

Abstract. Recently, many software engineers have drown their attentions on software process improvement and many research approaches have been proposed, but only few of them have been applied to industrial practice. There are still many significant challenges for our further success. For many years, we are supposing to develop a method which can make the Software Development Process (SDP) as efficient as the Hardware Production Line (HPL). In this paper, we discussed how to apply the successful mechanism (ANDON-CORD) in Toyota to the software development process. Finally, we highlight the importance of every member in the software development process for assuring the high quality of software products.

Keywords: Hardware assembly line, software development process, software quality assurance.

1 Introduction

In the world famous automobile company, Toyota, there is a special rope, called ANDON-CORD, along the whole production line. Everyone who works on the assembly line can haul the ANDON-CORD as soon as he finds something wrong with the product. If the rope is hauled by someone, the whole production line will be stopped until the issue is corrected, in order to avoid leaving defects to next stages. The right and the obligation to haul the ANDON-CORD to stop production when a defect is found makes the workers not just a part which can be replaced any time but a person who is valued. The famous management scientist OHMAE KENICHI concluded that the reason for the success of Japanese corporations is that they attached great importance to the employees. Is there an invisible ANDON-CORD along the software production line? And who has the right to haul it?

Software organizations cast their whole attentions on developing products to fulfill the needs of their customers. This is accomplished by means of processes, which can be defined as sequences of activities carried out by functions (performed by staff) with the use of tools [1]. In some organizations, the software processes are

Y. Yuan, X. Wu, and Y. Lu (Eds.): ISCTCS 2012, CCIS 320, pp. 714–720, 2013.
© Springer-Verlag Berlin Heidelberg 2013

under-taken by only one department. However, as the high development of software industry, the software processes become more and more complicated. Software is developed in teams within larger organizational structures. Generally, the software processes are composed of software development process, software testing process and software quality assurance process. The processes are becoming increasingly large and complex, so they are always performed by groups comprised of members from several departments. One implicit assumption in software process research is that improving the software processes will improve the software product quality and better control of the software processes will increase project success [2]. Then, how to manage all these processes to not only maximize the effectiveness but also improve the quality of the products become much more essential. In this paper, we discuss the characteristics of both the hardware production line and the software development process, and analyze the differences between them. Then we discuss how to apply the successful mechanism in Toyota to the software development to achieve higher qualities of the software products.

This paper is organized as follows: Section two briefly discusses related work. Section three describes how to apply the mechanism to the software development processes. Section four highlights the personal value in the software processes. Section five is conclusion and future work.

2   Related Work

A software process is a set of sequenced tasks (some tasks may execute in parallel) leading to design, development or maintenance of a software product [3]. ISO 12207 Software Life Cycle Processes Standard [4] is one of the most comprehensive documents. It defines many processes in the whole life cycle of a software product and all the activities that should be included in each process.

After many years of research, the development process, the testing process and the quality assurance process are highly developed. A multitude of different approaches and languages for process modeling have been developed [5], such as Waterfall Model, Rapid Prototype Model, Incremental Model, Spiral Model in software development process; V-Model, W-model, H-Model and X-Model which integrates testing process into development life cycle model; Capability Maturity Model Integration (CMMI) and ISO 9001 in software assurance process. All these processes and models have continuously been improved for achieving higher software quality.

People often confuse software quality assurance with software testing. However, software quality assurance is much more complicated. The ISO Standard 12207 defines quality assurance process this way: "The quality assurance process is a process for providing adequate assurance that the software products and processes in the product life cycle conform to their specific requirements and adhere to their established plans." QA is performed through all stages of the project, not just slapped on at the end [6]. QA provides assurance and credibility that the product will work accurately. It sounds like testing but more than testing.

3   The Invisible ANDON-CORD in SDP

3.1   Differences between HPL and SDP

An assembly line is an arrangement of workers and machines in a factory. Each worker deals with only one part of a product, and the product passes from one worker to another until it is finished. After the modern assembly line was first introduced by Ford, it has made the industrial output achieve a great leap forward, and the traditional industrial production has undergone a dramatic change.

On the assembly line, the product passes from one worker to another, so all the processes will be done sequentially. That's why the ANDON-CORD mechanism is so successful in Toyota. If one employee, who works on the assembly line, hauls the ANDON-CORD, then the whole production line will be forced to stop. Toyota adopts this mandatory way to avoid leaving mistakes to the next stage and to get higher quality of the products. The core idea is that whenever a mistake is found, bucket stop here.

Having researched for many years, experts found that in the software development process the cost and difficulty for resolving a defect left over will be higher and higher as the process moving on [7]. Therefore we propose to detect and correct the mistakes in the software as soon as possible. This core idea in software is the same as at Toyota. In order to get higher quality, the software testing process and quality assurance process has been introduced and is kept on improving.

However, the sequential feature does not always exist in the software development process. In fact, many tasks are executed in parallel. For example, in the coding phase, most of the engineers always develop a relatively independent module, and all these modules will be integrated nearly at the end of this phase. For example, parallelism, which is one of the most important characteristics of object-oriented technology, becomes more and more common.

Then, after losing the sequential feature, is there still an invisible ANDON-CORD in the software development process?

3.2   ANDON-CORD in the Top-Level Processes

In the typical software development process models, the top-level sub processes are normally executed sequentially. In order to find the invisible ANDON-CORD in SDP, the main attention will be drawn on the top-level processes. In ISO 12207, software implementation process is refined into six sub processes, including: software requirements analysis process, software architecture design process, software detailed design process, software construction process, software integration process and software qualification process. In order to better describe the topic of this paper, a software delivery & maintenance process is added. Figure 1 shows all the 7 sub processes, but also includes some other information which will be used to describe how to build an invisible ANDON-CORD along the software development process.

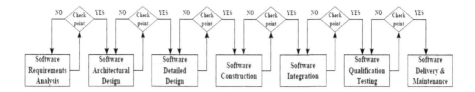

Fig. 1. Top-Level processes

As is shown in Figure 1, the software development process begins at software requirements analysis stage and ends at the software delivery & maintenance stage. In the hardware production line, products are assembled in sequence. One staff member could not start his work until all the processes before him are completely finished (the assembled product is flowing in front of him). However, in the software development process, many tasks are always executed in parallel. We can start on the next phase before one phase is fully accomplished. For example, in the detailed design process, the whole system is always divided into many modules. Then, after the design of one module is completely finished, it can be handed over to the construction process. So in Figure 1, some processes may be implemented at the same time.

When a task is delivered from one stage to another stage, the invisible ANDON-CORD becomes to appear. As is said in the previous section, the core idea of both the HPL and the SDP to achieve higher quality is to assure that no defect is left to the next stage. So at the top-level processes, a special check group is organized. The main duty for this group is to check whether a task can be delivered to the next stage. This is often called a milestone review.

The top level group may be composed of the project manager, the R&D manager, the testing manager, the QA manager, and even some higher managers for some important tasks. The managers' main duties are shown below:

- The R&D manager needs to report the development process, the personnel and time invested in, the coverage of the requirements, and particular problems encountered during the process.
- The testing manager has to illustrate the testing report, including the amount of the test cases, the coverage of the test case, the pass rate of the test cases, and so on.
- The QA manager should summarize whether the organization quality management policies, standards and procedures are followed, the quality management goals and objectives are achieved, and customers' satisfaction is assessed, and so on.

After the reports given by those three managers, all the group members need to discuss whether the result of the process can be delivered to the next stage. If the work is well done, it can be handed over. If the members think there are still some problems with it, then the work has to be returned back just like the ANDON-CORD is hauled.

Compared with the ANDON-CORD in Toyota, the only difference is that the whole software development process does not need to stop, but just some work needs to be modified.

In the top-level processes, only the department managers have the right and the obligation to check whether a task can be moved on to the next stage.

3.3   Refine, Down to Low-Levels

The top-level processes illustrate an overview of the software development process, but only those are not enough.   Actually, some more detailed sub processes need to be defined to guide practice. In ISO 12207 and some other international standards, the above top-level processes are refined into many detailed sub activities. For example, as is illurstrated in Figure 2, the software requirements analysis process is always divided into many sub activities. And each activity can also be refined into many tasks. In ISO/IEC 15288 [8], the first three phases in Figure 2 are defined as Stakeholder Requirements Definition Process, and the last two are difined as Requirements Analysis Process. But in practice, these phases are always called Requirements Analysis Process in general.

Fig. 2. Sub activities in software requirements analysis process

After years of research, experts found that most of the defects in a software product is introduced during the requirements analysis process [9]. Therefore, more attentions become to be drawn on this initial process. And the invisible ANDON-CORD will still be refined in this special stage.

As to achieve the customers' requirements as detailed as possible and to avoid any confusion, the requirements analysis process can be devided into many activities (As is shown in Figure 2). Firstly, the stakeholders need to be identified, and requirements need to be elicited from the identified stakeholders. Secondly, a set of activity sequences and constraints should be defined. Thirdly, the complete set of elicited requirements should be analyzed and fed back to stakeholders to ensure that the needs have been adquately captured. Then, the requirements need to be transformed into a technical view of the required product.

When a result flows from one stage to another, a low-level check group needs to be organized to decide whether it can be handed over. This check group may be composed of the project manager, the requirements analyst, the system architectural designer, the testing manager and the QA manager. A group meeting will be hold when a milestone is assessed to discuss whether it can be delivered. The check will be as careful as possible to avoid missing any deffect.

Furthermore, the activities in Figure 2 can also be refined into many sub tasks. For example, the elicit stakeholder requirements activity can be refined into two tasks, as is shown in Figure 3. Then a third level check group will be organized. With the refining process going on, a process can be divided into many activites, and an activity can be divided into many tasks. More and more check groups will be coming into existance.

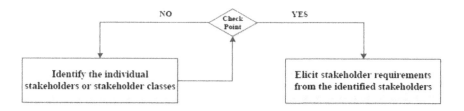

Fig. 3. Sub tasks in the elicit stakeholder requirements activity

With the flow of the results in the software development process, the other top-level processes will be refined. And more and more staffs will be included in the lower-level check groups, and everyone becomes a quality assurance member. An invisible ANDON-CORD appears in the software development process.

4   Everyone is a Hero

With the rapid development of software industry, software development is no longer as simple as twenty years ago. Software is developed in teams within larger organizational structures. We have proposed many complicated process models to assure the quality of the products, but that is not enough. James Bath has authored articles [10-11] insisting that the quality of the people is the primary driver for software quality. We need to let the members know that each of them is valuable.

As we mentioned before, the reason for the success of Japanese corporations is that they attached great importance to the employees. The same thing can also happen in software industry if everyone is valued as a hero for the success for the product quality.

The behavior of the members in different teams is often determined by their position within the organization. The structure and the dynamics of an organization can influence the way projects are handled [12]. That is why we want to introduce the ANDON-CORD mechanism into the software development process. With the check groups organized during the process refining, more and more staffs become members of the quality assurance. Everyone has the obligation to stop the defect delivering to the next stage. They are just like the managers in the top-level group. Everyone is a hero for achieving higher qualities of a product, and hence for the success of a product.

5   Conclusion

In this paper, the success of using ANDON-CORD to achieve higher product quality in Toyota is discussed. In order to get higher software product quality, the feasibility for applying this mechanism into the software development process is discussed.

Firstly, the differences between the HPL and the SDP are figured out. Secondly, the attention is paid to the top-level processes. A check group composed of managers is organized and a top-level ANDON-CORD is introduced. Then, the top-level processes are refined. As the refining process going on, the low-level check groups are organized, and more and more staffs are included in the check groups. The whole invisible ANDON-CORD becomes to appear. Finally, the importance of every staff member for achieving higher product qualities is highlighted.

References

1. Davenport, T.H., Short, J.E.: The New Industrial Engineering: Information Technology and Business Process Redesign. Sloan Management Review, 11–17 (1990)
2. Huo, M., Zhang, H., Jeffery, R.: An Exploratory Study of Process Enactment as Input to Software Process Improvement. In: Proceedings of the International Workshop on Software Quality, pp. 39–44 (2006)
3. Jonathan, E.C., Alexander, L.W.: Discovering models of software processes from event-based data. ACM Trans. Software. Eng. Methodology 7, 215–249 (1998)
4. Systems and software engineering – Software life cycle processes. ISO/IEC 12207 (2008)
5. Ambriola, Conradi, V.R., Guggetta, A.: Assessing process-centered software engineering environments. ACM Transactions on Software Engineering and Methodology (TOSEM) 3, 283–328 (1997)
6. Feldman, S.: Quality Assurance: Much More than Testing. QUEUE, 27–29 (February 2005)
7. Boehm, B.W.: Software Engineering Economics. IEEE Transactions on Software Engineering SE-10, 4–20 (1984)
8. ISO/IEC 15288 Systems and software engineering - System life cycle processes (2008)
9. THE STANDISH GROUP: Chaos Report (1995)
10. Bach, J.: Enough About Process: What We Need Are Heroes. Computer 12, 96–98 (1995)
11. Bach, J.: What Software Reality Is Really About. Computer 32, 148–149 (1999)
12. Dalcher, D.: Agility and Software Teams: The future of Software Process Improvement, 219–221 (2007)

Research and Implement of Security Situation Awareness System YH-SSAS

Weihong Han, Qingguang Wang, and Yan Jia

School of Computer Science, National University of Defense Technology
Changsha Hunan 410073
hanweihong@gmail.com

Abstract. The security situation awareness system for large-scale network YH-SSAS is oriented the large-scale network environment, such as national backbone network, large network operators and large enterprises. It acquires, understands and displays the security factors which cause changes of the network situation, and predict the future development trend of these security factors. The system implements important technologies of network security monitoring and becomes the focus of attention of major network security manufacturers. Research and development of security situation awareness system for large-scale network are very important to improve emergency response capabilities of national backbone network as well as large network operators and large enterprises, and to mitigate the harm caused by network attacks.

Keywords: Security Situation Awareness System, association analysis, multi-dimensional analysis, data flow.

1   Introduction

With the increasingly development of information technology, the Internet is becoming the national critical information infrastructure, and a variety of network-based applications are more and more widely used. Network security is related to the national and social interests. In recent years, with the global Internet being attacked frequently, the network security threats are a growing problem and important information system security is seriously threatened. The growing network security events have become the key factors restricting our country's economic development, and even threating to the social stability and national security.

In order to meet the challenges of network security, VPN, IDS, anti-virus system, identity authentication, data encryption, security auditing, and other security and management products have been widely used. But most functions of these products are dispersive and running in separate ways in the implementation of large-scale network security management. If we just take a simply aggregation analysis of data reported by these security products which are deployed in the network, it takes a huge storage and computational cost. Seriously, the truly useful threat information will be submerged by the mass of useless information. Finally, managers can't get the overall network security situation, so that it is difficult to make correct security decisions and

Y. Yuan, X. Wu, and Y. Lu (Eds.): ISCTCS 2012, CCIS 320, pp. 721–729, 2013.
© Springer-Verlag Berlin Heidelberg 2013

emergency response. We are facing with a series of important and challenging issues in terms of the security of national backbone network, large network operators and large enterprises: How to deal with the endless stream of network attacks, how to reduce false positive rate and false negative rate of the network security events and accurately find the important ones, how to realize real-time calculation of the network security situation based on massive data, how to formulate an accurate, understandable network security indicators system, how to predict network security situation effectively, and so on.

Security Situation Awareness System (YH-SSAS) is developed for national backbone network, large network operators, large enterprises and other large-scale network. The system acquires, understands and displays the security factors which cause changes of network situation, and predict the future development trend of these security factors. This paper describes its architecture and key technologies: security data integration technology for distributed heterogeneous network, association analysis technology oriented the major network security events, real-time analysis technology based on the data flow and multi-dimensional analysis for network security data, network security situation predictit6on technology, and so on. The performance tests show that YH-SSAS has high real-time and accuracy in security situation analysis and trend prediction. The system meets the demands of analysis and prediction for large-scale network security situation.

2   Related Research

Around the research of security situation awareness system for large-scale network, the USA, Japan, China and other countries have established national network security event monitoring systems. Among them, the USA has developed the Global Early Warning Information System (GEWIS) [1], and Japan has developed Internet Scan Data Acquisition System (ISDAS) [2], as well as China has established 863-917Network Security Monitoring Platform. These systems are self-contained, monitoring and early warning for specific problem areas. In research, there has been some latest representative work of the backbone network using real-time monitoring of security events. Kim, from University of Nevada proposed a DDoS detection methods based on PacketScore [3]. Ashwin Lall, from University of Rochester, proposed anomaly detection algorithm [4] based on the network traffic of entropy estimates. Chen, from University of Southern California, proposed distributed change point-based DDoS detection methods [5], and Min Cai developed WormShield [6] system. Currently, there is lack of overall architecture of security situation awareness system for large-scale network in the real mass data environment.

3   System Architecture

The system architecture of YH-SSAS is showed in Figure 1. The system consists of a front-end data integration subsystem, association analysis subsystem, network security event analysis and statistics subsystem, network security index computation subsystem and network security situation display subsystem. Data integration subsystem is responsible for collecting various types of network security events from heterogeneous network security products, and then these events are integrated into the system of uniform standards. In association analysis system, the association analysis is carried out between network security events and network assets, network vulnerability, and the events themselves. The association analysis system removes false alarms and increases the alert level. It is convenient for users to deal with high-risk network security events priority. Network security event analysis and statistics subsystem is responsible for making network security data with multi-dimension and multi-granularity statistics in real-time, and let the user access to the network security situation information clearly. According to user's configurations, Network security index subsystem is responsible for doing real-time calculation of the current network security index in the system of uniform standards. Network security situation display subsystem provides a visualization platform for users having an intuitive understanding of the current network security situation.

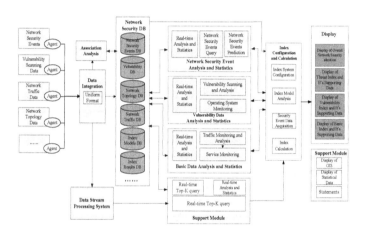

Fig. 1. The System Architecture of YH-SSAS

4   Key Technologies

We will describes the main features and key technologies of subsystems in YH-SSAS Below.

4.1   Real-Time Heterogeneous Data Integration Technology Combined Passive Acquisition and Active Query

Data integration subsystem provides basic information for the whole system. In order to make a more comprehensive and objective display and prediction of the overall

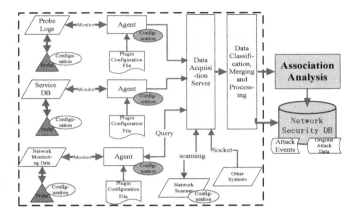

Fig. 2. Architecture of Data Integration Subsystem

network security situation, a scalable distributed data integration subsystem is designed in YH-SSAS. Subsystem architecture is shown in Fig 2. It consists of three modules: front-end probe module, data collection module and data merge module.

There are two data acquisition methods of traditional data integration technologies. One is passive data acquisition method that the latest data is pushed to the top from the underlying data source and the top receives the data passively. The other one is active data acquisition method that the top-layer database gets the latest data by using real-time query to the underlying data source. The system is mainly used in large-scale network. In order to make display and predictions of the large-scale network security situation, the system need gets network data information comprehensively in real-time. For data sources integrated in the system are diverse and numerous, we have designed and implemented the real-time heterogeneous data integration technology combined passive acquisition and active query.

Firstly, in order to achieve the integration of network event monitoring data, we have proposed passive data collection technology based network security logs. The core nodes collect network security events from the real-time detection log information generated by the network security equipment. These security events are packaged into an object in accordance with pre-defined technology, and then they are sent through the socket to a central database server for storage and pretreatment. The events provide complete foundation data for the subsequent correlation analysis of events and calculation of network situation. Secondly, we have adopted the active query technology to collect inherent network data, such as basic traffic information, network topology information, and vulnerability information. Because of facing with large-scale network, we can't collect all of the basic information of each part of network at beginning, so we design active query technology based on the request and put the whole option of network scale to the administrators. Administrators start the security equipment which is deployed in a critical network, and then the network information will be collected. Network administrators send request commands through the socket to the security equipment. The security equipment starts to collect information after receiving parameters from the servers. The operating results are sent to the server in the prescribed form at the end of run.

Our system achieves an effective integration of the massive, multi-source and heterogeneous network security data through the above technologies, while effectively reducing the network overhead and making sure the data acquisition in real time.

4.2   Rule-Based Multi-dimensional Cross-Association Analysis Technology

Network security alarms occur in different locations, different time and different levels of network security. We make an association analysis of the alarm events to dig out the real security events and to identify the real security risks. YH-SSAS system uses multi-dimensional correlation analysis technology, combined with the association between vulnerabilities, assets, and a variety of security incidents. We'll have a comprehensive grasp of the overall network security situation. The architecture shows in Fig 3.

At present, the system has been made an association analysis of the event source: network security event data produced by HIDS (snare) and NIDS (snort), security event data produced by the statistical packet anomaly detection engine (Spade), vulnerability data produced by network vulnerability scanning tools (Nessus) , traffic data produced by network traffic monitoring tools (Ntop), data produced by active detection tools (Arpwatch, Pof, Pads) , network topology data produced by network scanner (Nmap), the Open Source Vulnerability Database (OSVDB).

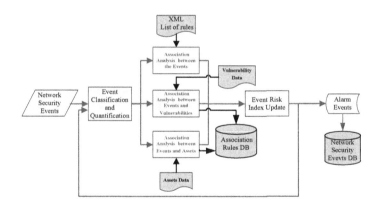

Fig. 3. Structure Chart of Association Analysis Subsystem

YH-SSAS uses tree rules to describe the relationship between the attack steps. It implements the functions of warning, aggregation and confirmation by multi-dimensional cross-association analyzing. By integrating three parts of functions, it forms a fully functional system of network security events association analysis. It mainly includes:

1) Association between Security and Vulnerability: The system adopts a proactive approach to scan and manage network vulnerabilities. After detecting the target events whether exists vulnerabilities, it filters false alarms to a great extent, reduces follow-up costs and improves efficiency.

2) Association between Security and Assets: The key protection of assets without Vulnerabilities, we also consider the probability of successful attack in the assets operating environment.

3) Association between the Events: The security events are described in a uniform format and alarms are confirmed by the tree detection rules. Not only the accuracy is improved, but also, according to the related events information what is saved in the matching process of tree rules, it's easy for administrators to restore the attack scene and to find attack information.

The original network security events are effectively analyzed and aggregated by the above algorithms. It alarms the real threats to network security and reduces the false alarms, at the same time laying the groundwork for network security situation.

4.3   Time Series Prediction Based On Multi-granularity

Multi-granularity time series prediction subsystem consists of data module, forecast module and user interface module. The system structure is shown in Fig 4.

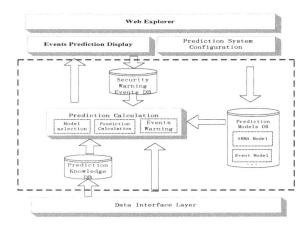

Fig. 4. Prediction Subsystem

Data module completes the input of network security events data. The data interface layer is mainly responsible for data communication with OLAP. Prediction module is divided into four sub-modules: Prediction Models DB, Prediction Knowledge DB, Security Warning Events DB and Prediction Calculation.

Node scale increases in the large-scale network, and the frequency of security events also have a great growth. At the same time the data changes from isolation to continuous events stream.

It is possible to predict the law that security incidents will occur for some time to come. The prediction of the law of continuous events stream provide basis for administrators. The traditional prediction methods attempt to create a single global prediction model. As the network security events are diverse, these models are localized and multi-mode. The frequency of network security events is an important factor for network security situation prediction. According to the requirements of network security situation prediction, YH-SSAS studies this factor as predicted object. We analyze a certain type of network security events for their frequency, that the number in a time granularity. According to the sequential characteristic of events, we propose an algorithm for network security situation prediction combined with a variety of prediction methods.

Short-term prediction (per minute) can catch the short-term exceptions of security events. It can catch paroxysmal exceptions, comparing the frequency of short-term events with the actual frequency. Short-term prediction has some significance to the real-time response to security events. The medium-term prediction (per hour) can find the changes in the law of events. It contributes to the timely adjustment of the prediction model. Long-term prediction (weekly) analyses the long-term trends of security event stream. Users a longer time scale of security incidents can have a general judgment, in order to make treatment decisions. We can have a general judgment with security events for a longer period of time and to make treatment decisions.

YH-SSAS uses related technologies of time series prediction in the field of network security. It chooses reasonable prediction model according to the characteristics and applications of different network security data requirements and uses the historical security event data to build models, and thus it makes multi granularity prediction according to those models and security data sources. For short-term forecasts, we mainly consider the law of development of the recent historical data, but for medium- and long-term forecasts, mainly considering the seasonal factors and the overall long-term trend of the historical security events. Meanwhile, the integration of several prediction models is also an important point to analyze. In this system, it combines the autoregressive model, moving average models and autoregressive moving average model to make prediction in three time dimensions of short-term, medium-term and long-term. Autoregressive moving average model uses small slope decomposition to predict in the time domain and frequency domain.

5   Performance Analysis

A Comparison of prediction accuracy between Short-term prediction and long-term prediction based on UCI data set is shown in Fig 5(a) and Fig5 (b). In the case of the single-step prediction, the regression-based method considers the continuity of data, which has a good effect in the short-term prediction. But its advantage reduces with the increases of prediction length. The errors of these prediction methods are all at a lower level. For the long-term projection, the data fitting curve can't accurately reflect the data law after a period of time. At this time, regression-based prediction error increases rapidly and predictions based on wavelet neural network and frequent item sets are suitable for this prediction scene. Prediction accuracy has been significantly improved compared to a regression-based method. Because YH-SSAS integrates several different prediction methods, the short-term prediction accuracy is not less than 95% and the long-term forecast accuracy is not less than 90%.

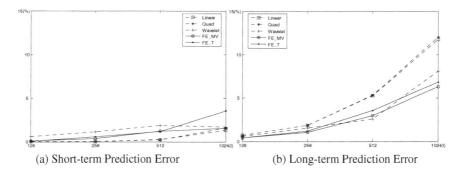

(a) Short-term Prediction Error   (b) Long-term Prediction Error

Fig. 5. The Prediction Error Based on UCI Data Set

6   Conclusion

YH-SSAS is developed for national backbone network, large network operators, large enterprises and other large-scale network. The system acquires, understands and displays the security factors which cause changes of the network situation, and predict the future development trend of these security factors. This paper describes its architecture and key technologies : security data integration technology for distributed heterogeneous network, association analysis technology oriented the major network security events, real-time analysis technology based on the data flow and multi-dimensional analysis for network security data, network security situation prediction technology, and so on. The performance tests show that YH-SSAS has high real-time and accuracy in trend analysis and prediction. The system meets the demands of analysis and prediction for large-scale network security situation.

The next work will continue to focus on YH-SSAS. At present the analysis and prediction technology has been developed well, but we need further study of the processing and tracing of major network and security events and the multi-dimensional visualization display of network security situation.

References

1. GEWIS (Global Early Warning Information System),
   http://www.acronymfinder.com/Global-Early-Warning-Information-System-%28GEWIS%29.html
2. JPCERT/CC, ISDAS (Internet Scan Data Acquisition System),
   http://www.jpcert.or.jp/isdas/

3. Kim, Y., Lau, W.C., Chuah, M.C., Chao, H.J.: Packetscore: Statistics-based overload control against distributed denial-of-service attacks. In: Proceedings of INFOCOM, HongKong (2010)
4. Lall, A., Sekar, V., Ogihara, M., Xu, J., Zhang, H.: Data streaming algorithms for estimating entropy of network traffic. ACM SIGMETRICS Performance Evaluation Review 34(1) (June 2011), doi:10.1145/1140103.1140295
5. Chen, Y., Hwang, K., Ku, W.-S.: Collaborative Detection of DDoS Attacks over Multiple Network Networks. IEEE Transaction on Parallel and Distributed Systems (2009) (accepted and to appear)
6. Cai, M., Hwang, K., Pan, J., Papadopoulos, C.: Wormshield: Fast Worm Signature Generation with Distributed Fingerprint Aggregation. IEEE Transaction on Dependable and Secure Computing (TDSC) (submitted December 2005 and revised July 2010)

A Reliable Query Scheme for Outsourced Data in Cloud

Junchao Wu, Panpan Li, Hongli Zhang, and Binsheng Chu

School of Computer Science and Technology at Harbin Institute of Technology, Harbin,
Heilongjiang, China
{wujunchao2011,lipan}@pact518.hit.edu.cn,
zhanghongli@hit.edu.cn,
chubinsheng@yahoo.com

Abstract. Cloud computing allows data owner to outsource its whole information infrastructure to cloud service provider (CSP).Authorized users can search
the data they want through cloud. However malicious CSP may not execute the
users' query but returns that there is no result matches the query condition for
economic benefit .In this paper, we propose a mechanism to solve this problem
in owner-write-user-read applications. We propose to add redundant data generated by a hash function to original data. When adding redundant data to users'
query, the cloud cannot return empty result because of there must exist redundant data in cloud. Through the adoption of key derivation method, the owner
needs to maintain only a few seeds. Analysis shows that the key derivation procedure using owner's data and users' information will introduce limited data
owner's storage overhead.

Keywords: cloud computing, data outsourcing, DaaS, reliable query.

1 Introduction

Cloud computing [1] has become increasing popular in recent years. As its key application, Data-as-a-Service (DaaS) [2-3] free the data owner from the burden of data
management. In this environment, cloud allows data owner to outsource its data storage, information processing, or even the whole information infrastructure to cloud
service provider (CSP). In this way, the data owners optimize the allocation of
resources and reduce hardware and software investment costs. It makes data owners
to focus more on their core business and leave the data operation to CSP.

While cloud computing takes so many advantages, it also brings new security
threats. Since data owners no longer physically possess the storage of their data, it is
unknown for the cloud users whether the query result from CSP is reliable. For
economic benefits, there exist a large number of motivations for CSP to behave un-
faithfully towards the cloud users. For example, in order to save storage space,
CSP may discard data that has not been or is rarely accessed [4-6]. In conclusion,
although outsourcing data into the cloud is economically attractive for the cost
and complexity of large-scale data storage, it does not offer any guarantee on data

Y. Yuan, X. Wu, and Y. Lu (Eds.): ISCTCS 2012, CCIS 320, pp. 730–736, 2013.
© Springer-Verlag Berlin Heidelberg 2013

integrity and availability [7]. Obviously, this problem will impede the development of the cloud.

Several papers have been made to protect the data security and users' privacy-preserving (see Section 2). In this paper, we mainly solve the problem that the malicious CSP does not execute the users' query operation but directly return that there is no result match the query. The cloud users can not verify whether the CSP execute the query operation because of neither data owner nor users have the original data. A basic idea is to add redundant information to the original data. When an authorized user executes a query operation on the cloud, his query includes not only his interesting information but also redundant data. CSP cannot return an empty result because at least there are redundant data in cloud. However, malicious CSP may falsify result to cheat users. So it calls for the query result must be verifiable. A simple method is the data owner store copies of redundant data and sends them to cloud users as soon as CSP return a result. By verifying correctness of the redundant data, users can judge whether CSP is faithful. But in order to prevent CSP from speculating redundant data, data owner must store a large amount of redundant data, which against the original intention of cloud computing. In this paper, we introduce a method that data owner only needs a small storage to get a large amount of redundant data.

The rest of the paper is organized as follows. We discuss related works in Section 2. Section 3 presents models and assumptions of our proposed scheme. In Section 4 we illustrate the detailed description of our scheme. Section 5 gives the analysis of our proposed scheme. Finally, we give our conclusions in Section 6.

2   Related Work

Several search reports have been performed on outsourcing data security. We will discuss the achievements in two research directions: data encryption and users' access control, from which our approach benefits.

Since CSP is untrusted, the data stored in cloud must be encrypted to prevent cloud servers leaking information to data owners' competitors. Many encryption schemes [8-10, 12] have been given to ensure data security. [12] encrypt data with a single key only. Sabrina De Capitani di Vimercati encrypts different data with a different key in [10]. He looks at the problem of defining and assigning keys to users by exploiting hierarchical key assignment schemes, and of efficiently supporting policy changes. Our scheme learns its thinking that the key is created by both data owner and cloud user.

Cloud users with different access rights need to read different data. There are lots of papers about access control method. [13] define and enforce access policies based on data attributes, on the other hand, allowing the data owner to delegate most of the computation tasks involved in fine-grained data access control to untrusted cloud servers without disclosing the underlying data contents.

3   Models and Assumptions

3.1   System Models

Our system is composed of the following parties: the data owner, a large number of users, clusters of cloud servers. The data owner creates original data. For data security concerns, data owner may encrypt original data with the scheme in section 2. Data owner also needs to create redundant data and add it to original data, then upload to the cloud servers. The users could make query on cloud servers and have the ability to judge the correctness of the result. The cloud servers are always online and they are assumed to have abundant storage capacity and computation power.

3.2   Security Models

We assume the data being stored in the cloud servers are lean to suffer from some inner attacks. The communication channel between the data owners, cloud users and cloud servers are assumed to be secured. For simplicity, we assume the data are stored in plaintext and all the users are supposed to have the same access rights. The only access privilege for users is data file reading. We assume the cloud owner have strategy to control users' access right. To coincide with the actual situation, we assume both the number of owner's original data and users are huge.

3.3   Design Goals

Our design goal is to implement that when malicious CSP do not execute the query operation or return a fake result, the users can judge the truth of the result according to the redundant data. In order to achieve the goal, there must be a large amount of redundant data. We also want to make the data owner store redundant data as little as possible. All these design goals should be achieved efficiently in the sense that the system is scalable.

4   The Proposed Schemes

In this section, we present the detail of the proposed approach. We first introduce our redundant data generation method which prevents malicious CSP from cheating users. The method can also effectively reduce the overhead on the data owner. Taking into account the situation of CSP using data mining method to speculate users' redundant data, we propose a neighbor key generation algorithm to solve this problem.

4.1   Determining Keys for Produce Redundant Data

Firstly, we randomly generate a set of values which we called keys. Then, we choose a hash function (for example, we can choose a secure hash function just like the hash function used in [10]). Finally, for each key, we define hash (key) as a redundant data block and add it to original data. For the purpose of the cloud cannot distinguish which is redundant data, the number of redundant data must be very huge. So there must be a large amount of keys. However, this brings a new situation that to store a large amount of keys is contrary to the original intention of using cloud to save data owner's storage. We propose a scheme that data owner and cloud users cooperate to store the keys to reduce the overhead of data owner.

For each user, we assign several labels which are related with his personal information. Then we use a random function to generate a set of random number which we called redundant seed. We redefine the key as label $\oplus$ seed, where $\oplus$ is the bit-a-bit xor operator. In this case, every cloud user stores his labels. Seeds are stored in data owner. When users need to query, firstly, he has to send a message including his identity information and a subset of his labels, for example n labels, to data owner. The data owner verifies the identity of the user. If it is a legal user, the data owner random choose several seeds (less than or equal to n) to xor with the user's labels to create keys and send them to the user. After the user receives the keys, he will add part of the hash (key) value to his query and send them to the cloud servers. Figure 1 shows the detail of the procedure.   If the cloud servers return an empty result, we can judge the CSP did not execute the query operation or delete our data. If the cloud servers return a result not matches the hash (key), we consider the CSP falsify data to users.

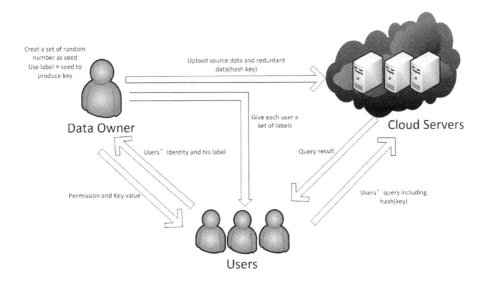

Fig. 1. Key generation and users' query procedure

4.2   Neighbor Key Generation Algorithm

In the above method, for each cloud user the number of redundant data is limited and fixed. Because of CSP has abundant computation, it may count each user's frequently access data other users have not accessed before and consider this data as this user's redundant data. Then CSP creates a redundant table to record the relation between users and their redundant data. When a cloud user executes a query on the cloud, CSP only need to search the relevant redundant table and merely return this user's redundant data. Obviously, in this situation, cloud users can not verify the correctness of the result.

In order to solve this problem, we change the key distribution scheme. We set a label register in data owner side to store the latest cloud users' label. When a user A delivers his identity and labels to data owner for cloud access permission, the owner take out label register's values(for example, it comes from user B), xor them with random seeds to create keys, then send it to A . Then it replaces the label register with A's labels. In this case, we can guarantee that each user's redundant data are not fixed, which prevent the cloud from speculating each user's redundant data. This method takes another advantage is that the user itself cannot get the seed by key xor his label that protect the system security.

5   Analysis of Our Proposed Scheme

5.1   Security Analysis

Our scheme is aim to protect data owners and users' right from malicious CSP who do not execute cloud users' complete query. The reason causing this secure problem is data owner does not save source data and the query result cannot be verified. By taking our redundant data search scheme, we make sure the query result can be verified for the users have hash key to regenerate the redundant data. If CSP do not execute the users' query and only return an empty result or fabricated data to users, the users can use the hash (key) to verify whether CSP is malicious. IF CSP execute only a part of query under condition that he does not know which the redundant is, it is possible for CSP to discard redundant data query. In this case, its malicious behavior can be identified by cloud users. Even if the CSP did not discard the redundant data query, it also cost CSP computing resource to make the query. We consider that CSP do everything for benefit. So it is impossible for CSP to risk perceiving by users to only save a little computing resource.

5.2   Performance Analysis

Because of there is no related scheme to solve this problem. So in this part, we follow the scheme description in Section 4 and analysis the storage overhead of the data owner. We assume that the size of the original outsourced data is 1PB and each data block size is 1KB. Therefore, we have 10^{12} original data blocks. We make an experiment about the impact of the number of users on data owner's storage overhead. So we totally need 10^{10} redundant data blocks. That is 10^{10} keys. We assume the system ask for the redundant account for 0.1% of the total data. We respectively select 100, 1000 and 10000 users. For each size, we choose 10, 100 and 1000 labels. The corresponding owner's storage overhead shows in Table 1.

Table 1. Data owner's storage overhead in different user size or label size

Label size / User size	10	100	1000
100	10000000	1000000	100000
1000	1000000	100000	10000
10000	100000	10000	1000

From the result we can get the conclusion that with the increase of user size, the data owner share storage overhead with cloud users, which largely reduce cloud users' storage overhead. For example, when there are 10000 cloud users and each store 1000 labels, the data owner only need to store 1000 keys, much smaller than 10^{10}. It shows that our scheme will introduce very limited overhead.

6   Conclusion

As the outsourced data storage services have become more and more popular, the concerns about cloud reliability have increased. In this paper we propose a mechanism to prevent CSP cheating users by returning an empty result or falsifying data. We propose to add redundant data to original data blocks to make the cloud query result be verifiable. Through the adoption of key derivation method, the owner needs to store only a few seeds. The key derivation procedure using the bit-a-bit xor operation will introduce very limited computation overhead. The future research direction will focus on combining our redundant data scheme with data encryption.

Acknowledgement. This work is partially supported by the National Grand Fundamental Research 973 Program of China (Grant No. 2011CB302605); High-Tech Research and Development Plan of China (Grant No. 2010AA012504, 2011AA010705); the National Natural Science Foundation of China (Grant No. 61173145).

References

1. Mell, P., Grance, T.: Draft nist working definition of cloud computing
2. Carey, M.: Declarative data services: This is your data on soa. In: Proceedings of the IEEE International Conference on Service-Oriented Computing and Applications, p. 4. IEEE Computer Society, Washington, DC (2007)
3. Truong, H.L., Dustdar, S.: On analyzing and specifying concerns for data as a service. In: 2009 IEEE Asia-Pacific Services Computing Conference, Los Alamitos (2009)
4. Ateniese, G., Burns, R., Curtmola, R., Herring, J., Kissner, L., Peterson, Z., Song, D.: Provable data possession at untrusted stores Cryptology ePrint Archive, Report 2007/202 (2007)
5. Shah, M.A., Swaminathan, R., Baker, M.: Privacy-preserving audit and extraction of digital contents.Cryptology ePrint Archive, Report 2008/186 (2008)

6. Wang, Q., Wang, C., Li, J., Ren, K., Lou, W.: Enabling Public Verifiability and Data Dynamics for Storage Security in Cloud Computing. In: Backes, M., Ning, P. (eds.) ESORICS 2009. LNCS, vol. 5789, pp. 355–370. Springer, Heidelberg (2009)
7. Wang, C., Wang, Q., Ren, K., Lou, W.: Privacy-Preserving Public Auditing for Data Storage Security in Cloud Computing. In: Proc. of IEEE INFOCOM 2010, San Diego, CA, USA (March 2010)
8. Wang, W., Li, Z., Owens, R., Bhargava, B.: Secure and Efficient Access to Outsourced Data. In: CCSW 2009 (2009)
9. Yang, M., Liu, F., Han, J.-L., Wang, Z.-L.: An Efficient Attribute based Encryption Scheme with Revocation for Outsourced Data Sharing Control. In: VLDB 2007 (2007)
10. di Vimercati, S.D.C., Foresti, S., Jajodia, S., Paraboschi, S., Samarati, P.: Over-encryption: Management of Access Control Evolution on Outsourced Data. In: VLDB 2007 (2007)
11. Atallah, M., Frikken, K., Blanton, M.: Dynamic and efficient key management for access hierarchies. In: Proc. of the 12th ACM CCS 2005, Alexandria, VA, USA (2005)
12. Ceselli, A., Damiani, E., di Vimercati, S.D.C., Jajodia, S., Paraboschi, S., Samarati, P.: Modelingand assessing inference exposure in encrypted databases. ACM TISSEC 8(1), 119–152 (2005)
13. Yu, S., Wang, C., Ren, K., Lou, W.: Achieving secure, scalable, and fine-grained data access control in cloud computing. In: Proceedings of the 29th Conference on Information Communications, INFOCOM 2010, pp. 534–542. IEEE Press, Piscataway (2010)

Author Index